Globalization and Labour Rights

Abdullah Al Faruque

Globalization and Labour Rights

Lessons from the Experiences of Bangladesh

palgrave
macmillan

Abdullah Al Faruque
Department of Law
University of Chittagong
Chattogram, Bangladesh

ISBN 978-981-92-3660-2 ISBN 978-981-92-3661-9 (eBook)
https://doi.org/10.1007/978-981-92-3661-9

This Palgrave Macmillan imprint is published by the registered company Springer Nature Singapore Pte Ltd.
The registered company address is: 152 Beach Road, #21-01/04 Gateway East, Singapore 189721, Singapore

Dedicated to
Dr. Shahdeen Malik
Eminent jurist, constitutional expert of Bangladesh and my mentor

Preface

Globalization, fostered by trade and investment liberalization, capital flows, and rapid technological changes, has led to the greater integration of economies and labor markets, is changing the nature of work and reshaping the landscape of industrial relations and labor rights in many developing countries, including Bangladesh. Globalization and technological changes are also seen as an important source of inequality in employment relations with distributional effects in society. This transformation has profoundly challenged traditional industrial actors, labor rights, and the nature of work in Bangladesh. Traditionally, state, employers, trade unions, and workers are considered the most important actors in industrial relations. As the globalization process deepens with increasing connectivity and networking, transnational alliances, facilitated by the international labor movement, have emerged as a powerful new governance trajectory, paving the way for workers and unions to organize and act transnationally to express solidarity and to protect collective rights of workers. The global economy's integration, driven by foreign investment and trade, has also changed the nature and scope of activities of multinational corporations and led to the growth of the global supply chain, undermining the capacity of states to regulate their labor markets. Furthermore, due to large-scale privatization of the economy over the last five decades, the share of the public sector in employment has been continuously reduced. On the other hand, with the availability of extensive surplus labor, there has been a substantial increase in subcontracting, outsourcing, temporary and casual work, causing flexibilization in the employment scenario. Such a feature contributes to informalization, vulnerability, and insecurity among the workforce. All the above factors have impacted the industrial relations in Bangladesh in significant ways like many other developing countries. However, over the past decades, economic globalization, driven by foreign investment and free trade, has enhanced employment opportunities and has accelerated the integration of the global labor rights regime established by the ILO within the national legal framework.

This book takes into account the most diverse influences of globalization, including transnational actor constellations and emerging transnational practices and institutions and the book draws lessons from the impact of globalization on the industrial relations system of Bangladesh, which is characterized by the huge presence of informal workers, fragmented unions, weak labor institutions, and lack of enforcement of labor laws. In particular, the Ready-Made Garment (RMG) industry in Bangladesh, which is now the second largest in the world, has been profoundly shaped by the economic globalization process and is a crucial part of the global supply chain. While the RMG is a key driver of the economic growth and retaining its competitiveness is critical for the Bangladeshi economy, precarious forms of work and labor rights violations are also frequently surfaced in this sector. Globalization has also impacted the traditional role of trade unions and the outcome and process of collective bargaining. Due to the globalization process, national trade unions and systems of collective bargaining have lost some of their capacity to protect the interests of workers and regulate the labor market. In this context, transnational systems of labor market regulation are now increasingly gaining prominence to address inequality of bargaining power, which can prevent workers from obtaining fair contract terms. Transnational collective bargaining agreements are now shaping many agendas of decent work globally. Bangladesh is no exception to this trend as many transnational initiatives by multi-stakeholders are currently regulating the safety and security of workers in the RMG sector.

Long working hours, low wages, unsafe working conditions, suppression of labor rights and non-payment of minimum wages often cause unrest in the RMG sector, leading to factory closures and disruption of production. The book attempts to explore the following intriguing questions: What are the challenges that globalization poses in industrial relations in developing countries like Bangladesh? How are labor rights violated in a global supply chain, and what are the emerging international standards that can address the issue of human rights and labor rights in such a global supply chain? What are the functions of labor law in the globalized world? How is globalization impacting trade union rights, collective bargaining, and minimum wage-fixing? What is the role of international labor standards in dealing with onslaughts of globalization? What are multi-stakeholders' initiatives taken after the Rana Plaza collapse in Bangladesh and what are the impacts of such initiatives on improving safety and security in the RMG sector? To what extent can social dialogue promote decent work agendas and what lessons can be learned from Bangladesh? How is globalization influencing international labor migration and to what extent is the international legal framework developed by the ILO and UN effective in protecting the rights of migrant workers, including irregular and undocumented migrants from developing countries?

Popular critiques of globalization often allege that free trade and multinational companies increase international inequality and have negative effects on working conditions and labor rights in developing countries. In this context, globalization requires a system of effective international labor standards to regulate working conditions and to counter such negative impacts. Apart from these, the international labor standards serve many purposes, such as they can be used as tools for governments to formulate and implement labor laws and labor policy in conformity with internationally accepted standards. They can also be used as tools for harmonizing national laws and practices on labor rights and to improve various administrative structures such as labor administration, inspection, and social security. Bangladesh has ratified most of the core conventions adopted by the ILO. While most of the international labor standards are legally recognized in Bangladesh through various labor laws, the implementation of these standards remains a daunting challenge due to the presence of large-scale informal economy, weak enforcement mechanisms, high prevalence of precarious work, and inadequate resource allocation for their implementation. Many existing labor law provisions need to be reformed to make them fully aligned with international standards.

The book also examines the issue of setting minimum wages and their distributive function. Since globalization is producing many unequal and unjust results, setting a minimum wage often has a potential redistributive effect. A participative process for setting minimum wage in which workers' and employers' representatives have equal bargaining power can produce an agreed minimum wage. Thus, a minimum wage that is the outcome of a consensus-oriented bargaining process between social partners, rather than being fixed top-down by the government, has redistributive effects and can fulfill the legitimate demands of workers. However, industries in Bangladesh, including the RMG sector, are typically characterized by low wages, excessive overtime, and poor working conditions. In many cases, even the legal minimum wages set for workers in the apparel industry fail to provide enough income to maintain a life with dignity.

This book also addresses the labor dispute settlement process in Bangladesh and identifies the spectrum of labor disputes that are settled by both adjudicatory and non-adjudicatory mechanisms. Then, it proceeds to examine the effectiveness of such non-adjudicatory and non-adjudicatory dispute settlement mechanisms and identifies challenges of traditional dispute settlement mechanisms to address new forms of labor disputes.

The book also focuses on social dialogue—one of the four pillars of the decent work paradigm set by the ILO. The aim of the decent work paradigm is to help ensure that tripartite dialogue occurs widely in policy-making, labor law reform, and implementation, to assist employers and workers to develop strong and representative organizations and to build their capacity to influence socio-economic policies. The 2008 ILO Declaration on Social Dialogue for a Fair Globalisation strongly reaffirms the universality of the relevance of social dialogue to the pursuit of employment and social policy objectives. The practice of well-crafted social dialogue can also promote sustainable socio-economic growth, sound industrial relations and improved productivity and decent work. In Bangladesh, social dialogue has been embodied in laws and regulations and institutionalized through the establishment of a number of bipartite and tripartite mechanisms, though its application in practice remains weak.

The Rana Plaza collapse in 2013, the deadliest industrial accident in Bangladesh, which caused the deaths of more than one thousand workers, led to a huge public outcry about workplace safety and security and warranted legal and institutional reform due to the intense pressure from the international buyers and labor organizations. The book explores the effectiveness of multi-stakeholder initiatives such as the Accord and the Alliance on safety of buildings of the RMG industry concluded after the Rana Plaza collapse. The emergence of this multilevel governance mechanism with transnational effect is described as private regulatory initiatives for ensuring the safety and security of the RMG workers. These transnational safety initiatives engaged a diverse group of actors, including foreign buyers, the ILO, and national and international unions and emerged as alternative to the traditional corporate self-regulation. This book evaluates these multi-stakeholders' initiatives as co-governance system and regulatory and institutional responses to the Rena Plaza collapse in Bangladesh.

This book also sheds light on international labor migration as an intrinsic feature of globalization, highlights the plight of temporary migrant workers, and explores international norms on migrant workers and their integration into domestic law of Bangladesh. While the causes of international labor migration are numerous and complex, tighter border control and increasingly restrictive immigration policies led to an increase in temporary, undocumented, or irregular migrant workers, who are often deprived of legal protection in host states.

In brief, this book attempts to analyze the impact of economic globalization on labor rights including trade unions, collective bargaining and minimum wage, highlights the emergence of transnational labor governance, explores the role of social dialogue in ensuring decent work, examines the distributive function of minimum wages, and emphasizes functions of international labor standards in offsetting negative impacts of globalization. This book critically investigates how far international labor standards have been integrated in the labor laws of Bangladesh, examines the issues of labor governance and labor rights in EPZs, and highlights challenges of the application of international labor standards in Bangladesh.

I am grateful to Mr. Syed Sultan Uddin Ahmed, Executive Director of the Bangladesh Institute of Labor Studies (BILS), Dhaka, for his useful comments on some chapters of this book. I am also thankful to Shushmita Ahmed, Senior Assistant Judge, and Hossain Md. Reza, Senior Assistant Judge for their support in completion of this book.

Chattogram, Bangladesh Abdullah Al Faruque

Contents

1	**Globalization and Changing Landscape of Industrial Relations in Bangladesh**		1
	1.1	*Context and Background*	1
	1.2	*Defining Industrial Relations (IR)*	3
	1.3	*The Impact of Globalization on Labor Rights in Developing Countries*	4
	1.4	*Changing Perspective of Industrial Relations in the Globalized World*	9
	1.5	*Labor Rights in Global Supply Chain*	12
	1.6	*Challenges of Integration of Due Diligence Regulations in Bangladesh*	14
	1.7	*Labor Market Scenario in Bangladesh*	18
	1.8	*Formalization of the Informal Sector*	19
	1.9	*Role of the RMG Sector*	21
	1.10	*Search for Sustainability of the RMG Sector*	23
	1.11	*Informal Workers in the Labor Market in Bangladesh*	24
	1.12	*Impact of the Coronavirus Pandemic on Labor Rights in Bangladesh*	25
	1.13	*Rana Plaza Disaster and Transnational Alliance*	27
	1.14	*Emergence of Transnational Labor Governance*	28

1.15 *Institutions, Power Relations, Competitiveness: Diverse Influences of Globalization* 32
1.16 *Conclusion* 33
Bibliography 34

2 Legal and Institutional Design of Industrial Relations in Bangladesh 43
2.1 *Introduction* 43
2.2 *Functions of Labor Law in the Age of Globalization* 44
2.3 *Evolution of Labor Law in Bangladesh* 47
2.4 *Constitutional Framework on Labor Rights* 48
2.5 *Critical Analysis of Legal Framework on Industrial Relations* 49
2.5.1 *Defining a Worker* 49
2.5.2 *Regulating Conditions of Employment* 51
2.5.3 *Social Security Measures for the Workers* 51
2.5.4 *Prohibition of Child Labor: Still a Reality* 54
2.5.5 *Health, Safety, and Welfare Measures* 56
2.5.6 *Welfare Fund and Insurance Scheme* 57
2.6 *Forgotten Domestic Workers* 58
2.7 *Rights of the Tea-Garden Workers—A Neglected Issue* 60
2.8 *The Bangladesh Labor Welfare Foundation Act 2006* 61
2.9 *The Bangladesh Labor Rules 2015* 62
2.10 *The Bangladesh Labor (Amendment) Act 2026: A Long-awaited Reform Agenda* 63
2.11 *Challenges of the Implementation of Labor Laws* 64
2.12 *Institutional Framework on Labor Relations* 64
2.13 *Compliance with Labor Laws Through Labor Inspection* 66
2.14 *Role of Employers' Organizations* 68
2.15 *Global Influences on the Design of Labor Laws in Bangladesh* 70
2.16 *Regulating the Gig Economy* 71
2.17 *Conclusion* 71
Bibliography 72

3 Economic Globalization and Export Processing Zones in Bangladesh 77

3.1 Introduction 77
3.2 Economic Globalization and EPZs 78
3.3 Significance of EPZs in the Economy of Bangladesh 81
3.4 Legal Framework of EPZs in Bangladesh 82
3.5 A Critical Assessment of Industrial Relations in EPZs 84
3.6 Conclusion 87
Bibliography 88

4 Challenges of Globalization and Regulation of Trade Unions in Bangladesh 91

4.1 Introduction 91
4.2 Changing Role of Trade Unions in the Globalized World 92
4.3 Legal Basis of Trade Union 93
4.4 Regulating Trade Unions in Bangladesh 94
4.5 Structure of Trade Unions in Bangladesh 96
4.5.1 Basic Trade Union 97
4.5.2 Industrial Federation 97
4.5.3 National Trade Union Federation 97
4.5.4 National Confederation 98
4.6 Trade Unions in the Public Sector 98
4.7 Trade Unions in the RMG Sector 98
4.8 Legal Restrictions on Trade Unions 100
4.9 Activities, Effectiveness, and Challenges of Trade Unions 100
4.10 Conclusion 104
Bibliography 105

5 Collective Bargaining in Bangladesh: Rhetoric and Reality 109

5.1 Introduction 109
5.2 Importance of Collective Bargaining 111
5.3 Impact of Globalization on Collective Bargaining 113
5.4 Preconditions for Successful Collective Bargaining 114
5.5 Law and Practice on Collective Bargaining in Bangladesh 115

5.6 *Right to Strike and the Role of Collective Bargaining* 117
5.7 *Collective Bargaining in the Export Processing Zones (EPZ)* 120
5.8 *Conclusion* 120
Bibliography 121

6 Fixing Minimum Wages: Issues and Challenges 125
6.1 *Introduction* 125
6.2 *Coverage of Minimum Wages* 127
6.3 *Process of Fixing Minimum Wages* 128
6.4 *Criteria for Fixing Minimum Wages* 129
6.5 *Distributive Justice Function of Minimum Wages* 131
6.6 *Challenges of Implementation of Minimum Wages* 132
6.7 *Setting Minimum Wages in Bangladesh* 133
6.8 *Minimum Wages in the RMG Sector* 136
6.9 *Minimum Wages for Tea-Garden Workers* 138
6.10 *Minimum Wages for EPZ Workers* 139
6.11 *Minimum Wages in Other Sectors* 139
6.12 *Exploitative Sourcing Price and Minimum Wages* 139
6.13 *Conclusion* 140
Bibliography 142

7 Labor Disputes Settlement Mechanisms: Search for Labor Justice in Bangladesh 147
7.1 *Introduction* 147
7.2 *Grievance Procedure* 148
7.3 *Bipartite Negotiation* 149
7.4 *Conciliation* 150
7.5 *Arbitration* 151
7.6 *Adjudication* 151
7.7 *Labor Appellate Tribunal* 153
7.8 *Preventive Measures for Avoiding Industrial Disputes* 154
7.9 *Dispute Settlement in Export Processing Zones* 154
7.10 *Role of ADR in Labor Dispute Settlement* 155
7.11 *Court-Sponsored ADR in Labor Dispute Settlement* 157
7.12 *Addressing Sexual Harassment in the Workplace* 158
7.13 *Internal Grievance Mechanism* 158
7.14 *Informal Mechanisms of Settlement of Labor Disputes* 159

	7.15	*Conclusion*	159
	Bibliography		160
8	**Implementation of International Labor Standards and Fair Globalization**		163
	8.1	*Introduction*	163
	8.2	*The Role of International Labor Standards for Offsetting Negative Effects of Globalization*	164
	8.3	*Labor Rights as Human Rights*	166
	8.4	*Contours of International Labor Standards*	168
	8.5	*The Universality of International Labor Standards*	175
	8.6	*Promoting Decent Work Agenda*	176
	8.7	*Process of Implementation of International Labor Standards*	178
	8.8	*Challenges of Implementation of International Labor Standards in Bangladesh*	180
	8.9	*Conclusion*	183
	Bibliography		185
9	**Practice of Social Dialogue in Industrial Relations: Evidence from Bangladesh**		191
	9.1	*Introduction*	191
	9.2	*Enabling Conditions of Social Dialogue*	193
	9.3	*Nature and Types of Social Dialogue*	194
	9.4	*The Role of Government in Social Dialogue*	195
	9.5	*Legal and Institutional Framework of Social Dialogue in Bangladesh*	196
	9.6	*Composition and Mandate of Bipartite and Tripartite Bodies*	197
	9.7	*Necessity of Social Dialogue in the RMG Sector*	201
	9.8	*The Practice of Social Dialogue in Bangladesh*	202
	9.9	*Challenges of Social Dialogue in Bangladesh*	204
	9.10	*Suggestions for Strengthening Institutional Framework*	205
	9.11	*Conclusion*	206
	Bibliography		207

10 An Evaluation of Multi-Stakeholders' Initiatives on Safety of Workers after the *Rana Plaza* Collapse 211
10.1 Introduction 211
10.2 The Accord 212
10.3 The Alliance 215
10.4 Evaluation of the Accord and the Alliance 216
10.5 Institutional Reform Initiatives 218
10.5.1 The Bangladesh Sustainability Compact 218
10.5.2 National Tripartite Action Plan on Fire Safety and Structural Integrity 219
10.5.3 Remediation Coordination Council (RCC) 220
10.5.4 RMG Sustainability Council (RSC) 221
10.6 Regulatory Reforms 221
10.7 The Rana Plaza Compensation Scheme 222
10.8 Conclusion 224
Bibliography 226

11 Protection of Migrant Workers' Rights: A Bangladesh Perspective 229
11.1 Introduction 229
11.2 Plight of Irregular Migrant Workers 231
11.3 Nexus between Irregular Migration and Human Trafficking 234
11.4 Labor Law, Migration Law, and Human Rights Framework: Complexities and Intersections 235
11.5 ILO Conventions on Rights of Migrant Workers 236
11.6 Convention on the Protection of the Rights of all Migrant Workers and Members of their Families, 1990 238
11.7 Plight of Migrant Workers of Bangladesh 239
11.8 Legal Framework on Migrant Workers in Bangladesh 243
11.9 Role of Bilateral Agreements on Labor Migration Governance 245
11.10 Conclusion 246
Bibliography 248

12 Conclusion 253

Index 261

CHAPTER 1

Globalization and Changing Landscape of Industrial Relations in Bangladesh

1.1 Context and Background

Globalization, technological changes, and the privatization process are continuously shaping the landscape of labor rights and industrial relations across many developing countries. Globalization facilitated by trade liberalization, investment protection regime, increasing interconnectedness, cross-border mobility of capital, goods, and services has led to the growth of global production networks, and the rapid transnationalization of corporate operations that have a profound impact on the state-centered labor regulatory regime and have challenged traditional industrial relations in many ways.

In fact, globalization as a process has generated multiple and opposite effects on labor rights and has created both opportunities as well as threats for actors in the labor markets. While economic globalization has created employment opportunities due to accelerated inward foreign investment and capital flight in developing countries and the expansion of the global economy, it has often led to a situation where multinational corporations exert significant influence on decision-making in areas of investment, production, employment, labor standards and industrial relations at the national level, which has created power asymmetry in global supply chains (Anner 2020). Globalization in the form of liberalized trade and investment has the potential to raise labor standards (Flanagan 2006) while it is

A. Al Faruque, *Globalization and Labour Rights*,
https://doi.org/10.1007/978-981-92-3661-9_1

often alleged that the ongoing economic globalization process has weakened domestic labor protections, labor rights and national trade union movements, which is typically explained as "the race to the bottom" situation (Stiglitz 2002). The race-to-the-bottom scenario is usually explained by the lowering of labor standards and relaxing national laws by developing countries in order to remain internationally competitive (Neumayer and Soysa 2007; Blanton and Blanton 2012). In fact, many developing countries attract foreign investment, especially in labor-intensive sectors like apparel, with promises of low labor costs and lowering labor standards with the resultant race-to-the-bottom situation, worsening labor rights, leading to poor working conditions, minimal labor rights, and diminished collective bargaining capacity. Heightened competition among developing countries for attracting foreign investment often forces them to lower labor costs and labor standards and creates scope for exerting influence of multinational corporations over domestic labor policies (Fick 2015, xiii). For example, many developing countries established and expanded export processing zones where international labor standards are hardly applied (Fick). In this way, the globalization process undermines national regulatory approaches to governing and labor relations (Bereusson and Estlund 2008, 2). Declining trends in the application of labor standards in many developing countries reflects the erosion of their power to regulate the labor market in line with such standards (Chan and Nadvi 2014, 516). The apparel sector has become the archetype of labor-intensive industry that demonstrates how globalization is influencing the application of international labor standards in Bangladesh.

During the 1980s, Bangladesh initiated steps for economic reform for moving away from command economy to a market economy and attempted to integrate into global economy by adopting the neoliberal model of liberalization, and privatization. Bangladesh embraced economic globalization and has been pursuing a liberal economic and trade policy since 1990s, when it joined the WTO for integration into global economy. The trade and economy of Bangladesh since then have undergone major structural transformation due to the economic globalization process that has also impacted its industrial relations and labor market. Following such an accelerated process of economic globalization, there has been a shift in the country's economic activity from agriculture to export-oriented industries and it has witnessed transformational changes in the labor market. Bangladesh adopted an export-led growth strategy to be spearheaded by the private sector replacing the earlier public sector dominated import substitution strategy.

One of the important consequences of economic globalization based on a neoliberal economic system is the large-scale privatization, which results in reduction in the demand for labor and consequent increase in unemployment. Bangladesh started privatization as a part of its economic liberalization policy, which resulted in economic growth but at the same time, it caused significant worker layoffs, retrenchment, and unemployment. Similarly, the process of technological change requires more and more skilled workers, with a consequent fall in the demand for less skilled workers, which can lead to unemployment and a huge pay gap between skilled and low-skilled workers (Chan and Nadvi 2014). In recent times, technological changes have necessitated skill upgrading of a large number of workers in apparel and other sectors to remain competitive and increased job insecurity and income inequality.

The emergence of the global supply chain is another manifestation of the economic globalization process and it has generated new actors, such as production- and consumption-based actors, who are shaping global labor governance. In this way, globalization also poses challenges to national regulation of the supply chain where many goods are manufactured in different countries and marketed globally by multinational corporations, who are not amenable to national jurisdiction. As a result, in the global supply chain, employers are hardly bound by the international labor standards applicable to production. Rather, labor standards of different countries may be applicable in such situations. In this way, globalization tends both to undermine international labor standards and to weaken the control of national authorities on market activity (Bereusson and Estlund 2008).

1.2 Defining Industrial Relations (IR)

IR usually refers to relationships between labor and employer that grow out of employment. It is the outcome of the process of power and control in workplace relations, and interaction between different industrial institutions, actors, and a product of the broader socio-economic structure in a country. IR is also concerned with the determination of wages, collective bargaining, safety of the workplace, dispute settlement, and conditions of employment. Harmonious relationships in the industrial sector are essential for both employers and employees to safeguard their mutual and collective interests, economic development, and the overall welfare of workers (Arumugam and Balasundaram 2010). But IR is generally characterized by a hierarchical relationship between employers and workers where, according to Kahn-Freuds, "the individual worker is subordinated to the power of management, but that power of management is coordinated with that of organized labor" (Kahn-Freuds 1983, 22). Sound industrial relations necessitate peaceful relations between labor and management where both parties can realize their mutual obligations toward each other. But industrial relations are increasingly becoming complex as many actors are becoming involved in the process of forming such relationships. In modern times, industrial relations are seen as an intricate mixture of many influences: interaction between labor and management, the informal understanding that develops between different groups, and the formal agreements between different actors (Benson 1988, 3).

Kaufman argues that the emergence of industrial relations is shaped by both negative and positive impulses (Kaufman 2004, 1–2). According to Kaufman, in its negative impulses, industrial relation evolved in order to address "human suffering" and "social injustice" caused by unrestrained profit-making of employers in the nineteenth century and the early twentieth century (Kaufman 2004, 1–2) while in its positive aspect, industrial relations is a response to the demand of improving the conditions of work and the relations between employer and worker through a combination of legal and institutional reform, education and training, institutions building, and a set of ethical standards and social responsibility (Kaufman 2004, 1–2). In fact, both impulses are continuously shaping industrial relations in modern times.

1.3 The Impact of Globalization on Labor Rights in Developing Countries

The globalization process accompanied by trade and investment liberalization, technological advancement has become a significant feature of the world economy, transforming the landscape of labor rights and industrial relations and integrating labor markets by increasing mobility of workers across borders. Growing importance of the WTO in promoting rule-based trade system and financial institutions like the World Bank and IMF in the global economic policies, and expansion of multinational corporations have reconfigured the traditional state-centric notion of the international order and emerged as pivotal actors in global economy. These factors, coupled with delocalization of production to developing countries in manufacturing sector, allowed multinational corporations to access skilled labor fostered the international division of labor. On the other hand, mobilization of labor across border reflects employment opportunity for surplus labor in developing economies. The question of whether economic globalization deteriorates or improves labor rights in developing countries has drawn sharp attention and generated many scholarly debates. Although it is well-established that globalization affects labor rights and industrial relations, level of such impact may vary from country to country depending upon its state of industrialization, general level of technology adoption, the current state of labor market, and the current state of education or human capital development (Hahn and Narjoko 2012, viii).

Various studies and research findings provide evidence that economic globalization has produced both positive and negative impacts on labor rights. According to an ILO study, some of the positive benefits of globalization include the reduction of extreme poverty, the development of social protection systems, the increased presence of women in the labor market, and the creation of job opportunities in the private sector, which have resulted in improved labor rights (ILO 2019a, 9). It also has many negative effects; for example, the globalized economy has resulted in precarious working conditions for migrant workers, major social upheavals leading to high unemployment in some parts of the world, financial instability, and violation of labor rights in the global supply chain (ILO 2019a). Foreign direct investment, a key driver of economic globalization, may create more employment opportunities in developing countries. However, FDI increases wage inequality as the capital-intensive production in foreign-owned firms generates greater demand for skills, pushing relative wages up for higher skilled workers, and reducing demand for less skilled worker (Do et al. 2024; Figini and Görg 2006).The income inequality between skilled and unskilled workers also tends to widen in firms that upgrade technology with the increase of demand for skilled workers (Hahn and Narjoko 2012, vii). Such gap could be further widened if all firms do not respond to the liberalizations by upgrading their technology capability (Hahn and Narjoko 2012, vii).

Globalization is also affecting national labor governance mechanisms, such as trade unions and collective bargaining, as the last decades witnessed declining in unionization and a weakening of bargaining capacity of workers. On the other hand, transnational trade unionism has emerged as a crucial element of labor governance facilitated by increased connectivity and networking of global trade unions. Globalization has also contributed to changes in the nature of the labor force, caused erosion of the standard employment relationship, and increased fragmentation of the workforce (Bereusson and Estlund 2008, 5). The international financial institutions, such as the World Bank and International Monetary Fund, also foster global economic integration and provide loans and development funding with political conditionalities constraining policy autonomy of developing countries (Blanton et al. 2015). The international financial institutions have been criticized for their policy reform prescription by labor rights advocacy networks claiming that the intrusive nature of such conditionalities attached to loans, which often mandate sweeping macroeconomic policy changes within recipient countries may harm workers' rights. Their policy prescriptions embodying the neoliberal norms may negatively affect labor rights, including freedom of joining trade union and collective bargaining.

Over the last few decades, globalization has also increased the degradation and objectification of workers in apparel and manufacturing industries in the Global South, despite the increasing number of international instruments adopted for expanding international labor standards. Labor rights in many developing countries have continued to decline, represented by widespread privatizations and exploitation of employees (Bereusson and Estlund 2008). It has been argued that in an increasingly globalized world, the employment relationship is changing, which tends to undermine the role of national trade unions (Hartzén 2018). According to the 2026 Global Rights Index report of the International Trade Union Confederation (ITUC)—the largest trade union organization—violation of workers' rights has increased as 72 percent of 151 countries surveyed denied workers' access to justice, and the right to strike was violated in 87 percent of countries. Globalization is also sometimes blamed for the increase of poverty and inequalities in many parts of the world, rising insecurities of workers, and "the growing power of capital" at the expense of labor (Keune and Schmidt 2009). Negative impact of globalization has led to instability in labor market, rising precariousness of working conditions and growing informalization of employment relations that limit collective representation (Keune and Schmidt 2009). It is also often contended that compliance with the higher level of labor standards raises the costs of labor, rendering the country less competitive and eventually less attractive to foreign investors This view is sometime contested as some experts found that countries with higher labor standards attract more foreign investment and the countries that are more open to foreign investment and trade have experienced fewer violations of labor rights than the closed ones (Neumayer and Soysa 2005). Some scholars argue that there is no clear-cut positive or negative co-relationship between globalization and higher labor standards as the effect of labor rights on foreign direct investment can depend on various factors, for example, the labor-intensity or skills-intensity of production of different industries (Kucera and Sari 2022, 29). In fact, neither proposition is supported by empirical evidence.

In order to attract foreign investment, many developing countries have created special industrial zones such as EPZs, which are often either under-regulated or difficult to regulate. Working conditions in EPZs are typically characterized by temporary contracts, subcontracting, long working hours, unrealistic production quotas, incentives, and low wages. Bangladesh is also not an exception to this trend, as EPZs are operating outside of the general labor law framework and many labor standards are not applicable there. A massive influx of women into low-wage industrial production process in Bangladesh like many other developing countries has become an essential part of the industrial relations. Profound rural poverty, the desire for economic independence, the perceived cheapness of women workers, and lack of ability to negotiate terms and conditions of employment explain such demand for their labor (Smith 2014).

On the other hand, globalization with its attendant social connectivity also has some positive aspects. It has been claimed that globalization has spurred transnational cooperation between national trade unions, which has resulted in a number of campaigns on improving labor standards and working conditions, including non-traditional issues such as protection of the environment, promotion of fair trade or social compliance (Smith 2014). Such transnational cooperation has also popularized the concept of the global justice movement. It has been claimed that foreign direct investment in least developed countries can raise the productivity of workers and their wages through transferring technology, management skills, and capital to these countries (Dadush and Shaw 2012). The proponents of globalization are optimistic and argue that globalization has expanded the world's production, wealth, income, and employment, which have increased the aggregate well-being of the people around the world. Globalization also provides new avenues for workers and unions to organize themselves transnationally to realize their demands and to create a fairer world order, where labor rights will be protected. It has been argued that globalization may exert important competitive pressure on labor standards in developing countries to improve labor standards (Banks 2006, 78) and the increased opening of countries to free market economies is likely to reduce violations of labor rights rather than to enhance them (Neumayer and Soysa 2005). Some experts claim that access to cheap labor is not the sole consideration that shapes corporate investment decisions. In investment decision-making, MNCs also consider a host of issues including the location of production that is close to markets, and stable political environment in host countries for investment (Aguirre Jr. and Ellen Reese 2004, 13). Deregulation of the labor market is also sometimes promoted by developing countries to attract FDI (Zandvliet 2022). In fact, lowering labor standards and labor rights can act as a barrier sometimes to attracting foreign investment (Rodrik 1996, 35). A plausible explanation for this is that the costs of high labor standards are often offset by positive externalities that help create a conducive climate for trade or investment (Kucera 2002, 63; Deakin 2011, 73–74). For example, it is argued that allowing the right to freedom of association and collective bargaining contributes to the political and social stability of a country, and the abolition of child labor and ensuring occupational safety enhances a country's human capital (Kucera 2002, 37). Such a trend is reflected in some trade agreements. For example, the EU-Canada Comprehensive Economic and Trade Agreement (CETA) states that a state party shall not waive or otherwise derogate from its labor law and standards to encourage trade or investment in its territory (Art 23.4.2 CETA). Sachs and Warner argue that globalization is about more than just market integration and it also leads countries to harmonize institutional and other regulatory arrangements (Sachs and Warner 1995, 1). This assertion also holds true for the harmonization of labor standards that is facilitated by trade and investment agreements as increasing number of these agreements incorporate provisions for enforcement of labor standards as a preconditions for free trade and attracting investment. Economic globalization might improve labor rights conditions when increased economic openness is regulated by enforceable measures, such as trade and investment agreements that integrate core labor standards, environmental obligations, and human rights norms (Peksen and Pollock

2021, 280). Conversely, it is posited that an unregulated economic globalization driven solely by market forces and competitive advantage is like to have negative impact on labor rights conditions (Peksen and Pollock 2021, 280). Thus, economic globalization in general is not inherently negatively or positively associated with labor rights.

1.4 Changing Perspective of Industrial Relations in the Globalized World

Due to the globalization process accompanied by delocalization and international migrations, the labor market and the organization of work have undergone a profound transformation over the last few decades. This has been reflected in the unification of the global labor market like the integration of the global economy. The idea of the labor market implies interactions of workers and employers, demand and supply of labor, the presence of the institution of wage labor, and the contract of employment (Deakin and Wilkison 2005, 1). The impact of globalization on industrial relations and labor market can be conceptualized in many ways: flexibilization of employment relationships where firms can increase or decrease their workforce has raised widespread concerns regarding employment protection, social rights, training opportunities, and income inequality. Technological changes and innovation have a dramatic impact on the labor market as many traditional jobs have disappeared and new forms of employment have been created. Most of these new forms of employment are part-time and contractual. These part-time and contractual workers neither have a fixed workplace like an office nor are they covered by labor laws or other legal instruments. Technological change has also precipitated the rise of digital labor platforms and flexible forms of employment contracts such as online freelancing, outsourcing, ride-sharing, and delivery services of what is known as the gig economy. While this gig economy in the form of digital labor platforms has transformed traditional work structures, it has also raised concerns about fair wages, employment rights, and social security. An increasing number of workers are now part of this gig economy around the world facilitated by easy access to the internet and digital technologies. The workers engaged in the gig economy are usually the unprotected workforce and have no fixed wage or salary. However, work patterns in the gig economy vary significantly across countries, depending on internet access, regulatory frameworks, economic factors, and level of skills specialization (ILO 2025).

As a result of technological change, the demand for unskilled labor has been reduced and consequently, the traditional nature of "work" has undergone fundamental changes in most developing economies, which were unable to adapt to the new technologies. On the other hand, demand for skilled labor has increased. The emergence of artificial intelligence (AI) is perhaps, the most dramatic aspect of this change as it is rapidly impacting and reshaping the job market globally and is creating new work opportunities while replacing some old ones with automation. The AI-led automation will require workers to continuously upskill and adapt to automation and demand for new skills (ILO 2025).

Flexibilization of employment relationships can lead to substandard and exploitative working relations, which are characterized by acceptance of longer working hours and substandard conditions by the workers who work outside of the legal requirements vis-à-vis benefits. This remains a significant aspect of migrant and female workers in many developing countries (Yimprasert and Petter Hveem 2005, 33). Sub-contracting and outsourcing have emerged as significant trends and symbols of the new forms of employment and a massive source of employment for migrant workers, and have played a leading role in the transformation of production, in the organization of global commodity chains, and in lowering the costs of production (Perocco 2018, 9). Secondly, casualization or informalization of the labor market, usually manifested in the transition from formal to informal employment relationships, has contributed to the growth of informal employment in the last couple of decades. The casualization of the labor market tends to exploit workers by maximizing profits through combining flexible forms of employment and production.

The trend of informalization of workers is the most significant one that is defining the changing landscape of the labor market in the globalized world. Informal employment is the informality of a job that is determined by the particular category of the worker's status in employment (Fudge 2012, 10). Incomes are generally much lower in the informal economy than the formal economy. There has been a significant increase of the engagement of workers in informal sectors in many parts of the world. A significant number of workers in the informal sector are either self-employed or contractually employed. Informal economies include small and micro-enterprises (MSEs). Self-employed workers, who are engaged in small or unregistered enterprises, are generally independent. Informal workers include dependent workers—paid or unpaid, contract labor, apprentices, homeworkers, and paid domestic workers (Kaufmann 2007, 5). Usually, women make up a larger part of the informal labor force compared to that in the formal sector.

Workers in the informal sectors are usually outside government regulation and the formal system of labor and social protection. Informal sectors are characterized by a lack of protection, rights, and representation. In informal sectors, lower incomes, low productivity, less job security, exclusion from social benefits, and lack of opportunities to participate in formal education and training programs have remained defining features of informal sectors and these, in turn, deprive them of decent work opportunities. Due to a lack of regulation, the informal sector sometimes turns into an exploitative one. They frequently face a precarious working environment. Informal sector is precipitated by increased competitiveness, together with technological innovation that has led to fragmentation and relocation of the production process and to deregulation of labor markets (Kaufmann 2007, 4). Moreover, the transformations in the nature of work, changing organizational forms, the introduction of new technologies and the integration of export-oriented sectors of the economy into global value chains have also contributed to the increase of the informal sector (ILO 2019b, 35–36). Typically, they are not covered by collective bargaining agreements. In general, informal workers experience lower wages, long working hours, and less favorable working conditions than their counterparts in formal employment (ILO 2019b). Informal employment is also intrinsically linked to the inferior status of workers (ILO 2019b) as informal workers generally have no power to negotiate pay and service conditions. On the other hand, there are some other negative consequences of the high informality such as widening inequality, and low labor productivity (Dallakoti 2024).

Informal sectors thrive in many developing countries with a large labor force but with a high rate of unemployment, poverty, and limited opportunity to be absorbed in the formal sector. In such circumstances, the informal sector is a significant source of employment generation because of the low requirements for education, skills, technology, capital, and relative ease of entry. However, such informal sectors hardly meet the criteria of decent work.

Many types of informal work are typically irregular and seasonal in nature. In the hiring practices of informal workers, employers are unaccountable to the law or employees. Furthermore, informal workers can hardly afford with low wages to acquire generic skills that can be used to be employed in the formal sector (Bacchetta et al. 2009). The informal economy of a country also harbors most child labor. Scholars argue that investments in human capital, training, and active labor market policy would be a response to the labor market challenges of globalization, technological change, flexibilization, and informality (Vliet et al. 2021).

1.5 Labor Rights in Global Supply Chain

Globalization has also led to the growth of global supply chain (GSC). Global supply chains explain the fragmentation of production across multiple economies and firms. The study of GSC is a valuable tool to understand the impact of economic globalization on labor standards as it explains some of the dynamics of contemporary global capitalism. GSC remains an important avenue through which multinational corporation of developed states "extract products" from low-wage workers by migrating their production processes to developing countries (Smith 2014). The GSC approach has been described as "trans-border value creation and distribution" in the production and commercialization process (Parrilli et al. 2013, 973) that reflects the growing diversification of production sources across the world. This diversification of global production networks, which are usually facilitated by multinational lead firms, aims to reduce production costs and to improve profit margins (Vadlamannati 2015, 7). This mobility of production base and processes in order to reduce cost constitutes the central dynamic of the global supply chain. In this process, many big firms employ their third-party contractors in low-wage countries that, in turn, lower the labor standards and rights of their employees that create power imbalance between employers and workers (Bulut and Lane 2011, 42). In the GSC, global brands and retailers exert more control over production networks and supply chains than local manufacturers (Bulut and Lane 2011) and lead firms subcontract production to independent suppliers that are mostly located in developing countries. In GSC, thus, multiple contracts involving both buyer and supplier firms are operational to implement multiple private governance standards, that leads to fragmentation of labor governance (Reinecke and

Donaghey 2023, 155) in geographically dispersed areas. In this fragmented operation of GSC, workers are mainly organized at the national level and they can hardly exercise any influence on the international flow of capital (Keune and Schmidt 2009, 14–15). In such situations, MNEs can gain an advantage from poor labor standards in host countries while evading liability (Prentice 2021, 5).

One of the manifest consequences of such a fragmented production process or GSC is reflected in the apparel or garment industry as firms in industrialized countries have shifted manufacturing of this industry to developing countries to access lower-waged labor (Edwards, Hunt and LeBaron 2019, 7). Anner contends that the apparel industry, thus, epitomizes this global supply chain, characterized as a "buyer-driven sourcing squeeze", has pushed prices down, shortened lead times, and contributed to low wages, health and safety concerns, and violations of freedom of association rights (Anner 2018). Supply chains in the garment industry are often described as the "archetypal buyer-led supply chains" or "global labor arbitrage", which refers to the intense competition among MNCs to accrue sizable profit through monopolistic control over the global labor market, that reinforces and seeks to profit from countries' "comparative advantage" of low wages and minimal labor rights. These long and complex supply chains comprise multiple firms which often spread across several countries (Edwards et al. 2019). Such complexity of the global supply chain is explained by the fact that multinational corporations control the highest value-added parts of the supply chain, without having direct ownership of manufacturing and without incurring legal liability for non-compliance with labor standards by outsourcing production to suppliers (Edwards et al. 2019). On the other hand, many developing countries' participation in global value chains remains narrow and concentrated in low-value segments. For example, while Bangladesh is deeply embedded in the global apparel chain but largely in its lowest-value stages; that is, cutting, making, trimming, and shipping, much of the value—in fiber development, design, branding, logistics, and retail intelligence—is created elsewhere (Selim 2026). Despite that Bangladesh participates in the global value chain, it does not yet exercise much influence over how the chain is organized (Selim 2026).

GSCs have facilitated many countries to industrialize by integrating into global production networks, attracting investment, technology, and export opportunities. GSCs have many benefits as they create employment opportunities, and help to alleviate poverty (Dijk and Trienekens

2012, 10). But they are not inherently inclusive, and their developmental impact relies on whether participation is accompanied by upgrading, knowledge diffusion, and broad-based domestic value capture (ADB 2026, 80). While GVCs can generate substantial employment and raise wage, they can create uneven outcomes that favor skilled, urban workers while leaving women and low-skilled workers concentrated in lower-paid, less protected, or informal roles (ADB 2026, 80). GSCs are also associated negatively with labor rights such as freedom of association and collective bargaining as globalized production networks reduce workers' bargaining power by putting downward pressure on wages and working conditions (ILO 2019a, 7 and Kuruvilla and Li 2021) and may generate new forms of poverty of workers (Selwyn 2018).

GSCs pose a particular challenge to traditional forms of labor regulations (Reinecke and Donaghey 2015, 721) as firms have to engage with multiple, overlapping, and often conflicting local, national, regional, and transnational legal regimes, soft-law normative orders, and private ordering mechanisms (The IGLP Law and Global Production Working Group 2016). GSC also contributes to the complexity of labor laws, and state institutional systems often face difficulty in monitoring and enforcing laws against firms involved in GSC (Akorsu 2018, 170).

1.6 Challenges of Integration of Due Diligence Regulations in Bangladesh

The concept of human rights due diligence (HRDD), an element of the broader notion of corporate responsibility, has emerged as a powerful tool to protect and respect human rights in business operations. The HRDD, grounded in the UN Guiding Principles on Business and Human Rights 2011, requires business enterprises to "identify, prevent, mitigate and address" potential and actual impacts on human rights caused by activities of business entities or such impacts are "directly linked to their operations, products or services by their business relationships" (UN General Assembly Resolution, A/73/163, 16 July 2018). It also mandates the integration of social and human rights impact assessment in their operation, and communicating with stakeholders on how impacts are being addressed (UN General Assembly Resolution, A/73/163, 16 July 2018). Most multinational enterprises are part of a global supply chain, either directly or indirectly, through their operations and they are invariably exposed to the risk of human rights violations and environmental pollution throughout their supply-chain operations. A number of risks in which business enterprises may be involved in their supply chain include child labor, forced labor, discrimination against women, migrant workers, and lack of fair wages. In global supply chains where transnational or multinational enterprises rely on contractors and suppliers in developing countries to produce and transport their products, may obscure employment relations in a way that increases the chances of consumers and companies being implicated in modern slavery practices like forced labor, debt bondage, child labor, and exploitation of workers. In fact, the necessity for prevention of the risk of modern slavery in the global supply chain prompted for adoption of human rights due diligence guidelines by the UN and the ILO, and laws and regulations by some developed countries and the European Union. For example, the ILO adopted a resolution concerning "decent work in global supply chains" (ILO 2016). While the resolution highlights many positive contribution of global supply chains in economic growth, job creation, and poverty reduction, also acknowledges weaknesses of GSCs that have caused deficits in decent working conditions such as in the areas of occupational health and safety, wages and labor rights. According to the Resolution, informality, child labor, forced labor, precarious working conditions, and the use of intermediaries are common in some GSCs (ILO 2016). The HRDD, ILO resolution, and national laws on HRDD require companies to adhere to human rights and environmental standards in their own operations and their global value chains. However, the UNGPs and the ILO resolution and corporate initiatives are voluntary in nature. It is against this background that several developed countries have enacted specific legislation to integrate HRDD into their national legal framework which requires corporations to comply with it in their sphere of operation. For example, the Modern Slavery Act 2015 of the UK aims to prevent forced labor and trafficking in the supply chains. The French Corporate Duty of Vigilance Law of 2017 requires French business enterprises to be "vigilant in order to prevent environmental and human rights harm caused by their subsidiaries and through their business relationships" (The French Vigilance Law of 2017). The Modern Slavery Act 2018 of Australia requires companies to report on how they manage modern slavery risks in their own operations and supply chains. *Germany's the Supply Chain Due Diligence Act 2023 requires large* companies, whether they are headquartered in Germany or have a branch there, to carry out HRDD in the supply chain to prevent "forced labor, child labor, environmental pollution and unsafe working conditions". Such legal developments also ask for meaningful disclosure of information and greater transparency relating to their operations. These national public regulatory initiatives are largely influenced by the UN Guiding Principles on Human Rights Due Diligence and effectively supplement the voluntary initiatives of the multinational enterprises on corporate social responsibility.

The EU Directive on Corporate Sustainability Due Diligence (CSDD) 2024 is seen as a groundbreaking and level playing field regulation that requires large companies operating in the EU to identify adverse human rights and environmental impacts throughout their global value chains and to "adhere to human rights and environmental standards in their own operations and their global value chains". The EU Directive is applicable to any EU-based company that has more than 1000 employees on average and an annual global turnover of more than 450 million euros. The EU CSDD aims to increase transparency and accountability across global supply chains by ensuring the application of such standards by the companies that manufacture their products in countries like Bangladesh. With the EU CSDD and other national diligence laws, the guidelines and standards for responsible business will no longer be voluntary for many companies, particularly those in the EU. The Directive has introduced sanctions for its non-compliance by companies, which include civil liability and fines. The EU Directive also asks brands to "meaningfully engage" with stakeholders, workers, and communities, to adopt their due diligence measures. The EU Sustainability Regulations are another dimension of growing corporate accountability mechanism by seeking sustainable corporate practices through increasing transparency in corporate sustainability reporting and integrating sustainability metrics within business operations. The EU Sustainability Regulations mainly include the **Corporate Sustainability Reporting Directive** (CSRD), which requires companies to disclose their environmental, social, and governance (ESG) impacts and risks and the **European Sustainability Reporting Standards** (ESRS) mandate companies to report on the impact of their operations on people, the environment, and how sustainability issues affect their financial performance.

Many national legislation and the EU CSDD and the EU Sustainability Regulations will apply to Bangladesh's RMG factories being part of the value chain of global brands and retailers. These rules significantly impact developing countries by requiring manufacturing industries in Bangladesh to comply with enhanced transparency standards to maintain access to the EU market.

The EU CSDD is particularly important for Bangladesh as it requires all member countries of the EU to regulate the human rights and environmental aspects of thousands of large corporations across various sectors, including those manufacturing their products from developing countries (Kashyap 2024). Global brands and retailers that will be affected by the EU Directive must review their due diligence efforts and incorporate measures for improving their compliance with human rights and environmental standards. These initiatives will demand that global brands identify and prevent environmental and human rights risks across their supply chain, and consequently, they will restrict the import of products into the EU and home countries of brands in order to prevent profiting from a race to the bottom in labor standards. The implementation of these initiatives will require EU companies to ensure transparency, monitor the effectiveness of their efforts, and embed responsible business practices into their operations. The implementation of the Directive will also require host countries like Bangladesh to initiate reform of labor laws and laws governing special economic zones in order to bring manufacturing factories of RMG and textile in line with international human rights, labor rights, and environmental standards.

As a whole, the process of HRDD needs to be institutionalized in the RMG sector of Bangladesh. This requires ensuring compliance with the national laws, EU CSDD, EU Sustainability Regulations, which will necessitate the infrastructure and resources to implement and awareness building and understanding about these regulations by factory owners. It will involve the RMG factory owners bearing increased administrative, operational, and monitoring costs to comply with these EU standards on HRDD. The Human Rights policy commitments of the RMG factories should be aligned with the national laws, the EU Directive and the UNGPs for the integration of HRDD. The RMG factories will increasingly be subject to scrutiny to address the problems of delayed or non-payment of wages, forced labor, child labor, and environmental pollution. However, it is believed that compliance with due diligence regulations will facilitate to improve social and environmental conditions of the RMG sector and establish a fair value chain. Bangladesh's RMG sector and other export-oriented industries must adapt to this global shift, actively participate in sustainability initiatives, and engage in dialogue to remain competitive in the global market. In order to comply with the

EU Directive and other diligence regulations, factories in Bangladesh must review their entire supply chain and identify risks, strengthen their internal system to align with these standards, adopt environmentally friendly production methods, and eliminate forced labor. The government of Bangladesh also has a crucial role to play in ensuring compliance with these regulations through strengthening labor and environmental laws.

1.7 Labor Market Scenario in Bangladesh

Labor market scenario depends on perceptions and norms of social justice of a country and is intrinsically linked to each country's social and political history. Bangladesh is not an exception in this regard. Bangladesh has the advantage of a huge and cheap labor force. Bangladesh has a high degree of informal employment, which accounts for 80 percent of total employment. According to the Bangladesh Bureau of Statistics' Labor Force Survey 2022, 84.9 percent of employed people are engaged in the informal sector, where workers do not enjoy labor rights including the minimum wages, fixed working hours, paid leave, and occupational safety. Technological change, the globalization of economic relations, and the entry of women into the labor force in very large numbers have shaped the labor market and changing industrial relations in Bangladesh over the last few decades. Feminization of the workforce, another significant trend of globalization, is also evident in Bangladesh. During the 1990s, the participation of the female labor force increased significantly in the labor market, in particular, in the RMG sector and this largely unorganized female labor force had migrated from the agricultural sector. A race to the bottom has been perpetuated by using the abundant supply of female labor force from rural areas for employment in the RMG sector, where women are willing to work under exploitative conditions.

On the other hand, suppression of movement for minimum wages, disregard of occupational safety and political instability contributed to uneasy and confrontational relations between labor and management across all sectors of the economy in Bangladesh that characterized the industrial relations over the last decades. These factors also led to a "vicious cycle of low pay, low skill and low productivity" (Raihan 2022). Precarious working conditions, high rates of rural–urban migration of labor force with a significant concentration of migrant workers in urban informal service sectors, and migration of low-skilled labor abroad are other significant features of the labor market in Bangladesh (Raihan 2022). Informalization of the formal sector is another trend in labor market in Bangladesh. Many workers who used to work in the formal sector have been informalized because of failure of employers to issue appointment letters and hiring casual workers for filling up of permanent posts of workers. Widespread prevalence of outsourcing and contractual employment has also contributed to informalization of workers.

It must be acknowledged that Bangladesh has made significant economic progress and witnessed a steady growth in industrial sectors over the last decades. As a result, the average share of the agriculture sector in total employment has gradually declined with the increase of the share of the service and the industry sector that led to the transformation of the labor market in Bangladesh. Among the industrial sectors, the Ready-made Garment (RMG) sector has emerged as the largest industrial sector both in terms of the number of people it employs and the contribution it makes to the national export earnings. The RMG sector is the largest formal sector in Bangladesh, which currently employs more than 4.0 million workers, about 45 percent of total formal sector employment. The RMG is a mainly export-oriented industry. There are other sectors such as construction, leather, pharmaceutical, or inland water transport employing a sizable number of workers with an important contribution to the national economy.

In recent years, the labor market of Bangladesh has witnessed a significant rise in the gig economy with the increasing use of digital platforms. In Bangladesh, the gig economy is driven by sectors such as ride-sharing, freelancing, food delivery, and e-commerce as many people are now engaged in these sectors to earn a living. While the gig economy offers autonomy and flexibility in employment relations, it also raises concerns about job security, social benefits, and labor rights as the workforce in this economy is yet to be recognized by the legal framework.

1.8 Formalization of the Informal Sector

The necessity of formalization of informal sectors is emphasized by the fact that an informal labor market usually worsens workers' rights, social protection, working conditions, and hinders inclusive economic growth and development. The persistence of informality also reduces public revenues and exacerbates inequality and poverty. Formalization of the informal sector is seen as a pivotal for ensuring decent working conditions, improving labor rights and standards, and increasing social protection. However, there are no universal criteria for the formalization of the informal sector. It requires specific attention to a state's level of economic development, the importance of the economic sector, and attention to other context-specific issues. There are two dominant theoretical lens of viewing formalization of informality: capital view and labor view. Capital considers inclusion of enterprises in the formal tax and financial systems; and labor view considers inclusion of workers in the social protection system. While capital view is merely concerned with inclusion of enterprises in formal accountable and traceable systems through incorporating them in tax or licensing system, labor view has wider implications of redistribution, tackling poverty, inequality, and vulnerability (Unni 2018).

The ILO adopted a specific recommendation on "Transition from the Informal to Formal Economy" (No. 204) in 2015 that provides guidelines for transitioning from the informal to the formal sector. Article 5 of the Recommendation defines the term "informal economy" as: "all economic activities by workers and economic units that are-in law or in practice-not covered or insufficiently covered by formal arrangements; and does not cover illicit activities...". It focuses on creating decent jobs in the formal economy, transitioning workers and enterprises from the informal to the formal economy, and preventing the informalization of formal jobs (ILO 2015). The ILO Recommendation 204 on "Transition from the Informal to the Formal Economy" has broadly included both the capital and labor views of formalization.

Apart from registration and licensing, formalization can also occur through legal recognition of workers. Such legal recognition can be done through their incorporation in laws or regulations, or even by issuing appointment letters through which they can seek legal protection. Formalization of the informal sector through legal recognition is vital for a country to achieve economic diversification and modernization of the private sector and to become competitive globally. Formalization is often accompanied by a long struggle of workers for legal recognition and protection of their rights.

In Bangladesh, the prevalence of large-scale informality poses significant challenges to achieving sustainable economic growth, social equity, and the promotion of decent work. The growing rate of informality brings many negative consequences, including a low-tax to-GDP ratio, widening inequality, stagnant industrial competitiveness in sectors other than the RMG and low labor productivity (Dallakoti 2024). It also hinders the potential of the industrial sector to participate and benefit from growing global GSC and export market opportunities (Dallakoti 2024). However, the process of formalization of informal sector is currently limited in Bangladesh due to the ineffectiveness of public services like registration, licensing and tax processing of businesses, lack of clear incentives to formalize, limited understanding of the process of formalization, and limited employment opportunities (Dallakoti 2024). Formalization of the informal sectors is imperative for Bangladesh to achieve the goal of economic diversification and modernization of the private sector to become competitive globally. Formalization of informal sector requires an integrated effort from the government, the private sector, and workers' organizations (Dallakoti 2024).

In Bangladesh, there is a discernible trend of formalization of some informal sectors through legal recognition for providing social protection to workers. Over the few last decades, many informal sectors like the ship-breaking industries and the shrimp industry, which were previously outside the scope of labor laws, have gradually been included in the formal sector through their recognition by the Bangladesh Labor Act 2006. This formalization process takes place through legal recognition of informal workers with social benefits and protection measures. The National Industrial Policy of Bangladesh 2022 recognizes the contribution of the informal sector in the economic growth and underscores the necessity of registration of entrepreneurs in informal sector and providing incentives to this sector. However, this policy framework does not adequately address the "labor view" of formalization adopted by the ILO Recommendation.

1.9 Role of the RMG Sector

The RMG sector has remained the leading employment sector in Bangladesh since the early 1990s. Bangladesh's recent economic growth is rooted in its success in export earnings from the RMG industry. It also crucially contributes to job opportunities. The RMG sector has also created indirect employment through backward linkage industries from the knitwear sector and other associated industries and service providers who are substantially dependent upon the RMG sector. There is no denying the fact that Bangladesh enjoys a comparative advantage in this industry because of low-cost labor and preferential market access.

Bangladesh occupies the second position in the export of apparel products in the global market. While retaining its second position globally, Bangladesh's share in global apparel trade is growing. It exemplifies the global supply-chain model where the lack of regulation and exploitation of labor is pervasive. However, the RMG sector workers face intense pressure to meet very high and rising productivity targets, shorter delivery times, at the lowest possible price with poor working conditions. Thus, while the RMG sector has been perceived as a route to economic development progress, it is also exploitative for workers as insecure contracts, low wages, excessive working hours, and few benefits are rampant in this sector that epitomizes this sector as "race to bottom". Workers in the RMG sectors receive minimum wages that are grossly insufficient to meet the living costs that compel them to undertake large amounts of overtime, work long working hours and endure precarious working conditions. All these make Bangladesh an example of "the hypercompetitive market dynamic of globalized, industrial capitalism" (Reinecke and Donaghey 2023, 160) where capitalist exploitation of workers is facilitated through competition for inward investment by offering cheap labor and lax regulation to keep prices low. These conditions are driven by the competitive pressures of the global buyers who demand lower prices and higher quality.

Undoubtedly, the RMG sector witnessed a phenomenal growth in the few last decades. Women make up the vast majority of the RMG workforce. More than 3 million women are currently employed in this sector. The RMG sector has had a number of beneficial effects on women workers in Bangladesh, such as access to income, support of families in rural areas through remittances, and increased household status, which resulted in empowering them, increasing their mobility and expanding their individual choice. Since most of the women workers, who were previously engaged in agricultural and household work, migrated from rural areas, employment in the RMG sector has provided them with an opportunity to enter the formal sector that has had profound implications for their economic and social empowerment (Uddin 2024). The RMG employs mostly female workers as more than 80 percent of the garment sector's total employees were females and most of them migrated from rural areas. However, the ratio of female workers in the RMG sector is declining in the recent time due to automation, lower wages, and opportunities in other sectors and many women are more interested in going to school or pursuing higher education (Mirdha 2024).

Like other countries, the labor market of Bangladesh is vulnerable to both external events such as global recession caused by the pandemic or the Ukraine-Russia war and internal events, such as labor unrest, social upheaval, and political instability. Such events have produced many negative effects on labor markets in Bangladesh. For example, reduction of demand for RMGs in the international market may lead to a reduction in sales and production that may force the owners to retrench the number of workers and even shut down the factories. On the other hand, a deteriorated law and order situation in the country, coupled with labor unrest, may force international buyers to cancel work orders due to disruption of production and uncertainty associated with supply of apparel products.

1.10 Search for Sustainability of the RMG Sector

The growing pressure from global buyers to achieve sustainability in production process in the RMG sector makes it imperative that this sector must embrace rapidly changing technology and adapt with it to produce sustainable products that are more environmentally friendly. Recently, due to pressure from global buyers, BGMEA, the largest employers' association in the RMG sector, has made significant investments in this sector to make it a sustainable, energy-efficient, and eco-friendly industry, on the realization that deteriorating environmental and climate conditions can adversely impact overall production. As a result, the RMG industry has moved toward green technology and renewable energy. The RMG industry is currently undergoing transformative changes toward sustainability through green practices such as sustainable manufacturing, promoting energy efficiency, waste reduction, and responsible water management (Rubel 2024). Some of the sustainability practices include rainwater harvesting, installing water-efficient equipment, waste management, and reusing or recycling of products (Rubel 2024). As a result, until now, the apparel industry in Bangladesh has achieved 171 US Green Building Council's (USGBC) Leadership in Energy and Environmental Design (LEED) certified green factories, which is the highest in the world (Hossain 2022). Through getting these green certificates, the apparel sector of Bangladesh is addressing the growing challenges to achieve sustainability, address the adverse impact of climate change, groundwater depletion, and energy efficiency (Hossain 2022). This international recognition has helped the RMG sector to regain its image to a certain extent after the Rana Plaza tragedy in 2013, and to ensure workplace safety by compelling the factory owners to follow regulations and codes in the construction of the buildings. These marketing strategies driven practices are also giving the RMG sector some competitive advantage in access to the global market.

However, as climate change intensifies, workers need protection from rising temperatures on factory floors. While the RMG factories' efforts to meet the sustainability targets of global brands are a step in the right direction, workers' well-being should not be overlooked.

1.11 Informal Workers in the Labor Market in Bangladesh

Bangladesh, being a developing country, is no exception to the trends of globalization. The scenario of the labor market has been changed in Bangladesh to a significant extent due to economic globalization, increased level of flexibility and informalization of work that have taken place in recent years. A significant number of workers are employed in Bangladesh on a temporary basis, and outsourcing, which leads to their exclusion from the scope of labor protection (Fudge 2012).

In Bangladesh, like many other developing countries, the informal sector dominates the employment scenario. The agricultural sector is the largest informal sector in Bangladesh. Only around 20% of the labor force in Bangladesh works under the formal labor market framework (Chowdhury 2019). Of these, 20 percent are employed in the public sector. Thus, the government as an employer generates only a small proportion of employment opportunities. Workers in the informal sector are not covered by labor laws, and hence, they are unregulated and unrecognized by the legal system and hence, they do not enjoy legal and social protection and benefits. Workers in the informal sector include wage laborers, self-employed persons, domestic workers, blacksmiths, carpenters, rickshaw-van pullers, transport workers, shopkeepers, temporary tea workers, workers engaged in hotel, restaurant, construction, electric, shoe, steel and engineering sectors, welding workers, security guards, cleaners, tailoring workers, and hawkers. Workers in the gig economy are another dimension of the informal sector as the number of workers on digital platforms and apps is increasing significantly due to the flexibility of work settings and the opportunity of being self-employed or independent contractors and earning income without a fixed salary or long-term employment contract. Access to the internet and digital technologies is facilitating workers to engage in gig economy.

While agriculture continues to remain the main source of the vast majority of the labor force in the informal sector in Bangladesh, industrial and service sectors also absorb a significant number of informal workers. Employment in agriculture is typically dominated by self-employment.

As informal workers usually do not get any appointment letters or a fixed salary, they have to depend on the whims of the owners or employers. They are low-skilled with no opportunities to receive training. Due to a lack of legal recognition, workers in the informal sector cannot organize themselves and are deprived of freedom of association and collective bargaining. They also face difficulty in accessing the legal and judicial system to enforce contracts, which eventually exclude them from public benefits.

The current labor market scenario of Bangladesh is reflected in a shift from regular to casual employment, declining of the share of the organized section of employment and growth in informal sector employment; a significant number of unskilled workers are working on contract labor with no job security. There is also the practice of engaging contract or seasonal workers, which has a long history in Bangladesh in its rural areas. With the availability of extensive surplus labor, there has been an increase in subcontracting, temporary, and casual work. However, data on the share of the informal sector is not always available. Reliable and timely labor market data is vital for accurately reflecting employment scenario, understanding vulnerability of workers in informal sector and essential for adopting evidence-based social policy for this sector (Raihan 2022). Exclusion of informal workers from the legal framework as workers is the main hurdle in ensuring the rights of informal workers. Although the National Labor Policy 2012 of Bangladesh emphasizes establishing a decent workplace for both formal and informal workers and formulating laws for the informal sector workers, large-scale informality poses informidable challenges to ensuring decent work conditions in this sector.

1.12 Impact of the Coronavirus Pandemic on Labor Rights in Bangladesh

The outbreak of Coronavirus pandemic in 2020, with the resulting economic downturn and global fall in demand, caused the loss of job and livelihoods of millions of workers worldwide. The COVID-19 pandemic also disrupted the lives of thousands of workers engaged in both formal and informal sectors in Bangladesh due to lockdown and closure of industries, which led to severe violations of labor rights, exacerbating vulnerability of workers. The adverse effects of the pandemic were being transmitted to the labor market through domestic and external channels (Islam 2020, 4). At the domestic level, the shutdown of public life resulted in a complete stoppage of economic activities during the period which in turn led to loss of jobs and livelihoods for many daily, casual laborers employed in transport, manufacturing, construction and service sectors. On the external side, Islam observes that the global recession caused by the pandemic resulted in a steady decline in demand for RMG products as orders were being canceled and new orders dried up, resulting in the closure of many factories. The pandemic caused temporary as well as permanent job loss of many workers bringing a substantial adverse impact on the existing poor state of labor rights and working conditions in Bangladesh. In particular, the pandemic further exacerbated the existing problems of long working hours, insufficient pay, untimely disbursement of wages, and weak collective bargaining capacity of workers of the RMG sector as many American-European buyers canceled orders putting workers in vulnerable positions. On the other hand, trade unions also largely failed to safeguard the interest of the workers throughout the crisis (Hassan et al. 2022). On the other hand, the pandemic changed the nature of some forms of work significantly as many workers were forced to work remotely using digital technologies.

Given the lack of legal protection and social benefits for workers engaged in the informal sector, the impact of the pandemic was also severe on the workers in this sector. Although the Government of Bangladesh provided a stimulus package for workers of the RMG workers, the effectiveness of the stimulus package was limited due to the lack of efficiency and transparency in the disbursement process. During the pandemic, a significant number of workers were laid off, subjected to widespread retrenchment and forced leave, but they were hardly compensated according to the labor law of Bangladesh. The informal sector workers suffered most as many informal workers lost their livelihood or were compelled to change their occupation, or migrated to other parts of the country (Siddiq and Sharif 2023). Their vulnerability was aggravated by the lack of formal contracts, which made them largely ineligible for getting any livelihood support from the employers or the government (Hassan et al. 2022).

Given its unprecedented nature, the COVID-19 pandemic has raised critical questions about the adequacy of labor laws regarding the protection of workers' rights and well-being in the pandemic situation throughout the world, including Bangladesh. The urgency of dealing with the pandemic situation pushed some countries to amend their labor laws to prevent precariousness and inequalities in the labor market. The existing labor laws of Bangladesh were found to be deficient in addressing the pandemic situation. Such inadequacy could be addressed through initiating legal reforms for ensuring a special compulsory paid leave for all non-essential workers, long-term employment protection, reduced and flexible working hours, and enhanced social security. However, Bangladesh took a more short-term approach to deal with pandemic situation than initiating legal reforms for long-term protection of workers.

1.13 Rana Plaza Disaster and Transnational Alliance

While industrial accidents are not new in Bangladesh, the Rana Plaza factory collapse on 24 April 2013 that claimed the death of 1100 and injury of more than 2,500 workers was the deadliest one to date in the world. The Rana Plaza disaster caused the unprecedented global outcry about workplace safety and security in Bangladesh and the immense pressure on international brands to improve safety in the RMG sector. As an aftermath of the incident, global retailers joined by international and national unions and NGOs launched a campaign for safety in the RMG sector. Before the Rana Plaza collapse, the *Tazreen* factory accident also claimed the lives of more than one hundred workers. Both incidents had helped mobilize national and international organizations to campaign for improving safety in the RMG sector in Bangladesh. These incidents were largely attributed to the negligence of factory owners, weak enforcement of labor laws, lack of institutional capacity of government agencies to monitor and implement such laws, poor resource allocation to the regulatory authorities and institutions concerned, and a lack of auditing and inspection of the RMG factories (Rahman and Moazzem 2017, 82). These incidents also underscored the necessity for initiating fundamental reforms relating to safety measures, inspection, and compliance in the RMG sector and highlighted the need for longer-term processes to enhance the capacity and accountability of the regulatory bodies responsible for inspection and compliance.

In particular, after the Rana Plaza disaster, more than 150 large retailers, brands, and buyers from Europe and North America took initiatives for ensuring the safety and security of RMG workers and undertook immediate steps of structural, fire and electrical safety inspections of 3,508 export-oriented RMG factories (Bossavie et al. 2019) that resulted in two multilevel initiatives—"the Accord on Fire and Building Safety in Bangladesh" and "Alliance". While "the Accord" was developed by the European retailers and brands, "Alliance" was also largely formed by North American retailers. Both initiatives were buyer-led and involved multilevel actors such as Global union federations, local unions, brands, ILO, and social movement organizations that developed a coalitional power for achieving a shared objective of ensuring safety in the RMG sector which is typically known for precarious working conditions and lack of compliance. These initiatives were taken in response to the inadequacy of laws and regulations and lack of compliance with the safety and security of workers in Bangladesh. On the other hand, the government of Bangladesh took several initiatives on regulatory and institutional reforms for safety in the RMG sector mediated by huge international pressure and on the realization that ensuring safety in this sector is necessary to remain competitive in the global supply chain. While these initiatives led to significant improvements in building safety of the RMG sector, they were not emulated and replicated in other sectors to address the safety concerns.

1.14 Emergence of Transnational Labor Governance

Traditionally, state, employers, trade unions, and workers remain the most important actors in industrial relations. But this traditional industrial relations landscape has undergone fundamental changes through the emergence of a transnational labor governance framework based on a private regime and contractual arrangements that are not guided by public regulation (Liukkunen 2021, 37). The globalization process has changed the role and relevance of these national actors, who are facing challenges of the process of transnationalization of labor law that affects the traditional labor law framework. Globalization also provides a common platform for workers and unions to develop networks in order to pursue their shared interests and goals of social justice and in particular, unions are forging alliances at trans-border and transnational levels (Hardt and Negri 2001). The predominantly national nature of trade unions and collective bargaining is increasingly under pressure from global circumstances and trends. The rise of globalization has prompted rapid transnationalization of labor governance mechanisms based on multilevel approaches to regulation. Transnational organizations like global and regional trade unions have emerged as new actors and are leveraging a unique form of influence over nation-states with regard to workplace rights and standards through facilitating rapid information exchange among workers across borders and coordinating international solidarity campaigns (Hardt and Negri 2001). For example, the International Trade Union Confederation (ITUC), along with other international sectoral unions, is playing an important role in shaping global labor relations through assisting national unions, organizing international campaigns to denounce child labor, forced labor, and violation of the ILS, advising national unions to respect ILO standards and exchanging and sharing information. IndustriALL is another global union that represents 50 million workers in 130 countries in the mining, energy, and manufacturing sectors and it has the capacity to mobilize workers for better working conditions, challenge the power of multinational companies, and negotiates with them on a global level (IndustriALL Global Union). Many such global and regional unions forged together to deal with the challenges of globalization, promote social justice for workers and build global solidarity for improving labor standards. Many unions have established transnational alliances with non-union actors, with the global justice movement, in order to express solidarity to promote their shared objectives of fairer globalization. For trade unions, alliances with this global movement provide them opportunities to reach out to wider stakeholders, and to strengthen their transnational mobilization capacity. Concerted industrial action, campaigning and solidarity strikes, and coordinating collective bargaining at the national and regional levels are also seen as outcomes of this global movement.

Traditionally, systems of industrial relations are predominantly based on national regulations, trade unions, and tripartite arrangements negotiated by the government, employers, and workers. But the national legal regime on industrial relations is increasingly shaped by the following factors: first, the national industrial relations systems have been gradually complemented by emerging transnational industrial relations systems and this evolving transnational dimension of industrial relations is providing a new normative basis for international labor law and cross-border collective contractual arrangements (Liukkunen 2021, 18). Second, in many areas of industrial relations, nongovernmental organizations (NGOs) are playing an active role in transnational industrial relations systems through networking and forging alliances with international trade unions. Third, there is a shift from a legally based industrial relations system to voluntary governance (Egels-Zandén 2009, 169–170). This transnational labor governance poses a considerable challenge to national trade unions and state-centered national governance.

The transnational labor governance has the following impacts: first, cross-border collaborative activities among the international trade unions have increased significantly. In order to address the challenges of globalization, cross-border collaborative activities have increased significantly through the conclusion of international or global framework agreements (GFAs) between global union federations (GUFs) and multinational enterprises (MNEs) over the last few decades (Luterbacher et al. 2017, 310). International or Global Framework Agreements are generally agreed between a multinational corporation and global unions and many of them refer to respect of international labor standards such as freedom of association, collective bargaining, non-discrimination, forced labor, and child labor throughout their supply chains in all the different countries in which they operate (Sengenberger 2005, 116). GFA refers to a negotiated agreement between a multinational enterprise and a Global Union Federation (GUF) to ensure that the company respects the ILO standards in all the countries where it operates. The objectives of GFAs are to promote labor relations at the national, sectoral, and enterprise level. GFAs also commonly refer to provisions for respect for these principles embodied in an agreement by MNE with their subcontractors and/or suppliers. Many GFAs also address workplace health and safety, minimum wages and working hours, and environmental issues (Luterbacher et al. 2017, 313). However, GFAs are voluntary instruments and hence, are not binding. Nevertheless, these agreements reflect a formal recognition of social partnership at the global level and they reflect a commitment to observe core international labor standards.

The growing number of GFAs clearly demonstrates new pattern of transnational labor relations that is based on respect for workers' rights in global supply chains. These global collective agreements are adopted as a response to the rising influence of global production networks.

Secondly, in order to offset the negative consequences of globalization and improve labor standards in sweatshop conditions at manufacturing industries, there was a growing call by labor rights activists and NGOs for integrating labor rights in global trade policies for ensuring accountability for worker rights violations (Fick xiv). Many bilateral and regional trade agreements now make reference to core labor standards.

Third, the emergence of codes of conduct of MNEs in unilateral forms of corporate self-regulation is another aspect of transnational labor governance. Such codes of conduct are seen as an outcome of pressure from labor rights activists and consumer groups, which represents a neoliberal embrace of market-based solutions to labor standards. Codes of conduct are different from labor provisions in trade agreements because the former are non-binding and non-enforceable, made by individual companies but labor provisions in trade agreements are negotiated by the government and have mandatory elements. The growing influence of MNEs since the 1980s and the concomitant criticisms of MNEs coupled with pressure from media, trade unions, civil society, and public entities to improve the labor conditions of workers in global supply chains (GSCs) have been key driving factors behind the development of such voluntary codes of conduct (Posthuma and Bignami 2014). These are mainly private regulations but can play a crucial role in promoting compliance with labor standards in global supply chains where government regulation is limited and public enforcement capacity is weak (Posthuma and Bignami 2014, 346). These codes of conduct are a reflection of corporate social responsibility initiatives of the MNEs by which they promote fundamental labor rights throughout the production and service networks (Droiin 2010, 591). This rapid proliferation of codes of conduct is also attributed to the wide dissemination of fundamental labor rights and their successful application by diverse social actors (Droiin 2010, 591). Some of the codes of conduct are company-specific and are articulated in the concept of CSR. These CSR norms and private regulatory initiatives have sought to constrain management practices. The multinational firms, who make investments in labor-intensive industries, enjoy higher bargaining power vis-a-vis some of the host country governments to negotiate on issues related to production costs that can force the host country governments to relax labor standards (Vadlamannati 2015). Some experts argue that MNEs attempt to uphold labor standards through codes of conduct because of the fear of loss of reputation as a result of either international criticism of corporate practices (Levi, et al.). They remain largely ineffective to prevent the violation of labor rights. Other experts argue that global buyers use voluntary codes of conduct and practice monitoring of labor standards to enhance their brand image among consumers and confront the corporate risk of negative publicity or legal liability for labor and human rights violations in their value chain (Posthuma and Bignami 2014, 349). Hence, many experts believe that they are used to provide legitimacy to MNEs and their effectiveness in improving labor standards is limited (Bulut and Lane 2011).

The Rana Plaza disaster and subsequent buyer-led multi-stakeholders' initiatives—"Accord" and "Alliance" have emerged as transnational governance mechanism that significantly shaped the landscape of labor regulations in Bangladesh through building collective action and collaboration of global labor actors and helped overcome governance gaps inherent in the traditional regulatory system that emphasizes individual actions. The institutional design of this transnational governance mechanism is molded by voluntary commitment, legally enforceable contractual obligations, leverage through collective action, accountability through collective oversight, and pooling of resources (Reinecke and Donaghey 2023). This collaborative governance mechanism also demonstrates the ineffectiveness of the prevailing practice of the corporate self-regulation in the form of voluntary codes or global framework agreements in time of crisis (Reinecke and Donaghey 2023).

1.15 Institutions, Power Relations, Competitiveness: Diverse Influences of Globalization

The impact of globalization on labor markets is a multifaceted and diverse process that intertwines institutions, power relations, competitiveness, technological advancement, and public and private regulations. Globalization has exposed labor market institutions of Bangladesh to these challenges and spurred the establishment of diverse forms of worker organizations beyond national traditional trade unions. There is a widespread concern that globalization erodes labor market institutions, which, in turn, decreases employment and wages (Potrafke 2013). However, it does not essentially induce governments to de-regulate labor markets (Potrafke 2013). Globalization has changed power dynamics and fostered competitiveness for market and resources, where corporations exert influence over decision-making processes in developing countries, that also shape labor markets and legal design of industrial relations. The flow of capital, technology, and information has sometimes created power imbalances in labor relations as globalization accelerated the growth of global supply chains, which allows for the fragmentation of production processes. Globalization has intensified competitiveness, which has resulted in the widening of the wage differences between highly skilled and lowly skilled workers in Bangladesh. The influence of globalization can also be seen in the institutional design of global labor policy, which is profoundly shaped by the ILO conventions and recommendations of what is known as the international labor standards.

1.16 Conclusion

The impact of globalization on industrial relations is multifaceted and multidirectional. Although in Bangladesh, employment contracts and relationships have been strengthened in recent years, informal employment continues to be the mainstay in the labor market. Despite the significant progress Bangladesh has made in economic growth rates, the labor market and industrial relations are still facing numerous challenges in securing the benefits of GSCs as workers employed in labor-intensive, lower-skill segments of GSCs have limited opportunities for skill development. Skill-development of workers through training is essential for them to integrate into GSCs. However, any skill-development system must adjust to the needs and the evolving demand of changing labor market. Bangladesh also needs strategies that combine upgrading with measures to promote the inclusion of marginalized groups—such as women, informal workers, and small firms in GSCs to reap the benefits of such GSCs. Growing demand for responsible business conduct from the industries and factory owners requires them to integrate HRDD in their operations to remain competitive in the global market. As the gig economy will continue to grow due to lack of formal job opportunities, it is expected that more workers in this sector will be absorbed in the labor market of Bangladesh. The labor market must also address challenges posed by the increasing use of artificial intelligence (AI) and digital transformation that will replace many old types of employment in the near future.

Bibliography

Books

Benson, Edward. 1988. *The Law of Industrial Conflict.* Macmillan Press.

Bereusson, Brian, and Cynthia Estlund. 2008. *Regulating Labour in the Wake of Globalization: New Challenges, New Institution.* Hart Publishing.

Deakin, Simon, and Frank Wilkison. 2005. *The Law of the Labour Market.* Oxford University Press.

Dijk, Meine Pieter van, and Jacques Trienekens, eds. 2012. *Global Value Chains, Linking Local Producers from Developing Countries to International Markets.* Amsterdam University Press.

Flanagan, Robert J. 2006. *Globalization and Labor Conditions: Working Conditions and Worker Rights in a Global Economy.* Oxford University Press.

Hardt, M., and A. Negri. 2001. *Empire.* Harvard University Press.

Kahn-Freuds. 1983. *Labour and the Law.* 3rd ed., Stevens and Sons.

Kaufmann, Christine. 2007. *Globalization and Labour Rights.* Hart Publishing.

Stiglitz, Josheph. 2002. *Globalization and Its Discontents.* W.W. Norton.

Zandvliet, R. 2022. *Trade, Investment and Labour: Interactions in International Law.* Brill–Nijhoff.

Chapters in Edited Books

Banks, Kevin. 2006. "The Impact of Globalization on Labour Standards: A Second Look at the Evidence." In *The Future of Labour Law*, edited by John D. R. Craig, 77–107. Cambridge University Press.

Campling, Liam, and Benjamin Selwyn. 2018. "Value Chains and the World Economy: Genealogies and Reformulations." In *Handbook of the International Political Economy of the Corporation*, edited by Andreas Nölke and Christian May, 416–434. Edward Elgar Publishing.

Deakin, Simon. 2011. "The Contribution of Labour Law to Economic and Human Development." In *The Idea of Labour Law*, edited by Guy Davidov and Brian Langille, 156–176. Oxford University Press.

Fick, Barbara J. 2015. "Introduction." In *International Labour Law*, edited by Barbara J. Fick, i–xxi. Edward Elgar Publishing.

Fudge, Judy. 2012. "Blurring Legal Boundaries: Regulating Decent Work." In *Challenging The Legal Boundaries of Work Regulation*, edited by Judy Fudge, Shae McCrystal and Kamala Sankra, 1–20. Hart Publishing.

Kucera, David, and Dora Sari. 2022. "Globalization and Freedom of Association and Collective Bargaining Rights." In *Handbook on Globalisation and Labour Standards*, edited by Kimberly A. Elliott, 13–35. Edward Elgar.

Liukkunen, Ulla. 2021. "The ILO and Transformation of Labour Law." In *International Labour Organization and Global Social Governance*, edited by Tarja Halonen and Ulla Liukkunen, 17–49. Springer.

Rahman, Mustafizur, and Khondaker Golam Moazzem. 2017. "The Legacy of Rana Plaza: Improving Labour and Social Standards in Bangladesh's Apparel Industry." In *Governing Corporate Social Responsibility in the Apparel Industry after Rana Plaza*, edited by A. Hira, M. Benson-Rea, 81–109. Palgrave Macmillan.

Reinecke, Juliane, and Jimmy Donaghey. 2023. "The Politics of Collaborative Governance in Global Supply Chains: Power and Pushback in the Bangladesh Accord". In The Evolution of Transnational Rule-Makers Through Crises, edited by Panagiotis Delimatsis, Stephanie Bijlmakers, M. Konrad Borowicz, 154–173. Cambridge University Press.

Rodrik, Dani. 1996. "Labor Rights in International Trade: Do They Matter and What Do We Do about Them?" In *Emerging Agenda for Global Trade: High Stakes for Developing Countries* edited by Robert Lawrence, Dani Rodrik, and John Whalley, 35–80. Johns Hopkins Press for the Overseas Development Council.

Smith, John. 2014. "The Globalisation of Production and the Challenges Facing International Solidarity (with Special Reference to Bangladesh)." In *Polarising Development—Alternatives to Neoliberalism and the Crisis*, edited by Lucia Pradella and Thomas Marois, 51–61. Pluto Press.

Srinivasan, T. 1996. "International Trade and Labor Standards from an Economic Perspective." In *Challenges to the New World Trade Organization*, edited by P. van Dijck and G. Faber, 219–243. Brill–Nijhoff.

Vliet, O. Van, Vincent Bakker, and L. Van Doorn. 2021. "From Social Protection to Social Investment: European Responses to Globalization, Technological Change, Labour Market Flexibilization, and Migration". In: *Europe's Income, Wealth, Consumption, and Inequality*, edited by G. Fischer and R. Strauss, 343–394. Oxford University Press.

Journal Articles

Aguirre Jr., Adalberto, and Ellen Reese. 2004. "Introduction: The Challenges of Globalization for Workers: Transnational and Transborder Issues." *Social Justice* 31 (3): 1–20.

Akorsu, Angela Dziedzom. 2018. "Labour Standards Regulation in a Globalised Economy: A Review of Existing Paradigms." *Ghana Journal of Development Studies* 15 (2): 70–90.

Anner, Mark. 2020. "Squeezing Workers' Rights in Global Supply Chains: Purchasing Practices in the Bangladesh Garment Export Sector in Comparative Perspective." 27 (2): 320–347.

Arumugam, Subramaniyam, and Nimalathasan Balasundaram. 2010. "Industrial Relation System: Lessons for Bangladesh and Sri Lanka from Japanese Perspective." *Petroleum-Gas University of Ploiesti Bulletin* 52 (1): 52–60.

Barrientos, Stephanie, and Sally Smith. 2007. "Do Workers Benefit from Ethical Trade? Assessing Codes of Labour Practice in Global Production Systems." *Third World Quarterly* 28 (4): 713–29.

Blanton, Robert G., Shannon Lindsey Blanton, and Dursun Peksen. 2015. "The Impact of IMF and World Bank Programs on Labor Rights." *Political Research Quarterly* 68 (2): 324–336.

Blanton, Robert, and Shannon Lindsey Blanton. 2016. "Globalization and Collective Labor Rights." *Sociological Forum* 31 (1): 181–202.

Blanton, Robert, and Shanon L. Blanton. 2012. "Labor Rights and Foreign Direct Investment: Is There a Race to the Bottom?" *Journal of International Interactions* 38 (3): 267–273.

Bulut, Tugce, and Christel Lane. 2011. "The Private Regulation of Labour Standards and Rights in the Global Clothing Industry: An Evaluation of Its Effectiveness in Two Developing Countries." *New Political Economy* 16 (1): 41–71.

Chan, Chris King-Chi, and Khalid Nadvi. 2014. "Changing Labour Regulations and Labour Standards in China: Retrospect and Challenges." *International Labour Review* 153 (4): 513–534.

Do, Q. A., A. D. Do, M. H. Doan, Q. H. Le, A. D. Le, and T. T. D. Nguyen. 2024. "Spatial Effects of Foreign Direct Investment on Wage Inequality in Vietnam." *Cogent Economics & Finance* 12 (1): 2293297.

Droiin, Rene-Claude. 2010. "Promoting Fundamental Social Rights through International Framework Agreements: Practical Outcomes and Present Challenges." *Comparative Labour Law and Policy Journal* 31: 591–617.

Egels-Zandén, Niklas. 2009. "Transnational Governance of Workers' Rights: Outlining a Research Agenda." *Journal of Business Ethics* 87: 169–188.

IGLP Law and Global Production Working Group. 2016. "The Role of Law in Global Value Chains: A Research Manifesto." *London Review of International Law* 4 (1): 57–79.

Keune, M., and V. Schmidt. 2009. "Global Capital Strategies and Trade Union Responses: Towards Transnational Collective Bargaining?" *International Journal of Labour Research* 1 (2): 9–26.

Kucera, David. 2002. "Core Labour Standards and Foreign Direct Investment." *International Labour Review* 141: 31–63.

Kuruvilla, Sarosh, and Chunyun Li. 2021. "Freedom of Association and Collective Bargaining in Global Supply Chains: A Research Agenda." *Journal of Supply Chain Management* 57 (2): 43–57.

Luterbacher, Urs, Andrew Prosser, and Konstantinos Papadakis. 2017. "An Emerging Transnational Industrial Relation? Exploring the Prospects for Cross-Border Labour Bargaining." *International Labour Review* 156 (3–4): 310–329.

Neumayer, Eric, and Indra De Soysa. 2005. "Globalization and the Right to Free Association and Collective Bargaining: An Empirical Analysis." *World Development* 34 (1): 31–49.

Neumayer, Eric, and Indra De Soysa. 2007. "Globalisation, Women's Economic Rights and Forced Labour." *The Journal of World Economy* 30 (10): 1510–1535.

Parrilli, Mario Davide, Khalid Nadvi, and Henry Wai-Chung Yeung. 2013. "Local and Regional Development in Global Value Chains, Production Networks and Innovation Networks: A Comparative Review and the Challenges for Future Research." *European Planning Studies* 27 (7): 967–988.

Peksen, Dursun, and Jacob M. Pollock. 2021. "Economic Globalization and Labor Rights: A Disaggregated Analysis." *Human Rights Review* 22: 279–301.

Perocco, Fabio. 2018. "Posted Workers between Work Casualisation and the Precarisation of Migration." *Journal of Two Homelands* 48: 7–21.

Posthuma, Anne, and Renato Bignami. 2014. "'Bridging the Gap'? Public and Private Regulation of Labour Standards in Apparel Value Chains in Brazil." *Journal of Competition and Change* 18 (4): 345–364.

Prentice, Rebecca. 2021. "Labour Rights from Labour Wrongs? Transnational Compensation and the Spatial Politics of Labour Rights after Bangladesh's Rana Plaza Garment Factory Collapse." *Antipode* 53 (3): 1–25.

Reinecke, Juliane, and Jimmy Donaghey. 2015. "After Rana Plaza: Building Coalitional Power for Labour Rights between Unions and (Consumption-Based) Social Movement Organisations." *Organization* 22 (5): 720–740.

Selwyn, Benjamin. 2018. "Poverty Chains and Global Capitalism." *Journal of Competition and Change* 23 (1): 1–27.

Siddiq, A. B., and S. M. Sharif. 2023. "Impact of COVID-19 on the Rights of Informal Workers in Bangladesh." *Society & Sustainability* 5 (1): 1–15.

Unni, Jeemol. 2018. "Formalization of the Informal Economy: Perspectives of Capital and Labour." *The Indian Journal of Labour Economics* 61 (1): 87–103.

Uwadinma, Alex Iloba. 2023. "Effects of Globalization on Labor Standards and Working Conditions." *Dhaka University Journal of Law* 34 (2): 133–151.

Vadlamannati, Krishna Chaitanya. 2015. "Rewards of (Dis)integration: Economic, Social, and Political Globalization and Freedom of Association and Collective Bargaining Rights of Workers in Developing Countries." *International Labour Review* 68 (1): 3–27.

Reports

ADB. 2026. *Global Value Chains and Inclusive Development*, May. Asian Development Policy Report, Manila.

Anner, Mark. 2018. "Binding Power: The Sourcing Squeeze, Workers' Rights, and Building Safety in Bangladesh since Rana Plaza." Center for Global Workers' Rights, Penn State University.

APEC Policy Support Unit. 2012. "Concepts and Trends in Global Supply, Global Value and Global Production Chains." Issues Paper no. 1, May.

Bacchetta, Marc, Ekkehard Ernst Juana, and P. Bustamante. 2009. "Globalization and Informal Jobs in Developing Countries." A joint study of ILO and WTO (Geneva). https://researchrepository.ilo.org/esploro/outputs/encyclopediaEntry/Globalization-and-informal-jobs-in-developing/995238293102676#file-0.

Bossavie, Laurent, Yoonyoung Cho, and Rachel Heath. 2019. "The Effects of International Scrutiny on Manufacturing Workers: Evidence from the Rana Plaza Collapse in Bangladesh." Social Protection and Jobs Global Practice (November), 1. Policy Research Working Paper 9065.

Boudreau, Laura, Rachel Heath, and Wahedur Rahman. 2022. "Economic Impacts of Coronavirus-19 on Workers in Bangladesh's Garment Sector," January. https://www.theigc.org/sites/default/files/2025-03/Boudreau%20et%20al%20Final%20Report%20January%202022.pdf.

Chowdhury, Philip. 2019. "Informal Sector: Early Experiences of Work." *The Daily Star* (Dhaka), July 2. Accessed on July 22, 2024. https://www.thedailystar.net/star-weekend/news/informal-sector-early-experiences-work-1763122.

Dadush, Uri, and William Shaw. 2012. *Globalization, Labor Markets, and Inequality*. Carnegie Endowment for International Peace, February 2.

Dallakoti, Gunjan. 2024. "For Shared Prosperity, Formalization of Work Is Vital". The Daily Star (Dhaka), June 26. Accessed on April 11, 2025. https://www.thedailystar.net/opinion/views/news/shared-prosperity-formalisation-work-vital-3642226.

Edwards, Remi, Tom Hunt, and Genevieve LeBaron. 2019. *Corporate Commitments to Living Wages in the Garment Industry*. Sheffield: SPERI & University of Sheffield.

"Exploring the Gig Economy: Challenges and Opportunities", A Self-Guided Resource, ILO. 2025. https://www.ilo.org/sites/default/files/2025-06/ILO%20-%20Mini%20Guide_%28Digital%29_13jun.pdf.

"Female Workforce in Garment Industry Slips to 53%." 2024. *The Daily Star* (Dhaka), December 9. Accessed on February 12, 2025. https://www.thedailystar.net/business/news/female-workforce-garment-industry-slips-53-3771696.

Figini, Paolo, and Holger Görg. 2006. "Does Foreign Direct Investment Affect Wage Inequality? An Empirical Investigation." Research Paper, No. 2006/29. Leverhulme Centre for Research on Globalisation and Economic Policy, University of Nottingham.

Hahn, Chin Hee, and Dionisius A. Narjoko. "Impact of Globalization on Labor Market," ERIA Research Project Report 2012, No. 4.

Hartzén, Ann-Christine. 2018. "Globalisation of Labour Markets and International Systems of Industrial Relations." The Nordic Work Life Conference 2018, Oslo, Norway. Accessed on April 12, 2024, https://lucris.lub.lu.se/ws/portalfiles/portal/99073756/FULLTEXT01.pdf.

Hassan, Mirza M., Syeda Salina Aziz, Raeesa Rahemin, Insiya Khan, and Rafsanul Hoque. 2022. "Impact of COVID-19 on Labour Rights and Working Conditions in Four Selected Sectors," April. https://bigd.bracu.ac.bd/wp-content/uploads/2022/04/Revised_clear_scoping_Impact-of-COVID-19-on-Labour-Rights-and-Working-Conditions-in-Four-Selected-Sectors.pdf.

Hossain, Saddam. 2022. "Bangladesh Boasts 171 LEED-Certified Green RMG Factories Now." *Dhaka Tribune*, September 22. Accessed on June 22, 2024. https://www.dhakatribune.com/business/276737/bangladesh-boasts-171-leed-certified-green-rmg.

https://carnegieendowment.org/2012/02/02/globalization-labor-markets-and-inequality-pub-47028.

IndustriALL Global Union. https://www.industriall-union.org/who-we-are.

International Labour Organization. "Compilation of International Labour Conventions and Recommendations." Meeting Document WCMS_377774. Accessed on March 2024, https://www.ilo.org/sites/default/files/wcmsp5/groups/public/@ed_norm/@relconf/documents/meetingdocument/wcms_377774.pdf.

International Labour Organization. 2019a. *The Rules of the Game: An Introduction to the Standards-Related Work of the International Labour Organization.* Geneva: ILO.

International Labour Organization. 2019b. *What Works: Promoting Pathways to Decent Work.* Geneva: ILO. https://www.ilo.org/global/publications/books/WCMS_724049/lang--en/index.htm.

International Trade Union Confederation (ITUC). 2026 Global Rights Index. file:///C:/Users/LENOVO/Downloads/global_right_index_2026_en.pdf.

Islam, Rizwanul. 2020. "The Impact of COVID-19 on Employment in Bangladesh: Pathway to an Inclusive and Sustainable Recovery." Bangladesh Institute of Labor Studies, Dhaka, (September): 4.

Kashyap, Aruna. 2024. "What Does the EU Due Diligence Directive Mean for Bangladesh?: It Paves the Way for Progressive Reforms." *The Daily Star*, May 31. https://www.thedailystar.net/opinion/views/news/what-does-the-eu-due-diligence-directive-mean-bangladesh-3622991.

Kaufman, Bruce E. 2004. *The Global Evolution of Industrial Relations: Events, Ideas and the IIRA*. Geneva: International Labour Organization.

Khan, Shahiduzzaman. 2018. "Pension: A Dream for Informal Sector Workers." *The Financial Express* (Dhaka), December 22.

Labor Force Survey 2022 Bangladesh. https://bbs.portal.gov.bd/sites/default/files/files/bbs.portal.gov.bd/page/b343a8b4_956b_45ca_872f_4cf9b2f1a6e0/2023-10-25-07-38-4304abd7a3f3d8799fbcb59ff91007b1.pdf.

Levi, Margaret, et al. 2013. "Aligning Rights and Interests: Why, When and How to Uphold Labour Standards." *World Development Report*. Washington, DC: World Bank.

Mirdha, Refayetullah. 2024. "Ratio of Female Workers in RMG on the Wane." *The Daily Star* (Dhaka), June 28. Accessed on January 21 2025. https://www.thedailystar.net/business/news/ratio-female-workers-rmg-the-wane-3643721.

Potrafke, Niklas. 2013. "Globalization and Labor Market Institutions: International Empirical Evidence" IFO Working Paper No. 154, February. Accessed on March 9, 2024. https://www.ifo.de/DocDL/IfoWorkingPaper-154.pdf.

Raihan, Selim. 2022. "How Should We Address Our Core Labour Market Challenges?" *The Daily Star* (Dhaka), November 6. Accessed on May 3, 2024, https://www.thedailystar.net/opinion/views/news/how-should-we-address-our-core-labour-market-challenges-3161181.

Rubel, Md Mohiuddin. 2024. "BGMEA Turning RMG Industry into Global Sustainability Leader." *The Daily Star* (Dhaka), January 10. Accessed on February 23, 2025, https://www.thedailystar.net/opinion/views/rmg-notes/news/how-our-rmg-industry-empowered-women-3657121.

Sachs, Jeffrey D., and Andrew Warner. 1995. "Economic Reform and the Process of Global Integration." *Brookings Papers on Economic Activity* 1995 (1): 1–118.

Selim, Raihan. 2026. "Bangladesh Needs to Move Up in Global Value Chains Through Industrial Upgrading." *The Daily Star* (Dhaka), May 17. Accessed on June 1, 2026, https://www.thedailystar.net/opinion/views/news/bangladesh-needs-move-global-value-chains-through-industrial-upgrading-4177356.

Sengenberger, Werner. 2005. *Globalization and Social Progress: The Role and Impact of International Labour Standards*. 2nd revised and extended edition. Report prepared for the Friedrich-Ebert-Stiftung. Bonn, July.

Uddin, Mostafiz. 2024. "How Our RMG Industry Empowered Women." *The Daily Star* (Dhaka), July 15. Accessed on August 22, 2024, https://www.thedailystar.net/opinion/views/rmg-notes/news/how-our-rmg-industry-empowered-women-3657121.

Yimprasert, Junya, and Petter Hveem. "The Race to the Bottom: Exploitation of Workers in the Global Garment Industry." Norwegian Church Aid Occasional Paper Series, no. 01/2005.

Legislation and International Instruments

The EU Directive on Corporate Sustainability Due Diligence 2024. https://eur-lex.europa.eu/legal-content/EN/TXT/HTML/?uri=OJ:L_202401760.

The French Vigilance Law of 2017, https://respect.international/french-corporate-duty-of-vigilance-law-english-translation/.

The ILO's Recommendation on Transition from the Informal to Formal Economy (No. 204) 2015. https://www.ilo.org/sites/default/files/wcmsp5/groups/public/%40ed_norm/%40relconf/documents/meetingdocument/wcms_377774.pdf.

The Modern Slavery Act 2015 of the UK.

The Modern Slavery Act 2018 of Australia, https://www.legislation.gov.au/C2018A00153/latest/downloads.

The Supply Chain Due Diligence Act 2023 of Germany, https://www.bmz.de/resource/blob/154774/lieferkettengesetz-faktenpapier-partnerlaender-eng-bf.pdf.

CHAPTER 2

Legal and Institutional Design of Industrial Relations in Bangladesh

2.1 Introduction

In general, labor law regulates industrial relations. Labor law is viewed as "collective laissez -faire" (Kahn-Freund 1972, 3) as it deals with collective rights and well-being of the workers. Labor law, being deeply embedded in normative understanding of institutional setting of labor market, has both individual and collective dimensions as it protects individual rights and collective capacity of workers to bargain with employers. In this context, labor law is also seen as a "complex bundle of restraints on freedom of contract" that constrains the unbridled behavior of employers in the labor market (Spector 2006, 1120) and strikes a greater balance of power in the labor market by providing protection to workers who are generally weaker than employers. Labor laws provide social protection measures for workers in order to offset the negative effects of economic globalization. The intrinsic value of labor law lies in its potential to protect workers' rights. It encompasses rules and principles of industrial relations regulating workers' collective welfare and collective action relating to organizing trade unions, participating in collective bargaining and calling strikes. It also sets standards on minimum wage, safety, overtime limits, and protection against discrimination in the workplace. Labor law is also concerned with setting social security measures for workers, like insurance, pensions, and workers' compensation for injury

A. Al Faruque, *Globalization and Labour Rights*,
https://doi.org/10.1007/978-981-92-3661-9_2

and dispute settlement. Labor law acts as a precondition for the realization of international labor standards at the national level.

Traditionally labor law is seen as the rules and principles developed in a country for regulating industrial relations and it is tailored to the domestic needs, conditions, and demands. However, the landscape of national labor laws is gradually expanding with the need for integration of the evolving international standards on labor rights. National labor law is traditionally oriented toward policy objectives, interests, and the building of labor institutions in domestic setting, but it is now subject to diverse influences. It has become increasingly complex because of the multiplicity of its sources, such as constitutions, Acts, judicial decisions, international standards, and non-legal norms that shape its contours and involvement of various actors in the implementation of labor laws. Although national labor laws are mostly shaped by international labor standards and enactments, they are often interpreted and applied by courts and government agencies and judicial interpretations are informed by non-legal norms (Arthur 2011, 16).

Labor law is not static as it evolves in historical process. Labor legislation is best understood as the outcome of a process of struggle between different social groups (Coutu et al. 2023, 9). As labor law needs to respond to the changing needs of workers and society, it often needs reform and hence, it is dynamic. Reforms in labor laws are often needed to respond to rapid changes in labor market conditions, to adapt with new forms of employment, and to reflect developments in international labor standards, and to address the challenges of globalization (Davidov 2016, 15–16). According to Fredman, the urgent need for transformation of labor law is widely accepted to assert the importance of labor or social rights in the face of competitive pressures caused by globalization (Fredman 2004, 32).

2.2 Functions of Labor Law in the Age of Globalization

The functions of labor law are often contested. Globalization, technological changes, changing patterns of work, and the search for decent work have brought new perspectives on the understanding of labor law (Hendrickx 2012, 108). In the context of globalization, labor laws can offset many of its negative effects. According to Charnovitz, national labor law aims at achieving three distinct objectives: correcting market failure, protecting workers from discrimination and mistreatment by government, and enhancing equity through addressing inequalities and imbalances in bargaining power between workers and employers (Charnovitz 2005, 161–162). However, the most compelling function of labor law in the context of globalization is to correct market failures caused by poor information about workplace hazards, imperfect competition in labor markets, and child labor (Charnovitz 2005). In this context, labor laws intervene in the free market to prevent market failures. Simon Deakin argues that labor law is an "inseparable part of the market" constituting it rather than limiting it (Deakin 2011, 162). Brian Langille contends that "markets are just an aspect and means of human freedom" and labor law, on this view, is also an inseparable aspect of markets necessary to achieve the broad goal of promoting freedom in labor relations (Langille 2015, 257).

Labor law is traditionally seen as a mechanism to address inequality manifested in the bargaining power of workers and employers in the negotiation and establishment of working conditions in labor relations, in which workers are "legally subordinated to the authority of the employer" (Hendrickx 2012). In this sense, the primary function of labor law is, in the words of Freund, to act as a countervailing force to reverse the inequality of bargaining power which is inherent in the labor relations (Kahn-Freund 1972, 8).

Labor law also performs an "ordering" function, as it seeks to establish social justice by providing for maximum working hours, minimum wages, occupational health and safety regulations, and other welfare measures for workers. Labor law also provides procedural protection when it protects rights to a fair bargaining process (Langille 2005). On the other hand, it also has the integrative function, which refers to the relationship between the workers and the larger society to which they belong. In this way, labor is not merely an "individual activity", but is also an inherently "social activity" (Langille 2005). According to Hepple, the main proponent of the integrative function of labor law (Hepple 1995), argues that the labor law must strike a balance between the individual and the collective responsibility in industrial relations. An integrative function of labor law unifies diverse socio-economic interests by balancing the inherent power imbalance between employers and workers. Finally, labor law fulfills an intermediary function which requires labor law to be connected with the broader social context. The necessary interdependence between labor law and social policy is recognized in the intermediary function. According to this function, labor law needs to mediate between reality in the ground, policy, and social aspirations and as such, it has to respond to changes and dynamics of societal reality (Hendrickx 2012).

Guy Davidov offers a multi-layered approach to understanding of labor law. According to him, at the highest level, labor laws refer to abstract values in the sense that they aim to protect or promote equality, autonomy, human dignity, social inclusion, and distributive justice (Davidov 2016, 31). At the second level, labor law regulates the core issues of labor markets, such as the market failures, inequality of bargaining power, the commodification of labor, or obstacles to the realization of human capital. At the third level, labor law focuses on the unique feature of employment relationships that put the worker in a vulnerable position, for example, "subordination" and "dependency". On this third view, the goals of labor law are to minimize these vulnerabilities (Davidov 2016).

The above analysis reveals that labor law serves protective, distributive, integrative, and intermediary functions. McCurdy presents three categories of labor law: protective, distributive and permissive (McCurdy 1998, 190–191). Protective legislation includes laws and regulations on the prohibition of child labor, prescribing maximum working hours, and health and safety provisions, prohibition of sexual harassment in the workplace and non-discrimination in recruitment and hiring. Distributive legislation deals with minimum wage, social security measures, and compensation for arbitrary dismissal or discharge of workers. Finally, permissive legislation facilitates the creation of institutions for concerted workers' action such as trade unions, collective bargaining, and labor dispute settlement mechanisms (McCurdy 1998).

Labor law also promotes harmonious industrial relationships between employers and employees by maintaining continuity of production, resolving conflicts, and providing for collective bargaining (Atleson 1983, 7–9). There are also three other ways in which the labor law plays a role in harmonious industrial relationships: providing workers' rights such as trade unions and collective bargaining, establishing machinery to assist in the smooth running of collective bargaining and constraining the combined power of a workforce by outlawing certain forms of industrial action (Benson 1988, xxxiv). The development of labor law is often seen as a political process, a product of the formulation and application of governmental economic and social policies in the sphere of industrial society (Davies and Freedland 1993, 7). As a political process, labor laws mediate between different kinds of power relations, seeks to promote fair labor standards on rights of representation and participation of workers in decision-making process.

Labor law has undergone a profound transformation in the last decades. Traditional labor law was mainly concerned with the protection of the workers rather than their rights. According to protective view, all workers must be given a minimal level of protection from unfettered managerial control. But there has been a shift of labor law from its focus on the "protective" purposes of labor law toward an emphasis on the rights-based approach through conferring rights on workers. Rights-based approach is increasingly gaining recognition for its correlative legal obligations for states and non-state actors for redressing the inequality in bargaining power between employer and worker (Hepple and Veneziani 2009, 15). Now the effectiveness of labor law is measured not only by the protection it might offer to individual workers (Hepple and Veneziani 2009, 23), but also by the extent to which it ensures welfare rights of the workers. From the perspective of a rights-based approach, labor law is not merely "protective law" for the advantage of the workers; its foundation is based on the concepts of "human dignity" and "social justice" (Hendrickx 2012, 110). Social justice, in other words, pays attention to the societal dimension of labor law, in which labor is inherently seen as a social activity. Social justice provides the main foundation of labor law (Hendrickx 2012, 116).

2.3 Evolution of Labor Law in Bangladesh

Labor laws play a pivotal role in maintaining sound industrial relations in any country. In Bangladesh, current corpus of labor laws are largely seen as an outgrowth of the struggle against employers by workers for realizing their legitimate demands. The origin of labor law in Bangladesh can be traced back to the Workmen Compensation Act 1923, the Trade Union Act, 1926, the Factories Act 1934, but these colonial legislation did not contain provisions for worker safety or minimum wages and recognize the collective bargaining of worker. For example, the Trade Union Act 1926 that aimed to provide for the registration of trade unions, but it did not contain any provision regarding collective bargaining or strikes. In the British colonial rule, while the registration of trade unions was allowed, strikes were forbidden in public services. After the partition of

India in 1947, the then-Pakistan government mostly adopted the colonial legacy with regard to labor laws. However, some laws were adopted during the Pakistan regime, such as the East Pakistan Trade Unions Act, 1965 and the Labor Disputes Act 1965. But these laws could not facilitate the healthy growth of sound industrial relations because of their restrictions on the freedom of association and right to organize (Khan 1997). In the Pakistan period, labor organizations' movement for trade unions and collective bargaining was generally suppressed. Subsequently, the Labor Disputes Act 1965 and the Trade Union Act 1965 were amalgamated in the Industrial Relations Ordinance 1969, which recognized collective bargaining in industrial relations, permitted the formation of trade unions at the factory level and allowed workers to strike.

After the emergence of Bangladesh, the evolution of labor law progressed from an exploitative colonial framework to a protective framework, though it suffered from the imposition of martial laws several times, the proclamation of a state of emergency for a prolonged period, and corresponding restrictions on trade union activities and collective bargaining.

2.4 Constitutional Framework on Labor Rights

As constitutional guarantees are of great importance for the protection of labor rights, the constitution of Bangladesh has provided a basic foundation of the same by incorporating several provisions on the right to organize and value of labor. The preamble of the Constitution of Bangladesh, 1972 envisages the establishment of a society free from exploitation as one of the fundamental principles of state policy, while Article 14 of the Constitution takes a corrective justice approach by pledging of the emancipation of the peasants and workers, including backward sections of the people, from all forms of exploitation. On the other hand, Article 20 of the Constitution of Bangladesh is deeply grounded in distributive justice as it proclaims that "work is a right,... and everyone shall be paid for his work on the basis of the principle—"from each according to his abilities, to each according to his work". The constitution of Bangladesh also requires the government to create conditions in which "human labor in every form shall become a fuller expression of creative endeavor and of the human personality". Apart from these fundamental principles of state policies, the constitution of Bangladesh has incorporated some rights such as freedom of form associations (Art.

38) and freedom from forced labor (Art. 34) as fundamental rights, which have a direct bearing on labor rights, especially, on the formation of trade unions.

2.5 Critical Analysis of Legal Framework on Industrial Relations

The post-independence legal framework of industrial relations was fragmented and piecemeal as it consisted of a number of overlapping enactments and Ordinances, which largely failed to aligned with international labor standards on protection of workers' rights, welfare and social security. The Bangladesh Labor Act 2006 remains the main piece of legislation that consolidated many labor laws to avoid overlapping and inconsistencies, as it amalgamated twenty-five of the prevailing enactments on the industrial relation system. Before the enactment of the Bangladesh Labor Act 2006, there were 46 laws to deal with labor and industrial sectors, but many of these laws were found to be backdated and inadequate in view of the changing labor relations and the international labor standards. The Bangladesh Labor Act (BLA) 2006, an umbrella legislation, was adopted in response to the growing demands of stakeholders for improving the legal framework in conformity with international labor standards. This enactment incorporated many international labor standards such as the right to organize, collective bargaining, minimum wage, as Bangladesh ratified most of the core ILO Conventions, bringing fundamental changes in the industrial relations system. The comprehensiveness and consolidated nature of this enactment is also demonstrated by its protective coverage of workers' rights, provisions for health and safety conditions in the workplace, introduction of identification cards and appointment letters for workers, prohibition of child labor, provisions for payment of compensation, enhanced social security, and overtime allowance for workers. Its scope includes all establishments, such as commercial and industrial establishments, factories, and tea plantations.

2.5.1 Defining a Worker

The definition of a worker is especially important to circumvent the legal uncertainty. The Bangladesh Labor Act 2006 takes a broader approach in defining "worker" as it covers those employed "directly or through contractors" and where the terms of employment are "either express or implied" (Section 2.2(65) of the Bangladesh Labor Act 2006). The Act has recognized workers of some of the most vulnerable industries, including ship-breaking, ship-building, security services, mobile phone companies, shrimp vessels and shrimp processing by bringing them within formal sector (Section 2.2 (61) of the Bangladesh Labor Act 2006). However, this definition expressly excludes employees primarily functioning in a "managerial, administrative or supervisory capacity". It also excludes some other categories of workers from the scope of application of the Bangladesh Labor Act 2006 as it is not applicable in certain establishments or workers such as government offices, security printing press, ordnance factory, and non-profitable organizations. The Act is also not applicable to workers engaged in the informal sector. Similarly, the Act is not applicable to workers engaged in some formal sectors like railway, postal, telegraph and telephone department; roads and highways department; the public works and public health engineering department; and the Bangladesh Government printing press except for the purpose of organizing and joining trade union. The Act has classified workers into six categories according to the nature and condition of work, namely: (a) apprentice; (b) substitute; (c) casual; (d) temporary; (e) probationer; (f) permanent; and (g) seasonal worker (Section 2.4 of the Bangladesh Labor Act 2006). Previously, seasonal workers were not recognized. But they were added to the category of workers through an amendment made to the Act in 2013 (Section 2.6(c) of the Bangladesh Labor (Amendment) Act 2013) that widened the definition of worker.

Through recent amendments made in 2013 and 2018 to the Labor Act 2006, workers in more industries have been formally recognized, as the definition of industrial establishment has been expanded to include contractor or sub-contractor establishments engaged in construction works, ship-building, and ship-breaking (Section 2.3 (f) of the Bangladesh Labor (Amendment) Act 2013) and ocean-going vessels (Section 2.3 (g) of the Bangladesh Labor (Amendment) Act 2018). However, in some aspects, the amendments and the Bangladesh Labor Rules 2015 further restrict the definition of workers by excluding supervising officers of any institutions or industrial enterprises.

2.5.2 Regulating Conditions of Employment

The Bangladesh Labor Act 2006 sets out conditions of employment and service by requiring factory owners to formulate service rules, to set standards of benefits, to arrange a service book for workers for inspection purposes. The Act also requires employers to provide an appointment letter and an identity card to the workers, which is considered crucial for the protection of their rights and getting remedies in case of unlawful termination and retrenchment by the employers and claiming their relationship with the appointed factories or firms. In fact, appointment letters act as an employment contract that enables workers to claim their legal rights and compensation for laying off or retrenchment of workers, or in case of death or injuries. Without written formal contracts and appointment letters, workers can be vulnerable to exploitation and their jobs can be terminated at any time without notice. Workers without written contracts usually remain in constant fear of losing their jobs and lack of alternative job opportunities may compel them to engage in precarious work. Therefore, an appointment letter serves as an employment contract that provides legal safeguards for the protection of workers and employment security and as a way of formalization of informality.

However, in order to obviate this legal requirement, factory owners sometimes employ temporary workers or daily basis workers or contractual workers in the post of permanent workers. This practice makes workers vulnerable to the whim and caprice of employers.

2.5.3 Social Security Measures for the Workers

Getting compensation for the injury or death of workers in the course of employment, layoff, and retrenchment is one of the fundamental labor rights. The Bangladesh Labor Act 2006 makes provisions for social security measures including paid sick leave, casual leave, and festival holiday and compensation for workers in the above-mentioned circumstances. But due to complex legal procedures and lack of compliance with the law, workers do not enjoy these legal entitlements. For example, due to the legal requirement of working continuously for one year for getting compensation for layoff under the Bangladesh Labor Act 2006, many laid-off workers are being left without any kind of compensation. Compensation for workers in Bangladesh is governed by the Fatal Accidents Act 1855 and the Bangladesh Labor Act 2006. Although the Bangladesh Labor Act 2006 establishes employer's liability to pay compensation for workplace injury or death of a worker, workers or heirs of deceased workers could hardly extract the compensation. The Act was amended in 2018 to provide compensation benefits to workers' families in case of their death. Previously, upon a worker's death, compensation was paid by the employer to a Labor Court but now, upon the death of a worker or if the worker's whereabouts is not being known, the compensation money must be given directly to a nominee of the deceased worker or his/her legal heir (Section 131 of the Bangladesh Labor Act 2006 as amended in 2018). If it is not possible, then it must be deposited to a workers' benefit foundation, and in such circumstances, if the worker is not found within 10 years, the money shall be utilized for the benefit of the foundation's beneficiaries (Section 131 of the Bangladesh Labor Act 2006). This new provision aims to ensure that the compensation directly reaches nominee or legal heir of a deceased worker or it can be utilized for the welfare of other workers and their families through the foundation.

According to the Bangladesh Labor Act 2006, any agreement as to indemnity from payment of compensation or reduction of liability will be void (Section 165 of the Bangladesh Labor Act 2006). The Labor Courts are entrusted to decide on the questions relating to employer's liability to pay compensation, the amount or duration of compensation, and any question as to the nature or extent of disablement. Apart from provision for extracting compensation through the Labor Court, this law requires the introduction of a compulsory group insurance scheme by the employer in any establishment where at least 100 workers are working (Section 99 of the Labor Act 2006 as amended by Section 32 of the Labor Amendment Act 2013). Group insurance policy is applicable in case of the death of workers and their permanent disabilities.

Inadequacy of this statutory compensation, legal complexities involved in the process of getting compensation prompted the emergence of private initiatives for awarding compensation to the workers, particularly to the victims of major industrial accidents. In the wake of the *Spectrum* Sweater factory collapse in April, 2005 caused by substandard building construction that led to 64 deaths, national and international trade unions along with international organizations, like the Clean Clothes Campaign (CCC) and Worker Rights Consortium (WRC) and international brands established a voluntary scheme of compensation—the Spectrum Relief Fund, for deceased and injured workers. The compensation fund known as the "Spectrum formula" was the first initiative of this kind to be developed in Bangladesh, and was a landmark private initiative of the global labor movement for providing financial support to the families of deceased workers in view of the fact that the traditional legal scheme for compensation is inadequate and involves a lengthy process (Sumon et al. 2017, 151).

Additional mechanism for compensation was developed under the Bangladesh Labor Rules 2015, namely the Central Fund for export-oriented sectors. This Fund is financed through a 0.03 levy on export orders and voluntary contributions (Rules 212–215). Another supplementary support is provided under the Bangladesh Workers Welfare Foundation Rules 2010 that allow certain financial assistance for death or permanent disability, for medical treatment and educational stipends for workers' children. However, these arrangements are inadequate, capped, and one-time payment, with no guaranteed system for long-term income replacement (Nasim 2026). In practice, these arrangements are not effectively implemented as the payment of these benefits are often delayed, sometimes industrial accidents are not reported or employers settle the amount informally below legal entitlements and workers face procedural barriers to access these funds (Nasim 2026). Furthermore, most benefits under Rule 4 and Central Fund provisions are discretionary and application based, making them inaccessible to workers. In view of shortcomings of the existing framework on compensation, the Bangladesh Labor (Amendment) Act 2026 introduced the Employment Injury Scheme—a more structured approach to compensation—which was long advocated by NGOs and the ILO. The scheme envisages a monthly pension payment as income replacement, to be calculated based on the worker's age and previous earnings, rather than relying solely on lump sum compensation.

Previously, there was no legal restriction on the employment of persons with disabilities in hazardous work. But an amendment made in 2018 to the Bangladesh Labor Act, 2006 prohibits their employment in dangerous machines or hazardous work (Section 44 of the Bangladesh Labor Act 2006). These amendments have bolstered labor welfare in the industry of Bangladesh and are expected to decrease the unrest among the labor and encourage more productivity. However, in many cases, laid-off workers are deprived of legally entitled compensation and other benefits due to lack of willingness or inability of employers to pay the same. To address the plight of laid-off workers, the establishment of a dedicated fund to provide financial benefits to the laid-off workers can ameliorate their conditions.

The Act also confers maternity benefits on women workers, such as paid maternity leave to a certain limit, as well as puts restrictions on the engagement of women workers during their pregnancy (Section 45 of the Bangladesh Labor Act 2006). Section 46 of the Bangladesh Labor Act 2006 entitles every woman worker to get maternity benefits from her employer for the period of eight weeks of pregnancy. But a woman worker will not be entitled to such benefit unless she has worked under her employer for a period of not less than six months immediately preceding the day of her delivery. The Bangladesh Labor Act 2006 also puts restrictions on the termination of employment of a woman during pregnancy through the requirement of giving notice before such termination, although it does not wholly prohibit termination during pregnancy (Section 50 of the Bangladesh Labor Act 2006). Amendments made in 2018 to the Bangladesh Labor Act 2006 facilitated some more benefits to woman workers in case of pregnancy by making provision that the post-birth leave period must be paid along with other benefits. The Bangladesh Labor Rules 2015 also were amended in 2022 to bring changes, *inter alia*, in the maternity provisions of the Bangladesh Labor Act 2006. The amendment of the Rules introduced a provision that allows four weeks' leave in the event of miscarriage. The Bangladesh Labor Act 2006 also prohibits employment of women in work of "arduous nature", on night shift or which involves long hours of standing or which is likely to adversely affect her health.

Despite these beneficial provisions, deprivation of women workers from maternity benefits is widespread, especially in the RMG sector and in many instances, women have been compelled to work night shifts or work of an arduous nature in violation of labor law due to pressure from employers.

2.5.4 Prohibition of Child Labor: Still a Reality

Child labor is generally exploitative in nature as it deprives children of health, education, and development. Child labor also manifests in forced labor. In Bangladesh, the problem of child labor is deeply entrenched in the social structure. Under the Bangladesh Labor Act 2006, child labor has been prohibited (Section 34 of the Bangladesh Labor Act 2006) except in some situations. For example, it is allowed for a child of twelve years of age in "a light work that does not hinder their education or development" (Section 35 of the Bangladesh Labor Act 2006). But this Act fails to clearly define what constitutes "light work". For school-going children, the working hours must be arranged in a way that it does not interfere with their attendance in school. Apart from these, the law prescribes that no handicapped worker shall be employed in the operation of a "dangerous machine" or "hazardous work" (Section 44(3) Bangladesh Labor Act 2006). Bangladesh also adopted the National Child Labor Elimination Policy in 2010, setting a goal to eliminate all forms of child labor by 2015. The Policy intends to make meaningful changes in the lives of the children by withdrawing them from all forms of child labor including the hazardous work and worst forms of child labor and by involving parents of working children in income generating activities with a view of getting children out of the vicious circle of poverty. In case of adolescents, the Bangladesh Labor Act, 2006 also puts restrictions on their employment as it requires by certificate of fitness by a registered medical practitioner to work in any occupation or establishment. This law prohibits employment of adolescents in hazardous work, underground and under water and limits their overtime work.

However, despite this legal prohibition, economic development and robust policy on elimination of child labor and exploitative practices, according to the National Child Labor Survey 2022, child labor has increased by 4.5 percent over the last decade due to weak implementation and lack of political will. According to the survey, child labor increased from 1.70 million in 2013 to 1.78 million in 2022. Out of 1.78 million, 1.07 million children are engaged in hazardous work according to a survey of the Bangladesh Bureau of Statistics. The government has categorized 43 types of work as hazardous for children which threaten their physical and mental development. Some of the most hazardous work where children are engaged include motor vehicle maintenance and welding, transportation, brickfields, footwear manufacturing, iron and steel casting, household good repair, tobacco and battery factories and fish processing. Most of the child labor is engaged in the informal sector. While poverty remains a fundamental reason behind child labor in Bangladesh, income inequality, economic injustice and discriminatory social structures are also the root causes that drive children into the workforce. The traditional mindset that child labor is normal, a lack of awareness about these legal provisions and lack of implementation of laws are also responsible for the practice of child labor (Hassan 2021, 11–12).

A significant number of children work as domestic servant who are often the least paid in society. Although the child domestic service is widespread in Bangladesh, it is not on the hazardous work list. It needs to acknowledge that many child domestic workers are abused and denied access to education, healthcare and protection. Child domestic workers must be categorized as hazardous work. It is needless to say that child labor, especially, in hazardous conditions, adversely affects children's health and education, subsequently affecting their future earning opportunities.

2.5.5 *Health, Safety, and Welfare Measures*

Health, hygiene, safety, and welfare issues of workers are receiving increasing attention along with the economic security of workers. The collapse of the Spectrum sweater factory in Bangladesh in 2005, the *Tazreen Fashions* factory fire of 2012 that claimed the lives of more than 112 workers, brought the safety and security issues of workers into sharp focus and acted as an impetus to incorporate adequate provisions on it in the Bangladesh Labor Act 2006 on health, hygiene and safety measures for the workers. The Act also provides detailed rules on daily working hours, intervals for rest and meals, weekly working hours, compensatory holidays, night shift, extra allowance for overtime, limited hours of work for women, special age limit for road transport workers, closure of shops, casual leave, sick leave, festival holidays and calculation of wages during the holidays. This law makes it mandatory for owners to provide personal safety equipment to every worker, to make workers aware of the hazards of work through imparting training in order to ensure protection of his health and safety. These obligations have strengthened safety measures for workers. The Bangladesh Labor Act 2006 also requires factory owners to take necessary steps for remediation of a building, or its machinery and plant that poses a serious threat to workers (Section 61 of the Bangladesh Labor Act 2006). The inspector may prohibit the use of any building, machinery or plant of any establishment if it appears dangerous to human life or safety (Section 61(2) of the Bangladesh Labor Act 2006). The Bangladesh Labor Act 2006 also requires that every establishment is equipped with firefighting apparatus and a fire exit (Section 62 of the Bangladesh Labor Act 2006), machines in motion or in use be securely fenced by the safeguards of substantial construction (Section 63 of the

Bangladesh Labor Act 2006), and the working environment of an establishment should not be overcrowded (Section 56 of the Bangladesh Labor Act 2006).

According to the Bangladesh Labor (amendment) Act 2013, the formation of a safety committee consisting of management and union/worker has been made compulsory in every factory that has 50 or more workers. A Safety Committee has a duty to assist the employer in maintaining a safe workplace and to monitor safety conditions and to conduct training.

However, due to the absence of monitoring and an effective compliance mechanism, lack of awareness of workers, financial pressure on factory owners that prioritize profit over safety of workers, the above-mentioned legal provisions relating to occupational safety and health, and welfare measures are frequently ignored and violated, leading to many industrial accidents in Bangladesh. These are evident from many subsequent industrial accidents that claimed lives of hundreds of workers.

2.5.6 *Welfare Fund and Insurance Scheme*

The Bangladesh Labor Act 2006 establishes a Workers Welfare Fund and Workers Participation Fund for those companies or establishments that meet either of the two criteria: the amount of its paid-up capital exceeds BDT ten million or the value of its permanent assets exceeds BDT twenty million and engage at least 100 workers (Section 232 of the Bangladesh Labour Act 2006). Workers' participation fund and welfare fund have been established to ensure that workers get a share in the profits of a company (Section 234 of the Bangladesh Labour Act 2006). It also obliges employers meeting certain minimum conditions to subscribe to a group insurance scheme covering all their employees and specifically for 100% export-oriented establishments and companies to establish a Central Fund from where payments can be made in the event of a death or injury of a worker. Companies in this category are required to establish the Participation Fund, Welfare Fund under the Bangladesh Labor Act 2006 and Workers Welfare Foundation Fund established under Section 2.14 of the Bangladesh Workers Welfare Foundation Act, 2006 within one month from the passing of the Act and deposit five percent of their net profit therein at a ratio of 80:10:10 within nine months from the year-end. It needs to be mentioned that all three funds are funded by a portion of a company's net profit for the welfare of workers. However, the effectiveness of these funds is undermined by low contribution rates from companies, their poor administration and administrative hurdles in delivering benefits to workers.

The Bangladesh Labor Act 2006 also introduces a "compulsory group insurance" scheme which must be implemented "under the existing insurance laws" by any establishment where at least one hundred permanent workers are employed (Section 99 of the Bangladesh Labor Act 2006). The group insurance policy covers financial benefits to be given in case of workers' deaths and permanent disabilities (Section 98(2) of the Bangladesh Labor Act 2006). For workplace deaths, it is the responsibility of an employer to pay insurance money to the dependents of the deceased worker. It also needs to be mentioned that the insurance premiums are to be solely paid by the employer on an annual basis and such premiums cannot be deducted from workers' wages (Rule 98(4) of the Bangladesh Labor Rules 2015). However, the Group Insurance scheme will not be necessary if a Central Fund is established by the government for workers in hundred percent export-oriented industrial sectors or hundred percent foreign exchange investing sectors (Section 99 (3) of the Bangladesh Labor Act 2006 as added by the Labor Amendment Act 2018).

2.6 Forgotten Domestic Workers

Domestic workers are one of the most vulnerable groups among the workers in Bangladesh and they often suffer harassment, physical torture and verbal abuse. Most of the domestic workers migrate from rural areas to urban areas because of poverty and they take household services as a way of their livelihood. There is no law to protect domestic workers in Bangladesh except the Domestic Servants' Registration Ordinance of 1961, which merely requires registration of domestic workers with the police. However, in practice, they are hardly registered with the police. A significant number of domestic workers are children. However, the Bangladesh Labor Act 2006 is silent about the recognition and protection of domestic workers. As such, domestic workers are not given any written employment contract defining their rights and roles, leaving them unprotected and deprived of any legal remedies in case of their abuse and exploitation. Their recruitment mostly occurs informally, as currently there is no legal requirement of involvement of a recruiting agency for their employment.

In 2010, the National Child Labor Elimination Policy of Bangladesh placed domestic workers as part of the informal sector. Domestic work is to be recognized as a formal sector in the Bangladesh Labor Act 2006. Domestic workers being engaged in the private sphere and being excluded from the public domain and the formal sector, they are not entitled to have the benefits of workers entitled under the formal sector. The Government of Bangladesh adopted a National Policy on Protection and Welfare of Domestic Workers in 2015 to protect two million domestic workers, the majority of whom are women and children, by recognizing them as workers and outlining 16 provisions for their rights and welfare, including requirements for registration, written contracts, and government support, defining responsibilities of employers and the government. However, the 2015 policy has been criticized for its silence about the role of recruiting agencies, the minimum wage of domestic workers, and migrant domestic workers, despite the fact that Bangladesh is a source country of a significant number of migrant workers.

Domestic workers get wages, which are invariably below the minimum wage of other sectors. They do not get any compensation for injury or death. Many domestic workers are subject to abusive working conditions, amounting to forced labor. Although workers in some informal sectors have been included in the welfare fund, there is no such fund for domestic workers. There is no complaint mechanism for domestic workers to lodge a complaint if they are oppressed. The absence of any authority to monitor the situation of domestic workers in the protection system, non-binding nature of the policy, their reluctance to report the various forms of abuse due to fear of social stigma, and the absence of a trade union contribute to their vulnerability (Khan et al. 2021). Moreover, there is no monitoring mechanism to supervise the recruiting practice of domestic workers by private employment agencies.

The 2015 Policy needs to be turned into law to afford legal protection to domestic workers. The supervision of law-enforcing agencies regarding their recruitment and registration is also needed to ensure their safety and security. A central monitoring cell has been established under the Policy. But the monitoring cells that were supposed to be formed at the city corporation, district and sub-district levels, have not yet been established. Bangladesh is yet to ratify key international instrument on domestic workers—the ILO Convention concerning Decent Work for Domestic Workers of 2011. Ratification of this Convention by Bangladesh can help protect domestic workers. Due to persistent demands of rights bodies and the ILO, the Bangladesh Labor (Amendment) Act 2026 has incorporated domestic workers in the formal sector, allows them to organize and form trade unions and introduced remedies for violation of their rights through establishing workplace complaint committees and grievance redressal procedure. However, this new law fails to make provision for issuing appointment letters, identification cards and other benefits of workers in the formal sector, making it difficult for them to organize and join trade unions.

2.7 Rights of the Tea-Garden Workers—A Neglected Issue

Tea-garden workers, predominantly women from ethnic minorities and lower-caste communities, are the most deprived and are neglected in the discourse of industrial relations due to their marginalized status in society. According to some estimates, there are about 7,00,000 tea workers in 168 tea gardens in Bangladesh (Ahsan and Chowdhury 2021). Because of a poor pay structure, most of them live below the poverty line. According to the data from the Statistical Handbook on Bangladesh Tea Industry 2019, there are 166 tea gardens in the country where 103,747 permanent workers and 36, 437 temporary workers are involved. The Bangladesh Labor Act 2006 creates obligations for employers to arrange entertainment, educational and housing facilities for tea-garden workers (Sections 95 and 96 of the Bangladesh Labor Act 2006). The tea-garden sector is semi-formal in nature as despite they are recognized as workers under the Bangladesh Labor Act 2006, they do not enjoy many benefits provided under this Act relating to leave and compensation. The exploitative attitudes of the tea-garden authorities contribute to isolation and vulnerability of tea-garden workers. The conditions of their work and wages are determined by the agreement that the Bangladesh Tea Association (BTA) and *Bangladesh Cha Sramik Union* (BCSU) that is signed every two years. While the BTA represents owners of the tea gardens, BCSU is the only trade union for around 1,38,000 tea workers and their combined bargaining agent (Gain 2023). However, this biannual agreement is never signed on time. As such, payment of arrears has become part of the culture in Bangladesh's tea gardens (Gain 2023).

Because of persistent reluctance of the BTA's in increasing wages, the tea workers went for street agitations and strike from August 9 to 27 in 2022(Gain 2023). It needs to be mentioned that the three minimum wage boards set up for tea-garden workers for the tea industry have fixed minimum wages which is much lower compared to other industries. Temporary tea-garden workers are paid around 30 to 50 percent lower wages than permanent workers. As per government directives, a permanent tea-garden worker is now paid BDT 170 per day, but the wages of many temporary workers were not raised, though according to the Bangladesh Labor Act 2006, workers must be paid equal wages for equal work.

Despite tea gardens as a labor-intensive industry, the workers get minimum wages and fringe benefits compared to other sectors, excluding them in economic, political, social, and cultural aspects of society (Dey and Uddin 2025). With a high rate of illiteracy, inadequate health care system, poor housing and living conditions, they remain marginalized from mainstream society.

2.8 The Bangladesh Labor Welfare Foundation Act 2006

The Bangladesh Labor Welfare Foundation Act 2006 was enacted to establish a Labor Welfare Foundation in order to ensure the welfare of the workers employed in both the formal and informal sectors. Section 2.2(a) of the Bangladesh Labor Welfare Foundation Act 2006 defines informal sector as the private sector where conditions of work or employment are not regulated by the existing labor laws or rules and where the opportunity to organize is very limited. The main functions of the foundation are to ensure the welfare of workers and their families by taking various welfare projects for the workers, providing financial assistance to the disabled workers and the families of a worker in case of his death by accident, providing medical services to sick workers, providing scholarships and stipends to the meritorious children of workers and by introducing collective insurance for the life of workers (Section 2.5 of the Bangladesh Labor Welfare Foundation Act 2006).

The fund of such foundation will be drawn from the grants of the government, the employer and other recognized sources (Section 2.14 of the Bangladesh Labor Welfare Foundation Act 2006). According to the Labor Welfare Rules 2010 formulated under this Act, informal workers outside the purview of the existing labor law will be entitled to a provident fund facility, which was a long awaited welfare measures for them. The Rules also provide for detailed provisions for administering such fund, introduction of group insurance for the firm where more than two hundred workers—formal or informal—are engaged to ensure their economic security. The Rules have been further amended in 2015 to include more welfare and beneficial provisions for the workers, dependents of such workers and families of workers in case of their death and provide for welfare measures for maternity benefits for women workers in the informal sector (Rule 4).

While enactment of this law is a welcome development for extending social benefits to the informal sector, the foundation remains largely dysfunctional because most of the employers, driven by self-interest and profit maximization, are reluctant to contribute to this fund and they often devise tactics to avoid their contribution. An effective implementation of this law depends considerably upon the willingness of employers.

2.9 The Bangladesh Labor Rules 2015

The Bangladesh Labor Rules 2015 formulated under the Bangladesh Labor Act 2006 elaborated the provisions to supplement the latter and have introduced some positive changes in industrial relations as they contain provisions relating to employment policy or service rules of an establishment, prescribe the process and forms for the registration of manpower supply agencies, clarify and remove ambiguities regarding issuing appointment letter of workers, provide detailed guidelines regarding provident fund, holidays, clarify the provisions related to compensatory weekly holiday, and provide detailed guidelines on health and fire safety. Under the Rules, clarification is provided for the mechanism of calculating wages for a fraction of a month and deduction from wages. The Rules also outline some prescribed forms for filing cases in the Labor Court and provide detailed guidelines on how approval of the factory plan and any extension thereof should be obtained. The Bangladesh Labor Rules 2015 also deal with retrenchment of workers during factory takeovers, and clarify provisions relating to maternity benefits.

2.10 The Bangladesh Labor (Amendment) Act 2026: A Long-awaited Reform Agenda

In the wake of criticism of the labor law framework by human rights bodies buyers, global labor federations, the ILO, the EU and USA, the Bangladesh Labor Act 2006 has undergone many reforms in 2026 in a number of areas that include lowering trade union-registration requirement, expanding the definition and categories of worker and workplace, introduction of new safety, hygiene requirements, and enhanced maternity-related obligations for employers. The expanded definition of worker includes care-givers employed in hospitals, clinics and diagnostic centers. The amendment also recognizes domestic workers, self-employed persons and individuals involved in digital platform as workers but only for limited purpose, e.g., domestic workers for getting compensation for workplace injuries and joining trade unions, while self-employed persons and digital platform workers only for joining trade union. The amendment also prohibits the blacklisting of workers by any factory, forced labor, discrimination against workers and sexual harassment in factories, and makes formation of "safety committee" mandatory for every establishment with fifty or more than fifty workers. It also establishes "Employment Injury Scheme Fund", allows workers of non-profit institutions to claim their labor rights, contains provision for reducing gender pay gap, defines direct and indirect pattern of discrimination and widens the scope of social dialogue through formation of tripartite consultative council at national and sectoral level. The Act also bars the employers from preparing and maintaining a list or database of workers ineligible for re-employment after termination for any other reason. Although ILO Conventions prohibit discrimination in employment, there was no explicit provision in labor laws of Bangladesh prohibiting discrimination in employment. By prohibiting discrimination against workers, this amendment closely aligns with international labor standards. This Act also defines and prohibits forced labor. Overall, these reforms are significant positive steps in view of the fact that despite the constitutional provisions on equality, non-discrimination and prohibition of forced labor, labor laws were deficient to address specific cases of discrimination in employment and occupation and did not elaborate on what constitutes forced labor.

The need for these legal reforms was underpinned for aligning labor law with the international labor standards to sustain the country's trade benefits, especially in the European Union and the USA. This reform initiative is seen as a major effort to ensure decent work, improve industrial relations and align labor law with international standards. However, success of these reform initiatives will largely depend on overcoming hurdles like enforcement gaps, capacity constraints, and employer resistance to embrace these reforms.

2.11 Challenges of the Implementation of Labor Laws

While the regulatory framework on labor relations has been improved by adopting many laws in the last two decades, labor laws are routinely breached by employers and sometimes by government. This remains the main hurdle for workers for gaining the benefits of such improved labor standards. Some of the challenges can be attributed to a lack of accountability for such breaches and fear of employers of loss of competitiveness as most of them believe that compliance will increase production cost. One significant challenge of the implementation lies with an entrenched culture of negligence of employers toward safety. Although fire incidents occurred in many industries, causing loss of lives, only a few factory owners have been held liable for negligence in ensuring worker safety (Sumon, Shifa, and Gulrukh 2017, 151–152).

Weak enforcement, lack of awareness among workers about their legal rights, unrealistic penalties, limited resources, and lack of database of workers also contribute to poor implementation of labor laws. Lack of willingness on the part of employers, inadequate human resources, and lack of institutional capacity and monitoring of enforcement are the main reasons for the non-implementation of labor laws.

2.12 Institutional Framework on Labor Relations

A sound institutional framework plays a pivotal role in the enforcement and implementation of labor laws. Like many developing countries, the government is the key actor in industrial relations in Bangladesh as it formulates law and policy on labor issue and establishes institutions to enforce laws and administer labor administration of justice, determine wages, protect the rights of workers and promote a balance between the interest of different stakeholders. First, it is responsible for creating legal and regulatory structure through enacting law and ratifying ILO conventions and transposing the ILS into national legal framework. Second, it controls employment in public sector enterprises and influences labor relations in the private sector by shaping laws and policies. Third, the government is mainly responsible for creating an enabling environment for facilitating collective bargaining and protecting freedom of association to prevent interference in the bargaining process from any political party, government agency or the employer. Fourth, the government also plays a predominant role in coordinating among trade unions, employers' organizations, and international agencies like the ILO and facilitating meeting of tripartite bodies in order to address the labor rights and problems of workers. The success of tripartite consultation or negotiations largely depends on the responsiveness of the government to meet the demands of both employers and workers. Fifth, the government is responsible for establishing different institutions and agencies for labor administration and the resolution of labor disputes. There are various government authorities and agencies entrusted with the responsibility of labor administration in Bangladesh.

In Bangladesh, the Ministry of Labor and Manpower is the apex body of government agencies and institutions on labor administration and is responsible for policy formulation, establishing minimum wage boards, collection of labor statistics, reaching agreements with international labor organizations, coordinating with other government agencies, and overall supervision of the government agencies under it such as the Department of Labor, the Department of Inspection for Factories and Establishments; the Bureau of Manpower, Employment and Training (BMET); and the Minimum Wages Board.

However, the Department of Labor remains the main government agency to deal with labor administration and governance and implementation of labor laws and policies and is responsible for registration of trade unions and federations of trade unions, determination of collective bargaining agents under the Bangladesh Labor Act 2006. It also acts as a conciliation machinery to address labor disputes, including strikes and lock-outs, to ensure industrial peace, holds tripartite conciliation meetings of the management and workers both in the public and private sectors, lodges legal proceedings on behalf of the government in civil courts, labor courts, and labor appellate tribunal, and provides advisory services to employers' organizations and trade unions on the interpretation and application of labor laws.

However, the DOL's capacity to carry out its wide-ranging functions effectively is constrained by a lack of adequate human and financial resources. Its effectiveness is limited due to the lack of accountability of its conciliators and other key personnel.

2.13 Compliance with Labor Laws Through Labor Inspection

The system of labor inspection plays an important role in securing compliance with labor law in relation to the safety and security of workers. Labor inspection is carried out by a variety of approaches, which include compliance and enforcement measures. According to an ILO study, a labor inspection system has a two-fold purpose—firstly, it supervises and monitors the enforcement of provisions such as building codes, and occupational health and safety. Secondly, it provides training, advisory services and information to workers, employers, and their representatives (Vega and Robert 2013, 3). However, compliance strategies alone are not sufficient to prevent violations of labor laws. There must be appropriate sanctions for non-compliance with labor laws. In this context, imposition of sanctions for non-compliance is considered as complementary to the overall purpose of holding accountable for violations (Vega and Robert 2013).

In any country, institutions of inspection for factories and establishments play a critical role in enforcing labor laws and regulations. Labor inspectorates present substantial institutional heterogeneity across countries (Kanbur and RonconI 2018, 333). In Bangladesh, the Department of Inspection for Factories and Establishments (DIFE) is entrusted with responsibilities for inspection of factories, and establishments for enforcement of labor laws in order to ensure safety, health, hygiene, approval of layout and design of factories, monitoring the compliance with working hours, payment of wages and compensation as prescribed by labor laws. It is also responsible for monitoring the enforcement of provisions relating to occupational health and safety, social security and welfare measures for workers; filing cases for the violations of labor laws in labor courts; approval of construction factory building and compliance with building codes; issue of registration and licenses of factories, and coordination with different government agencies, employer's organizations and trade unions regarding enforcement of labor laws. The Bangladesh Labor (Amendment) Act 2026 has further expanded the scope of activities of the inspectorate by delineating its detailed functions.

However, the Department of Inspection is not well-equipped with manpower and financial resources. Fire safety certificates are not renewed regularly. Sometimes, the owners of the factories are not aware of the building codes. Labor inspection offices require significant public investment and resources to ensure compliance with building and safety codes.

According to the Bangladesh Labor Act 2006, although prior written approval from the Chief Inspector of factories is mandatory for constructing a factory or its expansion, there is no provision for inspecting the construction works of a factory by the Chief Inspector of factories. To secure safety of the factory workers, submission of a certificate from the concerned authorities following the approval of the building plan can be made mandatory.

The Inspection Office lacks adequate manpower. There are only a few inspectors for around 40,000 factories, 168 tea gardens, 60 ship-breaking industries, two dockyards in the country. On the other hand, there is no provision for holding the Chief Inspector and other inspectors accountable for their failings or violation of labor law. Lack of a complaint mechanism at the Inspection Office regarding non-compliance with its decisions or inaction or omissions of the inspection office is the main barrier in holding accountability of inspectors. A robust complaint mechanism with definitive and transparent rules, including the fixation of time for the disposal of complaints by workers concerning the safety of the factory, should be introduced.

Thus, the ineffectiveness of the Inspection Offices in Bangladesh can largely be attributed to a lack of adequate inspectors and logistic support, insufficient budgetary allocation, inadequate punishment for negligence in performing duty of inspectors, lack of training of inspectors and absence of complaint mechanism. In order to enable labor inspection office in enforcement of labor law effectively, inspectors need to be authorized to record instances of violations and to impose a fine for non-compliance with the labor laws. The Bangladesh Labor Act 2006 needs to be amended to allow any individual or organization to report violations of any labor law relating to safety to the office of inspection. Capacity building of the inspection office in terms of equipping labor inspectors with sufficient knowledge and training to perform their role properly needs to be given priority for ensuring effective compliance (Vega and Robert 2013, 43).

Although amendments made in 2013 to the Bangladesh Labor Act 2006 have strengthened the Department of Inspection by equipping it with more powers and enhancing its legal status, it needs an adequate number of inspectors and logistic support to function effectively.

2.14 Role of Employers' Organizations

The traditional role of eEmployers' associations includes protecting and defending their common interests in collective bargaining with workers' union and raise their collective viewpoints to government. The Bangladesh Labor Act 2006 confer on the right of employers to establish and to join associations of their own choosing in order to regulate the relations between employers and workers or employers and employers. In this regard, the law does not make any distinction between the procedures of registration of trade unions of workers and trade unions of employers. Therefore, procedures for registration and cancelation of trade unions are equally applicable to employers' organizations. However, due to asymmetrical power relations in the labor market, employers' organizations exert a much broader range of influence and exercise power over production compared to that of workers' organization.

The Bangladesh Employers Federation (BEF) is the main federation of employers' associations and the main members of this federation are: Bangladesh Garments Manufacturing and Exporters Association (BGMEA), Bangladesh Textile Mills Association (BTMA), Bangladesh Knitwear Manufacturers and Exporters Association (BKMEA), Bangladesh Jute Mills Association (BJMA), and Bangladesh Finished Leather, Leather goods and Footwear Exporters Association. Established in 1998, BEF "represents nearly 90 per cent of the established employers in the private sector, all the public sector corporations and autonomous bodies". It participates in ILO activities, representing the employers of Bangladesh and provides multiple services to members, including capacity building, advisory services, and training.

The Bangladesh Garment Manufacturers and Exporters Association (BGMEA), a trade association of 4,524 garment factory owners founded in 1983, is one of the most influential employers' organizations in terms of economic and political leverage that it exerts. While BGMEA is mainly concerned with the promotion of the export of garment products, it also provides advisory services to its members, facilitates compliance with labor law and promotion of labor welfare. It also attempts to ensure workers' rights and social compliance at factories, collaborates with local and international stakeholders, including brands and development partners, to facilitate the development of the Bangladesh apparel industry. Over the years, the BGMEA has also undertaken initiatives for social dialogue in both formal and informal manner. The BGMEA has adopted its Sustainability Strategic Vision 2030, which sets targets for improving environmental, social and governance aspects of the RMG industry, aligning with global concerns and SDGs. The Vision commits to address climate change, circularity, water use, energy conservation, deforestation, gender equality, workplace safety, skills development, community well-being, data reporting, industry growth, green infrastructure, innovation, global reach and good governance (Rubel 2024). In the competitive global market, employers' associations must embrace accountability, transparency, ethical conduct and responsible business practices in order to ensure sustainable growth of the industrial relations in Bangladesh. Two major employer associations—BGMEA and BKMEA are responsive to international pressure and to the demands of buyers in the area of social compliance. Rahman observes that the employer association is more active to respond the buyers' concerns rather than the concerns of the workers (Rahman 2013, 35). Apart from protecting their collective interests in industrial relations, they have a vital role to play in applying the international labor standards, implementing national labor laws and emerging human rights due diligence norms to remain competitive globally. The employer organizations also need to develop strategy for workforce transitions towards artificial intelligence and digital transformation.

However, the employers' organizations are fragmented and are facing many challenges posed by globalization. In the globalized world, the growing presence of multinational firms, which are often outside the membership of employers' organizations are posing formidable challenges to such organizations at the national level.

2.15 Global Influences on the Design of Labor Laws in Bangladesh

Over the last years, the labor laws of Bangladesh are increasingly subject to scrutiny and criticisms from rights bodies, buyers, ILO, the EU, and USA because of their perceived inadequacy of the international labor standards. As a result, the Bangladesh Labor Act 2006 underwent a series of legal reforms in 2013, 2018, and 2023 for improving labor rights, safety, and security of workers. The need for reform was underpinned by pressure from these actors for aligning labor law with global standards to sustain the country's trade benefits, especially in the European Union and access to the USA market. These reform initiatives—an outcome of persistent and collaborative efforts of various stakeholders—are seen as a major shift toward aligning labor law with international standards. Thus, the globalization process and external pressures from buyers and international organizations for incorporating international standards are continuously shaping the changing landscape of labor laws of Bangladesh. The changing power relations in bargaining capacity, the necessity to remain competitive in the global market, and technological changes have provided an impetus to bringing recent changes in labor laws. The labor law of Bangladesh has been designed in a way to reduce huge and long-standing asymmetry in the bargaining power between employers and employees. The increasing importance of international labor standards promoted by the ILO and obligations of Bangladesh to adhere to these standards is another pivotal factor that underpins the improvement of labor standards.

The collapse of the Rana Plaza building on 24 April 2013 was a turning point in initiating crucial legal reforms on workers' safety. The labor law and institutional reforms initiated after the *Rana Plaza* collapse are largely mediated by the demands of the international community and stakeholders for improving labor rights and occupational safety in the RMG sector. The trade liberalization and increasing reference to labor standards in investment and trade agreements have also influenced the improvement and design of labor laws (Sheffer 2011). A review by the ILO in 2022 found that about 30% of new Bilateral Investment Treaties (BITs) include references to labor standards. This trend signals a departure from earlier treaty practices and reflects a growing recognition of labor rights as fundamental values. Similarly, inclusion of social clauses in trade agreements aims to discourage developing countries to lower labor standards. Many social clauses seek to eliminate the worst form of workers' exploitation (Berik and Rodgers 2010). This growing trade-labor-investment nexus reinforces that both host states and investors are obligated to adhere to the international labor standards. Bangladesh, being a developing country and party to many BITs and trade agreements, is under international obligation to align its labor law with the ILS.

The above discussion reveals that the influence of global actors is evident in the legal design of labor market and institutions of Bangladesh that have been developed drawing lessons from the international labor standards and upward harmonization is reflected in the recent amendments of the Bangladesh Labor Act 2006. Another noticeable trend is that Bangladesh has gradually adopted stronger regulations for labor market instead of de-regulating it.

2.16 Regulating the Gig Economy

As mentioned in Chapter 1, Bangladesh is experiencing a significant increase in employment in the gig economy, characterized by using online platforms to match workers with short-term jobs and flexible work arrangement that suits their needs. However, the gig economy poses challenges for application of traditional labor laws, which have traditionally been focused on protecting workers in traditional workplaces. However, these new forms of work have also raised questions about the application of labor laws to gig workers as there is no defined and clear employer-employee relationship in gig economy (Singh and Bhushan 2023, 23). Addressing these challenges brought by changes in employment relationships requires reform in labor law in Bangladesh to ensure that legal framework is adapted to the changing nature of work.

2.17 Conclusion

Labor laws and their recent reforms must be understood as an outcome of workers' struggles for realizing their legitimate claims against the state and employers. Labor laws of Bangladesh have undergone profound transformation toward progressive changes in the last decades that reflect shifting dynamics of labor relations. While previously it was mainly concerned with the protection of the workers, over the last decades, there has been a shift of labor law from its focus on the "protective" purposes of labor law toward an emphasis on "right" to decent conditions of work, fair pay, job security, participation in trade union, and collective bargaining through progressive reforms. However, a wide gap between the rhetoric and the reality of the implementation of labor laws persists in Bangladesh as many reform initiatives have been undermined by lack of enforcement, capacity constraints, and employer resistance to embrace the changes not been able to bring the desired changes due to its in-built weaknesses, and lack of institutional capacity to implement the laws. Such a gap persists in a range of issues, including minimum wages, collective bargaining, trade union, decent work, and safety, security of workers. Social safety net programs, such as employment injury insurance and unemployment benefits are largely missing for workers in Bangladesh. Despite recent changes, Bangladesh is facing the challenge of keeping labor law abreast with international labor standards and modern trends in labor market regulation. With the advent of automation, artificial intelligence, the rise of gig economies, and the rise of the global supply chain, the legal framework on labor relations in Bangladesh are being challenged to adapt to these new realities. The enforcement of labor law is always a daunting task, which is partially attributed to a lack of knowledge and awareness about labor laws and public functions of labor institutions among workers, and partially it can be traced to lack of institutional capacity to implement laws. A low level of legal literacy among workers is one of main obstacles to the application of labor law.

Bibliography

Books

Atleson, James B. 1983. *Values and Assumptions in American Labor Law*. University of Massachusetts Press.

Benson, Edward. 1988. *The Law of Industrial Conflict*. Macmillan Press.

Davidov, Guy. 2016. *A Purposive Approach to Labour Law*. Oxford University Press.

Davies, Paul, and Mark Freedland. 1993. *Labour Legislation and Public Policy*. Clarendon Press.

Hepple, Bob, and Bruno Veneziani. 2009. *The Transformation of Labour Law in Europe*. Hart.

Kahn-Freund, O. 1972. *Labour and the Law*. Stevens.

Chapters in Edited Books

Arthur, Harry. 2011. "Labour Law after Labour." In *The Idea of Labour Law*, edited by Guy Davidov and Brian Langille, 13–29. Oxford University Press.

Charnovitz, Steve. 2005. "The Labour Dimension of the Emerging Free Trade Area of the Americas." In *Labour Rights as Human Rights*, edited by Philip Alston, 143–176. Oxford University Press.

Deakin, Simon. 2011. "The Contribution of Labour Law to Economic and Human Development." In *The Idea of Labour Law*, edited by Davidov and Langille, 156–176. Oxford University Press.

Fredman, Sandra. 2004. "The Ideology of Labour Law." In *The Future of Labour Law: Liber Amicorum Bob Hepple*, edited by Catherine Barnard, Simon Deakin, and Gillian S. Morris, 1–21. Hart Publishing.

McCurdy, Charles W. 1998. "The 'Liberty of Contract' Regime in American Law." In *The State and Freedom of Contract*, edited by Harry N. Scheiber, 193–207. Stanford University Press.

Sumon, H., Nazneen Shifa, and Saydia Gulrukh. 2017. "Discourses of Compensation and the Normalization of Negligence: The Experience of the Tazreen Factory Fire." In *Unmaking the Global Sweatshop: Health and Safety of the World's Garment Workers*, edited by Rebecca Prentice and Geert De Neve, 147–172. University of Pennsylvania Press.

Journal Articles

Ahsan, F. W., and P.A. Chowdhury. 2021. "Modern Day Slavery in the Tea Gardens of Bangladesh: Abolished in Law, Persisting in Fact." *Journal of International Law and Comity* 2 (1): 1–28.

Berik, Günseli and Yana van der Meulen Rodgers. 2010. "Options for Enforcing Labour Standards: Lessons from Bangladesh and Cambodia." *Journal of International Development* 22 (1): 56–85.

Coutu, M., R. Dukes, and G. Murray. 2023. "Labour Law and Industrial Relations: Toward Renewal?" *Relations industrielles/Industrial Relations* 78 (4). https://doi.org/10.7202/1111504ar.

Dey, Goutam Dey, and Mahabuba Uddin. 2025. "Social Exclusion of Tea Plantation Workers: A Study on Moulvibazar District, Bangladesh." *Social Science Review* 3 (3). https://ssr.gstu.edu.bd/page13.html.

Hendrickx, Frank. 2012. "Foundations and Functions of Contemporary Labour Law." *European Labour Law Journal* 3 (2): 108–133.

Hepple, Bob. 1995. "The Future of Labour Law." *Industrial Law Journal* 24: 303–322.

Kanbur, Ravi, and Lucas Ronconi. 2018. "Enforcement Matters: The Effective Regulation of Labour." *International Labour Review* 157 (3): 331–356.

Khan, B. U. 1997. "The Development of Right to Freedom of Association in Pre-independence Bangladesh (1919–1971): An Analysis of Legislation and Policy." *Bangladesh Journal of Law* 1 (2): 182–220.

Langille, Brian. 2015. "'Take These Chains from My Heart and Set Me Free': How Labor Law Theory Drives Segmentation of Workers' Rights." *Comparative Labor Law & Policy Journal* 36: 257–282.

Langille, Brian. 2005. "Core Labour Rights—The True Story (Reply to Alston)." *European Journal of International Law* 16 (3): 428–433.

Rahman, Kazi Mahmudur. 2013. "Governing Mechanisms for Controlling Labour: The Case of the Ready-Made Garments Industry in Bangladesh." *International Journal of Political Science and Development* 1 (2): 3–15.

Sheffer, Megan Wells. 2011. "Bilateral Investment Treaties: A Friend or Foe to Human Rights?" *Denver Journal of International Law and Policy* 39: 483–511.

Singh, Ruchi, and Dr. Vani Bhushan. 2023. "The Global Workforce Revolution: Exploring Digital Labour Platforms and the Gig Economy in the Era of Globalization." *International Journal of Civil Law and Legal Research* 3 (2): 19–27.

Spector, Horacio. 2006. "Philosophical Foundations of Labor Law." *Florida State University Law Review* 33: 1119–1148.

Reports

Bangladesh Employers' Federation. https://bef.org.bd/.

BGMEA at a Glance. https://www.bgmea.com.bd/page/aboutus.

Constitution, Legislation and Policy.

Domestic Workers Protection and Welfare Policy. 2015. https://bef.org.bd/wp-content/uploads/2021/08/Domestic-Workers-Protection-and-Welfare-Policy-2015.pdf.

Gain, Philip. 2023. "No Justice in Paying Tea Workers' Arrears." *The Daily Star* (Dhaka), January 29. Accessed on February 3, 2024. https://www.thedailystar.net/opinion/views/news/no-justice-paying-tea-workers-arrears-3232926.

Hassan, Kashfeea. 2021. "Breaking the General Perception: How Far Is Poverty the Main Cause of Child Labour?" In *An Analysis of Perception, Cause, Impact and Relevant Laws/Policies*, December. Dhaka: Bangladesh Institute of Labour Studies (BILS).

Nasim, AKM. 2026. "Compensation Falls Short and Fails Workers, It Needs Urgent Reform". *Interview with the Daily Star* (Dhaka) April 25: https://www.thedailystar.net/slow-reads/slow-reads-special/price-labour/news/compensation-falls-short-and-fails-workers-it-must-change-4159021.

National Child Labour Elimination Policy 2010, Ministry of Labour and Employment Government of the People's Republic of Bangladesh. https://file-khulna.portal.gov.bd/files/iri.khulna.gov.bd/notices/d096fb5b_f22a_4091_88bb_b5d6d79c09fb/ed4f342be9069c852569c159e78829cb.pdf.

Rubel, Md. Mohiuddin. 2024. "BGMEA Transforming RMG Industry into Global Sustainability Leader." *The Daily Star* (Dhaka), January 10. Accessed on May 3, 2024. https://www.thedailystar.net/business/news/bgmea-transforming-rmg-industry-global-sustainability-leader-3515336.

Sarwar, Mohammad Golam. 2021. "Mainstreaming Human Rights in Business to Protect Workers' Rights." *The Daily Star* (Dhaka), May 4. Accessed on May 22, 2024. https://www.thedailystar.net/law-our-rights/news/mainstreaming-human-rights-business-protect-workers-rights-2087989.

The Bangladesh Labor (Amendment) Act 2026.

The Bangladesh Labor Act 2006.

The Constitution of Bangladesh 1972.

Vega, Maria Luz, and René Robert. 2013. *Labour Inspection Sanctions: Law and Practice of National Labour Inspection Systems*. Labour Administration and Inspection Programme (LAB/ADMIN). Geneva: International Labour Office.

Zakir Hossain Khan, M., et al. 2021. "Assessment of the Implementation Status of the Domestic Workers Protection and Welfare Policy and way forward." Bangladesh Institute of Labor Studies, May, Dhaka. http://bilsbd.org/wp-content/uploads/2021/08/Assessment-of-the-implementation-status-of-the-Domestic-Workers-Protection-and-Welfare-Policy-and-way-forward.pdf.

CHAPTER 3

Economic Globalization and Export Processing Zones in Bangladesh

3.1 Introduction

The rapid expansion of Export Processing Zones (EPZs) or sometimes also called Special Economic Zones (SEZs) across both developed and developing countries has been a catalyst for economic globalization over the past few decades, shaping flows of global trade and investment. The global growth of EPZs can be attributed to their potential for promoting industrialization, technology transfer, economic development, and creation of employment opportunities. EPZs in developing countries are mostly designed to attract FDI and to boost export-led economic growth. The rapid expansion of these zones has been constructed as a part of promoting capitalist development policies in developing countries that began in the era of decolonization (Neveling 2015). EPZs are also seen as a process of liberalizing trade and integrating national economies into the global economy. Employment in EPZs can—in the right circumstances—lead to a broad "upskilling" of the workforce of the host country, as employees of foreign firms operating within the EPZ learn new skills on the job (Aggarwal 2007). EPZs have fostered the growth and expansion of the global supply chains, further integrating the global economy (Braga et al. 2023). An increasing number of developing countries promote EPZs for acquiring industrial skills and resources necessary to compete in the global economy. EPZs may also create a positive impact on the economy of a country through their backward and forward linkages.

A. Al Faruque, *Globalization and Labour Rights*,
https://doi.org/10.1007/978-981-92-3661-9_3

EPZs operate in specialized and fenced-in industrial enclaves with distinct operational rules and principles, which are usually different from those that prevail outside of such zones. An increasing number of EPZs are also open to domestic investor participation. Similarly, not all EPZs are exclusively export-oriented. In some countries, EPZs have been established in some countries to meet the needs of domestic demand. While in the large majority of cases, EPZs have had a positive impact on host economies, they are sometimes fiercely criticized for poor working conditions and violation of international labor standards. For example, inadequate health and safety standards, deficient enforcement of health and safety standards, excessive working hours, job insecurity, low wages, and breaches of trade union rights are reported in many EPZs in developing countries (Binder 2010, 101). While some of the problems are due to explicit exemptions of EPZs from the application of certain national legislation, others relate to general deficiencies in legislation or to a poor enforcement of the relevant laws (Binder 2010, 101). Although it is generally found that minimum wages for EPZ workers are higher than those of workers outside of EPZs, it does not necessarily imply that such wages are decent or livable wages (Lang 2010, 20).

Bangladesh started establishing EPZs in the early 1980s when it enacted a special law for this purpose and since then, it has experienced rapid expansion of EPZ as a way to attract foreign direct investments, to increase export earnings, to boost employment opportunities and to diversify its export portfolio.

3.2 Economic Globalization and EPZs

Critics of globalization often claim that the governments of developing countries limit the application of labor law and labor standards in an effort to stimulate exports through these zones. In fact, the setting up of EPZs has been seen as the main investment and trade facilitation policy of many developing countries. EPZs are seen as a quid pro quo between governments and investor companies: in exchange of the job creation, technological transfer, economic development, and compliance with export performance requirements, investor companies receive substantial fiscal incentives, such as tax and tariff exemptions. Apart from tax exemptions, relaxed regulatory environment, liberal profit repatriation regulation, and easing of foreign ownership regulations provide a comparative advantage to foreign firms for investing in EPZs, which enable them to provide access to world markets by raising industrial output, and upgrading production standards to a point that domestic firms cannot accomplish this. Large corporations that govern global production chains continue to invest in and produce in EPZs with preferential trade and input price conditions and the relatively lax labor standards that allow greater control of the production process (Milberg and Amengual 2008, 3). Apart from the above, EPZs offer other benefits to international firms, such as infrastructure, special administrative supports and subsidized utilities, and unlimited duty-free imports of raw and intermediate goods needed for production (Madani 1999). These special administrative arrangements and differential rules regulate investment conditions, customs, and taxation in order to create a favorable business environment for investors (Farole and Akinci 2011, 23). Through the export-led growth policies pursued for EPZs, many developing countries have integrated into the global market (Farole and Akinci 2011, 23). EPZs in developing countries, thus, have a distinctive model of governance and are regulated by a set of laws and norms that are different from mainstream labor laws. Over the years, EPZs have become more attractive for multinational firms as they prefer to invest in these zones for the lax legal framework and for producing labor-intensive goods through "subcontracting" and "outsourcing industries" (Vadlamannati 2015, 8).

The EPZs have undoubtedly paved the way for industrialization, economic development, and growth in developing countries by attracting foreign investment and generating earnings of foreign exchange, and enhancing exports (Nigar 2020). Moreover, EPZs have also facilitated much-needed transfer of technology and knowledge, creating employment opportunities and upgradation of skills of workers in most developing and emerging economies (Nigar 2020). The EPZs have also contributed to improving the local infrastructure and local wealth creation in host countries.

While in many countries EPZs have contributed to economic development and transformed their economies, they are criticized for poor working conditions and the absence of labor rights. There are also growing social and environmental concerns as setting up these zones requires the acquisition of large areas of land which leads to dispossession of agrarian community, forced relocation, livelihood destruction, and causes environmental damage. Sometimes, environmental standards are relaxed to attract investment in these zones at the expense of severe environmental damage. These relaxed environmental standards act as an incentive for relocating production to zones (Arnold 2017, 5). These social and environmental costs associated with the establishment of EPZs often outweigh the economic gains from these zones (Arnold 2017, 5). Although it is generally found that minimum wages for EPZ workers are higher than that of workers outside of EPZs, it does not necessarily imply that such wages are decent or livable wages (Lang 2010, 20).

EPZs in Bangladesh have attracted investment in labor-intensive industries like RMG due to the abundant supply of cheap labor, favorable investment climate, and enabling legal framework. EPZs are particularly attractive to investors because of labor-intensive industries such as RMG, footwear and assembling of electronic components, which do not require high technological knowledge and as such, a low-skill workforce meets the requirement of employment in EPZs. In terms of exports, manufacturing employment and the attraction of foreign investment, the EPZs are vital for the economy of Bangladesh. Bangladesh has adopted special labor legislation for its EPZs.

Special treatment of labor may be of particular concern in export processing zones (EPZs) in which governments provide basic infrastructure and tax concessions to attract foreign investment. While EPZs frequently offer a higher level of wages and other benefits compared with other sectors of the economy (Richardson and Harrison 2017, 10), they are often characterized by longer compulsory working hours and inadequate safety measures (Richardson and Harrison 2017). According to Richardson and Harrison, work in EPZ involves repetitive manual labor, which consequently leads to serious occupational health and safety risks (Richardson and Harrison 2017, 10). EPZs are typical examples of earning foreign exchange with the low cost of production through the availability of cheap labor and tax and tariff exemptions, and the flexibility of labor laws (Vadlamannati 2015, 8). Since the enactment of the EPZ law in the early 1980s in Bangladesh, activity in the EPZs has experienced rapid expansion and witnessed a significant increase in the employment of workers given the fact that export-producing firms are allowed to produce goods at the lowest possible cost, which gives them a competitive advantage in the global market (Vadlamannati 2015). In many developing countries, such zones are regulated by separate laws and norms of enforcement (Vadlamannati 2015). However, such a special legal regime on EPZs may fall below international legal standards because freedom of association and collective bargaining are hardly allowed in

EPZs. Even when freedom of association and collective bargaining activities are legally permitted in the zones, such activities can be seriously restricted and undermined in practice. Limited rights of workers to redress their grievances, excessive working hours, absence of minimum wages, the gender pay gap, and inadequate safety measures can further worsen the rights of workers. The legal regime of EPZ is sometimes criticized for its excessive focus on securing profit margins for investors rather than on the safety and welfare of workers.

3.3 Significance of EPZs in the Economy of Bangladesh

In Bangladesh, there are eight export processing zones. The export of products of EPZs constitutes 18% of the total volume of national export. As per BEPZA data, around 0.52 million workers are employed in the EPZs, of which 66% are women and they facilitate economic well-being and empowerment for women. Exports from EPZs accounted for 11 percent of total foreign exchange earnings in the fiscal year 2022–2023, making a valuable contribution to the economy of Bangladesh by employment generation, export, and industrialization. In order to attract foreign direct investment, Bangladesh offers income and other tax concessions and tax holidays to firms in EPZs, following global trends. Such tax concessions are important for foreign firms, especially those that are subsidiaries of a foreign company, are operated as cost centers and generate no profits that can be taxed. Therefore, the foreign firms in EPZs enjoy certain facilities that are not available to similar firms outside the EPZs.

Two-thirds of the total workers in EPZs are engaged in garments. Other factories in the EPZs include agro-based industries, chemicals, backward and forward linkage industries, and electrical equipment and components. The RMG industry located in the EPZs has developed direct links with international buyers, modern equipment, a relatively skilled workforce, and better working conditions (Khanna 2011). The growing importance of the EPZs lies in the fact that over the last years, they have contributed to diversifying the export products making the economy of Bangladesh less vulnerable to adverse changes in commodity prices as well as to export market restrictions.

3.4 Legal Framework of EPZs in Bangladesh

In line with global trends, Bangladesh has enacted separate laws for establishing EPZs and these laws intend to attract foreign investment, create employment opportunities, and to promote export for earning foreign exchange. The first law is the Bangladesh Export Processing Zone Authority (BEPZA) Act 1980, which establishes the Bangladesh Export Processing Zones Authority for the development, operation, management, and control of export processing zones. EPZ started its operation in 1983. The general direction and administration of the affairs of the Authority have been vested in the Executive Board of the BEPZA and it is guided by the Board of Governors of the Authority (Section 3.3A of the Bangladesh Export Processing Zone Authority (BEPZA) Act 1980). The Executive Board is entrusted to diversify the sources of foreign exchange earnings, to foster the establishment and development of industries and commercial enterprises in EPZs, to generate to upgrade labor and management skills (Section 3.4A of the BEPZA Act 1980). On the other hand, the function of the Board includes the formulation of the policies for the operation and management of the Authority and the zones, and reviewing the activities of the Executive Board and the zones (Section 3.5A of the BEPZA Act 1980).

The main functions of the Authority are acquisition or requisition of land for the purpose of development of a zone; granting permission to set up an EPZ; providing infrastructure, and customs bonded facilities for importation of building materials for construction; allowing import of raw materials required for use in the zone and export of semi processed, processed or other goods; providing necessary banking facilities within the zone; establishing liaison with the port, municipal authorities to make arrangement for transportation of imported raw materials; and sanctioning employment of foreign nationals (Section 7 of the BEPZA Act 1980). The BEPZA Act exempted such zones from the operation of certain laws and entrusted the Bangladesh Export Processing Zones Authority (BEPZA) with the responsibility of ensuring compliance on social and labor issues within EPZs.

EPZs in Bangladesh have their own labor relations officials, the labor inspectors, and counselors. These counselors worked like facilitators and informal arbitrators between management and workers to resolve grievances. The Foreign Private Investment Act of 1980 provides protection to foreign investors, which is applicable for EPZs. The Act makes provision for adequate compensation for the expropriation of property of foreign investors. Foreign investors are also allowed to repatriate profits and capital to their home country.

Another important piece of legislation is the Bangladesh Private Export Processing Zone Act, 1996, which aims to enable foreign and local investors to set up Private EPZs in Bangladesh. The Act establishes a Governing Board, an Executive Cell, Committees, and exempts the private EPZs from the operation of certain laws and offers some other facilities for investors.

A comprehensive law titled the Bangladesh Economic Zones Act was enacted in 2010 to accelerate economic development and growth by increasing productivity, employment creation, industrialization and growth of export through the establishment of economic zones. The Bangladesh Economic Zones Act 2010 aims at establishing economic zones (EZ) in potential areas including backward and underdeveloped areas and development, operation, management and control of such zones. This Act provides for public–private partnership for establishing both public economic zones and private economic zones by domestic and foreign investors; procedures of site selection and acquisition of land, the appointment of economic zone developers, and special financial incentives to the investors. The Act envisages four categories of EZs in Bangladesh: public–private partnership EZ, private economic zones established individually or jointly by local, non-resident Bangladeshis or foreign investors, government economic zones, and special economic zones for the establishment of any kind of specialized industry (Section 3.4 of the Bangladesh Economic Zones Act 2010). This Act exempts the application of some tax laws and local government laws in economic zones in order to attract foreign investment (Section 13 of the Bangladesh Economic Zones Act 2010). It authorizes the government to provide special tariff benefits, financial and other benefits for EPZs (Sections. 10, 11, and 12 of the Bangladesh Economic Zones Act 2010) and establishes an Authority called the Bangladesh Economic Zones Authority (BEZA) with a broader mandate and functions than BEPZA. The Act also establishes a Governing Board, Executive Board and formation of committees for the management and operation of EPZs. Although the Bangladesh Economic Zones Act 2010 imposed some environmental obligations on firms operating in the EPZs (Section 30 of the Bangladesh Economic Zones Act 2010), it did not contain any provisions relating to industrial relations, labor rights, trade union activities, collective bargaining, wages, compensation to workers and settlement of disputes. In view of mounting criticisms by the labor rights groups and in response to international pressure, this Act was amended in 2013 to incorporate l*abor rights mentioned in the Bangladesh Labor Act 2006 and to allow trade union activities in the EZs.*

3.5 A Critical Assessment of Industrial Relations in EPZs

In EPZs of Bangladesh, the formation of trade unions and collective bargaining was not generally allowed on the grounds that introducing trade unions in such areas would create instability and undermine the flow of capital and foreign investment. EPZ employers were also hostile toward the trade union movement. After long struggles of civil society organizations and demands of international buyers and developed countries, EPZ workers in Bangladesh gained freedom of association at limited scale in July 2004 through the enactment of the EPZ Workers Association and Industrial Relations Act 2004, which recognized the right of the workers to form association. However, this Act was repealed and currently, industrial relations in EPZs is governed by the EPZ Labor Act 2019, which provides that the workers in industrial units of an EPZ shall have the right to form association and join the Workers' Welfare Association in order to engage in industrial relations. Like the Bangladesh Labor Act 2006, the EPZ Labor Act 2019 makes provisions for the appointment letter and identity cards for workers, conditions of employment and service, classification of workers, service book, registration of workers, procedures of leave, shut down of establishment, layoff, compensation for laid-off workers, discharge and dismissal of workers, compensation for death of workers, and grievance procedure. It also lays down provisions relating to the determination of minimum wages, compensation for injuries to workers during working hours, maternity benefits, health, and safety issues. The EPZ Labor Act 2019 defines a "worker", but unlike the Bangladesh Labor Act 2006, this Act classifies workers into five categories: apprentice, casual, temporary, probationer, and permanent. It excludes seasonal workers from the ambit of the scope of the definition of worker.

While the EPZ Labor Act 2019 does not expressly mention trade unions, it allows the formation of the Workers' Welfare Association in Export Processing Zones and collective Bargaining by the Workers' Welfare Association. According to this Act, the Collective Bargaining Agent in an EPZ is entrusted with the right to negotiate with the employer on wages, working hours, and other terms and conditions of employment, to undertake collective bargaining with the employer, to represent workers in any legal proceedings, and to declare a strike. Although the scope of collective bargaining is severely limited by absence of trade unions in these zones, an agreement concluded between any Workers' Welfare Association and the employer shall be binding upon both parties and it shall be enforceable through the EPZ Labor Court. This is an innovation of this law, as there is no similar provision under the Bangladesh Labor Act 2006.

For the formation of a Workers' Welfare Association, the application of not less than 20% of the permanent workers of the industry is required (Section 94(2) of the EPZ Labor Act 2019). In any enterprise where the Workers' Welfare Association is formed, this law requires that a minimum 30% posts of the Executive Council shall be filled up by permanent female workers (Section 94(5) of the EPZ Labor Act 2019). The Act also allows the formation of a federation of the Workers' Welfare Association if 50% of the Workers' Welfare Association in any Zone agrees (Section 113 of the EPZ Labor Act 2019). But WWA federations are not permitted to associate with federations beyond their zone or from other zones. This Act also allows the formation of the Employers' Association if the majority of the employers of industries in any EPZ agree to work as representatives of employers to engage in industrial relations. According to the Act, the Workers' Welfare Association does not have the same rights as trade unions. It also forbids workers from associating with trade unions or workers' organizations outside the EPZ. In practice, the workers' welfare association is virtually non-existent in EPZs, which prevents unionization of workers in these zones.

The EPZ Labor Act imposes liability on the employer to pay compensation for death or injury to workers in the course of their employment. This Act also confers maternity benefits on women workers like the Bangladesh Labor Act 2006 and puts restrictions on the termination of employment of a female worker during the maternity period. Following the Bangladesh Labor Act 2006, the EPZ Labor Act 2019 requires employers to introduce a system of compulsory group insurance in all enterprises where at least twenty-five permanent workers are employed and also contains provisions for daily working hours, extra allowances for overtime work, and prescribes limited hours of work for female workers. This Act establishes the Minimum Wages Board for the purpose of fixing the minimum wages of the EPZ workers and lays down factors to be considered in making recommendations, such as the minimum wages or scale of salary of the industries located outside the Zones and other relevant factors. The EPZ Labor Act also provides for periodical review of minimum rates of wages if any change in the factors and other relevant factors demand so. The Act prohibits payment of wages at a rate lower than the minimum rates of wages by the employer and it prescribes sanction for payment of wages less than the declared minimum wages. The last minimum wage board for EPZ workers was formed in 2013, setting the minimum monthly wage at BDT 5,600. In 2018, BEPZA revised it to BDT 8,200.

The Act also contains a list of unfair practices on the part of employers. These include restrictions on workers joining any Workers' Welfare Association, refusing to continue in employment of any worker for being a member of such Association, dismissal, discharge, or removal of a worker for being a member of the Workers' Welfare Association (Section 115 of the EPZ Labor Act 2019).

Like the Bangladesh Labor Act 2006, the EPZ Labor Act 2019 provides for the participatory committee in any enterprise where there is no Workers' Welfare Association or the Workers' Welfare Association is dissolved. Such a participatory committee shall consist of with equal number of the representatives of both employers and workers. The functions of the Participatory Committee include promoting mutual trust, understanding, and cooperation between the employers and the workers; fostering discipline, improving and maintaining safety, occupational health and working conditions; and taking steps for the improvement of welfare measures for the workers and their families.

For settlement of industrial disputes in EPZs, the Act provides for negotiation, conciliation, arbitration mechanisms, the EPZ Labor Court and EPZ Labor Appellate Tribunal. The BEPZA is entrusted to appoint the required number of conciliators, arbitrators, and counselors for negotiation and settlement of disputes in the EPZs. The EPZ Labor Act 2019 also provides for the Constitution of a Provident Fund by each employer of each enterprise for its workers and the formation of an Employer-buyer-worker Participatory Fund for the welfare of workers employed in the EPZ (Section 172 of the EPZ Labor Act 2019). The fund shall be used for bearing the expense of emergency assistance, social security, the expense of administrative, developmental, and other related expenditures. Indecent behavior with female workers in EPZs is also prohibited (Section 189 of the EPZ Labor Act 2019). In order to reduce gender parity in the payment of wages, the Act contains the principle of payment of equal wages for work of equal nature and value and prohibits gender-based discrimination in payment of wages. The overall responsibility of implementation of this Act vests with the BEPZA and inspection and supervision of safety aspects has been entrusted to the Chief Inspector and other inspectors of the EPZs. However, the Act has failed to prohibit child labor explicitly as it only mentions that an underage worker shall not be employed in an industry (Section 175 of the EPZ Labor Act 2019).

The industrial relations are sometimes strained by hostile attitudes of EPZ investors toward trade unions and their strong opposition to international labor standards (Jauch 2009, 75). Scholars argue that EPZs can deepen developing countries' dependency on foreign capital and can have a detrimental effect on national industries (Jauch 2009, 83). Experiences elsewhere have shown that compromises on social, environmental, and labor standards in the name of international competitiveness lead to a "race to the bottom" in EPZs (Jauch 2009, 82). Therefore, a holistic approach to EPZs needs to be adopted in the context of universally applicable human rights and labor standards and the need for export earnings, which will have truly positive effects on national economies and sustainable growth stimulation (Binder 2010, 101).

3.6 Conclusion

In Bangladesh, EPZs have become an engine of economic growth and development, having a positive impact on employment and poverty alleviation. However, poor working conditions and the lack of application of labor standards in EPZs have been raised in the context of sustainable economic growth. The EPZ laws in Bangladesh have been reformed several times to bring them in line with international standards. In this regard, the EPZ Labor Act 2019 is a significant step for recognizing the rights of workers in EPZs. However, this legislation is yet to be fully consistent with international standards, particularly, in the areas of trade union and collective bargaining, creating significant gaps between EPZ workers and workers outside the zones. The dichotomy between the general labor law framework and the EPZ-specific regime further raises the question of uniformity and consistency in the application of labor rights for workers. Based on its competitive advantage of having cheap labor, Bangladesh has renewed efforts for the expansion of EPZs as it decided in 2015 to set up one hundred more such zones across the country to attract both foreign and local investments for accelerating industrialization, creating more job opportunities, and exporting goods and services from such zones. For this purpose, the government has offered extensive tax exemptions and other incentives to investors. However, there is a growing concern of poor working conditions, non-compliance with international labor standards, and negative impact on environment and displacement and marginalization of local communities. Human rights and environmental due diligence and social impact assessment need to be pursued by Bangladesh while establishing such zones to prevent any negative effect on the environment and society. It is expected that ensuring an adequate protection of labor standards in these zones will be conducive for attracting investment and achieving sustainable development in Bangladesh. EPZ labor laws also need to be harmonized with the general legal framework on labor relations applicable in the rest of the country. Labor inspection must be adequately resourced and trained to effectively implement and enforce labor market regulation in EPZs.

Bibliography

Chapters in Edited Books

Arnold, Dennis. 2017. "Export Processing Zones." In *International Encyclopedia of Geography: People, the Earth, Environment, and Technology*, edited by Douglas Richardson, Noel Castree, Michael F. Goodchild, Audrey Kobayashi, Weidong Liu, and Richard A. Marston. Wiley.

Neveling, Patrick. 2015. "Export Processing Zones, Special Economic Zones and the Long March of Capitalist Development Policies During the Cold War." In *Negotiating Independence: New Directions in the Histories of the Cold war and decolonization*, edited by Leslie James and Elisabeth Leake, 63–84. Bloomsbury.

Journal Articles

Binder, Christina. 2010. "Economic Growth at the Price of Human Rights Violations? The Protection of Human/Labour Rights in Export Processing Zones." *City University of Hong Kong Law Review* 2 (1): 99–116.

Braga, Helson, Raul Gouvea, Margarida Gutierrez. 2023. "Brazilian Export Processing Zones & Green Powershoring: Challenges & Opportunities." *Modern Economy* 14: 1–27.

Jauch, Herbert. 2009. "Attracting Foreign Investment at All Costs? *The Case of Export Processing Zones (EPZs) and Ramatex in Namibia." International Journal of Labor Research* 1 (1): 73–84.

Khanna, Pragya. 2011. "Making Labour Voices Heard During an Industrial Crisis: Workers' Struggles in the Bangladesh Garment Industry." *Labour, Capital and Society* 44 (2): 106–129.

Nigar, Neelum. 2020. "Special Economic Zones for Growth and Competitiveness in Pakistan's Economy." *Strategic Studies* 40 (4): 42–59.

Vadlamannati, Krishna Chaitanya. 2015. "Rewards of (Dis)Integration: Economic, Social, and Political Globalization and Freedom of Association and Collective Bargaining Rights of Workers in Developing Countries." *International Labour Review* 68 (1): 3–27.

Reports

Aggarwal, Aradhna. 2007. *Impact of Special Economic Zones on Employment, Poverty, and Human Development*, 12ff. Available at http://www.icrier.org/pdf/Working_Paper_194.pdf.

Farole, Thomas, and Gökhan Akıncı. 2011. *Special Economic Zones: Progress, Emerging Challenges, and Future Directions*. Washington, DC: World Bank.

Madani, Dorsati. 1999. "A Review of the Role and Impact of Export Processing Zones." Policy Research Working Paper WPS 2238, November. Washington, DC: World Bank Group. http://documents.worldbank.org/curated/en/789981468766806342.

Milberg, William, and Amengual, Matthew. 2008. *Economic Development and Working Conditions in Export Processing Zones: A Survey of Trends*. ILO.

Richardson, Benjamin, and James Harrison. 2017. "Labour Rights in Export Processing Zones with a Focus on GSP+ Beneficiary Countries." Directorate-General for External Policies, Policy Department, European Parliament.

Lang, Andrew. 2010. "Trade Agreements, Business and Human Rights: The Case of Export Processing Zones." Corporate Social Responsibility Initiative Working Paper No. 57, April. Cambridge, MA: John F. Kennedy School of Government, Harvard University.

Legislations

Bangladesh Export Processing Zone Authority Act, 1980 (Act No. XXXVI of 1980).

Bangladesh Private Export Processing Zones Act, 1996 (Act No. 20 of 1996).

Bangladesh Economic Zones Act, 2010 (Act No. 42 of 2010).

Export Processing Zones Labour Act, 2019 (Act No. 2 of 2019).

Foreign Private Investment (Promotion and Protection) Act, 1980 (Act No. XI of 1980).
Export Processing Zone Labour Act 2019.

CHAPTER 4

Challenges of Globalization and Regulation of Trade Unions in Bangladesh

4.1 Introduction

The trade unions have historically played a pivotal role in protecting the rights of the workers, promoting their collective welfare, and constraining the employer's unscrupulous behavior. Trade unions are considered the main institutional means for workers "to influence not only their own working conditions but also the legal regime governing working conditions" (Bereusson and Estlund 2008, 5). A trade union is considered an instrument for balancing "unequal power relations" in the workplace as it restrains the unlimited powers of employers. The collective action of trade unions also exemplifies the solidarity of workers as it gives an individual worker organizational support for representing and safeguarding his rights and interests, which he himself is unable to raise either for fear of termination or for lack of knowledge (Nimalathasan and Taher 2012). The trade union bargains and negotiates with the employer on behalf of workers regarding the terms and conditions of their employment, and workplace safety, minimum wages, complaint procedures, upgradation of workers, and social benefits. They also make workers aware of labor laws and their rights under existing laws and international labor instruments and improve their skills through training programs. It is well-established that through joining and becoming members of trade unions, workers can protect their rights effectively and collectively advance their interests, including better wages and safe working conditions.

A. Al Faruque, *Globalization and Labour Rights*,
https://doi.org/10.1007/978-981-92-3661-9_4

4.2 Changing Role of Trade Unions in the Globalized World

Globalization, accompanied by a proliferation of global supply chains and networks of transnational actors, has challenged the traditional system of industrial relations and the role of different actors including trade unions. Schnabel shows that trade unionization and bargaining coverage have fallen in most countries in the last decades, which can be partially attributed to the forces of economic globalization (Schnabel 2020, 32). The operation of trade unions, being largely circumscribed by national boundaries, has little influence over global supply chains. Due to globalization and the emergence of transnational governance systems, trade unions have been weakened and there has been a shift in the regulation of labor from the national level to the transnational level (Meardi and Marginson 2014), where production activities are distributed across global supply chains and relocated across national borders, but not labor itself. Uncontrolled mobility of capital and growth of global supply chain cause significant changes in the bargaining capacity of labor and thus, undermine trade unions. It is argued that globalization reduces the bargaining power of workers as lead firms can suppress the voice of trade union effectively by threatening to outsource their production to countries where labor is cheaper, and the labor market is less regulated (Hessami and Baskaran 2015, 1883).

Trade unions must respond to the changing needs of globalization and the dynamics of the global supply chain. These factors have led to the internationalization of labor movement and have influenced the sphere of activities of national trade unions (Munck 2008). It has been correctly observed that globalization is commonly linked to the decrease in public sector employment, which undermines the strength of trade unions (Ebbinghaus 2002).

Furthermore, the trade unions have to develop a clear understanding of the implications of technological changes generated through the 4th industrial revolution. The rise of automation through the 4th industrial revolution can make many workers vulnerable and may be subject to layoff or retrenchment on the grounds of redundancy. In this circumstance, trade unions have to embrace the challenges of rapid technological changes to protect the workers. Trade unions need to evaluate the effectiveness of traditional bargaining strategies to address these issues and focus on adapting to the challenges and developing innovative strategies to deal with technological changes (Mamun 2022).

In the age of globalization, it is trite to say that trade unions need to be affiliated with international workers organizations in order to keep abreast of developments at the international level, and build networking and solidarity with the latter to draw strength in times of their crises. The legal framework needs to be supportive to enable trade unions affiliated with international unions. The role of trade unions is changing globally to meet the needs of workers in the globalized world and in view of technological changes. Trade unions should also be equipped with a greater level of bargaining power to negotiate with employers on terms and conditions of work and to prevent exploitation in global supply chains. The weak bargaining power of workers in any sector leaves them vulnerable to unfair practices of employers.

4.3 Legal Basis of Trade Union

The legal basis of trade unions derives from the right to freedom of association in labor relations, which implies that workers can form, join, or belong to a trade union of their choice and engage in collective bargaining. The right to freedom of association is considered a process or an enabling right for the realization of all other labor rights, including the formation of and joining in trade unions. This right purports to increase the power of workers relative to governments and employers to enable workers to establish a legal framework on working conditions and wages and to secure their effective application (Kucera and Sari 2022). The right to freedom of association is widely acknowledged as one of the core international labor standards and has been incorporated in the ILO Convention on the Freedom of Association and the Protection of the Right to Organize 1948 (No. 87), the ILO Convention on the Right to Organize and Collective Bargaining 1949 (No. 98) and human rights treaties including the International Covenant on Economic, Social and Cultural Rights (ICESCR) 1966, and the International Covenant on Civil and Political Rights (ICCPR) 1966. These international instruments ask state parties to ensure freedom of association in their national territory and to incorporate in national laws to facilitate the formation of trade unions.

The constitution of Bangladesh guarantees the freedom of association, which provides the legal basis for the formation of trade unions by workers and organizations by employers. However, states may prescribe requirements and legal formalities for the establishment and membership of trade unions. While states are allowed to impose some reasonable restrictions on the right to freedom of association, such restrictions should not be obstacles to the formation of trade unions, and their operation and organizational structure. Some well-established limitations are acceptable, such as the requirement that trade unions have a minimum number of members in order to be recognized. The requirement of a minimum number of members must be reasonable so that it does not create an obstacle to the formation of a union. On the other hand, trade unions should be representative organizations in an establishment. The determination of representativeness should be based on objective, pre-established, and well-defined criteria. The legal framework of trade unions must allow the trade unions to draw up their constitution and operational rules, elect their representatives freely, carry out administrative and usual activities, and formulate their programs. In a broader sense, the practice of democracy and respect for civil liberties are necessary preconditions for the effective exercise of freedom of association in a country.

4.4 Regulating Trade Unions in Bangladesh

The Bangladesh Labor Act 2006 remains the main statutory framework for regulating trade unions, and it recognizes both the right of workers to join trade unions and the right of employers to join associations. The Act does not distinguish between the public and private sectors in relation to trade unions. However, trade unionism has been more active in the public sector in Bangladesh because management in the public enterprise has been much more tolerant of trade unionism. The Bangladesh Labor Act 2006 requires the registration of trade unions that enables them to acquire legal status and certain benefits. The registration of a trade union confers on it a legal entity that is separate from its members so that they can engage in collective bargaining. A trade union also means a federation of trade unions. Registration has been made compulsory for the formation of a trade union (Section 192 of the Bangladesh Labor Act 2006). The Bangladesh Labor Act 2006 mentions necessary requirements for registration of trade unions. The most important requirement is the minimum number of workers who want to be members of a trade union. Previously, in order to be registered, it was required that a trade union must have a minimum membership of 30% of the total number of workers employed in any establishment. After the amendment in 2018, this requirement of a minimum membership was lowered to 20%. Still this requirement of minimum membership fixed by law was criticized as too high to hinder the establishment of a trade union at the enterprise level and as inconsistent with international labor standards. The recent amendment made in law in 2026 has withdrawn this restricted legal requirement for the establishment of a trade union and it allows the establishment of a trade union with the consent of 20 workers in an establishment having 20 to 300 workers. This new threshold for trade union registration is a significant legal step to align with the ILS.

Trade unions are required to be registered with the Registrar of Trade Unions after fulfilling the requirements under the Labor Act, and a registered trade union is a statutory body and endowed with the privilege of "body corporate" and enjoys legal capacity to own property, and enter into contract, which are essential for its effective functioning (Section 194(1) of the Bangladesh Labor Act 2006). Thus, registration of a trade union ensures its legal recognition and confers some rights upon itself and its members as well as vests the officials with some duties. Therefore, registration procedures must not be complicated and lengthy. The imposition of a legal requirement of prior authorization from government agencies for registration under the existing labor law often makes such a process difficult. As per the law, for the purpose of formation of a trade union, more than one establishment of the same employer would be taken as one establishment when the establishments are of the same nature and work together in the same industry (Section 179(2A)) as amended by the Bangladesh Labor (Amendment) Act 2013). However, not more than three registrations would be given within one establishment or group of establishments. Recently, in order to improve transparency around the process and reduce the complexity and lengthy process of registration, the registration process of trade unions has been simplified in Bangladesh by introducing Standard Operating Procedures (SOPs). The SOPs provide timelines for registration and specify persons responsible at each step of the registration process. The SOPs aim to prevent unfair labor practices and ease the complexity of the system. But the SOPs fail to address the many barriers workers face in the registration process (Vogt 2017, 82).

In order to prevent harassment of workers for becoming members of a trade union, Section 186 of the Bangladesh Labor Act 2006 guarantees that the conditions of service of trade union officials must not be changed pending registration of a trade union and an employer cannot change such conditions to the disadvantage of workers or officers. This provision aims to safeguard the interests of workers during the pendency of registration. Furthermore, imposition of any restrictions on the employment or discrimination or discharge of any worker or refusal of employment to any worker on the grounds of his membership of a trade union has been declared as unfair labor practice and has been prohibited (Section 195(1) as amended by the Bangladesh Labor (Amendment) Act 2018). Provision on anti-trade union discrimination has also been incorporated in the Bangladesh Labor Act 2006 in 2018, which strengthens the workers' rights regarding trade union. It implies that if, during the process of trade union registration, or pending the application for registration of trade union, or after registration, an employer violates any terms and conditions of service of a worker or takes any retaliatory measures against any workers, such actions will be treated as anti-trade union discrimination (Section 196(A) as amended by the Bangladesh Labor (Amendment) Act 2018).

In order to enhance women's participation in trade union activities, the Bangladesh Labor Act 2006 requires that at least 10% of female members shall be included in the executive committee of the union if there is 20% of the total workforce is female during the registration process (Section 176(e) as amended by the Bangladesh Labor Amendment Act 2013).

The Bangladesh Labor Act 2006 also lays down the procedure of the cancelation of registration of trade union and authorizes the Director of Labor to cancel the certificate of registration under well-defined circumstances. However, such a procedure has been often used to harass trade unions, and sometimes, registration of trade unions has been canceled without furnishing any reasonable grounds.

Despite an enabling legal framework and recent reforms for bolstering trade union activities, only around 10 percent of the total workforce is unionized and most of the unions are limited to the public sector or state enterprises. The private sector is less unionized compared to the public sector due to various constraints. Trade unions are also not allowed in some sectors, such as the Export Processing Zones (EPZ), which is exempt from the application of certain labor laws.

4.5 Structure of Trade Unions in Bangladesh

There is a four-tier structure of trade unions in Bangladesh:

4.5.1 *Basic Trade Union*

Usually, the trade unions formed at the plant or enterprise level are called basic trade unions. A basic trade union is a primary organization of workers at any establishment as this union is formed by the direct participation of the workers at the grassroots level. They are formed at the plant or enterprise level with the membership of workers in the particular unit or enterprise. Basic trade unions work as a Collective Bargaining Agent. Such a body, at the grassroots level, has the advantage of being close to the workers and they can deal with their day-to-day problems.

4.5.2 *Industrial Federation*

An industrial federation consists of all trade unions of the same industrial sector. Section 200(1) of the Bangladesh Labor Act 2006 provides that any five or more registered trade unions formed in an establishment carrying on the same type of industry may constitute a federation if a proposal to that effect is passed by their general meeting and they execute an instrument of federation. Usually, an industrial federation raises collective demands of workers to owners or the management and negotiates with the owners on a range of issues, including minimum wage.

4.5.3 *National Trade Union Federation*

It is constituted of at least twenty basic trade unions from more than one establishment (Section 200(5) of the Bangladesh Labor Act 2006). A national federation generally extends organizational and advisory support and services to its affiliated enterprise union federations. Political affiliation is an important feature of all national trade union federations. National-level trade unions formed a grand alliance under the *Sramik Karmachari Oikya Parishad* (SKOP) in 1983 to articulate their voice and raise their demands to the government. It is now composed of sixteen national federations which represent ninety percent of the total workers in Bangladesh. Since 1983, most of the trade union movements have been organized under SKOP and it submitted a charter of demands for improving the rights of workers but it failed to achieve any tangible results in realizing the demands for workers because it was weakened gradually due to the political affiliation of trade union leaders.

4.5.4 National Confederation

At least ten national trade union federations are needed to constitute a national confederation (Section 200(6) of the Bangladesh Labor Act 2006). A national confederation usually represents the total workers of the country.

Currently, there are more than 9,000 enterprise-level trade unions, and these trade unions are organized into more than 190 sectoral workers' federations. These federations are clustered into 37 national federations.

4.6 Trade Unions in the Public Sector

Since the Bangladesh Labor Act 2006 is not applicable to offices of the government, security printing presses, ordinance factories, non-profitable caregiver organizations, retailer shops, non-profitable educational and research institutions, student hostels, hospitals, and diagnostic centers (Section 4.1(4) of the Bangladesh Labor Act 2006), the concept of a trade union is not applicable to these offices, institutions and firms. However, trade unions are allowed for workers of publicly owned corporations, railways, telephone and postal services, roads and highways, public works, public health engineering, and the government printing press (Section 4.1(4)(J) of the Bangladesh Labor Act 2006). In fact, workers of state-owned oil and gas companies, banking, and transport sectors are reasonably organized in Bangladesh (Faruque 2009). Apart from these institutions and offices, trade union is not allowed in other institutions and offices in the public sector and state enterprises. Explicit statutory restrictions are another barrier in realizing trade union activities in the public sector. For instance, the Essential Service (Maintenance) Act, 1952 prohibits trade union activities and strikes in certain essential services.

4.7 Trade Unions in the RMG Sector

Since a significant number of workforce in Bangladesh are employed in the RMG sector, it is vitally important that workers are organized in this sector to realize their rights and collective welfare. The presence of trade unions in the RMG sector also carries special significance due to the sector's economic importance. However, trade unions in this sector were a neglected issue for long time. Recognition of trade union in the RMG sector is the outcome of a long struggle of the workers to organize to raise their voices to be heard. Although the RMG sector started its journey in the early 1980s, the RMG workers' movement to organize trade unions faced resistance from both owners and the government (Faruque 2009). Since its recognition by the Bangladesh Labor Act 2006, trade unions gradually increased in this sector and after the Rana Plaza collapse, the number of trade unions has increased significantly in the RMG sector due to sustained demand from international buyers, developed countries and federations.

Currently, there are a total of 56 registered federations in the garments sector and these federations have 329 registered basic unions as affiliates in Bangladesh (Hassan et al. 2022). In addition, about 40 to 50 unregistered federations are also active in the RMG factory regions, namely *Savar Ashulia, Tejgaon-Baddha-Mirpur, Narayanganj, Gazipur, and Chittagong* (Hassan et al. 2022). However, till now, only 5% of the RMG workers are unionized. Nearly 70 percent of about 4,000 garment factories in the country do not have registered trade unions. In the absence of trade union, participation committees in these industrial units are responsible for the well-being of workers. However, the Participation Committee is not required once a trade union is formed in an establishment (Section 205(12) of the Bangladesh Labor Act 2006). Currently, two national RMG federations are registered with the Department of Labor. The RMG trade union federations maintain direct relationship with government agencies, and factory owners to realize different demands of workers and tend to be affiliated with political parties, international unions and federations, and associations to form alliance and network for various kinds of support for workers (Hassan et al. 2022). The international organizations and alliances support the federations mostly through extensive capacity building training and awareness campaigns (Hassan et al. 2022) and work as a pressure group through their linkages to improve working conditions in this sector (Hassan et al. 2022). These international networks and alliances also collaborate to ensure the fundamental worker's rights including the right to organize, the right to collective bargaining, protection from discrimination, and the elimination of child labor and forced labor (Hassan et al. 2022).

4.8 Legal Restrictions on Trade Unions

The Bangladesh Labor Act 2006 does not cover a large number of workers in informal sectors such as workers of EPZs, and agricultural workers. Even the workers employed in some government sectors, educational institutions, nursing, health sector, rural electrification, private security services, workers in security printing press, and ordnance factory are still outside of the purview of the provisions on the formation of trade unions. In some sectors, the Bangladesh Labor Act 2006 recognizes limited trade union rights. For example, a trade union was allowed in the civil aviation industry if such a trade union was necessary for affiliation with international organizations. Similarly, only one trade union was allowed for the workers in ocean-going vessels. But these restrictions are now withdrawn by the Bangladesh Labor (Amendment) Act 2026. Still only one trade union is allowed for workers employed in different port authorities in Bangladesh.

The Act needs further amendment to lift several restrictions on the right to strike, such as the prohibition of strikes in a new establishment or an establishment owned by foreigners for two years (Sec. 211(8) and 227 (c) of the Bangladesh Labor Act 2006), and the prohibition of strikes on the grounds of national interest (sec. 211(3) of the Bangladesh Labor Act 2006). The government can prohibit a strike or lock-out at any time before or after its commencement in case of any public utility service (Section 211(4) of the Bangladesh Labor Act 2006). Such public utility service may include the power generation, production and supply of gas and oil, railways, airways, road and river transport, ports, and banking, where a significant number of workers of the total workforce of the country are working.

Besides the above-mentioned legal restrictions, administrative regulations and intimidation by the owners, especially in private industries, prevent the workers from organizing, forming, and joining a trade union.

4.9 Activities, Effectiveness, and Challenges of Trade Unions

In Bangladesh, trade unions are not only a crucial labor institution for the protection of workers' rights, but historically they have played a vital role in political movements. Trade unions in Bangladesh are generally concerned with collective bargaining, improving working conditions, providing input on legislation and policy design, ending violence and harassment against workers, promoting occupational safety and health (OSH) awareness, capacity, upgrading workers' skills, and mainstreaming gender issues in all policies and programs to promote women workers' rights (ILO 2014). Over the last few years, the trade unions of Bangladesh have also been organized to engage in social dialogue and enter into framework agreements, and address social issues in the workforce, such as gender inequality in payment of wages, child labor, and occupational safety in the factories. Emphasizing the role of trade unions in ensuring workers' safety, Anner and Bair explain, "The threat posed by safety hazards is greater in the absence of an empowered workforce that is organized and protected by trade union representation" (Anner and Bair 2022, 417).

The Bangladesh Labor Act 2006 allows trade unions or federations of trade unions to be affiliated with international labor unions such as ITUC and confederations of workers' organization (Section 176(c) of the Bangladesh Labor Act 2006). Such organizations and confederations collaborate with their affiliated unions and federations of unions to improve work conditions, and protect their rights and offer advisory services to them. Some of the national federations of trade unions in Bangladesh are affiliated with international unions. The ILO offers many services to activate trade unions and facilitate their affiliation with international trade unions. However, the effectiveness of trade unions in promoting and protecting workers' interests through international affiliation is still limited for various reasons discussed below.

The effectiveness of a trade union depends on its autonomy, legitimacy, and representativeness. Autonomy refers to the free will of workers to join a trade union. The legitimacy of trade unions depends on the fairness of the election process for trade unions and whether the trade union leaders have the consent of the common workers. Accountability of the trade union leaders must be ensured through devising appropriate mechanism of checks and balances between labor institutions and performance standards for trade union leaders. Representativeness does not imply mere membership of a union; rather it must be inclusive so that workers can trust it as a credible vehicle for articulating their demands. Trade Unions' existence and their political and economic influence crucially depend on their ability to attract membership and to successfully represent their members' interests in collective bargaining (Schnabel 2020). The effectiveness of trade unions also depends on the bargaining and negotiation skills of the trade union leaders, which involve their capacity to raise and articulate their demands, make decisions without external pressure, and implement the decisions effectively.

Trade unionism in Bangladesh faces many challenges, as the number of trade unions in Bangladesh is still inadequate compared to the total labor force in the country. In particular, the presence of trade unions in the export-oriented sectors such as RMG, EPZs, and shrimp exporting firms is very poor. Many trade unions in the RMG sector operate outside the factories and therefore lack the active participation of the general workers in the affairs of trade unions (Faruque 2009). Many factors, such as a lack of enforcement of labor laws, legal restrictions, and widespread practice of contract labor, are responsible for reduced trade union membership in these sectors (Mondal 2002, 125). Application for trade union registration is sometimes rejected on technical or vague grounds or grounds not specified in the law to keep the industry union-free. Sometimes trade union registration is denied arbitrarily without showing any adequate justifications.

Trade unions working at plants as well as at the industry level also suffer from a lack of funding to run their activities, poor organizational strength, reluctance of workers toward union activities, ideological division, and intra-union rivalries. Trade unions' effectiveness in delivering their stated goals is also hampered by punitive management actions for union activities, and frequent changes of unions both by leaders and workers. Government intervention in trade unions also remains a persistent feature of the industrial relations system in Bangladesh.

The trade unions as a collective bargaining agent have to act in opposition to both the employers and the state. It has been observed that the behavior of trade unions has been motivated most of the time by political objectives rather than the interests of the working class. The political parties sometimes consider trade unions as their source of power, which creates fragmentation among trade unions and mistrust among workers. In fact, mistrust among trade union leaders, their political affiliation on ideological grounds, employer's unwillingness to cooperate with trade unions and their efforts for undermining the activities of unions, failure of trade unions to represent the interest of the workers, are some of the major problems that reduce their effectiveness in Bangladesh (Allen 1975, 10; Sinha and Shekhar 2004, 156). Their affiliation with the ruling party and acting in favor of employers instead of realizing the demands of workers is a major hindrance to the effectiveness of trade unions (Nimalathasan and Taher 2012). State machineries sometimes favor employers to suppress trade unions and they fails to play a neutral role between the employers and workers (Islam and Asaduzzaman 2015) Trade union leaders also face intimidation, arbitrary arrest, and legal proceedings that deter them from securing better wages or improved working conditions.

Building cohesion among trade unions, which are divided into many federations with diverse ideological and political philosophies, is a necessary condition in order to minimize fragmentation and maximize workers' welfare and to strengthen their associational power. In fact, the politicization of trade unions represents a persistent challenge for strengthening the labor movement in Bangladesh as it prevents the ability to raise their voice collectively (Zajak 2017, 13), to become strong partners in collective bargaining. It is imperative for the trade unions to be free from influences from political groups, government influence, and owners to protect the rights of workers. Only a few trade unions have effective bargaining capacity.

There are some other reasons for the ineffectiveness of trade unions. For example, in the public sector, it has been observed that trade unions are often unable to exercise collective bargaining because of highly centralized management, direct participation of government in wage-setting, and restrictions on collective bargaining (Hossain et al., 1998).

Imposition of formal and informal restrictions on freedom of association, blacklisting and repression by government and employer resistance in the form of intimidation, violent attacks, or dismissal of workers also act as hindrances to the proper functioning of trade unions (Zajak 2017). Use of laws of dissent, sedition charges against labor organizers, rejecting registrations of undesirable trade union applicants by the government has created a culture of fear limiting the growth and institutionalization of trade unions (Hassan et al. 2022). In addition, trade unions in Bangladesh suffer from a low level of social acceptance due to the detachment of trade union leaders from common workers (Rahman and Langford 2012, 99). As a result, the roles of union leaders remain insignificant during the crisis period. Gaining recognition and acceptance from workers is crucial for the credibility of this power source (Zajak 2017, 10). The recent reforms in labor law attempt to address some of these pressing problems. The Bangladesh Labor (Amendment) Act 2026 makes worker blacklisting illegal in order to protect workers from retaliation or discrimination by employers. It states that workers who have been terminated or laid off or gone to retirement must not be incorporated in a database for the purpose of making them ineligible for new employment in an establishment. It also allows a trade union for administrative, managerial, and supervisory personnel to form and join an association. These changes reflect an attempt to strengthen the legal protection of workers and their freedom of association.

The gender representation gap is another challenge of trade unions to be inclusive. For example, despite the fact that women make up 80% of the workforce of the RMG sector, their representation in the trade unions is very poor because the percentage of women joining trade unions remains generally lower than the percentage for men (Hossain and Afroza Akter 2022, 7).

4.10 Conclusion

Trade unions have played an important role in the implementation of labor standards and decent work conditions in many countries (Wälde 2012). Currently, there are over 9,000 trade unions in the country, but many of them are dysfunctional. Also, trade union presence is generally higher in export-oriented industries than in industries meeting demands for domestic markets. Although the existing labor laws of Bangladesh substantially reflect the fundamental principles of freedom of association of workers and employers, there are still some legal and administrative barriers to form trade unions and the right to organize. The registration process for trade unions is still cumbersome and politicized needs to be eased further. Currently also, a large number of workers in the informal economy, and in EPZs are not unionized mainly due to the lack of a legislative framework on trade unions in these sectors because the enabling rights, such as the right to freedom of association, are not recognized. Moreover, violence against workers and the criminalization of trade union activities are other obstacles to the smooth functioning of trade unions. Thus, the mere presence of trade unions does not guarantee their effectiveness. It depends on whether they can work without political, administrative, and legal barrier, their ability to engage in genuine collective bargaining, enforce workers' rights, and ensure meaningful improvements in working conditions. The trade unions of Bangladesh must address the problems of organizing informal workers, their legitimacy crisis, challenges of globalization, and adapt to new forms of work and must raise their collective voice for the vulnerable groups and gain legitimacy. Furthermore, they have to develop a clear understanding of the implications of technological changes on employment opportunities.

Bibliography

Books

Allen, F. 1975. *Industrial Relations: What Is Wrong with the System*. Faber.

Bereusson, Brian, and Cynthia Estlund. 2008. *Regulating Labour in the Wake of Globalization: New Challenges, New Institution*. Hart Publishing.

Khan, A. A., and M. A. Taher. 2009. *Human Resources Management and Industrial Relations*, 3rd ed. Abir Publication.

Sinha, P. R. N., B. Sinha, P. S. Shekhar. 2004. *Industrial Relations, Trade Unions, and Labour Legislation*. Pearson Education.

Chapters in Edited Books

Anner, Mark, and Jennifer Bair. 2022. "The Bangladesh Accord and Alliance: Addressing Building Safety Through Global Supply Chain Co-governance." In *Handbook on Globalization and Labour Standards*, edited by Kimberly A. Elliott, 416–431. Elgar Edward Publishing.

Kucera, David, and Dora Sari. 2022. "Globalization and Freedom of Association and Collective Bargaining Rights." In *Handbook on Globalisation and Labour Standards*, edited by Kimberly A. Elliott, 13–35. Edward Elgar.

Mondal, Abdul Hye. 2002. "Globalisation, Industrial Relations and Labour Policies: The Need for a Renewed Agenda." In *Bangladesh: Economic and Social Challenges of Globalisation*, edited by Muhammed Muqtada, Andrea M. Singh, and Mohammed Ali Rashid, 21–35. University Press Limited.

Rahman, Zia, and Tom Langford. 2012. "Why Labour Unions Have Failed Bangladesh's Garment Workers." In *Labour in the Global South: Challenges and Alternatives for Workers*, edited by Sarah Mosoetsa and Michelle Williams, 87–112. ILO.

Schnabel, Claus. 2020. "Union Membership and Collective Bargaining: Trends and Determinants." In *Handbook of Labor, Human Resources and Population Economics*, edited by K. F. Zimmermann, 1–37. Springer Nature.

Journal Articles

Ebbinghaus, Bernhard. 2002. "Globalization and Trade Unions: A Comparative-Historical Examination of the Convergence Thesis." *International Journal of Economic Analysis* 55 (2): 121–139.

Hessami, Zohal, and Thushyanthan Baskaran. 2015. "Has Globalisation Affected Collective Bargaining? An Empirical Test, 1980–2009." *The World Economy*, 1880–1911.

Islam, Farmin, and Md. Asaduzzaman. 2015. "Legal Framework for Trade Unionism in Bangladesh." *IOSR Journal of Humanities and Social Science* 10 (2): 13–19.

Meardi, G., and P. Marginson. 2014. "Global Labour Governance: Potential and Limits of an Emerging Perspective." *Work, Employment and Society* 28 (4): 651–662. https://doi.org/10.1177/0950017014534007.

Munck, Ronaldo. 2008. "Globalisation and Trade Unions: Towards a Multi-level Strategy?" *Work Organisation, Labour & Globalisation* 2 (1): 11–23.

Nimalathasan, Balasundaram, and Abu Taher. 2012. "Situation Analysis of Trade Unions and Industrial Relations in Bangladesh: A Country Profile." *Manager Journal* 16 (1): 55–67.

Vogt, Jeffrey S. 2017. "The Bangladesh Sustainability Compact: An Effective Tool for Promoting Workers' Rights?" *Politics and Governance* 5 (4): 80–92. https://doi.org/10.17645/pag.v5i4.1093.

Zajak, Sabrina. 2017. "International Allies, Institutional Layering and Power in the Making of Labour in Bangladesh." *Development and* Change 48 (5): 1–24, 13. https://doi.org/10.1111/dech.12327.

Reports

Donado, Alejandro, and Klaus Wälde. 2012. "Globalization, Trade Unions and Labour Standards in the North." Employment Sector Employment Working Paper No. 119, ILO.

Faruque, Abdullah Al. 2009. "Current Status and Evolution of Industrial Relations in Bangladesh." Accessed on July 23, 2025. https://www.ilo.org/sites/default/files/wcmsp5/groups/public/%40asia/%40ro-bangkok/%40sro-new_delhi/documents/publication/wcms_123336.pdf.

Hassan, Mirza M., Syeda Salina Aziz, Raeesa Rahemin, Insiya Khan, and Rafsanul Hoque. 2022. "The Political Economy of the Landscape of Trade Unions in Bangladesh: The Case of the RMG Sector," July.

Hossain, Jakir, and Afroza Akter. 2022. "Trade Union Organizing in Bangladesh's Ready-Made Garment Sector Amidst Covid Pandemic: Status, Challenges and Scope." Workers Resource Centre-WRC, June.

Hossain, M. Ismail, Sayed A. Hye, and M. Ali Amin. 1998. "Structural Adjustment Policies and Labour Market in Bangladesh." CIRDAP, Dhaka, July.

Mamun, Md Yousuf Al. 2022. "How Do We Protect Workers' Rights in the Age of 4IR?" *The Daily Star*, December 22. Accessed on October 24, 2024. https://www.thedailystar.net/opinion/views/news/how-do-we-protect-workers-rights-the-age-4ir-3202061.

Walde, Alejandro Donado Klaus. 2012. "Globalization, Trade Unions and Labour Standards in the North." Employment Sector Employment Working Paper No. 119, ILO.

"Trade Unions in Bangladesh: Promoting Safe and Healthy Workplaces in the Ready-Made Garment (RMG) Sector." 2014. International Training Centre, ILO. Accessed on October 23, 2024. https://www.ilo.org/wcmsp5/groups/public/---asia/---ro-bangkok/---ilo-dhaka/documents/publication/wcms_615874.pdf.

International Instruments

ILO Convention on the Right of Association (Agriculture), 1921 (No. 11). Accessed on October 22, 2024. https://normlex.ilo.org/dyn/nrmlx_en/f?p=NORMLEXPUB:12100:0::NO:12100:P12100_INSTRUMENT_ID:312156:NO.

ILO Convention on the Right of Association (Non-Metropolitan Territories) Convention, 1947 (No. 84). Accessed on October 22, 2024, https://normlex.ilo.org/dyn/nrmlx_en/f?p=NORMLEXPUB:12100:0::NO:12100:P12100_INSTRUMENT_ID:312229:NO.

ILO Convention on the Workers Representatives 1971 (No. 135). Accessed on October 22, 2024, https://normlex.ilo.org/dyn/nrmlx_en/f?p=NORMLEXPUB:12100:0::NO:12100:P12100_INSTRUMENT_ID:312280:NO.

ILO Convention on Rural Workers' Organisations 975, (No. 141). Accessed on October 22, 2024, https://normlex.ilo.org/dyn/nrmlx_en/f?p=NORMLEXPUB:12100:0::NO::P12100_ILO_CODE:C141.

ILO Convention on Labour Relations (Public Service) 1978 (No. 151). Accessed on October 22, 2024, https://normlex.ilo.org/dyn/nrmlx_en/f?p=NORMLEXPUB:12100:0::NO:12100:P12100_INSTRUMENT_ID:312296:NO.

Legislation

The Bangladesh Labour Act 2006 (Act No. XLII of 2006).

The Bangladesh Labour (Amendment) Act 2018 (Act No. LVIII).

The Bangladesh Labour (Amendment) Act 2013(Act No. XXX)

The Essential Services (Maintenance) Act 1952 (Act No. LIII of 1952)

The EPZ Workers Association and Industrial Relations Act, 2019

CHAPTER 5

Collective Bargaining in Bangladesh: Rhetoric and Reality

5.1 Introduction

Collective bargaining, a power of collective mobilization and institutional articulation of labor, remains a pivotal instrument to raise and realize the collective interests of the workers. Collective bargaining has been defined as the process of voluntary negotiation between trade unions and employers, where the interests of the workers are commonly presented by representatives of a trade union for reaching agreements for regulating working conditions (Brandl 2013). According to Kahn-Freuds, collective bargaining makes a balance of "the collective forces of management and organized labor" (Kahn-Freund 1983, 12). Ideally, the collective bargaining process leads to conclusion of collective bargaining agreements, which are binding on management and trade unions for a specified period. Collective bargaining acts as a mechanism for accommodating conflicting interests and economic and social concerns of workers through consultation and negotiation and in this way, it serves as a formal channel for dispute resolution based on law or agreement and works through addressing the discontents of workers. In case of discontent in industry, workers tend to resort to informal, clandestine, often violent action to express their grievances and discontent with perceived injustices. Collective bargaining agreements act as a preventive mechanism for dispute resolution by fixing the terms of employment and the conditions of work and redressing the grievances of workers. Through channeling the

A. Al Faruque, *Globalization and Labour Rights*,
https://doi.org/10.1007/978-981-92-3661-9_5

grievances of workers and protecting the rights of workers, collective bargaining also enhances the productivity, performance, and competitiveness of firms or industries. At the national level, organized or coordinated collective bargaining has been associated with reduced strike rates, high productivity, fair wage-setting, and distributional outcomes within firms and societies (Doellgast and Benassi 2020, 239). Doellgast and Benassi focus on the distributional benefits of collective bargaining as it allocates the distribution of economic gains from productivity improvements, the distribution of risks resulting from fluctuations in the business cycle, and the broader distribution of economic and political power within workplaces or in society (Doellgast and Benassi 2020, 250).

The legal basis of collective bargaining is deeply grounded in the ILO Convention on the Right to Organize and Collective Bargaining, 1949 (No. 98), which sets standards for collective bargaining at the national level. According to the ILO Collective Agreements Recommendation 1951, collective bargaining agreements will have binding force and prevail over individual contracts of employment (Gernigon et al. 2000, 35). The Labor Administration Convention, 1978 (No. 150) reinforces the importance of collective bargaining by providing that the relevant authorities of labor administration of the state parties must support and promote the implementation of the terms and conditions of employment reached by means of collective bargaining (Article 5 of the Convention).

Generally, the collective bargaining process is facilitated by trade unions. Therefore, a collective bargaining agreement needs well-informed trade unions that have a comprehensive understanding of the needs of the workers, and a strong relationship with management. Effective collective bargaining is essential for sound industrial relations in any country. However, it will be effective only when the bargaining power of the trade unions is equal to that of the management. The collective bargaining agreements reached by these negotiations usually cover the issue of minimum wages, working hours, training of workers, overtime payment, grievance mechanisms, and rights to participate in a trade union. Such agreements also set out work schedules, safe working environments, and a fair share in the benefits of increased productivity of an industry (Hayter and Visser 2018, 1). While traditionally, collective bargaining is seen as a voluntary process, depending on the level of maturity of industrial relations in a country, the state may compel workers and employers to bargain on a range of issues relating to employment in order to institutionalize collective bargaining (Kahn-Freund 1983, 8). A legally enforceable duty to bargain enables unions to demand it as a right that is not possible to secure through persuasion (Kahn-Freund 1983). The organization and structure of collective bargaining show a high degree of variation across countries, as it evolved historically in distinct national socio-economic environments (Brandl 2013). This also holds true for Bangladesh, where the functioning and the socio-economic impact of collective bargaining are deeply embedded in distinct institutional and organizational structures.

5.2 Importance of Collective Bargaining

Collective bargaining has many important bearings on the industrial relations system. First, collective bargaining agreements have emerged as an alternative form of dispute resolution, as parties to the agreement generally remain committed to complying with certain terms and conditions mentioned in the agreement. Through setting out procedures for labor dispute settlement, these agreements prevent conflicts and reduce confrontational attitudes associated with the employment relationship (Khabo 2008, 1).

Second, collective bargaining coverage represents the power dimension of the bargaining system (Traxler et al. 2001) because collective bargaining is based on the premise that employers enjoy greater social and economic leverage than individual workers. In this way, collective bargaining involves correcting a basic power imbalance in the employment relationship through legal intervention and collective action (Doellgast and Benassi 2020, 250). Generally, employment contracts are heavily imbalanced in favor of employers due to the fact that its terms and conditions are largely determined by the employer because of controlling the means of production, which places him in a stronger bargaining (Traxler et al. 2001). The weak bargaining power of workers can prevent them from getting fair contract terms on welfare provisions and safety conditions or protection against wrongful discharge (Spector 2006, 1133). It is against this background that collective bargaining agreements act as a "countervailing force against the powers of management" (Spector 2006, 1133) and address the inequality of bargaining power between employers and workers (Spector 2006, 1132).

Third, collective bargaining agreements are seen as key private regulatory mechanisms that influence the outcomes of social policy of government. Collective bargaining agreements may address traditional social policy issues such as minimum wage, safety, and security of workers to complement the welfare state (Glassner and Kwune 2012).

Fourth, the importance of collective bargaining can be viewed from both micro and macro perspectives. From a micro perspective, collective bargaining is a voluntary exchange between different actors because the relationship is dependent on the willingness of actors to participate and negotiate over wages and working conditions (Glassner and Kwune 2012). On the employee's side, collective bargaining strengthens their voice to articulate their interests and promote their demands. On the employers' side, collective bargaining enables them to maintain social peace, ensure the legitimacy of managerial control, and reduce the costs of employment regulation (Glassner and Kwune 2012). From a macro perspective, collective bargaining can be seen as a societal institution for ensuring certain societal and economic goals, such as realizing a fairer distribution of benefits of productivity, promoting the dignity of workers, and resolving industrial conflicts between employers and employees (Brandl 2013). It has been argued that coordinated bargaining systems are associated with higher employment, better integration of vulnerable groups and reduction of wage inequality (Garnero 2021).

Collective bargaining power of labor is typically categorized as both associational and structural power. Association power refers to the density of unionization, the coverage of the collective agreements or the participation of labor collectives in firm and non-firm decision-making while structural power implies the capacity of workers to mobilize economic resources within a key industrial sector (Iliopoulos 2026, Wright 2000). While associational power denotes a capacity to act collectively, structural power implies disruption capacity of workers in production network (Ahumada 2021, 87). Iliopoulos argues that the bargaining power of labor is not merely rooted in the organizational strength of its unions or the institutional influence of the working class, but also in the structural power embedded in interdependent systems of production—global value chain, and it influences distributional outcomes, conditional on institutional and political context (Iliopoulos 2026, 15). By understanding and utilizing the structural power inherent in global value chains, Iliopoulos claims, "unions can better navigate the complexities of the world economy,... and secure more favourable outcomes for labour" (Iliopoulos 2026, 15). These different forms of power are interrelated in the sense that workers are more likely to succeed in protect their interests when they are strong in both power relations. In other words, when their associational power is weak, the power of mobilization of economic resources is less likely to be effective (Ahumada 2021, 88).

5.3 Impact of Globalization on Collective Bargaining

The globalization process has brought drastic changes in both the formal and informal sectors of work, with an increase in precariousness of working conditions, which has far-reaching implications for collective bargaining. The last decades witnessed the diversification of works and a reduction of the average size of enterprises through a restructuring that resulted in the erosion of the power base of trade union organizations and their traditional collective bargaining power (Cunniah 2009, 5). The liberalization of trade, deregulation, and privatization—the main instrumentality of economic globalization—strained the traditional collective bargaining process because all these changes have contributed to shifting the balance of power between employers and workers (Cunniah 2009, 5). Globalization has reduced workers' bargaining power due to capital's increased mobility, which has made it easier for firms to relocate their business and put downward pressure on outcome-related labor standards (Elliott and Freeman 2003). Fudge and Shamir's influential critique of the expansion of the global supply chains highlights that outsourcing and subcontracting enabled key firms to disperse different elements of supply and production to different countries and by taking advantage of this geographic dispersion of production, multinational enterprises have undermined workers' traditional power resources (Fudge and Shamir 2025).

Collective bargaining is also strained by the dramatic increase in precarious work conditions that is accelerated by the growth of casual work and temporary employment contracts (Gernigon et al. 2000, 33). In the globalized labor relations, the scope of collective bargaining has been diminished significantly due to high levels of unemployment, the growth of the informal sector, widespread practice of subcontracting of workers and use of the various forms of non-standard employment relationships, which make unionization and collective bargaining more difficult (Gernigon et al. 2000, 33). In developing countries, one of the main challenges of collective bargaining is formalizing the informal labor sector in order to ensure that workers in the sector can be covered by collective bargaining agreements.

On the other hand, in response to the increasing internationalization of the economy and the consequent delocalization of MNE's activities, transnational collective bargaining has emerged as a new tool to overcome the difficulties brought by globalization. Transnational collective bargaining generally results in transnational collective bargaining agreements (Marassi 2015, 22). It is undeniable that national systems of collective bargaining with reduced power and authority have lost some of their capacity to protect the interests of workers and regulate the labor market. These factors have underpinned the need for transnational systems of labor market regulation and collective bargaining (Hartzén 2024). Over the last decades, the transnational labor movement has built up strong international solidarity and international cooperation that resulted in conclusion of transnational collective bargaining agreements. However, transnational collective bargaining is not without problems. As there is no domestic and international legal framework to regulate such bargaining and make these agreements enforceable (Keune and Schmidt 2009, 24), most of these collective bargaining agreements are voluntary in nature, resulting in minimal compliance.

5.4 Preconditions for Successful Collective Bargaining

Presence of strong and representative trade unions, an enabling legal framework, and a cooperative attitude to negotiation are essential conditions for effective collective bargaining. Since trade union strength plays a decisive role for bargaining outcomes, lower unionization rates may reduce bargaining power of workers. A collective bargaining to be successful, it must be "sufficiently representative" in order to be acceptable to all stakeholders, guided by the principle of the independence and autonomy of the parties, and the negotiation must be voluntary (Gernigon et al. 2000, 36). Similarly, in order for trade unions to be able to achieve the interests and rights of workers by collective bargaining, they must be independent and must have the right to organize their activities without any interference from the public authorities that would impede the legal exercise of that right (Article 3 of the ILO Convention on the Freedom of Association and Protection of the Right to Organize). The effectiveness of the collective bargaining agreement also depends on the minimum level of interference by the government in bipartite negotiations and ensuring "primacy to employers' and workers' organizations as the parties to the bargaining process" (Gernigon et al. 2000, 34). The collective bargaining process should also be molded by the principle of good faith. Success in collective bargaining also depends upon the flexibility of the process, careful preparation and building a constructive attitude so that parties can discuss mutual problems and reach an agreement.

5.5 Law and Practice on Collective Bargaining in Bangladesh

The collective bargaining in Bangladesh is governed by the Bangladesh Labor Act 2006. Generally, trade unions act as a collective bargaining agent in Bangladesh. Where there is only one trade union in an establishment, the trade union shall act as the collective bargaining agent for such establishment (Section 202 of the Bangladesh Labor Act 2006). But where there is more than one registered trade union in an establishment, a collective bargaining agent will be elected by the majority of workers in the enterprise, and it will have the exclusive right to bargain in that enterprise (Section 202(2) of the Bangladesh Labor Act 2006). While availability of a registered trade union in an establishment or industry is essential for functioning of a collective bargaining agent, there is no legal obligation to register collective bargaining agents or collective bargaining agreements. According to the Act, in order to conduct collective bargaining activities, the employer or collective bargaining agent may take the assistance of experts (Section 202A as added by the Labor (Amendment) Act).

The scope of collective bargaining has been elaborately spelled out in the Bangladesh Labor Act 2006. A collective bargaining agent is entitled to raise labor disputes on behalf of the workers (Section 209 of the Bangladesh Labor Act 2006), to bargain with the employer regarding joblessness, conditions of work or environment of work; to represent workers in any legal proceedings; to declare a strike; and to nominate representatives of the workers in any welfare fund for workers. Therefore, CBA does not deal with a dispute if it does not affect the collective interest of workers. For example, the issue of unfair treatment of an individual worker, harassment of a worker by a co-worker, non-payment for overtime work, pressure on a worker to complete his work at an unreasonable speed, punishment of a worker for alleged misconduct, withholding of increment for a certain period, these cannot be addressed by the CBA.

Similarly, if an individual worker is laid off or retrenched, discharged, or terminated, CBA cannot intervene. In all these circumstances, an aggrieved worker can resort to the grievance procedure under section 33 of the Bangladesh Labor Act of 2006. According to section 203, a federation of trade unions may be the exclusive bargaining agent for all federated unions within a "group of establishments" if a majority of the members of the federated unions authorize this through a vote.

The role of the trade union as a collective bargaining agent has been undermined to some extent by the legal requirement of the establishment of a workers' representative committee in factories, which is known as the Participation Committee. As per the 2013 amendments made to the Bangladesh Labor Act 2006, in an establishment where there is no trade union, the workers' representatives in the Participation Committee shall run activities related to workers' interests in the concerned establishment until a trade union is formed (Section 205(6)(a) of the Bangladesh Labor Act 2006). However, the Participation Committee is not authorized to negotiate with employers about the interests of workers and to conclude any collective bargaining agreement.

Collective bargaining coverage depends more on the level at which collective bargaining takes place than on trade union density (Schnabel 2020, 33). As per the Bangladesh Labor Act 2006, collective bargaining with employers was not allowed at the sectoral level; it was only allowed at the enterprise or plant level. The practice of collective bargaining in Bangladesh was, thus, highly centralized and limited as there is no legal provision for collective bargaining at the sectoral or national levels. The Bangladesh Labor (Amendment) Act 2026 now allows collective bargaining at the sectoral and national level. This amendment makes a fundamental shift from enterprise level collecting bargaining to mult-layered collective bargaining, which means that not only individual trade union, but also even federations and confederations are allowed to bargaining at sectoral and national level. As per the ILO's Social Dialogue (SD) Report 2022, in Bangladesh, the collective bargaining agreement (CBA) coverage rate is 1.5%, with only 499 enterprise-level CBAs recorded in the manufacturing sector (ILO 2022). Furthermore, there is limited data on the number of active and effective collective agreements in the country at enterprise and sectoral levels. The 2024 report of the ILO Committee of Experts on the Application of Conventions and Recommendations (CEACR) highlights that collective bargaining primarily takes place at the enterprise or industry level, with sectoral bargaining limited to the tea and shipping sectors. It also notes that although the Bangladesh Labor Act 2006 mandates submission of bipartite CBAs to the Department of Labor (Section 210(3) of the Bangladesh Labor Act 2006), employers often fail to comply, resulting in poor statistical tracking.

In the private sector, the scope of collective bargaining is wider than in the public sector since the determination of minimum wages of workers, and terms and conditions of employment constitute the core issues of collective bargaining. Collective bargaining occurs occasionally in large private enterprises in sectors such as RMG, pharmaceuticals, jute or textile industries due to limited level of unionization of workers. Collective bargaining in small private enterprises is virtually non-existent for similar reasons. Collective bargaining has been rarely resorted to the private sector enterprises due to the unwillingness of employers to recognize the CBA leaders as equal partners in the negotiation process. Since 2013, an estimated 51 collective bargaining agreements have been signed in the apparel sector (Country Information & Practical Advice on Freedom of Association (FoA) & Collective Bargaining (CB): Bangladesh 2025).

5.6 Right to Strike and the Role of Collective Bargaining

A strike, an institutional power of labor, is usually taken to consist of the simultaneous and coordinated withdrawal of labor by workers to disrupt production (Novitz 2003, 38). But neither the ILO constitution nor any ILO Convention explicitly recognizes the right to strike. However, the right to strike is a necessary element of the right to organize and bargain collectively. Strikes may be organized through trade unions or may be the result of a joint but informal decision to work outside an institutional framework. In either case, the persuasive power of a strike usually lies in collective action, which has more impact than the withdrawal of labor by a solitary worker (Novitz 2003). Strikes are usually concerned with such matters as pay, safety, and job security. The right to strike is intertwined with the right to free speech, freedom of association, or even freedom from forced labor and in this way, it has assumed the status of a fundamental civil liberty (Novitz 2003).

The right to strike is a concerted collective stoppage of work- a weapon of employed workers to achieve certain goals. Strike is a form of political or economic freedom. In this way, a strike is considered an "economic weapon" in industrial relations or an "industrial sanction" to realize legitimate collective rights of workers or enforce existing rights (Freund and Hepple 1972, 6). The right to strike serves the purpose of dispute settlement mechanism since it is resorted to in circumstances when parties have failed to negotiate on an issue of industrial relations (Khabo 2008, 17). The right has been "justified as a countervailing force to the power of capital" (Freund and Hepple 1972, 6) and it is an ultimate means of persuasion to bring the workers and employers in the negotiation process and sanction for the enforcement of collective bargaining agreements. It should be acknowledged that strikes occur when collective bargaining fails to address working conditions or workers' rights. However, the use of this economic power should be used sparingly, and it should be used as a last resort because of its potential adverse effects on the economy. The right to strike is therefore regulated by a set of procedural limitations in all countries.

The Bangladesh Labor Act 2006 prescribes that before resorting to a strike, parties have to exhaust negotiation and conciliation efforts to try and solve the dispute amicably and avoid industrial action as much as possible (Section 211 of the Bangladesh Labor Act 2006). A strike can be called by the Collective Bargaining Agent (CBA) or employer after serving seven days' notice to either party. Previously, before serving any such notice by CBA, it had to obtain the consent of three-fourths of its members through a secret ballot, a stringent procedure that virtually curtailed this right. Through an amendment made in 2018 to the Labor Act 2006, the requirement of obtaining the consent of three-fourths of its members has been reduced to 51% of workers' consent. However, obtaining consent through secret ballot is often a time-consuming process, which provides employers ample scope to intimidate workers to prevent their participation in strikes. During the strike, the dispute can be referred to the labor court for judicial settlement. No party can serve a notice of strike or lock-out while conciliation is going on or during the pendency of proceedings before the Labor Court or Labor Appellate Tribunal (Section 225 of the Bangladesh Labor Act 2006). The Labor Court and the Labor Appellate Tribunal can prohibit any strike or lock-out during the pendency of any proceeding before it (Section 226 of the Bangladesh Labor Act 2006). If a strike or lock-out continues for more than 30 days, the government may prohibit the strike or lock-out (Section 211(3) of the Bangladesh Labor Act 2006). Even the government may prohibit a strike or lock-out at any time before the expiry of thirty days if it is satisfied that the strike is causing serious hardship to public life or is contrary to the national interest (Section 211(3) of the Bangladesh Labor Act 2006). In the case of any of the public utility services, the government may prohibit a strike or lock-out at any time, either before or after the commencement of a strike or lock-out (Section 211(4) of the Bangladesh Labor Act 2006). Moreover, the strike or lock-out is prohibited in an establishment for a period of three years from the date of commencement of production therein, if such establishment is a new one or is owned by foreigners or is established in collaboration with foreigners (Section 211 (8) of the Bangladesh Labor Act 2006). A strike can be considered illegal if it is called without following the above procedures (Section 227 of the Bangladesh Labor Act 2006). The government can prohibit it at any time on the ground of national interest, which can be broadly interpreted. Moreover, a penalty has been prescribed for illegal strikes and instigating illegal strikes (Section 294 and 295 of the Bangladesh Labor Act 2006) that can effectively prohibit workers from calling strikes and can be used unreasonably against the workers.

Thus, the Bangladesh Labor Act 2006 lays down numerous stipulations that workers would have to meet in order to conduct a lawful strike and elaborates various circumstances in which the strike could be ordered to cease. In fact, the right to strike is practiced rarely in industries in Bangladesh.

Restriction on the right to strike can also be found in the Bangladesh Nationalized Enterprises and Statutory Corporations (Prohibition of Strikes and Unfair Labor Practices) Order 1972, which provides that no worker or trade union shall resort to any strike by using intimidation, coercion, pressure, threats, confinement to a place, physical injury, disconnection of telephones, water, or power facilities (President's Order No. 55 of 1972). While the Bangladesh Labor Act 2006 allows workers to organize and strike, such a right is hardly exercised due to the pressures of powerful factory owners. As a result, Bangladeshi workers have remained vulnerable to exploitation by employers, without sufficiently robust protections to organize and strike for better working conditions.

5.7 Collective Bargaining in the Export Processing Zones (EPZ)

The EPZ Labor Act 2019 does not recognize trade unions in the EPZs, but it allows collective bargaining by any Workers' Welfare Association. Under this Act, the Collective Bargaining Agent in EPZs shall have the right to negotiate with the employer on the issue of wages, working hours and other terms and conditions of employment, to represent workers in any legal proceedings; and to declare a strike (Section 119(2) and 119(3) of the EPZ Labor Act 2019). However, in the absence of trade unions in the EPZs, the practice of collective bargaining is severely restricted and ineffective. Lack of collective bargaining has exacerbated the violation of labor rights in these zones, as there is no sufficient legal protection against forced or compulsory labor and against discrimination in recruitment and employment, and poor and unsafe working conditions there.

5.8 Conclusion

The above analysis reveals that while there are some enabling provisions under labor laws to facilitate collective bargaining at the enterprise level to improve the rights and welfare of workers. It is not widely practiced due to various constraints such as lack of awareness among workers about the right to collective bargaining, weak unionization, employers' resistance, limited government oversight, and intimidation by employers. In Bangladesh, the scope of collective bargaining is limited as there is no enabling provision for collective bargaining on a sectoral and national level. The practice of collective bargaining is also very limited in the public sector enterprises since the government often determines the wage levels for workers of these enterprises. In order to make collective bargaining effective, the autonomy of parties, especially, workers, must be safeguarded through legal provisions. Collective bargaining agreements, which are negotiated by independent, autonomous, and representative trade unions and employers' organizations in a particular sector or occupation, enjoy more legitimacy and acceptability and can contribute to improving labor condition and advance stability in the workplace by reducing the likelihood of strikes or other disruptions (Hayter and Visser 2018, 2). The representatives of trade unions, e.g., unions' executive committee, need to be equipped with knowledge and skills about collective bargaining. They must have strong knowledge and understanding of laws and international standards on collective bargaining and prioritize the needs of workers.

Bibliography

Books

Kahn-Freund, O. 1983. *Labour and the Law*, 3rd ed. Stevens and Sons.

Kahn-Freund, O., and B. Hepple. 1972. *Laws Against Strikes*. Fabian Society.

Marassi, Stefania. 2015. *Globalization and Transnational Collective Labour Relations: International and European Framework Agreements at Company Level*. Wolters Kluwer.

Novitz, Tonia. 2003. *International and European Protection of the Right to Strike*. Oxford University Press.

Chapters in Edited Books

Brandl, Bernd. 2013. "Collective Bargaining." In *Sociology of Work: An Encyclopedia*, edited by Vicki Smith, 99–103. Sage Publications.

Doellgast, Virginia, and Chiara Benassi. 2020. "Collective Bargaining." In *Handbook of Research on Employee Voice*, edited by Adrian Wilkinson, Jimmy Donaghey, Tony Dundon, and Richard B. Freeman, 239–258. Edward Elgar Publishing.

Hayter, Susan, and Jelle Visser. 2018. "The Application and Extension of Collective Agreements: Enhancing the Inclusiveness of Labour Protection." In *Collective Agreements: Extending Labour Protection*, edited by Susan Hayter and Jelle Visser, 1–27. ILO.

Schnabel, Claus. 2020. "Union Membership and Collective Bargaining: Trends and Determinants.". In *Handbook of Labor, Human Resources and Population Economics*, edited by K. F. Zimmermann, 1–37. Springer Nature.

Traxler, Franz, Sabine Blaschke, and Bernhard Kittel. 2001. "The Coverage of Collective Bargaining." In *National Labour Relations in Internationalized Markets: A Comparative Study of Institutions, Change and Performance*, edited by Franz Traxler et al., 194–210. Oxford University Press.

Journal Articles

Ahumada, Pablo Pérez. 2021. "Why Is It So Difficult to Reform Collective Labour Law? Associational Power and Policy Continuity in Chile in Comparative Perspective." *Journal of Latin American Studies* 53: 81–105.

Cunniah, Dan. 2009. "Preface." *International Journal of Labour Research* 1 (2): 1–5.

Fudge, Judy, and Hila Shamir. 2025. "Strike Law and Workers' Power Resources in Global Supply Chains and Platform Giants." *Comparative Labor Law & Policy Journal* 45 (2): 370–397.

Garnero, Andrea. 2021. "The Impact of Collective Bargaining On Employment and Wage Inequality: Evidence From a New Taxonomy of Bargaining Systems." *European Journal of Industrial Relations* 27 (2): 185–202.

Gernigon, Bernard, Alberto Odero, and Horacio Guido. 2000. "ILO Principles Concerning Collective Bargaining." *International Labour Review* 139 (1): 33–55.

Glassner, Vera, and Maarten Kwune. 2012. "The Crisis and Social Policy: The Role of Collective Agreements." *International Labour Review* 151 (4): 351–375.

Iliopoulos, Panagiotis. 2026. "Globalization and Income Distribution: What Is the Role for Workers' Structural Bargaining Power?." *British Journal of Industrial Relations*: 1–17.

Keune, Maarten, and Verena Schmidt. 2009. "Global Capital Strategies and Trade Union Responses: Towards Transnational Collective Bargaining?." *International Journal of Labour Research* 1 (2): 9–26.

Spector, Horacio. 2006. "Philosophical Foundations of Labor Law." *Florida State University Law Review* 33: 1119–1148.

Wright, Erik O. 2000. "Working-Class Power, Capitalist-Class Interests, and Class Compromise." *American Journal of Sociology* 105 (4): 957–1002.

Reports

Country Information & Practical Advice on Freedom of Association (FoA) & Collective Bargaining (CB): Bangladesh, accessed on May 13, 2024, https://www.imvoconvenanten.nl/-/media/imvo/files/kleding/child-labour/association/country-information-bangladesh.pdf.

Elliott, K. A., and R. B. Freeman. 2003. *Can Labor Standards Improve Under Globalization?*. Institute for International Economics, Washington, DC.

Hartzén, Ann-Christine. "Globalisation of Labour Markets and International Systems of Industrial Relations." A Conference Paper. Accessed on May 13, 2024. http://www.diva-portal.org/smash/get/diva2:1236764/FULLTEXT01.pdf.

Khabo, Fumane Malebona. 2008. "Collective Bargaining and Labour Disputes Resolution: Is SADC Meeting the Challenge?." ILO Sub-Regional Office for Southern Africa (Issue paper No. 30). ILO, Harare.

The ILO Social Dialogue Report 2022. ILO, 63. Accessed on June 12, 2025. https://www.ilo.org/sites/default/files/wcmsp5/groups/public/%40dgreports/%40dcomm/%40publ/documents/publication/wcms_842807.pdf.

International Instruments

ILO Collective Agreements Recommendation. 1951 (No. 91). Accessed on March 17, 2024. https://normlex.ilo.org/dyn/nrmlx_en/f?p=NORMLEXPUB:12100:0::NO::P12100_ILO_CODE:R091.
The Right to Organise and Collective Bargaining Convention. 1949 (No. 98). Accessed on March 17, 2024. https://normlex.ilo.org/dyn/nrmlx_en/f?p=NORMLEXPUB:12100:0::NO:12100:P12100_INSTRUMENT_ID:312243:NO.
The Labour Administration Convention. 1978 (No. 150). Accessed on March 17, 2024. https://normlex.ilo.org/dyn/nrmlx_en/f?p=NORMLEXPUB:12100:0::NO:12100:P12100_INSTRUMENT_ID:312295:NO.
ILO Collective Agreements Recommendation, 1951 (No. 91).

Legislation

President's Order No. 55 of 1972.
The EPZ Labor Act 2019.
The Labour Administration Convention. 1978 (No. 150).
The Bangladesh Labor Act 2006.

CHAPTER 6

Fixing Minimum Wages: Issues and Challenges

6.1 Introduction

The minimum wage, a cornerstone of labor market policy, is one of the crucial elements of distributive justice pertaining to the collective welfare of labor and the enhancement of their capability to attain social goods. The minimum wage has a profound distributive function in the labor market as it aims to ensure a fair distribution of wealth between workers and employers by specifying a legally mandated minimum price for labor. Most countries have a minimum wage system for workers, although its coverage and degree of implementation may vary depending on the level of socio-economic development of a country (Benassi 2011, 2). The main goal of the minimum wage is redistribution of resources from employers to workers (Davidov 2016, 30). Setting a minimum wage is not only an economic issue; it has broader effects on labor flows, productivity, firms' profits, and their connection with the state of the economy (Wang 2025). Setting a minimum wage is, sometimes, also subject of political debate as the government, workers' organizations and employers have to reach a consensus on it, find an appropriate method of fixing, and agree on the redistribution of wealth (Benassi 2011, 2). Setting a minimum wage is considered essential for the protection of the dignity of workers (Davidov 2016, 23), and is one of the preconditions of ensuring decent work and is inextricably linked to workers' well-being (Merk 2009, 7). However, fixing minimum wages is often a complex process. There is diversity in

A. Al Faruque, *Globalization and Labour Rights*,
https://doi.org/10.1007/978-981-92-3661-9_6

approaches to setting minimum wage. Some countries adopt national minimum wages that apply to all workers. This type of minimum wage is applied by mostly developed countries like the USA, the UK, and France (Belser and Sobeck 2012, 109). On the other hand, many developing countries fix the minimum wage at the sectoral level and public authorities in these countries determine minimum wages for different economic activities (Belser and Sobeck 2012). In these countries, different levels of minimum wages apply to different groups of workers due to the diversity and complexity of economic conditions that makes it impossible to formulate one precise standard of minimum wage for all industries.

The objective of minimum wages is to reduce discrimination and the gender pay gap and provide social protection to workers. In many countries, it is designed as a policy tool to alleviate poverty (Rani et al. 2013, 381). Minimum wages are commonly set by governments in both developed and developing countries in order to prevent exploitation of workers, to prohibit "unfairly low pay" (Wascher 2015, 561), to ensure that workers receive a "fair" wage for their work and they are not discriminated in work place and to raise the wages of many low-skilled workers (Wascher 2008). However, some critics of minimum wage argue that minimum wages do not reduce the poverty of low-income families if they are not regularly adjusted to reflect inflation in the market (Neumark and Wascher 2008, 6).

The globalization process has also negatively impacted the setting of minimum wages due to the increasing competition between countries for investment and trade that pushed them to lower minimum wages to reduce labor costs for foreign investors. Outsourcing of jobs in manufacturing industries to countries with lower labor costs and the increasing trend of casualization of work have also contributed to lowering the minimum wage in many developing countries.

Setting a fair minimum wage is a long-standing contested issue in Bangladesh, especially in the RMG sector, where the owners compete for orders from brands and retailers by continuously lowering production costs to remain competitive.

6.2 Coverage of Minimum Wages

The term "minimum wage" is not defined by any ILO Conventions. However, it refers to the minimum sum payable to a worker for work performed or services rendered, within a given period, and it is guaranteed by law to cover the minimum needs of the worker and his or her family, in the light of national economic and social conditions (the Minimum Wage Fixing Convention, 1970 (No. 131) and the Minimum Wage Fixing Recommendation, 1970). The binding nature of minimum wages has been reflected in its legal recognition in numerous countries. The minimum wage is different from the low wage that is set even below the minimum wage. Low wages are generally a reflection of negative conditions in labor markets for example, the repression of unions, massive unemployment and underemployment, extreme rural poverty, and manipulation of gender and ethnic divisions. On the other hand, the minimum wage is different from the "living wage". "Living wage" implies the wage by which workers and their families can lead a decent life in light of the level of economic development of a country (Anker 2011, 1; Lawton and Pennycook 2013, 10). By earning a "living wage", it is expected that workers can live above the poverty line, participate in social and cultural life, and attain a minimum standard of living (Anker 2011, 5). The concept of a "living wage', therefore, refers both to the existence of a minimum level of wage that ensures an acceptable standard of living (Anker 2011, 5). According to the International Labor Organization, as of 2023, more than 90% of countries of ILO member states have some type of minimum wage, although the specific levels of minimum wages, their coverage, and the processes for determining wages can differ substantially across these countries (ILO 2024).

In terms of coverage of minimum wage, the Minimum Wage Fixing Convention, 1970 (No. 131) requires the establishment of a system of minimum wages for covering all groups of wage earners and it lays down that every country should have a mechanism to fix a minimum wage for workers to "prevent unduly low wages". However, this Convention also accommodates flexibility for a state party to exclude certain groups of wage earners from the coverage of its minimum wage system. In fact, many state parties to this Convention have excluded workers in informal sectors, e.g., agricultural, domestic workers, family businesses, small enterprises, apprentices and trainees, and workers with disabilities using this flexibility.

6.3 Process of Fixing Minimum Wages

There are two opposing viewpoints in setting minimum wages: The first is that a minimum wage can be set by the government through enacting a law, while the second proposition is that setting minimum wages should entirely rest on the supply and demand scenario and thus, may be set through collective bargaining, not by legislation or other regulatory measures (Saget 2008, 25). However, in most countries, minimum wages are set by either legislation or a wage board. Only in a few countries, it is set by collective bargaining. Some countries have separate legislation on minimum wages and some other countries have incorporated it in labor legislation, e.g., Bangladesh. For example, India has separate minimum wage legislation called the Minimum Wage Act of 1948. Minimum wages can also be set by giving legal effect to provisions of collective agreements. The genesis of setting up an institutional mechanism for fixing minimum wage lies in the ILO Minimum Wage Fixing Machinery Convention, 1928, which provides for creating machinery for fixing minimum rates of wages in industries where no arrangement exists for the regulation of wages by a collective agreement. Article 10(1) of the ILO Social Policy (Basic Aims and Standards) Convention, 1962 emphasizes fixing minimum wages by "freely negotiated collective agreements", or by any other appropriate arrangements through consultations with employers' and workers' representatives. Article 10(3) of the Convention also requires that workers must be kept informed of the minimum wage rates applicable to them and about the procedure to enforce it.

Sectoral-level collective bargaining plays a critical role in fixing minimum wages. The fixing of minimum wage is also considerably shaped by the strength and capacity of trade unions to bargain about wage-setting (Grimshaw 2013, 19). The importance of collective bargaining in setting minimum wages lies in the fact that most individual workers do not hold bargaining position to employers regarding wage-setting (Kaufman 2009). More importantly, employers are typically resistant to minimum wage legislation, and they oppose law or policy interventions that raise the minimum wage (Grimshaw 2013, 24). It is widely acknowledged that the effective participation of the workers and social partners in the decision-making process relating to the fixation of minimum wages increases the probability of adoption of a fair degree of minimum wage, enhances the application of the minimum wages, and therefore contributes to greater compliance. On the other hand, inadequate consultation with the stakeholders in fixing the minimum wage contributes to setting low levels of minimum wage. The process of setting minimum wages by collective bargaining and consultation with stakeholders makes the wage-setting process more transparent and participatory. Thus, the relationship between minimum wages and collective bargaining is well-established, as it is evident that a stronger collective bargaining system enhances the level of minimum wage even in countries with a statutory national minimum wage (Grimshaw and Bosch 2013, 51). It is also demonstrated that weak collective bargaining practice is responsible for setting low minimum wages (Saget 2008, 26). Although there is no minimum wage for the informal sectors in many countries, in certain situations, the minimum wage fixed by collective bargaining is used as a reference wage in the bargaining between an individual worker and an employer in the informal sector (Saget 2008, 35).

Generally, the minimum wage that is fixed by law should be set after consultation with relevant stakeholders in the concerned industrial sector. According to Davidov, a minimum wage, which is an outcome of participative and consensus-oriented negotiations between social partners, is more acceptable to the stakeholders and employers are more likely to comply with it than the minimum wage fixed by a top-down process by the government (Davidov 2016, 35).

6.4 Criteria for Fixing Minimum Wages

Legislation may set certain criteria for fixing minimum wages reflecting both the needs of workers and their families, and economic considerations. Eyraud and Saget have identified some common criteria in the minimum wage legislation that include “the basic needs of workers and their families, the increase in the consumer price index, productivity, the level of employment, and the levels of wages and of social security benefits” (Eyraud and Saget 2005, 35). There are two main approaches to setting minimum wages: a balanced approach and an evidence-based approach. The Minimum Wage Fixing Convention, 1970 takes a balanced approach to setting minimum wages as it requires that in determining the level of minimum wages, “the needs of workers and their families, the general level of wages in the country, the cost of living, social security benefits, and the relative living standards of other social groups” must be taken into account (Article 3 of the Convention). On the other, these individual needs should balance with “economic factors, including the requirements of economic development, the level of productivity, and the desirability of attaining a high level of employment" (Article 3b of the Convention).

The ILO Minimum Wage Fixing Recommendation, 1970 (No. 135) also incorporates the same criteria for fixing minimum wage as the ILO Convention (131). It further provides that the minimum wage must be able to provide necessary social protection for the workers. Both the ILO Convention 131 and the ILO Minimum Wage Fixing Recommendation, 1970 (No. 135) ask state parties to set the minimum wage at a certain level that allows workers and their families to meet their basic needs though they do not mention precise indications on the amount of the minimum wage. This omission reflects that state parties have flexibility and discretionary power to set minimum wage rates in full consultation with the workers' representatives and social partners, taking into account the needs of workers and their families and the level of economic development of each country.

On the other hand, an evidence-based approach requires that in determining minimum wages, statistical indicators should guide the fixation of the level of minimum wages and inform the social partners in their deliberations (ILO 2016). Statistical indicators include the general level and distribution of wages, cost of living as well as national or sectoral levels of labor productivity and rates of economic growth (ILO 2016). Both the balanced and evidence-based approach is important in one way or another in fixing minimum wages by the national authorities, though the exact interpretation and relative importance of each of the criteria are not clearly defined (Belser and Sobeck 2012, 114). Consultation with social partners, coupled with statistical indicators, can contribute to a balanced approach to setting minimum wages.

The above discussion of the ILO Conventions reveals that in determining minimum wage, the standard of living that takes into account basic needs should be considered as a yardstick. According to Anker, any definition of minimum wage must incorporate the concept of meeting the basic needs of a worker and his/her family and provide some discretionary income (Anker 2011, 23). Basic needs mean more than the bare necessities of life—food, clothing, and shelter and they also include "clean water, healthcare, childcare, transportation, education, energy and some discretionary income or savings" (Anker 2011, 95). In this context, the concept of a living wage is closely related to the setting of minimum wage.

A living wage supports a satisfactory standard of living for workers and their families and fulfills their "basic needs".

The effectiveness of minimum wages depends on many factors, such as broad coverage, adequate level, compliance, and monitoring of compliance. In terms of coverage, minimum wage must be extended to all workers in an employment relationship, regardless of their contractual arrangements, as well as all industries and occupations in a country (Minimum Wage Policy Guide). So far as the level is concerned, it needs to be set and adjusted at an adequate level, taking into account economic factors such as the needs of workers and their families. Compliance refers to the proper and full implementation of minimum wages by employers.

6.5 Distributive Justice Function of Minimum Wages

According to the ILO Minimum Wage Fixing Recommendation, 1970 (No. 135), one of the objectives of fixing minimum wages is to overcome poverty and to ensure the satisfaction of the needs of all workers and their families. It is the distributive justice functions of a minimum wage that are most valued (Grimshaw and Rubery 2013, 82). According to Sidney Webb, a minimum wage can reduce the "parasitic" exploitation of low-wage employers and prevent the risk of discrimination, especially against women (Grimshaw and Rubery 2013, 84). From the context of distributive justice, the minimum wage must be set to reflect fairness and efficiency. Setting minimum wages too low increases poverty and vulnerability of the workers, contributes to inequality, reduces social cohesion, and results in unrest in a country (Merk 2009, 7). On the other hand, if the minimum wage is set too high, it will be poorly complied with. A high minimum wage can reduce demand for labor and have a negative impact on employment opportunities. Therefore, minimum wage must be set at a level that is adequate to maintain a reasonable standard for living for workers, as this is understood in their time and country. It must also ensure equality for lower-income groups. The minimum wage also has a gender dimension. An important purpose of fixing minimum wages is to reduce wage inequality, especially between men and women. If there is no minimum wage, female workers' income can actually be lower compared to male workers' income due to gender stereotype and discrimination. In this sense, gender pay equality is one of the basic indicators of minimum wage. In many developing countries, gender discrimination is apparent in the informal sector, which is not covered by minimum wage and where women are still paid less than male employees.

Setting a fair minimum wage is also linked to enhancing the productivity of labor. In Bangladesh, according to a report by the Global Alliance for Improved Nutrition in 2023, about 43 percent of garment workers in Bangladesh were suffering from malnutrition (Hassan 2023). Malnutrition is closely linked to low wages that prevent workers from affording nutritious food, which can eventually reduce productivity.

Setting minimum wages below the inflation rate can worsen the poverty situation as many workers will be compelled to cut their basic necessities. Therefore, minimum wage levels need to be adjusted periodically to reflect inflation and economic factors. A hike in inflation can reduce real income, may lead to wage inequality and increase the poverty level. Therefore, minimum wage must be set and adjusted above the average inflation rate.

6.6 Challenges of Implementation of Minimum Wages

Minimum wage coverage and compliance are treated as an effective tool of protection provided to low-paid workers and their families. A comprehensive strategy for the implementation of the minimum wage is needed. Several strategies have been suggested for the implementation of the minimum wage. First, a persuasive approach that builds public support for the minimum wage through consultation with the relevant stakeholders, which persuades employers to comply with it voluntarily. Second, both employers and workers must be kept informed about the minimum wage so that employers can apply it in their industries and workers can demand it from employers. Third, a monitoring system should be in place in order to identify any non-compliance with the minimum wage. Fourth, a grievance mechanism should exist in order to empower the workers to lodge complaints about violations of the minimum wage law and seek remedies for such violations. Fifth, effective sanctions against employers should be set for non-compliance with the minimum wage and such sanctions can act as an effective deterrent for employers (Merk 2009, 34).

Thus, compliance with minimum wage should not be taken for granted. It requires both "soft" approach, such as persuasion, and "hard" approach, such as sanctioning, for the implementation of a minimum wage. In Bangladesh, enforcement of minimum wages presents a serious challenge due to the lack of a sufficient number of labor inspectors, weak sanction mechanisms, lack of awareness among workers, and a weak trade union movement (Rani et al. 2013, 382).

Implementation of minimum wage is not only a matter of the presence of an institution and the process of compliance; it also depends on the determination of the right level and structure of minimum wage that is fixed in consultation with employers' and workers' organizations. Countries that set minimum wages at a lower level may have higher levels of compliance by employers. However, such minimum wages can become ineffective as a "re-distributive policy instrument" and as a means of improving the welfare of the working class at large (Rani et al. 2013, 403). Conversely, countries that set the level of minimum wage too high may have lower compliance rates (Rani et al. 2013, 403). But where minimum wages are set by agreements set by negotiations between unions and employers' associations with the passive role of the government that only provides legal status to these agreements (Boeri 2012, 282), these are more likely to have higher degree of compliance. Similarly, countries that have a simple national minimum wage system have higher compliance rates than those with minimum wages set at the sectoral level (Rani et al. 2013, 402). Awareness among the workers about the minimum wage is also crucial for its implementation.

6.7 Setting Minimum Wages in Bangladesh

Bangladesh follows statutory minimum wages set through government and has industry-specific minimum wages, which result in more than one minimum wage. Minimum wage rates for workers are declared by the government on an industry basis following recommendations by the Minimum Wage Boards (Section 140 of the Bangladesh Labor Act 2006). The Minimum Wage Board, a tripartite and statutory body, was established in 2004 in Bangladesh in accordance with the Minimum Wage Ordinance 1961 under the Ministry of Labor and Employment to govern and fix minimum wages. The Minimum Wages Ordinance 1961 had been consolidated with the Bangladesh Labor Act 2006, and hence the erstwhile Minimum Wages Board is now operative under this Act. The main function of the Minimum Wage Board is to fix minimum wages for workers in the industrial sector with the consultation with the concerned industrial sector. The Board sometimes consults with NGOs and social partners in fixing minimum wages. As of now, the Minimum Wage Board has fixed minimum wages for 42 industries. Some of these industries with minimum wages are informal economy as they are not covered by the Bangladesh Labor Act 2006. The Board has fixed the minimum wages for the following sectors: aluminum and enamel industry, Bakery Biscuit and Confectionary industry, Jute press and Belling industry, privately owned jute machinery industry, rice mill, plastic industry, construction and wood, cold storage, and rubber industries.

In most cases, the decisions on minimum wages are made consensual basis. Decisions reached through consensus are considered more effective in terms of compliance than those reached by the majority. The minimum wage structure in Bangladesh consists of four components: basic allowance, housing allowance, medical allowance, and transport allowance (Moazzem et al. 2023, 5). Apart from basic allowance, housing and other allowances are currently fixed amounts. But these should be calculated as a percentage of the basic wage in view of changing levels of such allowances.

A proper definition of minimum wage in the national legal framework is critically important for fixing it. Although "wage" has been defined in the Bangladesh Labor Act 2006, the term "minimum wage" is not defined by it. Rather, the Bangladesh Labor Act 2006 sets out criteria and procedures for fixing minimum wage industry-wise minimum wage rates. According to section 138 of the Labor Act, minimum wages are to be recommended by the Minimum Wage Board for workers of all types of industry except newspaper workers. In its recommendation, the Wage Board indicates whether the minimum rates of wage shall be adopted uniformly throughout the country or with variations for local areas (Section 139(5) of the Bangladesh Labor Act 2006). Minimum wage rates are set on an industry basis and minimum wage rates declared by the government are binding on all employers concerned and every worker shall be entitled to be paid wages at a rate not less than the declared rates of wages (Section 148 of the Bangladesh Labor Act 2006). Correspondingly, the Act prohibits employers from paying wages to any worker at a rate lower than the rates declared to be the minimum rates of wages (Section 149 of the Bangladesh Labor Act 2006).

In making recommendations, the Wages Board considers the cost of living, the standard of living, production cost, productivity and price of products, inflation, the nature of work, the risk involved, business capability, socio-economic conditions of the country, and other relevant factors (Section 141 of the Bangladesh Labor Act 2006). However, in practice, these factors are often disregarded when setting minimum wages in Bangladesh. The "considerations" under the Act do not include the relative living standards of other social groups and social security benefits mentioned in the ILO Recommendation 135. However, "other relevant factors" can be broadly interpreted to include criteria mentioned in the ILO instruments. The Minimum Wages Board (MWB) is obliged to review periodically the recommendations on minimum rates of wages and revise its recommendations, if any of the aforementioned criteria change within one to three years (Section 142 of the Bangladesh Labor Act 2006).

Section 345 of the Bangladesh Labor Act of 2006 adopts the principle of equal wages for male and female workers for work of "equal nature or equal value" for eliminating gender pay gap. The newly adopted the Bangladesh Labor (Amendment) Act 2026 also bans gender-based wage inequality to promote fairness and equal opportunity across work places. However, gender pay gap exists in the informal sector and unorganized small enterprises, which are not covered by minimum wages.

The Minimum Wage Board faces some challenges in setting a minimum wage. Moazzem and Raz mention three important concerns in this regard: first, there is no proper definition of the minimum wage under the Bangladesh Labor Act 2006; second, there is a lack of a standard methodology which could be followed by the Board for estimating the minimum wage; and third, dearth of available sector-specific and macroeconomic data on key indicators in the public domain makes it difficult to capture the real scenario (Moazzem and Raz 2014, 1). As a result, these gaps in negotiation and discussion on the minimum wage result in setting a minimum wage that may not be fair and acceptable to the stakeholders of the concerned sector (Moazzem and Raz 2014, 1). It needs to be highlighted that an evidence-based discussion and negotiation supported by sector-specific data and an appropriate methodology can contribute in setting a fair minimum wage for that sector.

Section 143 of the Bangladesh Labor Act 2006 provides for the formation of a separate Wage Board for newspaper workers and mentions some considerations in making recommendations for the fixation of minimum wage. Such "considerations" include "the cost of living, the prevailing rates of wages of equal nature of employment in Government, corporation and private sectors, the conditions of the newspaper industry in different regions of the country, and any other relevant factors" in making recommendations for minimum wages for them (Section 143 of the Bangladesh Labor Act 2006).

Currently, the Minimum Wage Board can only determine minimum wages, but it has no mandate to implement it. The implementation of minimum wages largely depends on the willingness of employers. Labor inspectors are authorized to ensure the implementation of minimum wage provisions. Furthermore, a worker may also resort to the Labor Court if he is paid less than the declared minimum wage. Payment by an employer to his workers' wages at a rate below the minimum wages has been made a punishable offense under the Bangladesh Labor Act 2006 (Section 289 of the Bangladesh Labor Act 2006). But this provision is hardly enforced by the government as no punitive measures are taken against factories in case they are non-compliant in the enforcement of the minimum wages.

6.8 Minimum Wages in the RMG Sector

Traditionally, the RMG industry around the world is widely known for low wages, excessive overtime, and poor working conditions. Setting minimum wage for the RMG sector is always a contentious issue and has generated considerable debate because this sector attracts a significant number of workers in Bangladesh. Low wages in the RMG sector have been a major factor that has triggered worker movement and industrial unrest in Bangladesh. In the RMG sector of Bangladesh, it is evident that the minimum wage has always been set after political agitation of the workers and demands for an increase in minimum wage and it is realized through protests, blockades, boycotts, and attacks on the workers. It is also alleged that tripartite consultation is largely absent in fixing minimum wages as it is mainly fixed by the government on the basis of proposals made by the RMG owners. Sometimes, minimum wages were increased nominally after the agitation of workers. For example, in response to workers' agitation after the Rana Plaza collapse, the minimum wage was increased.

Factory owners sometimes argue that an increase in minimum wages would hamper the competitiveness of the RMG sector of Bangladesh. As the international RMG market is highly competitive, employers are generally reluctant to increase minimum wages in the RMG sector due to fear of losing competitiveness. As such, employers face the challenge of producing apparel at lower costs while improving working conditions.

However, the RMG is one of the few sectors that has had a statutory minimum wage since 1985. The government of Bangladesh reviewed the minimum wage rate for the RMG workers in 2018 and fixed the minimum wage of an entry-level worker at BDT 8000. After a violent protest campaign by the RMG workers in 2023, the minimum wages for the RMG workers were reviewed and the new minimum wage was raised to BDT 12,500 after consultation with the RMG factory owners. Although RMG workers' minimum wage from 1985 to now has increased manifold, such increased minimum wages are still one of the lowest in the world and is inadequate to maintain a minimum standard of living due to the high rate of inflation and the rising price of essentials (BILS 2018). The current minimum wage also does not reflect the market's growth or the factory owners' profit. In many cases, the current minimum wage set for workers in the RMG sector fails to provide enough income to maintain a family of four above the nationally defined poverty level (Merk 2009, 7) and fulfill their basic needs of food, housing, and healthcare. Therefore, a balance must be made between staying competitive by lowering minimum wage and cost of living and a rise in inflation and prices of basic essentials. Minimum wages set for each sector need to be periodically reviewed and increased, taking into account productivity, wages in other countries, owners' profits, inflation, and living expenses.

Under the market dynamics of demand and supply, the near absence of collective bargaining, coupled with a low level of unionization and the collective power of factory owners contribute to the fixing of lower wages (Mustafa 2023). In fact, RMG workers in Bangladesh are getting lower minimum wages in comparison with the competing countries in Asia (BILS 2018). In the RMG sector, minimum wages set by the Minimum Wage Board often fall below the expectations and demands of workers. Moazzem mentions several factors behind this: "lack of proper definition and method for calculating minimum wages; limited access to technical knowledge of the Board members about different aspects related to skill, productivity, costs and returns, competition in the global market, price offered by brands/buyers; lack of competency of some members of the Board; unwillingness of parties to negotiate concern issues; and weak negotiating capacity of workers' representatives" (Moazzem 2019, 10). The minimum wage in the RMG sector needs to be fixed by considering the necessity of fulfilling the basic needs of workers and their family members, and their required calorie intake (BILS 2018). In fixing or increasing minimum wage, inflation of currency and an increase in commodity prices also need to be considered. Workers must also benefit from the sustained growth of GDP of the country to which export earnings from the RMG sector make an important contribution. Similarly, they must be benefited from the robust growth of export earnings from this sector and this needs to be reflected in setting their minimum wage (BILS 2018).

6.9 Minimum Wages for Tea-Garden Workers

Minimum wage set for tea-garden workers in Bangladesh exemplifies a low-wage structure that is set below the poverty line. The Minimum Wage Board 2019 published a gazette on tea workers' wages in 2019, but it failed to frame acceptable recommendations on the tea workers' wage structure. Due to the persistent movement of tea-garden workers, the government fixed a daily minimum wage of BDT 170 per day for A-class gardens, BDT 169 for B-class, and BDT 168 for C-class gardens, which went into effect in August 2022 (Gain 2023). Even this daily minimum wage was not adequate for tea workers, given the increase in prices of all essential goods and fell short of the poverty threshold. This extremely poor rate of daily minimum wage also creates a scope for the owners to exploit workers (Pal 2022).

However, tea workers get some other benefits. For example, unlike workers in other industries, tea workers get rations at a subsidized price and some fringe benefits, including housing, and very basic health care. Still, these are grossly inadequate for them to maintain a living standard above the poverty line. The role of the Minimum Wage Board in the tea industry remains insignificant as it does not sit regularly for the wage negotiations and it has been formed three times so far to fix the tea workers' wages. It is also because the wages in the tea industry used to be set based on labor agreements between the *Bangladesh Tea Association* (BTA) and the tea workers' union- the *Bangladesh Cha Sramik Union* (BCSU). In order to secure more welfare for the tea workers, workers' representation in the Minimum Wage Board needs to be strengthened, gratuity benefits need to be paid to them as per the Labor Act 2006 and workers' access to shares in the company's profits needs to be ensured.

6.10 Minimum Wages for EPZ Workers

There is a separate minimum wage board for the EPZ workers. In November 2023, a minimum wage board was formed for the workers of the EPZs and Economic Zones (EZs) under the Bangladesh EPZ Labor Act 2019. The last minimum wage board for EPZ workers was formed in 2013, setting the minimum monthly wage at BDT 5600. In 2018, BEPZA revised it to BDT 8200. The government declared in December 2023 a new minimum wage of 12,800 for workers in EPZs (*The Daily Star*, December 11, 2023).

6.11 Minimum Wages in Other Sectors

Workers in other sectors get a minimum wage of less than half of an RMG worker's minimum wage (Islam and Mollah 2023). Workers in most of these sectors in the past have not had any national trade union representatives raising a voice for them in the wage boards formed to set their minimum pay (Islam and Mollah 2023). The latest minimum wage in these sectors was set in 2018 or before (Islam and Mollah 2023). For example, according to data from the Minimum Wage Board, minimum wages were fixed in 11 sectors, including hotels and restaurants, iron foundries, and engineering workshops, Ayurvedic medicine factories, match factories, tea gardens, and tailoring workshops are less than BDT 5000 (Mustafa 2024), which is too low to afford the basic needs of a worker. Meanwhile, the minimum wages in salt crushing, cold storage, soap and cosmetics, cotton textile, bakeries and confectioneries, automobiles workshops, and shrimp processing have been fixed between BDT 5000 to BDT 7000 (Mustafa 2024). Thus, there is a huge disparity in the level of minimum wages for workers in Bangladesh. Many other industries are not still covered by the minimum wages.

6.12 Exploitative Sourcing Price and Minimum Wages

In a competitive market conditions, brands and retailers demand lower prices, shorter lead times, longer payment terms to maximize their profits. This downward pressure on prices and labor costs, unreasonable lead times and subcontracting often leads to exploitative sourcing price under garment production system. It is demonstrated by trade patterns that show that buyers of garment products have shifted sourcing toward locations that offer the lowest prices at scale with the consequence of setting a minimum wage which is far below a living wage. Bangladesh has become the global hub of import of large-volume, low-price knitwear in the EU. According to a recent report, titled "Squezzed Dry", the sourcing price after adjusting to global inflation, have fallen by half in real terms for Bangladeshi RMG products, producing negative consequences on wages and working conditions (Public Eye and Clean Clothes Campaign 2026). The report shows that many European buyers still source a standard cotton T-shirt at around USD 2–3 per piece, with unit prices below USD 1 persisting in parts of the market. This sustained erosion of sourcing price in real terms undermines suppliers' economic resilience and depresses wages. This persistently low sourcing prices have become a central feature of the RMG industry in Bangladesh structurally locking-in poverty wages and precarious working conditions. Therefore, brands and buyers have a crucial role in increasing minimum wages by offering fair prices to Bangladesh RMG exporters (Khatun 2023). International brands and buyers need to pay a price that absorbs any increase in statutory minimum wages for reducing pressures on owners and covering the increased production cost. Adopting an ethical sourcing pricing by international buyers can support fair wages for workers. Current sourcing pricing system also does not cover the costs of sustainable production system (Public Eye and Clean Clothes Campaign 2026). Therefore, this pricing system needs a revision to include cost of environmental and social improvements made in the production system by the owners.

6.13 Conclusion

A decent minimum wage at the sectoral level remains a far cry in Bangladesh due to low levels of unionization, absence of effective collective bargaining, lack of government initiative, and the excessive profit motives of factory owners. There is no national minimum wage in Bangladesh. The Bangladesh Labor Act 2006 contains provisions relating to setting the sector-wise minimum wage. Since a large number of sectors are still out of the purview of the minimum wage structure and a huge disparity exists across the sectors, the introduction of a national minimum wage may be a useful way to end disparity and cover all sectors of the economy in Bangladesh. For this purpose, the Bangladesh Labor Act

2006 needs an amendment to incorporate a provision on the determination of the national minimum wage. The link between ensuring living wages and decent work is now well-established. Better wages or fair minimum wages are also linked to better productivity. Very often, minimum wages are not enough to cover basic needs of the workers. In particular, widespread gender discrimination in the informal sector leads to the employment of relatively more women at lower wages than would be paid to men for the same work (Merk 2009, 13).

In Bangladesh, in fixing minimum wage, the criteria and standards set out in the ILO Conventions and the Bangladesh Labor Act 2006 are not followed. Minimum wages fixed for various sectors are not regularly adjusted to reflect the rising cost of living (Merk 2009, 13). But both the ILO Convention (131) and the ILO Recommendation (131) ask state parties to adjust minimum wage rates from time to time to take into account changes in the cost of living and other economic conditions. Wage adjustments that align with GDP and inflation can make wage changes more transparent and prevent abrupt demands for wage hikes due to inflationary pressures. Non-adjustment of minimum wages at regular intervals may negatively affect both workers and employers, as workers do not know how long price inflation will reduce their purchasing capacity while employers might suddenly face an abrupt increase in their labor costs (ILO 2016). An increase in the general level of prices and the cost of living should be a determining factor in minimum wage adjustments. This is because inflation erodes the real value of the minimum wages over time (ILO 2016, 5). Currently, minimum wages are not consistently fixed in terms of price hike and are inadequate to meet the needs of the workers because minimum wages are not adjusted sufficiently to maintain the workers' purchasing power. If minimum wages are not regularly adjusted to take into account the rise in living expenses, workers' income progressively falls. This is evident from the fact that the workers' standards of living have not significantly improved despite the increase in minimum wages due to persistent inflationary pressure.

Even the existing minimum wages are not properly implemented due to a lack of monitoring, and a lack of accountability of employers. There is a need to raise awareness among workers about their entitlement to minimum wages that they are entitled to according to the law, as they are often uninformed about the government-set minimum wages, which makes it difficult for many of them to raise formal complaints regarding non-payment or underpayment of minimum wages. Training should be imparted for workers to create awareness among them regarding their legally entitled wages. Such awareness is the first step to wage compliance, which increases the scope of the owners' accountability. Weak enforcement of provision on minimum wage in Bangladesh is a barrier to its full realization.

Due to a lack of a strong enforcement mechanism, deviations in minimum wage payments and delays in timely payments are a regular phenomenon in many sectors in Bangladesh that often leads to street agitation. Weak enforcement of the minimum wage gives employers more opportunities to deprive workers of their rights (Merk 2009). In this regard, labor institutions such as trade unions and collective bargaining can play a critical role in pressurizing employers to enforce the minimum wages. Sometimes minimum wages are not enforced due to lack of inspection. The Department of Inspection for Factories and Establishments (DIFE) should increase its inspections of industries for monitoring compliance with minimum wages at the sectoral level and produce a progress report on the compliance level. In order to increase workers' knowledge of their grades, wages, and other financial benefits, factories should set up effective communication mechanism with workers to inform them about different changes in wages and other facilities (Moazzem 2019, 14). Sometimes, wage irregularities and underpayment of minimum wage occur because the employers face financial difficulty that can be caused by a global crisis or by cancelation of orders (Merk 2009, 22). In contrast to the current five-year review system of minimum wages, a regular annual minimum wage review mechanism should be introduced in order to respond to prevailing economic circumstances without imposing sudden and huge burdens on employers.

Fixing minimum wage is a multi-stakeholder activity. Especially in the RMG sector, ensuring fair minimum wages should be a shared responsibility of factory owners, government, brands, and buyers.

Bibliography

Books

Davidov, Guy. 2016. *A Purposive Approach to Labour Law*. Oxford University Press.

Neumark, David, and William Wascher. 2008. *Minimum Wages*. The MIT Press.

Chapters in Edited Books

Grimshaw, Damian. 2013. "Minimum Wages and Collective Bargaining: A Preliminary Characterisation." In *Minimum Wages, Pay Equity, and Comparative Industrial Relations*, edited by Damian Grimshaw, 19–50. Routledge.

Grimshaw, Damian, and Gerhard Bosch. 2013. "The Intersections between Minimum Wage and Collective Bargaining Institutions." In *Minimum Wages, Pay Equity, and Comparative Industrial Relations*, edited by Damian Grimshaw, 50–80. Routledge.

Grimshaw, Damian and Jill Rubery. 2013. "The Distributive Functions of a Minimum Wage: First- and Second-Order Pay Equity Effects." In *Minimum Wages, Pay Equity, and Comparative Industrial Relations*, edited by Damian Grimshaw, 81–110. Routledge.

Wascher, William. 2015. "Minimum Wages." In *International Encyclopedia of the Social & Behavioral Sciences*, edited by James D. Wright, vol. 1, 2nd ed., 561–565. Elsevier.

Journal Articles

Belser, Patrick, and Kristen Sobeck. 2012. "At What Level Should Countries Set Their Minimum Wages?." *International Journal of Labour Research* 4 (1): 105–120.

Boeri, Tito. 2012. "Setting the Minimum Wage." *Labour Economics* 19: 281–290.

Cunniah, Dan. 2009. "Preface." *International Journal of Labour Research* 11 (2): 1–6.

Garnero, Andrea. 2021. "The Impact of Collective Bargaining on Employment and Wage Inequality: Evidence from a New Taxonomy of Bargaining Systems." *European Journal of Industrial Relations* 27 (2): 185–202.

Iliopoulos, Panagiotis. 2026. "Globalization and Income Distribution: What Is the Role for Workers' Structural Bargaining Power?." *British Journal of Industrial Relations*: 1–17.

Kaufman, B. 2009. "Promoting Labour Market Efficiency and Fairness Through a Legal Minimum Wage: The Webbs and the Social Cost of Labour." *British Journal of Labour* 47 (2): 306–326.

Rani, Uma, Patrick Belser, Martin Olez, and Setareh Ranjbar. 2013. "Minimum Wage Coverage and Compliance in Developing Countries." *International Labour Review*, 152 (3–4): 381–410.

Saget, Catherine. 2008. "Fixing Minimum Wage Levels in Developing Countries: Common Failures and Remedies." *International Labour Review* 147 (1): 25–42.

Wang, Tong. 2025. "Labour Market Outcomes of Minimum Wage Changes: A Behavioural Perspective." *Labor Economics* 97: 102824.

Reports

Anker, R. 2011. *Estimating a Living Wage: A Methodological Review*. Conditions of Work and Employment Series No. 29. Geneva: International Labour Organization (ILO).

Benassi, Chiara. 2011. "The Implementation of Minimum Wage: Challenges and Creative Solutions." International Labour Office. Geneva: ILO, 57 (Global Labour University Working Papers; No. 12).

"Determining Wage for RMG Workers: Basis, Situations and Considerations." Policy Brief, BILS, 2018.

Elliott, K. A., and R. B. Freeman. 2003. "Can Labor Standards Improve Under Globalization?." Institute for International Economics, Washington, DC.

Eyraud, Francois, and Catherine Saget. 2005. *The Fundamentals of Minimum Wage Fixing*. Geneva: ILO.

General Survey of the Reports on the Minimum Wage Fixing Convention, 1970 (No. 131).

Gain, Philip. 2023. "Tea Workers' Wages Finalised: Owners Win, Workers Lose." *The Daily Star*, August 25. Accessed on May 3, 2025. https://www.thedailystar.net/opinion/views/news/owners-win-workers-lose-3402171.

Hartzén, Ann-Christine. "Globalisation of Labour Markets and International Systems of Industrial Relations." A Conference Paper. Accessed on April 22, 2025. http://www.diva-portal.org/smash/get/diva2:1236764/FULLTEXT01.pdf.

Hachfeld, David, and Christian Eckerlein. "Squeezed Dry—Pricing Pressure in the Global Fashion Industry." A Public Eye Report, May 2026. https://www.publiceye.ch/fileadmin/img/Mode/2026_Squeezed_Dry/PE_Report_CCC-Pricing_5-26_E.pdf.

Hassan, Sajjadul. 2023. "The Minimum Wage—The Way Forward." *The Daily Star*, November 23. https://www.thedailystar.net/business/column/news/minimum-wage-the-way-forward-3476251.

Islam, Zyma, and Shaheen Mollah. 2023. "May Day: Even Minimum Wage Eludes the Workers." *The Daily Star*, May 1. Accessed on May 24, 2024. https://www.thedailystar.net/news/bangladesh/news/may-day-even-minimum-wage-eludes-the-workers-3308256.

Khatun, Fahmida. 2023. "What's Stopping RMG Workers from Getting Higher Wages?." *The Daily Star*, November 20. Accessed on March 12, 2024. https://www.thedailystar.net/opinion/views/macro-mirror/news/whats-stopping-rmg-workers-getting-higher-wages-3473661.

Lawton, K. and M. Pennycook. 2013. "Beyond the Bottom Line: The Challenges and Opportunities of a Living Wage." Institute for Public Policy Research/Resolution Foundation, London.

Merk, Jeroen. 2009. "Stitching a Decent Wage Across Borders: The Asia Floor Wage Proposal 2009." Asia Floor Wage Campaign.

"How Many Countries Have a Minimum Wage?." Accessed on March 21, 2024. https://www.ilo.org/global/topics/wages/minimum-wages/definition/WCMS_439073/lang--en/index.htm.

"EPZ Workers See Over 50% Hike in Minimum Wage." *The Daily Star*, December 11, 2023. Accessed on May 22, 2024. https://www.thedailystar.net/business/economy/news/epz-workers-see-50-hike-minimum-wage-3491041.

"Minimum Wage Systems." General Survey of the Reports on the Minimum Wage Fixing Convention, 1970 (No. 131).

Minimum Wage Policy Guide, ILO (2016).

Moazzem, Khondaker Golam, and Saifa Raz. 2014. "Minimum Wage in The RMG Sector of Bangladesh: Definition, Determination on Method and Levels." CPD Working Paper 106.

Moazzem, Khondaker Golam, Tamim Ahmed, and M. M. Fardeen Kabir. 2024. Revisions of the Minimum Wage of RMG Workers in 2023. Centre for Policy Dialogue, 5. https://cpd.org.bd/resources/2024/03/Revision-of-the-Minimum-Wage-of-RMG-Workers-in-2023.pdf.

Moazzem, Khondaker Golam. 2019. "New Minimum Wage of The RMG Sector Addressing the Issues of Non-Compliance in Implementation." CPD Working Paper 129. CPD.

Mustafa, Kallol. 2023. "The Minimum Wage Question: Owner's Profit Versus Worker's Survival." *The Daily Star*, August 5. Accessed on July 4, 2024. https://www.thedailystar.net/opinion/views/news/the-minimum-wage-question-owners-profit-versus-workers-survival-3385501.

Mustafa, Kallol. 2024. "Bangladesh's Ever-Neglected Working Class." *The Daily Star*, May 21. https://www.thedailystar.net/opinion/views/news/bangladeshs-ever-neglected-working-class-3599646.

Pal, Tapas. 2022. "Government Must Ensure Living Wage for Tea Workers." *The Daily Star*, August 15. Accessed on March 22, 2024. https://www.thedailystar.net/letters/ensure-minimum-wage-tea-workers-1581511.

International Instruments

ILO Minimum Wage Fixing Convention, 1970 (No. 131).

ILO Minimum-Wage Fixing Machinery Convention, 1928 (No. 26).

ILO The Social Policy (Basic Aims and Standards) Convention, 1962 (No. 117).

The Minimum Wage Fixing Recommendation, 1970 (No. 135).

The ILO Minimum Wage Fixing Convention, 1970 (No. 131).

The ILO Minimum-Wage Fixing Machinery Convention, 1928 (No. 26).

The ILO The Social Policy (Basic Aims and Standards) Convention, 1962 (No. 117). Minimum Wage Policy Guide, ILO (2016).

CHAPTER 7

Labor Disputes Settlement Mechanisms: Search for Labor Justice in Bangladesh

7.1 Introduction

Labor disputes are inevitable features of industrial relations because of the conflicting and divergent interests of workers and employers in such relations. The spectrum of labor disputes covers wide-ranging issues, including disagreements between the employer and the workers regarding working conditions, wages, and compensation in the course of employment. Generally, a labor dispute may be divided into two categories, namely: disputes of an individual in nature and industrial disputes, which are collective in nature. Both kinds of disputes arise in different ways and for different reasons. Generally individual dispute is raised by a worker in their individual capacity for violation of labor rights. Individual disputes mostly cover disputes arising out of dismissal, discharge, termination, non-payment of compensation, non-payment of wages, termination without notice, and non-payment of termination benefits, while industrial dispute arises due to differences between workers and employers with regard to collective demands of workers. Threats and intimidation, refusal to allow maternity leave, and seizure of ID card are also cited as causes of individual disputes (BILS 2020). Widespread prevalence of termination of workers without notice, unlawful denial of social security benefits, deprivation of termination benefits, withholding or delayed or partial payment of minimum wages, abuse of workers, arbitrary dismissal, sudden layoff, or closure of factories are also sources of industrial disputes.

A. Al Faruque, *Globalization and Labour Rights*,
https://doi.org/10.1007/978-981-92-3661-9_7

Dispute settlement mechanisms are essential for addressing grievances of workers because when working conditions become too exploitative or oppressive or when there is no scope for collective bargaining or channeling their legitimate demands through formal or informal mechanisms, workers can resort to protest, which can ultimately erupt into violence and street agitation.

However, in the case of individual disputes in Bangladesh, due to the complicated, costly, and lengthy procedure, the workers are usually reluctant to make formal complaints to avoid a bitter relationship with the management or due to fear of losing their job (BILS 2020).

Again, the reasons for labor disputes may include both economic and non-economic. While economic reasons involve issues like non-payment of wages, bonuses, allowances, overtime work, working hours, leave and holidays without pay, unjust layoffs and retrenchments, the non-economic issues include unfair treatment of workers, poor conditions of work and employers' negative attitude toward workers (Hossain and Akter 2016, 13). Although both kinds of labor disputes are prevalent in Bangladesh, the majority of labor disputes are concerned with economic reasons.

One of the main objectives of the Bangladesh Labor Act, 2006 is to settle industrial disputes in order to promote industrial peace and harmonious relationships between labor and management. For this purpose, the Bangladesh Labor Act, 2006 contains dispute settlement by both non-adjudicatory and adjudicatory mechanisms and establishes labor administrations such as the Department of Labor. While non-adjudicatory mechanisms include negotiation, participation committees, conciliation, and arbitration, the adjudicatory system is mainly based on judicial procedures and bodies such as labor courts. Most of the individual disputes are resolved by labor Courts, while industrial disputes are mainly settled by bipartite negotiation and conciliation.

Different forms of dispute settlement mechanisms have been discussed below at length.

7.2 Grievance Procedure

The grievance procedure is generally applicable when workers' rights and entitlements guaranteed under laws, employment contracts, and collective agreements are violated. The ILO Examination of Grievances Recommendation, 1967 (No. 130) recognizes workers' right to submit a grievance, which must be examined by an effective, fair and open procedure. The grievance procedure has been designed under the Bangladesh Labor Act 2006 to address individual disputes concerned with the violation of the statutory rights of an individual worker. Section 33 of the Bangladesh Labor Act 2006 empowers any aggrieved worker who has been laid off, retrenched, discharged, dismissed, removed, or terminated from employment to lodge a complaint with their employer for getting redress. Upon receiving the complaint, the employer is obliged to investigate the complaint and provide an appropriate remedy to the aggrieved worker. However, in rare cases, this mechanism produces desired results, as in most cases, upon receiving such a complaint, the employer disposes of the same in a slipshod manner without providing any meaningful remedies to the concerned worker (Meahzi 2022).

7.3 Bipartite Negotiation

Bipartite negotiation as a means to prevent and solve disputes has long been considered an amicable way of settling industrial disputes, as it helps maintain sound industrial relations without the intervention of any third party. In this way, it is a convenient tool for developing a harmonious relationship between the management and workers. Bipartite negotiation usually takes place between the employers and collective bargaining agents (CBAs)—elected representatives of workers. The scope of bipartite negotiation has been expanded with the growth of industrialization, trade union activities, and the evolution of the enabling legal framework (Faruque 2009).

For bipartite negotiation, a trade union, which is elected as the CBA, can raise a dispute before the management for settlement. Similarly, the employers can also raise a dispute and place it before the CBA for negotiation. Though the law provides a favorable environment for bipartite negotiation, the scenario is different in practice. The effectiveness of bipartite negotiation as a dispute settlement system is limited as it cannot protect the interests of the workers due to the unfavorable and authoritarian attitude of employers toward trade unions, the lack of experience of the trade union officials to negotiate, the interference of the government in the settlement of industrial dispute, political affiliation of trade unions, and lack of bargaining capacity of trade unions (Faruque 2009).

7.4 Conciliation

When a bipartite negotiation fails, some mechanisms must be in place to which an aggrieved party can resort to. Conciliation is a tripartite mechanism, is such an option in case of failed bipartite negotiation (Section 210(4) of the Bangladesh Labor Act 2006). In conciliation, conciliator, a third-party neutral person having expertise on labor law tries to help the conflicting parties resolve their disputes amicably in order to restore good relationships between the disputing parties, which is essential for sound industrial relations. The Department of Labor, the main labor administration institution in Bangladesh also acts as a conciliator. The conciliation for settlement of labor disputes has been made compulsory by the Bangladesh Labor Act 2006 before resorting to industrial action, such as strike or lock-out. Thus, neither the workers nor the employers can go for direct industrial action such as strike and lock-out without first going through conciliation. A conciliator can suggest or recommend solutions for facilitating a compromise between workers and the employers. However, the success of conciliation depends considerably on the willingness of the workers and employers to cooperate to reach a solution and implement the negotiated agreement.

One new area of dispute resolution by conciliation in Bangladesh was added in 2013 through the amendment of the Bangladesh Labor Act 2006. According to this amendment, disputes involving outstanding payments of workers (including wages) can now be resolved through conciliation (Section 124A of the Bangladesh Labor Act 2006). Conciliated decisions are binding on the parties. If the parties do not agree to follow the conciliator's decision, they can file a case in the Labor Court.

Despite the above-mentioned enabling provisions, only a few disputes are settled through conciliation annually. Though the conciliation is an important tool for amicably settling of industrial disputes, its effectiveness is limited as employers do not often implement them. Poor accountability of conciliation officers, biased attitude, and inefficiency of some conciliators to persuade the disputants to reach an agreement, have been cited as some of the reasons for the ineffectiveness of conciliation (Faruque 2009, 54).

7.5 Arbitration

Arbitration is another non-adjudicatory process for the settlement of labor disputes and it is usually initiated on the basis of a joint written request by the disputing parties in case of failure of conciliation. An arbitrator can be appointed from the panel of arbitrators nominated by the government or can be appointed by the parties themselves. The award of the arbitrator is final and no appeal shall lie against it. An arbitral award remains valid for two years.

The effectiveness of arbitration as a labor dispute settlement mechanism is limited due to the length and complexity of its procedure. Furthermore, due to the weak bargaining power of the workers, sometimes they do not get appropriate legal remedies through arbitral decisions. Sometimes, the settlement agreements reached through arbitration are not registered and complied with by the employers.

In practice, very few disputes are referred to the Arbitration as in most cases, they are settled at the time of conciliation or in the case of failure of conciliation, the parties feel more interested to go to the Labor Court rather than going for arbitration (Faruque 2009).

7.6 Adjudication

After exhaustion of bipartite negotiation and conciliation, the disputant parties may refer their dispute to the arbitrator or resort to the adjudicatory mechanisms such as Labor Court. Under the Bangladesh Labor Act, 2006, the adjudication mechanism has been strengthened to protect the rights of workers by entrusting labor courts to adjudicate all issues under labor law, allowing all appeals from the decisions of the labor courts to the labor appellate tribunal, by fixing a time-frame for every stage of the proceedings in the labor court for the speedy disposal of the disputes. Labor Court is a tripartite adjudicatory mechanism for the settlement of industrial disputes. An industrial dispute may be lodged to the labor court in any of the following ways: If a strike or lock-out continues for more than 30 days, the government may prohibit such strike or lock-out and in that case, the government must refer the dispute to the Labor Court (Section 211 of the Bangladesh Labor Act 2006). Secondly, in case of failure of the employer to render any decision or if the concerned worker is dissatisfied with any decision given by the employer under the "Grievance Procedure", the Labor court may be approached by the concerned aggrieved worker. Under this procedure, disputes arising out of layoff, dismissal, discharge, retrenchment, or removal from employment by other means may be referred to the Labor Court, which may, direct the reinstatement of the complainant in service, and convert the order of dismissal, removal or discharge to any minor punishment (Section 33(5) of the Bangladesh Labor Act 2006). Apart from the above, the following kinds of the disputes may also be lodged before the Labor Court: deduction from the wages of an employee, non-payment or delay in payment of wages or gratuity or provident fund (Section 132 of the Bangladesh Labor Act 2006); compensation for injury or death of worker caused by accident (Sections 150, 151, 158, 168 of the Bangladesh Labor Act 2006); offenses relating to violation of the provisions of the Labor Act, 2006 (Section 307 of the Bangladesh Labor Act 2006); and application by any collective bargaining agent, or any employer or worker for enforcement of any right, or any award or settlement or contract guaranteed under the Labor Act (Section 213 of the Bangladesh Labor Act 2006).

However, since most of the cases could not be resolved within the mandatory time-frame, creating a backlog of cases, the amendment to the Labor Act 2006 in 2013 extended such time-frame and now a dispute must be resolved by taking another 90 days (Section 216(13) added by the Bangladesh Labor (Amendment) Act 2018). This additional period of 90 days encourages the Court to dispose of cases more expeditiously.

Nevertheless, currently a huge number of cases are pending before the labor court and tribunals due to an inadequate number of courts as there are only ten labor courts, three in Dhaka, two in Chattogram, and one each in Khulna and Rajshahi and one labor appellate tribunal operating in Bangladesh for all workers in the formal sector and no penalty exists for exceeding this time-frame. Consequently, the needs of the vast workforce of the country to access to justice remain unmet. Moreover, their geographical distribution is also unbalanced, which does not cover many densely populated industrial regions. This geographical distance from other districts to lodge complaints and financial constraints, such as lawyers' fees and court expenses, inhibit most of the workers' access to the labor courts (Meahzi 2022). Lack of training of judges on labor laws or lack of prior experience in dealing with labor issues, and the frequent absence of members of courts, especially of representatives of owners, often causes unnecessary delay in disposing of the labor disputes. The other reasons behind the backlog of cases in the labor courts include an inadequate number of judges, critical shortages of staff and resources in labor courts, inadequate budgetary allocation, absence of plaintiff workers due to their engagement in work, delay in issuing summons, frequent time petitions by the lawyers in submission of their reply, and reluctance of witnesses to appear before the labor courts (Faruque 2009, 57).

According to a study conducted by the Bangladesh Legal Aid and Services Trust (BLAST) in 2019 (Huda 2020), the average time taken to dispose of a labor case was 630 days for awarded cases and 571 days for dismissed cases. The long delay bears unequal significance to the disputing parties. Workers are more affected than employers in attaining justice due to delay (Kadir 2024). This chronic delay is one of the main hurdles to access to justice for workers, and it sometimes compels workers to pursue alternatives, often disadvantageous solutions to workers. They often settle for ADR, which pressurize them to accept meager settlements rather than pursue their rightful dues through the court system (Ratan 2024). Because of this protracted delay, many workers lose interest in continuing the cases (Ratan 2024). Consequently, the labor courts, which are considered as a last resort for workers, fail to deliver justice and significantly fewer cases are submitted before them than there are actual disputes (Ratan 2024). The power imbalance between owners and workers within the labor court system also discourages the latter to resort to the court. The owners' financial advantages allow them to hire better lawyers, further limiting workers' access to legal representation (Ratan 2024).

However, among the different mechanisms for settlement of labor disputes, labor courts remain the preferred option for the workers for addressing their grievances and interests as it is revealed that most of the judgments in labor cases go in favor of the workers.

7.7 Labor Appellate Tribunal

Any party aggrieved by an award, decision, or judgment of the labor court may file an appeal to the Labor Appellate Tribunal and the decision of the Tribunal in such appeal shall be final (Section 217 of the Bangladesh Labor Act, 2006). The Labor Appellate Tribunal on appeal may set aside, vary, or modify any award, decision, judgment, or sentence given by the Labor Court or send the case back to the Court for re-hearing (Section 218(10) of the Bangladesh Labor Act, 2006).

Like the delay in the labor court, the Labor Appellate Tribunals also face backlog of cases. Insufficiency of benches of the Appellate Tribunal is one of the main reasons behind the backlog of cases in such a tribunal. At present, only two benches exist, which are inadequate to deal with the large volume of appeals from the labor courts. Lack of infrastructural support is also a barrier in smooth functioning of the tribunal.

7.8 Preventive Measures for Avoiding Industrial Disputes

The Bangladesh Labor Act 2006 contains some preventive measures for avoiding industrial disputes. The Participation Committee is such a mechanism for minimizing industrial disputes at the very initial stage as it can take measures to prevent industrial dispute. The Participation Committee, a bipartite mechanism comprising an equal number of representatives of workers and employers, is formed in an establishment where fifty or more workers are employed. One of the important functions of the Participation Committee is to prevent industrial dispute by inculcating and developing a sense of belonging among workers, promoting mutual trust, understanding and cooperation between the employer and the workers, ensuring the application of labor laws and fostering a sense of discipline among workers. The employer of the concerned establishment shall take necessary measures to implement the specific recommendations made by the Participation Committee within the time prescribed by it (Section 208(1) of the Bangladesh Labor Act, 2006).

However, the role of the Participation Committee is very limited as such a committee exists only in a very few industries and establishments. Some of them do not even operate regularly.

7.9 Dispute Settlement in Export Processing Zones

The EPZ Labor Act 2019 establishes a complaint procedure like "grievance procedure" for any worker who has been laid off, retrenched, discharged, dismissed, removed, or otherwise terminated from employment and intends to get redress for this. It also contains provisions relating to bipartite negotiation, conciliation, arbitration, and adjudication of a labor dispute; and requires appointment of conciliator, arbitrator, and counselor and establishes the EPZ Labor Court and EPZ Labor Appellate Tribunals for the EPZs. The Act lays down that if a dispute is likely to arise between an employer and worker, employer or collective bargaining agent shall communicate with other party to reach an agreement to settle the dispute through dialogue (Section 124 of the EPZ Labor Act 2019). When negotiation fails, any of the parties can request to the conciliator to conciliate the dispute (Section 126 of the EPZ Labor Act 2019). If the conciliation process fails, the parties to the dispute are entitled to go for a strike or lock-out (Section 127(1) of the EPZ Labor Act 2019). However, for serving any notice of strike, consent of two-thirds of the members of the Executive Council of the Workers' Welfare Association is needed through secret ballots (Section 127(2) of the EPZ Labor Act 2019). If the conciliation fails, the Conciliator shall persuade the parties to refer the dispute to an Arbitrator, and if the parties agree, an arbitrator can be appointed from the panel of arbitrators. The award of the arbitrator shall be final and binding on the parties to the dispute (Section 130 of the EPZ Labor Act 2019).

A dispute can also be referred to the EPZ Labor Court in several ways. If the parties do not refer to the arbitrator, they may go for strike or lock-out and may even refer the dispute to the labor court either before or after the commencement of a strike or lock-out (Section 131 of the EPZ Labor Act 2019). The EPZ Labor Court can also try any offenses under the EPZ Act 2019. The EPZ Labor Appellate Tribunal may hear appeal from the decisions of the Labor Court and can uphold, amend, modify, or set aside the award of an EPZ Labor Court (Section 137 of the EPZ Labor Act 2019).

In practice, it is revealed that there are only few conciliators, counselors, and arbitrators appointed in the EPZs in Bangladesh that undermines the redressal of grievances of workers.

7.10 Role of ADR in Labor Dispute Settlement

The resolution of labor disputes requires a consensual and informal mechanism for avoiding costs and lengthy procedures. Therefore, an adjudicatory system with an adversarial nature should be approached minimally in the industrial relations context. Less formal, bipartite negotiation and voluntary processes such as collective bargaining should be preferred as an ideal forum for labor dispute settlement, as there are no losers, but a win–win situation because parties often reach a compromise under this process (Khabo 2008, 13). In the context of labor disputes resolution, the practice of alternative dispute resolution (ADR) contributes to the promotion of collective bargaining as it facilitates the voluntary, informal, accessible, and speedy resolution of such disputes. Since the traditional litigation system is costly, lengthy, and inaccessible to a large number of people and working class, ADR is increasingly recognized as one of the instrumentalities to facilitate access to justice for them. The "all or nothing" approach of litigation in terms of its outcome is now considered inappropriate for resolving all kinds of disputes (Sampath 1991, 3–4). This proposition holds particularly true in labor disputes where workers with weak bargaining power and few financial resources can hardly afford to litigate, which is a costly and time-consuming process.

Among the ADR strategies, mediation is considered the most appropriate one and widely practiced for resolving labor disputes in many countries. The popularity of mediation can be attributed to the following reasons:

First, in mediation, parties need not adhere to legal technicalities, procedures of evidence, and witnesses while they can control the process and influence the outcome that meets their needs.

Second, the autonomy of parties in the mediation process has great potential to empower the disputant parties who are more likely to comply with mediated settlement than "all or nothing" approach of traditional litigation (Nolan-Haley 1991, 58).

But the success of mediation may depend on the nature of disputes, the type of legal and institutional arrangement and the attitude of judges and cooperation of parties. Some experts have suggested the establishment of an independent ADR Commission for resolving labor disputes to address the unique challenges faced by workers and employers and the chronic delay in settling such disputes by labor courts (Kadir 2024). It is also suggested that an independent ADR Commission should consist of labor experts, who will be better equipped to handle complex disputes more effectively and efficiently (Kadir 2024). Several countries around the world have established such independent and separate institutions for resolving labor disputes through ADR. In a significant move, the Bangladesh Labor (Amendment) Act 2026 has introduced alternative dispute resolution mechanisms for resolving labor disputes and for this purpose, it requires the establishment of an Alternative Dispute Resolution Authority.

7.11 Court-Sponsored ADR in Labor Dispute Settlement

There is a discernible trend toward integration of elements of the informal justice system with the formal one. Norms of the informal justice system have been transplanted in the formal justice system through the amendment of relevant procedural rules of what is known as court-sponsored mediation or judicial mediation. Given the existing backlog of cases, and for increasing access to justice, Bangladesh has initiated a legislative scheme toward pretrial mediation in order to make the formal justice system more accessible and fair as mentioned above. Such much-needed legal reform was not only necessary to overcome the problem of accessibility in the formal justice system, but was also needed to generate confidence in the common people about the fairness and ability of the court to deliver justice, which has eroded in recent times. ADR has now been institutionalized in Bangladesh in many areas of dispute settlement, such as family disputes, civil disputes, criminal disputes, and commercial disputes. Court-sponsored ADR differs from traditional mediation in the sense that while the latter is based on purely voluntary third-party-assisted negotiation, the former is court-assisted, and a formalized process, which is mandatory for disputing parties to some extent (Yu 2009). In contrast to traditional mediation, court-sponsored ADR or judicial mediation occurs within the framework of law and existing judicial structure. While in traditional mediation, there is the possibility of coercion, unfairness, and bargaining imbalance between the parties, these problems do not arise in judicial mediation. There are two types of court-sponsored mediation: The first type is compulsory, while the second type is mediation following an application made by the parties.

In order to reduce the backlog of the labor cases and to ensure access to justice for workers, court-annexed mediation system can be introduced in labor disputes by bringing some amendments to the relevant provisions of the Bangladesh Labor Act 2006. Such a court-annexed mediation can be made mandatory since labor disputes are relatively simple in nature.

Currently, there is no formal procedure for ADR for settling any dispute pending before the labor court or labor appellate tribunal. Therefore, the introduction of compulsory and time-bound court-sponsored ADR for settling labor disputes can make a major breakthrough to address the existing problem of delay and consequent backlog of labor dispute settlement.

7.12 Addressing Sexual Harassment in the Workplace

Despite the widespread practice of sexual harassment in factories and establishments in Bangladesh, there was no explicit provision for submitting or processing sexual harassment-related complaints. Section 332 of the Bangladesh Labor Act 2006 only prohibits behavior that is "indecent or unmannerly or which is repugnant to the modesty or honor" of any woman. This prohibition is enforced by the general penalty of imprisonment or fine. The High Court Division of the Supreme Court of Bangladesh also issued guidelines in 2009 on the prevention of violence against women in the workplace and these guidelines stipulate the establishment of complaint committee headed by women, to receive and investigate the complaints on sexual abuse and harassment of women in workplaces. However, in reality, even after 14 years have passed, only a few factories have formed such committee. Most of the workers are not aware of these guidelines, resulting in fewer complaints being lodged and investigated.

The newly adopted Bangladesh Labor (Amendment) Act 2026 has introduced a detailed definition of sexual harassment in the workplace and established a compliant committee with female representation in the workplace that establishes an organizational accountability framework.

7.13 Internal Grievance Mechanism

An internal grievance mechanism refers to a mechanism by which factories attempt to solve issues within their own structures and processes (Sharon 2022, 12). Factories or companies bear the primary responsibility of setting up such mechanism, investigating, and settling disputes and their internal management staff process the complaint formally or informally to provide a remedy (Sharon 2022). Suggestion boxes and written grievance registers are some of the examples of the internal grievance mechanism (Sharon 2022). Although these mechanisms are highly accessible, as workers have multiple avenues to submit grievances, workers have low acceptance of the internal grievance management system, as it is perceived to be power imbalanced to the advantage of management (Sharon 2022, 14).

Another example of such an internal grievance mechanism is Arbitration-cum-conciliation committee of BGMEA, established in 1998 in accordance with Industrial Relations Ordinance (IRO) 1969 with equal representation from BGMEA and RMG registered trade unions (Sharon 2022, 22). It provides alternative dispute resolution services to workers free of cost to resolve cases of disputes and grievances (Sharon 2022, 23). The committee resolves the disputes between the owner and the employees of the factory before referring the matter to court, which is time-consuming and costly (Sharon 2022, 23).

7.14 Informal Mechanisms of Settlement of Labor Disputes

There are some informal practices of resolving labor disputes. Many cases filed before the labor courts are withdrawn subsequently and compromised by the parties and thus settled informally and outside of the courts. Another common informal means is the settlement of disputes with the help of workers' federation where the aggrieved worker serves notice to the factories through the federation. Then federation contacts factory management to settle the dispute (BILS 2020). Dispute settlement by federation is mainly used in the RMG sector. The individual member of a federation can submit his/her grievance to that federation's office in person or via phone call. Generally, federation offices provide informal, formal, and legal support to submit grievances and remedies. When a worker submits a grievance to the federation office, the office contacts the factory to resolve the issue. If the factory is non-responsive and does not commit to resolving issues, federations try to engage the brand that produces in that factory for leverage (Sharon 2022). A significant number of labor disputes are also settled by NGOs, trade unions, and employers' organizations. They have developed informal procedures and norms to settle labor disputes. Moreover, some NGOs also provide legal aid to the poor workers in cases before labor courts.

7.15 Conclusion

Peaceful resolution of labor disputes is essential for the smooth functioning of the labor market and stability in industrial relations. A fair, cost-effective, and efficient labor dispute resolution system that ensures speedy disposal of cases can facilitate access to justice for workers. The labor court is the pioneer adjudication body in settling labor disputes.

It has an important role to play in applying the international labor standards. The need for reform initiatives for introducing a court-sponsored mediation system is more felt in labor disputes than in other kinds of disputes because workers are among the most vulnerable group of people and the relatively simple nature of labor disputes. Effective and speedy labor dispute settlement requires an increasing number of labor courts, enhancing the capacity of staff, establishing oversight and monitoring of the implementation of judgments of labor courts, and legal reform for addressing weaknesses of labor courts. A scheme of court-sponsored mediation can be introduced in the Bangladesh Labor Act 2006 to make the labor courts and tribunals more accessible to workers and employers. However, it is not enough to bring some changes in procedural laws to facilitate access to justice through mediation. Rather, it requires considerable reorientation of judiciary toward mediation, efficient administration and adequate institutional support and motivation and skill development of a large number of judges and lawyers.

With the advent of rapid technological change, new forms of disputes are emerging, particularly in relation to automation, AI, and the gig economy. Traditional dispute settlement methods must be adapted to address these new challenges. Strengthening worker representation and voice in the dispute settlement process is also crucial in protecting their rights in new forms of disputes.

Bibliography

Books

Sampath, D. K. 1991. *Mediation*. National Law School of India University.

Nolan-Haley, Jacqueline M. 1991. *Alternative Dispute Resolution*. West Publishing Company.

Journal Articles

Yu, Hong-Lin. 2009. "Is Court-annexed Mediation Desirable?." *Civil Justice Quarterly* 28 (4): 515–646.

Reports

"Neglect of Workers Mirrors the Neglect of Labour Courts." Interview with Razekuzzaman Ratan. *The Daily Star*, February 7, 2024. Accessed on March 2, 2025. https://www.thedailystar.net/tags/labour-courts.

Faruque, Abdullah Al. 2009. "Current Status and Evolution of Industrial Relations System in Bangladesh." ILO, 18. Accessed on January 12, 2024. https://www.ilo.org/sites/default/files/wcmsp5/groups/public/@asia/@ro-bangkok/@sro-new_delhi/documents/publication/wcms_123336.pdf.

The High Court Division Guidelines on Violence Against Women in Workplace. https://file-dhaka.portal.gov.bd/files/seo.kishoreganjsadar.kishoreganj.gov.bd/notices/e60762d4_cb8b_466a_bb35_79a19fdbaeca/27d0127926ff9978bbf4413860477865.pdf.

Hossain, Jakir, and Afroza Akter. 2016. "Bangladesh Garment Sector Tripartism and the Scope of Harmonious Industrial and Labour Relations." Bangladesh Institute of Labour Studies (BILS).

Huda, Taqbir. 2020. "Tire Them Out: Challenges of Litigating Compensation Claims Under the Bangladesh Labour Act 2006." Bangladesh Legal Aid and Services Trust, Dhaka. https://www.blast.org.bd/content/report/Challenges-of-litigating-compensation-claims-under-the%20Bangladesh-Labour-Act-2006-(2020).pdf.

Kadir, Chowdhury Albab. 2024. "We Need an Independent Commission to Resolve Labour Disputes." *The Daily Star*, September 20. Accessed on July 12, 2025. https://www.thedailystar.net/opinion/views/news/we-need-independent-commission-resolve-labour-disputes-3707026.

Khabo, Fumane Malebona. 2008. "Collective Bargaining and Labour Disputes Resolution: Is SADC Meeting the Challenge?." ILO Sub-Regional Office for Southern Africa. Harare: ILO (Issue Paper No. 30).

Meahzi, Kamal Hossain. 2022. "To Improve ADR System Under the Labour Law in Bangladesh." *The Daily Star*, April 23. Accessed on September 11, 2024. https://www.thedailystar.net/law-our-rights/law-reform/news/improve-adr-system-under-the-labour-law-bangladesh-3010506.

Policy Brief on "Industrial Dispute Settlement in the RMG and Inland Water Transport (IWT) Sectors of Bangladesh: Present Situation and Recommendations for Comprehensive Approach." Bangladesh Institute of Labour Studies (BILS), March 2020.

Sharon, Md. Nazmus Sayeed. 2022. "Existing Complaints Structures for Workers in the Export-Oriented Textile and Garment Sector in Bangladesh." Deutsche Gesellschaft für, Internationale Zusammenarbeit (GIZ) GmbH, Dhaka.

Legislation

The Bangladesh Labor Act 2006.
The Labour (Amendment) Act 2018 (Act No. 58 of 2018).
The EPZ Labor Act, 2019.

CHAPTER 8

Implementation of International Labor Standards and Fair Globalization

8.1 Introduction

The International Labor Standards (ILS) refer to the well-known set of universally recognized labor rights, principles for the protection of workers and welfare measures established by the ILO, and they represent the universal consensus on minimum best practices on industrial relations. International labor standards consist of numerous legal instruments such as Conventions, Protocols, Declarations, and recommendations adopted by the ILO, designed to eliminate unjust labor practices and to improve working conditions. Such legal instruments are developed by the ILO's three main constituents—governments, employers and workers, and they embody international standards, basic principles, and rights at work (ILO 2019). While the ILO Conventions and Protocols are legally binding instruments that need to be ratified by member States of the ILO, Recommendations are non-binding in nature and supplement these Conventions by providing more detailed guidelines on how they could be applied at the national level. Since its establishment in 1919, the ILO has not only adopted international labor standards, but also promoted their application through supervision and monitoring the progress of their implementation in its member states. As of now, the ILO has adopted more than 188 Conventions and over 190 Recommendations, which collectively set international labor standards that encompass the freedom of association, the right to collective bargaining, the abolition of forced

A. Al Faruque, *Globalization and Labour Rights*,
https://doi.org/10.1007/978-981-92-3661-9_8

labor, non-discrimination in employment opportunity, equal treatment in employment, equal wages for men and women, minimum age for employment, and the elimination of the worst forms of child labor. These are now universally recognized core labor standards and also constitute basic human rights. The other substantive standards deal with hours of work, occupational safety and health, labor inspection, employment security, social security, holidays, and settlement of labor disputes.

The ILS play a crucial role in the promotion of social justice, contribute to the social and human objectives of economic development, and harmonize national labor legislation with such standards. The scope of the ILSs is both normative and prescriptive as they lay down the contents of rights and detail the provisions relating to their implementation.

Bangladesh has accepted the ILS by ratification of most of the core ILO conventions to improve labor rights and working conditions of the formal sectors. The current labor framework of Bangladesh is considerably shaped by the ILS.

8.2 The Role of International Labor Standards for Offsetting Negative Effects of Globalization

In order to counter the negative impacts of globalization, it is often suggested that a system of effective international labor standards should be in place to establish a just labor order and decent work conditions. The implementation of international labor standards is often seen as an important tool to achieve fair globalization and a catalyst for improving working conditions and living standards of workers. The ILS set a minimum standard that aims to create a level playing field in the global economy by persuading governments and employers not to lower such standards to gain a greater comparative advantage in international trade, which creates "race to the bottom" conditions in developing countries (ILO 2019, 14). International labor standards play an important role in the design of laws, regulations, and policies on labor issues at the national level. In fact, the ILS serves many purposes, such as they can be used as a yardstick for governments to harmonize national laws and practices with such standards and to improve various labor administration systems such as government agencies, labor inspection, and social security administration. The ILS are also increasingly applied by labor dispute resolution bodies, and as models for reaching collective bargaining agreements.

However, sometimes it is argued that the implementation of the ILS is costly and can hinder the economic development of poor countries. But there is no empirical evidence to support this claim. On the other hand, it is clearly established that foreign investors tend to invest in countries with strong labor rights (Busse 2002, 1; Kucera 2002). Some recent studies suggest that a positive and significant relationship exists between FDI and overall labor standards and FDI flow is connected positively with the protection of collective labor rights (Messerschmidt and Janz 2023). Although the implementation of the ILS increases labor cost, it does not negatively affect FDI because the ILS facilitates the development of human capital and political and social stability, e.g., ensuring freedom of association increases political stability and the reduction in child labor increases human capital, which acts as an incentive for attracting FDI (Kucera 2002, 35). Similarly, the realization of minimum wages and securing occupational safety may involve a cost factor. But it is also well-established that the observance of international labor standards is often accompanied by improvements in productivity and increased performance of workers that contribute to accelerating the economic development of a country (ILO 2019, 14). The implementation of labor standards is now considered indispensable for achieving sustainable development. The participatory process embedded in the ILS such as freedom of association, collective bargaining, and collective action gives credibility and sustainability to development (Novitz 2010).

The implementation of international labor standards also plays a catalytic role in the promotion of social justice, decent work, preservation of human dignity and facilitating the social and human objectives of economic development in a country. In fact, the idea of social justice figures prominently in the whole discourse of international labor standards. The ILO Declaration on Social Justice for a Fair Globalization 2008 presents a vision of globalization and stresses the importance of compliance with the ILS to meet the universal aspiration for social justice. Promoting fair globalization is one of the core strategies of the ILO addressed in its activities and agendas in its programs across the world over the last few years.

Another significant rationale for pursuing international labor standards relates to the prevention of social dumping, or "race-to-the-bottom", e.g., lowering labor standards to remain competitive for attracting foreign investment, which eventually leads to downward trend for wages and other labor conditions that lead to vulnerability of workers (Sengenberger

2005, 10). In this context, the value of the ILS has become more important in the course of accelerating economic globalization during the last three decades as it has witnessed the opening of national markets to the international economy. In view of the economic globalization that weakened state authority, the need to apply ILS has increased in order to fill the regulatory vacuum (Sengenberger 2005, 11). The instrumental role of the ILS can be attributed to attaining a "fair degree of wage and income equality", which is necessary for economic development, eradication of poverty, and social cohesion (Sengenberger 2005, 13). Respecting the ILS is now considered a crucial element in attracting foreign investment and countries that do not respect the ILS receive a very small share of global foreign investment flows (Sengenberger 2005, 13).

8.3 Labor Rights as Human Rights

International labor standards are firmly based on the idea of labor rights, which postulate that although labor has a productive function, it is not a commodity rather "it gives persons a sense of identity and meaning, allowing them to secure their self-respect and self-esteem" (Beatty 1980, 324). In this sense, respecting labor is an element of human dignity that furnishes the foundation of the notion of human rights. In this context, workers' rights must be viewed as human rights and respected as such, regardless of their economic value. This right-based approach in the labor context challenges the arguments of the neo-classical idea that the free market economy maximizes the social welfare of the workers. Labor rights are claimed as human rights that human beings have in their capacity as workers. As such, they are collective in nature.

Labor rights are usually categorized into the following types: *political rights* such as the right to freedom of association, the right to collective bargaining, the right against involuntary servitude, the right against exploitative use of child labor, and the right to lodge grievances. *Survival rights* include the right to a fair wage, the right to information about hazards of working conditions, the right to compensation for accident and the right to limited hours of work. *Security rights* encompass the right against arbitrary dismissal, the right to retirement benefits and the right to social security benefits. Apart from covering general issues relating to labor rights, some ILO Conventions address special rights of some specific category of workers such as seamen, domestic workers and migrant workers.

Claiming labor rights as human rights is justified on the ground that in addition to the ILO conventions, the sources of international labor standards also derive from core human rights treaties, such as the International Covenant on Civil and Political Rights (ICCPR) 1966, the International Covenant on Economic, Social and Cultural Rights (ICESCR) 1966, the Convention on the Elimination of All Forms of Discrimination Against Women (CEDAW) 1979 and the Convention on the Rights of the Child (CRC) 1989. While the ICCPR prohibits slavery, servitude, forced labor, and discrimination and protects the freedom of association and the right to join trade unions; the ICESCR protects the right to work and choice of employment, and the right to "just conditions of work", the right to join trade unions, and the right to "an adequate standard of living". The CEDAW asks states to abolish discrimination against women in employment, and to ensure safe and healthy working conditions and to grant maternity leave with pay. The CRC requires state parties to protect children from child labor, abuse, or exploitation.

Labor rights as human rights have been categorized into three groups: rights regarding access to work, rights to decent conditions at work, and the right to form and join unions and collective bargaining. Again, access to work has been explained to include opportunities for people to work, employment at their choice and security of employment (Gilabert 2018).

Despite these similarities, human rights and labor rights conceptually differ from each other in three important ways on the basis of the sphere of operation of the state and the private actors, their engagement at the individual versus collective level and processes versus outcomes (Kolben 2010). First, while labor rights primarily affect private actors and require state intervention in the private sphere, human rights primarily affect states (Kolben 2010). Within the private sphere, labor rights serve at least two important economic functions (Kolben 2010). The first function is protection since labor rights provide guarantees to workers in the context of an economic relationship between the employer and employee, which is based on unequal bargaining power. A second economic function of labor rights is facilitative since these rights enable workers to engage fairly with employers in the marketplace (Kolben 2010).

Secondly, while human rights are the rights of individuals in society, labor rights are particularly associated with the collective or group rights of the workers. Third, some labor rights such as forming and joining trade unions and collective bargaining are called process rights that enable workers to negotiate and access other entitlements, and conditions of employment, such as health and safety policy, living wages, and working hours. These kinds of labor help mobilize workers for the realization of these entitlements. On the other hand, human rights are a set of guarantees and safeguards for individuals against the state (Kolben 2010). In brief, while human rights aim primarily to limit the power of the state, labor rights are primarily oriented toward limiting the power of private actors, e.g., employers in the market (Kolben 2010, 452). Despite these major differences, core labor rights are treated as human rights and labor rights organizations have increasingly utilized human rights law and discourse to fight for the realization of labor rights. The labor rights norms embedded in human rights instruments also serve legitimacy of such claim.

8.4 Contours of International Labor Standards

International labor standards, as elaborated by the ILO Conventions, can cover the following aspects of labor relations:

i. **Freedom of Association and Collective Bargaining**

Freedom of association and the right to organize play a pivotal role in the formation of trade unions and in enhancing the bargaining power of workers. The ILO Declaration of Philadelphia 1944 affirms that the ILO is based on the fundamental principle of freedom of expression and association. The concept of fundamental human rights of workers includes the rights of workers and employers to join trade unions or other types of representative organizations. It also includes the right to freedom from forced labor, slavery, and servitude, and the right to collective representation. They are often referred to as "enabling rights" because the protection of these rights is essential in order to enable workers to realize other labor rights. Two important legal instruments in this regard are the ILO Convention concerning Freedom of Association and Protection of the Right to Organize (No. 87) that focuses on freedom of association and the ILO Convention concerning the Application of the Principles of the Right to Organize and to Bargain Collectively 1949 (No. 98), which outlines the right to organize and the right to collective bargaining. The ILO Convention concerning the Promotion of Collective Bargaining

1981 (No. 154) asks state parties to take measures for promoting collective agreements between employers and workers by engaging themselves freely. It also calls for a progressive extension of collective agreements to cover working conditions. This Convention requires governments to consult employer organizations and workers before adopting any measure of collective bargaining. The Tripartite Consultation (International Labor Standards) Convention 1976 (No. 144) asks for the establishment of tripartite consultative procedures with a view to improving the application of international labor standards through consultation and discussion. The Convention on the Right to Organize and Collective Bargaining, 1949 (No. 98) is an instrument for "the shaping of norms for the extension of collective agreements" (Hayter and Visser 2018, 5). Bangladesh has ratified all of these ILO Conventions and incorporated most of the underlying principles in its domestic legislation.

ii. **Protection of Wages**

A number of ILO Conventions establish the principle of minimum wages and lay down the conditions for the protection of wages. For example, the Protection of Wages Convention, 1949 (No. 95) elaborates specific guarantees for the protection of wages, prohibits the payment of wages in kind and provides that wages shall be paid at regular intervals. The Equal Remuneration Convention, 1951 (No. 100) lays down the principle of "equal remuneration for men and women workers for work of equal value" while the Convention on Fixing Minimum Wages of 1970 (No. 131) asks the state parties to fix procedure and machinery to fix minimum wage through legislation, to create a system of inspection and sanctions for the enforcement of such legislated minimum wage and to periodically review and adjust minimum wage rates.

iii. **Social Security**

As social security issues have always been at the forefront of the concerns of the ILO, many ILO Conventions have elaborated provisions on social security for workers. The ILO Convention on Social Security (Minimum Standards) 1952 (No. 102) lays down the minimum standards of nine branches of social security namely medical care, sickness benefit, unemployment benefit, old-age benefit, employment injury benefit, family benefit, maternity benefit, invalidity benefit, survivors' benefit; sets out "a socially acceptable minimum level of protection and requires state parties to gradually raise the basic parameters of the social security programs to higher levels. The Convention also establishes the principles and rules of financing, governance, and management of social security systems. It adopts a holistic and comprehensive approach to social security by covering nine branches of social security and taking an approach of minimum level of protection.

Compensation for the injury or death of workers in the course of employment is a crucial element of labor rights. The ILO Convention on Social Security (Minimum Standards) 1952 also deals with employment injury benefits and specifically lays down guidelines on how employment injury benefit is to be ensured. According to article 32 of this Convention, the right to employment injury benefit is recognized in four circumstances that arise due to an "accident or a prescribed disease resulting from employment". The first three circumstances deal with varying degrees of injuries, where the worker must either suffer from a "morbid condition", face incapacity for work leading to suspension of earnings or face total or partial loss of earning capacity which is likely to be permanent. The fourth situation deals with the death of a worker who acted as the sole earner in his family, so his widow or child suffers the loss of support (Article 32(d)).

However, compensation standards and social security have been significantly improved by the ILO Convention on Employment Injury Benefits Convention, 1964 (Convention No. 121) and its accompanying Recommendation, No. 121, which comprehensively deal with social security for workplace injuries and deaths. The ILO Convention No. 121 creates an obligation for payment of compensation for workplace injuries and deaths as a component of social security and it must be realized through a centralized insurance scheme. It requires State parties to enact legislation on employment injury benefits and to provide compensation to "prescribed categories of beneficiaries." It retains the four circumstances recognized by Convention No. 102, and similarly entitles a worker to adequate medical care in respect of a morbid condition while requiring periodical cash benefits for all the remaining circumstances (Article 6). However, Bangladesh has not yet ratified this Convention.

The ILO Convention on Termination of Employment 1982 (No. 158) is an instrument of employment security for workers as it sets out explicit conditions under which employment contracts can be terminated. The Convention covers all workers except those under fixed-term contracts, casual, and probationary workers. According to the Convention, employers are required to give a valid reason for the termination of any employment (Article 4), and aggrieved workers must have legal recourse to any unjust termination (Article 8). This Convention obligates state parties to impose adequate safeguards against the use of fixed-term contracts as a means of obviating rules of protection under employment law and protection against arbitrary termination of workers.

iv. **Prohibition of Forced Labor**

According to the ILO, about 13 million people across the world are victims of forced labor. Forced labor is a severe violation of human rights. It is deeply rooted in poverty, entrenched discrimination and the absence of a legal framework against it. Forced labor mostly occurs in the private sector. The ILO Convention on Forced Labor 1930 (No. 29) defines forced labor as the involuntary exaction of work or service from any person under the menace of any penalty (Article 2) while using forced labor for the purpose of economic development or as a means of political education, discrimination, labor discipline, or punishment for having participated in strikes has been prohibited by the ILO Convention on Abolition of Forced Labor 1957 (No. 105). The ILO has developed some indicators for identifying forced labor, which include "abuse of vulnerability, deception, restriction of movement, isolation, physical and sexual violence, intimidation and threats, retention of identity documents, withholding of wages, debt bondage, abusive working and living conditions, and excessive overtime" (ILO 2024). The existence of forced labor may be implied even by the presence of a single indicator in a given situation. A Protocol was adopted in 2014 to the Forced Labor Convention 1930 to require States to prevent forced labor, to give protection and remedy to the victims of forced labor.

v. **Elimination of Discrimination in Employment**

Many ILO Conventions aim to eliminate discrimination in the workplace, stipulate minimum working hours, and regulate the night work of young persons. The Convention on Hours of Work (Industry), 1919 was the first ever legal document adopted by the ILO, and it established "the principle of a maximum 48-hour work week in industry" while working time will not exceed 8 hours a day. The ILO Equal Remuneration Convention 1951 (No. 100) is the first binding international treaty to prohibit gender discrimination in employment by requiring equal payment between men and women. The ILO Convention on Holidays with Pay (Revised) 1970 (No. 132) lays down that workers are entitled to "a minimum of three weeks' paid holiday for one year of service". The ILO Convention on Minimum Age for Employment 1973 aims to prevent child labor by setting a minimum age for admission to employment. According to this Convention, "the minimum age for admission to employment should not be less than 15 years" (Article 2(1)), and in case of heavy or dangerous work, "it should not be less than 18 years" (Article 3). This Convention allows children aged 13 years and over to engage in light work, provided it is not harmful to their health and does not hamper their education. Some flexibility is made in the Convention to allow developing countries, whose economy and educational facilities are not well-developed, to temporarily set the minimum age for admission to employment at 14 years (Article 2(4)).

vi. **Labor Market and Social Policies**

Many ILO Conventions aim to improve the living standards of workers. For example, in order to raise levels of living, overcome unemployment and underemployment, the ILO Convention on Employment Policy 1964 (No. 122) asks state parties to adopt a policy to promote freely chosen productive employment for all people seeking work (Article 1). The ILO Convention on Social Policy (Basic Aims and Standards) 1962 (No. 117) sets out basic standards of social policy that aim for the welfare of workers. It highlights that the improvement of living standards shall be the main objective in the planning of the economic development of each country (Article 2). Especially, it emphasizes enhancing the productive capacity and improving the standards of living of agricultural workers (Article 4). The Convention on Human Resources Development (No. 142) of 1975 puts emphasis on adopting a comprehensive system of vocational training for workers in the relevant sectors (Article 1).

vii. **Elimination of Worst Forms of Child Labor and Hazardous Work**

Prohibition of child labor and elimination of the worst form of child labor has been one of the core concerns of the ILO since its establishment in 1919 and several Conventions have been adopted to this effect to regulate child labor. For example, the Minimum Age Convention 1973 aimed at the progressive elimination of child labor, while the Worst Forms of Child Labor Convention, 1999 focuses very specifically on the worst forms of child labor and highlights the necessity to take immediate and effective measures to prohibit and eliminate it by enacting laws. The definition of the worst forms of child labor comprises: "(a) practice of slavery and forced labor, including child trafficking, debt bondage and forced recruitment of children for armed conflict; (b) child prostitution and pornography; (c) the use of children in illicit activities, in particular for the production and trafficking of drugs; and (d) work likely to harm the health, safety or morals of children" (Article 3). This Convention mandates State parties to design programs of action in consultation with the relevant stakeholders to eliminate the worst forms of child labor on a priority basis (Article 6).

The ILO's Worst Forms of Child Labor Recommendation, 1999 (No. 190) elaborates "hazardous work" as the exposure of children to "physical, psychological or sexual abuse, work underground or underwater, work at dangerous heights or confined spaces, work with dangerous machinery, work in unhealthy environments, unnecessarily long work hours, or work that confines the child to the premises of the employer". This Recommendation emphasizes the reduction of hazardous work for children and the prevention of the engagement of children in the worst forms of child labor.

viii. **Occupational Safety and Health**

Several ILO Conventions deal with occupational safety and health. The ILO Convention on Working Environment (Air Pollution, Noise and Vibration) 1977 (No. 148) aims to protect workers from "occupational hazards in the working environment" caused by air pollution, noise or vibration. The Occupational Safety and Health Convention, 1981 (No. 155) elaborates on detailed norms relating to occupational safety and health in factories and workplaces. The Convention applies to all branches of economic activity such as maritime shipping or fishing, in respect of which special problems of a substantial nature arise (ILO 2024, 2). Article 4 of the Convention requires the ratifying states to formulate law and policy on “occupational safety, occupational health and the working environment” and periodically review such law and policy while Article 9 provides that the enforcement of such laws must be secured by an adequate and appropriate system of inspection and penalties.

The Promotional Framework for Occupational Safety and Health Convention, 2006 (No. 187) asks each state to develop a national policy, program and system for “continuous improvement of OSH to prevent occupational injuries, diseases and deaths” and periodically review national program on OSH in consultation with stakeholders. The national system for occupational safety and health, according to Art. 4, shall comprise of laws and regulations, collective agreements, a designated national authority, compliance mechanisms including systems of inspection, preventive measures, and the provision of occupational safety and health training. The core provisions of Conventions Nos. 155 and 187 are complementary and set out the principle of prevention for sustained improvements toward safe and healthy working environment.

Finally, the Convention on Safety and Health in Construction 1988 (No. 167) requires State parties to take health and safety measures for workers in the construction sector and to adopt law and enforce existing laws for compliance with the provisions of the Convention on the basis of an assessment of the safety and health hazards involved. Bangladesh needs to ratify this Convention to strengthen its national system of OSH.

ix. **Prevention of Violence and Harassment**

Violence and harassment at the workplace is a widespread phenomenon in many countries that negatively affects workers’ well-being, the work environment and productivity. In 2019, the ILO Convention on Violence and Harassment (No. 190) and Recommendation (No. 206) were adopted with the aim of preventing and eliminating violence and harassment in the world of work. The Convention recognizes that violence and harassment of workers is a violation of human rights violation or abuse and requires member states to adopt an inclusive, integrated, and gender-responsive approach to prevent and address these problems by enacting appropriate laws.

8.5 The Universality of International Labor Standards

The universality of some core labor rights and standards is now well recognized. Out of 188 ILO Conventions, the ILO Declaration on Fundamental Principles and Rights at Work 1998 identifies eight core Conventions that all ILO member States have agreed to respect, promote, protect, and realize in good faith. As such, this Declaration recognizes freedom of association, the right to collective bargaining, elimination of forced labor, abolition of child labor, and the elimination of discrimination in respect of employment and occupation as core labor standards and universal and requires Member States of the ILO to respect and promote these standards, irrespective of the fact that the States have not ratified the relevant Conventions. The Declaration confirms the universality of these standards, which are applicable to all people in all States—regardless of the level of economic development, and must be respected in all working relations.

The international labor regime is increasingly shaped by this 1998 Declaration and it has been reflected in both regional and bilateral free trade agreements. They have also been incorporated into the wide range of labor-related provisions in soft-law instruments such as the UN's Global Compact, the OECD guidelines, as well as the policies of the World Bank, IFC, and corporate code of conduct (Alston 2004, 518).

According to Alston, the 1998 Declaration has transformed the international labor rights regime through the widespread use of the concept of "core labor standards" (Alston 2004). Alston also opines that the Declaration, by asking a diverse range of actors including transnational corporations and consumers to promote and enforce these core standards, has laid the basis of a decentralized system of labor standards implementation (Alston 2004, 460). However, he has also criticized this declaration for its focus on a limited range of process rights, its neglect of substantive norms such as those relating to safety and health, minimum wages, and reasonable conditions of work' (Alston 2005) and its excessive reliance on "principles rather than rights", and 'voluntarism' in relation to implementation and enforcement (Alston 2004).

8.6 Promoting Decent Work Agenda

In recent years, the concept of "decent work" has gained increasing attention from the ILO. "Decent work" is a multi-dimensional concept that encompasses a set of norms and aspirations concerning workplace safety, social security, social protection, fair wages, right to participate in the decision-making process, equality of opportunity, and non-discrimination. It was first formulated through the adoption of the ILO's Decent Work Agenda in 1999, which has added a new dimension to the growing body of international labor standards. It was developed in response to the significant changes that took place in the standard employment relationship, especially the widespread practice of informal employment (ILO 1999). The "decent work agenda" aims to remove the root causes of informal work and for this purpose, it sets four preconditions—generating opportunities for employment and income, enhancement of rights at work, improvement of social protection, and strengthening representation and engaging with the informal economy through social dialog. In the context of a decent work agenda, employment covers work of all kinds, both in the formal and informal sectors and refers to adequate opportunities for work, living wages, safety at work, and healthy working conditions (Ghai 2003, 113). Social protection includes "social security and income security defined according to each society's capacity and level of development" (Ghai 2003, 113). Worker rights refer to the fundamental rights of workers such as freedom of association, non-discrimination at work, and the absence of forced labor and child labor; while social dialogue implies a process in which workers articulate their views and interests and negotiate on a range of issues relating to work conditions with employers and government (Ghai 2003, 113). These objectives of decent work are interconnected and mutually reinforcing.

The Decent Work Agenda constitutes a fundamental shift from the ILO's traditional focus on workers of the formal sector to the protection of workers engaged in the informal sector. Its goal is to enhance opportunities for workers to obtain decent and productive work in conditions of freedom, equity, and security and human dignity. It promotes the application of international labor standards in both formal and informal economies.

In 2008, the ILO adopted a Framework of Decent Work Indicators linking the four strategic pillars of the Decent Work Agenda. The main indicators include the ILS and fundamental principles and rights at work, employment generation, social protection, social dialog, employment opportunities, adequate earnings and productive work, decent working time; stability and security of work, equal opportunity and treatment in employment, safe work environment, social security and workers' representation (ILO 2013). These indicators reflect "the structural dimensions of the decent work measurement" through which implementation of "decent work agenda" will be assessed.

The ILO Decent Work for Domestic Workers Convention 2011 remains the first ever legally binding document on decent work and it has been formulated in view of the vulnerability of domestic workers to discrimination in respect of conditions of employment and of work, and to other abuses of human rights. The preamble of the ILO Decent Work for Domestic Workers Convention 2011 recognizes that despite the fact that the significant contribution made by domestic workers to the global economy, their work is often undervalued and invisible. It also highlights that in developing countries where opportunities for formal employment are very limited, domestic workers constitute a significant proportion of the national workforce. Article 3 of the Convention asks each member state to take measures to protect the human rights of all domestic workers, as set out in this Convention. Article 4 requires state parties to set a minimum age for domestic workers consistent with the provisions of the Minimum Age Convention, 1973 (No. 138), and the Worst Forms of Child Labor Convention, 1999 (No. 182). According to the Convention, each state shall ensure that "domestic workers enjoy effective protection against all forms of abuse, harassment and violence" (Article 5), they enjoy "fair terms of employment" as well as "decent working conditions'" (Article 6), they are informed of terms and conditions of their employment in written contracts (Article 7) and they are "free to reach agreement with their employer" (Article 9). Article 10 requires state parties to take measures for ensuring equal treatment between domestic workers and general workers regarding normal hours of work, overtime payment, periods of daily and weekly rest and paid annual leave in accordance with national laws, or collective agreements. Article 11 provides that domestic workers should be given a minimum wage if it exists in a given country.

Decent work is also one of the important goals of the UN SDGs. Especially, Goal 8 of the 2030 Agenda calls for the promotion of decent work and productive employment for all for sustained, inclusive and sustainable economic growth. Decent work and the four pillars of the Decent Work

Agenda—"employment creation, social protection, fundamental rights at work and social dialogue" are the central elements of the Sustainable Development Agenda 2030. Ensuring decent work requires not only productive work with sufficient wage income, but also adequate social protection for the workers.

8.7 Process of Implementation of International Labor Standards

The implementation of the ILS depends on their integration of the ILS within the national legal framework, and placing an institutional framework for enforcing them. A number of domestic political and economic factors may also influence implementation of the ILS. For example, countries with higher levels of democracy and strong democratic institutions such as independent judiciary are more likely to protect collective labor rights (Neumayer and Soysa 2007). Similarly, economic development has a positive correlation with improved labor rights as countries with higher levels of economic development have more resources to establish and enforce robust labor laws, provide stronger social safety nets and are likely to have greater respect for labor rights (Blanton and Blanton 2012).

The implementation mechanisms of the international labor standards encompass both public and private regulatory instruments. While the public regulatory mechanisms include ratification of ILO conventions, promulgation and enforcement of national labor laws, global enforcement of labor standards, private regulatory mechanism refers to corporate self-regulation through codes of conduct. While countries vary in applying labor standards, ratification of the ILO Conventions creates a level playing field across countries to protect workers' rights and promote decent work, social justice, and sustainable development by promoting universal application of the ILS (ILO 2024, 6). The ILO Conventions represent benchmarks of global labor standards which countries must implement them by enacting and enforcing national laws. At the national level, ratification of the ILO Conventions by the member states is first step for creating legal obligations to implement labor standards. In second step of implementation, states must adopt appropriate legislative and administrative measures or amend existing law to comply with the ILO convention in question. Given the fact that states have very different levels of economic development and diverse legal approaches, the ILO

Conventions have considerable flexibility for states to comply with the Conventions.

At the international level, implementation of labor standards is backed by a supervisory system of the ILO as mentioned above. The ILO has developed three main types of supervisory mechanisms by which it examines the status and level of compliance with obligations of member states deriving from ratified Conventions. The first type of supervision is conducted through the submission of annual reports, which is known as a regular procedure, (Article 22 of the ILO Constitution), second, through special procedures based on complaints or representations to the Governing Body made by ILO constituents (articles 24 and 26 of the Constitution). Third, there is a special complaint procedure relating to freedom of association which is referred to the Committee on Freedom of Association of the Governing Body (Alston 2004, 518).

Although the ILO Recommendations are not binding and cannot be ratified, states are obliged to inform the ILO on the actions that have been taken in pursuit of the recommendation's objectives and on "the position of the law and practice in their country in regard to the matters dealt with in the Recommendation ..." (Art. 19.6 of the ILO Constitution..

The ILO regularly reviews the application of the ILS in member states and makes recommendations for reforming relevant labor laws. The system of supervision is based on the examination of reports submitted by member states on the application of the ILS and on observations by workers' organizations and employers' organizations on compliance with the ILO Conventions. The examination is done by two ILO bodies, namely—

- The Committee of Experts on the Application of Conventions and Recommendations (CEARC)
- The Conference Committee on the Application of Standards (CAS)

After reviewing and strunizing state reports, the CEARC publishes two annual reports: the "General Report", which contains observations and a "General Survey" which provides a broad overview of one specific theme.

The CEACR reports are submitted to the CAS, which is a tripartite standing committee of the International Labor Conference. The CAS examines individual cases concerning the application of ratified Conventions, which have been the subject of observations by the Committee of Experts. While the CEARC only communicates with member states in writing, the CAS invites these states to appear at its session and comment upon the alleged failure to comply with the ILO convention in question (Zandvliet 2019, 50). However, the ILO's supervisory mechanism has been best described as persuasive and its capacity to enforce treaty obligations by member states is always contested.

Despite the fact that the international labor standards have been included in many instruments including international trade and investment agreements, in practice these standards have not been translated into action at the national level. They remain largely rhetorical (Levichristopher et al. 2013, 15). The gap between labor standards in law and labor standards in practice emerges either because many states lack political willingness to enforce them, or because they lack the power to enforce them. Trade unions can play an important role in implementing labor standards through campaigns for labor rights, collective bargaining but unions are declining in many developed and developing countries as the percentage of workers represented by unions is very low. Although labor standards originate from international norms, their implementation is generally dependent on domestic laws and enforcement mechanisms. Enforcement of the ILS largely depends on their incorporation in national laws and policies, the quality and capacity of domestic institutions to apply them, an adequate inspection system, and strong implementation mechanisms. Since the ILO has limited power to enforce its conventions and recommendations, their implementation largely depends on national machineries. The ILO's main means of enforcement of ILS are moral persuasion and providing technical assistance to countries to foster their adoption and implementation. On the other hand, many developing countries face resource constraints in implementing these standards.

8.8 Challenges of Implementation of International Labor Standards in Bangladesh

Bangladesh has ratified thirty-nine ILO Conventions including all of the eight core conventions on freedom of association, the right to join trade and collective bargaining, discrimination and equal remuneration, child labor and forced labor. It has also ratified the Protocol of 2014 to the Forced Labor Convention 1930. Bangladesh has also accepted a number of recommendations including the ILO Declaration on Fundamental Principles and Rights at Work 1998. Recently it has ratified the ILO Minimum Age Convention 1973 (No.138), the Occupational Safety and

Health Convention 1981 (No. 155), Promotional Framework for Occupational Safety and Health Convention 2006 (No. 187) and Convention on Violence and Harassment 2019 (No. 190), signaling its willingness for further improving the labor rights including occupational safety and security of workers and prevention of harassment.

Implementation of the ILS is facing many challenges in Bangladesh. One of the important reasons for the non-implementation of labor rights is that many labor rights are widely seen as less enforceable or justiciable than other types of human rights. Since the ILO has no direct implementation authority to enforce its Conventions at the national level, it depends on government agencies and local stakeholders to ensure that these are implemented. While Bangladesh has ratified the ILO Conventions, it has yet to transpose many of the obligations under those conventions into national law. Even when some of these obligations have been transposed to national laws, enforcement of those laws is more challenging as enforcement of labor rights is also dependent on employers, rather than the state or government. For example, despite having ratified most of the core conventions and enabling legislation, children in Bangladesh are subjected to the worst form of child labor in the drying of fish and the production of bricks, footwear, *Bidi* factories, furniture, glass, shrimp, soap, textiles, and jute sectors. Economic hardships force many school-age children to take on temporary jobs in factories. Although child labor has been officially eliminated from the RMG sector in 2004 in consultation with ILO, child labor still exists in the subcontracting factories and the informal sector.

The main instruments of application of the ILO standards in Bangladesh include labor legislation, institutional frameworks such as government agencies, judiciary, and non-state actors NGOs. Bangladesh has adopted many laws to implement international labor standards. The Bangladesh Labor Act 2006 remains the main legal framework for labor standards and labor rights. This Act envisages several institutions to implement the labor standards such as the Department of Labor, Labor Court, the Chief Inspector of Factories and Establishments, and National Council on Occupational Health and Safety. The Director of Labor is responsible for labor administration and has wide powers to interfere in the internal affairs of trade unions and can enter union premises and inspect documents, which may hamper the independence of trade unions (Report for the WTO 2012). The Director may also cancel the registration of a union, with the approval of Labor Court.

The weak labor administration is also responsible for the lack of implementation of the ILS. For example, the Office of the Chief Inspector of Factories and Establishments is responsible for enforcing the provisions relating to the inspection of working conditions and filing complaints against employers in case of non-compliance. But most of the inspectorates are under-resourced and lack the technical capacity to enforce the ILS. Export Processing Zones (EPZs) are regulated by special labor legislation whereby basic rights are not permitted and workers are unable to join trade unions and bargain collectively. As such, many of the ILS are not applicable for the EPZs.

Many important provisions of the Bangladesh Labor Act 2006 still do not meet the ILS standards. For example, section 20 of the Bangladesh Labor Act 2006 allows the employer to terminate a worker under the ground of retrenchment giving a one-month notice indicating the reason for retrenchment. However, the requirement of giving notice can be waived by paying wages in lieu of such notice. The optional nature of the requirement of giving notice creates scope for instant termination without giving reasons. On the other hand, imposing lenient punishments and low compensations for violation of labor laws allows employers to enjoy impunity and disregard the international labor standards (Syed 2024).

There are also practices of delayed wage payments, long working hours, discrimination, unsafe working conditions, and poor work environment in violation of labor standards and existing labor laws. Workers are mostly unorganized and face many barriers in union formation. Though the law has made it mandatory for employers to provide appointment letters and identity cards to the workers, a large number of RMG workers are still deprived of appointment letters and identity cards from their employers. Dismissal of workers without notice is also common practice.

There is also a lack of compliance with the provisions relating to weekly rest days and leaves, and overtime rules. Legal provisions on casual leave, sick leave, and annual leave are not fully complied with by employers due to weak enforcement mechanisms. Health and safety facilities are also inadequate in the RMG and other industries. Reporting of industrial accidents and death or injury of workers needs to be a mandatory requirement for holding employers accountable.

The Bangladesh Labor Act, 2006 fails to include a large number of workers—domestic workers, workers engaged in health care and education, agricultural workers in farms with less than 10 employees, and workers in shops and restaurants. Many employers hire irregular workers to escape payment of various workers' benefits and avoid trade unionism. Getting financial benefits in case of termination are quite a lengthy process (Hossain et al. 2010). To get financial benefits for retrenchment and discharge, a worker must show proof of a minimum one-year service. The establishment of a provident fund is not made mandatory (Hossain et al. 2010). It is dependent on the demand of a prerequisite number of workers. The introduction of "group insurance" is also dependent on the number of workers and the prerequisite number is quite high (Hossain et al. 2010).

The amount of compensation given to workers due to work-related injury, disability, and death is grossly inadequate for the worker and his/her family. In this regard, the ILO Convention No. 121 which sets a global standard on compensation, is not yet ratified by Bangladesh. Instead, compensation for workers in Bangladesh is governed by some statutory laws and rules. The current levels of compensation for workplace injuries and deaths set out in these laws are grossly inadequate to properly compensate workers and their families.

There are other challenges and problems that need to be addressed to apply labor standards in Bangladesh. Labor laws of Bangladesh do not adequately provide for freedom of association, the right to collective bargaining and the right to strike. The law does not protect unions from interference by employers and has excessive requirements for the registration of trade unions. Frequent denial of appointment letters to the workers, absence of effective bargaining power, lack of regular inspection of establishment, excessive working hours, lack of implementation of minimum wages, and frequent non-compliance with health and safety regulations are impediments to the implementation of the international labor standards. Finally, implementation of the ILS also depends on a well-informed judiciary on international labor instruments, which can apply these norms in the settlement of labor disputes. As such, labor dispute settlement mechanisms in Bangladesh need to be well-equipped through training and capacity building to apply these standards.

8.9 Conclusion

The horizon of international labor standards is expanding. While most of the international labor standards are legally recognized in Bangladesh through various labor laws, the implementation of these standards faces numerous challenges. Extending these standards to workers in informal sector remains a major hurdle for their effective implementation. Although the recent legal reforms have significantly improved the regulatory framework, still there are some needs of further reform to make it fully consistent with international standards. In order to remain globally competitive, Bangladesh needs to adhere to international labor standards and implement these in its national legal framework to offset the negative impacts of globalization on labor rights. There is a well-established linkage between greater respect for collective labor rights and improvements in working conditions. It is widely believed that the implementation of these standards promotes better jobs, higher wages, safer workplaces, and less forced and child labor. In Bangladesh, institutional mechanisms for the implementation of international labor standards need to be strengthened further through enhancing capacity building of existing labor institutions including labor courts, the Department of Labor, and office of inspections. Many developing countries, including Bangladesh, hold the view that adoption of higher labor standards creates rigidities in the labor market and as a result, hinder the foreign investment and economic development (Howse et al. 2006, 159). But it is not proven that higher labor standards hamper the inflows of investments and economic development (Lim 2001). In fact, there is no causal link between the implementation of core labor standards and labor costs (Lim 2001). Rather, it is well-established that compliance with ILO standards can enhance productivity, they further enhance equality of employment and income opportunities, and at the same time it can afford social protection to workers. The reasons for non-adherence to the ILS can be largely attributed to primarily political one because there is no compelling reason for failing to comply with them on economic grounds. Compliance with ILS also prevents downward trends in setting minimum wage. Apart from government agencies, the implementation of ILS also depends on the collaborative efforts of other relevant actors, including trade unions, NGOs, and social partners.

Bibliography

Books

North, Douglass. 1990. *Institutions, Institutional Change, and Economic Performance*. Cambridge University Press.

Chapters in Edited Books

Alston, Philip. 2005. "Labour Rights as Human Rights: The Not So Happy State of the Art." In *Labour Rights as Human Rights*, edited by Alston Philip, 1–24. Oxford University Press.

Beatty, David M. 1980. "Labour is Not a Commodity." In *Studies in Contract Law*, edited by Barry J. Reiter and John Swan, 314–331. Butterworths.

Gilabert, Pablo. 2018. "Labor Rights." In *Human Rights and Human Dignity*, edited by Pablo Gilabert, 229–260. Oxford University Press.

Hayter, Susan, and Jelle Visser. 2018. "The Application and Extension of Collective Agreements: Enhancing the Inclusiveness of Labour Protection." In *Collective Agreements: Extending Labour Protection*, edited by Susan Hayter and Jelle Visser, 1–27. ILO.

Howse, Rober, Brian A. Langille, and Julien Burda. 2006. "The World Trade Organization and Labour Rights: Men Bites Dog' in Virginia." In *Social Issues, Globalization and International Institutions: Labour Rights and the EU, ILO, OECD and WTO*, edited by A. Leary and Daniel Warner, 157–231. Martinus Nijhoff Publishers.

Novitz, Tonia. 2010. "Core Labour Standards Conditionalities: A Means by Which to Achieve Sustainable Development?." In *International Economic Law, Globalization and Developing Countries*, edited by Julio Faundez and Celine Tan, 234–251. Edward Elgar Publishing.

Journal Articles

Alston, Philip. 2004. "Core Labour Standards' and the Transformation of the International Labour Rights Regime." *European Journal of International Law* 15 (3): 457–521.

Blanton, Robert G., and Shannon L. Blanton. 2012. "Labor Rights and Foreign Direct Investment: Is There a Race to the Bottom?." *International Interactions* 38 (3): 267–294.

Busse, Matthias. 2002. "Foreign Direct Investment and Fundamental Workers' Rights." *Journal of International Relations and Development* 5: 143–155.

Ghai, Dharam. 2003. "Decent Work: Concept and Indicators." *International Labour Review* 142 (2): 113–145.

Kolben, Kevin. 2010. "Labour Rights as Human Rights." *Virginia Journal of International Law* 50 (2): 450–472.
Kucera, David. 2002. "Core Labour Standards and Foreign Direct Investment." *International Labour Review* 141 (1–2): 31–68.
Messerschmidt, Luca, and Nicole Janz. 2023. "Unravelling the 'Race to the Bottom' Argument: Foreign Direct Investment and Different Types of Labour Rights." *World Development* 161: 106097.
Syed, Robayet Ferdous. 2024. "Labor Standards, Labor Policy, and Compliance Mechanism: A Case Study in Bangladesh." *Labor History* 65 (2): 256–272.

Reports

ILO. "Applying and Promoting International Labour Standards." Accessed on January 12, 2024. http://www.ilo.org/global/standards/applying-and-promoting-international-labour-standards/lang--en/index.htm.
ILO. 2013. *Decent Work Indicators: Guidelines for Producers and Users of Statistical and Legal Framework Indicators. ILO Manual: Second Version.* Geneva: International Labour Office (ILO).
Sengenberger, Werner. 2005. "Globalization and Social Progress: The Role and Impact of International Labour Standards." A Report Prepared for the Friedrich-Ebert-Stiftung, 2nd Revised and Extended Revision Bonn.
"Internationally Recognised Core Labour Standards in Bangladesh." Report for the WTO General Council Review of the Trade Policies of Bangladesh, Geneva, 2012. Accessed on July 8, 2025. http://www.ituc-csi.org/IMG/pdf/bangladesh-final.pdf.
ILO. 2019. "Rules of the Game: An Introduction to the Standards-Related Work of the International Labour Organization." International Labour Office, Geneva, 12, 14. Accessed on January 13, 2024. https://www.ilo.org/sites/default/files/wcmsp5/groups/public/%40ed_norm/%40normes/documents/publication/wcms_672549.pdf.
ILO. 2024. "Understanding the Ratification and Implementation Process of the Fundamental Conventions on Occupational Safety and Health." Geneva, 2.
ILO. "Universal Social Protection to Achieve the Sustainable Development Goals." World Social Protection Report (2017–19) 58.
ILO. 2013. *Decent Work Indicators: Guidelines for Producers and Users of Statistical and Legal Framework Indicators: ILO Manual: Second Version.* Geneva: International Labour Office.
General Observation on the Application of the Worst Forms of Child Labour Convention, 1999 (No. 182). Adopted By the Committee of Experts on the Application of Conventions and Recommendations (CEACR) at Its 91st Session (November–December 2020).

Hossain, Jakir, Mostafiz Ahmed, and Afroza Akter. 2010. "Bangladesh Labour Law: Reform Directions." Dhaka. Accessed on March 8, 2024. http://www.ituc-ap.org/wps/wcm/connect/18bf80804c4b9364a854e9074f891cc1/report-of-the-baseline-study-on-bangladesh.pdf?MOD=AJPERES.

Levichristopher, Margaret, Adolphdaniel Berlineraaron, Erlichanne Greenleafmilli, and Lakejennifer Noveck. 2013. "Aligning Rights and Interests: Why, When and How to Uphold Labor Standards." Background Paper for the World Development Report, 15.

Lim, Hoe. 2001. *The Social Clause: Issues and Challenges*. ILO.

The Director-General's Programme and Budget Proposals for 2014–15, Report, II (Supplement). International Labour Conference, 102nd Session, Geneva: ILO. (2013a, para. 49).

Zandvliet, R. 2019. *Trade, Investment and Labour: Interactions in International Law*. https://scholarlypublications.universiteitleiden.nl/access/item%3A2977127/view.

International Instruments

Declaration Concerning the Aims and Purposes of the International Labour Organization. Accessed on May 13, 2024. https://webapps.ilo.org/static/english/inwork/cb-policy-guide/declarationofPhiladelphia1944.pdf.

ILO Convention Concerning Freedom of Association and Protection of the Right to Organize (No. 87). Accessed on May 12, 2024. https://webapps.ilo.org/static/english/inwork/cb-policy-guide/freedomofassocandrighttoorganiseno87.pdf.

ILO Convention Concerning the Application of the Principles of the Right to Organize and to Bargain Collectively 1949. Accessed on March 3, 2024. https://normlex.ilo.org/dyn/nrmlx_en/f?p=NORMLEXPUB:12100:0::NO::P12100_INSTRUMENT_ID:312243.

ILO Convention Concerning the Promotion of Collective Bargaining 1981. Accessed on March 3, 2024. https://webapps.ilo.org/static/english/inwork/cb-policy-guide/collectivebargainingconvention1981No154.pdf.

ILO Convention on Abolition of Forced Labour 1957 (No. 105). Accessed on March 20, 2024. https://normlex.ilo.org/dyn/nrmlx_en/f?p=NORMLEXPUB:12100:0::NO:12100:P12100_INSTRUMENT_ID:312250:NO.

ILO Convention on Decent Work for Domestic Workers (No. 189). Accessed on May 19, 2024. https://normlex.ilo.org/dyn/nrmlx_en/f?p=NORMLEXPUB:12100:0::NO::p12100_ILO_CODE:C189.

ILO Convention on Employment Injury Benefits Convention, 1964 (No. 121), Art. 4. Accessed on March 12, 2024. https://normlex.ilo.org/dyn/nrmlx_en/f?p=NORMLEXPUB:12100:0::NO:12100:P12100_INSTRUMENT_ID:312266:NO.

ILO Convention on Employment Policy 1964. Accessed on March 23, 2025. https://normlex.ilo.org/dyn/normlex/en/f?p=NORMLEXPUB:12100:::NO:12100:P12100_ILO_CODE:C122:NO.
ILO Convention on Forced Labor 1930. Accessed on March 12, 2024. https://normlex.ilo.org/dyn/nrmlx_en/f?p=NORMLEXPUB:12100:::NO:12100:P12100_ILO_CODE:C029:NO.
ILO Convention on Holidays with Pay (Revised) 1970. Accessed on March 20, 2024. https://normlex.ilo.org/dyn/normlex/en/f?p=NORMLEXPUB:12100:0::NO::P12100_ILO_CODE:C132.
ILO Convention on Hours of Work (Industry), 1919. Accessed on March 21, 2024. https://file.portal.gov.bd/files/dife.sylhet.gov.bd/files/8bfa08b7_1040_4e10_85ec_160a802b170a/065c19c71031c8dffd4f8dc57762b136.pdf.
ILO Convention on Human Resources Development 1975 (No. 142). Accessed on April 1, 2024. https://normlex.ilo.org/dyn/nrmlx_en/f?p=NORMLEXPUB:12100:0::NO:12100:P12100_INSTRUMENT_ID:312287:NO.
ILO Convention on Safety and Health in Construction 1988. Accessed on July 10, 2024. https://normlex.ilo.org/dyn/normlex/en/f?p=NORMLEXPUB:12100:0::NO::P12100_ILO_CODE:C167.
ILO Convention on Social Policy (Basic Aims and Standards) 1962. Accessed on March 27, 2024. https://normlex.ilo.org/dyn/normlex/en/f?p=NORMLEXPUB:12100:0::NO::P12100_ILO_CODE:C117.
ILO Convention on Social Security (Minimum Standards) 1952. Accessed on March 3, 2024. https://normlex.ilo.org/dyn/nrmlx_en/f?p=NORMLEXPUB:12100:0::NO:12100:P12100_INSTRUMENT_ID:312247:NO.
ILO Convention on Termination of Employment 1982. Accessed on March 12, 2024. http://ilo.org/dyn/normlex/en/f?p=NORMLEXPUB:51:0::NO:51:P51_CONTENT_REPOSITORY_ID:2543200:NO.
ILO Convention on the Minimum Age, 1973 (No. 138). Accessed on March 23, 2024. https://normlex.ilo.org/dyn/nrmlx_en/f?p=normlexpub:12100:0::no::P12100_ilo_code:C138.
ILO Convention on Working Environment (Air Pollution, Noise and Vibration) 1977. Accessed on April 22, 2024. https://normlex.ilo.org/dyn/normlex/en/f?p=NORMLEXPUB:12100:0::NO::P12100_ILO_CODE:C148.
ILO Convention on Worst Forms of Child Labour, 1999 (No. 182). Accessed on March 23, 2024. https://normlex.ilo.org/dyn/nrmlx_en/f?p=NORMLEXPUB:12100:0::NO::P12100_ILO_CODE:C182.
ILO Declaration on Social Justice for a Fair Globalisation, 2008. Accessed on May 11, 2024. https://www.ilo.org/sites/default/files/2024-12/ILO-Declaration-2008_En.pdf.

ILO Indicators of Forced Labour. Accessed on March 20, 2024. https://www.ilo.org/sites/default/files/wcmsp5/groups/public/@ed_norm/@declaration/documents/publication/wcms_203832.pdf.

ILO Occupational Safety and Health Convention, 1981. Accessed on March 23, 2024. https://normlex.ilo.org/dyn/normlex/en/f?p=NORMLEXPUB:12100:0::NO::P12100_ILO_CODE:C155.

Tripartite Consultation (International Labor Standards) Convention 1976. Accessed on March 3, 2024. https://normlex.ilo.org/dyn/nrmlx_en/f?p=NORMLEXPUB:12100:0::NO::P12100_ILO_CODE:C144.

"The ILO Declaration on Fundamental Principles and Rights at Work and Its Follow-Up." Adopted by the International Labour Conference at Its Eighty-Sixth Session, Geneva, 18 June 1998.

CHAPTER 9

Practice of Social Dialogue in Industrial Relations: Evidence from Bangladesh

9.1 Introduction

Social dialogue constitutes one of the pillars of the ILO Decent Work Agenda, along with fundamental rights at work, employment opportunities, and social protection. There is no universal model or definition of social dialogue. Generally, social dialogue is the process through which key actors in industrial relations, such as governments, trade unions, employers, and workers negotiate or consult on labor issues, labor market policies, economic policy, and social protection. In social dialogue, various actors in industrial relations inform each other of "their intention and capacities, elaborate information provided to them, and clarify and explain their assumptions and expectations" (EU 2002, 25). In this way, it is different from collective bargaining process. Social dialogue promotes the legitimacy of decisions taken in a collective manner, reduces conflict in industrial relations, replaces hostile relationships with collaborative partnerships, and develops a shared understanding of industrial or social problems.

The aim of the social dialogue as a decent work paradigm is to help ensure that policy-making and labor law reform take place through tripartite dialogue, and to build the capacity of workers to influence and shape socio-economic policies (Minet 2008). The 2008 ILO Declaration on Social Justice for a Fair Globalization strongly reaffirms the necessity and the relevance of social dialogue in the pursuit of the achievement of

A. Al Faruque, *Globalization and Labour Rights*,
https://doi.org/10.1007/978-981-92-3661-9_9

employment and social policy objectives, translating economic development into social progress, facilitating consensus building on employment and decent work strategies and making labor law and institutions more effective.

Another objective of promoting social dialogue in industrial relations is to minimize labor disputes, to reduce labor unrest and to establish harmony between employers and workers. The practice of well-crafted social dialogue can also promote sustainable socio-economic growth, sound industrial relations and improved productivity and decent work.

Social dialogue promotes cooperative industrial relations and improves labor market performance (Feldmann 2009). Such cooperative relations offer many benefits over confrontational industrial relations. In cooperative relations, the workers tend to become "more willing to invest in their own human capital", and foster positive work environment that increases productivity (Feldmann 2009). Social dialogue carried out through tripartite structures provides a forum for mutual discussion, review of labor legislation, information and knowledge sharing, and updating and awareness about developments in the labor market (Khabo 2008, 21). Social dialogue may prevent labor unrest, agitation, and conflicts by reaching acceptable solutions on conflicting issues and can replace "adversarial relationships" with collaborative partnerships(Feldmann 2009). Workers' participation in social dialogue on equal footing enhances their sense of self-worth, gives them an opportunity to raise their voice for meeting their needs and paves the way for inclusiveness in industrial relations. Social dialogue is considered an effective means to address economic and social tensions during periods of economic crisis or transition and has the potential to combat different forms of inequality in industrial relations and in this way, it can develop a "shared understanding of problems" through facilitating discussion on contested issues by involving stakeholders in key aspects of industrial relations. In many countries, social dialogue is used as "consensus-building mechanisms", which has enabled the social partners to develop solutions to changing needs and to address new challenges in industrial relations. In this way, it is different from the traditional bargaining process. According to Ghai, social dialogue between different economic groups and the public authorities in a cooperative framework is an essential attribute of a democratic society and can promote equity, efficiency and sustain economic progress (Ghai 2003, 134).

Social dialogue is not a static concept. Rather, it is a flexible and dynamic concept to be adapted to the most diverse situations. The content of national social dialogue is shaped by the economic realities and changing needs of industrial relations and hence, it may therefore differ at different stages of economic and social development (Ghai 2003, 134).

The necessity of social dialogue in industrial relations in Bangladesh can hardly be overemphasized as it has moved from an agriculture-based economy to an industrial society. This transformation requires government labor administration mechanisms and industries to engage in social dialogue at the factory, sectoral, and national levels to address numerous issues of industrial relations. It also emphasizes the need for integration of social dialogue in the legal framework and strengthening existing social dialogue institutions as a strategy to improve industrial relations in Bangladesh through reaching consensus on issues of common concerns.

9.2 Enabling Conditions of Social Dialogue

Effective social dialogue is dependent on a number of conditions that can create an enabling environment for it. The main enabling conditions for social dialogue include respect for and implementation of freedom of association, the right of workers and employers to form and join trade unions, and the free functioning of tripartite organizations. The promotion of social dialogue also requires the strong political will of all parties involved, a pluralist democracy, a market economy, a sound legal framework, efficient institutions, independent representatives of employers and technical competency of all stakeholders (Ghai 2003, 134). An enabling legal framework on the right to freedom of association and collective bargaining is essential for social dialogue. Effective social dialogue depends on the legitimacy of the social partners in the sense that both employers' and workers' organizations need to be representative and reflect the interests of the members. The social partners should participate in social dialogue on an equal footing. It is equally important that all social partners should have mutual trust in and commitment to the process of social dialogue and have the necessary technical capacity and knowledge to engage in debate on wider social issues beyond their immediate interests (Ghai 2003, 134). It is also important that agreements reached through social dialogue is implemented and monitored by the governments and employers. Social partners should ensure their accountability, transparency and cohesiveness in their engagement in social dialogue (Ishikawa 2003, 5). The involvement of NGOs and civil society in social dialogue can also play an important role in making it more effective by providing the necessary expertise and knowledge.

In brief, the main preconditions for making social dialogue successful are the presence of independent, broad-based and representative workers' and employers' organizations having the technical capacity and access to the relevant information to participate in social dialogue, their commitment to engage in social dialogue, respect for the fundamental rights of freedom of association and collective bargaining and appropriate institutional support (Sivananthiran & Ratnam 2003, 1). But many of these enabling conditions are largely absent in Bangladesh.

9.3 Nature and Types of Social Dialogue

Social dialogue may take many forms, ranging from the sharing of information about the labor conditions to consultation and negotiation. It may also involve discussion about the general prospects of the enterprise, changes in the methods of production, and workers' participation in the decision-making process (Chowdhury 2004). Social dialogue can take place at three levels: national, sectoral, and enterprise level. Social dialogue at the national level can play an important role in addressing broader issues related to the economic and social policies of a country (Ishikawa 2003, 15). It can address wider economic and social policy issues such as macro-economic policy framework, wage increase, employment policy, gender equality, education and vocational training, productivity, social welfare, security and protection, and labor and industrial issues such as wage-setting, labor legislation, working conditions, labor market policy, labor dispute settlement, and occupational safety and health. The outcome of social dialogue can also vary, ranging from binding agreements to recommendations, consultation, or merely information sharing. Social dialogue on labor relations issues has been categorized into the following types:

Narrow social dialogue: Social dialogue in a narrow sense takes place when employers' and workers' organizations deliberate on core issues of workers' rights, such as wages, terms and conditions, and rights at work, social security of workers.

Broad social dialogue: This form of social dialogue takes place when social partners discuss broader social issues such as job creation and employment policy.

Wider social dialogue—It comprises tripartite and other relevant interest groups including NGOs and negotiation takes place on legal and policy reform and wider social and economic issues of industrial relations (Ishikawa 2003, 17).

For social dialogue to be effective, social partners should be actively involved not only in different stages of the social dialogue processes that lead to agreements, but also be actively involved in the implementation and monitoring stages of the agreements reached (Ishikawa 2003, 22).

Social dialogue can take place on an informal, ad hoc basis or institutionalized form. Ad hoc social dialogue can take place during labor unrest or transition periods or in the case of temporary economic crises. But formally established and permanent institutions are needed for organizing national social dialogue (Ishikawa 2003, 23). A well-developed institutional framework is pivotal in facilitating the process of social dialogue.

Social dialogue is mainly practiced at the bipartite and tripartite level. At the bipartite level, dialogue occurs only between trade unions and employers' organizations with or without indirect government involvement. On the other hand, tripartitism refers to labor relations in which the State, employers and workers take part in social dialogue, but they are autonomous and interdependent from each other forging common interests (Thamarajakshi 2003, 1). In the tripartite social dialogue process, the government acts as an official party to the dialogue.

While social dialogue of tripartite level is recognized as an effective means for the protection of the rights of the workers and settlement of industrial disputes and maintaining industrial relations, bipartite negotiation cannot always protect the interests of the workers for various reasons, such as unfavorable and authoritarian attitude of management toward trade unions, lack of relevant skills of trade union leaders, and inefficiency in applying bargaining techniques.

9.4 The Role of Government in Social Dialogue

Government, as a key factor in industrial relations, plays a critical role in the advancement and success of social dialogue at the national level. In Bangladesh, the government remains the main actor in tripartite social dialogue. In general, government, in consultation with other social partners, shapes the content of the tripartite agreements and finances the tripartite institutions and to a large extent determines their agendas. In order to make social dialogue effective, it is necessary that the government should respect and give due consideration to the recommendations that emerge from social dialogue. The government should consult effectively with social partners or the national tripartite bodies, before making any decision. In order to promote social dialogue, the government should strengthen the existing institutions of social dialogue at the various levels and recognize legitimate workers' and employers' organizations as valuable partners capable of making contributions to economic and social policy formation. Government's support in the tripartite consultation process can encourage the proactive participation of social partners in policy-making processes, and make social dialogue successful (Ishikawa 2003, 5).

Among the government agencies in Bangladesh, the Ministry of Labor is mainly responsible for the promotion of tripartite or bipartite social dialogue. In order to promote social dialogue, the government should establish an appropriate legal framework and institutions of social dialogue at the national, sectoral, and plant level. In the social dialogue process, the government has to play a strong and effective role in both the public and private sectors. In public sector social dialogue, the government engages with its own employees, while in social dialogue of the private sector, the government takes part in it as a full partner or as a facilitator.

9.5 Legal and Institutional Framework of Social Dialogue in Bangladesh

A sound legal framework is essential for promoting and establishing social dialogue. The legal framework of social dialogue not only refers to ratification of the relevant ILO conventions, but it also means the presence of enabling provisions. Bangladesh ratified the main international instrument on social dialogue—the ILO Convention concerning Tripartite Consultations to Promote the Implementation of International Labor Standards, 1976 (No. 144) in 1979. Since then, social dialogue has been institutionalized through the establishment of a number of bipartite and tripartite mechanisms in Bangladesh, although its application in practice remains weak as it has not yet adopted specific legislation to implement the convention. Even the Bangladesh Labor Act, 2006 does not provide any definition of or any explicit provision on social dialogue.

Given the ineffectiveness of the existing social dialogue mechanisms, the Bangladesh Labor (Amendment) Act 2018 introduced a tripartite advisory council to advise the government on matters relating to law, policy, and labor. The Bangladesh Labor (Amendment) Act 2026 has further expanded the scope of social dialogue by establishing a Tripartite Consultative Council at the national and sectoral level for advising government on the above matters and provides for formation of a National Social Dialogue Forum to determine social and labor relations, to formulate collective bargaining agreements and their enforcement. It is expected that this new legal arrangement will bolster the institutionalization of social dialogue in Bangladesh.

In terms of legal mandate and authority, there are three types of social dialogue institutions in Bangladesh: first type of institution includes those established under the ILO Conventions, such as the Tripartite Consultative Council (TCC) and second type of institutions includes those established under the Bangladesh Labor Act, 2006, such as Collective Bargaining Agents, Participation Committees, Safety Committee and the Minimum Wage Board. The third category refers to institutions established outside the Bangladesh Labor Act, 2006 and includes the Social Compliance Forum, the Crisis Management Committee, etc.

There are four main regular tripartite institutions at the national level in Bangladesh: the Tripartite Consultative Council (TCC), the Minimum Wage Board (MWB), the Tripartite Productivity Committee (TPC), and the National Council for Skill Development and Training (NCSDT). There are some ad hoc tripartite institutions convened at irregular intervals, such as the National Wages and Productivity Commission (NWPC). Apart from these, there are some sector-based tripartite bodies for engaging in social dialogue and monitoring of social compliance such as the Social Compliance Forum for the RMG sector.

9.6 Composition and Mandate of Bipartite and Tripartite Bodies

Tripartite Consultative Council (TCC).

It is the oldest tripartite body consisting of 60 members (20 each representing the government, employers, and workers group). The TCC is the main institution for initiating social dialogue in Bangladesh and discusses various issues of national importance, such as the formulation of labor policy, the amendment of the existing labor laws, the elimination of child labor, the adoption of the ILS, and the overall improvement of industrial relations. After examination of the texts of ILO Conventions and Recommendations and reviewing existing labor laws and practices prevailing in Bangladesh, the TCC recommended to the government the ratification of some of the ILO Conventions. Based on its recommendation, the government made some amendments to the Industrial Relations Ordinance 1979 and ratified ILO Conventions Nos. 144 and 149 (relating to tripartite consultation and nursing personnel). It has also contributed to formulation of the National Labor Policy 2010, the amendment of the Bangladesh Labor Act, 2006, and adoption of the Policy on Prohibition of Hazardous Works by Children. However, the TCC does not have the mandate to deal with a crisis situation or crisis management. Since its establishment, it has made only a few attempts to arrange social dialogue. Irregular meetings, lack of human and financial resources, antagonistic attitude of employers and reluctance of the government to make TCC functional are the main obstacles to its effectiveness. Constant change in the composition of the TCC is another hurdle in making this body an effective institution.

In 2017, the government formed a separate Tripartite Consultative Council for the RMG Sector with representatives from workers, employers, and the government to review the industrial relations, to advise the government to take measures for developing harmonious industrial relations and increasing productivity in the RMG sector.

Participation Committee.

It is a bipartite institution comprising an equal number of representatives of workers and employers for worker-management dialogue. Participation Committee remains an important tool for the bipartite mechanism of social dialogue under the Bangladesh Labor Act, 2006 for maintaining harmonious relationships between workers and employers and minimizing industrial disputes at the very initial stage. It is provided under the Bangladesh Labor Act that the employer and the trade union of the establishment shall take necessary measures to implement the recommendations made by the Participation Committee within the prescribed time-frame. Workers elect their representatives to the Participation Committee, which then meets with management once every month or two to discuss worker concerns. But the role of the Participation Committee is very limited, as such committee exists only in a very few industries and establishments. Only four or five percent of the existing establishments have such Participation Committees. Even these are not working properly due to the fact that there is no adequate and effective representation of workers. Many of them do not even operate regularly. Another criticism is that these Participation Committees have been formed to avoid trade unions in the establishment or factories. One of the main limitations of the Participation Committee as a mechanism of social dialogue is that it has no mandate to raise any demand relating to the rights of the workers. While these committees create space for workers to raise their voice, lack of bargaining capacity of the workers makes them powerless and have no leverage when dealing with management. There are also instances of management influencing the selection of worker representatives to the participation committees. The effectiveness of these committees is also questioned on the grounds of a lack of trust between workers and employers, and "the quality of discussion and implementation of the decisions made" (Hossain and Akter 2021, 20). In fact, participation committees are not a substitute for genuine trade unions or collective bargaining in a factory.

Safety Committee.

The Safety Committee is another forum for employer-worker relations that can initiate social dialogue at the factory level. The Bangladesh Labor Act 2006 makes it compulsory to establish a Safety Committee with the equal participation of management and workers' representatives in every factory where 50 or more workers are employed. The Safety committee is responsible for advising employers on OSH, assisting them in implementing relevant regulations on OSH, monitoring the implementation of OSH regulations, organizing training for various groups in the factory, and liaising with employers, workers, and the Labor Inspectorate to implement such regulations.

National Wages and Productivity Commission (NWPC).

Constituted in 1984, this tripartite body is mandated to make recommendations on the wage structure and other benefits of various categories of workers in various industries on the basis of the productivity of such industries. The Commission, in making recommendations, takes into account the cost of living of workers, the productivity, resources and economic viability of industries, the desirability of fairness and efficiency with reference to the nature of the work, and the need for removal of disparities in wages, if any, between workers of the same category in different units of the same industry. Currently, this commission is mainly engaged in wage-setting of workers in state-owned industries.

Tripartite Productivity Council.

The council, established in 1983, is responsible for formulating policies, plans, and programs on different issues of productivity in the industrial sector through social dialogue. It is headed by the Minister in charge of the Ministry of Industry and comprises 37 members, including secretaries of different ministries, representatives of different chambers, workers federations, and the representatives of education, professional and research institutions. However, so far, its activities are limited to organizing training programs only.

Crisis Management Core Committee.

This tripartite body was established in 2010 in order to resolve industrial unrest in the RMG sector. It was a ten-member tripartite body headed by the State Minister of Labor and Employment. In 2021, this Committee was restructured, and it now comprises 25 members, to look into the overall labor situation and resolve labor unrest in the RMG and other industrial sectors.

Social Compliance Forum for the RMG sector.

Social Compliance Forum, a multi-stakeholder organization, was established in 2005, comprising government representatives, industry associations, buyers, development partners, and civil society. This tripartite forum aims to ensure social compliance in export-oriented industries such as RMG. It also coordinates with the Ministry of Works and the Ministry of Home affairs, BGMEA and BKMEA, buyers, donors, NGOs, and international labor organizations. The main objective of the Social Compliance Forum is to review existing policies on occupational safety and labor welfare aspects of the RMG sector and to provide guidelines for implementing them. The Forum has undertaken some steps for building awareness about laws and developing database on the information of factories.

Currently, the composition of many institutions of social dialogue is narrow and dominated by government officials. The composition of social dialogue institutions, which is broad-based and socially inclusive, tends to be more effective and representative. The existing laws and procedures do not allow NGOs and experts to be partners in social dialogue. Although in some countries, social dialogue institutions include NGOs or experts as partners, which is typically known as tripartite plus membership, this is yet to be accepted as the norm in Bangladesh.

9.7 Necessity of Social Dialogue in the RMG Sector

So far as social dialogue is concerned, the RMG sector needs special attention as it constitutes the main export-earning industry and employs the largest number of workers in Bangladesh. Establishing, reviewing and adjusting minimum wages in the RMG sector remains the most important agenda for social partners and social dialogue is considered the most important avenue to realize it. According to existing law, trade union is allowed in the RMG sector. Both bipartite and tripartite social dialogue mechanisms exist in the RMG sector. But in the RMG sector, social dialogue is not practiced widely, mainly because there are only a few trade unions for more than four thousand RMG factories. Absence of an adequate number of participation committees, trade unions and tripartite mechanisms in most of the factories also prevents social dialogue in this sector.

In recent times, the RMG sector has suffered from increasing labor unrest and serious industrial accidents. Although the Social Compliance Forum and the Crisis Management Committee have been formed to prevent labor unrest, these forums have been largely unsuccessful in mitigating the grievances of the workers due to lack of meaningful social dialogue, except for a few. In 2010, a dialogue was held between the government, BGMEA and the workers to allow trade unionism in the RMG sector to prevent labor unrest. But the recommendations have not been implemented yet. However, there is a clear understanding of the urgency of social dialogue in the RMG sector to meet the prevailing problems in this sector, especially on health and safety issues. Urgency of social dialogue in the RMG sector must be appreciated by government and factory owners given the size of and recurring unrest in the industry. In view of diverse interests involved, RMG is not merely a tripartite, but rather it should be considered as a multi-stakeholder sector. There is widespread support for the belief that social partners in the RMG sector should also include buyers. Therefore, the RMG sector needs a permanent and separate multi-stakeholder mechanism for social dialogue involving the government, employers, buyers, and workers.

9.8 The Practice of Social Dialogue in Bangladesh

The concept of social dialogue is a relatively new one in Bangladesh and is now increasingly practiced in industrial relations in the country as in recent years several processes of social dialogue have taken place. The main issues in the agenda of the social dialogue in Bangladesh include labor law reform, protecting workers' rights from abuse, elimination of child labor, working hours, setting minimum wages, payment of overtime, improving occupational safety and health, social security and rights of women workers. The practice of bipartite negotiation is well-developed in pharmaceuticals and multinational enterprises. While some progress has been made, the practice of social dialogue is still limited in terms of achieving decent work and occupational safety in other sectors. In Bangladesh, social dialogue at the national level is mainly practiced for reforming labor laws, policy and regulations, and addressing critical labor issues. For example, in June 2006, stakeholders in the RMG sector initiated a social dialogue that resulted in the signing of Memorandum of Understanding among the government, the BGMEA and the leaders of the workers. This tripartite MoU was aimed at ending labor unrest in the RMG sector through addressing long-standing grievances of the workers (the National Tripartite Meeting on Social Compliance 2007, 69). The main agendas of MoU were: issuing appointment letters and identity cards to the workers, enhancing bargaining powers of the workers with owners, a one-day weekly holiday for workers, fair trade union practice in the RMG sector, overtime allowances, maternity leave with pay, and formation a Minimum Wage Board to fix minimum wages. The formulation of the Bangladesh Labor Act, 2006 was greatly influenced by the outcome of this social dialogue and many points of MoU had been incorporated in the Act. The 2013 and 2018 amendments to the Bangladesh Labor Act 2006 were adopted on the basis of considerable tripartite consultation.

Social dialogue sometimes occurs in Bangladesh after a major industrial accident that creates public outcry. For example, in November of 2012, a fire in the *Tazreen Fashions* factory in Dhaka killed 113 workers and injured many led to a tripartite social dialogue brought together government, labor, and employers to construct a plan to improve factory fire safety. After the Rana Plaza accident, stakeholders agreed to develop, promote and implement collaborative and participatory mechanisms to ensure fire safety in Bangladesh. In the face of labor unrest and violent protest in the RMG sector for raising wages and other benefits, in September 2024, factory owners in Bangladesh, worker organizations and the interim government signed a tripartite agreement to meet 18 demands of workers including the demands for timely payment of wages, and raising workers' attendance bonus. Similarly, in the wake of widespread persistent industrial unrest across various sectors, the government of Bangladesh, the Bangladesh Employers' Federation and workers represented by the National Coordination Committee for Workers' Education (NCCWE) jointly adopted a declaration on an "Improved and Harmonious National Industrial Relations System in Bangladesh" on December 2024 to work collaboratively to build stable industrial relations system in Bangladesh and to promote harmonious relations between workers and employers for sustainable and resilient economic growth. This significant step undertaken through social dialogue reiterates its importance for harmonious industrial relations and its recognition as a key tool to achieve social justice.

Social dialogue can be channeled into both formal and informal processes. In the absence of a formal institutional framework, informal negotiation can play a key role in resolving a crisis. The opportunity for informal process or channel of social dialogue involving workers, employers, and government, civil society organizations can avoid labor unrest that can erupt into violent conflict. While some progress has been made regarding the collective welfare of workers through social dialogue, it's utility has not yet been fully explored due to a lack of effective legal and institutional arrangement. The potential of social dialogue needs to be fully harnessed for achieving decent work environment and addressing disputes early to prevent them from escalating into violence. It should be acknowledged that while there is a practice of social dialogue at the national and sectoral level, there is hardly any social dialogue at the plant level. In Bangladesh, the social dialogue is also not carried out on broader social and economic issues. The ILO plays a crucial role in initiating social dialogue in Bangladesh and it has identified five areas that requires social dialogue: wage structure and policy reform, labor law reform and strengthening legal protections, a strong national industrial system, social protection and occupational safety and health (ILO 2024).

9.9 Challenges of Social Dialogue in Bangladesh

Social dialogue faces many challenges in Bangladesh, such as, restriction on the formation of trade union, inadequate knowledge about benefits of social dialogue, lack of trust among social partners and institutional deficit. The effectiveness of the tripartite institutions in promoting social dialogue is limited due to various factors. Although there are some tripartite institutions in Bangladesh, which are assigned different functions of industrial relations, only few of them are well-equipped to address the challenges of industrial relations. Moreover, the competence of many tripartite bodies is limited only to wage determination, which constitutes only one part of the problems of industrial relations. Many tripartite bodies suffer from inadequate staff and other logistic support, facilities, detailed rules for their operation and a lack of willingness to engage with workers and employers on regular basis. The predominant role of the government in all the tripartite bodies seriously limits closer "labor-management co-operation" (Mondal 2002, 127). Fragmentation among social partners is also responsible for absence of strong social dialogue practice. Social dialogue to be successful and effective, all the social partners—the government, the employers, and the trade unions must collaborate in good faith and be willing to implement the negotiated agreements. Effective social dialogue through tripartism can take place only if the results of the negotiations are respected by all parties.

The guarantee of freedom of association and the effective recognition of the right to collective bargaining are fundamental requirements for the presence of social dialogue. According to one study, "Autonomous, independent and strong workers' and employers' organizations are crucial for effective social dialogue. The quality of that dialogue is determined by the extent to which the social partners are able to negotiate collective agreements that govern the terms and conditions of employment and regulate labor relations" (Hayter and Stoevska 2011, 1), Generally, countries with high trade union density and collective bargaining density have higher level of social dialogue, restrictions on the formation of trade unions and the right to join trade unions, lack of trust among stakeholders, and inadequate knowledge about its benefits.

In Bangladesh, lack of democratic functioning of the constituents of social dialogue, lack of mutual respect, the mindset of employers, unfavorable attitude of government machinery create obstacles for meaningful social dialogue. Although employers are organized, trade unions are weak in terms of skill, capability, knowledge, and representation. Trade unions, which are important actors in social dialogue, are beset with problems of politicization or political affiliation, lack of legitimacy, patronage of vested interest groups and internal conflict. Thus, the three pillars of industrial relations are not equally strong, which is essential for effective social dialogue.

Exclusion of informal sector workers in the social dialogue process undermines its legitimacy as countries with a large unorganized and informal sector, where these workers cannot participate in trade unions, tripartite discussions cannot reflect the interest and concerns of the vast majority of the working population (Hayter and Stoevska 2011, 1). These views equally hold true for Bangladesh. Lack of initiative on the part of government for social dialogue and lack of awareness about the benefits of social dialogue are also responsible for absence of strong social dialogue practice in Bangladesh. Rahman and Moazzem have identified some reasons for limited success of social dialogue in Bangladesh: "lack of decision-making structures, absence of follow-up and a lack of trust between owners and workers, worker intimidation by owners and a lack of credibility of the government agencies with regard to their acting as honest brokers"(Rahman and Moazzem 2017, 87). Rapid technological changes and the rise of new forms of work due to automation also pose challenges to social dialogue in Bangladesh. Social partners need to realize the potential implications of technological innovation on labor market.

9.10 Suggestions for Strengthening Institutional Framework

Although there is an understanding among the stakeholders about the necessity of social dialogue for its potential role in enhancing productivity, the existing tripartite institutions are ill equipped to promote social dialogue. In this context, recent labor law reforms for establishing tripartite consultative council at the national and sectoral level are a welcoming development. Implementation of this reform initiative may pave the way for institutionalization of social dialogue and holding social dialogue on regular basis. Broadening the legal framework, developing internal rules, and procedures for convening and conducting social dialogue by different institutions, enhancing the capacity of social partners and making them aware of benefits of social dialogue can strengthen the practice of social dialogue. Currently, the scope of the legal framework of social dialogue is very narrow as it does not allow social dialogue in the informal sector. There is also a lack of adequate data, lack of institutional and individual capacity for promoting social dialogue. Most of the current practices of social dialogue are informal and take place outside the legal framework. There is no well-developed procedure or regulations on holding social dialogue. Content and detailed norms of social dialogue are yet to be developed. An action plan or charter of demands on social dialogue needs to be developed for strengthening it at the various levels. Increasing the frequency of meetings of existing institutions and logistical support of the government can further strengthen social dialogue in Bangladesh.

Social dialogue is a continuing process. It should not be conducted as a one-off process. Such dialogue should be based on an equal footing so that it becomes acceptable to all stakeholders. All the stakeholders of social dialogue need to understand that effective, meaningful social dialogue is essential for the sustainable development of the national economy, industrial growth, as well as increasing productivity to compete in the global market.

At the enterprise level, a bipartite mechanism should be used as a core forum for social dialogue. At the national level, the TCC should be used as a core forum for social dialogue. Social dialogue plays an important role in institutional designing of training programs for workers across different sectors. On the other hand, training programs should be undertaken for capacity building for all stakeholders to be engaged in social dialogue. Training programs on social dialogue needs to focus on the impact of digital technologies, automation and the use of artificial intelligence on employment structure. The social partners need a friendly attitude to settle their problems instead of a confrontational one. The broad-based social dialogue involving main stakeholders tends to be more effective.

9.11 Conclusion

Social dialogue is considered an effective strategy for maintaining harmonious industrial relationship, inclusive labor policy design and the realization of the demands of various stakeholders. Despite many potential benefits of social dialogue as mentioned above, it is yet to be fully explored to promote the industrial relation system in Bangladesh. It is also considered one of the foremost ways to achieve workers' right to decent work. In Bangladesh, some successes of social dialogue can be found in the efforts of elimination of child labor, minimum wage determination, occupational safety, and labor law reform. Importance of regular social dialogue on key labor policy and social issues should be particularly highlighted in view of the recurring industrial unrest in the RMG sector and weak government machinery to deal with such unrest and lack of willingness of employers to ensure fulfilment of the genuine and lawful demands of the workers. Despite its proven worth, potential of social dialogue is far from being fully utilized in Bangladesh. Since current mechanisms and practices of social dialogue are not fully effective, the legal and institutional framework on social dialogue should be improved and strengthened. It should be promoted for protection of workers' rights, harmonious relationship between employers and workers, sustainable economic growth, and productivity in the country. The role of social dialogue needs to be appreciated by all stakeholders including government to address the pressing problems in industrial relations in Bangladesh.

Bibliography

Books

Sivananthiran, A. and Ratnam, C.S. Venkata. eds. *Best Practices in Social Dialogue*, ILO Sub-regional Office, New Delhi, 2003.

Chapters in Edited Books

Mondal, Abdul Hye. "Globalisation, Industrial Relations and Labour Policies: The Need for a Renewed Agenda". In *Bangladesh: Economic and Social Challenges of Globalisation*, edited by Muhammed Muqtada, Andrea M. Singh and Mohammed Ali Rashid. University Press Limited. (2002):125-154.

Rahman, Mustafizur and Khondaker Golam Moazzem. "The Legacy of Rana Plaza: Improving Labour and Social Standards in Bangladesh's Apparel Industry". In *Governing Corporate Social Responsibility in the Apparel Industry after Rana Plaza* edited by A. Hira, M. Benson-Rea. Palgrave Macmillan, (2017): 81–109..

Thamarajakshi, R. 2003. "Overview". In *Best practices in social dialogue*, edited by A. Sivananthiran and C. S. Venkata Ratnam, 1–16. New Delhi: ILO Sub-regional Office.

Journal Articles

Feldmann, Horst. 2009. "The quality of industrial relations and unemployment in developing countries". *Review of Development Economics* 13 (1): 56–69.

Ghai, Dharam. 2003. "Decent work: Concept and indicators". *International Labour Review* 142 (3): 113–145.

Reports

Bangladesh: Labour Rights in the supply chain and corporate social responsibility, Report of a FIDH Mission to Bangladesh, June 2008.

Chowdhury, Kabir Ahmed. "Innovative approaches to institutionalize social dialogue, which can benefit workers and employers". A paper presented at workshop on tripartism and social dialogue, organized by ILO area office, Dhaka, 16–17 August 2004.

Hayter, Susan and Stoevska, Valentina. "Social Dialogue Indicators". Technical Brief, ILO, Geneva, November, 2011.

Hossain, Jakir, and Afroza Akter. "Social Dialogue In The 21st Century: Mapping Social Dialogue In Apparel: Bangladesh". Cornell University School of Industrial and Labor Relations & The Strategic Partnership for Garment Supply Chain Transformation. January 2021.

"Improving industrial relations: The importance of social dialogue in Bangladesh", Statement of the ILO, 24 September 2024., https://www.ilo.org/resource/statement/improving-industrial-relations-importance-social-dialogue-bangladesh.

Ishikawa, Junko. 2003. *Key features of National Social Dialogue*. ILO, Geneva: A Social Dialogue Resource Book.

Khabo, Fumane Malebona. "Collective bargaining and labour disputes resolution: Is SADC meeting the challenge?", ILO sub-regional Office for Southern Africa, Harare: ILO, 2008, (Issue paper No. 30).

Minet, Georges. "Some aspects of social dialogue from an ILO standpoint', 24–25 July 2008.

"Social Compliance & Decent work: The Bangladesh Perspective". A collection of Papers and Proceedings of the National Tripartite Meeting on Social Compliance in the RMG Sector, Dhaka, (July 18, 2007).

Social Dialogue Statistics, accessed on http://www.ilo.org/global/statistics-and-databases/statistics-overview-and-topics/social-dialogue/lang%2D%2Den/index.htm.

The 2002 Industrial Report, *EU Report of the High-Level Group on Industrial Relations and change in the EU*, 2002.

The Joint Declaration for "Improved and Harmonious National Industrial Relations System in Bangladesh" https://www.ilo.org/sites/default/files/2024-12/Joint%20Declaration%20on%20National%20IR%20System_1%20December%202024.pdf.

International Instruments and Legislation

The 2008 ILO Declaration on Social Justice for a Fair Globalization., https://www.ilo.org/sites/default/files/2024-12/ILO-Declaration-2008_En.pdf.
The Labour (Amendment) Act 2018 (Act no. 58 of 2018).

CHAPTER 10

An Evaluation of Multi-Stakeholders' Initiatives on Safety of Workers after the *Rana Plaza* Collapse

10.1 Introduction

The Rana Plaza disaster highlights the limits of traditional models of labor regulation in global supply chains and witnessed the emergence of two transnational alliance agreements for the safety of the RMG sectors—"The Accord on Fire and Building Safety in Bangladesh" and "Alliance", that involved multiple actors at diverse levels of governance. The Rana Plaza disaster also exposed a deep crisis in the traditional voluntary code of conduct and audit model, given that garment factories in Rana Plaza and elsewhere had been officially certified despite unsafe working conditions or repeated violations of fundamental worker rights (Vogt 2017, 87). These transnational safety initiatives developed, therefore, an innovative solution combining both voluntary commitments and binding regulations, provided necessary financing for inspection and remediation and monitoring mechanisms. The Rana Plaza disaster demonstrated that shifting production to contractors based in low-income countries with weaker labor standards, limited collective bargaining coverage, and poor enforcement can lock workers in life-threatening working conditions and expose them to an extremely vulnerable situation. These private regulatory initiatives created structures and processes for collective action for collaborative governance to improve labor conditions in the RMG factories. The Rana Plaza disaster also triggered some national initiatives on

A. Al Faruque, *Globalization and Labour Rights*,
https://doi.org/10.1007/978-981-92-3661-9_10

institutional reform, measures such as the formation of the "Sustainability Compact", the adoption of the "National Tripartite Plan of Action of Fire Safety and Structural Integrity", the "Remediation Coordination Council" and reforms of the existing labor laws.

10.2 The Accord

The "Accord", which was signed on May 13, 2013, three weeks after the Rana Plaza collapse, was largely seen as a collaborative effort to create a legally binding agreement, focusing on three overarching areas—inspection, remediation, and workers' empowerment. The Accord mandated the brands to provide funding for independent factory inspection, repair, fire safety training, required factories to establish safety committees, and to prevent unsafe working conditions. The Accord was a ground-breaking tripartite agreement between government, corporations, and workers to create a system of a multilevel governance mechanism that designed innovative legal solution to labor regulatory vacuum. The Accord was a negotiated settlement reached after an intense discussion between NGOs, international union federations (IndustriAll and UNI Global Union), and representatives of over 40 global fashion brands, which are mainly Western clothing giants. Nearly 200 clothing brands and buyers from 20 countries in Europe, Asia, and Australia had signed the Accord. Other signatories include two global trade unions, IndustriALL and UNI, and many Bangladeshi unions. The Accord has been described as a prime example of "the complementarity of consumption- and production-based actors" forging to create innovative governance mechanisms to govern the global supply chain (Reinecke and Donaghey 2015, 724). This role of "complementary capacities" of multiple private actors in generating governance solutions through exercising coalitional power must be understood in light of the dynamics of the global supply chain.

By February 2014, the Accord covered 1600 factories that employ more than 50 percent of the Bangladeshi workers engaged in the RMG sector. The Accord spanned five years. The Accord required mandatory safety inspections of factories by independent experts, public disclosure of inspection reports, and asked suppliers to implement repairs and renovations as determined in the inspections. According to the Accord, workers who refused to work based on a reasonable fear for safety could not be discriminated against or forced to work. Companies were asked to terminate business with any factory that does not comply with the measures required by the Accord. The Accord contains 25 Articles focusing on the safety of workers, creating an independent inspection program, public disclosure of information, dispute settlement, the establishment of new institutions and reform of existing institutions and training.

An important aspect of the Accord was the governance structure of a three-person "steering committee" consisting of an equal number of members representing the signing retailers and trade unions. This Steering Committee was entrusted to develop the standards of the Accord and implement it in collaboration with the Bangladesh Ministry of Labor and Employment. In addition to the steering committee, there was an "advisory committee" that included brands and retailers, suppliers, unions, governments, and nongovernmental organizations. The advisory committee was formed to ensure that a wide range of stakeholders' views are represented in the implementation of the program under the Accord (Rahman 2014, 71).

The signing retailers provided funding for the administration of the Accord. Funding was made through a subscription of each brand, related to the size of its business in the country. The Accord was an important step toward "responsible labor practices" in Bangladesh as it shared the responsibility of improving labor conditions between the government and private actors (Evans 2015, 597).

The Accord was legally binding as by signing it, company signatories made legally binding commitments that were enforceable in the national courts in the country within which they were registered. The legally binding nature of the Accord was tested in two arbitral proceedings brought by the global union signatories—IndustriALL Global Union and UNI Global Union against brand signatories in 2016 and 2018 before the Permanent Court of Arbitration to account for failing to meet Accord terms. The two cases were consolidated in a single proceeding. In both cases, the unions argued that the signatories failed to ensure remediation within the time-frame required by the Accord. In both cases, settlement was reached with lead firms for a considerable amount of money to be expended for fixing safety hazards in more than 150 factories in Bangladesh.

The Accord was designed in a way that it would be implemented in cooperation with the Government of Bangladesh and the ILO. Article 5 of the Accord contained a legally binding international arbitration procedure as a mechanism for the settlement of disputes arising out of its interpretation. It made provisions for hotlines for workers to report safety violations; ensured stronger worker representation in the Steering Committee. The Accord required the parties to complete an initial inspection of each factory within the first two years of its signing and publication of safety reports, remediation, and safety training. The Accord also ensured a high level of transparency by requiring the publication of all inspection reports.

It can be fairly argued that the Accord emerged as a new form of supply-chain governance mechanism that directly engaged buyers in protecting supplier employees, setting, monitoring, and enforcing standards in areas which were traditionally regulated by employers, and governments (Salminen 2018, 415–416). In this way, the Accord represented a "new model of accountability" as it was designed to hold international retailers accountable for the conditions of the workers (Salminen 2018, 620). The Accord's inspection team was also made accountable to workers and retailers (Salminen 2018, 622). The Accord has been viewed as an institutional innovation to trans-national labor governance because, for the first time in the history of industrial relations, such a multi-stakeholder initiative between international trade unions, apparel companies, and trade unions was established (Donaghey and Reinecke 2017). The process of this new governance initiative resembles "transnational collective bargaining" (Donaghey and Reinecke 2017). The Accord has also facilitated the building of associational power of trade unions as "external allies" supported their capacity building by providing funding, training, and organizational space (Zajak 2017, 14). In this way, the Accord, by its very design, represented an important source of "institutional power" (Zajak 2017, 15).

The Accord has facilitated the advancement of the trade union movement in a number of ways, such as by sharing information, by providing a complaint mechanism, and by raising their voice in case of any injustice to workers (Zajak 2017, 14). The number of trade union registrations also increased after the signing of the Accord. The Accord has been described as a significant achievement in respect to improving workers' safety and the working conditions in Bangladesh, as it has addressed some significant issues including transparency and public documentation of inspection results, making them subject to scrutiny of unions, labor rights groups, and mass media (Rahman 2014, 70).

The Accord represented a paradigm shift in the governance of the global supply chain by introducing legally enforceable contractual obligations for remediation efforts, which depart from voluntary corporate social responsibility (CSR) standards. This structural difference between the Accord and traditional CSR initiatives reflects lead firms' seriousness to implement their obligations for remediation and safety measures. Another defining structural characteristic of the Accord is that it is a multi-stakeholder initiative that included both buyers of the developed world, trade unions of Bangladesh and international unions, which truly reflected it as an example of transnational private regulation. The inclusion of worker representatives acts as an important legitimizing factor for the Accord. In fact, the Accord has demonstrated a "paradigm shift", due to its coverage, including 200 member brands, its legally binding nature, the inclusion of unions and sourcing guarantees for manufacturers.

The five-year-long Accord expired in May 2018, and it was succeeded by the 2018 Accord on Fire and Building Safety in Bangladesh on May 31, 2018, and this was continued until May 31, 2021. The new Accord of 2018 extended the program for completion of required remediation work. In 2020, however, after a protracted legal battle, the functions of the Accord were transferred to a national regulatory body that includes the employer association and the government of Bangladesh.

In order to continue and replicate the success of 2013 and 2018 Accords, the a framework agreement was developed titled "International Accord for Health and Safety in the Textile & Garment Industry" containing the same principles of the Accords such as respect for freedom of association, independent labor inspection program, transparency and accountability, provisions for remediation, establishment of safety committee, training and worker awareness program, and an independent complaints mechanism. Currently, it has been replicated in Pakistan.

In November 2023, a "Country Specific Safety Program on Health and Safety in the Bangladesh Textile and Garment Industry" was established under the International Accord of 2023. As of January 2024, a total of 102 global brands and retailers have so far signed this Bangladesh Safety Agreement to continue the inspection and remediation program.

10.3 The Alliance

Although few major U.S. retailers have signed onto the Accord, the majority of the US retailers, most notably, Gap and Walmart have declined to join the Accord, arguing that its binding nature could result in incurring liability in U.S. courts for factory disaster (Greenhouse

2013). Therefore, U.S. and Canadian retailers signed the Alliance—another transnational private regulation and multi-stakeholder initiative. The Alliance focused on compliance with three areas of building safety: electrical, fire, and structural. In contrast to the Accord, the "Alliance" is not legally binding. But like Accord, it called for retailers to fund factory inspections (Greenhouse 2013). The Alliance is based on the voluntary approach, focusing on the traditional corporate social responsibility model instead of highlighting workers' rights.

10.4 Evaluation of the Accord and the Alliance

The Accord and the Alliance were developed as a response to the crisis generated from the Rana Plaza disaster and were never intended to be a permanent solution to the problems of worker safety. Both the Accord and the Alliance formally ended their operations in Bangladesh but established innovative models for transnational labor governance. The Accord and the Alliance are unique, but they are structurally different from each other as models of supply-chain governance. While the Accord creates legally binding obligations as it is an enforceable contract between buyer companies and the global and local representatives of their suppliers' workers, the Alliance is a voluntary arrangement based on CSR mechanism to coordinate funding for inspection and remediation ((Salminen 2018, 415–416). Both the Accord and Alliance initiatives focused on occupational safety and health in the RMG sector and were successful in taking significant efforts for the safety and security of the RMG workers. From June 2013 to September 2018, 91 percent of factory remediation was complete across all Alliance factories, which is 84 percent overall in the Accord factories September 2018 (European Commission 2018, 4). However, the Accord and Alliance have been criticized sometimes for their limited focus on overseeing the safety conditions of workers in the RMG sector and they did not address the deeper and structural issues, such as labor rights, corporate commitment for economic empowerment and fair wages for workers Khan 2020, 2–3).

These initiatives did not all workers and not all manufacturers have made the necessary remedial steps to comply with the Accord and the Alliance. Banerjee and Alamgir argue that these multi-stakeholder initiatives provide legitimacy to multinational corporations and their global brands but they do not address the structural problems of exploitative pricing and procurement process, which are one of the key reasons for deplorable working conditions in the apparel industry (Banerjee and Alamgir 2018). Another criticism of both the Accord and the Alliance is that they did not prohibit unauthorized subcontracting by the supplier factories. However, according to Reinecke and Donaghey, such a narrow focus was necessary for implementing the Accord as an agreed-upon common standard across all factories that wished to supply for any Accord brands (Reinecke and Donaghey 2023, 160). They observe that wide-ranging approaches such as the UN Global Compact or global framework agreements, which cover a wider variety of industrial relations issues, are difficult to implement due to the lack of expertise required and the monitoring involved (Reinecke and Donaghey 2023, 167). On the other hand, the targeted focus of the Accord enabled the stakeholders to implement it effectively, as over 90% of the safety hazards originally identified by the Accord inspectors were eliminated.

Despite some limitations, the Accord and Alliance offered many new opportunities to improve the safety and security of the workers. According to Zajak, despite the Accord's embeddedness in supply-chain capitalism, it facilitated trade unions to develop "their associational capacities, improve their social acceptance, and increase local leverage and protection" (Zajak 2017, 21). The collaborative approach taken in both agreements not only provides collective leverage against those who may seek to free-ride, it entails a mechanism through which diverse actors can be guided to achieve common goals (Zajak 2017, 25). The factory owners complied with the terms and conditions stipulated in the Accord and Alliance and realized that in order to remain internationally competitive and attractive to foreign buyers, it is necessary to ensure safety in the RMG sectors, though they resisted core labor rights.

Anner and Bair correctly claim that while both the Accord and the Alliance expired, they left important legacies in the areas. First, the traditional concerns of working conditions were mainly limited to focusing on the rights of workers. But the Accord and Alliance highlighted the importance of health and safety, and more specifically, they provide crucial guidance on how the difficult issue of building safety might be addressed (Anner and Bair 2022). Second, although these initiatives formally ceased their operation in Bangladesh, the model of collaborative governance by private regulation can inform other efforts to improve labor standards in global supply chain programs, especially on several key principles: enforcement, including binding arbitration, co-governance, and transparency.

10.5 Institutional Reform Initiatives

The *Tazreen* and Rana Plaza disasters revealed the weak capacity of the factories in general and the RMG sector in particular in Bangladesh to effectively ensure safety and proper working conditions. These accidents also underlined the need for strengthening the labor inspectorate. Therefore, apart from the Accord and the Alliance, due to pressures from the international community, the government of Bangladesh had undertaken some measures to provide institutional support to enhance safety in the RMG sector. For example, the upgradation of the Department of Chief Inspector of Factories and Establishment to the Directorate of Industrial Establishment and Factories (DIFE), updating the Fire Service and Civil Defence Department (FSCD) in order to enhance their capacity to carry out inspections and respond to accidents. After the Rana Plaza collapse, the capacity of the DIFE regarding its technical and institutional capacity has been enhanced through the appointment of more skilled inspectors. The Labor Inspection Management Application—a digital inspection application of the DIFE, has been introduced. However, there are some concerns about the quality of safety inspection. Irregular inspection, non-disclosure of information by the DIFE, under-reporting of accidents, injuries, and deaths of workers in the RMG and other industries, absence of internal evaluation of performance of DIFE and weak management of safety-related data are also major problems regarding safety inspection (Moazzem and Ahmed 2023).

After the expiry of the Accord and Alliance in 2018, some transitional steps were taken by the government and the ILO to continue the efforts for factory inspection and remediation. One such initiative is the government of Bangladesh's National Initiative, supported by the ILO. Under the NI, 1549 factories were inspected with the support of the ILO (EU Commission 2018, 29). The establishment of the Bangladesh Sustainability Compact, National Tripartite Action Plan on Fire Safety and Structural Integrity, Remediation Coordination Council (RCC), and RMG Sustainability Council are notable instances of institutional building and reforms.

10.5.1 The Bangladesh Sustainability Compact

As a part of a government initiative after the Rana Plaza disaster, consultations between representatives of the European Union, ILO, the United

States, Canada, and the government of Bangladesh led to the adoption of the Sustainability Compact, another innovative and multilateral approach, for continuous improvements in the protection of labor rights and safety in the RMG and Knitwear Industry in Bangladesh in July 2013. The Compact was built on short and long-term commitments related to three inter-linked pillars: "respect for labor rights; structural integrity of buildings and occupational safety and health; and responsible business conduct". Representatives from industry, including brands, and retailers, employers, trade unions, and other key stakeholders also supported the initiative. According to the Compact, the government of Bangladesh committed to fulfil several time-bound measures including measures to ensure fire and building safety in the RMG sector, measures to protect the right to freedom of association and to bargain collectively, including labour law reform and enforce its labor laws. (Vogt 2017). Unlike the Accord and the Alliance, the government of Bangladesh is responsible for the implementation of the "Compact" with technical assistance from the ILO. But the Sustainability Compact could not accomplish its stated goals due to lack of political willingness of government to implement it and hostile attitude of employers (Vogt 2017).

10.5.2 National Tripartite Action Plan on Fire Safety and Structural Integrity

A National Tripartite Action Plan on Fire Safety was adopted by the Ministry of Labor and Employment of Bangladesh on March 24, 2013, in response to the fire at *Tazreen* Fashions. But after the Rana Plaza disaster, a new component called "Structural Integrity" was added to this Action Plan following consultation with the ILO and the original Action Plan was renamed as the "National Tripartite Plan of Action (NTPA) on Fire Safety and Structural Integrity" in the Ready-Made Garment Sector in Bangladesh. This Action Plan, a time-bound program, was an important outcome of the Sustainability Compact to ensure the long-term sustainability of the RMG sector of Bangladesh through improving fire safety conditions and structural integrity of factory buildings in the RMG sector. It contained the legal, institutional and operational commitments made by the government to be implemented by a set of detailed measures to improve safety in RMG factories. It included worker organizations and employer representatives including BGMEA. The ILO has an advisory role and it offers technical assistance to implement NTPA. The NTPA is closely tied to the Accord. But unlike the Accord, the NTPA is an agreement only between Bangladeshi entities and does not include retailers. In order to facilitate the implementation of the NTPA, the government of Bangladesh formed a High-Level Tripartite Committee. Under the NTPA and Sustainability Compact, a unified fire safety checklist was introduced for use by all relevant government agencies, a workers' safety hotline through the FSCD and a one-stop shop for fire safety licensing and certification, factory-level fire safety needs assessment, delivery of safety related training, and strengthening the capacity of FSCD were established for continuous improvement of workers' safety (Rahman and Moazzem 2017, 95–96).

10.5.3 Remediation Coordination Council (RCC)

After the Rana Plaza collapse, the immediate priority was to inspect all of the RMG factories to address safety concerns. While factories covered under the Accord and the Alliance were inspected, the next step was remediation of factories on the basis of inspection reports. However, financing the cost of remediation was a major obstacle for many factories. It is against this background that the RCC was established as a part of the National Initiative in 2017 with a view to remediating factories based on the findings of the inspection reports. It is a specialized temporary unit of DIFE and was initiated to oversee the remediation of 1549 identified National Initiative factories. The RCC carried out its oversight with financial and technical support from donor countries and the ILO. Although the formation of the RCC was a major step toward improving workplace safety in the RMG sector, it has made little progress in fixing safety issues in the RMG factories. The slow progress of remediation of NI factories can be attributed to lack of cooperation from the factory owners (The Business Standard, 2021), most of the NI factories operating in rented buildings, lack of adequate funding, and the financial emergency induced by the pandemic (Moazzem and Ahmed 2023).

Subsequently, the responsibility of overseeing the remediation of NI factories had been shifted from RCC to the Industrial Safety Unit (ISU)—a newly formed unit of DIFE. Unlike the RCC, the ISU is a permanent unit, and its role includes not only monitoring the remediation of NI factories but also conducting safety inspections in non-RMG factories (Moazzem and Ahmed 2023). However, detailed modalities are yet to be developed regarding its prescribed functions.

10.5.4 RMG Sustainability Council (RSC)

As mentioned above, RSC—a national tripartite initiative, was established to carry forward the principles incorporated in the safety Accords of 2013, 2018, 2021, and 2023 and continue the progress made on inspection and remediation measures under such accords. It is responsible for conducting structural, electrical, fire and life safety and boiler safety inspections, supporting and monitoring the remediation process, arranging safety training, and operating an independent occupational safety and health complaints mechanism for workers in RMG factories. As of January 2023, the RSC covered a total of 1828 factories (Moazzem and Ahmed 2023). However, only 500 RSC-covered factories have completed full initial remediation (Moazzem and Ahmed 2023). It is alleged that the lack of coordination between the RSC and other government agencies slowed down its function (Moazzem and Ahmed 2023). In addition, according to Moazzem and Ahmed, "indirect pressure from employers and government agencies on the RSC staff also prevents them from conducting independent assessments and resolving complaints actively" (Moazzem and Ahmed 2023). However, unlike the Accord, this transitional arrangement is not legally binding and it lacks the legal authority to force brands to implement safety standards.

10.6 Regulatory Reforms

Before the *Rana Plaza* accident, factory owners were generally reluctant and resistant to any effort to improve working conditions and raise wages, and as a result, workers and unions resorted to demonstrations, strikes, and violence very often to realize their demands. The Rana Plaza disaster sparked huge demands for improving the regulatory framework on fire and safety, which resulted in a number of amendments in 2013 to the Bangladesh Labor Act 2006. The amendments reformed the provisions relating to freedom of association and collective bargaining, and improved the legal obligations of factory owners to ensure workers' safety and security as well as workers' rights at the workplace. The 2013 amendments required the election of worker representatives in trade union by secret ballot, ensured the smooth registration of trade unions, established Health and Safety Committees in factories with more than 50 workers and elaborated collective bargaining rights. These favorable changes were accompanied by support from international donor agencies and trade unions through funding for trade union development (Zajak 2017, 6).

After the Rana Plaza disaster, regulatory reforms and changes also included an increase in the minimum wage of the RMG workers. Overall, regulatory reforms as demanded by international retailers and European and US governments after the Rana Plaza disaster were indeed successful in improving working conditions of the RMG workers in Bangladesh (Zajak 2017, 25). These reform initiatives were not limited to ensuring workers' safety as they also addressed the demands for an increase in minimum wage and reducing barriers in forming trade unions.

10.7 The Rana Plaza Compensation Scheme

The existing legal framework on compensation in Bangladesh is grossly inadequate for injured workers or family members of the deceased workers who died due to industrial accidents. The *Tazreen* Fashions Fire accident, followed by the Rana Plaza collapse, highlighted the need for an effective compensation scheme to be in place for those workers, who were injured or killed in such horrific industrial accidents. In order to provide compensation to the Rana Plaza disaster survivors, an Agreement was signed in November 2013 between the government, leading buyers, employers' and workers' organizations as well as NGOs for establishing a trust fund called "The Rana Plaza Donor Trust Fund". The Fund was constituted with contributions from companies to provide compensation to victims and their families and injured workers. The agreement was based on principles outlined in the ILO Convention No. 121 on Employment Injury Benefits (1964). A compensation formula was calculated to ensure payments were sufficient to provide an income for the lifetime of all beneficiaries, taking into account different individuals' needs and circumstances. The agreement known as the "Rana Plaza Arrangement" has been described as a "hybrid mechanism" that recognizes "workers' right to compensation for injury or death but relies on the voluntarism of corporate social responsibility for funding" as global apparel companies donated funds voluntarily (Prentice 2021, 2). The amount of compensation paid to injured workers and families of deceased workers met the international standards of worker compensation for occupational injury or death specified in the ILO Convention No. 121. The arrangement of compensation after the Rana Plaza accident was based on the right-based approach. This was a significant step toward providing effective compensation for the workers. According to Prentice, by calculating claims for compensation in line with the ILO standards, the "Rana Plaza Arrangement" recognized workers' entitlement to rights that had been denied earlier (Prentice 2021, 2). This reflected a shift from previous approach taken in the *Spectrum* accident compensation scheme (Spectrum factory collapse 2005) where family members of the deceased workers received lump sum amount of compensation relinquishing their legal right to sue. As the amount of compensation under the existing labor law is grossly inadequate, the Rana Plaza survivors were compensated using a different approach called "meaningful" compensation as it is based on the international standards set by the ILO in its Employment Injury Benefits Convention No. 121(Prentice 2021). They got compensation from the Rana Plaza Donor Trust Fund without impacting their statutory rights of compensation under the existing laws in Bangladesh.

However, the above-mentioned donor-led funds were ad hoc and short-term in nature. It has been argued that while such initiatives have been able to meet the immediate needs of victims and their families, such monetary compensation initiatives have been criticized on the ground that they prioritized compensation over criminalizing the global and local actors involved in such incidents (Prentice 2021). Both payment of compensation to workers on the basis of international standard and accountability of factory owners' should guide the future development of law for long-term solution Needless to say, that the amount of compensation under the Bangladesh Labor Act 2006 is inadequate and should be increased to reflect the ILO Convention 121, the Fatal Accident Act 1855 and the examples of standard of compensation paid to the victims of the Rana Plaza disaster. Although Bangladesh is yet to ratify the convention, compensation standard set by the Rana Plaza donor trust fund can be replicated in case of other industrial accidents in Bangladesh.

Since the Rana Plaza collapse, an Employment Injury Insurance scheme in Bangladesh has been proposed to provide compensation to workers in event of workplace accident or disease. Such a scheme, if materialized, will supplement the compensation provisions under the Bangladesh Labor Act which is grossly inadequate. However, in the aftermath of Rana Plaza, the government amended section 232 of the Bangladesh Labor Act 2006 to constitute a fund specifically for workers engaged in hundred percent export oriented such as the RMG or foreign exchange industrial sectors, which will be used for the benefit of those working in these sectors. The Bangladesh Labor Rules 2015 elaborated the functions, formulation, and administration of this "central fund" for the hundred percent export-oriented industry (The Bangladesh Labour Rules 2015, rules 212–226). A tripartite framework comprising of representatives from the government, workers, and employers was prescribed for management of this fund (The Bangladesh Labour Rules 2015, rule 212 (2). The fund is to be mainly sourced from a mandatory contribution of 0.03% of the total amount of work order along with any profit made from investment of the fund (The Bangladesh Labour Rules 2015, rule 214). It also has three other sources which are voluntary in nature: donations made by the buyers, the government, and foreign individuals or organizations (The Bangladesh Labour Rules 2015, rule 214). This fund would then be split equally across two accounts: Beneficiaries Welfare Account and Emergency Account (The Bangladesh Labour Rules 2015, rule 214). It is expected that effective operation of this fund will be useful for promoting welfare of workers of these sectors.

10.8 Conclusion

The aftermath of the Rana Plaza collapse witnessed the emergence of private regulatory initiatives on safety and security of workers in the RMG sector that supplemented public regulation. The Rana Plaza disaster exposed inadequacy of both public regulation and traditional CSR model to ensure health and safety issues and to prevent accident of catastrophic scale. In this regard, the Accord and Alliance, contractual arrangements supported by legally enforceable mechanisms, represent a major shift in supply-chain governance. The main goals of these initiatives were factory inspection, remediation efforts, safety training programs, and compensation to the workers. Although these private regulatory initiatives faced resistance from the factory owners because of fears of loss of competitive advantage, and they were never intended to be a permanent solution to the governance of worker safety, they left a legacy of collective action and collaborative governance model that supplemented public regulation in effective way and were leveraged to develop nationally based institutions such as Sustainability Compact, Tripartite Plan of Action of Fire Safety, and Structural Integrity (NTPA), Remediation National Coordination Cell (RCC), and RMG Sustainability Council.

The Accord and Alliance have made provisions for remediation financing to make improvements in safety of RMG sector, which led to an increase in compliance-related cost but despite these compliance cost RMG sector has thrived. Inspection, monitoring, and remediation are continuing process and RMG factories need to be continually monitored, inspected, and remedied to avert industrial accident. The success of the Accord and Alliance demonstrates that in view of the weak regulatory capacity of the nation-state, transnational forms of labor governance through multi-stakeholders' initiatives can fill the regulatory vacuum at the domestic level. Labor movements have traditionally relied on domestic legislation to improve labor standards, but transnational governance in the form of Accord and Alliance can strengthen labor's power in collective bargaining.

These multi-stakeholder initiatives, though they are legally different, have also brought significant institutional changes in corporate responsibility from purely voluntary nature of CSR to legally binding arrangement in global supply chain. These initiatives were also successful in creating greater awareness of the responsibility of global brands to engage in ethical sourcing practices and in improving working conditions. Despite these transnational governance initiatives' substantial achievements in improving workplace safety, government and industry actors in Bangladesh tried to resist them fearing that improved labor standards would threaten managerial control over labor forces (Bair, Anner, And Blasi 2020). However, due to persistent campaign of unions and pressure from international actors, the government of Bangladesh initiated institutional and regulatory reforms. Alongside these private and public initiatives, Rana Plaza's owner, and factory managers faced criminal prosecution for failures of exercising due diligence in ensuring safety of workers.

After the Rana Plaza collapse and the subsequent changes to Bangladesh's labor laws, the RMG sector continues to thrive making the country the second largest garment producer in the world, after only China. This is due to the fact that collaborative governance approach of brands and buyers with suppliers and Bangladeshi entrepreneurs helped improve compliance with standards on health and safety aspects of industry. Most of the RMG owners now have accepted compliance as an integral part of their business to survive and remain competitive.

Despite many initiatives taken after the Rana Plaza tragedy, however, there are still some obstacles hindering the improvement of workers' safety in Bangladesh. In fact, the government-led initiatives have limited success in ensuring the safety due to lack of effective monitoring, inadequate capacity of safety monitoring entities (e.g., DIFE and ISU), non-disclosure of information, and lack of accountability of its inspectors as individuals and the DIFE as an institution. In this regard, initiatives need to be undertaken to increase the capacity building of inspectorate, involvement of the workers representatives in the safety committees of factories, enhance collaboration between DIFE, RSC, and other agencies and ensure accountability of all stakeholders (Moazzem and Ahmed 2023) because improving occupational safety and health and labor rights is a shared responsibility of governments, manufacturers, brands, buyers, workers, unions, and consumers. Making information about the safety conditions of factories, including fire safety and building codes, readily available to workers and placing robust grievance redressal mechanisms in all factories is essential to ensure compliance with safety measures and accountability of DIFE, RSC, and other agencies (Moazzem and Ahmed 2023).

Since the Rana Plaza disaster, Bangladesh has made progress in improving occupational safety and health in the RMG sector, but there are many challenges lie ahead in extending the framework in other sectors including the informal economy.

Bibliography

Chapters in Edited Books

Anner, Mark, and Jennifer Bair, "The Bangladesh Accord and Alliance:addressing building safety through global supply chain co-governance" in: *Handbook on Globalization and Labor Standards,* ed., K. A. Elliot, Edward Elgar Publishing (2022): 416–431.

Rahman, Mustafizur, and Khondaker Golam Moazzem. "The Legacy of Rana Plaza: Improving Labour and Social Standards in Bangladesh's Apparel Industry". In *Governing Corporate Social Responsibility in the Apparel Industry after Rana Plaza* edited by A. Hira, M. Benson-Rea. Palgrave Macmillan, (2017): 81–109..

Reinecke, Juliane and Donaghey, Jimmy, "The Politics of Collaborative Governance in Global Supply Chains: Power and Pushback in the Bangladesh Accord" in Panagiotis Delimatsis, Stephanie Bijlmakers, M. Konrad Borowicz (eds.), *The Evolution of Transnational Rule-Makers through Crises,* Cambridge University Press, (2023):154–173, 160.

Journal Articles

Bair, Jennifer, Mark Anner, and Jeremy Blasi. 2020. The political economy of private and public regulation in post-Rana plaza Bangladesh. *International Labour Review* 73 (4): 969–994.

Banerjee, S. B., and F. Alamgir. 2018. Contested compliance regimes in global production networks: Insights from the Bangladesh garment industry. *Human Relations* 72 (2): 272–297. https://doi.org/10.1177/0018726718760150.

Donaghey, Jimmy, and Juliane Reinecke. 2017. When industrial democracy meets corporate social responsibility - a comparison of the Bangladesh accord and Alliance as responses to the Rana plaza disaster. *British Journal of Industrial Relations.* 56 (1): 14–42.

Evans, Benjamin A. 2015. Accord on fire and building safety in Bangladesh: An international response to Bangladesh labor conditions. *North Carolina Journal of International Law* 40:597–626.

Khan, Zobaida. 2020. Rethinking post-Rana plaza transnational labour governance: A proposal for a transformative governance model. *University of Western Ontario Law Journal* 10 (2): 1–41. https://doi.org/10.5206/uwojls.v10i2.9445.

Prentice, Rebecca. 2021. Labour rights from labour wrongs? Transnational compensation and the spatial politics of labour rights after Bangladesh's Rana plaza garment factory collapse. *Antipode* 53 (6): 1767–1786.

Reinecke, Juliane, and Jimmy Donaghey. 2015. After Rana plaza: Building coalitional power for labour rights between unions and (consumption-based) social movement organisations. *Organization* 22 (5): 720–740.

Salminen, Jaakko. 2018. The accord on fire and building safety in Bangladesh: A new paradigm for limiting buyers' liability in global supply chains? *American Journal of Comparative Law* 66:411–451.

Vogt, Jeffrey S. 2017. The Bangladesh sustainability compact: An effective tool for promoting workers' rights? *Politics and Governance* 5 (4): 80–92. https://doi.org/10.17645/pag.v5i4.1093.

Zajak, Sabrina. 2017. International allies, institutional layering and power in the making of labour in Bangladesh. *Development and Change* 48 (5): 1007–1030.

Zillur, Rahman, Md. 2014. Accord on "fire and building safety in Bangladesh": A breakthrough agreement? *Nordic Journal of Working Life Studies.* 4 (1): 69–74.

Reports

"2018 Accord on Fire and Building Safety in Bangladesh: May 2018", accessed on May 5, 2025., https://docs.pca-cpa.org/2016/02/2018-Accord-full-text.pdf.

"Bangladesh Agreement on Health And Safety In The Textile And Garment Industry", Addendum To The International Accord For Health And Safety In The Textile And Garment Industry, 1 November 2023, accessed on May 7, 2025., https://internationalaccord.org/wp-content/uploads/2023/11/CSSP-Bangladesh-Agreement_public-version.pdf

Bossavie, Laurent, Yoonyoung Cho, and Rachel Heath. "The Effects of International Scrutiny on Manufacturing Workers: Evidence from the Rana Plaza Collapse in Bangladesh", Social Protection and Jobs Global Practice (November 2019), 1. Policy Research Working Paper 9065.

Greenhouse, Steven, "U.S. retailers see big risk in safety plan for factories in Bangladesh", New York Times, May 22, 2013, accessed on May 7, 2025, http://www.nytimes.com/2013/05/23/business/legal-experts-debate-us-retailersrisks-of-signing-bangladesh-accord.html?pagewanted=all.".

http://trade.ec.europa.eu/doclib/docs/2013/july/tradoc_151601.pdf.

Implementation of the Bangladesh Compact Technical Status Report, European Commission, September 2018, accessed on May 15, 2024, https://www.europarl.europa.eu/meetdocs/2014_2019/plmrep/COMMITTEES/INTA/DV/2018/11-19/Sustainable_Compact_EN.pdf.

International Accord on Health and Safety in the Textile and Garments Industry, accessed on May 6, 2025., https://internationalaccord.org/about-us/.

Moazzem, Khondaker Golam and Ahmed, Tamim. "How are local monitoring agencies faring 10 years after Rana plaza?". *The daily* The Star, 5 May 2023, accessed on August 22, 2024, https://www.thedailystar.net/opinion/views/news/how-are-local-monitoring-agencies-faring-10-years-after-rana-plaza-3311051.

"Over 100 brands sign the Bangladesh Safety Agreement", accessed on May 7, 2025., **https://internationalaccord.org/over-100-brands-sign-the-bangladesh-safety-agreement/**.

"RCC factories remediation sees slow progress", *The Business Standard,* December 02, 2021, accessed on September 22, 2024, https://www.tbsnews.net/economy/rmg/rcc-factories-remediation-sees-slow-progress-338023.

Sustainability Compact for Bangladesh., http://trade.ec.europa.eu/doclib/docs/2013/july/tradoc_151601.pdf.

Legislation

Bangladesh Labour (Amendment) Act, 2013 (Act No. 30 of 2013).

The Bangladesh Labour Rules 2015, rules 212–226.

CHAPTER 11

Protection of Migrant Workers' Rights: A Bangladesh Perspective

11.1 Introduction

The mobility of people across international borders, whether for trade or protection from persecution or work, has become an intrinsic feature of globalization. The dynamics of labor migration can be partially explained by competition among states for both demand and supply for labor. Globalization has created a strong global demand for skilled workers in labor markets due to the unequal allocation of skills on the global market (Panizzoni 2011). On the other hand, the abundance of cheap labor in many developing countries explains the supply side of labor migration. International migration has been described as one of the major driving forces shaping processes of reorganization of production in global supply chains and the acceleration of international trade (Triandafyllidou 2024, 6). In this way, the economic globalization process has significantly changed the patterns of international migration (Triandafyllidou 2024, 6). This cross-border mobility of people has been accelerated by the economic globalization process and is a part of global integration that is facilitated by movements of commodities, capital and improved communication (Casdes and Miller, 2003, 4).

The causes of international labor migration are numerous and complex and are popularly explained by both "Push" and "Pull" factors. "Push factor" is characterized by poor living conditions, lack of employment opportunities, burden of paying family debt and abject poverty in the

A. Al Faruque, *Globalization and Labour Rights*,
https://doi.org/10.1007/978-981-92-3661-9_11

country of origin such as Bangladesh that drive large number of people to leave in search for better life, economic security, and decent life. International labor migration is also driven by "pull factor" that refers to the availability of well-paid work, economic security, and a higher living standard in developed countries, which attracts people from developing countries to migrate (Cholewinski 1997, 18). Migration process has also been analyzed and conceptualized as a "function of aspirations and capabilities" of peoples to migrate within given sets of perceived geographical opportunity structures" (Haas 2021, 2). This framework, closely aligned with the pull factors, and it views "human mobility as people's capability to choose where to live – including the option to stay"(Haas 2021, 2). The labor migration from Bangladesh is intertwined with the forces of globalization and both push and pull factors.

Migrant workers are often exposed to vulnerable situations in host states not only because of precarious working conditions and lack of legal recognition (Guchiten and Pecoud 2009, 2), but also because they are, to a large extent, perceived negatively in countries of destination as they are often seen as potential competitors by the domestic labor force. Many of them reach destination countries after embarking on perilous journeys in which some of them may fall prey to organized criminal groups, including smugglers, and become victims of trafficking. They also face many social problems in host states as sometimes they become victims of anti-immigrant rhetoric from right-wing political parties, and sometimes they are blamed for the rise in criminal activities and are considered to be a threat to social order and stability in the host states. Migrant workers are also harassed or pushed into an economically vulnerable position and are often denied medical care and other social goods. Migrant workers receive legal treatment in host states, which is generally less than the treatment enjoyed by the citizens regarding employment, access to justice, labor rights, and access to health care and education.

Ensuring the safety and well-being of migrant workers in host countries remains a great concern. In particular, female migrants often face various gender-specific discrimination during their recruitment as gender norms and common perceptions of typical roles of women and men in the division of labor often determine their employment in the domestic and care-giving services and the agriculture sector (CREST and IOM 2020). While labor migration often enhances women's economic empowerment, many women migrant workers, particularly those in the informal sector with low-wage and low-skill jobs, face unique barriers to decent work and social protection (CREST and IOM 2020, Sargean 2014). Sometimes, they do not get promised wages and other benefits. As most women migrate abroad as domestic workers, they are subject to discrimination, sexual harassment and are paid low wages since many destination countries have not yet ratified the ILO Domestic Workers Convention in 2011.

11.2 Plight of Irregular Migrant Workers

While all migrant workers are at risk of discrimination in destination countries, specific groups of migrant workers, such as temporary, irregular migrant workers, and migrant domestic workers, are particularly vulnerable to such risk. The recent years have witnessed a significant increase in temporary and irregular migrant workers in host states, partly due to the "push" factor and partly due to the strict control of borders. Irregular migration arises from the unlawful crossing of a border of a state without appropriate documentation. Strict regulation of population movement across national boundaries remains a fundamental contradiction of contemporary globalization that promotes free borders for the movement of people, goods, capital, services and information (Bedford 2022, 22). Tighter border control, restrictive immigration policies of destination countries, and deliberate misinformation about employment opportunities and living conditions in destination countries have resulted in illegal cross-border movement of a large number of undocumented migrants who are paid lower wages, and put in precarious working conditions characterized by inadequate safety and security, suppression of labor rights, and erosion of collective bargaining power. As restrictions on legal entry become tighter, more people are seeking opportunities for work in developed countries through illegal means.

Temporary and irregular migrant workers are also exposed to the risk of arbitrary detention, physical or sexual abuse, the risk of statelessness, forced labor, restrictions on freedom of movement, and criminalization of their situation. As non-nationals of host countries, temporary or irregular migrant workers are sometimes subjected to deportation. They are often compelled to work in informal sectors of the economy, consequently, they are not being protected by labor law (Guchiten and Pecoud 2009, 2). In fact, irregular migrant workers are exposed to downward pressure on wages and benefits or face unemployment. As significant numbers of migrant workers are undocumented, temporary, and irregular in nature, which is often categorized as illegal migration. The informalization of the economy has a nexus to a persistent lack of rights of irregular migrant workers. For example, they are not given a written job contract. Engaging irregular migrant workers in informal sectors also results in irregular and delayed payment, and physical abuse. These vulnerability of irregular migrant workers compel them to accept extremely precarious living and working conditions that perpetuate discrimination and exploitation and lock them in a position of what is known as profound commodification of labor (Rosewarne 2010). They are treated as a source of cheap labor and resultantly, they do not get the protection of law and their rights are hardly respected (Guchiten and Pecoud 2009). Public concerns over the economic and social impacts of irregular migrants have also influenced many countries to restrict the movement and rights of irregular migrants.

The desperation of people of developing countries to seek job in abroad often manifests in their intense competition to engage with intermediaries and they become susceptible to abuses in the recruitment process. Being charged with excessive fees in sending countries and lured by non-existent jobs, they often land in detention centers in destination countries. An unregulated sponsorship system that requires employers to sponsor migrant workers tends to be exploitative and migrant workers' travel and identification documents are withheld, and original employment contracts are substituted. The sponsorship system also limits the ability of migrant workers to change their employers, sponsors, or workplaces as in some destination countries, creates risks of labor exploitation, and restricts their internal labor market mobility (ILO 2023). In other situations, migrant workers may be terminated without notice and may remain unprotected by laws of such countries. In this way, this sponsoring system creates "unequal power dynamic between the employer and the migrant worker" that eventually leads to a high level of dependency of migrant workers and makes them vulnerable to discrimination.

Apart from recruiting agencies, there are many types of sub-agents involved in international labor migration, whose services are generally not registered and their services are informally procured by the recruiting agencies. This allows for fraud and corruption in the recruitment process. In particular, many fake recruiting agencies are involved in such fraud and corruption. Migrant workers, who suffered from ill-treatment, discrimination and abuse, may be reluctant to lodge complaints and seek redress from employers due to fear of retaliation, including termination or non-renewal of the employment contract.

For example, according to a study, a significant number of the victims of forced labor in the UK are irregular migrant workers who have ended up vulnerable to trafficking and exploitation due to restrictions on foreign unskilled workers' access to the UK's labor markets (Crane, LeBaron, Allain and Behbahani 2017). Forced labor is also evident in other developed countries.

Pervasive discrimination and exploitation also exist in the context of migrant domestic workers. Women constitute the majority of domestic workers. Like irregular migrant workers, domestic workers are frequently excluded from the scope of labor laws of host states, leaving them in a vulnerable and unprotected condition. In some countries, however, the legal framework has been improved through the adoption of special laws and regulations or developing model contracts for the employment of domestic workers, though these may fall short of providing a full level of rights and protections under national laws. Absence of adequate legal safeguards for migrant domestic workers, informal or semi-formal nature of the employment relationship, stereotyped views regarding gender roles and the undervaluation of their work lead to multiple forms of discrimination and vulnerability.

Recent years have witnessed a significant increase in labor migration along the migration "fault lines", which implies an economic disparity between poor countries and developed countries that trigger migratory flows through clandestine journeys along dangerous sea and land routes (Grant 2011, 48). Many illegal migration flows take place across these "fault lines" and eventually reach destination countries. According to Grant, "The concept of fault line is a useful way of thinking about individual protection needs, and also about the wider asymmetries in human development, human security and human rights which drive irregular migration" (Grant 2011, 49). Three of these fault lines that attracted global attention, run along the land border between Mexico and the United States, the maritime borders between North Africa and Southern Europe, and between the Horn of Africa and the southern Arabian Peninsula (Grant 2011, 48). In recent years, frontier deaths have increased on the "fault lines" exposing the risk and vulnerability of irregular migrant workers to life-ending situations.

Over the last years, in a desperate move for migration, many Bangladeshi people are taking deadly risks of crossing the sea by boats, or desert and forest to reach some European Countries or the USA in search of better opportunities. In particular, the migration from Bangladesh to

Italy through Libya by boat using the dangerous route of the Mediterranean Sea through Libya often led to the death of many Bangladeshi people (The Business Standard 2024).

11.3 Nexus between Irregular Migration and Human Trafficking

The international migration process has a highly exploitative criminal dimension that is exemplified by the smuggling of people and human trafficking. The desperation of people living in abject poverty, or under repressive political regimes or conflict zones caused by violent internal armed conflict or international armed conflict try to escape such situations and fall prey to human traffickers. Some criminal organized groups take advantage of this desperation and traffic them to another country in exchange for extortion of significant sums of money (Bedford 2022, 22). Although it is very difficult to obtain data on smuggling, it is now widely recognized that human trafficking is a very profitable business in most parts of the world. Human traffickers take advantage of a desire by increasing number of people to escape human rights abuses, armed conflict, civil unrest, environmental degradation, and poverty by moving to another State where opportunities for a safe and better life are perceived to exist. Another dimension of irregular migration is that they are often tapped in human trafficking, which is often clandestine in nature and it involves the violation of basic human rights and is commonly identified with sexual exploitation. Unlike smuggling, trafficking involves exploitation of women, men, and children who are often "sold" for sexual services, bonded labor, domestic servitude, forced marriage, organ trading, and begging (Bedford 2022, 22). Victims of trafficking are sometimes stripped of their travel documents and kept in isolated places so as to make escape difficult and end up in debt bondage. Combating human trafficking in the guise of migration is often very difficult as it thrives in conditions of labor market exclusion and disempowerment in the country of origin, demand for illegal labor in destination countries, and the lure of well-paid jobs abroad (Bedford 2022, 22).

11.4 Labor Law, Migration Law, and Human Rights Framework: Complexities and Intersections

Generally, migrants and their status are dealt with predominantly by the legal system of the receiving state that regulates the process of migration. The labor law of a receiving country is also relevant to migrant workers in different ways: it may define their rights, affect the supply of workers, increase the control of employers over the supply of labor and especially, control over migration status; determine access to legal system, and increase the temporariness and precariousness of work relations (Freedland and Costello 2014). On the other hand, national migration laws and policies determine migrant workers' status, define their conditions of entry and stay, employment relations, and access to social entitlements and public services (Diller 2022, 85). Migration law may restrict migrant workers' labor rights by placing high legal hurdles in the entry of migrant workers in various ways, such as putting restrictions on irregular migrants seeking to join or form trade unions, and thereby further exacerbating the plight of migrant workers (Freedland and Costello 2014). Labor or migration laws of host countries may also restrict access to the labor market and social security protection to certain categories of migrants such as undocumented migrants. The restrictive migration laws constraining conditions of entry, and employment relations, and strict administrative measures may serve to legitimize the precariousness that contributes to migration vulnerability and may institutionalize insecurity (Diller 2022, 86).

Migrant workers' rights are now firmly grounded in human rights law. Initially, migrant workers' rights were not recognized by international human rights law. This traditional approach of international human rights law toward migrant workers stems from the fact that, generally, the notion of human rights is intractably bound up with the structure of the nation-state and citizenship and human rights are applied to citizens within the state territory. This inherent link between human rights and the territorial notion of the nation-state excluded migrants from the universal norms of human rights for a long time (Cholewinski 1997, 6). It has also been reflected in the Universal Declaration of Human Rights (UDHR) 1948, which recognizes the right to leave a country, but does not recognize the right to enter any particular state.

But this traditional state-centric notion of human rights in relation to migrant workers began to change with the increasing integration of migrant rights within the international treaties on human rights. The migrant workers' rights as human rights have been gradually recognized by international human rights law and their rights are now treated as a group rights. The overarching principle of states' obligation to protect human rights implies that states have an obligation to protect "everyone", including migrants, regardless of their immigration status(Grant 2011, 56). The intrinsic value of the human rights framework suggests that in the absence of a national regulatory framework or in the case of a deficient legal framework on migrant workers' rights, it can enable the protection of migrant workers, and inform the policies of receiving states. It also posits that rights of migrant workers be grounded in the universality of human rights, which postulates that their rights is based on a "sense of shared humanity" rather than membership of a specific political community (Dembour and Kelly 2011, 1–2). According to Weissbrodt, the duty of states entails them to protect migrants as international human rights law requires "the equal treatment of citizens and non-citizens" with regard to political rights and economic and social rights (Weissbrodt 2003). Similarly, the principle of non-discrimination, a crucial element of protection of migrant workers, is deeply embedded in human rights norms. On the same vein, it has been claimed that migrant workers are entitled to the benefits of social security in the same manner as citizens enjoy (Lamarche 2014, 14). Human rights framework provides, thus, a normative basis of state' obligation's protect any person and to prevent harm and deprivation directly or by the action of others (Diller 2022).

11.5 ILO Conventions on Rights of Migrant Workers

The main ILO Conventions relating to migrant workers' rights include the 1949 Migration for Employment Convention (ILO Convention 97) and 1975 Migrant Workers (Supplementary Provisions) Convention (ILO Convention 143). The 1949 Migration for Employment Convention (ILO Convention 97) aims to facilitate the movement of labor and to ensure equality of treatment between regular migrant workers and nationals regarding remuneration, hours of work, overtime arrangements, holidays with pay, minimum age for employment, apprenticeship and training, membership of trade unions, collective bargaining, accommodation and social security. The Convention No. 97 also spells out measures to regulate the conditions in which labor migration should occur. For example, it requires state parties to take measures for free services of assistance and accurate information to migrant workers, and to take steps against misleading information on the migration process (Article 7).

On the other hand, Convention No. 143 asks state parties to respect the basic human rights of migrant workers, to take measures to prevent and suppress the abusive migration process, and the "illegal" employment of migrant workers. Like Convention No. 97, Convention No 143 contains a number of provisions regarding equality of treatment of migrant workers with nationals and citizens in respect of guarantees of security of employment. Provides protection against irregularity of migrant workers who have lost their job and calls upon states to formulate a national policy on equality of opportunity and treatment between migrant workers and nationals (Article 10). Such national policy on equal opportunity may cover educational programs, and equal treatment in working conditions. While under international law, there is no obligation on states to regularize migrant workers, Convention No. 143 expressly allows state parties to regularize illegal migrants and to provide them with employment.

However, both ILO Conventions No. 97 and 143 exclude temporary migrant workers and domestic workers from the scope of their application. In this context, the adoption of the Domestic Workers Convention No. 189 and its supplementing Recommendation No. 201 was a significant step toward recognition of the value of domestic work and the rights of these workers who also include migrant workers. Thus, these instruments aim at the protection of all domestic workers as they do not distinguish between nationals and non-nationals employed as domestic workers. These instruments impose some specific obligations on the ratifying states to ensure that migrant domestic workers receive a written job offer or employment contract before departing for the destination country, and effective protection for migrant domestic workers from abusive recruitment practices. They also aim to ensure equal treatment between domestic workers and workers generally in relation to work hours, overtime compensation, rest and leave periods, and provisions of social security.

The ILO Protocol 2014 to the Forced Labor Convention also requires states to prevent abusive practices in the recruitment process and to ensure migrant workers' access to appropriate and effective remedies, including compensation.

11.6 Convention on the Protection of the Rights of all Migrant Workers and Members of their Families, 1990

The Convention on the Protection of the Rights of All Migrant Workers and Members of their Families, 1990 (CMW) is specifically designed as a human rights treaty for the protection of the rights of migrant workers It sets out a "rights-based approach" to labor migration and protection of migrant workers. This Convention lays down a comprehensive set of civil, political, economic, and social rights for migrant workers, including the right to equal protection under labor laws, non-discrimination laws, and family laws (Ruhs 2017, 172–176). It has been asserted that this Convention has been formulated to protect one of the most vulnerable groups of people. It sets the international standard in terms of migrants' access to fundamental rights, the labor market, education, and health systems in a host country (Guchiten and Pecoud 2009, 1). The countries that have ratified the Convention have to make coordinated efforts to implement the standards of the Convention in those different sectors (Guchiten and Pecoud 2009, 16).

Based on international human rights instruments, the Migrant Workers Convention merely reaffirms existing human rights norms without developing new ones. Therefore, the ICRMW is not considered to establish wholly new rights. Art. 5 of the CMW provides for two categories of protected migrant workers— regular or documented and undocumented or irregular migrant workers. It imposes obligations on host states or country of origin to provide all prospective migrant workers with information on their rights (Art. 33 and 37), to ensure that migrant workers are recruited only by private recruitment agencies that are licensed and supervised by government (Art. 66), to prevent private agencies and others from confiscating worker's identity documents (Art. 21); to ensure all migrant workers have access to consular assistance and protection abroad if their rights under the convention are impaired (Art. 23) and to ensure migrant workers have access to effective remedies including compensation and to enforce those remedies (Art. 83). Thus, the CMW is more detailed than other Conventions and extends fundamental human rights to all migrant workers, both regular and irregular while it provides additional rights for regular migrant workers and members of their families to discourage illegal migration.

It has been argued that the CMW rests on the principle of equal treatment of migrants and nationals rather than on a "minimum standards" approach, which characterizes many other international legal instruments (Ruhs 2017, 172–176). However, as of July 2024, only 59 countries have ratified the Convention. The countries that have ratified the CMW are predominantly migrant-sending rather than migrant-receiving countries (Ruhs 2017, 172–176). This inadequate number of ratifications limits the effectiveness of the Convention in protecting migrant workers in practice. The great majority of high-income countries that receive migrant workers, have not yet ratified this convention. There is considerable evidence to suggest that the main reason why these countries have not ratified the CMW is that they consider the ratification of the convention will create huge negative economic and social impacts on them and put additional burden on the population of these host countries (Ruhs 2017, 172–176). Another barrier to ratification is that the Convention explicitly grants right to irregular or undocumented migrants. While the Convention does not encourage irregular migrants or recommend their regularization, it asks state parties to prevent irregular migration and put an end to the existence of irregular migrants. The CMW considers eight different categories of migrant workers but it does not explicitly protect domestic workers and it restricts the protection of asylum seekers, refugees and stateless persons to what is provided for by national law.

Despite the recognition of migrant workers' rights as human rights, they are deprived of the enjoyment of these rights in host states due to non-ratification of this crucial treaty. The effective protection of migrant workers in the host country depends not only ratification of ILO Conventions and the CMW and elimination of the legal hurdles to access to the labor market and on the recognition of labor rights, but also on a comprehensive recognition of their rights under national legal framework. But many host countries like Saudi Arabia and other Middle East Countries have no well-developed legislation on migrant workers' rights and social security.

11.7 Plight of Migrant Workers of Bangladesh

Bangladesh is a significant source of migrant workers in the Middle East and Southeast Asian countries like Malaysia and Singapore. Like the previous years, Saudi Arabia, Qatar, Malaysia, Singapore, and Kuwait have been the top destinations for Bangladeshi workers in 2024. However, monopoly of few employment agencies over appointment of workers, breach of contract, allegation of human trafficking, false promise of job, and exploitation of migrant workers remain main obstacles to the safe and orderly migration from Bangladesh. Most of the migrant workers from Bangladesh are unskilled or low-skilled and temporary and they are involved in risky and difficult laborious jobs in precarious working conditions in the host states. According to a 2022 International Organization for Migration report, Bangladesh is the sixth largest labor sending country and the seventh largest in terms of remittance earnings and most migrant workers are staying in the Middle East and Malaysia. Plight of migrant workers begins with their journey from Bangladesh to destination countries through involvement of intermediaries such as *dalals* (local informal brokers) in the recruitment process and a significant portion of recruitment costs is spent on bribes, illegal fees to recruitment agencies (Rahman 2023). As a result, according to the various reports, among the South Asian countries, migrant workers from Bangladesh have to bear the highest migration cost due to fraudulent practices of recruiting agents and their informal intermediaries which lead to a huge gap between the official cost and actual cost of migration. Needless to say, high migration costs not only push workers into debt bondage but also negatively impact migrant workers'well-being. Developing online platforms and end-to-end digitalization of services can reduce dependency on intermediaries (Hasan 2024). In the destination countries, their suffering is exacerbated due to a lack of information about the availability of employment opportunities, lack of knowledge about their rights and legal remedies for deception by recruiters and employers (Abrar 2023). Lack of accurate and reliable information about the migration process makes migrant workers more vulnerable to exploitation and the risk of trafficking or irregular migration (Hasan 2024).

A large number of the migrant workers are subjected to various forms of discrimination and abuse in destination countries. The Kafala- a sponsoring system used by employers in the Middle East countries appears to be a tool of abuse and exploitation of workers, as under this system, workers are unable to change jobs or leave the country without their employer's permission. This Kafala labor system is utilized foreign knowledge workers as a temporary tool to build local human capital in receiving countries and to ensure flexible access to foreign workers and exercise maximum control (Ewers, Khattab, Babar and Madeeha 2022, 278). The migrant workers are also harassed in the hiring process by the recruiting agencies in destination countries because they sometimes charge additional fees from workers, creating a vicious circle of debt and thereby forcing workers to work longer hours. The hostile environment, confiscation of passports, long duration of daily work routine, absence of rest periods during extended shifts, poor and unhygienic living conditions, separation of relatives for a long time, and mental stress are common scenarios for most Bangladeshi workers abroad. Constant stress, oppression by employers, pressure to send money home for payment of debt are also contributing factors to their plight. In host states, especially in the Middle East, workers are sometimes deprived of due wages or paid less than what was promised. Irregular and undocumented migrant workers of Bangladesh abroad are often deprived of legal protection. Non-payment or irregular payment of wages and other entitlements, systemic wage theft of migrant workers is often reported. Although a formal written contract by employers is considered a core element of protection of migrant workers, it is common practice that many workers are compelled to destination countries without such written contracts or sometimes the contract offered before departure is substituted with an inferior one offering lower wages and poor working conditions (ADB 2016). For example, according to the UN experts' findings, many Bangladeshi migrants upon arrival to Malaysia do not find their promised jobs and are often forced into overstaying their visas (OHCHR 2024). Consequently, they face the risk of arrest, detention, ill treatment, and deportation (OHCHR 2024). The experts also found that members of criminal networks operating in Malaysia and Bangladesh earn a huge sum of money through the fraudulent recruitment practice (OHCHR 2024). On the other hand, deception of employers, closure of companies, change of employer, non-renewal of visa can turn a regular migrant worker into an irregular one.

Women migrant workers from Bangladesh, who mostly work as domestic workers, are particularly vulnerable to abuse in destination countries as they are often subjected to abusive practices by employers, such as retention of passports, non-payment of wages, overwork, deprivation of liberty, denial of access to health care, and physical and sexual abuse, which can amount to forced labor (Kamruzzaman 2021, Kanya 2021). Overall, the vulnerability of women migrant workers is attributed to a number of factors including the isolated nature of their work, their level of dependence on their employer for income, accommodation, and immigration status, lack of legal framework regulating their work, and non-ratification of the relevant ILO Conventions.

Over the last 15 years, nearly one million migrants have returned as deportees, almost empty-handed (Hasan 2024). According to the Wage Earners' Welfare Trust Board data, 4552 migrant workers returned home as corpses in 2023—the highest figure in a decade. In 2024, 4, 813 bodies of Bangladeshi migrants were brought to Bangladesh and most of them died due to accidents, suicides, or suspected homicides. Most of the deaths of migrant workers from Bangladesh occur in the Middle East countries and in many cases, the causes of death of migrant workers every year remain unexplained or sometimes shown as "natural causes". However, these unusual deaths are mainly caused by unsafe working environments, extreme heat and humidity, overwork, pollution, psychological stress and the workers' lack of access to health care (Mustafa 2024). Many migrant workers in the Middle East have to work in the infrastructure sector amid extreme heat during the day time and without having adequate safety equipment. In destination countries in the Middle East, it is very difficult to hold employers liable for compensation for workers' deaths due to a lack of adequate protection through national law or legal support.

Both Bangladesh and some destination countries are heavily dependent on migrant workers, albeit, for different purposes. While migrant workers fill the labor force shortages in the destination countries, Bangladesh is also heavily dependent on the remittances sent by migrant workers. Therefore, both origin and destination countries have a shared responsibility to ensure safe working conditions for migrant workers and the protection of their rights (Mustafa 2024). Especially, the destination countries need to ratify international instruments on migrant workers' rights, to adopt appropriate laws and administrative measures to ensure a safe working environment for migrant workers, properly investigate workers' death and identify any link between the workers' deaths and unsafe working and living conditions (Mustafa 2024).

The plight of migrant workers is exacerbated by the lack of adequate support in destination countries from the government agencies of Bangladesh. There are a lot of challenges in providing support to migrant workers in the destination countries as extending such support is largely dependent on laws and policies in the concerned destination countries (Abrar 2023). Although the labor wings of the Bangladeshi embassies are mainly responsible for such support, they often lack the necessary human and financial resources to carry out their responsibilities. Resource mobilization for the offices of labor attached to destination countries is critically important for equipping them for assistance and support to migrant workers. The lack of cooperation, coupled with the limited capacity of Bangladesh missions, the absence of bilateral agreements and the absence of strong human rights organizations in most destination countries, make the workers vulnerable to exploitation and abuse (Abrar 2023). Moreover, the workers' inability to understand the local language, lack of financial capacity to secure services of interpreters and legal counsels, as well as the non-availability of legal aid support, can deprive them of access to justice in destination countries (Abrar 2023). Another challenge of returning of temporary migrant workers, who are largely low-skilled, is how to re-integrate in labor market in Bangladesh as there is no national strategy yet.

11.8 Legal Framework on Migrant Workers in Bangladesh

Restrictive migration law and policies of host states can play a formative role in creating and sustaining precarious working conditions by downgrading migrant status. In this context, the presence of well-designed laws and policies of sending countries can ensure orderly and safe migration of workers and reduce precariousness and their vulnerability. Migrant workers from Bangladesh have to rely on the legal system of the host countries and Bangladeshi overseas missions for their protection. Bangladesh enacted the Overseas Employment and Migrants Act (OEMA) in 2013 for orderly and safe migration of workers, but it has no extra-territorial effect and as such, it cannot afford protection to the workers abroad. Bangladesh has also formulated Rules and set up institutional facilities for workers in destination countries. The OEMA 2013 establishes the regulation of recruitment agents to ensure a "safe and fair system of migration, and to ensure rights and welfare of migrant workers and members of their families". The OEMA requires written employment contracts for the safeguarding of migrant workers against exploitative practices, establishes Labor Welfare Wings in receiving states to redress workers "grievances and forbids fraudulent recruitment activities. It recognizes migrant workers" right to information about the "migration process, employment contract, and the terms and conditions of the work overseas" to allow them to lodge complaints regarding employment contract, such as unpaid wages, excessive working hours and any other precarious working conditions. To prevent illegal activities of intermediaries, the OEMA 2013 requires that a recruiting agency must hold a license issued by the government to perform migrant recruitment activities. This provision aims to ensure that workers are required to use only formal streams of migration via registered and licensed recruitment agencies. The OEMA 2013 affirms the principle of non-discrimination to be applied at all times for overseas employment and return of migrant workers. The OEMA also elaborates on the eligibility of the recruiting agent for granting a license in favor of them, their roles and responsibilities, the provision for license renewal and the cases for suspension and cancellation of the license to establish accountability of recruiting agencies. No brokers, sub-agents or intermediaries, who have no license to act as recruiting agents, are legally empowered to do this recruitment work. Section 15 of this law lays down the duties of recruitment agents to ensure safe migration and protection of the workers' interests. For example, the recruitment agent shall employ the migrant worker in the job offered, provide wages, and other benefits and ensure good working conditions in accordance with the terms and conditions of the employment contract, and maintain communication with the employers for these purposes; and agent will give proper information as to the salary and wages, other terms and conditions of job to the potential migrants in their advertisements. Section 16 places a responsibility on the government to establish a performance-based grading system for the classification of recruitment agents. But there is no implementation of this provision.

In order to protect the rights and interests of the migrant workers, Section 22 of the OEMA Act mentions the basic terms and conditions, wages, accommodation facilities, duration of the contract, and compensation in case of death or accident, to be incorporated in an employment contract. It also empowers the labor welfare wing of Bangladeshi embassies to enter into a MoU or bilateral agreement with the host country with the purpose of increasing opportunities for overseas employment, improving the management of labor migration, repatriation and reintegration of the migrant workers in the home country and ensuring the welfare and the rights of migrants' workers including the members of their families. This Act elaborates the guiding principles for the government for the execution of such MoU or bilateral agreement (Sections 23, 24, and 25 of the Overseas Employment and Migrants Act 2013). The OEMA discourages unlawful migration. It contains a specific provision for female migrant workers to enable the government to implement welfare programs or initiatives for ensuring the dignity, rights, safety and security of the female migrant workers.

However, the OEMA 2013 does not ensure access to justice for irregular migrant workers and does not regulate *Dalals*—local intermediaries, and as such they are not registered. As a result, the victim of irregular migration is deprived of the right to get a remedy against fraudulent practices of the broker, middlemen or *dalals* who link migrants with recruitment agencies. Migrant workers are very much ignorant about those rights. The OEMA 2013 has been supplemented by the 2017 Overseas Employment and Migrants' Management Rules, which regulate the obtaining of passports, visas, and predeparture training. The newly enacted law—the Prevention and Suppression of Human Trafficking and Smuggling of Migrants Act 2026—criminalizes both smuggling and organized smuggling of migrants and lays down several provisions on prevention of smuggling of migrants and protection from physical abuse and violence on migrants. This law has extra-territorial application and takes an integrated transnational approach to the prevention of smuggling of migrants through exchange of information, criminalizing advertisement of migrant smuggling by both conventional and digital platform.

11.9 Role of Bilateral Agreements on Labor Migration Governance

Recently, there has been a resurgence of bilateral labor migration agreements and Memorandum of Understanding between sending and receiving countries because formal migration laws often fail to regulate migration effectively. Given the ineffectiveness of international legal framework, these agreements spell out the rights of migrant workers, obligations of recruiting agencies, host states and sending states in order to ensure safe, orderly and regular migration. Bilateral agreement between sending and receiving country as a legal arrangement has emerged as a pivotal framework of migration governance to regulate and manage migration flow in an orderly manner to ensure that migration takes place on the basis of agreed principles. Such agreements create a framework for partnership in order to facilitate safe and orderly migration so that workers can live and work with dignity and without discrimination. Bilateral arrangements can include application of international labor standards, provisions on decent work conditions, payment of fair wages, freedom of association and collective bargaining and address the issues of human trafficking and exploitation. Such agreements can minimize the risk of vulnerability of temporary and low-skilled migrant workers by providing a framework for fair treatment of migrant workers and protection of their rights. As authorized by the OEMA 2013, the labor welfare wings of Bangladeshi embassies have concluded several MoU with several destination countries including countries in Southeast Asia, Europe and the Middle East, for fixing quotas of the maximum number of manpower who can migrate every year, duration of their contracts, and increasing protection and welfare of migrant workers and improving the immigration process. Such agreements also deal with meeting the needs of the labor market for temporary seasonal workers, enhancing cooperation between sending and destination countries on the return of migrant workers, and regularization of undocumented Bangladeshi migrant workers (Eurofound 2025).

However, several gaps exist in such agreements, as many of these agreements fail to incorporate international labor standards and social protection measures. Bangladesh needs to negotiate for more robust bilateral agreements that align with international labor standards. Low ratification of the ILO Conventions and CMW in the destination countries is another obstacle to the implementation of these bilateral agreements (OHCHR 2017). A bilateral labor migration agreement or memorandum of understanding, which is based on international labor standards, properly implemented and monitored, can enhance the protection of the rights of migrant workers significantly and contribute to labor governance.

Apart from these legal arrangements, protecting migrants against vulnerabilities also requires the coordination of numerous actors involved in the migration process, including destination countries (Bossavie 2023).

11.10 Conclusion

The need for greater protection of migrant workers is highlighted in view of increasing precarity and exploitation in host states, perpetuated by the absence of a robust legal framework. International migration poses transnational governance challenges that go beyond national legal and institutional frameworks and require bilateral agreements, regional and multilateral cooperation between receiving, transit, and sending countries. The main challenge for international instruments on migrant workers' rights is their poor implementation in both sending and receiving countries. As mentioned above, migrant workers can be vulnerable in destination countries due to their undocumented status, economic crises, lack of legal protection, absence of a written contract and bilateral agreements. Given the fact that the availability of decent work becomes increasingly scarce in destination countries adds to the plight migrant workers. Governance of temporary and irregular labor migration has emerged as one of the most significant social, economic and human rights challenges of this century. Needless to say, irregular migrants, low-skilled temporary workers, and migrant domestic workers are often exposed to the risk of poor working conditions and exploitative treatment. Female migrants, in particular, experience gender-specific vulnerabilities and exploitation. In this context, clearly defined legal rights, accessible and effective complaint procedures and means of redress and remedies, availability of adequate information, opportunities of counselling, and legal assistance are crucially important for their protection in destination countries. Similarly, the recognition of the right of freedom of association and collective bargaining is essential for migrant workers in ensuring their rights and in improving terms and conditions of their employment. To secure the protection of migrant workers, the rights, enshrined in the ICRMW, need to be recognized and ensured by the host or receiving countries. But till now, the major destination Countries from Bangladesh, e.g., the Middle East countries, Malaysia, the Republic of Korea have not ratified this Convention. Besides international obligations, freedom of association and the right to collective bargaining for migrant workers are not generally recognized by the law of the countries of destination, which inhibits them from establishing their own unions, and the right to organize, and consequently, they have little bargaining power.

In order to avoid recruitment agencies, which act as intermediaries but control the recruitment process as a syndicate, the government should directly contact employers in home countries for the appointment of migrant workers in proper jobs. Migration insurance may be introduced for migrant workers from Bangladesh to ensure medical treatment and legal support for their proper rehabilitation. Bangladesh should adopt the International Recruitment Integrity System developed by the International Organization of Migration (IOM) to facilitate ethical recruitment and transparency in the recruitment process. A certification system can be introduced in Bangladesh by following this model for recruiting agencies. It is imperative that Bangladesh digitizes the whole process of migration to make information relating to selection of workers, employment contract, information about employers, visa processing and statement of costs of migration available to workers. Opening these information can help them to make informed decision and to avoid intermediaries.

Since currently, most of the migrant workers from Bangladesh are low-skilled, they are compelled to work with lower wages and precarious working conditions, which makes them vulnerable to ill treatment and abuse. To upgrade the skills of the migrant workers, Bangladesh needs to make significant investment in this sector for their training in order to enable them to get better jobs in destination countries and cope with the changing demands of labor market in these countries. Identifying skills demand in major destination countries, reducing high costs of labor migration, ensuring decent work through bilateral agreements, strengthening the institutional arrangement for orderly migration, the prevention of fraudulent practices in the recruitment process, establishing a transparent migration process, making available consular services in remote areas of destination countries and addressing the issue of abuse of migrant workers in bilateral agreements can enhance the protection of Bangladeshi migrant workers. A comprehensive strategy and policy framework is needed to support return migrants' reintegration into domestic labor markets. Developing a multilevel governance of migration involving international organizations, private sectors, and NGOs is also essential for complementing the national governance framework on labor migration.

Bibliography

Books

Casdes, Stephen, and Mark J. Miller. 2003. *The age of migration.* 3rd ed. Guilford Press.

Cholewinski, Ryszard. 1997. *Migrant Workers in International Human Rights law.* Clarendon Press.

Chapters in Edited Books

Bedford, Richard. 2012. Contemporary patterns of international migration. In *Foundations of international migration law*, edited by Brian Opeskin, 17–55. Richard Perruchoud: Jillyanne Redpath-Cross. Cambridge University Press.

Guchiten, Paul De and Pecoud, Antoie. "Introduction: The UN Convention on migrant Workers' rights". In Migration and human rights: The United Nations Convention on migrant Workers' rights, edited by Ryszard Cholewinski, Paul De Guchiten, Antoie Pecoud. Cambridge University Press, (2009):1–46.

Dembour, Marie-benedicte and Kelly, Tobias. "Introduction". In *Are Human Rights for Migrants? edited by* Marie-Benedicte Dembour and Tobias Kelly, Routledge, (2011): 1–15.

Diller, Janelle M., "Protecting the vulnerable: migration, work and human rights due diligence" in: *Handbook on Globalisation and Labour Standards*, ed. Kimberly A. Elliott, Edward Elgar (2022): 84–106..

Freedland, Mark and Costello, Cathryn. "Migrants at Work and the Division of Labour Law". In *Migrants at Work: Immigration and Vulnerability in Labour Law,* edited by Cathryn Costello and Mark Freedland. Oxford University Press, (2014): 1–26.

Grant, Stefanie. "Irregular migration and frontier deaths': Acknowledging a right to identity". In *Are Human Rights for Migrants?* edited by Marie-benedicte Dembour and Tobias Kelly. Routledge, (2011): 48–67.

Lamarche, Lucie. "Human rights, social security and migrant Workers". In Social security and migrant Workers edited by Pablo Arellano Ortiz, Marious Olivier and Gijsbert Vonk. Wolters Kluwer, (2014): 9–30.

Triandafyllidou, Anna "migration and globalization: Dynamics and contradictions", in Handbook of migration and globalization, 2nd ed. ed. Anna Triandafyllidou, Edward Elgar Publishing, (2024):1–24.

Journal Articles

de, Haas, Hein. 2021. "A theory of migration: The aspirations-capabilities framework", *comparative. Migration Studies* 9 (8): 1–35. https://doi.org/10.1186/s40878-020-00210-4.

Crane, Andrew, Genevieve LeBaron, Jean Allain, and Laya Behbahani. 2017. Governance gaps in eradicating forced labor: From global to domestic supply chains. *Regulation & Governance* 13 (1): 1–21.

Ewers, Michael C., Nabil Khattab, Zahra Babar, and Muznah Madeeha. 2022. Skilled migration to emerging economies: The global competition for talent beyond the west. *Globalizations* 19 (2): 268–284.

Panizzoni, M. 2011. Migration and trade: Prospects for bilateralism in the face of skill-selective mobility Laws. *Melbourne Journal of International Law* 11 (2): 1–46.

Rosewarne, S. 2010. Globalisation and the commodification of Labour: Temporary Labour migration. *The Economic and Labour Relations Review.* 20 (2): 99–110.

Ruhs, Martin. 2017. Rethinking international legal standards for the protection of migrant Workers: The case for a "Core rights" approach. *American Journal of International Law* 111:172–176.

Sargean, Malcolm. 2014. Domestic Workers: Vulnerable Workers in Precarious Work. *E-Journal of International and Comparative Labor Studies* 3 (1): 1–19.

Reports

"Committee on the Protection of the Rights of Migrant Workers considers initial report of Bangladesh: Report of Bangladesh" 4th April 2017., https://www.ohchr.org/en/press-releases/2017/04/committee-protection-rights-migrant-workers-considers-initial-report.

Abrar, C. R. "Challenges that our migrant workers face", *the daily* The Star, December 18, 2023, accessed on April 9, 2025, https://www.thedailystar.net/opinion/views/the-shores-injustice/news/challenges-our-migrant-workers-face-3496706.

ADB, "Overseas employment of Bangladeshi Workers: Trends, prospects, and challenges", ADB Briefs, No. 63, (August 2016) 6, https://www.adb.org/sites/default/files/publication/190600/overseas-employment-ban-workers.pdf

"Addressing Women Migrant Worker Vulnerabilities in International Supply Chains", A Report Prepared by CREST and IOM, accessed on March 12, 2025,

April 2023., https://thedocs.worldbank.org/en/doc/3ab0cffdc2e4621f8b5a70a0410213d5-0050062023/original/Bangladesh-case-study-FORMATTED.pdf.

Background paper to the World Development Report 2023: Migrants, Refugees, and Societies.

Bossavie, Laurent, "Low-skilled temporary migration policies: The case of Bangladesh".

Editorial, "A platform for systematically abused female migrant workers" the daily The Star, April 22, 2022, accessed on April 22, 2025, https://www.thedailystar.net/views/editorial/news/platform-systematically-abused-female-migrant-workers-3010176.

Eurofound. 2025. *Bilateral labour agreement between the governments of Greece and Bangladesh, measure GR-2023-26/3873 (measures in Greece).* Dublin:

EU PolicyWatch. https://static.eurofound.europa.eu/covid19db/cases/GR-2023-26_3873.html.

Hasan, Shariful. 2024. "Actions, not slogans, are needed for migrant workers' welfare", *the daily. The Star*. accessed on April 8, 2025.

https://roasiapacific.iom.int/sites/g/files/tmzbdl671/files/documents/addressing-women-migrant-worker-vulnerabilities.pdf.

https://www.thedailystar.net/opinion/views/news/actions-not-slogans-are-needed-migrant-workers-welfare-3778551.

ILO, "Sponsorship reform and internal labour market mobility for migrant workers in the Arab states", ILO, 23 July 2023., https://www.ilo.org/resource/other/sponsorship-reform-and-internal-labour-market-mobility-migrant-workers-arab.

Kamruzzaman, M. 2021., accessed on March 7, 2025, https://www.aa.com.tr/en/asia-pacific/bangladeshi-women-. "Bangladeshi women migrants working abroad face discrimination, deprivation" AA news broadcasting. *System*migrants- working-abroad-face-discrimination-deprivation/2451097.

Kanya, Promila. 2021., accessed on May 23, 2025, https://www.tbsnews.net/features/panorama/bangladeshi-. Bangladeshi female migrants and their struggle with children of abuse. *The Business Standard*female-migrants- and-their-struggle-children-abuse-304027.

"Malaysia: Bangladeshi workers must be protected from exploitation and criminalisation, say UN experts', April 19, 2024, accessed on May 19 2024, https://www.ohchr.org/en/press-releases/2024/04/malaysia-bangladeshi-workers-must-be-protected-exploitation-and.

Mustafa, Kallol. "Why do so many migrant workers die abroad?" *the daily star*, Dhaka, April 5, 2024, accessed on July 23, 2025, https://www.thedailystar.net/opinion/views/news/why-do-so-many-bangladeshi-migrant-workers-die-abroad-3582216.

Rahman, Sanjana Prachee. "From 'Act' to 'Action': Protecting migrant workers through the overseas employment and migrants act" The Business Standard, March 29 2023, accessed on March 22, 2024, https://www.tbsnews.net/features/panorama/act-action-protecting-migrant-workers-through-overseas-employment-and-migrants-act.

UN Commission on Human Rights, "Report on the Human Rights of Migrants submitted by the Special Rapporteur of the Commission on Human Rights" (22 September 2004) UN Doc A/59/377.

Weissbrodt, D. "Final Report on the rights of non-citizens", 2003, UN Doc E./CN.4/Sub.2/2003/23.

"What pushes Bangladeshis out to sea and possible death?" The Business Standard, Dhaka, 20 May 2024., https://www.tbsnews.net/features/panorama/what-pushes-bangladeshis-out-sea-and-possible-death-855381

World Bank. 2023. Background paper to the world development report 2023: Migrants. *Refugees, and Societies*. https://thedocs.worldbank.org/en/doc/3ab0cffdc2e4621f8b5a70a0410213d5-0050062023/original/Bangladesh-case-study-FORMATTED.pdf.

International Instruments

ILO Forced Labour Convention, (No. 29), 1930, accessed on February 17, 2024, https://normlex.ilo.org/dyn/nrmlx_en/f?p=NORMLEXPUB:12100:0::NO::P12100_ILO_CODE:C029.

Migration for Employment Convention (Revised), 1949 (No. 97) accessed on April 19, 2025, https://normlex.ilo.org/dyn/nrmlx_en/f?p=normlexpub:12100:0::no:12100:p12100_instrument_id:312242:no.

Migrant Workers (Supplementary Provisions) Convention, 1975 (No. 143), accessed on April 19, 2025, https://normlex.ilo.org/dyn/nrmlx_en/f?p=NORMLEXPUB:12100:0::NO::P12100_INSTRUMENT_ID:312288

Legislation

The Overseas Employment and Migrants Act 2013.

CHAPTER 12

Conclusion

The industrial relation system in Bangladesh is characterized by the predominant position of large-scale informal economy, precariousness of working conditions, fragmented trade unions, weak labor institutions, lack of enforcement of labor laws and conflict-ridden employer-worker relations. Economic globalization has precipitated changes in patterns of production and work, diminished the capacity of trade unions for collective bargaining in the country, that have worsened the protection of labor rights and accelerated the informalization process over the years.

Globalization continues to reshape labor market, creating new trends with profound regulatory implications in Bangladesh. It has a diverse impact on workers and industrial relations in Bangladesh. While the globalization process has accelerated "race to bottom" scenario, and weakened state authority, it has also enabled workers to organize transnationally and to negotiate with corporations on a global level to address global issues. Transnational labor governance has emerged as catalyst of this process and international unions and transnational labor institutions are the most important organized part of this labor movement around the world and play a key role in influencing, implementing, and enforcing international labor standards to achieve a fair globalization.

The role of labor law in the globalized world has assumed wider significance to enhance the realm of individual labor rights as trade unions become gradually weaker and as the scope of collective bargaining shrinks.

A. Al Faruque, *Globalization and Labour Rights*,
https://doi.org/10.1007/978-981-92-3661-9_12

Given the widespread informality and marginalization of workers, labor law must protect the most vulnerable and lowest paid workers to confront rising inequality. Bangladesh is facing many challenges in ensuring labor rights, regulating workers in gig economy, ensuring decent work conditions, and applying international labor standards. Although over the last decades Bangladesh has enacted many laws on labor rights and industrial relations, the laws are not fully congruent with the core ILO conventions and international labor standards. Even these laws are not properly enforced by labor institutions and implemented by employers. As industrial relations encompass industry owners, workers, government and trade unions, enforcement of labor law depends on adherence of all of these stakeholders to such law. Weak enforcement mechanisms, lack of compliance with safety and security regulations, lack of awareness about labor rights among workers, low wages, and appalling working conditions are formidable challenges in ensuring decent work conditions in Bangladesh. Lack of human resources, lack of inspection capacity, inadequate budgetary allocations and poor infrastructure of government labor institutions put severe constraints on the capacity of these institutions to implement the international labor standards. There is a well-known nexus between labor standards and economic progress. It is crucial to acknowledge that Bangladesh has made significant economic development and it needs to allocate adequate resources for the implementation of the international labor standards to improve labor rights. Currently a separate set of laws exist for regulating industrial relations in EPZs where international labor standards relating to freedom of association, and collective bargaining are not applied. This fragmented approach of labor law to deal with EPZs in Bangladesh creates obstacles in uniform application of labor laws and deprives EPZ workers from the benefits and rights guaranteed under the ILO Conventions and labor laws of Bangladesh. Therefore, a unified legal framework is essential for regulating all types of labor relations in industrial sectors. Although recent reforms of labor law, particularly, the amendment of the Bangladesh Labor Act 2006 this year has significantly broadened the scope of legal protection and provisions for benefits to workers covered under this law, similar initiative was not taken to reform the EPZ related laws, creating gaps in application of the international labor standards.

Non-payment of minimum wages, lack of regular adjustment of minimum wages on the basis of inflation, inadequate coverage of minimum wages remain a persistent problem in Bangladesh and is a significant source of discontent among workers that often leads to street agitations and closure of industries. Even when adjustments are made in minimum wages due to workers' agitation, such adjustments have always been insignificant against the demand of workers. A transparent and regular review of minimum wages should be incorporated in legal framework for ensuring fulfilment of basic needs of workers and their family members and it needs to be prioritized by the government and employers in Bangladesh.

After the Rana Plaza collapse, the landscape of industrial relations in the RMG sector has undergone significant transformation. Bangladesh has now the highest number of green RMG factories. Since Rana Plaza disaster, there have been improvements for workers in health and safety conditions, job security, and social benefits in Bangladesh facilitated by multi-stakeholder initiatives like the Alliance and the Accord—multi-stakeholder initiatives that involved different actors have created new processes of standard-setting, monitoring, benchmarking and enforcement, paving the way for transnational labor regulation and collaborative approach for implementation of the international labor standards. However, other industrial sectors have not experienced similar improvements. These initiatives set a benchmark that should be followed by other industries, which are still lagging behind regarding occupational safety and security of workers. However, successes of safety in the RMG sector achieved during the Accord-Alliance period depend on sustained actions on the part of government and employers through strengthening the monitoring and enforcement capacity of labor organizations and accountability of these institutions. It is crucial to recognize that improving occupational safety, health, and labor rights is a shared responsibility of both government and owners and hence they should be held accountable for lack of workplace safety and violations of labor rights.

There are some other new challenges, such as the graduation of Bangladesh from Least Developed Country (LDC) will move the RMG and other export-oriented industries from preferential treatment to competitive environment for market access. Therefore, the export-oriented industry, particularly the RMG sector, needs to increase competitiveness in the international market through robust compliance standards. Secondly, the emergence of global standards on, the adoption of laws by several developed countries and the EU directive on human rights due diligence have posed a significant compliance challenge for the RMG sector of Bangladesh to remain competitive by complying with them.

These "Due diligence" laws will significantly impact developing countries, which often serve as sources in global supply chains and governments in developing countries will be required to strengthen their own legal frameworks, enforcement mechanisms, and capacities to combat modern slavery. It is expected that compliance by multinational enterprises with these laws and regulations will improve labor standards by identifying and mitigating modern slavery risks in their supply chains, leading to better working conditions, wages, and human rights protection for workers in developing countries including Bangladesh. These will also promote greater transparency and accountability in supply chains, making exploitation harder to conceal, can lead to increased awareness and protection for vulnerable groups susceptible to exploitation. The implementation of these laws and regulations will also require host countries like Bangladesh to initiate reform of labor laws and laws governing special economic zones in order to bring manufacturing factories of RMG and textile in line with the international human rights, labor rights, and environmental standards.

Technological changes like the increased use of automation and Artificial Intelligence (AI) in both manufacturing and services have posed another significant challenge to industrial relations and labor rights because its application will result in the loss of jobs for many workers in Bangladesh like many other countries. But it may also generate demand for new specialized skills.

Therefore, workers need training and skill development so that they are familiar with AI and adapt to it. Lifelong learning and upskilling of workers need to be prioritized to embrace these new challenges. Labor laws and institutional design also need modification to adapt to these changes.

It is now widely recognized that presence of effective trade unions, wide coverage of collective bargaining, practice of social dialogue, presence of robust grievance redressal and dispute settlement mechanism to address workers' agitation for legitimate demands, strengthening bipartite and participation committees, ensuring labor rights and compliance with safety and security of workers can contribute to sound industrial relations in Bangladesh and enhancing productivity. Historically, trade unions have an important role to play in protecting workers' rights and demands, settling disputes between workers and fixing minimum wages by way of collective bargaining. However, political affiliation of trade unions, intimidation by owners, intervention by government, legal, and informal restrictions on formation and joining trade unions have hindered the growth of strong trade union movement in Bangladesh. As a result, workers in Bangladesh often find themselves in vulnerable situations and have reduced their bargaining capacity. Although in recent times the rate of unionization has increased in the RMG sector, trade union affiliation is still low in Bangladesh compared to many other developing countries due to legal restrictions, and increasing flexible types of employment relationships that contribute to the low rate of unionization. Similarly, collective bargaining has been considered a fundamental and long-standing institution of industrial relation for securing decent work, reducing wage inequality, stabilizing labor relations and inclusive labor governance and protection. However, coverage of collective bargaining is still very poor in Bangladesh.

Social dialogue as a voluntary negotiation and consultation process among stakeholders has appeared as an instrument of the democratic foundations of labor markets, containing recurring unrest and violence in industries and the implementation of the international labor standards. However, the social dialogue process in Bangladesh has only had limited success because of the lack of decision-making structures, the absence of follow-up and a lack of trust between employers and workers, and a lack of legitimacy of social partners. Social dialogue needs to be strengthened in Bangladesh to address pressing labor issues, grievances of workers, and resolution of discontents that often erupt into violent agitation and conflicts. Effective social dialogue requires trust building between the social partners and the government and improving negotiation techniques and knowledge base of trade union leaders and employers in Bangladesh. The presence of effective and strong labor institutions, e.g., trade unions and employers' association, is central to social dialogue by offering forums for consultations and negotiations. However, in Bangladesh, the ability of unions to represent and defend the interests of workers is constrained by many factors mentioned above.

It is widely believed that integration and implementation of international labor standards prevents "the race to bottom" scenario by upward harmonization of such standards. Although Bangladesh has ratified most of the important ILO Conventions, there are significant gaps in compliance with the ILO standards in number of areas including safety and security of the workplace, inspection, compensation, elimination of the worst form of child labor and forced labor, freedom of association, the right to organize and bargain collectively, labor relations in EPZs and prevention of discrimination in workplace. The labor laws of Bangladesh should be amended to bring them in fully consistent with the ratified ILO conventions and reflect international labor standards, and to adapt to new forms of work. In particular, vulnerable workers like domestic workers, workers engaged in informal sectors and tea-garden workers are deprived of the benefits of international labor standards and legal protection afforded under labor laws of Bangladesh. Workers engaged in informal sectors are also excluded from social protection scheme in Bangladesh. Extending social protection to all types of workers can significantly improve workers' health, income security, and productivity. Social protection helps increase access to opportunities for poor workers.

Legal recognition of workers engaged in informal sector is considered a key to transitioning from informal sector to formal one and ensuring universal application of labor rights guaranteed under the constitution of Bangladesh and the ILO conventions. On the other hand, lack of implementation of labor law can accelerate informalization of workers. For example, despite legal requirements, many employers still fail to provide workers with written employment contracts, and identity card, resultantly, their status is reduced to informal position without legal protection.

Persistently high rates of underemployment coupled with lack of decent work opportunities in Bangladesh compel many unemployed people to take a risky journey to seek jobs in the Middle East, Europe, and the USA and work in mostly informal sectors. Migrant workers from Bangladesh are often subjected to abusive practices, such as non-payment of wages, deprivation of liberty, physical abuse, and retention of passports. The international migration legal and governance framework does not offer adequate protection against these abuses in destination countries.

Industrial relations in any country are vulnerable to external events and give rise to temporary shocks that economies and labor markets fail to absorb properly. These shocks may take the form of a contraction in labor demand due to an economic or financial downturn. Contractions in labor demand following an economic downturn may, in turn, restrict access to decent work opportunities by tightening the labor market and encouraging the adoption of new, increasingly flexible working arrangements. This increases the risk of workers losing their jobs and turning to the informal labor market. Bangladesh is no exception to this trend. A policy initiative and contingency planning need to be in place for addressing such external shocks.

Industrial relations and labor rights in Bangladesh can be further improved through strengthening the institutional capacity of trade unions and federations to deliver effective services, institutionalizing the concept and benefits of social dialogue, formation of participation committees in all industries, and enhancing the capacity of the trade unions for the promotion of collective bargaining.

In order to improve labor market conditions in Bangladesh, development of necessary skill of workers must be emphasized as it is linked to productivity and efficiency. Low productivity and poor efficiency of workers are related to a lower level of their skill. An active labor policy that encourages life-long learning and skills development can support a just transition into decent employment and improve access to basic opportunities and adequate standards of living. This is particularly true for migrant workers from Bangladesh, majority of whom are low-skilled and are often compelled to work in precarious conditions in destination countries. As the nature of work is changing, Bangladesh needs urgent policy and legal reforms to prepare its workforce for the technological changes that are reshaping jobs rapidly.

Index

A

Accord on Fire and Building Safety in Bangladesh, 28, 211, 215
Adjudication, 151, 154, 159
Alliance, vii, x, 27–30, 32, 99, 132, 211, 215–220, 224, 255
Alternative Dispute Resolution, 153, 155–157, 159
Appointment letters, 19, 20, 25, 49, 51, 60, 182, 183, 202
Arbitration, 86, 148, 151, 154, 213, 217
Artificial intelligence, 10, 33, 72, 160, 256
Associational power, 103, 112, 113, 214

B

Bangladesh Cha Sramik Union (BCSU), 60, 138
Bangladesh Economic Zones Act 2010, 83
Bangladesh Employers Federation, 68
Bangladesh Export Processing Zone Authority, 81–83, 86, 87, 139
Bangladesh Garments Manufacturing and Exporters Association (BGMEA), 23, 68, 69, 158, 159, 200–202, 219
Bangladesh Knitwear Manufacturers and Exporters Association (BKMEA), 68, 69, 200
Bangladesh Labor Act 2006, 21, 49, 51–54, 56–63, 65, 67, 68, 70, 71, 84–86, 94–101, 115, 116, 118, 119, 133–136, 140, 141, 149–151, 154, 157, 158, 160, 181, 182, 199, 202, 221, 223
Bangladesh Labor (Amendment) Act 2013, 50, 95
Bangladesh Labor (Amendment) Act 2026, 53, 60, 63, 67, 100, 103, 116, 135, 156, 158, 197
Bangladesh Labor Rules 2015, 50, 53, 54, 58, 62, 224
Bangladesh Labor Welfare Foundation Act 2006, 61

A. Al Faruque, *Globalization and Labour Rights*,
https://doi.org/10.1007/978-981-92-3661-9

Bangladesh Nationalized Enterprises and Statutory Corporations (Prohibition of Strikes and Unfair Labor Practices) Order 1972, 119
Bangladesh Private Export Processing Zone Act, 1996, 83
Bangladesh Tea Association (BTA), 60, 138
Bangladesh Workers Welfare Foundation Act, 2006, 57
Bargaining power, viii, x, 14, 31, 45–47, 70, 92, 93, 110–114, 151, 156, 167, 168, 183, 231, 247
Basic trade union, 97
Bilateral Agreements on Labor Migration, 245
Bipartite negotiation, 148–151, 154, 155, 195, 202
Broad social dialogue, 194
Bureau of Manpower, Employment and Training (BMET), 65

C
Child domestic workers, 56
Child labor, 8, 12, 15, 17, 29, 30, 45, 46, 49, 54–56, 87, 99, 101, 164–167, 172, 173, 175, 176, 180, 181, 184, 198, 202, 207, 257
Civil society, 31, 84, 194, 200, 203
Codes of conduct, 31, 178
Collective bargaining, viii, ix, xi, 2, 3, 5, 6, 8, 11, 14, 25, 26, 29, 30, 43, 46–49, 65, 72, 80, 81, 83–85, 87, 93, 94, 99–104, 109–118, 120, 121, 128, 129, 137, 140, 142, 148, 149, 152, 155, 156, 163–169, 175, 180, 183, 191, 193, 194, 197, 199, 204, 211, 214, 221, 225, 231, 236, 246, 247, 253, 254, 256, 257, 259
Collective bargaining agent, 65, 102, 115, 116, 149, 152, 155
Collective bargaining agreements, viii, 11, 109–111, 113–115, 117, 118, 164, 197
Compensation, 43, 46, 49, 51–53, 59, 60, 66, 83–85, 147, 152, 166, 170, 183, 222–224, 237, 238, 242, 244, 257
Compulsory group insurance, 52, 58, 85
Conciliation, 65, 86, 118, 148, 150, 151, 154, 155, 158
Convention on the Elimination of All Forms of Discrimination Against Women (CEDAW) 1979, 167
Convention on the Protection of the Rights of All Migrant Workers and Members of their Families, 1990, 238
Convention on the Rights of the Child (CRC) 1989, 167
Coronavirus pandemic, 25
Corporate social responsibility, 16, 31, 215, 216, 222
Court-sponsored ADR, 157
Coverage of minimum wages, 127, 254
Crisis Management Core Committee, 200

D
Department of Chief Inspector of Factories, 218
Department of Inspection for Factories and Establishments, 65, 66, 142
Department of Labor, 65, 99, 117, 148, 150, 181, 184

Directorate of Industrial Establishment and Factories (DIFE), 66, 142, 218, 220, 226
Domestic Servants' Registration Ordinance of 1961, 58
Domestic workers, 11, 24, 56, 58–60, 127, 166, 177, 182, 231, 233, 237, 239, 241, 247, 258

E
Economic globalization, viii, xi, 1–3, 5, 9, 12, 24, 43, 77, 92, 113, 166, 229
Employers' organizations, 65, 68, 69, 120, 159, 179, 194–196, 204
Employment Injury Benefits Convention No. 121, 223
EPZ Labor Act 2019, 84–87, 120, 139, 155
EPZ Labor Appellate Tribunals, 154
EPZ Labor Court, 85, 86, 154, 155
EPZ workers, 78, 80, 84, 85, 87, 139, 254
EU Directive on Corporate Sustainability Due Diligence (CSDD) 2024, 16
European Union, 15, 63, 70, 218
EU Sustainability Regulations, 16, 17
Evolution of labor law, 47, 48
Executive Council of the Workers' Welfare Association, 155
Exploitative Sourcing Price, 139
Export Processing Zones (EPZ), 2, 77, 78, 80–82, 84–88, 96, 120, 139, 154, 155, 182, 254

F
Factories Act 1934, 47
Fair globalization, 164, 165, 253
Fault line, 233
Fire Service and Civil Defence Department (FSCD), 218, 220
Flexibilization of employment relationship, 9, 10
Forced labor, 15, 17, 18, 29, 30, 49, 54, 59, 63, 99, 117, 164, 167, 168, 171, 173, 175, 176, 180, 231, 233, 241, 257
Foreign direct investment, 5, 7, 78, 81
Foreign Private Investment Act of 1980, 82
Formal justice system, 157
Formal sector, 11, 12, 19–22, 50, 59, 60, 152, 176
French Corporate Duty of Vigilance Law of 2017, 15
Functions of labor law, ix, 44
  distributive, 46
  integrative, 45, 46
  intermediary, 45, 46
  protective, 46, 47, 71

G
Germany's the Supply Chain Due Diligence Act 2023, 15
Gig economy, 9, 19, 24, 25, 33, 71, 160, 254
Global economy, vii, 1, 2, 5, 9, 77, 164, 177
Global framework agreements, 30, 32, 217
Globalization, vii–ix, xi, 1–9, 12, 18, 24, 28–30, 32, 33, 44, 45, 69, 70, 78, 92, 93, 105, 113, 114, 126, 164, 165, 184, 191, 229–231, 253
Globalized world, ix, 6, 9, 10, 69, 92, 93, 253
Global labor governance, 3

Global supply chain, vii–ix, 3, 5, 12–15, 28, 72, 92, 212, 214, 217, 225
Grievance procedure, 84, 116, 148, 149, 154

H
Human rights, ix, 8, 14–17, 32, 63, 87, 93, 164, 166–168, 171, 174, 177, 181, 233–239, 243, 247, 255, 256
Human rights due diligence, 14, 15, 17, 33, 255
Human trafficking, 234, 246

I
Identification cards, 49, 60
ILO, viii–xi, 5, 10, 14, 15, 20, 21, 28–30, 33, 49, 53, 59, 63, 65, 66, 68, 70, 93, 101, 110, 114, 116, 117, 127, 128, 130, 131, 135, 141, 148, 163–181, 183, 184, 191, 196–198, 203, 213, 218–220, 222, 223, 231, 232, 236, 237, 239, 242, 246, 254, 257, 258
ILO Collective Agreements Recommendation 1951, 110
ILO Convention concerning Decent Work for Domestic Workers of 2011, 59
ILO Convention concerning the Promotion of Collective Bargaining 1981, 169
ILO Convention concerning Tripartite Consultations to Promote the Implementation of International Labor Standards, 1976, 196
ILO Convention on Abolition of Forced Labor 1957, 171
ILO Convention on Employment Injury Benefits Convention, 1964, 170
ILO Convention on Employment Policy 1964, 172
ILO Convention on Fixing Minimum Wages of 1970, 130, 169
ILO Convention on Forced Labor 1930, 171
ILO Convention on Holidays with Pay (Revised) 1970, 172
ILO Convention on Hours of Work (Industry), 1919, 171
ILO Convention on Human Resources Development (No. 142) of 1975, 172
ILO Convention on Migrant Workers (Supplementary Provisions) 1975, 236
ILO Convention on Migration for Employment 1949, 236
ILO Convention on Occupational Safety and Health 1981, 173, 181
ILO Convention on Protection of Wages 1949, 169
ILO Convention on Social Policy (Basic Aims and Standards) 1962, 172
ILO Convention on Social Security (Minimum Standards) 1952, 169, 170
ILO Convention on Termination of Employment 1982, 170
ILO Convention on the Freedom of Association and the Protection of the Right to Organize 1948 (No. 87), 93
ILO Convention on the Right to Organize and Collective Bargaining, 1949, 93, 110

ILO Convention on Violence and Harassment (No. 190), 174
ILO Convention on Working Environment (Air Pollution, Noise and Vibration) 1977, 173
ILO Decent Work Agenda in 1999, 191
ILO Decent Work for Domestic Workers Convention 2011, 177
ILO Declaration on Fundamental Principles and Rights at Work 1998, 175, 180
ILO Declaration on Social Justice for a Fair Globalization 2008, 165, 191
ILO Equal Remuneration Convention 1951, 172
ILO Examination of Grievances Recommendation, 1967, 148
ILO Minimum Wage Fixing Machinery Convention, 1928, 128
ILO Promotional Framework for Occupational Safety and Health Convention, 2006, 174, 181
ILO Recommendation on Transition from the Informal to Formal Economy' 2015, 20
ILO Social Policy (Basic Aims and Standards) Convention, 1962, 128
ILO Worst Forms of Child Labor Recommendation, 1999, 173
IMF, 4
Implementation of international labor standards, 164, 165, 178, 180, 184, 196, 257
Implementation of labor laws, 44, 64, 65, 72
Industrial Federation, 97
IndustriALL Global Union, 29
Industrial relations, vii–x, 1, 2, 4, 5, 7, 9, 18, 28–30, 32, 33, 43–45, 47–49, 60, 62, 64, 69, 83–85, 87, 92, 102, 110, 111, 118, 147, 149, 150, 155, 159, 163, 191–193, 195, 198, 202–205, 207, 214, 217, 253–256
Industrial Relations Ordinance 1969, 48
Informality, 10–12, 15, 19, 20, 25, 51, 254
Informalization, viii, 6, 10, 19, 20, 21, 232, 253, 258
Informal justice system, 157
Informal Mechanisms of Settlement of Labor Disputes, 159
Informal sector, 10, 11, 18–21, 24–26, 50, 55, 59, 61, 62, 100, 113, 127, 129, 132, 135, 141, 176, 181, 184, 205, 206, 230–232, 258
Inspection, ix, 27, 51, 66, 67, 87, 88, 142, 164, 169, 174, 180, 182, 183, 211–216, 218, 220, 221, 224, 254, 257
Institutional design, 32, 33, 256
Institutional framework, 64, 117, 178, 195, 203, 207
Internal grievance mechanism, 158
International Covenant on Civil and Political Rights (ICCPR) 1966, 93, 167
International Covenant on Economic, Social and Cultural Rights (ICESCR) 1966, 93, 167
International labor standards, ix, xi, 2, 3, 6, 30, 33, 44, 49, 63, 70–72, 78, 87, 88, 93, 95, 160, 163–165, 167, 169, 176, 178, 180–184, 246, 253–255, 257, 258

International Organization for Migration, 240
International Recruitment Integrity System, 247
International Trade Union Confederation (ITUC), 6, 29, 101
Irregular migrant workers, xi, 231–233, 238, 245
Italy, 234

J
Judicial mediation, 157

L
Labor appellate tribunal, 65, 86, 118, 151–153, 155, 157
Labor Court, 52, 62, 118, 136, 150, 151, 153, 155, 181
Labor disputes, x, 65, 115, 147, 148, 150–153, 155–157, 159, 160, 164, 183, 192
Labor Disputes Act 1965, 48
Labor disputes settlement mechanisms, 147
Labor justice, 147
Labor law, viii–xi, 7–9, 14, 17, 21, 24, 26–29, 43–49, 54, 61, 63–67, 69–72, 78–80, 88, 91, 95, 96, 102–104, 120, 150–152, 154, 178, 179, 182, 183, 191, 192, 197, 198, 202, 203, 205, 207, 212, 219, 223, 225, 231, 233, 235, 238, 253, 254, 256–258
Labor migration, ix, xi, 229, 230, 232, 233, 236, 238, 244–248
Labor rights, vii–ix, xi, 1, 2, 4–9, 13–15, 17–20, 26, 30, 31, 44, 48, 49, 51, 63, 65, 70, 79, 83, 84, 93, 120, 163–168, 170, 175, 178, 180, 181, 184, 214, 216, 217, 219, 226, 230, 231, 235, 239
Libya, 234
Living wage, 127, 130, 131
Lock-out, 65, 100, 118, 119, 150, 151, 155

M
Maternity benefits, 54, 62, 84, 85
Migrant domestic workers, 59, 231, 233, 237, 247
Migrant workers, ix, xi, 5, 10, 15, 18, 59, 166, 230–232, 235–247
Migrant workers' rights, 235, 236, 239, 242, 247
Migration law, 235, 243, 245
Minimum Age Convention 1973, 173, 180
Minimum wage, viii–xi, 18, 22, 30, 43, 45–47, 49, 59, 61, 65, 72, 78, 80, 81, 84–86, 91, 97, 110, 112, 117, 125–142, 147, 165, 169, 175, 177, 183, 184, 201, 202, 207, 222, 254–256
Minimum Wage Act 1948 of India, 128
Minimum Wage Fixing Convention, 1970, 127, 129
Minimum Wage Fixing Recommendation, 1970, 127, 130, 131
Minimum Wage Ordinance 1961, 133
Minimum Wages Board, 65, 85, 133, 135
Ministry of Labor and Employment of Bangladesh, 219
Modern Slavery Act 2015 of the UK, 15
Modern Slavery Act 2018 of Australia, 15

Multinational corporations, vii, 1–3, 5, 13, 216
Multi-stakeholders' Initiatives on Safety of Workers, 211

N
Narrow social dialogue, 194
National Child Labor Elimination Policy of Bangladesh 2010, 59
National Child Labor Survey 2022, 55
National Confederation, 98
National Council for Skill Development and Training (NCSDT), 197
National Policy on Protection and Welfare of Domestic Workers in 2015, 59
National social dialogue, 193, 195
National Social Dialogue Forum, 197
National trade union federation, 97, 98
National Tripartite Plan of Action of Fire Safety and Structural Integrity, 212
National Wages and Productivity Commission (NWPC), 197, 199
Negotiation, 45, 86, 101, 109, 114, 117, 118, 135, 148, 149, 155, 157, 194, 195, 203, 257
NGOs, 27, 30, 53, 133, 159, 181, 184, 193, 195, 200, 212, 222, 248

O
Overseas Employment and Migrants' Management Rules 2017, 245
Overseas Employment and Migrants Act (OEMA) 2013, 243, 244, 248

P
Participation Committee, 99, 116, 148, 154, 198, 199, 201, 256, 259
Participation Fund, 57
Preventive measures, 154, 174
Principle of non-discrimination, 236, 244
Private regulations, 31, 32
Privatization, vii, 1–3, 113
Protocol 2014 to the Forced Labor Convention 1930, 237
Public sector, vii, 3, 24, 65, 68, 92, 94, 96, 98, 103, 117, 120, 196
Pull factor, 230
Push factor, 229

R
Race to bottom, 22, 253, 257
Rana Plaza Arrangement, 222
Rana Plaza disaster, 27, 28, 32, 211, 216, 218, 219, 221–224, 226, 255
Rana Plaza Donor Trust Fund, 222
Ready-made Garment industry, viii
Remediation Coordination Council, 212, 218, 220
Right to freedom of association, 8, 93, 94, 104, 166, 193, 219
Right to strike, 6, 100, 117–119, 183
RMG industry, x, 21, 23, 69, 81, 136
RMG sector, viii, x, 17–19, 21–23, 26–28, 54, 70, 98, 102, 104, 126, 136, 137, 142, 159, 181, 198, 200–203, 207, 212, 216, 218–220, 224–226, 255, 257
RMG workers, xi, 26, 28, 99, 137, 182, 216, 222

S
Safety Committee, 57, 63, 197, 199, 215
Sexual harassment, 46, 63, 158, 231
Smuggling, 234
Social Compliance Forum for the RMG sector, 200
Social dialogue at enterprise level, 194
Social dialogue at sectoral level, 194
Social dialogue in industrial relations, 192, 193
Social security measures, 43, 46, 51
Special Economic Zones (SEZs), 17, 77, 83, 256
Sramik Karmachari Oikya Parishad (SKOP) *National Confederation*, 97
Standard Operating Procedures, 95
Structural power, 112
Sustainability Compact, 212, 218, 219, 224
Sustainability of the RMG Sector, 23, 219

T
Tazreen factory accident, 27
Tea Garden workers, 60
Technological changes, vii, 1, 3, 44, 70, 92, 93, 105
Technological transfer, 78
Temporary migrant workers, xi, 237, 243
The Accord on Fire and Building Safety in Bangladesh, 28, 211
The Committee of Experts on the Application of Conventions and Recommendations (CEARC), 179
The Conference Committee on the Application of Standards (CAS), 179, 180
Trade liberalization, 1, 70
Trade union, vii–ix, xi, 2, 5–7, 26, 28–32, 43, 46–50, 52, 59, 60, 63, 65, 66, 68, 72, 78, 83–85, 87, 91–104, 109, 110, 113–116, 119, 133, 139, 149, 195, 198, 201, 202, 204, 214, 221, 222, 257
Trade Union Act, 1926, 47
Trade Union Act 1965, 48
Transnational alliance, vii, 27, 29, 211
Transnational collective bargaining, viii, 114, 214
Transnational collective bargaining agreements, viii, 114
Transnationalization, 1, 28, 29
Transnational labor governance, xi, 28, 30, 31, 216
Tripartite Consultation (International Labor Standards) Convention 1976, 169
Tripartite Consultative Council, 63, 197, 198, 205
Tripartite Productivity Committee (TPC), 197
Tripartite Productivity Council, 200
Tripartitism, 195

U
UN, ix, 14, 175, 177, 217, 241
UN Guiding Principles on Business and Human Rights 2011, 14
United States, 219, 233
Universal Declaration of Human Rights (UDHR) 1948, 235

W
Wage Earners' Welfare Trust Board, 242
Welfare fund, 57, 59, 115
Wider social dialogue, 195
Worker, vii, viii, x, 3–16, 18–25

Workmen Compensation Act 1923, 47
World Bank, 4, 6, 175
Worst Forms of Child Labor Convention, 1999, 173, 177
WTO, 2, 4, 181

FSC
www.fsc.org
MIX
Papier | Fördert gute Waldnutzung
FSC® C083411

Kolibri 360 GmbH
Ferdinand-Jühlke-Straße 7
99095 Erfurt, Deutschland
produktsicherheit@kolibri360.de

The Gendered Landscape of Suicide

"Throughout history and across many cultures, men have been far more likely to take their own lives and in modern society, blue collar, less educated men are especially at risk. In this important new study of men who want to, try to and do commit suicide, the sociologist Anne Cleary discovers underlying feelings of anguish, desperation, and shame. Equally important, she astutely observes that *as men* they feel obliged to "bravely" cover such feelings from public view. This misplaced notion of male valor, she persuasively argues, has tragically escaped public notice, seen as "just how men are" and foreclosed the possibility of receiving vitally needed help. An important contribution to sociology and a revelatory book for policy-makers, men at risk of their male socialization—and everyone else."

—Professor Arlie R. Hochschild, *Professor Emerita, Department of Sociology, University of California, Berkeley*

Anne Cleary

The Gendered Landscape of Suicide

Masculinities, Emotions, and Culture

palgrave
macmillan

Anne Cleary
UCD Geary Institute for Public Policy
University College Dublin
Dublin, Ireland

ISBN 978-3-030-16633-5 ISBN 978-3-030-16634-2 (eBook)
https://doi.org/10.1007/978-3-030-16634-2

Cover illustration: Khurshid Dustmurodov/EyeEm

This Palgrave Macmillan imprint is published by the registered company Springer Nature Switzerland AG
The registered company address is: Gewerbestrasse 11, 6330 Cham, Switzerland

For David

Acknowledgements

Chapter 2 draws on material originally published in:

Cleary, A. (2012). Suicidal action, emotional expression, and the performance of masculinities. *Social Science & Medicine, 74*, 498–505.

Chapter 5 refers to material originally published in:

Cleary, A. (2017). Help-seeking patterns and attitudes to treatment amongst men who attempted suicide. *Journal of Mental Health, 26*(3), 220–4.

This research was funded by the Irish Research Council and the National Disability Authority and facilitated by an award from the Fulbright Commission (Ireland).

The author would like to thank the men who participated in this study and record her gratitude to the staff of the hospitals and services involved in the research as well as to the staff of the Central Statistics Office, Cork.

Contents

1 Introduction: The Gendered Landscape of Suicide 1

2 Masculinities, Emotions, and Culture 35

3 Growing Up Male 61

4 The Meaning and Context of Suicidal Action 97

5 Survivors and Casualties 137

6 Conclusions: The Social and Emotional Landscape of Suicide 171

7 Postscript: Lessons for Prevention 189

References 197

Index 209

1
Introduction: The Gendered Landscape of Suicide

Why Study Suicide?

Suicide has been identified by the World Health Organisation (2014) as a global health problem and the fact that an estimated 800,000 people kill themselves each year receives considerable media and public attention. Yet suicide has always exerted a particular fascination for people. This might be attributed to the existential threat implied by suicide, which is effectively a public statement that life is not worth living (Baechler 1979). When a young person completes suicide this effect is probably intensified. Individual suicides are generally the focus of public attention but patterns of suicide are considered by sociologists to be indicative of societal currents or trends—a kind of barometer of wellbeing in a society. Consequently, the distribution of suicide can shed light on critical and or destabilising elements within a culture and in this way map the socioemotional landscape of a society at a particular point in time. The study of suicide therefore extends beyond the examination of a health-related issue, makes visible the '*…circumstances of individuals caught in life's troubles*' (Weaver 2009: 345) and helps to explain the

A. Cleary, *The Gendered Landscape of Suicide*,
https://doi.org/10.1007/978-3-030-16634-2_1

relationship between the person and his/her society. This is an important objective of sociology and of this book which explores how social and emotional issues are implicated in suicidal action.

Defining Suicide

Although suicide appears to be a clear and conclusive action, defining a death as suicide is problematic and this has significant implications for research in the area. Suicide is only categorised as such when there is clear intent and this is generally only possible to confirm from written information left by the deceased and or the lethality of the method used. Notes are left by a minority of those who kill themselves (O'Donnell et al. 1993) and the fact that national statistics often contain an additional mortality categorisation of 'undetermined death' indicates the challenges of defining suicide. Cultural aspects (for example, a religious prohibition on suicide) as well as coroners' practices also influence whether a classification of suicide will be made (Atkinson 1978). In addition, there are philosophical issues concerning the delineation of suicide, whether it is a distinct action or a behaviour, for, as Baechler (1979) noted, suicide is rarely circumscribed by the precise moment when it is accomplished.

The meaning of suicide is contested across cultures and time because suicide is a culturally constructed act performed in the context of a cultural system of meaning (Counts 1991). MacDonald and Murphy (1990) have described how every era and society has its own way of identifying and assigning meaning to deaths by suicide and over time attitudes to suicide have been influenced by shifts in religious, political and philosophical thinking. Until the 1700s suicide was considered both an immoral and a criminal act as people were viewed as the property of God and or of the state. As MacDonald and Murphy (1990) suggest, the move towards greater understanding for suicide followed a shift from a religious to a secular worldview and a change in the relationship between the individual and the state. In these circumstances, suicide could take on an entirely new perspective, for example, as an indicator of human freedom. From the nineteenth century explanations for suicide moved towards psychological and social explanations and with the rise of literacy, suicide could be an expression of one's life and feelings (MacDonald and Murphy 1990). Suicide could also absorb a variety of meanings (both religious and secular) within a single society, as Paperno (1997) demonstrates in her study of suicide in Russia. Explanations for a reputed epidemic of suicides in nineteenth-century Russia centred on the rise of secularisation while in the twentieth century the Soviet Government cast rising rates of suicide as a residue of the old bourgeois order (ibid.: 15).

Culture exerts a considerable influence on suicide rates particularly in terms of the society's overall attitude or script in relation to suicide. Western society, operating within a similar religious milieu, has tended to label suicide as deviant either in a religious, social, or psychological sense but there are societies where suicide is condoned or even valorized. There are also cultures where ambiguous attitudes to suicide exist, where the practice is permitted in certain circumstances. This can occur in societies where suicide is strongly prohibited and disguised forms of suicide are required to transform the deed into a positive action or into a feat of individual or political bravery. Political hunger strikes in Ireland and the practice of Jihad in Muslim culture are examples of this practice (Andriolo 1998). Cultural ideas are interwoven with beliefs about gender and class and these factors have an important influence on suicide patterns.

Since the twentieth century, mental illness has become the dominant paradigm for understanding suicide. Within the biomedical framework suicide results primarily from mental illness, particularly depression, but social factors are increasingly cited in these explanations to address high levels of suicide outside the clinical domain (Hamdi et al. 2008; Owens et al. 2003). Sociology made an early contribution to knowledge about suicide with the publication of Durkheim's (1951) Le Suicide in the late nineteenth century and there were some important studies in the 1960s and 1970s but thereafter sociological interest in the topic decreased.

The Sociological Understanding of Suicide

Sociological understanding of suicide began in the nineteenth century with Durkheim's (1951) analysis of the phenomenon and Le Suicide remains one of the best known and most referenced texts on this topic. His choice of subject was deliberate in that he sought to challenge the prevailing nineteenth-century view of suicide as shaped by personal factors including mental illness. Durkheim's aim was to move the explanatory framework for suicide from the individual to the group and in this way establish the credentials of the emerging discipline of sociology. He used national statistical data, newly introduced in Europe, to map suicide patterns across nations and explained variations in terms of sociocultural factors. Durkheim focused on suicide rates which he believed were social facts reflecting suicidogenic currents or trends in a society. He proposed that each society had a specific tendency towards suicide which is a function of collective consciousness, social relationships and the shared beliefs that bind people together. According to Durkheim the collective tendencies in a society towards suicide dominate the consciousness of individuals and these currents are variously felt across a society. He developed four types of suicide—anomic, egoistic, altruistic and fatalistic—which he maintained were symptomatic of different types of social structure. He attributed egoistic suicide to lack of integration within a society and altruistic suicide to over-integration; anomic suicide as representative of a society lacking regulation and fatalistic suicide to over-regulation in society. His central thesis was that societies require a critical level of integration and or regulation to provide protection from suicide. When levels of integration or regulation are too low, or too high, members of the society lack the necessary social rules or goals, their social-psychological identity is impaired and the most vulnerable among them commit suicide. He examined factors such as the family and religion and concluded that suicide varies inversely with the degree of integration of the religious and domestic groups of which the individual forms a part. He theorised that Catholics were members of a more integrated religion and therefore had lower rates of suicide than Protestants and that family membership also conferred protection from suicide.

Durkheim believed that suicide would increase as societies moved towards modernisation and greater complexity when institutions such as religion and the family would be less important. Suicide rates were also likely to rise during periods of rapid change as people struggled to cope without the protection of weakened social institutions. This 'fear of the modern' was a feature of the social sciences in the nineteenth century (and intensified towards its end) and is similarly illustrated by Tönnies' (1957) work on the transition from collective or Gemeinschaft environments to the less communal Gesellschaft settings. In line with these developments, Durkheim anticipated that suicide rates would rise exponentially in the twentieth century but the scenario that did emerge diverged in a number of ways from his predictions.

Suicide rates increased in the twentieth century, particularly from the mid-century, but not to the extent Durkheim envisaged and changes were not uniform in that patterns of suicide across and within regions varied considerably. Russia moved from the lowest to the highest position in terms of international suicide rates and suicide levels in Scandinavia rose considerably but at a different pace across the region with Finnish rates quadrupling during this period (Helliwell 2007). Elsewhere, suicide rates in countries such as France, Austria and Germany remained stable but high relative to countries such as Great Britain (ibid.). The end of the twentieth century was a period of transformative change with diminishing adherence to traditional values, factors which Durkheim linked to rising levels of suicide. His underlying thesis was that people would be overwhelmed as they sought to negotiate the uncertainly of an increasingly fragmented society and the variety of life choices offered. Yet change evolves in an uneven way with quite different implications for regions, groups and individuals and in line with this suicide rates increased in some, but not all, countries at this time and there were variations across and within regions. This is typified by the former Eastern Bloc region which experienced very similar social and economic upheavals in the late 1980s but which emerged with quite diverse suicide patterns across the region (Mäkinen 2000, 2006).

In the twenty-first century the international pattern remains diverse. Globally, there is a noticeable difference between suicide levels in the East and West and there are significant discrepancies in suicide rates between regions and countries. Rates are highest in China, Japan and Russia and within Europe rates are highest in the Eastern and Northern countries and lowest in the Mediterranean regions (Pritchard and Baldwin 2002; Marusic et al. 2008). Within the Eastern European region levels of suicide differ between individual countries (Mäkinen 2000, 2006) and variations within countries are also evident with suicide rates generally higher for minority groupings. In the United States, suicide is a leading cause of death among Native American (Wissow et al. 2001) and indigenous Alaskan people (Wexler 2006) while African-American males have higher levels of suicide than their White counterparts (Willis et al. 2002). High rates are also evident among some, but not all, First groups in Canada where prevalence appears to relate to levels of self-governance (Chandler and Lalonde 1998). These variations support Durkheim's basic thesis regarding the sociocultural underpinnings of suicide rates but challenge some of his ideas about the links between suicide and values and beliefs (specifically the idea that Catholics nations had lower rates than Protestant groups), urbanisation and age. In the twentieth century, cultural factors continued to influence suicide rates but it appeared that these features were shifting as society changed.

Durkheim's view that traditional values and beliefs protect from suicide continues to have empirical validity but the association is complex. Moving away from tradition in religious terms does increase the suicide rate which helps to explain why suicide rates remain high in developed countries (Helliwell 2007). Yet, paradoxically, freedom from religious and other forms of regulation increases wellbeing in a society (ibid.). The fact that the removal of traditional certainties increases the suicide rate while freedom from traditional constraints paradoxically reduces the suicide rate is probably explained in terms of differential access to opportunities (Baudelot and Establet 2008; Helliwell 2007). The exact mechanism by which religion reduces risk in terms of suicide is unclear. Being part of a religious community may have a general protective effect (Van Tubergen et al. 2005) or reduced risk may be related to more specific features of a religion (Pencosolido and Georgianna 1989). Other factors cited by Durkheim as reducing susceptibility to suicide, such as the family, can have positive but also negative effects as instanced in Wu's (2009) study of suicide in China.

As these developments imply, new cultural forms of integration emerged in the twentieth century which compensated for lessening adherence to traditional values. The safeguards which accrued from adherence to religion were counterbalanced by new forms of integration such as the rise of values associated with self-realisation and creative individualism (Helliwell 2007; Baudelot and Establet 2008). The transformation of the work environment from a place linked to survival into a space which facilitated the development of a positive social identity changed its association with suicide. Higher status, professional work and the positive capital which accrued from this, emerged as a protective feature in terms of suicide from the twentieth century on. Education, particularly at higher levels, offered protection from suicide, and the opposite became true for those lacking educational resources (Baudelot and Establet 2008). These developments contributed to falling or stable suicide rates in some countries from the mid-twentieth century which was contrary to Durkheim's predictions. Changes also occurred relating to the socioeconomic, age and geographical distribution of suicide from the twentieth century.

The socioeconomic distribution of suicide changed in the twentieth century when being in possession of economic resources became a protective feature (Baudelot and Establet 2008). Contrary to Durkheim's thesis that poverty protected from suicide, wealth is now a much greater defence in terms of self-killing and those at the top of the socioeconomic ladder in rich countries are the most shielded group in terms of suicide (Helliwell 2007). Conversely, those in low socioeconomic groupings are the most vulnerable category in terms of suicide (Lorent et al. 2005). Socioeconomic discrepancies in suicide rates are evident across Europe and in the United States where, for example, explanations for rising rates among young African-American men implicate more extreme poverty and extensive underemployment among this population (Joe and Kaplan 2001). Lower socioeconomic groupings have higher rates of unemployment, educational disadvantage and poverty, all of which increase the risk of suicide. People in these social categories also lack access to effective prevention and treatment and, more generally, to the protective environment afforded to the better off via the opportunities offered by well-paid, secure, professions (Baudelot and Establet 2008). The affluent, as Baudelot and Establet (2008) have suggested, have more control over their lives and better access to health knowledge and interventions than those in lower socioeconomic groups. In contrast, poverty can accumulate risk across a number of areas and in the context of increasingly unstable social environments some groups possess more economic and social capital to withstand these changes (Bourdieu 1998). In wealthier countries, which experience relatively high suicide rates, those with high educational and economic status have comparative protection from suicide (Helliwell 2007).

From the mid-twentieth century, suicide became prominent among younger as well as older people (Baudelot and Establet 2008). This increase is generally attributed to a rise in suicides among young males (although internationally this trend was uneven) but the age-related change may also have been associated with enhanced social and economic conditions for older people, factors which have an important impact on suicide rates among this grouping (Baudelot and Establet 2008). In relation to geographical location, urban rates were much higher than rural rates at the beginning of the twentieth century but levels equalised during that century and since then urban rates have been declining relative to rural rates across the world (Helliwell 2007; Baudelot and Establet 2008). Durkheim considered that urbanisation contributed to rising suicide rates because cities were less integrated than rural settings. While this thesis may well have applied to the rapidly growing, disorganised and unhealthy conurbations of the nineteenth century new forms of social existence and solidarity emerged in cities in the twentieth century which offset the negative aspects of urbanisation. There were similar transformative changes in rural life in the twentieth century which made these environments less positive places to live in compared to urban areas (Ní Laoire 2001).

This summary of suicide patterns and the factors which influence suicide rates provides support for Durkheim's general thesis that cultural elements have a decisive influence on levels of suicide. Integration, in the form of adherence to religious or traditional values, continues to reduce risk but the link is not straightforward and new protective, integrative, features have surfaced since the twentieth century. Economic factors have emerged as key in explaining variations in suicide rates, but now wealth, rather than poverty, protects. Similarly, old age is no longer as risk-laden in relation to suicide as Durkheim predicted. Durkheim's achievement was to demonstrate the sociocultural basis to suicidal behaviour but his work has proved difficult to replicate. Concepts such as integration and regulation are difficult to operationalise as they are not strictly defined in his work. Durkheim was prone to redefinition when findings did not comply with his overall framework, for example, he categorised suicides in the military as altruistic when high rates of suicide in the army did not fit with his integration thesis (Kushner 1995). He also made broad claims, for example, about the protective effect of marriage, without explaining how to test these assertions (Weaver 2009). More critically, he made far-reaching assumptions about individual suicides without empirical support (Douglas 1967; Jacobs 1967). Durkheim produced a convincing theory of suicide but, prompted by his desire to launch a sociological account of the phenomenon, he downplayed the contribution of individual-level factors.

Sociological inquiry in this area of study has tended to follow Durkheim (1951) in adopting a quantitative, macro-level, approach but Sociology makes a relatively small contribution to the investigation of suicide which is primarily undertaken by disciplines such as medicine and psychology. Some investigators suggest that adhering to the Durkheimian model is preventing sociologists from advancing in this field of study and that a new research direction is needed (Nolan et al. 2010). Within sociology there has always been an alternative line of theory and enquiry relating to this topic. Halbwachs (see Travis 1990), writing early in the twentieth century, rejected Durkheim's sharp division of social and psychological explanations and later Cavan (1965) suggested combining a societal and individual focus in the study of suicide. After the mid-twentieth century Douglas (1967), drawing on Weber rather than Durkheim, attempted to move the focus towards suicide as a form of meaningful action. These approaches have rarely been used and qualitative research on this topic accounts for a very small proportion of published material (Wray et al. 2011). In light of the societal changes and shifts in suicide patterns experienced since the nineteenth century a sociological framework which permits a more realistic understanding of suicide is required.

Gender and the Gendered Construction of Suicide

A gender pattern in suicide rates has been evident from the earliest studies with male rates generally exceeding female rates. Yet a male preponderance in terms of suicide is not universal and is more representative of the Western World. China, which internationally has a very high rate of suicide, has a gender configuration which is the reverse of trends in the West (Lee 2000). Women in Asian countries complete suicide at a proportionately higher rate than males and more than half of female suicides worldwide occur in China (Pritchard and Baldwin 2002). There are other significant exceptions, including India, where male and female suicide rates are similar (Mayer and Zaian 2002). Gender ratios therefore vary greatly across, as well as within regions, of the world as do explanations for these differences. Suicide in China is primarily explained in terms of sociocultural factors rather than psychiatric factors and the preponderance of suicides among women is viewed as arising from the over-regulation of Chinese females by both the family and the State (Wu 2009). Wu (2009) has attributed high female rates to the powerlessness of women in the context of the destabilisation of the traditional Chinese family as well as to a cultural script which regards suicide as preferable to losing one's honour. His account resonates with other findings showing that higher suicide rates for women in China are confined to rural areas where traditional ways of life are more in evidence (Phillips et al. 2002) and also reflects Pearson and Liu's (2002) ethnographic account of the suicide of an individual Chinese woman.

Despite these noteworthy exceptions the idea that men are especially vulnerability to self-destruction persists and is combined with an historical notion that suicide is a masculine act. This theme is evident in Durkheim's (1951) work which abounds, as Kushner (1995) has noted, with essentialist ideas about men and women. Durkheim explained higher male rates of suicide in terms of men's superior intellectual and moral capacity and women's comparative immunity to suicide to their instinctive and caring qualities. His account of suicide is essentially a narrative of male suicide which he considered to be an indicator of national economic and social wellbeing while suicide among females was framed as an individual, personal, act. These views, originating in the nineteenth century, implied that there was a particular connection between men and suicide and that suicide was a socially significant and sometimes a positive, even courageous, action for a man. These ideas have persisted up to the present time and the most recent example of this thinking emerged at the end of the twentieth century in the form of a thesis linking high rates of male suicide to presumed societal challenges men were encountering at that time. These theories represent stereotypical, gendered, beliefs about men in that they are predicated on the idea that men are a singular category. This unitary notion of men underpins prevailing research frameworks in the study of suicide, specifically sex-difference type research. Sex refers to biological features while gender denotes the attributes assigned by a culture to biological characteristics and therefore provides a wider and more fluid explanatory framework. Sex-difference constructions are intrinsic to the disciplines, notably medicine and psychology, which dominate the study of suicide and sociology has similarly followed a narrow empirical and theoretical pathway in this subject area. Within sex-difference frameworks variations are examined via unitary as well as binary classifications of males and females and higher male rates of suicide have been attributed to biological-related factors, for example, to higher levels of aggression and impulsivity among men, compared to women. These explanatory frameworks reveal little of the subtleties of gender and its association with suicidal behaviour.

There is a paradox in statistical terms (at least in the West) in that men are more likely to complete suicide and women are more likely to engage in self-harm but the categorisation of attempted suicide as a typically feminine action and the completion of suicide as resonant of men is an example of gendered thinking. The image of the typical self-injurer in the psychiatric literature is female although levels of self-harm are rising among men and gender norms may conceal the true prevalence of this behaviour among men (Inckle 2014; Griffin et al. 2018). The gendering of suicidal behaviour continues in the allocation of feminine and masculine type causation for suicide, that women complete suicide for reasons connected to relationships and men kill themselves for economic reasons although this has been refuted (Cleary 2012). These ideas about suicidal behaviour are widely held in the general population with males who attempt suicide viewed as more feminine than men who complete suicide and those who complete suicide for economic reasons rated more highly than those who suicide for relationship reasons (Canetto 1997). These narratives surrounding suicide influence suicidal behaviours in that they provide scripts which people draw on when considering this action. Gendered ideas also extend to emotions and the emotional lives of men and women.

Masculinities, Emotions and Suicidal Behaviour

The narrative of men and their relationship to wellbeing and health presented in the academic literature and the media tends to represent men as emotionally inexpressive and stoical in the face of challenges, features which have been identified as contributing to suicide risk (Courtenay 2000). This scenario represents some but not all men and the form of masculinity associated with these attributes is typically referred to as hegemonic masculinity (Connell 1995; Connell and Messerschmidt 2005). Kimmel (1994) and others have described how the traditional or hegemonic definition of manhood connects masculinity to strength and discourages the display of feelings such as sadness which imply weakness, while other emotions such as anger, are permitted. According to Kimmel (1994), these behavioural and expressive rules are inculcated in males from an early age and are maintained via surveillance from peers and family and form part of a more general process of rejecting feminine discourse and developing a contrasting socioemotional persona. The result is the concealment of these feelings as boys grow into adulthood when this containment becomes increasingly more entrenched and out of consciousness.

Hegemonic-type masculinity has its historical and cultural provenance in nineteenth-century Western society and implies a unitary and binary notion of maleness, that all men are the same and share similar lives and attitudes which are fundamentally different to that of women (Shields 2007). In the latter part of the twentieth century, as the diversity of male lives and experiences became more visible, this type of manhood was referred to as hegemonic or conventional masculinity (Connell 1995; Connell and Messerschmidt 2005). The term was developed by Connell (1995) to shift attention from singular accounts of masculinity but probably attained a more fixed quality than she intended and the validity of the concept has been questioned (Southworth 2016). Critics maintain that few men embody all its ideals and that there are multiple, context-dependent, strategies for doing this type of masculinity (Wetherall and Edley 1999; Jefferson 2002).

In reality, there are many types of men and diverse examples of masculinity and it is a changing concept as men are continually constructing gender. Attempting to understand men's emotional lives using singular and static constructions of man is therefore problematic as is employing binary categorisations of male and female emotions. Men vary in terms of the expressive space available to them and there are identifiable differences in emotional practices and attitudes across groups of men. These trends follow cultural, socioeconomic and or ethnic lines and practices have been identified which conform to the rubric of hegemonic masculinity (Cleary 2012). These beliefs are evident in studies which examine men's help-seeking practices in relation to physical and psychological conditions (Seymour-Smith et al. 2002; O'Brien et al. 2005; Emslie et al. 2007). Men consult health professionals less often than women and reporting psychological distress appears to present particular challenges as it is perceived by certain men as implying weakness (O'Brien et al. 2005). These attitudes are not shared by all men nor by men within similar environments. Some men willingly admit to psychological difficulties and even among men who adhere to a hegemonic-type stance various approaches to health and help-seeking are discernible which are hegemonic in certain situations but not in others (Robertson 2006). Some groups of men do endorse traditional practices in relation to the disclosure of distress, or at least feel constrained to follow prevailing gender norms relating to the expression of suffering, and these men have a heightened risk of suicide (Cleary 2012). In this way, the concept of hegemonic masculinity, while not a rigid categorisation, is useful in classifying attitudes and behaviour.

If males are socialised to believe a strong front or performance is synonymous with masculinity they are less likely to disclose difficulties and seek help and if emotional pain is suppressed it is liable to increase distress and could move the person towards suicide (Brownhill et al. 2005; Cleary 2012). Undisclosed pain can be channelled in other ways, for example, into violent behaviour (Scheff 1997) and significantly higher male (compared to females) rates of substance misuse suggest that alcohol and or drugs may be a culturally acceptable method of coping with distress for men (Cleary 2012). While men's health and expressive behaviours need to be understood as a complex cultural and socioeconomic issue, environments that adhere to relatively narrow, binary, views of gender behaviour, are more likely to give rise to these practices. In this respect, there is evidence that working-class communities are more likely to affirm conventional types of masculinities and help-seeking practices than their more affluent counterparts who access a wider variety of masculine identities and practices (Joe and Kaplan 2001). In this way, the emotional context or community which the man is part of has an important influence on his wellbeing and particularly how his emotions are expressed.

An analysis of emotion and emotional cultures is surprisingly absent from most investigations of suicide and, with the exception of Hochschild's (1979) work, is relatively underdeveloped within sociology despite the fact that meaning and the intersection of structure and biography are central to the discipline (Mills 1959). Yet, emotions form the background to much work related to suicide and are powerfully present in studies such as Weaver's (2009) historical account of suicides in

Australia and New Zealand which illustrates how emotions are contextualised within particular cultural settings.

> *The men who committed suicide in New Zealand and Queensland wanted 'to finish the business' or 'get out of it.' It was consistent with a cultural conditioning that they would follow a script which represented masculine conduct as decisive, brave, and unequivocal. …They had motives and pain but they needed justification, rooted in cultural beliefs of self-sacrifice…* (Weaver 2009: 215/269)

Understanding the link between emotions and suicide is problematic because the notion of gender-specific feelings is deeply entrenched in the scientific literature (Shields 2007). The origins of these beliefs can be traced to Western ideas about the dualisms of body and mind, emotion and reason, the allocating of these traits to male or female and the concept of complementarity, that the traits of males are compensated for by the traits of females. Within this construction, the traits of each sex were viewed as a consequence of biology and the female reproductive physiology was central to explaining women's distinctive emotional character (Shields 2007). These ideologies were used in the nineteenth century to justify the division of labour between men and women, and in the twentieth century underpinned ideas about men's and women's respective family roles. In the nineteenth century sociologists such as Durkheim and Spencer described female reasoning as intuitive, in contrast to rational, intellectually superior, male reasoning and in the following century Parsons and Bales (1955) built on the notion of gender-specific emotional attributes to develop their theory of family cohesion. These ideas are embedded in sex-difference research frameworks which adopt oppositional concepts of masculinity and femininity and a unitary notion of men and male emotions. Historically, beliefs about emotions included class and racist ideas, for example, 'rational man' was white and educated and the emotions of the lower classes were described as crude and instinctive (Shields 2007: 107). As Shields (2007) suggests, these gender and class-linked constructions of emotions define who is 'permitted to speak from the heart' (ibid.: 107).

The ability to express feelings is related to the emotional culture or community men inhabit as people within similar emotional communities share a common discourse relating to feelings and expression (Tarlow 2000). Emotions are constructed within particular sociocultural settings which specify the emotions which are valued and those which should be avoided and how emotions are to be experienced, interpreted and expressed. These emotional cultures are not static but differ across time and place as they exist only through cultural meaning. Elias (1939) identified a general trend of increasing emotional restraint from the middle ages and the emotional culture which emerged in response to industrialisation in the nineteenth century changed with the rise of a consumer society in the twentieth century (Sterns 1994). At this point, according to Sterns (1994), emotional restraint became a key task for men (at least in the United States) and public displays of emotion were discouraged. There were further gender-related transitions in emotional discourses later in the twentieth century in response to changing family needs as gender distinctions around emotional expression reduced (but did not disappear) (Sterns 1994). Yet, despite the view that a more flexible, mutually negotiated, type of emotional culture is now in place (Wouters 2007), emotion norms, as Hochschild (2012) maintains, continue to shape how we feel. Emotion regimes vary in terms of the degree of conformity required and tensions can arise if there is a strong disjoint between felt and expressed emotion, when people are forced to feel in constrained ways (Reddy 2001). The contention of this book is that men in some communities are restricted in terms of their ability to express feelings, especially emotional pain, and that this has a significant impact on levels of risk in relation to suicide.

Gender remains an important differentiating factor in society and while adherence to gender-specific social roles are less in evidence today gendered attitudes to emotions have proved more resistant to interrogation. Individuals acquire gender-linked knowledge about emotions in childhood and this process, and the way males and females respond to stressful, emotion-eliciting, situations tends to be in line with the gender and social class expectations of their particular community (Hochschild 1979; Kemper 1981). Research findings imply that the emotional lives of men and women are not dissimilar but the expression of emotions varies between the sexes (Simon and Nath 2004). Although females report more psychological difficulties similar levels of psychological distress are evident across genders if both depression and substance misuse are taken together and substance misuse may be a masking diagnosis for depression in men (Cochran and Rabinowitz 2000). In this way, emotional pain may be channelled in culturally prescribed ways and could account for higher reported levels of psychological distress for women yet higher rates of suicide for men (Van de Velde et al. 2010, 2013).

Based on this evidence, men's emotionality is unlikely to be a biological or psychological given but rather influenced by culture and therefore diverse in terms of felt and expressive practices (Holmes 2015). Men develop their emotional lives within a specific community and draw on the feeling rules of that community to guide them and in this way emotions, and especially the expression of emotions, vary across groups of men. Emotions such as shame, guilt and anger feature prominently in studies of suicidal behaviour and these sentiments may be more heavily concentrated in some cultural groupings (Scheff 1997). Studies of non-clinical populations, from which the majority of suicides emerge, suggest that suicidal behaviour results from unbearable emotional pain, when people believe this action is one of the few options available and or from efforts to control stressful feelings (Shneidman 1991). Suicide may therefore be a way of discharging painful emotions in a culturally constricted environment when using the body to express distress is the only available narrative (Frank 1996).

A Socioemotional Framework for Understanding Suicide

The summary of suicide-related research presented here signals considerable changes in society as well as in suicide trends since Durkheim (1951) produced his analysis in the nineteenth century. There is now a consistent association between low socioeconomic status and suicidal behaviour (Lorent et al. 2005; Baudelot and Establet 2008) and since the mid-twentieth century younger as well as older people are likely to complete suicide (see Middleton et al. 2006). Suicide is more prevalent among men but specifically men from lower socioeconomic groupings and this is frequently combined with educational deficits and unemployment (Lorent et al. 2005). In this way, cultural and economic factors are critically related to suicide and account for variations across and within societies as they influence how people experience and channel emotional distress. Emotions coalesce around strongly defined themes and values within a society and feeling rules may restrict emotional expression in some male groupings (Hochschild 1979; Kemper 1981). Emotions may therefore be viewed as forming a conceptual bridge between individuals, their decision-making around suicide and the larger social milieu in which they are located (Abrutyn and Mueller 2014; Mueller and Abrutyn 2016).

This research seeks to address a gap in the sociological literature by examining the meanings and emotions involved in suicidal behaviour for men. The study draws on the narratives of a sample of young men who made a serious suicide attempt, recounted in interviews carried out shortly after the suicide attempt. Over four decades ago, Douglas (1967) remarked that the meaningful analysis of suicide should be based on the definitions supplied by the social actors involved and this sample is the closest approximation to this population. The study follows Douglas (1967) in focusing on the subjective meanings and patterns generated by these stories of suicidal action. The aim is to profile the men and their feeling narratives, to chart the growth of their emotional turmoil and their response to this and in this way explicate the issue of emotional cultures and their link to suicide. In seeking to understand why these men moved towards suicidal decisions, I draw on concepts and knowledge from gender and masculinity studies as well as the sociological study of emotions. My aim in this text is to develop an approach to suicide that includes an exploration of how gender and specifically masculinities and emotional cultures interact and how these are linked to structural factors to increase vulnerability to suicide. Suicide is grounded in individual action and meaning but individuals share cultural meanings, even when these meanings have become part of their unconscious as Bourdieu (1998) suggests. The stories on which this analysis is based are all different but they combine to support the idea that suicide is, as Durkheim theorised, a very sociological story. But while he identified themes prevalent in the nineteenth century these men's stories exemplify vulnerable lives in the twenty-first century. This vulnerability is not conclusive or fixed as indicated by the participants in this study who survived and moved on with their lives. At the same time, the fact that a number of these men later completed suicide allows us to follow a line in some men's lives from distress to a point of unbearable emotional pain and to suicide.

The initial sections, Chapters 2 and 3, examine the gender and emotional biographies of the study participants. In Chapter 2 the focus is on the feelings the men incorporated into their stories to illustrate the sociocultural background they emerged from. Chapter 3 describes their experiences growing up, how they acquired ideas about masculinity and the ways in which gender was regulated within their communities. Chapter 4 details the suicide attempts and Chapter 5 examines how these men's lives evolved over subsequent years. The final sections (Chapters 6 and 7) summarise the main findings and provide some recommendations for prevention.

Methodology and Details of the Study

This programme of study was carried out over a period of fifteen years with the baseline interviews conducted over two and one-half years. The participants consisted of fifty-two men who made a clinically serious suicide attempt. The objective of the initial investigation was to explore the motivations and meanings involved in the suicidal behaviour. The follow-up studies were carried out to establish outcome for these men, particularly in terms of subsequent episodes of suicidal behaviour. The initial follow-up inquiry was undertaken seven years after the baseline interviews and involved analysis of national mortality data from the Central Statistical Office (CSO) as well as hospital and outpatient data to determine health status and service take-up in the interim period. A small number of interviews with the original participants were also carried out at this time. Eight years later a further examination of National Mortality (CSO) data was conducted to determine outcome at the fifteen year point.

The Baseline Study

Participants consisted of fifty-two men who were interviewed following a suicide attempt over a period of two and one-half years. The group represent a consecutive sample of men who made a clinically serious suicide attempt and who were admitted to three hospitals in the Dublin (Ireland) area over the study period. The sample can be regarded as representative due to the seriousness of the attempts and because these hospitals were likely to receive all such admissions from this area over the period of the study. Two of the hospitals are district or catchment area hospitals (and include Accident and Emergency and psychiatric units) and the third a psychiatric unit which admits patients from a nearby general hospital. Inclusion criteria included gender (male), age (18–30 years) and, intent, in that all those included in the study had made a suicide attempt with definite intent to die and which required hospital treatment. This age and gender group was chosen to reflect the population category with the highest rate of suicide in Ireland and other Western countries. Participants were referred by the liaison psychiatric team working in the Accident and Emergency Departments of the hospitals.

When a subject presented or was admitted to the hospital I was usually contacted but I also telephoned the agreed liaison person on a daily basis. The men were initially given information about the study from the liaison team and agreed in principle to participate. One man refused to be interviewed. All interviews were carried out by the author (AC). When I met the potential participants I gave them more detailed information, answered any questions they asked and again sought their permission to include them in the study. If they agreed to proceed they signed a consent form to participate in the project before the interview commenced. Separate consent was obtained relating to the audio-taping of the interviews and two men did not agree to this. In these instances I took notes. The men were almost always interviewed within twenty-four hours of the suicidal action but in some cases interviews were not possible within this time frame because of the level of injuries sustained. The majority of the interviews took place in a room arranged for this purpose in the hospitals and the sessions generally lasted between one and two hours but some were considerably longer. No details other than the name and age of the respondent were referred to prior to interview and hospital notes were not consulted. The methodology for the original study was primarily qualitative and data collection was based on an unstructured interview in order to explore the motivations and circumstances involved in the suicidal behaviour.

Interviews and the Interviewing Experience

The interview schedule used in the session consisted of one introductory question:

Can you tell me how you came to be admitted here?

Thereafter, no further pre-set questions were asked but questions were asked in response to issues raised by the respondent. This approach was adopted to avoid pre-categorisation of actions or motives and allowed the subject to define the action himself, i.e. whether he regarded it as a suicidal attempt. Thereafter, the aim was to allow the subject to tell his story in his own way and the interviewing style was informal with an emphasis on listening. As described by Goffman (1968) the interviewer can be a 'sympathetic other' with whom the subject can discuss their situation in a non-judgemental way and this was the role I played. It was not difficult to feel sympathy as the stories were replete with very human experiences of pain and disappointment. The fact that I was female was, I think, an advantage as females had provided the only confiding experiences for these men. I viewed the interviews as co-constructions between interviewer and interviewee but this did not imply uncritical acceptance of their accounts of themselves. My position was that of an academic researcher from a university and I emphasized both verbally and in the consent form that I had no connection with the study hospitals. I wanted the participants to see me as someone separate from hospital personnel and I emphasised that our discussion would not be disclosed in any way to the staff.

The beginning of the interviews were usually tentative, for both of us, but a common feature was a verbal outpouring after the initial question. The majority of the men had little experience of speaking about themselves and they often professed themselves to be lacking in these skills. Yet the level of engagement and fluency demonstrated by these men indicated their ability and willingness to discuss sensitive, personal, matters. They generally welcomed the opportunity to talk after such a traumatic event and a common response to being asked to participate was that they were glad to do so if it helped someone else in a similar situation. In almost all cases they developed the narratives themselves and required little prompting. Many of the interviews could have gone on longer and pauses were generally very brief. Common themes among the men's stories quickly emerged which was, of course, partly due to the fact that they had a very specific issue in common but they spontaneously raised other similar topics. After each interview I wrote up notes on the encounter which also involved tracking my response to the session and the subject. The respondents were generally interesting, engaging and reflective and even, on occasions, funny but some opinions were distasteful and occasionally horrifying, for example, when violent actions were described.

The majority of the interviews could be classified as successful encounters in that there was an acceptable level of engagement, both interviewer and respondent were relatively relaxed and the encounter resembled an ordinary conversation, but this didn't always occur. Some respondents were interested in the research which helped the interview relationship but others showed little interest in the study. Interviews were difficult for a variety of reasons. Sometimes participants were not forthcoming and a small number were intent on controlling the interview session. There was an element of performance in some interviews and a few encounters were quite instrumental. These men saw me as part of the hospital system, despite my clarifications, and thought that speaking to me would help them in some way. Although the majority of the men did not have serious psychiatric difficulties one interview session was disrupted due to acute symptoms. There were also practical problems when a man refused to be taped or, as happened on a few occasions, the tape machine failed or malfunctioned.

My interview with Jack was one of the most testing encounters. He was extremely agitated and didn't want to engage in any conversation which did not focus on his symptoms. The interview with Myles was the most challenging encounter of all and came almost at the end of the fieldwork. He appeared detached and suspicious and observed me intently throughout the session. Once his short summary of what had happened was over and I mentioned some of the points he had raised he became angry and brought the interview to an end. Rory was a difficult subject to engage with and when he completed suicide some months after I interviewed him (while the fieldwork was still ongoing) the encounter took on an added significance and made me revisit and reflect on the transcript and notes of the interview.

Follow-Up Studies

In the first phase of follow-up, data relating to the fifty-two men were obtained from hospital (In-patient, Accident & Emergency and Outpatient) records and Central Statistics Office (CSO) (Ireland) mortality data. Information was collected on subsequent admissions and presentations to hospital and attendance at Out-Patient Departments; reasons for these admissions; subsequent evidence of suicidal behaviour and self-harm; diagnosis of mental disorder and present/most recent mental health status. Any relevant additional information relating to the subsequent life of the participants was also recorded. CSO records for suicide and undetermined deaths for the twenty-six counties of Ireland were also examined to establish the prevalence of completed suicides for the sample of fifty-two men over the study period. A small number of interviews ($n=4$) were also undertaken with participants about their health and treatment experiences since the index episode. It was not possible to interview more of the men primarily due to ethical considerations around re-establishing contact with them but there may also have been a reluctance to re-engage with the study. The majority of the participants had not maintained contact with the services and letters inviting participation in these interviews were only forwarded (via the relevant clinical team) if a current address was verified. It was only possible to establish contact addresses for twenty-four of the participants and of these four men agreed to be interviewed, one refused, and there was no reply from the remaining nineteen. The follow-up interviews were audiotaped.

At the fifteen-year follow-up CSO mortality data only was examined with the aim of identifying men who had completed suicide in the interim period.

Data Analysis

The interview tapes and field-notes were transcribed and the analysis carried out via computer and manual methods. The data were analysed using a modified version of grounded theory (Strauss and Corbin 1998) and guided by Douglas's (1967) general methodological approach. I read all transcripts and field-notes numerous times to obtain a comprehensive picture of the data. From the beginning some regularities were identifiable—not surprisingly constructed around explanations for the suicidal behaviour and the way in which the suicidal pathway developed—but also relating to childhood and family factors. Themes related to the suicide attempt included enduring emotional pain, inability to disclose pain and the reasons for this. Sub-themes relating to the man's background included childhood adversity and father–son relationships. These thematic concepts form the basis of the account presented in this book. I also used a computer programme for qualitative data analysis (NUD*IST) to identify frequently occurring words and phrases linked to these themes and produced a summary relating to each participant based on the transcript and field-notes. Following this stage I reread the transcripts, field-notes and individuals' summaries continually to establish themes. I then examined relevant literature and moved back and forth between the literature and transcripts to develop the thematic analysis. Theoretically the analysis was driven by a social constructionist framework and more specifically by the work of writers such as Connell (2002) and Hochschild (1979). Participants' constructions of masculinity were central to the analysis of the data but while their narratives contained frequent references to what men do, think and feel none specifically mentioned this term. In writing up the findings I have used verbatim quotations when appropriate to stay as close as possible to the meanings the men attached to their actions.

Ethical Considerations

Consent for the baseline and the initial follow-up study was obtained from the Hospitals' Ethics Committees and the hospitals provided significant support for the research. A protocol was developed on each occasion to deal with the various issues and stages of the research. In the baseline study, potential recruits were provided with information about the study by hospital personnel and asked if they would like to participate. They were informed that the study was completely separate from their treatment regimes and that participation was entirely voluntary. If a man agreed to participate I then met with him and explained the nature of the study in greater detail and again emphasised the voluntary, confidential and independent (of treatment) aspect of participation. If he agreed to proceed with the interview at this point he signed a consent form. Potential recruits therefore had a number of opportunities to decline an interview which represented an important safeguard for them at a vulnerable time. The data was anonymised before it was removed from the hospitals and the list of participants, to which only the author had access, was kept in a locked environment in the university.

The follow-up study which took place seven years after the baseline inquiry was primarily based on documentary methods and data collected were anonymised before information was removed from the hospital or service setting. The same step-wise procedure was followed in relation to gaining consent from the participants (i.e. they were contacted by the clinical team initially) and the protocol for this study included service support for participants, if required, following the interview.

In writing up the details of this study care has been taken to remove any features which might identify the participants. All names provided are pseudonyms and identifying details have also been removed from the narratives. As the group who completed suicide are relatively small in number particular care has been taken to conceal specific details of these men's lives.

Background Details of the Participants

The mean age of the participants when they were first interviewed was 23 years and the range was 18–30 years, in line with the study criteria. The majority (94%) were single and they were all born in the Republic of Ireland. The most commonly used method in the suicide attempt was an overdose of drugs (58%) and the remaining cases featured methods generally categorised as particularly lethal (hanging, shooting, etc.). Almost half (48%) worked in unskilled jobs and they came primarily (88%) from unskilled and skilled manual backgrounds. Less than forty per cent had a Leaving Certificate (the examination taken in Ireland at the completion of second level schooling), which implies that their average level of educational attainment was considerably lower than the national average (Clancy and Wall 2000). Over one quarter (27%) of the participants had been in trouble with the law and they tended to come from neighbourhoods consisting predominantly of public housing and a concentration of lower socioeconomic groupings.

Summary

The demographic profile of suicide has changed since Durkheim produced his seminal book in the nineteenth century and some of these changes have cast doubt on both his theoretical and methodological approach. In contrast to Durkheim's findings, suicide is now more a rural than an urban phenomenon, is prevalent among younger as well as older people and occurs more often in lower socioeconomic groupings. There is still convincing evidence of the sociocultural underpinnings of suicide but it appears that the factors which impact on suicide rates have changed over time. Significant cross cultural disparities exist in relation to suicide patterns and there are also variations between groups within particular societies. Differing male and female rates of suicide have been an enduring feature of suicide but contrary to a prevailing idea, men do not always predominate in terms of completed suicide and internationally there are considerable gender variations. Within the Western world, where men tend to have higher rates of suicide, there are differences between groups of men based on socioeconomic, ethnic and other factors. The idea that all men are vulnerable to suicide is predicated on a notion that men are a unitary group and this idea is incorporated into many studies of suicide behaviour.

This study examines suicide from a gender perspective and focuses on the emotions involved in this behaviour. The theoretical framework incorporates emerging ideas about gender and emotions in an attempt to produce a socioemotional understanding of suicide. Culture has an important impact on emotions and communal feeling rules guide how emotions are felt and, in particular, expressed. These feeling rules have gender and class elements so that men in particular communities may be restricted in terms of demonstrating specific sentiments. The contention is that the true nature of men's emotions may not be apparent in conventional studies due to normative constraints operating in particular environments. Methodologically, this study departs from the dominant, statistical-based, research paradigm used in investigations of suicide in employing a qualitative design which draws on the narratives of a sample of young men who made a serious suicide attempt. These stories were recounted in interviews carried out shortly after the suicide attempt and the approach follows Douglas's (1967) contention that a meaningful analysis of suicide should be based on the definitions of the actors involved. Those who engage in medically serious, near-fatal, suicide attempts are the closest approximation to the population of those who end their lives. The aim is to profile the men and their feeling narratives, to chart the growth of, and their response to, emotional anguish and in this way explicate the issue of emotional cultures and their link to suicide.

References

Abrutyn, S., & Mueller, A. S. (2014). The socioemotional foundations of suicide: A microsociological view of Durkheim's suicide. *Sociological Theory, 32*(4), 327–351.

Andriolo, K. R. (1998). Gender and the cultural construction of good and bad suicides. *Suicide and Life Threatening Behaviour, 28*(1), 37–49.

Atkinson, J. M. (1978). *Discovering suicide*. London and Basingstoke: Macmillan.

Baechler, J. (1979). *Suicides* (B. Cooper, Trans.). New York: Basic Books.

Baudelot, C., & Establet, R. (2008). *Suicide: The hidden side of modernity*. Cambridge: Polity Press.

Bourdieu, P. (1998). *Practical reason: On the theory of action*. Stanford, CA: Stanford University Press.

Brownhill, S., Wilhelm, K., Barclay, L., & Schmied, V. (2005). Big build: Hidden depression in men. *Australian and New Zealand Journal of Psychiatry, 39*(10), 921–931.

Canetto, S. S. (1997). Meanings of gender and suicidal behaviour during adolescence. *Suicide and Life-Threatening Behaviour, 27*(4), 339–351.

Cavan, R. S. (1965). *Suicide*. New York: Russell and Russell.

Chandler, M. J., & Lalonde, C. E. (1998). Cultural continuity as a hedge against suicide in Canada's First Nations. *Transcultural Psychiatry, 35*(2), 193–211.

Clancy, P., & Wall, J. (2000). *Social background of higher education entrants*. Dublin: Higher Education Authority.

Cleary, A. (2012). Suicidal action, emotional expression, and the performance of masculinities. *Social Science & Medicine, 74*(4), 498–505.

Cochran, S. V., & Rabinowitz, F. E. (2000). *Men and depression*. San Diego, CA: Academic.

Connell, R. W. (1995). *Masculinities*. Berkeley: University of California Press.

Connell, R. W. (2002). *Gender: Short introduction*. Cambridge: Polity Press.

Connell, R. W., & Messerschmidt, J. W. (2005). Hegemonic masculinity: Rethinking the concept. *Gender & Society, 19*, 829–859.

Counts, D. S. (1991). Suicide in different ages from a cross-cultural perspective. In A. A. Leenaars (Ed.), *Life-span perspectives on suicide*. Boston, MA: Springer.

Courtenay, W. H. (2000). Constructions of masculinity and their influence on men's well-being: A theory of gender and health. *Social Science and Medicine, 50*(10), 1385–1401.

Douglas, J. D. (1967). *The social meanings of suicide*. Princeton, NJ: Princeton University Press.

Durkheim, E. (1951). *Suicide: A study in sociology* (R. Spaulding, Trans.). London: Routledge and Kegan Paul.

Elias, N. (1939). *The civilising process: Sociogenetic and psychogenetic investigations*. Oxford: Blackwell.

Emslie, C., Ridge, D., Ziebland, S., & Hunt, K. (2007). Exploring men's and women's experiences of depression and engagement with health professionals: More similarities than differences? A qualitative interview study. *BioMed Central Family Practice, 8*(1), 43.

Frank, A. (1996). Reconciliatory alchemy: Bodies, narrative and power. *Body & Society, 2*(3), 53–71.

Goffman, E. (1968). *Asylums*. Harmondsworth: Penguin Books.

Griffin, E., Dillon, C. B., McTernan, N., Arensman, E., Williamson, E., Perry, I. J., et al. (2018). *National self-harm registry Ireland annual report 2017*. Cork: National Suicide Research Foundation.

Hamdi, E., Price, S., Qassem, T., Amin, Y., & Jones, D. (2008). Suicides not in contact with mental health services: Risk indicators and determinants of referral. *Journal of Mental Health, 17*(4): 398–409.

Helliwell, J. F. (2007). Well-being and social capital: Does suicide pose a puzzle? *Social Indicators Research, 81*(3), 455–496.

Hochschild, A. R. (1979). Emotion work, feeling rules, and social structure. *American Journal of Sociology, 85*(3), 551–575.

Hochschild, A. R. (2012). *The managed heart: The commercialisation of human feeling*. Berkeley: University of California Press.

Holmes, M. (2015). Men's emotions: Heteromasculinity, emotional reflexivity, and intimate relationships. *Men and Masculinities, 18*(2), 176–192.

Inckle, K. (2014). Strong and silent: Men, masculinity, and self-injury. *Men and Masculinities, 17*(1), 3–21.

Jacobs, J. (1967). A phenomenological study of suicide notes. *Social Problems, 15*(1), 60–70.

Jefferson, T. (2002). Subordinating hegemonic masculinity. *Theoretical Criminology, 6*(1), 63–88.

Joe, S., & Kaplan, M. S. (2001). Suicide among African American men. *Suicide and Life Threatening Behaviour, 31*(Supplement) (Spring), 106–121.

Kemper, T. D. (1981). Social constructivist and positivist approaches to the sociology of emotions. *American Journal of Sociology, 87*, 336–361.

Kimmel, M. (1994). Masculinity as homophobia. In H. Brod & M. Kaufman (Eds.), *Theorising masculinities* (pp. 119–141). London: Sage.

Kushner, H. I. (1995). Women and suicidal behavior: Epidemiology, gender and lethality in historical perspective. In S. S. Canetto & D. Lester (Eds.), *Women and suicidal behavior* (p. 11). New York: Springer.

Lee, S. (2000, September 9). Suicide in China—International patterns (BMJ letter).

Lorent, V., Kunst, A. E., Huisman, M., Costa, G., & Mackenbach, J. (2005). Socio-economic inequalities in suicide: A European comparative study. *British Journal of Psychiatry, 187*(1), 49–54.

MacDonald, M., & Murphy, T. (1990). *Sleepless souls: Suicide in early modern England.* Oxford Studies in Social History. Oxford: Clarendon Press.

Mäkinen, I. H. (2000). Eastern European transition and suicide mortality. *Social Science and Medicine, 51*(9), 1405–1420.

Mäkinen, I. H. (2006). Suicide mortality of Eastern European regions before and after the Communist period. *Social Science and Medicine, 63*(2), 307–319.

Marusic, A., Petrovic, A., & Zorko, M. (2008). Does suicide know the points of the compass? *International Journal of Social Psychiatry, 54*(5), 387–389.

Mayer, P., & Ziaian, T. (2002). Suicide, gender, and age variations in India: Are women in Indian society protected from suicide? *Crisis, 23*(3), 98–103.

Middleton, N., Sterne, J. A., & Gunnell, D. (2006). The geography of despair among 15–44-year-old men in England and Wales: Putting suicide on the map. *Journal Epidemiology & Community Health, 60*(12), 1040–1047.

Mills, C. W. (1959). *The sociological imagination.* Oxford: Oxford University Press.

Mueller, A. S., & Abrutyn, S. (2016). Adolescents under pressure: A new Durkheimian framework for understanding adolescent suicide in a cohesive community. *American Sociological Review, 81*(5), 877–899.

Ní Laoire, C. (2001). A matter of life and death? Men, masculinities and staying 'behind' in rural Ireland. *Sociologia Ruralis, 41*(2), 220–236.

Nolan, P. D., Triplett, J., & McDonough, S. (2010). Sociology's suicide: A forensic autopsy. *The American Sociologist, 41*(3), 292–305.

O'Brien, R., Hunt, K., & Hart, G. (2005). 'It's caveman stuff, but that is to a certain extent how guys still operate': Men's accounts of masculinity and help seeking. *Social Science and Medicine, 61*(3), 503–516.

O'Donnell, I., Farmer, R., & Catalan, J. (1993). Suicide notes. *British Journal of Psychiatry, 163,* 45–48.

Owens, C., Booth, N., Briscoe, M., Lawrence, C., & Lloyd, K. (2003). Suicide outside the care of mental health services: A case-controlled psychological autopsy study. *Crisis: The Journal of Crisis Intervention and Suicide Prevention, 24*(3), 113–121.

Paperno, I. (1997). *Suicide as a cultural institution in Dostoevsky's Russia*. Ithaca, NY: Cornell University Press.

Parsons, T., & Bales, R. F. (1955). *Family, socialization and interaction process*. Glencoe, Illinois: The Free Press.

Pearson, V., & Liu, M. (2002). Ling's death: An ethnography of a Chinese women's suicide. *Suicide and Life-Threatening Behaviour, 32*(4), 347–358.

Pescosolido, B., & Georgianna, S. (1989). Durkheim, suicide and religion: Toward a network theory of suicide. *American Sociological Review, 54*(1), 33–48.

Phillips, M. R., Xianyun, L., & Yanping, Z. (2002). Suicide rates in China, 1995–99. *The Lancet, 359*, 835–840.

Pritchard, C., & Baldwin, D. S. (2002). Elderly suicide rates in Asian and English-speaking countries. *Acta Psychiatrica Scandinavica, 105*(4), 271–275.

Reddy, W. (2001). *The navigation of feeling: A framework for the history of emotions*. Cambridge: Cambridge University Press.

Robertson, S. (2006). Health an interdisciplinary 'not living live in too much of an excess': Lay men understanding health and well-being. *Health: In Interdisciplinary Journal for the Social Study of Health, Illness and Medicine, 10*(2), 175–189.

Scheff, T. (1997). *Emotions, the social bond, and human reality*. Cambridge: Cambridge University Press.

Seymour-Smith, S., Weatherall, M., & Phoenix, A. (2002). 'My wife ordered me to come!': A discursive analysis of doctors' and nurses' accounts of men's use of general practitioners. *Journal of Health Psychology, 7*(3), 253–267.

Shields, S. A. (2007). Passionate men, emotional women: Psychology constructs gender in the late 19th century. *History of Psychology, 10*(2), 92–110.

Shneidman, E. S. (1991). The commonalities of suicide across the life span. In A. A. Leenaars (Ed.), *Life span perspectives of suicide: Time-lines in the suicide process* (p. 39). New York: Plenum Press.

Simon, R. W., & Nath, A. (2004). Gender and emotion in the United States: Do men and women differ in self-reports of feelings and expressive behavior? *American Journal Sociology, 109*(5), 1137–1176.

Southworth, P. M. (2016). Hegemonic masculinity and suicide: A review of the literature. *The European Health Psychologist, 18*(1), 7–24.
Sterns, P. N. (1994). *American Cool: Constructing a twentieth-century emotional style*. New York: New York University Press.
Strauss, A., & Corbin, J. (1998). *Basics of qualitative research: Techniques and procedures for developing grounded theory*. Thousand Oaks, CA: Sage.
Tarlow, S. (2000). The archaeology of emotion and affect. *Annual Review of Archaeology, 41*(1), 169–185.
Tönnies, F. (1957). *Community and society: Gemeinschaft und Gesellschaft* (Charles P. Loomis, Ed. and Trans.). East Lansing: The Michigan State University Press.
Travis, R. (1990). Halbwachs and Durkheim: A test of two theories of suicide. *The British Journal of Sociology, 41*(2), 225–243.
Van de Velde, S., Bracke, P., & Levecque, K. (2010). Gender differences in depression in 23 countries. Cross-national variation in the gender gap in depression. *Social Science and Medicine, 71*(2), 305–313.
Van de Velde, S., Huijts, T., Bracke, P., & Levecque, K. (2013). Micro-level gender equality and depression in men and women in Europe. *Sociology of Health & Illness, 35*(5), 682–698.
Van Tubergen, F., Te Grotenhuis, M., & Ultee, W. (2005). Denomination, religious context, and suicide: Neo-Durkheimian multilevel explanations tested with individual and contextual data. *American Journal of Sociology, 111*(3), 797–823.
Weaver, J. C. (2009). *A sadly troubled History: The meanings of suicide in the modern age*. Montreal: McGill-Queen's University Press.
Wetherall, M., & Edley, N. (1999). Negotiating hegemonic masculinity: Imaginary positions and psycho-discursive practices. *Feminism & Psychology, 9*(3), 335–356.
Wexler, L. M. (2006). Inupiat youth suicide and culture loss: Changing community conversations for prevention. *Social Science and Medicine, 63*(11), 2938–2948.
Willis, L. A., Coombs, D. W., Cockerham, W. C., & Frison, S. L. (2002). Ready to die: A postmodern interpretation of the increase in African-American adolescent male suicide. *Social Science and Medicine, 22*(6), 907–920.
Wissow, L. S., Walkup, J., Barlow, A., Reid, R., & Kane, S. (2001). Cluster and regional influences on suicide in a Southwestern American Indian tribe. *Social Science and Medicine, 53*(9), 1115–1124.

World Health Organisation. (2014). *Preventing suicide: A global imperative.* Geneva: WHO.
Wouters, C. (2007). *Informalisation: Manners and emotions since 1890.* London: Sage.
Wray, M., Colen, C., & Pescosolido, B. (2011). The sociology of suicide. *Annual Review of Sociology, 37*, 505–528.
Wu, F. (2009). *Suicide and justice: A Chinese perspective.* Contemporary China Series. New York: Routledge.

2

Masculinities, Emotions, and Culture

Introduction

There are significant variations, including gender differences, in suicide rates across regions of the world as well as within countries and this diversity supports the sociocultural basis to suicidal action. That men are more likely to complete suicide is a frequently advanced, but not universal, feature of suicide and this idea is linked to a longstanding notion of suicide as a male practice. This study focuses on cultural factors and particularly the impact of emotional cultures, on male suicidal action. Emotions and emotion norms have obvious implications for suicidal behaviour yet the topic is underdeveloped in accounts of the phenomenon or referenced via stereotypical ideas about the emotional lives of men and women. The notion that men and women have different emotions, that these emotions are 'natural' or innate and channel males and females into various forms of behaviour, is deeply embedded in both public discourse and the academic literature (Shields 2007). These beliefs are grounded in Western ideas about the dualisms of body and mind, emotion and reason, and the allocation of traits based on biological sex with female reproductive physiology the

A. Cleary, *The Gendered Landscape of Suicide*,
https://doi.org/10.1007/978-3-030-16634-2_2

basis of women's distinctive emotional character (Shields 2007: 96). These ideas are embedded in sex-difference research frameworks, which adopt oppositional concepts of masculinity and femininity and a unitary notion of men and male emotions. The validity of these ideas is questionable as research suggests that male and female emotions are not particularly dissimilar although there are gender variations in relation to the expression of emotions (Simon and Nath 2004). Similarly, although females report more psychological difficulties, levels of distress across genders are comparable if both depression and substance misuse (which may represent disguised depression) (Cochrane and Rabinowitz 2000) are combined.

The ability to express feelings varies because emotions are constructed within particular sociocultural settings which specify how emotions are experienced, interpreted and expressed. In this way gender and social class influence the experience and the expression of emotions (Hochschild 1979; Kemper 1981). In some cultures, males are restricted in terms of expressing emotions, specifically sentiments relating to sadness and pain, and in this way men's so-called emotional inexpressiveness is likely to have a cultural basis. This feature is usually linked to hegemonic masculinity which is only one possible form of masculinity and may no longer be a singular or dominant type of manhood. The hegemonic definition of manhood connects masculinity to strength and discourages the display of feelings which imply weakness (Connell 1995; Connell and Messerschmidt 2005). According to Kimmel (1994: 119–141), this forms part of the development of a male socioemotional persona in contrast to that of the female. These gender-related ideas are introduced to boys from an early age and maintained via surveillance from other males with the result that the concealment of these feelings can become automatic. If males are socialised to believe a strong front or performance is synonymous with masculinity they are less likely to disclose difficulties and seek help and if emotional pain is suppressed it is liable to increase distress and may lead to suicidal action (Brownhill et al. 2005; Cleary 2012). Environments that adhere to relatively narrow views of gender behaviour are more likely to give rise to these practices. There is evidence that working-class communities are more likely to affirm conventional types of masculinities (Joe and Kaplan 2001) and this may form part of the explanation linking higher risk of suicide to low socioeconomic background. In this way, the emotional context or community which the man is part of has an important influence on his emotional life and particularly how his emotions are expressed.

Suicide is associated with intense emotional pain and the amelioration of this pain is dependent on the capacity to express these feelings and to receive an adequate response. The culture provides the background context and gender script which the man draws from when negotiating his emotional life and behaviour and provides guidelines for how to deal with distress. Suicide is more likely to happen in emotionally constricted environments and this type of emotional culture is more likely to occur alongside conventional ideas of masculinity (Cleary 2012). These issues are examined in this chapter, drawing on the narratives of men who made a serious suicide attempt and recounted in interviews carried out shortly afterwards. In this way men's lives and emotions are explored via their own accounts of what led to a suicide attempt in the belief that listening to men provides a more accurate explanation for male suicidal action and the way gender norms about emotions seep down into individual lives. Following Douglas (1967), the focus is on the subjective meanings and patterns generated by these stories of suicide. The aim is to profile the men and their emotional narratives, to chart the development of, and their response to, emotional turmoil and in this way explicate the association between gender and emotional cultures. The more general contention is that men's emotionality is not a biological or psychological given but influenced by cultural context and is subject to change (Holmes 2015).

Emotional Stories: A Narrative of Long-Term Pain and Distress

Although men are frequently constructed in the literature as emotionally inexpressive the evidence in this study is very much to the contrary. Profound feelings of sadness and desperation were evident and the participants made it clear that these painful emotions had been present but hidden for a long time—often since childhood. They were sad and dejected, fearful and (less often) angry and generally experiencing a sense of hopelessness that their lives had come to this point. Serious, ongoing, mental illness affected only a small minority of the men and therefore was not a major contributing factor in these stories. Having taken a decision to end their lives they had subsequently woken up in a hospital bed and in this context emotions were raw and generally unrestrained. As they recounted, these feelings had been contained, usually for a considerable time, and prior to the suicide attempt distress had reached an unbearable level of intensity. In the aftermath of the action however they felt free to tell their stories and express their emotions openly.

Fergus, Dara, Kieran and Ronan

At interview, Fergus appeared sad and dejected and spoke in a low voice throughout the session. Fergus had never self-harmed before, had a relatively good level of educational attainment and regular employment, and did not abuse alcohol or drugs. He was acutely aware of being in a hospital and ashamed of the action which had caused him to be admitted. The suicide attempt was related to the ending of a relationship but early in the interview he mentioned that his unhappiness predated this by many years. The break-up had revived childhood insecurities and feelings of rejection by his father and of being an outsider within his family and elsewhere. Fergus had struggled to cope with these emotions for many years but had always remained silent about them.

> *I suppose I've been depressed for a long time but a month ago I split up with my girlfriend. We've a baby and just my whole life was kind of based around them. Just been lonely ever since. We lived together at one stage. We haven't lived together for over a year. Since the time that we didn't live together it's kind of 'in there'. The more I think about it the more I think its always kind of 'in there'.*
>
> ***Do you remember when it started?***
> *I don't really remember to be honest. Yeah definitely the last few years anyway it's gotten worse.*

And how did it show itself?
Just days when I just wouldn't be able to function. Wouldn't be able to do anything. Like I go to work but I wouldn't get anything done. I would just be quiet. I've never been really good at communicating with people anyway.

You said that it's been a long time since you felt good?
Yeah I suppose it has. I never really got on too well at home and I moved out of home when I was very young and I suppose after I moved out of home for a while I felt happy that I'd kind of got away from home. After that I just wasn't happy anymore really.

Fergus related a story of long-term unhappiness which was exacerbated by his partner leaving him. His presentation was underpinned by a sense of hopelessness and incomprehension at why and how these events had unfolded. He implied that he had been a dutiful partner and provider and had taken the responsibilities of the relationship and fatherhood seriously. He had made sacrifices, returning reluctantly to live in his family home so that they could save for a house and 'be a family'. In return for this he had sought a loving, caring, relationship and had trusted his partner with his thoughts and feelings but, according to Fergus, she had failed to care for him and now she had rejected him completely.

I didn't get any explanation from her or anything like that. I just felt like I dedicated all my time to her and the whole time she just didn't want to be with me and I couldn't understand how someone could treat you like that. I gave her everything. I wasn't a bad boyfriend. We had arguments and fights like everybody else. I never hit her or I wasn't the type that would go out drinking all night and not come home or anything like that. I kind of knew myself. I knew at the back of my mind but I just didn't really want to face up to it. It just took her to come out and say it. She just said she didn't want to be in a relationship anymore. There's been no talking about it. That was it.

And did you try to talk to her?
Yeah I've tried and I realise now I'm just banging my head off a wall just trying to talk to her.

And how about the baby? Do you see much of her/him?
I do. I see a good bit of her/him. I just kind of feel I'm never going to be the father to her/him that I want. …I wanted to be a family. I wanted to be

> *there for her/him if she/he ever needed me. I don't think she ever loved me at all. It was good at the start. It was very good. Then just things changed. I kind of knew in myself. When we'd go out and I'd get drink on me and I'd say to her that she didn't love me. She'd always swear blind that she did. I just knew. You just know these things from the way people are with you. We tried to save for a house and I moved home and she went home. I wasn't kind of really welcome to come home so I moved to a rented house. She knew how lonely and all I felt because I didn't know anyone in the house and any time that I had to spare I was only with the baby. I had a lot of money worries at the time as well. I was paying for everything, absolutely everything. She just never made an effort. She never looked after me. I don't mean like make my dinner. She was never concerned about me or after I had the first attempt when I went to see a counsellor, she never came with me.*

Dara's suicide attempt was also preceded by the ending of a relationship and, as with Fergus, this re-ignited painful feelings which he had experienced when he was younger. The loss of the relationship and the child they shared evoked memories of abandonment as a child. Dara cried throughout the interview and exhibited a combination of feelings particularly sadness and anxiety. He was in his twenties and there was no history of self-harm in his background, he had a relatively high level of educational attainment and had regular employment. He didn't drink alcohol excessively but he did use non-prescribed drugs. His family background was one of loss and abuse. His parents had separated when he was young and thereafter he had infrequent contact with his father. His mother was dependent on alcohol and as the home situation deteriorated Dara spent some time in care. The care home he lived in did provide stability but he found the setting impersonal and he had not established a trusting relationship with any of the staff. Dara showed a good deal of resilience in coping with this adversity and successfully completed the Leaving Certificate but he had never been able to explore or express his feelings. As with Fergus, Dara linked his past and present difficulties and also felt that he was an outsider. He too sought emotional comfort in a relationship at a relatively young age and in doing so he had overcome a strong resistance to becoming emotionally dependent on another person. There was a further parallel in their stories in that they both concealed their unhappiness over time and felt a degree of self-blame for what had occurred in their lives. As Dara recounted the events which had preceded the suicide attempt the words rushed forth and he became visibly upset.

> *Yeah, it just started about six weeks ago. Oh God. Myself and my girlfriend, we live in the house together and we have a kid together and for the past three years and we've been just living for each other and I had an awful lot of problems before I met her. I just felt down and she came along and then about two months ago, probably six weeks ago, she started going out and meeting other people and coming back and I just felt like a whole part was after been reefed away – stabbed. I couldn't believe it. I was just devastated. She kept this up and she kept coming back for the past few weeks and saying she's sorry and she'll never do it again and everything else and the whole lot. Full of stories, and I kept believing and believing her different stories and then she'd fuck off the next day again and come back to me later on and say she didn't want to be with me or she'd be hiding down in the babysitters or something and I'd be just left there not knowing what the story is. And then last night or two nights ago she came in before she went out and started talking to me saying that everything was going to be alright and she was going to go back to me and I still couldn't understand it at this stage and I was just like 'okay' … and she comes back after she's been out and basically just humouring me and the next day she said she'd be back in ten minute. That was yesterday and three hours later she came back saying she didn't want to be with me anymore. And I really just fuckin had enough at that stage. I had had a few weeks of sitting in the house on my own. I was just cracking up. It took too much out of me. The past few weeks, just really fighting and fighting. I grew up in a hard enough life, I know what it's like, what a hard life is like and I'm a strong person. I've come through an awful lot. But I just can't cope with it. I really can't. I feel like I'm depressed. There's always something. It just like hit me yesterday. I was sitting in* (mentions site of suicide attempt) *and I kept getting these little feelings of just calmness and I just thought I was going to die. What's the point, what's the point? Tomorrow is just going to be the same, and the next day and the next day.*
>
> ***What do you think it was that made you feel like that?***
> *Emptiness. Nothing in the house, no one in the house. No one around me. The only person like I lived for, my little family, me, her and the baby.* (We)

> *were really struggling to make ends meet and she just fucks off and ruins that and that was all you had left at that stage. Just to be sitting there on my own and it just feels like I'm going nowhere and I just don't want to go anywhere and I'm just in bits and I need some sort of help and I don't believe that I can be helped and I don't know. We were inseparable. … It's only in the past few months that I've really settled down and now it's her turn to just fuck off or whatever. I don't see the point in anything. Talk to people, I've been doing that since …I really couldn't cope that night. Just feel like being eaten away on my own and no one understands because no one knows. Then I try to be happy for people and it really fucks me up. It's crazy. I just feel different to everyone.*

Kieran had attempted suicide some weeks after the break-up of a relationship following a chance encounter with his ex-partner. He described feeling overwhelmed by panic following this meeting, at the realisation that the relationship was over, and he made a sudden decision to end his life. Yet it quickly became apparent that the seemingly impulsive action was the culmination of a long period of unease and worry. As with Dara, he exhibited significant pressure of speech and anxiety during the interview.

> *Basically myself and my ex-girlfriend split up about three weeks ago and it was actually about, so it was six weeks after. I had a few drinks with her and I just couldn't handle it at all and I think we had a bit of a row. We were only in the place about twenty minutes and I left and a very good friend of mine, I was all upset and he was saying 'just go home, calm down' so I got into a taxi and I as soon as I went home I knew I was going to hang myself. And I was in the taxi and I was very upset and I said I just can't hack this anymore. I never reacted like that before.*

As with Fergus and Dara, Kieran had become involved in a relationship in his late teens and had become a father soon afterwards. This was the first time Kieran had self-harmed, he had never taken drugs and drank alcohol very infrequently. He had done well in school and had a stable work life and a large group of friends. He had experienced adversity in childhood in that his parents had separated when he was young and he was sexually abused by a relative, an experience which was a critical, but unspoken, part of his childhood and adolescence. Recently Kieran had confided for the first time about the abuse to his (now ex) partner who, he said, struggled to understand his ambivalent attitude towards the abuser. In Kieran's story there was similarly an expressed need for care to compensate for previous insecurity while in his narrative there was an attempt to retain elements of masculinity, specifically strength and resilience, in the midst of vulnerability.

> *The reason why I broke up with her was I needed her to be there for me and she was always letting me down. I felt sick, I had* (mentions physical condition) *and she didn't do anything. She wouldn't believe me at first and then I was in hospital. I had a car crash* (mentions when) *and she made no attempt to help me. I was having panic attacks getting back into the car and she wouldn't believe me, she thought I was just putting it on. We're together* (mentions number of years) *and she's seen me like pretty strong in reality and couldn't believe that I was reacting that way. That annoyed me. That was the reason I split up with her. …She was never there when you needed her. When I had my car crash it took me three months to get back in the car. I had a head on collision. It was pretty nasty. I was lucky to get out of it and I was scared. I still am getting into the car. I would not get into a car. Very rarely would you get me into it. I'm scared to drive over bridges. …It scared me. I was in (*mentions place*) a couple of months ago with a friend of mine and he was driving the car. …and I said 'stop' I'm going to have to get out of the car right in the middle of nowhere. I got out of the car. I couldn't do it. I had to drive the car then. I will not trust someone else with my life. That's the way it was. If I'm driving the car at least I have the control. …I've been upset for say the last five weeks or so. I know I've got upset in the last week or so and I felt like, I broke down crying in front of her a few weeks ago and she said 'what do you want' and I said….. 'we're supposed to be together'. She just started laughing and said it's not going to happen. That's the worst. I'm not handling this. I'm upset and if I see her I just break down and if I'm in* (mentions country he intends going to), *I'm not going to see her. I think that on the other side of the world that it would be easier over there. I'm not going to see her. I spent a year in care when I was* (mentions age). *I had been abused by* (names person). *Sexually abused by* (names person). *I never told her until last year and she lashed out about me being depressed and nobody ever told her and she couldn't believe that it took so long to tell her that. But she was really there for me.*

In these men's narratives similar themes emerged of unhappiness and vulnerability experienced over time as well as attempts to escape painful environments and seek emotional comfort in relationships outside their families. They shared other features in that they were relatively strong individuals with good educational and other resources. Despite their recent suicidal action they presented as friendly, engaging, people and it would have been difficult for those around them to guess the turmoil they were experiencing. They had rarely, if ever, spoken about their distress and the painful events in their lives and this concealment isolated them emotionally from families and friends. The relationships which these men had been involved in had offered emotional security and support but they found it difficult to trust people sufficiently to share sensitive, personal, issues (illustrated by the length of time it took Kieran to tell his partner about the sexual abuse he suffered as a child). As the stories demonstrate, they wanted to be cared for partly because they had lacked adequate care in their upbringing, and they had reacted strongly to what they perceived as abandonment by the person closest to them. Their expressions of vulnerability were interspersed by claims of strength and resilience, of how the present action was out of line with their usual behaviour. The juxtaposition of strength and weakness was a common feature of the narratives and illustrates, as Schwab et al. (2016) have noted, the strong pull of prevailing gender norms. Even in the context of emotional turmoil they felt they had to perform a competent masculinity.

In reality, these men were struggling to keep up with the normative masculinity and many spoke about their fears of not being 'typical' men. They believed that the majority of men were strong and competent in managing their lives and their emotions and in this context they sometimes referred to themselves as being 'softer' than other men (*I'm not a typical bloke, soft or whatever. …Nervous, just different and more quiet.* Dermot). They had worked hard at concealing any features which distinguished them from other men and some had disguised their true state of mind by affecting a completely carefree attitude among their peers. For these men the ending of a relationship had reinforced their sense of masculine incompetence as the break-up was frequently accompanied by a belief that abandonment by their partner was due to their failings as a man.

In this way, Ronan felt different from his male peers and believed he had been consistently victimised because of this. He recounted that he had always felt helpless and fearful and his background had contributed to these feelings in that he had had to cope as a child with a violent, erratic, father. The situation had isolated him socially in that his home was not a place where friends could visit, and emotionally, as he did not feel able to discuss family problems with his friends. As with the other men cited here, Ronan had attempted suicide when his partner ended their relationship.

> *I was just afraid to take a chance. I would worry about everything. I would always think of the worst thing that would happen and I would be afraid. …Just afraid to leave and look to the future and everything new. Afraid to start over again. Most would get up and go but I don't. …Because I'm quiet and put down and hurt. I've just been afraid. Afraid if I do something and it won't work out. Afraid to take a chance. What can you do? Regret not trying even but that's just the way I've always been.*
>
> ***Who put you down?***
> *Everyone. I guess I'm too trusting of people. It's nice to be nice and I just try to be nice and help people and make people happier and be friends and they just take advantage of you. That's always happened. People I've worked with, people I've known for years, school friends. …Because they know they'll get away with it. And slagging matches or slagging competitions, they just say something and I just let it roll off my cheek and try and laugh it off. I don't like putting people down because I don't like them doing it to me. I don't do things to people that I wouldn't like being done to myself. So basically they just take the piss.*

As the narratives imply, these men spoke readily and fluently about the emotional pain which resulted in the suicide attempt and related their present situation to past experiences. Distress had increased in intensity before the suicidal action and in its aftermath, at this critical moment, there was a space to speak about their suffering. The unhappiness they expressed was generally longstanding and frequently related to unresolved childhood experiences. These issues had not been addressed because they had insufficient knowledge to identify and deal with distressing feelings and symptoms and more particularly because they had never felt able to disclose painful emotions. In this, they adhered to the feeling rules prevalent in their homes and communities. They did not speak about these matters but rather worked hard at obscuring their difficulties and problems were compounded by the extent and duration of the concealment as well as by the methods they used to cope with ongoing anguish. This is examined in the following sections along with an exploration of the emotional cultures the men were part of.

Concealing and Containing Emotional Pain

These men were struggling with problems which did not appear to be very different from those experienced by young women and the storylines around their unhappiness (for example, relationships) did not seem gender-specific either. Yet they did not disclose their distress and typically linked their failure to communicate their feelings to norms of masculinity in their cultural environment. They were aware of the constraints relating to emotional expression for men in their community and of the negative implications of disclosing problems and did not consider an alternative way of responding. The practice of non-disclosure of distress was a widespread and prolonged pattern of behaviour among the men and they had not spoken to partners, family, or friends about the acute distress which led to the suicidal action. This admission was made very early in their narratives and formed an important explanatory element in terms of their pathway to suicidal action. Henry, who had a wide circle of friends and a caring family, illustrates this practice.

> *For two years when I did feel down, I didn't talk to anyone. I just kept it all inside. I just didn't tell anyone anything. I just didn't like talking about my feelings or anything. I just didn't want to involve anyone, I just didn't want anyone else to tell. Hoped that by just ignoring it and left it alone, it would go away but it didn't. … It's probably bottling things up because whatever stresses you out you might just not say it to anyone, just let it inside, hold it in kind of thing and if you keep holding things in it's just going to get worse*

> *and worse and then it escalates and you want to do something. You just can't handle it anymore.*

They explained their failure to communicate their feelings in terms of the norms of masculinity in their cultural environment and specifically to being exposed as weak and vulnerable. Concealing emotions and distress, they maintained, is what men do (*I'm not really like that. Talking about things. I don't really do that. Most men never talk.* Ben). According to these participants, appearing strong and being able to manage one's life were important elements of masculinity and if you failed to demonstrate this you would be perceived as weak. The power of this masculinity discourse was apparent when they reached a particularly critical level of desperation in the build-up to the suicidal action. At this point they considered seeking help but, as David relates, decided against doing so as it would imply failure.

> *I thought of it but I didn't do it. You're telling someone you failed. I feel like I failed. They (men) don't tell anyone about their problems. Men feel they have to be strong. Maybe you feel you have failed, that it's a failure. That you have to be able to manage when you are a man.*

Constraints relating to the expression of certain emotions are key to understanding their decisions relating to suicidal action. Concealing unhappiness had been an ongoing issue as they didn't feel they had safe channels of expression in the environment they lived in and feared that if their problems came to light it would endanger their masculine identity, an identity many were already unsure about. Distress was concealed to disguise vulnerability for in this cultural setting men were required to project an image of strength. This was evident in Matt's story.

Matt had had no previous episodes of self-harm, came from a relatively caring home background and had no alcohol or drug problems. He had completed second level schooling and was in a long-term relationship. He attempted suicide when he could no longer deal with mounting work problems, difficulties he had concealed from his partner and his family. Themes of strength and competence and maintaining a strong front were prominent as he described writing a note to his family prior to the suicide attempt.

> *And I sat there and I was sad, I was very depressed …and I wrote down what I thought. I think it was something about the world is a cruel place to live and it's very hard sometimes. People don't realise I'm not the strong man that everybody thinks I am and I do have problems but I'm very stubborn and I find it hard. I love my family, I love* (mentions partner's name) *and I feel everything gets too much for me sometimes and I don't know how I can go on anymore. Everybody sees me as the big guy, the strong fella, the strong type who never has a problem. I never did have any problems, I've always been able to kill them off. I just let it all go. I knew it was wrong what I was doing. …I said I'm tired and things are happening and I'm trying to keep up on it and I'm losing the fight. Everybody thinks I'm winning all the fights. I let them think I am. … I was crying all the time, constantly, and an emotional wreck. I felt sad because of what I was doing. I was embarrassed in a way as well to think what I was doing. …I was very, very, sad. …I realised that if I do this, look at what I'm leaving behind me and it was also going through my mind that I was so young and I had a rough time in life. Years ago I was in hospital. I was working too hard and I had* (mentions condition) *which causes tiredness. And that was that. That has been a chip on my side for years because I'm not the man I was when I first got into the* (mentions work) *and all that. It holds me back because I'm not at peak condition and I know I'm not. I was a very fit person. I was a lot bigger than I actually am now and I was doing the gym. I used to do training and I worked hard and I had cars, I had what I wanted. I had everything I wanted, not a care in the world. I felt a lot stronger then obviously but when that happened to me, since then I can't stand anything going wrong with me because I never had an ailment in my life and that happened. …I never tire. I could work long hours without feeling tired because I always stop to eat well and rebuild the batteries again and get going again. I start at eight in the morning and finishing time will be around six or could be around nine or ten, sometimes working Saturdays. …I'm very strong minded anyway, it takes a lot to knock me out. I was always strong minded and I fought back from it all.*

Matt related how he had been bullied in school (as had Ronan and Fergus) and this reinforced links between strength and masculinity. He tried to maintain a strong front and conceal his distress but this collapsed in the face of overwhelming anxiety and rather than tell his family about this he opted for suicide. His narrative refers to the emotional discourse within his home as well as to prevailing masculinity norms.

> *I have a habit of bottling things up and never saying anything to anybody but I found now over the last two weeks I've been saying that things are getting too much for me and it's wearing me down. …I haven't had many worries ever really. I've never felt that way, I've always been very strong. I do worry about things – little things. That's recently as well. Since I took on* (mentions work). *It wasn't so bad when you knew where you were at. I'd say men in general have a problem with that. Then again who am I to say but I find, in general I find it hard to express my emotions to anybody. I wouldn't even tell my mother if I had a problem or my father. I find it hard to speak to my father anyway. We never really talked about… Construction, building, and things like that, have a few pints and have a laugh, that's about it. You can never go deep into what's on your mind. Life was too tough for me and maybe that's the same way for most men out there because as time goes on things get harder to do and life gets harder. …I made a haims of everything really. I messed up my own life by trying to do this and I messed up people's lives around me as well. I managed to keep it going. I'm a strong man, fighting back, getting there, getting in, doing the work, two in the morning, get it done, it will be grand then, until it's bright. And I just can't do that anymore. I lost weight over two months, a lot of weight loss for a tall guy like me. I admit I was having problems but I'm strong minded. I put a front on always. Probably because I like to feel that I'm showing … always been careful… I always find that women are strong minded in regard to pressure. …I feel that women are better ….. the emotional pressure, I don't think they suffer from it as much. From my own point of view, (names partner), she'd always be the stronger one, she always will bounce back. …But I'm still bottled with problems.*

Another reason for not disclosing problems was that revealing distress was categorised as 'feminine' behaviour. Repudiating the feminine, defining oneself and one's behaviour in opposition to the female, is, as Kimmel (1994: 119–141) has said, key to understanding the performance of emotional inexpressiveness in men. Yet, for the majority of men in this study, this was a façade, a performance they knowingly enacted, as suggested by Adam, to align their behaviour with the prevailing masculinity.

> *I think because we're afraid to. Not to seem weak. We're afraid of seeming weak or something. Because we have to have this image of being macho, we have to have this image of not being girls.*

Locality was also important in terms of concealing vulnerability and men who lived in what they described as 'rough neighbourhoods' feared more serious retribution for non-adherence to masculinity norms. The rules of masculinity prevalent in their communities were clearly known to them but while they adhered to these norms they didn't necessarily endorse them and they were aware of the performative quality of men's behaviour.

> *The stereotype that are men. More powerful and all this crap. At the end of the day we're all the same.* —Christopher

These men conformed to gender norms, as Liam relates below, because this was the masculinity they were familiar with and because of the perceived implications of deviating from these norms. Liam's relationship had just ended due, in part, to his drug use and he was devastated by the loss of his partner and their child. Liam had been experiencing considerable distress for some time but did not disclose this to his partner because he felt this would have implied a lack of male competence. The normative male role was that of protector and women, as well as other men, expected this.

> *I never told anyone I was depressed. Nobody knew I was depressed. And that's because I was afraid…like I was afraid then, I was afraid either way she wouldn't want to have anything to do with me, you know that kind of a way.*
>
> ***Why did you think she wouldn't want anything to do with you if you were depressed?***
> *I don't know…She's only young, you know what I mean. She doesn't need any of that. On her shoulder, you know what I mean. She could easily go out and find someone else that hasn't got any problems like that and just have*

a normal life without any extra grief or any extra worry, you know. ...Just, some days, sometimes you're grand. There's other days you're not... There were times where you just wouldn't get out of bed, you know that way. Talking to the doctor yesterday...and he asked me to describe it in one word, and I just said, there's only one word, 'dark', you know that way. Not feeling that you've anyone to talk to. Not feeling...that there's anyone that you've anything in common, you know that way. Someone that can relate to you, you know that way. Just feeling isolated all the time, you know that way. Wanting to scream and shout but you can't say anything, you know that way.

And you never told anyone?
Nobody. I never told anyone. Never even went over to my doctor and said it to him, you know that way, like, to try and get something. You know, he's confidential, like. But I never opened my mouth, said anything.

Why do you think you didn't tell anyone?
I just, a weakness, showing people a weakness, you know that way.

You said earlier that depression might be a kind of a weakness.
Yeah. I meant that as in the way of...other people, other people would take it, you know what I mean, as being weak like and then try and use it against you, you know that kind of a way, like.

Do you think being strong is important?
Yeah. Well...I've always grown up in a bit of a rough area, you know what I mean. My whole life has been surrounded by drugs...So you don't like to leave out, don't like to give any sign of weakness or...tell your closest friend that you might be this or you might be that, you know what I mean. People can turn and use it against you, you know that way...That's why I wouldn't say anything to anyone.

Constant performative work and monitoring of behaviour was required to project this image of competence and avoid being unmasked in the context of underlying distress. At times an exaggerated display of behaviour or hyper-performance was required in order to ensure a successful level of concealment and the men were very aware of the contrast between this and their 'true' self, as recounted by Liam.

If there was someone who wanted to go out, or someone turned around and said, come on we'll do this for the weekend, or come and do that, you know

> *what I mean, the finger goes straight to me, you know. 'There you go, there's your man now, what do you want to do.' As long as it involved getting absolutely out of your mind. If you want an all-nighter, he'll sit up with you. If you want to go out for the whole week, he'll go out with you. No sleep, no nothing, he'll be there? That's the way people see me. That's not me. That's not me at all.*

Disclosing any kind of sensitive information was viewed as challenging but communicating psychological distress was regarded as particularly risky. These men did not regard themselves as having a mental illness and viewed those who exhibited psychological problems as an entirely different category of people—a scenario noted elsewhere (River 2018). This was evident in the obvious discomfort felt by these men if they were categorised as a 'psychiatric case' and visited by a psychiatrist in the main hospital or, even more fear-inducing, when they were transferred to a psychiatric unit or hospital. Men such as Ronan, who were admitted to a psychiatric unit, regarded this as a particularly low point in their lives. Substance misuse appeared to be a more acceptable diagnostic category but few, if any, had any real knowledge of psychiatric disorder. Yet, as Adam suggests, this may be part of a distancing and concealing process for in reality, he maintained, psychological distress was widespread among men, a kind of open secret among males in his age group.

> *Mental illness is very kind of hush-hush among young men. It's taboo. Any kind of mental illness seems to be taboo among young men, that's what I think. Just not discussed, not mentioned, not paid attention to.*
>
> ***Do you think some of them are in distress?***
> *Yeah, I think a lot of them are but they just don't admit it.*
>
> ***How would you notice another man is in distress, say someone your own age?***
> *You wouldn't, that's the weird thing, you wouldn't notice at all.*
>
> ***So how would it emerge then?***
> *Maybe when one of them tries to kill themselves or something.*

These men gave superficial allegiance to a view of masculinity which had many of the features of conventional or hegemonic masculinity.

These gender expectations constrained emotional expression and adherence to these masculinity codes was at the conscious and sometimes unconscious level. These rules were contested and the majority of the men were aware that there was a performative quality to these practices. Yet, they felt significant pressure to conform because there was surveillance of behaviour in their environment and they were conscious, and sometimes fearful, of the implications of performing differently to other men. Many were aware from past experiences that deviation from conventional behaviour was unsafe, and those who had been bullied in school were particularly mindful of this. Conformity to existing masculinity norms was also evident between friends. In this way, male friendship did not provide an outlet to express difficulties as there were clearly understood rules about communication between men.

> *Lads can't turn around and talk to their friends. If you turned around and gave a sign of being weak and stuff like that, you'd be ridiculed. There's no way you could show your emotions like that.* —Will

In this study male friends were regarded as unreceptive to emotional communication and speaking about psychological difficulties regarded as unacceptable and possibly risky. Male friendships were important in that they affirmed elements of masculinity but these relationships did not provide emotional intimacy. There were issues of trust and possibly specific difficulties surrounding same-sex friendships for the men, as Nardi (1992) suggests. The acknowledgement that certain subjects were off limits was effective in preventing meaningful emotional engagement between male friends. Participants recounted attempts to speak to friends about their distress and receiving definite signals that this type of communication was unwelcome. The disclosures that did occur between male friends usually took place in the context of drinking alcohol and were made tentatively to test out the ground and ensure the individual could be trusted but these encounters almost never involved communicating the extent of their unhappiness.

Conventional constructions of masculinity also influenced decisions not to disclose to one's family or partner. Difficulties were not discussed with fathers because they were perceived as emotionally distant or unresponsive and communication with mothers was impeded by a desire to protect them (*'I didn't want to upset or frighten her'* Leo). Protecting girlfriends and partners was also the motivating factor for failing to speak to them about difficulties, as well as a desire to project strong masculinity which they felt women preferred. There was some evidence that gendered expectations around behaviour were shared by family and partners but more usually the participants had developed a façade to disguise their true state of mind and some had become quite emotionally isolated from their families and partners. Concealing performances were enacted whether one was socially connected or not but social isolation added an additional defensive element to emotional concealment. What resulted was a series of barriers not only preventing disclosure but also inhibiting others from identifying and or responding.

Prolonging the Silence

Practices of concealment were widespread among this group of men but they usually broke down within the hospital and the interview process. However, a small number of participants, while willing to be interviewed, did not wish to discuss the suicidal action in any detail or framed it as something other than a suicidal action. Maintaining control over one's feelings in the midst of an emotional crisis has been noted elsewhere (Schwab et al. 2016) and these cases may be an extreme example of this. They all came from rural backgrounds which suggests there may be an added dimension to concealment and the performance of masculinity in these environments (Cleary et al. 2012). These men's suicide attempts had been particularly lethal and had resulted in serious injuries but they shared another feature, a desire to leave the hospital as quickly as possible.

Myles was one of these men. He was in his twenties, lived in the family home, and had a moderate level of educational attainment and irregular employment. He was visibly impaired by the suicidal action which he framed as an inexplicable and 'out of character' action. In this way, he described the suicide attempt as a sudden aberration which he could not explain and reported that there was nothing problematic about his life.

He had refused to discuss the background to the suicide attempt with hospital personnel and the referring doctor was surprised when he agreed to be interviewed for this study.[1] He proved to be a challenging, somewhat hostile, interviewee who seemed to want to control the encounter. He made it clear he did not want to engage in discussion about the event and ended the session abruptly.

> *Basically I tried to shoot myself, kill myself. Why I don't know. I don't remember. I don't remember any of it, barely. I don't know why it happened or how. …I remember bits of it like. I don't remember. The day is very vague like. … It's just I don't know now what I done. Just waking up here.*
>
> ***You woke up here?***
> *Mmm. Well I remember just barely waking up in the ambulance leaving* (mentions hospital) *but after that, from all the tablets and the drugs they gave me for the pain, I don't … Well I'm just lucky that I got a second chance, that it didn't go the other way. Thank God it didn't. I don't know after that. I don't know why or how or why it happened. There were no signs to it or symptoms. I don't know.*
>
> ***Have you any ideas about it?***
> *No, its still all a blank like. The day is just a blank. The weekend is just a blank. I can remember months before and after but I can't just put that, I don't know why that's been shut out but it just is. …Basically I went to shoot myself. Lucky enough it didn't work out that way, it went the other way, touch wood. …No more after that now. That's all I can tell you (laughs). That's all I know I suppose. Never, never crossed my mind or came into it. I don't know why it did that day but it just did. That's basically all I can tell you now. If that's any good to you. …Oh yeah they're trying to put together the pieces of the jigsaw but there's a piece missing and they can't. I can't remember and they're not going to, they can't put words into my mouth. That won't do any good. …I don't know. There's just that many people coming and going now I don't know. … There are people coming and going and asking questions. Social workers and whatever you call the other people, and they're asking questions, basically the same as you're asking. They're trying to put the jigsaw*

[1]The referral process, described in the Introduction required that the men were briefed on the research study and consented to be seen before I could meet them.

> *together. There's one peace missing. The piece in the middle. …Now I think we have enough. Now I think that's all I can tell you, all I can help you with.*

While these men shared some features they were quite different individuals and their motivations also probably differed. Myles presented as suspicious while the other two rural participants were the opposite in terms of emotional presentation. Robert appeared nervous and fearful and would reveal nothing about the suicide attempt other than it had resulted from a spontaneous thought which 'came into my head' following a party. He had suffered a major bereavement in recent times but denied any particular emotional distress connected to the death. The third participant in this category (Frank) had made the second of two near-fatal suicide attempts when I interviewed him. He was friendly and willing to share his story, up to a point, but he seemed uneasy at times during the interview and was vague about the reasons for his suicide attempt and his ongoing unhappiness, which he did acknowledge. Frank's story will be explored further in Chapter 5.

Along with the men who continued to guard their thoughts and feelings were others who did not recognise their distress as an emotional issue and or had reworked their difficulties as physical problems. This inability to recognise psychological difficulties has been identified in other studies (Addis and Mahalik 2003). The lack of knowledge may also reflect the participants' socioeconomic background as those in higher socioeconomic categories appear to draw on more diverse emotional and psychological discourses (Seale and Charteris-Black 2008). Knowledge about psychological issues was generally lacking and when participants drew on established frameworks they tended to reference depression which appeared to be the only psychological concept they were familiar with.

> *The pain, and I don't know whether it was depression. I was very sad, you know. … it's a very brutal feeling. I can't describe it. I wouldn't say its depression. I don't know what it is.* —Christopher

Mitch channelled his distress via physical illness. He had had a serious physical illness in the past and was convinced (despite test findings to the contrary) that the symptoms were returning. He could not countenance the idea that these symptoms might have a psychological basis and his anxiety increased when this was suggested by doctors and his family (*I don't feel right. No one can explain my symptoms. I don't understand it at all. I'm not functioning normally*). Jack was similarly enveloped in a world of fear about his symptoms. He had suffered his first panic attack in the context of recreational drug use some years before and the anxiety which resulted from this changed his life dramatically. He had been a successful professional and was now unemployed and addicted to alcohol.

> *It started out being anxiety but I don't know what it is now. It used to be anxiety and then it was depression and…now, well, now it's just completely messed……* [long pause]. *I cover it up quite well, because I've kind of learnt to cope with it. But it doesn't, it doesn't make it any easier. Those panic attacks are, they definitely pretty much finished, you know, the happy life I knew. Now I've got a crap life.*

Self-Medicating with Alcohol

Alcohol was the primary way of coping with uncomfortable feelings and stressful symptoms and the majority admitted that they self-medicated in this way. Almost two-thirds of the participants were using alcohol to some extent and a high proportion were also using non-prescribed drugs. There were variations in the type and level of dependency and this had important implications for outcome in terms of repeating and completing suicide (this will be addressed in Chapter 5). As these participants discovered, alcohol and drugs merely anaesthetised the feelings and they faced additional problems when dependency developed as Liam recounts.

> *I suppose, for the last four or five years, I've been, I've been hiding, if you want. Hiding from everyone else. Denying, denying to myself that, like I was depressed, you know? And I was using all sorts of drugs to, just kind of, to go out to enjoy myself basically, you know that kind of a way. To forget about everything, to forget about it, you know that's what I was doing. To basically

forget about it. And then I had a steady job. You wouldn't have been able to tell me any different from any other fella up and down the street. You know that kind of a way. Then I met a girl, had a baby. It was only then, when [name] was born, I was really... But I didn't look for help or anything but just thought right, I'll stop. It was only when I stopped that the depression started kicking in. You know that kind of a way, like. I wanted to stop taking the drugs. ...Things were just deteriorating, you know. But I was afraid to tell her about me, about me being depressed, you know. I was afraid to tell her in case she didn't want anything to do with me. I just hid it from her. Just never told her. ...I never told anyone. I never wanted to admit to myself that I was, you know what I mean. I just wanted to forget about it, get on with it, you know that kind of a way, like. Probably none of this would have turned out to where I am now, you know. I should have stopped lying to myself basically, you know that kind of a way, like. Pretending that there was nothing going on, when really, you know, there is something going on, and there's something not right.

Summary

These findings demonstrate high levels of psychological distress and the existence of long-term problems and emotional pain among a group of young men interviewed shortly after they had made a suicide attempt. Stress had increased in the build-up to the suicidal action but their unhappiness was usually of longer duration and frequently related to events or situations which had occurred earlier in their lives. These issues had remained unresolved as they lacked a space in which to express emotional difficulties and this was primarily due to gender constraints within their cultural environment. Up to the suicidal action these emotions were invisible as the participants had actively disguised specific feelings and their distress. In the aftermath of the suicide attempt and in the absence of these constraints these men, who spoke of never having divulged their feelings, produced long, emotion-laden, narratives. These men had experienced intense pain and despair and the array of emotions evident in their accounts challenge simple dualistic categorizations of male and female emotions. They had not disclosed their suffering because they felt such sentiments were inappropriate emotions for a man to display in their social environment and if revealed would have had negative implications for them. Emotions linked to strength were identified as acceptable while emotions implying weakness were unsuitable and viewed as female type emotions. They adhered, at least outwardly, to the prevailing masculinity rules because they recognized their local importance and because behaviour was monitored by other men. In this way, norms reflecting conventional, hegemonic-type, masculinity created barriers to knowledge about their emotional lives and prevented them from identifying symptoms and seeking help. Treatment was not sought because of the fear of exposure and because the men were unfamiliar with, or rejected, a psychological or illness discourse, themes which appear in other studies (Addis and Mahalik 2003; River 2018). In the absence of disclosure and or a treatment intervention alcohol provided a culturally acceptable form of masking problems which prolonged the men's denial and placed them at greater risk of suicidal behaviour. Within this scenario, painful feelings which could have been addressed grew into significant problems and accrued additional emotional weight over time.

References

Addis, M. E., & Mahalik, J. R. (2003). Men, masculinity, and the contexts of help seeking. *American Psychologist, 58*(1), 5–14.

Brownhill, S., Wilhelm, K., Barclay, L., & Schmied, V. (2005). Big build: Hidden depression in men. *Australian and New Zealand Journal of Psychiatry, 39,* 921–931.

Cleary, A. (2012). Suicidal action, emotional expression, and the performance of masculinities. *Social Science and Medicine, 74,* 498–505.

Cleary, A., Feeney, M., & Macken-Walsh, A. (2012). Pain and distress in rural Ireland: A qualitative study of suicidal behaviour among men in rural areas. *Teagasc* (Agriculture and Food Authority).

Cochrane, S. V., & Rabinowitz, F. E. (2000). *Men and depression.* San Diego: Academic.

Connell, R. W. (1995). *Masculinities.* Berkeley: University of California Press.

Connell, R. W., & Messerschmidt, J. W. (2005). Hegemonic masculinity: Rethinking the concept. *Gender & Society, 19,* 829–859.

Douglas, J. D. (1967). *The social meanings of suicide*. Princeton, NJ: Princeton University Press.
Hochschild, A. R. (1979). Emotion work, feeling rules, and social structure. *American Journal of Sociology, 85*, 551–575.
Holmes, M. (2015). Men's emotions: Heteromasculinity, emotional reflexivity, and intimate relationships. *Men and Masculinities, 18*(2), 176–192.
Joe, S., & Kaplan, M. S. (2001, Spring). Suicide among African American men. *Suicide and Life Threatening Behaviour, 31* (Supplement), 106–121.
Kemper, T. D. (1981). Social constructivist and positivist approaches to the sociology of emotions. *American Journal of Sociology, 87*, 336–361.
Kimmel, M. (1994). Masculinity as homophobia. In H. Brod & M. Kaufman (Eds.), *Theorising masculinities* (pp. 119–141). London: Sage.
Nardi, P. M. (1992). Seamless souls: An introduction to men's friendships. In P. M. Nardi (Eds.), *Men's friendships*. Newbury Park, CA: Sage.
River, J. (2018). Diverse and dynamic interactions: A model of suicidal men's help seeking as it relates to health services. *American Journal of Men's Health, 12*(1), 150–159.
Schwab, J. R., Addis, M. E., Reigeluth, C. S., & Berger, J. L. (2016). Silence and (in)visibility in men's accounts of coping with stressful life events. *Gender and Society, 30*(2), 289–311.
Seale, C., & Charteris-Black, J. (2008). The interaction of class and gender in illness narratives. *Sociology, 42*(3), 453–469.
Shields, S. A. (2007). Passionate men, emotional women: Psychology constructs gender in the late 19th century. *History of Psychology, 10*(2), 92–110.
Simon, R. W., & Nath, A. (2004). Gender and emotion in the United States: Do men and women differ in self-reports of feelings and expressive behavior? *American Journal Sociology, 109*(5), 1137–1176.

3

Growing Up Male

Introduction

The predominance of male suicide in the Western World has led to the belief that men are particularly at-risk of suicide and rising levels of male suicide have been linked to presumed challenges for men in contemporary society, notably the erosion of men's economic and family roles. The account of suicide patterns provided in the introduction to this text demonstrates that all men are not equally at-risk of suicide and the idea that men are particularly susceptible to suicide is connected to a historical construction of suicide as a male practice. This notion incorporates gendered, stereotypical, ideas about men and women and presumed differences between them as well as erroneous ideas about suicide. Masculinity is a diverse concept and male groupings vary greatly in terms of resources and power and these factors influence the level of suicide risk. Men vary in terms of the expressive space available to them and there are identifiable variations in attitudes and practices relating to emotions across different groups of men. People acquire ideas about gender within a particular cultural setting and, as the previous chapter outlined, the men in this study adhered to a conventional form of

A. Cleary, *The Gendered Landscape of Suicide*,
https://doi.org/10.1007/978-3-030-16634-2_3

masculinity in terms of emotional communication. Conventional or hegemonic concepts of masculinity emphasise strength and discourage behaviour which implies vulnerability. A feature of their narratives was that they had concealed their distress despite spiralling anguish and were motivated to do so by these gender expectations. In the aftermath of the suicidal action, expression was generally unconstrained and, as recounted in the previous chapter, emotional narratives emerged which included a wide range of feelings, from sadness to fear and desperation. Kimmel (1994) and others suggest that ideas about masculinity are introduced to boys from an early age, are maintained via surveillance from family and peers, and become increasingly more embedded and involuntary. This chapter explores the men's experiences growing up and the cultural and familial context in which they developed their early, formative, ideas about gender and masculinity and how this affected their ability to deal with their difficulties.

Families, Gender and Emotions

The family is generally the most influential social context for a child and adversity experienced during childhood can lead to psychological problems and create risk for suicidal behaviour. People who grow up within secure families are less likely to succumb to suicidal behaviour and conversely those who die by suicide experience child maltreatment more often than their peers (Dube et al. 2001; Enns et al. 2006). Specific types of childhood adversity are linked to suicidal behaviour and the risk of suicide increases substantially with the nature and extent of the negative experiences (Dube et al. 2001; Molner et al. 2001; Wagner et al. 2003; Afifi et al. 2009). Those who complete suicide are more likely to have been physically and or emotionally abused and the risk of suicide is particularly strong for males following sexual abuse (Afifi et al. 2009). Adversity in childhood is probably linked to suicide because it involves direct pain and also powerlessness, experiences which children cannot easily navigate. Yet, young people are generally resilient in the face of difficulties and adversity does not necessarily imply later risk of suicide. The association between early adversity and negative outcomes is related to a number of factors including the ability of the child to find alternative sources of support and affirmation and, in this way, educational attainment positively affects outcome even if significant levels of hardship are present. However, if the child cannot get respite from, or speak about, difficult experiences suppression of these issues will increase the psychological burden and this may explain the strong association between childhood abuse and suicide for men (Afifi et al. 2009).

A high proportion of the men in this study faced challenges growing up and approximately one half experienced significant adversity in childhood. These included either physical, psychological and or (less commonly) sexual abuse and over one-third experienced more than one of these challenges. There was a spectrum of family environments ranging from significantly dysfunctional families (which were comparatively rare) to relatively happy families which were also uncommon.

Dominic, who was in his early twenties, had a background which represented the more challenging end of the family spectrum. He had emerged from a family which had never been a cohesive unit and in which there were instances of serious drug addiction and sexual abuse. His biological parents had never lived together and both had had a number of other children with a series of partners. Dominic had lived with his mother for a relatively brief period and had inconsistent contact with his father. The only stability in his upbringing appeared to be supplied by a grandmother (with whom he lived sporadically) and the school environment, where he had received individual attention. His girlfriend became pregnant when he was in his late teens and they lived together for a period after the child was born, a time Dominic referred to as a happy, stable, phase in his life. This relationship had ended some months previously and his narrative reflected his sense of loss about this as well as indicating the wide-ranging nature of his difficulties and the hopelessness he was experiencing. (*I have a lot of problems at home. I've too many problems.*)

Dominic's home represented a particularly challenging environment in which to grow up and when prolonged economic insecurity is factored in it is clear that Dominic had faced considerable problems in his life. He attempted suicide followed a knife attack which occurred while he was living rough on the streets and he attributed the suicidal action to a combination of losing his partner and his job as well as to a general desperation about his life situation. With the ending of the relationship he had lost the security of a relationship as well as a place to live and thereafter life had become a matter of survival from day to day. He spent much of the day on suburban trains trying to keep warm and safe and the evening searching for somewhere to spend the night. He lacked family support, didn't appear to have many friends, and dabbled in drugs which increased his vulnerability on the streets. As time elapsed he found it increasingly difficult to cope as negative events (which he could see no solution to) became more frequent and he had come to the conclusion that ending his life was one of the few options available to him.

> *I'm walking around worrying the whole time. …About everything. Where I'm going to live, where I'm going to get work and all that. Like I'm not too good at that kind of stuff.*

Dominic's family situation was comparatively extreme as was his present life situation and the helplessness he was experiencing was understandable in this context. There were families which provided greater security but the majority of the participants lived in families where there were some challenges and the participants frequently cited the emotional impact of family issues as contributing to their present problems. Difficult family backgrounds affected their security and sometimes resulted in considerable suffering and an additional issue was the silence which surrounded these problems and the lack of a space to speak about them. In this chapter the men describe their experiences growing up and the prevailing gender and emotional discourse within the home. The aim is to explore the family environment and its gender and emotional culture and how this influenced the men's wellbeing and their ability to express emotional issues.

Learning About Masculinity and Emotions

The family was an important site for acquiring masculinity for these men and for receiving guidance on how to behave and express emotions. Fathers were usually the primary male figures who interpreted masculinity and exerted an important influence on the son's behaviour and his ability to express specific emotions. Fathers were influential whether they lived in or out of the family home and fathers outside the home shaped their sons' behaviour and emotional wellbeing long after they had been routinely part of their lives. Fathers were often important role models against which the men compared their own performance of masculinity and they generally wanted to emulate and gain the approval of their fathers. This is apparent in Alex's narrative as are the conventional masculinity values which he assigns to his father. Along with other participants, Alex linked acceptable manhood to strength and competence and, as he relates, his father demonstrated these qualities.

> *My da is everything to me. He's one of those people really I can look up to. He made himself into what he is and he's just great. My dad knows how to talk and he'll never blame anyone. He's so independent. He went out, he knew what he had to do and he did it. He went out into the world like that. I'm a grown man and he was* (mentions age) *years old and he was working. He was a child, a baby, and he knew what he had to do and he went out and he did it and he's done it every day since and that's something I look up to. God knows I've tried but I'm not his son at all, because his son would be able to go out and do that. That's what my father would do, not what I'm doing. I know he wouldn't think bad of me, no matter what. I know his attitude, I know he'd never talk bad of me. In my da's eyes we're all equal and no brother is more special than anyone. He knows some people have it tough so he'll never hold anything like that. You follow in your father's footsteps and you'll be better. If I was to follow his footsteps, be it the man he is, be the husband that he is to my mother and be the father that he is to us, I would be… …that's what you want and it's a horrible thing when you want something and you can't have it. It's just, it doesn't make you feel good anyway.*

The form of masculinity evident in these families was traditional in terms of behaviour and the expression of emotions. Guidelines concerning appropriate feeling norms were presented to the participants from an early age and the father was instrumental in imparting these ideas. In this way, the participants were aware of acceptable masculine behaviour and the risks of deviating from this from an early age.

> *I learned from an early age from my father that having problems is not a good thing to have. Well, just things that happened to me. I remember one time I got moderately upset about something and my mother and my mother's friend were being all mollycoddling to me and my father thought this was absolutely a big laugh, disgraceful, so he just gave me a look of severe disgust and embarrassment - that I had been allowing myself to be mollycoddled by females. I was about eight or something.* Guy

In these home environments, the prevailing emotional discourse among males was invariably lacking in intimacy and emotional engagement between fathers and sons was restricted. These modes of behaviour and expression within the home were reinforced by older male siblings and communication with fathers and brothers rarely diverged from a narrow, relatively impersonal, format. Male engagement generally focused on discussing mundane, everyday, matters and teasing or 'slagging' and the men were expected to enthusiastically participate in these encounters. Alex, who was the youngest male in the family, struggled to engage in this way and felt less competent than his brothers for his inability to do so. When he began to experience significant distress arising from a series of negative life events this bantering discourse proved even more difficult to cope with but Alex (and his father) felt he should be able to manage this. Despite Alex's contention that he was part of a 'close' family, in this household there were clear barriers to sharing any kind of sensitive information and he therefore lacked an outlet to express his anguish and the signals of his distress were ignored.

> *My brothers taught me an awful lot. I don't fight. I've never been much for fighting. I'm a real easy person to set off. My brothers tease me and all like that. In a way they upset me because my da says 'well they're your brothers*

and that's what your brothers do'. But yeah, they're my brothers but they know it upsets me. I generally really just can't take a joke. I could before but now it's like I'm looking for an excuse just to show anger. You think you feel better after but you don't and every night, every day, the same thing. You think you're better off to get it off your chest but you don't so every day you're just feeling even worse and they haven't done it in ages because I think they just know it's not funny with me. I talk to my brothers and I talk to my da. They thought I was just being too much of a whinger which I was. I was still whinging about it. They were joking and having a laugh but they didn't really realize the extent that I don't want to deal with that. They are supposed to love me. And they do. I know they do but I was twisting it and everything. I was trying to make something bad out of it.

When you told your dad about the teasing, what did he say?
'Stop whinging'. Stop your moaning about it and he was right and I should have because they all mess with each other. They have a laugh with each other and you want to be a part of that, have their little joke and that but I'll fucking ruin it and I'll just be a prick. I get unsettled too easily and take it out on them and because I'm not happy, you're not going to be happy, I'll ruin it for you. Making my problem everyone else's problem. You want to sit there and you want to have a laugh with them and have a joke with them and talk about things and tell jokes but you can't and you don't know why but you try and the more you try the worse it makes you because you're turning into something that's not there. And then it just gets to you. You can't do it. You cannot sit down and just talk to these people. …We're a very close family and that's what makes it very hard as well. I think the fact that we're so close makes it really hard. Because we're so close you hurt people even more.

There were numerous examples of fathers unable or unwilling to engage emotionally with their sons and this influenced the son's willingness to disclose distress. Participants often cited the father's tendency to avoid emotional closeness as a generational issue yet they still adhered to these practices. And, while fathers were the models for (non) expressive behaviour this emotional discourse was generally practised by other males within the family. Fathers and brothers were viewed as emotionally inaccessible figures who avoided displaying emotions such as affection and because of this fathers and brothers were almost never a source for disclosing personal matters. Paternal behaviours involving alcoholism and violence reduced the possibility of a close, confiding, relationship still further. This gender and emotional landscape, illustrated by Leo's account, helps to explain the men's reluctance to speak about their difficulties to their family. Leo had a number of older brothers whom he described as 'tough men' who personified strength. He described his relationship with his father as emotionally distant and, as in Alex's family, communication between males in the family was restricted to practical matters and 'kidding around' which Leo found similarly difficult to cope with.

> *It's hard to live up to your brothers. I felt that I didn't really belong. I don't know. I can't talk to them at all. I have said it to them. I don't know my brothers the way I should know them. Anytime we see each other we always start messing. No one is ever serious.*

Leo didn't want to be like his brothers but he was aware that they represented the normative masculinity in the neighbourhood and the fact that he had been bullied in school increased this conviction. In the aftermath of Leo's suicide attempt his siblings were sensitive and supportive and one of his brothers revealed that he had suffered from depression in the past. This suggests a divergence between performance and the reality of these men's lives but, as Leo implies, this information did not open his mind to the multiplicity of male experience. He maintained a brave front in front of his brother and he reframed the sibling who had shared knowledge of his own mental health problems as lacking the toughness displayed by his other brothers.

> *All my brothers were here. They knew there was something wrong. They said you can always talk. One of my brothers, he came in and he said 'what's wrong with you' and he started crying and I started crying as well. He's kinder with me in a sense and I put it down to him not being a Hard Chaw. All my brothers are big and he's not big but that's what I think. And he started crying and I started crying and he said 'just come on, we'll talk about it, it'll be alright' and I just told him 'it's hard enough but you get through it'.*

Families in which the men could express sensitive or personal issues were exceptional. Mothers overwhelmingly did the emotional work within families and mothers and sisters were more likely than fathers and brothers to be supports and confidants for the men. This provided a potential channel for disclosure but the prevailing masculinity script required the men to restrict signs of vulnerability and to protect, rather than seek assistance from, mothers and sisters because they were women. A similar barrier existed in terms of disclosing to a partner and there was the additional fear that she would opt for a stronger, more competent, male companion if the man revealed his 'weakness'. Although the men initially learned about masculinity within the home perhaps the most stringent regulation of masculine codes occurred in the neighbourhood and in the school and this will be addressed later in the chapter. These stories imply a performance of masculinity which silenced and made certain kinds of feelings invisible yet the narratives, as well as evidence from their fathers' lives, demonstrate an abundance of strong, but often repressed, emotions and of unhappiness channelled via alcohol and sometimes violence. And, while a hegemonic-type discourse constrained emotional expression in these men's families there was alongside this a clear desire to be loved and nurtured by the father.

Fathers and Sons

Fathers influence their children in important, and complex, ways and the existence (or non-existence) of an emotional bond between father and son has a significant impact on psychological wellbeing (Wagner et al. 2003; Videon 2005; Bronte-Tinkew et al. 2006; Booth et al. 2010). Yet, despite the importance of fathers to their children, the literature, including the sociological literature, is relatively sparse on the detail of father–child relations and especially father–son relationships. Models of fatherhood, which focused on moral leadership, changed to a view of the father as the economic provider for the family in post-industrial times (Lamb 2010). In the twentieth century, further iterations of the father's function emerged, for example, as a role model for sons and later, as an emotionally engaged parent (ibid.: 3). The role of the father continues to evolve and a nurturing function appears to be an important element in contemporary fatherhood (Pleck 2010).

Existing knowledge about father–son relationships indicates that the emotional dimension is more important for the children in terms of social and psychological outcome than the resident/non-resident status of the father (Pleck and Marsiglio 2010). Males who have close relationships with their fathers are more likely to be open about problems and to develop warm friendships with other males while destructive father–child relationships are associated with less positive outcomes including suicidal behaviour in offspring (Fergusson et al. 2000; Johnson et al. 2002; Wagner et al. 2003). It is the characteristics of the father as a parent rather than the gender-related characteristics which mediate his influence (Lamb 2010: 5). When relationships between conventionally masculine fathers and their sons are good, boys tend to follow this masculine pattern but sons also bond and model themselves on fathers who perform less conventional masculinity and there is no evidence that children do better with either version of fatherhood (Pleck and Marsiglio 2010). These findings, along with emerging evidence of fathers as carers and nurturers of their children, demonstrate the importance of emotional engagement and the father's ability to positively influence his child's social and emotional wellbeing (Hanlon 2009; Lamb and Lewis 2010; Moore 2018). An important theme in the present study concerned the men's desire for emotionally meaningful relationships with their fathers and the unhappiness which resulted if this was not forthcoming.

Fathers had a significant influence on these men and their narratives were replete with stories about the relationship, or lack of relationship, with their fathers. Love and affirmation was sought from fathers but rarely given in a demonstrable, consistent, way. Fathers were central figures in their lives but caring interactions between fathers and sons were exceptional. Relations with both parents were sometimes difficult but relationships with fathers tended to be more problematic and father–son conflict emerged as a prominent theme in the study. The majority of the men had difficult, even hostile, relationships with fathers and whether the father was resident or non-resident was not the critical factor in relation to this. Father–son difficulties related to the father's inability to affirm and or care for the participant and or to the disjoint between the father and normative markers of a good father. The most common criticism about fathers, as Larry's narrative demonstrates, was their lack of emotional engagement.

> *I don't get on with my father. I don't know. When I say I don't get on with him, I see him, I speak to him, I never talk to him. He never talked to us. He was just a normal sort of, go to work, come home, have dinner, watch a bit of telly, go to bed. I probably would have liked to have been closer to him when we were younger but it wasn't really an option. I certainly wouldn't call him warm. He was strict. I don't really remember an awful lot about him when I was younger. My father was a person who didn't show his feelings. He still doesn't even now. …My dad always drank a lot. He certainly wouldn't say he is an alcoholic but I'd say he is. …It was just a normal childhood. We had the strict side of it alright, very strict. Don't question it. If you did go against it you'd get a hiding. Not all the time, not to a serious extent. It probably seemed serious at the time. My dad used to slap us. Yeah, I was afraid of him, I suppose, in a way. If he said something you'd do it quicker than for my mam. … I suppose we were never asked for our opinion. Nothing was ever discussed. That's what it is, take it or leave it. Or you couldn't even leave it, you had to take it. I'd say that its more important to children that you talk to them in a proper manner like I talk to you or you talk to me and treat them like an adult. If you treat them like they have intelligence they'll use it at least.*

Larry described his childhood as a standard upbringing and as typical of the time but it was clearly deficient in emotional engagement and this set a pattern for how he dealt with issues in his own life. His resentment of his father's authority (which was shared by his siblings) had caused friction between them and had influenced Larry's life choices in significant ways. He refused a place in university when his father encouraged him to accept the offer and afterwards took a job well below his intellectual capability and began a long-term relationship primarily to leave the family home and avoid dependence on his father.

> *I had the chance but I didn't take it which didn't go down very well. I was at the point. I was going to do (*name of academic subject*) in* (name of university) *and I had the points and all but at that stage I had worked about three or four months in* (mentions employment). *I came home on Tuesday night about two in the morning. It was very late anyway and my Dad was there, still up, waiting up. Of course I got the letters* (from the university*)* *but didn't show anybody. And he was there with the cheque on the table saying 'you're going and that's it.' So I said 'no I'm not'. So that was it, end of conversation, never discussed again. This was a person who hadn't taken an interest in eighteen years. I had made up my mind I wasn't going. If I had gone, first of all I would have been very reliant on my parents. It would have meant another few years at home. I was gone a couple of months later. That had something to do with it. I had met my partner. She was my only girlfriend then but I knew I was going to live with her.*

Although Larry was highly critical of his father's lack of engagement he followed his father in developing a solitary lifestyle apart from his own family and, like his father, began to drink heavily until his drinking habit had escalated into alcoholism. He did not reveal his deepening unhappiness to his partner nor to his family (although he reported that he was close to his mother) and referenced the masculinity and authoritarian values he experienced growing up in explaining this. Larry considered his childhood to be normal and typical of the time but there were indications that he felt the loss of emotional connection to his father acutely and that communication was generally restricted in the family.

> *I wouldn't say it has a lot to do with my childhood really except that I was always a loner. Maybe not in primary school, but when I got to secondary, it was just very much on my own. Through my own choice again. Just that I arrived home and had my dinner, go to my room and listen to the radio and do work for school and go to bed. I would do that all the time. And I was quite happy doing that. Or I would go to the pictures and do whatever I did. That was my own choice.*

Seeking to develop a confident sense of self-identity in the context of an emotionally distant father was problematic for those who experienced it but there were instances of more obvious exclusion by fathers. Some of these narratives of rejection implied a communication blockage between father and son with neither having a language to express feelings. This was exemplified by Isaac's situation. Isaac had had a difficult relationship with his father for many years and related how his father visited him in the hospital after the suicide attempt and sat silently by his bedside. As he was leaving his father gave Isaac a note (which he asked Isaac to read after he had left the hospital) which contained the following sentence '*I hope you get better and that you'll be well soon*'.

Some of the father–son relationships were underpinned by more significant paternal rejection and Fergus's story demonstrates the long-standing distress this caused. Fergus desperately wanted his father to love him but he felt his attempts to attain this love were always rebuffed. He felt powerless to resolve the situation and experienced guilt that he was somehow responsible for his father's behaviour. The manner in which his father disclosed information about his parentage (when Fergus was about to leave the household to live elsewhere) exemplified the level of anger and sadness which permeated the relationship.

> *I just didn't get on at home. I suppose at the time mostly with my da. There's a bit of history behind it. I was in care for a couple of years when I was born and I only found out just before I moved out like, and it wasn't very nice the way I found out. My da told me. He was having a row with my ma, which is nothing new. He kind of told me just to, kind of, turn me against my mam. Oh I'll never forget that. There's always been a thing. Well not so much lately but when I was younger there was always a thing that my father wasn't my father. Not from my side but from his side.*
>
> ***Would he say that to you?***
> *Not directly to me but in an argument or whatever with my mam and I'd hear it. There's a long trail there believe me.*
>
> ***That goes back to your childhood?***
> *More or less yeah. I suppose when I first heard it and I kind of started thinking to myself, I would have been around twelve, thirteen, fourteen years of age. I think what actually clicked it for me first was I think I needed to get my birth cert or something for my confirmation or something like that and my birth cert, it wasn't like anybody else's. I always kind of noticed it. Even when I was very young I said the one thing I do before I die is move out of this house before*

> *I'm eighteen. There's be nights when he'd be drunk and I'd hear him slagging me off and saying really, really, hurtful things. He wouldn't be a violent man towards us. Now he's been violent towards my mam in the past but I shouldn't even say it because it's been drink orientated. There's never been any violence when he was sober. Just a man that's very kind of set in his ways and I was the oldest and I should have been doing this and I should have been doing that. I was never as close to them as anybody else in the family and we're only a small family. There's only* (number mentioned) *of us. I was never as close to them as any of the rest of them were. Always about me and never about anybody else, always about me. It's like he had some sort of a vengeance for me. I don't even know to this day whether he truly believes that I'm his son. That's half the reason why I didn't want to tell them anything. It's just being the oldest and I didn't want them to be ashamed of me. I loved him but couldn't understand what I needed to do to make him kind of love me. Like I know now that he loves me but what I had to go through to kind of find it out.*

These experiences affected Fergus's self-confidence which impacted negatively on his educational attainment and led him to believe that psychological survival involved trying to distance himself from this unhappiness. He left the family home and entered a relationship and became a father in early adulthood and while this was a fulfilling experience the emotional pain did not disappear. He felt unable to confide in his partner or family members and was constrained in speaking to friends as he described such disclosure as risky in the neighbourhood he lived in. Yet despite his inability to admit his distress, he was heavily dependent on his partner for emotional security and when she left the relationship with their child Fergus was devastated and made the decision to complete suicide.

Fergus's story concerned paternal rejection and cultural themes of shame and rigidity as well as signifying intergenerational male unhappiness due to emotional suppression. There were clearly unresolved issues between Fergus's father and mother, focusing on his birth and their subsequent marriage, which were channelled into negative emotions and behaviour. Both parents drank heavily, his father was physically abusive to his mother and Fergus seemed to have become the scapegoat for his father's unhappiness. He described a lonely childhood with few emotional links to anyone and it appeared his siblings were not treated in the same negative way by the father.

I was always the black sheep when I was at home. Didn't kind of interact with the family or kind of always felt a little bit set aside. But I'm close with my sisters and brothers. There's times I can remember when everybody else would be sitting out at the table and I'd be in the sitting room kind of away from everybody else. I suppose that was as much my choice as anything. I could have always joined them if I wanted to.

And why do you think you didn't?
Because I just felt out of place. Yeah, but you see you don't know what your feeling is actually the way it is or whether it's just the way you think about things. Like I'm a terrible thinker. I just think about everything and analyse every little small bit of it until I just drive myself insane.

And you think that's bad for you?
Yeah.

When you were young, were you ever able to talk to anyone about things that were troubling you?
No. It wasn't that kind of family that you'd kind of, you know, if you had something that was troubling you, you'd say it to somebody. No, and because I was the oldest.

His father's attitude and behaviour had affected Fergus's self-esteem and emotional security from an early age and he was bullied in school which added to his suffering growing up. These experiences had caused him considerable psychological distress throughout his life and the feelings returned as he recovered from the suicide attempt.

I used to have bad nightmares when I was a kid. I had it the other day. I had it on Monday. I woke up on Monday morning and obviously I wasn't well at all. I used to get this feeling when I was younger when I'd be lying in bed going asleep. It was like my whole body was swollen. I got the feeling there the other day. I hadn't felt that for a long time.

Despite the background of rejection, the reaction of Fergus's father to his suicide attempt tell a sad story of communication barriers, of the constriction and repression of feelings, and of the use of alcohol to suppress and dull emotional pain.

> ***How did your parents respond when they found out (about the suicide attempt)?***
> *I don't really know but I've only seen my dad for a few hours this morning. He didn't really say much. My ma came in last night and she was kind of tearful.* (She said) *My da kind of couldn't understand why we didn't talk to one other.*
>
> ***When your father came in what did you talk about?***
> *He didn't mention it. He's not good at that kind of thing. He was brought up in the country. He's one of those.*

Fergus's story contained themes which were common to many of the narratives but some of the specific details of his life resonated in Dermot's story. The precipitant of Dermot's suicide attempt was also the break-up of a relationship and he felt similarly isolated from, and different to, his siblings ('*like the odd one out …well not odd one but kind of left out of things*') and this extended to an idea that he was different from other men. His paternity was also in doubt and, as with Fergus, this had been communicated indirectly to him from childhood in the context of marital conflict. He wanted to be loved and accepted by his father but the innuendo about his paternity had recently emerged again. This had preoccupied him and contributed to his suicide attempt as it undermined the fragile identity he had developed and gave a sense of reality to one of his greatest fears—that he did not belong. This situation was exacerbated by the absence of support and someone to share these feelings with. He felt unable to talk to anyone within his family because he was '*…not close to my parents like that*' and felt he could not discuss it with his father 'as *it might hurt his feelings or whatever*'. Dermot, along with Fergus, had reservations about the authenticity of the normative masculinity but they still felt pressure to conceal their vulnerability and Dermot practised the concealment of emotional suffering to an extreme degree.

> *I'm outgoing as happy all the time. Put on a grin even when I'm sad or whatever. Just put a happy face on for everyone.*
>
> ***And do you feel happy?***
> *Well sometimes I don't but I still have to put it on.*
>
> ***Why?***
> *Well there's no point in dumping problems on other people.*

Kieran's story also exemplified marginalisation from the family and a desire for a nurturing father and has added complexity in that the person he regarded as a father figure sexually abused him. Yet this narrative did not proceed as one might expect. When the abuse was discovered Kieran's negative attitude to his father, with whom he had had a difficult relationship from an early age, hardened and his attitude to his abuser, while complicated, was more accepting. His parents were separated and according to Kieran, he disliked his father because of his behaviour and considered him to be an inadequate role model.

I didn't really like being there (home) *to be honest. I just didn't. I didn't like being there. That's the truth. I never have. That's the truth. Say from the age of* (mentions age) *I hated it. I didn't like it at all. I loved going to school and playing sports and stuff like that. I'd stay out of the house at much as I could because I hated being there.*

Do you know why you hated it?
No. I just never liked it. It never felt like home to me. ...I don't speak to him (father).

Why is that?
I just don't. ... I just never liked him. ...I remember one time when I was about fourteen and looking at him and saying "I'm going to get you eventually, you know that". I hate my father, hate him. I have no feelings at all for him. Literally nothing. I hate the man. I am not a fool, I am not a hypocrite. That's just the way I feel and that's the end of it. ...I was in the hospital the other night after that (suicide attempt) *happening and I woke up and he was there and he started talking to me. I just ignored him. Even in the state I was in. I don't care. I'm not a hypocrite. I'm not going to speak to the man ever again and that's the end of it. ...I can't respect him. I can't. I have no time for him. Other people might. I don't. Some people do. I don't.*

Kieran avoided home and spent time during his childhood in a relative's house where he was sexually abused. When this emerged he was taken into care but Kieran refused to admit that the person had abused him because, he said, he wanted to protect him. The experience of the abuse, and the complexity of his feelings for the perpetrator, were a hidden, unresolved, part of Kieran's life for a long time.

> *I know I used to have bad dreams and any time I stayed in* (name of relative) *house I would have really bad dreams. I used to have really really strange dreams. I used to have one recurring dream anytime I stayed in the house, it was real weird. All animals would be running over me. I used to have that dream all the time when I was in the house and I thought it was really strange. I always had that dream when I was there. A recurring dream of wildlife animals running over me.*
>
> ***Did you ever think what it might be?***
> *I thought it might be something to do with that, yeah. I only ever had it when I was there. I never had the dream anywhere else. …It was a strange one because I spent a lot of time with him* (names the perpetrator of the abuse) *and I liked being there. I knew that it was wrong but still I'd be there. …I wouldn't admit it to them because I didn't want to hurt* (names the perpetrator of the abuse). *I spent* (time mentioned) *in care but I just wouldn't admit what had happened. I wouldn't admit it to anybody. I didn't really tell anybody… I kept it inside me. I didn't want anyone to know. …The relationship was great. It was very good. That's why I protected him. That's why I never said anything. I've had endless social workers asking me did anything like that happen to me and I'm just saying no it didn't. They didn't know from where I was coming from. There was nothing they could do so I had to live with it. …I really cared about him. I knew what happened was wrong. He'd be there if I was playing a football match and come up and watch me and stuff like that. Just things. …He was a very hardworking man and that and far from my dad. He'd be more like he'd look after his family better and stuff like that. …That was my father figure as far as I am concerned.*

The issues around his abuse and his sense of abandonment as a child remerged following the ending of his relationship and is also mirrored in his reaction to his own child now that he intends to leave the country.

> ***Did you tell anyone about your childhood, the abuse?***
> *I don't know, it's tough. I just wouldn't. I probably would be ashamed of it probably - yeah. I don't think I really have worked it out to be honest with you. I don't think I have.*
>
> ***Why, do you think?***
> *I still don't, not saying nothing was wrong but I didn't see harm in it.*

> ***Are you okay with that?***
> *I shouldn't be okay with it. Maybe I am okay with it but I shouldn't be okay with that. I shouldn't be. I should know that's wrong. I should know like that is totally wrong and if anybody done that to one of my brothers or sisters or my daughter/son I would go mad so why am I not going mad because it happened to me. I don't know, I'm just very.... I don't think I have worked it out. I don't think I ever have. I don't think I've ever sat down and gone through the total story. I have to get over this and I'm not getting over it. I know it's respect for my life and I know it tends to be insecurity and where all of that is coming from. I don't think it's coming from that specific issue. The fact that I spent* (mentions time) *in care and I was going here, there and everywhere. ...I couldn't handle that again. ...There was nobody protecting me. It was even there the whole time of the break up. I don't see an end to this. I don't know, I don't see an end to actually getting over it, I wish I did but I cannot see it. I don't know. I don't know how I'm ever going to get over it. People say to me 'ah you will, you will in time' and I go yeah but I'm sure people break up every day but I don't see myself getting over this. It's the only major relationship I've had. ...I think the whole thing now with this break-up is that I, remember I told you how I used to go home some weekends and I'd have to go back to the care home after the weekend and how hard that was for me. Now I'm walking away from* (name of child*). I can't see her/him. I don't want to see her/him. I've tried to see her/her over the past few months but I've only seen the child three times. I can't do it. I had her/him out with me yesterday, I had her/him out for a few hours walking around. Crying, just walking around, playing with her/him and then crying. I can't go back or I'll go to bits. I can't do it. Too many bad memories. It's too hard.*

The events and experiences which Kieran recounted about his childhood represent significant challenges for any child and in his case it was compounded by suppression and a self-imposed silence. Yet his life story in other ways was one of relative stability, he did well in school and had a wide circle of friends and there was no economic deprivation in his background. He found emotional sanctuary in a relationship and fatherhood at a relatively young age and had never engaged in alcohol or drug misuse. He mentioned that his background had made him insecure, a feature he said he had always hidden. He implied that this insecurity probably prompted him to form a long-term relationship and become a father at a young age and also caused him to react so intensely when his partner ended the relationship.

> ***Do you feel you have adjusted to what happened to you?***
> *Maybe but I think I am very insecure. I put out a great confidence attitude but I'm not really. Like everybody that knows me would say yeah I'm very confident and one of my best mates in the hospital the other night said to me you're the last person in the world I'd expect to do it. I bottle things up.*

The most hostile father–son conflict generally occurred in families where there was paternal violence and in these situations anger was directed at the father's behaviour as well as his lack of love and care. Violence was a relatively common experience in that almost one-third of the men were raised in homes where this was a feature over a period of years. Generally, the mother was the victim but some of the men had been subjected as children to long-term physical abuse (in one case the perpetrator of the violence was a mother). Violence in the home was usually linked to alcoholism and when this occurred the participants described childhoods infused with fear and powerlessness as well as economic hardship. They also related attempts, especially if they were the eldest male, to adopt a role of responsibility within the family.

Nick was the eldest in his family and his father's alcoholism had resulted in a precarious economic situation for the family when he was younger. His relationship with his father growing up was fraught with conflict and, as the eldest child, Nick felt a responsibility to protect the family, and especially his mother, from his father's behaviour. While relations with his father had improved since he gave up alcohol they remained emotionally distant and the father's previous behaviour was rarely if ever mentioned in the household. The suppression or silencing of uncomfortable topics was a common theme in families previously affected by alcoholism and violence. Yet while Nick struggled to deal with his father's past he still sought his approval.

> *There's a bit of friction between the two of us. He used to be an alcoholic and he gave it all up years ago. He was pretty difficult. He drank a lot. I remember it but my other brother doesn't. Nothing I really like to remember. He was violent to my mother. He's a different person now. He was violent to me a couple of times. I was always in trouble. Every time he came in drunk*

I was in trouble. She had a hard enough life too. There was never any money there. I remember hating him when I was young. My younger brother was the pet. When he's come home I would have done all the work. He'd come in giving out, he'd be fighting with me over nothing and he would probably bring the other fella home sweets or something. He'd (brother) *play him along a bit. I wasn't able to do that. I remember when I was in primary school. I used to come home from school and she might only get dinner once or twice a week because there wouldn't be enough food. She would feed the children but she wouldn't have eaten for the day. My father was getting big money at the time from work and it was all going on drink. At the time when he had the problem I remember I had nothing but cheap clothes going to school. I was very sensitive about that and I'd blame it on him. I was never proud of my father. I'd be proud of him now the way he was an alcoholic and the way he turned himself around. I'd be proud of him now but back then no, I absolutely hated him. The other brother, when he'd came home he's run up to him and make up to him and he'd love that but I wouldn't. I hated him and I think he knew that as well.*

How is your relationship with him now?
Ok. He's a different person now.

Is he the kind of person you could talk to?
No. I don't think so, no. I couldn't talk to him anyway. I feel awkward with him. I talk to my mother alright.

Have the others in the family had the same difficulties?
No. They just laugh at my father. … They all get on great with him. They've never seen him drinking or anything.

Why do you think that is?
Probably because I remember when he used to drink and the fighting.

Have you and your brothers ever talked about that time?
No. I don't even think about when I was young to be honest. …There was a row in the house and someone confronted him about the drink. It nearly killed him. He went out of the room. …Yeah, he just had to go away.

It's not something you could discuss with him?
I'd never bring that up. Its in the past like, you know. He was a different person back then. He wasn't himself.

***Did you ever think of going to him* (before the suicide attempt)?**
No. When I was in the hospital I was told my father was down in the dumps because I hadn't told him. He said that he thought I could talk to him about everything.

But you didn't feel you could?
No, not really, no. I'd feel like I was letting him down, failing him again.

Narratives relating to the violent father reflected the suffering they, and frequently their mothers, had experienced. This was usually cloaked in silence and there was rarely a space to speak about such matters even when the father was transformed into a caring father having recovered from alcoholism. Ronan came from a home dominated by a violent, alcoholic, father (who had now ceased to drink). Ronan described the uncontrollable rages and the fear, as well as the emotional isolation, this caused in his family.

> *My father was an alcoholic most of my childhood. He'd go from being nice to someone totally different and then wake up in the evening shouting and hitting and kicking. He hit us all. Six nights a week he would come home and be a different person. Just afraid to do anything and I'd just go up to my room. If my sisters were downstairs he'd probably slap them or whatever. The oldest, he left home. I don't know if he ran away or just left home but he left home one night. He used to share the same room and I woke up and the wardrobe was empty and he'd moved.*

Paternal violence resulted in childhoods permeated by sadness as well as fear and there was often relief if the father departed the family home. Frank's father left having inflicted a particularly ferocious beating on Frank (which he described in detail).

> *He was an absolute bastard. I remember the beating. I can't remember how I felt. I think he'd beaten my mum just before he'd given me the hiding. …I was just delighted that he left.*

Parental alcoholism and violence is associated with suicidal behaviour in children as it has a significant impact on a child's sense of security and control (Whipple and Noble 1991; Loukas et al. 2001).

These features were evident among the men who had experienced paternal violence in that they had to contend with the constant fear of physical abuse and the economic deprivation which usually accompanied alcoholism as well as isolation from peers due to concealment of these issues.

Ronan lacked confidence and while his suicide attempt followed the break-up of a relationship he reported feeling unhappy for many years and he had always felt marginalised. In Frank's case, despite the relative stability which followed his father's exit from the home, the violence had had a major impact on his life. He recounted that he had always experienced low self-esteem, was fearful of taking on new challenges and had opted for work below his ability. Perhaps more seriously, he felt coerced into a relationship about which he had serious doubts and this partnership became a source of intense unhappiness and contributed to his suicide attempt. These home situations caused considerable psychological distress which was unlikely to be resolved in the context of the family suppression of painful memories and without support and counselling—which were unlikely options for these men. In this context, the physical abuse Adam suffered as a child became normalised.

> *They separated when I was about* (age mentioned). *It was a relief to be honest. My father was an alcoholic and he had violent tendencies towards me. He physically abused me as a kid. It was always just me.*
>
> ***How often would that happen?***
> *Once every few days*
>
> ***And how did that make you feel?***
> *Afraid. …I suppose resentful I guess now that I have gotten a bit older. I still talk to him. I'm going over to see him in (name of country) soon. It wasn't entirely his fault, he's* (mentions diagnosis) *and he's an alcoholic. I don't think it's entirely his fault.*
>
> ***But at the time?***
> *I was terrified.*
>
> ***You feel differently about him now?***
> *Yeah, I feel sorry for him.*

What kind of a father do you think he was?
He wasn't a very good one anyway. I don't know – he wasn't very responsible because he was always drinking.

When you were growing up, did you have someone to talk to about your problems?
No.

Did you ever tell anyone?
No.

Did you talk to your mum?
No.

Had you any close friends at that time?
A few, yeah, but I didn't talk to them about it because I thought it was normal, I thought it was like that in every house. I didn't think it was abnormal. When you grow up with things you think they're normal.

As these stories demonstrate, many of the men experienced significant challenges in their young lives. They were subjected to various forms of maltreatment and fathers were the usual perpetrators of the abuse. Paternal disengagement and abuse impacted negatively on their self-esteem and peer victimisation (which was commonly experienced by these men) added to this. The adversity experienced by these men would be difficult for any child but what compounded the issues in these men's lives was the lack of an outlet, a voice, to speak about their pain. They grew up in a cultural environment which favoured a rigid form of manhood, although, as is evident, they frequently received ambivalent messages about masculinity. They always rejected the father's violence but received little or no support in dealing with his behaviour or the suffering it caused. In this way pain was experienced silently and gave rise to helplessness as well as fear. Yet, despite the difficulties encountered the majority of the men sought emotional connection with their fathers and sometimes felt responsible if this was not forthcoming. A background narrative is the evident unhappiness of many of these fathers—implied by the men's stories as well as the level of paternal alcohol consumption which appeared to be an enduring narrative of unresolved emotional pain. These stories and themes had an intergenerational quality as Sean's account implies. His father was dependent on alcohol and was violent towards his family and Sean attributed this behaviour to the fact that his father had been abused by his own father. Sean suggests that his father needed help yet he himself had not sought assistance for his own problems.

> *I'd say my father was asked to go for help. I'd say he was. He had to be told he needed help at some stage in his life and I think that he probably did try at one stage and maybe didn't like it or something and that was it.*

A high percentage of fathers were absent from the home during these men's childhoods but relationships with fathers were not dependent on the presence or absence of the father. Non-resident fathers vary greatly in terms of engagement with their children as well as parenting characteristics and this makes it difficult to establish any direct association between type of fathering and childrens' wellbeing. While some research indicates no association between a father's absence from the family home and negative outcomes for the child, other studies infer an impact on socioemotional adjustment and increased risk of suicide for male children (Weitoft et al. 2003). Yet, the links between absent fathers and suicidal behaviour are likely to be complex and moderated by cultural and economic factors as well as by individual personality features. Positive outcomes and the development of a healthy masculinity for males is not dependent on having a father figure present during childhood (Pease 2000) but where orthodox ideas about gender exist the absence of a father may be more challenging for male children. For the men in this study, the challenges they encountered growing up left an emotional mark and led to sublimation of emotional pain if there was no one to confide in. If the father was outside the home he may have been less accessible in this respect.

Dara's father had maintained regular contact for some years after his parents separated but contact decreased considerably from this period. When Dara was going through difficult times he had reached out to his father for support but, according to Dara, his father had not responded to his plea for help.

> *I used to ring up from time to time. I saw him when I was* (mentions age) *over there, that's it. I don't ring him anymore.*
>
> ***Why not?***
> *Because he's a fucking asshole. I begged him to take me over about a year ago just for a while because I was really feeling shit and he started all this shit of what's coming over here going to help and what's coming over here going to achieve and what can I do? And I said you're my fucking father. So after that I just lost interest and it was like you're just a fucking asshole.*

The rejection experienced by many of these men in their early lives resulted in insecurity and self-blame and relationship loss, which precipitated the suicide attempt for Dara and others, had particular symbolic meaning as it resurrected these feelings.

> *There's always something. It's like inevitable that there's always going to be something. Me whole life revolves with some sort of fuckin tragedy. I bring it upon myself. Just like a magnet to fuckin shite and I don't feel good about myself because of that. That's why I feel different because I'm just fucking... Because of who I am more than the life I've had. I'm just so used to all of that sort of stuff. I end up attracting girls that have problems. I end up not having a job sometimes and then having a job and I don't know, it's just fuckin always.*

Fathers were influential even if they had never been part of one's life. Harry had not met his biological father who he regarded as irresponsible for deserting his mother. His suicide attempt followed the unexpected pregnancy of his girlfriend and the circumstances of his own birth had moved him to persuade her to proceed with the pregnancy although she had initially wanted a termination.

> ***Tell me about your biological father?***
> *I can't because I don't know anything about him. I know I've been given a description of him. I can't remember his name. ...I just know if I saw him I'd be angry. It wasn't like my ma got pregnant and he didn't know. He did know and then just left. ...This summer I was going off to* (names place) *to work but now I'm going to stay here and for the moment make sure I'm there for the kid's life anyway, the whole thing. Even if I don't stay with my girlfriend I'm going to be there for my kid. It's a simple fact that I didn't know who my da was and I wouldn't want this child to grow up with the same thing.*

The father was a significant influence on these men in terms of guiding their gender behaviour and their lives generally. They sought to engage emotionally with their fathers but generally this kind of support was missing whether the parent lived inside or outside the home. The prevailing masculine discourse did not facilitate close emotional relationships, other than as part of a heterosexual relationship and even then there was a perceived need to present a competent, resilient, front. These factors tended to ensure that hurt and emotional pain were contained and the model of masculinity prevalent in the neighbourhood contributed to this. In this way, the rules of masculinity implanted in the family were reinforced outside the home.

The Regulation of Masculine Behaviour

The main sites for the regulation of masculinity outside the family were the neighbourhood and the school. George, who had made a number of suicide attempts, provided an illuminating narrative about the regulation of masculine behaviour in his community. His account denotes a very rigid interpretation of masculinity with strong elements of surveillance and enforcement from childhood into adulthood.

> *Look at a group of three men and a group of three girls. One of the men is different and one of the girls is different. The girl will be taken into the group no matter what she looks like. The man will be shunned. They will turn their back on him if he's any way different. They'll give him the stick for it. It doesn't happen with girls, it happens with men. They just always turn their back on the black sheep. I was always more feminine than most fellas so that's why I don't think I had friends in school. …The fellas would just turn their back on you immediately. If your voice hadn't broken yet or anything like that, they don't want to know you and we will give you stick and that's what happens. … So you just get shunned if you're different. That's being a fag. When you're growing up there's a lot of pressure not to be gay. I'm not saying I am gay. I'm very comfortable with my sexuality. But if you're gay you get an awful time. Life should be wife and kids. That's life. A good job, engineer or something. You get your hands dirty. I've never seen a fella want to be a botanist. I think they're just afraid of what they could become and they're very insecure about their own sexuality. …Gay and feminine is the same.*

> *They just think that what you're wearing or the way you stand or the way you sit or your hands move when you talk that you're gay so you get punished for that in society especially when you're teenagers and I certainly did. You just get slagged for it and beaten up and thrown into the girls toilets with your trousers down. The way they see it a man would be a man who goes out and has a pint and watches the football match on a Sunday and goes out to work for the rest of the week and does nothing but talk about football. That's a man. If you ask me that's a very empty life. There are no men at my class that wanted to be like me, I wanted to be a* (career mentioned). *No one wanted to do that, they wanted to be mechanics and panel beaters and bricklayers and sparkies… …They will attack the weaker one. I don't know how they see it but they will attack them and the minute I arrived into that school, the secondary school, I was the weaker person and I got attacked. I got jumped on and bullied and it even got to the point where people in other years, the stronger people in the lower years, were bullying me. Just because you're that little bit different and it can have a detrimental effect on somebody's life. That's the way men are. …I have had a series of jobs. Most of them I've gotten bullied in as well which is getting a little bit tedious at this point. I have to change the way I talk to people in different situations like in a working situation. I have to change completely who I am. Like in the course I'm in at the minute I'm a lad. For some reason I'm hanging around with the lads. There's people there that listen to the same music as me. Well I'm not a lad, that's for one thing. I'm very sensitive especially to other people's emotions. I'm very sensitive to other people. Just caring. I love caring for all people and I love people caring for me. That's what I'm really like. That's not a lad. A lad is a pint of Guinness and watching the football. …Yes, they're normal. Well, in society's eyes they're normal because I was abnormal in school according to them.*

Having a gay identity in these environments was hazardous and being unable to come out as gay men was directly implicated in at least two of the suicidal actions. Alan described growing up with constant harassment and the ongoing fear of being identified as gay in a community where homosexuality was the moniker for unacceptable masculinity.

> *I really had a bad life. I know there's people worse off than me but to me it's just my life, it's not right. I think everything would be so much better if I wasn't here. I've always been bullied. I've always had my friends and I've always had people taking a dislike to me and I've actually been bullied*

badly. …I've always been bullied. I don't think I'm bullied that much now but as a young child I was bullied up to about thirteen. …Because of the way I talk. The way I talk, it's not a man's voice. I've always been squeaky. I never realised that I talk the way I talk until like sixth class …. in third class people would call me faggot and then I'd call them faggot back. I hadn't actually ever heard myself. The first time I did that I said 'shit'. … Before fifth class if someone called me names like queer, I'd call them queer back. And after fifth class, Jesus they can't call me queer anymore. It must be to do with the way I talk. You get used to it. Like now I'm a sixth year student – I'm walking down the corridor and a first year would go and call me a name, 'Queer! Faggot!' and I would turn around and say I'll fuckin' kill you. It's not as bad now. Now I'd easily go and give them a thump in the face and they'd shut up. …kids on the road, they just want a chase, they'll think I'll chase them but I just turn around and say I'll get you next day. Like you can't walk out on the road without someone calling you a name.

School was a key site for displaying and enforcing the prevailing masculinity and was a profoundly negative experience for some of the participants. Bullying was endemic in the (generally all male) schools they attended and while it did occur at primary level victimisation seemed to reach a peak of intensity in the initial years of secondary school. As implied in earlier sections of this chapter, a significant proportion of the men in the study had been victimised in school and for some men school became a psychological and physically abusive environment which continued to haunt them long after they had left as Matt's narrative attests.

It was down to someone who wears glasses. Someone with something that is different. If you're quiet that's it, you can't be quiet. You have to be some way outstanding or you don't survive. I was picked on a lot at school. I had an awful lot of torment in school over the years. I wasn't one of the strongest boys. But as I got older obviously I got bigger and bigger and was able to fight my own battles and I had friends and that was grand then. But before that I was tormented as a kid. Primary was hard. …I always had a good friend. I always had good friends wherever I was but the bullying aspect was always there and that used to get me. I think it was just generally picking on the weaker ones.

> ***How did you feel when you were bullied?***
> *Well you go home to your mother or father and you hate school. It made me hate school anyway and that's what I felt. But I could hate those people still and if I saw them on the street I'd jump on them. It was something that I learnt, that I was always the target. I was always a very small guy, I only started growing in second year at college and now I'm (gives height) and I've been in the (gives height) league for a long time now and being a lot bigger I never had a problem then.*
>
> ***Did it affect your self-esteem?***
> *It did yeah, that's why I'll never recover from it. That's the way I let it happen. It's probably up to me to face that but that's the way I let it happen. You don't feel as adequate as the others.*

As Matt suggests, they were targeted for a multiplicity of reasons but any display of difference or vulnerability was likely to result in victimisation. Victims were generally those who visibly departed from the dominant masculinity norms and difference was linked to homosexuality as Guy related.

> *Bullying started first day in school. I was flavour of the month. Yeah, like day one of secondary school and then I make the fatal mistake afterwards of saying 'can I be their friend' and they just thought it was hilarious and then passed it to the next guy who also thought it was funny and by the end of the day everyone thought I was a weak coward who deserved to be picked upon. …usually things about my sexuality and this kind of thing. They would try and embarrass me and it was just reference to my genetalia and to my alleged homosexuality and this sort of thing. I think they saw me as a sort of a weakling. Men are supposed to be strong and proud and independent and I'm not saying homosexual people can't be that way but generally they're seen as effeminate and submissive and weak so if you want to insult someone, especially their sexual integrity, you call them homosexual.*

The distress caused by family adversity often made one vulnerable to being bullied and made it less likely that the participant would report the victimisation. The misery and self-blame which resulted from bullying was therefore intensified by non-disclosure. Victimisation ended the academic aspirations of a number of the participants, including Guy, who intended to advance to third level but was forced to leave school early.

> *I didn't get to go to college because I was abused when I was in school and I left there without any qualifications. …everywhere I went in the entire school there was someone there to pick on me or call me some random name that they just felt inclined to …and by the time I got through that I was so messed up that I couldn't relate to anybody and I spent the whole year in isolation and I didn't get to do my Leaving Cert at the end of it.* Guy

Participants were aware that more flexible forms of masculinity existed elsewhere and was usually associated with higher socioeconomic status. In the same way, university was associated with more fluid gender practices and for this reason, a number of the participants desperately wanted to access third level education although the rarely succeeded. This denotes the link between socioeconomic status and educational outcome and demonstrates how educational routes out of these situations were not a feasible option for many of the men. Guy had moved to a school in a middle-class district near the end of his secondary school career and described stark differences between the two environments in relation to both the educational experience and to outcome. According to Guy education in lower socioeconomic areas is narrowly conceived and schools are viewed by students as places they have to endure and as academic endpoints. He contrasted this with schooling in middle-class areas, in particular private education, which he described as a preparation for further study, career and for life generally. In this way, middle-class education systems, underpinned by middle-class social and economic capital, facilitated academic advancement and self-confidence by providing better learning environments as well as offering a more fluid gender culture.

> *Success breeds success and middle class families all have middle class parents so when your father is an accountant or a doctor and your mother is a teacher or a lawyer that is an amazing advantage to you as a child. You could not quantify that type of intellectual capital that is being pumped into you as a child. Compared to the inner city school I went to where you get bullied at every location. You go to the toilet and you get bullied, you come out and you get bullied. Everyone does. Its like being prayed on by wolves. In an inner city school if you happen to be quite smart they really kind of dislike you for that and they make an effort to drag you down.*

The practice of bullying resulted in physical and psychological suffering and induced long-lasting insecurity and anger. Victimisation created a cycle which was difficult to break as it induced a feeling that one was different from, and weaker than, one's male peers and this perception was difficult to discard. Bullying experienced in this way caused suffering and social isolation and sometimes impacted significantly on the participants' academic careers and when they were aware of alternative masculinity settings they found what was available to them even more difficult to endure.

Summary

This chapter explored the men's experiences growing up and the cultural and familial context in which they developed their early, formative, ideas about gender and emotions. They came from a variety of backgrounds but the majority were from a broadly working-class background. Almost all the men emerged from families where the normative expectations were based on a hegemonic type of masculinity which defined manhood in narrow, conventional, terms emphasising strength and stoicism and restricting the expression of sentiments connected to weakness. This resulted in an emotional environment which was lacking in intimacy and communication between fathers and sons rarely diverged from a narrow, relatively impersonal, format—whether the father lives within or outside the family home. Fathers were central figures in their lives from whom love and affirmation was sought but rarely given in a demonstrable way and the most common criticism directed at fathers was their lack of emotional engagement. Paternal behaviours involving alcoholism and violence reduced the possibility of close, confiding, relationships still further. A background narrative is the evident unhappiness of many of the fathers. In this way, the stories had an intergenerational quality and presented a scenario of emotional pain and suppression passing from father to son. Many grew up in families in which there was significant adversity and these problems circumscribed the men's social, economic and emotional lives as they grew. Growing up in a problematic family impacted negatively on one's self-esteem and led to sublimation of emotional pain as restrictions on emotional expression prevented them from disclosing the suffering they had experienced.

The men generally rejected aspects of masculinity presented to them within the home and their communities but essentially it became the basis of their masculinity and the lack of socioeconomic and educational resources constricted their ability to explore alternative masculinities. There was little flexibility around masculine scripts and there was surveillance both within and outside the home and especially in the school where the masculine environment was even more rigid. The majority of the men did not feel they measured up to the prevailing version of masculinity and a substantial number of boys were victimised by peers which reinforced fears about their masculine identity. These findings illustrate how specific emotional cultures instilled early in life, linked to conventional masculinities, limited the expression of feelings and the working through of painful experiences. The result was the repression and prolongation of these distressing emotions and or their channelling into negative emotions or harmful forms of behaviour.

References

Afifi, T. O., Boman, J., Fleisher, W., et al. (2009). The relationship between child abuse, parental divorce, and lifetime mental disorders and suicidality in a nationally representative adult sample. *Child Abuse and Neglect, 33*(3), 139–147.

Booth, A., Scott, M. E., & King, V. (2010). Father residence and adolescent problem behaviour: Are youth always better off in two-parent families? *Journal of Family Issues, 31*(5), 585–605.

Bronte-Tinkew, J., Moore, K. A., Carrano, J., et al. (2006). The father-child relationship, parenting styles, and adolescent risk behaviours in intact families. *Journal of Family Issues, 27*(6), 850–881.

Dube, S. R., Anda, R. F., Felitte, V. J., et al. (2001). Childhood abuse, household dysfunction, and the risk of attempted suicide throughout the life span: Findings from the adverse childhood experiences study. *Journal of the American Medical Association 26, 286*(24), 3089–3096.

Enns, M. W., Cox, B. J., Afifi, T. O., et al. (2006). Childhood adversities and risk for suicidal ideation and attempts: A longitudinal population-based study. *Psychological Medicine, 36*(12), 1769–1778.

Fergusson, D. M., Woodward, L. J., & Horwood, L. J. (2000). Risk factors and life processes associated with the onset of suicidal behaviour during adolescence and early adulthood. *Psychological Medicine, 30*(1), 23–39.

Hanlon, N. (2009). Caregiving masculinities: An exploratory analysis. In K. Lynch, J. Baker, & M. Lyons (Eds.), *Affective equality: Love, care and injustice.* (pp. 180–198). London: Palgrave Macmillan.

Johnson, J. G., Cohen, P., Gould, M. S., et al. (2002). Childhood adversities, interpersonal difficulties and risk for suicide attempts during late adolescence and early adulthood. *Archives of General Psychiatry, 59*(8), 741–749.

Kimmel, M. (1994). Masculinity as homophobia. In H. Brod & M. Kaufman (Eds.), *Theorising masculinities* (pp. 119–141). London: Sage.

Lamb, M. E. (2010). *The role of the father in child development.* Hoboken, NJ: Wiley.

Lamb, M. E., & Lewis, C. (2010). The development and significance of father-child relationships in two-parent families. In M. E. Lamb (Ed.), *The role of the father in child development* (4th ed.). New York: Wiley.

Loukas, A., Fitzgerald, H. E., Zucker, R. A., et al. (2001). Parental alcoholism and co-occurring antisocial behavior: Prospective relationships to externalizing behavior problems in their young sons. *Journal of Abnormal Child Pschology, 29*(2), 91–106.

Molner, B., Berkman, L. F., & Buka, S. L. (2001). Psychopathology, childhood sexual abuse and other childhood adversities: Relative links to subsequent suicidal behaviour in the US. *Psychological Medicine, 31*(6), 965–977.

Moore, B. (2018). Transitions toward equality: A sociological analysis of contemporary fatherhood (Unpublished Doctoral thesis). University College Dublin, Dublin, Ireland.

Pease, B. (2000). Beyond the father wound: Memory-work and the deconstruction of the father–son relationship. *Australia and New Zealand Journal of Family Therapy, 21*(1), 9–15.

Pleck, J. H. (2010). Fatherhood and masculinity. In M. E. Lamb (Ed.), *The role of the father in child development* (5th ed., pp. 27–57). New York: Wiley.

Pleck, J., & Marsiglio, W. (2010). Fatherhood and masculinity. In M. E. Lamb (Ed.), *The role of the father in child development.* Hoboken, NJ: Wiley.

Videon, T. M. (2005). Parent-child relations and children's psychological well-being: Do dads matter? *Journal of Family Issues, 26*(1), 55–78.

Wagner, B., Silverman, M. C., & Martin, C. E. (2003). Family factors in youth suicidal behaviors. *American Behavioral Scientist, 46*(9), 1171–1191.
Weitoft, G. R., Hjern, A., Haglund, B., et al. (2003). Mortality, severe morbidity, and injury in children living with single parents in Sweden: A population-based study. *The Lancet, 361*(9354), 289–295.
Whipple, S. C., & Noble, E. P. (1991). Personality characteristics of alcoholic fathers and their sons. *Journal of Studies on Alcohol, 52*(4), 331–337.

4

The Meaning and Context of Suicidal Action

Culture exerts a considerable influence on suicide rates and while this has been evident since the nineteenth century the detail of how this operates is far from clear. Culture infiltrates at various levels but predominantly in terms of the society's overall attitude or script in relation to suicide. Cultural ideas are interwoven with beliefs about gender and class and these factors play out critically in relation to suicidal action. Explanations for male suicide range from essentialist, biological, arguments, such as men's alleged tendency to impulsivity, to predominantly social explanations. The main biomedical explanation for suicide—mental disorder—is contested as the diagnosis (depression) most frequently linked to suicide is statistically more prevalent among women and a considerable number of suicides take place outside the clinical domain (Owens et al. 2003; Hamdi et al. 2008). Sociological explanations have been equally deterministic, for example, Durkheim's suggestion that only men were intellectually capable of making decisions to suicide (Kushner 1995). While Durkheim's reasoning lacks credibility today a gendered perspective remains implicit in many investigations of suicidal behaviour and prevailing research paradigms facilitate this. The sex-difference framework, which is frequently used in suicide research,

A. Cleary, *The Gendered Landscape of Suicide*,
https://doi.org/10.1007/978-3-030-16634-2_4

divides male and female behaviour along binary lines and highlights differences rather than the similarities and points of confluence noted in studies of gender activity (Thorne 1993). Equally problematic is the fact that men in these studies are constructed as a single, cohesive, group. Higher rates of male suicide in the Western World have been linked to a so-called crisis of masculinity which suggests that the erosion of men's economic and family roles has had negative psychological repercussions for all men (Atkinson 2011). There have been major changes for men over recent decades across the domains of work and family but these changes have affected men differently depending on their socioeconomic, ethnic and other positions within society. Masculinities, ways of being a man, are always mediated through these social divisions and socioeconomic status is an important predictor of suicide (Lorent et al. 2005; Rehkoph and Buka 2006).

Existing research frameworks for understanding suicide support gendered profiles in suicide research and these ideas, in turn, have filtered through to the general population via the media and other channels (Coyle and MacWhannell 2002). These gendered themes portray the action as a significant even brave deed if undertaken by a man and imply that levels of male suicide are a kind of barometer of national economic and social wellbeing (Kushner 1995). The gendering of suicide extends also to the definition of suicidal action and to its causation. Completed suicide is constructed as a forceful, rational, male act undertaken in the face of external problems and attempted suicide as implying weakness, irrationality and personal pathology. In this way completed suicide remains attached to masculinity while attempted suicide is constructed as a feminine behaviour (Inckle 2014). The causes of male suicide are connected to external factors such as economic issues, while female suicide is associated with relationship issues (Canetto 1992). Motivations for suicide are largely unknown but emerging knowledge indicates that relationship loss is a significant element in male suicides (Fincham et al. 2011; Cleary 2012).

In contrast to Durkheim's (1951) findings in the nineteenth century, wealth now protects from suicide and the poorest groups in society, whom Durkheim believed were the least vulnerable in terms of suicide, are currently the most at-risk category (Page et al. 2014; Patterson and Holden 2012). Suicide rates among minority, ethnic, populations are generally high (Chandler and Lalonde 1998) as are rates for young LGBT people in the United States and elsewhere although levels for this grouping stabilise in adulthood (Russell and Toomey 2012). These findings demonstrate both the variability of suicide rates and the importance of culture in explicating the meanings of suicide across different social categories. It is some, rather than all, men who are at risk of suicide and this challenges a straightforward link between 'men' and the social changes which have occurred over recent decades.

This chapter contains the narratives of men who attempted suicide and presents their explanations for, and the meanings they attached to, their actions in interviews conducted a short time after the suicidal episode. The context and background to the suicide attempt are described in their own words and, in general, according to their sequencing as the men frequently intermingled issues as well as past and present experiences. The objective is to demonstrate how suicidal pathways are formed and while the focus is on the event it will become apparent how past issues and unresolved suffering and concealment are implicated in the process. More generally, these stories indicate how culture and structural factors impact on particular groups yet they remain individual stories emanating from men who came, via their own socioemotional routes, to a point where they decided to end their lives.

Despairing Narratives: The Long and Silent Road to Suicidal Action

These men's stories demonstrate that suicide is rarely, if ever, an impulsive action, despite the strong link between impulsivity and male suicide in the literature. In the context of the concealment of distress presented in previous chapters, it is easy to see why post hoc analysis of male suicides gives rise to this misperception. Neither is suicidal action generally a response to a particular issue or event, another predominant idea associated with suicide. Such events tend to act as precipitating rather than causal agents. For these men, the suicide attempt generally occurred in the context of long-term unease or unhappiness and within a period of intensified despair when they came to believe their pain could not be relieved. They couldn't see an end to the mental anguish they were experiencing and sought release from this. This perception sometimes had an element of objective reality in that these men lacked financial and other resources, as well as access to alternative views of masculinity, which would have increased the possibility of an intervention. Suicidal action also needs to be understood in the context of long-term suppression and concealment of suffering and in this way more accurately represents a long emotional journey incorporating the man's major life experiences and what his life had come to mean to him at that time.

When these men began to move towards suicide they had, in general, experienced considerable emotional pain over their lifetime and this had occurred in a socioemotional environment which required suppression of suffering. There were therefore unresolved issues and emotions and problems which they tended to view as part of a pattern, as confirmation of their inadequacy and powerlessness in terms of the prevalent masculinity. A common theme was that they were weaker than other men who, in contrast to them, were perceived as strong and adept in managing their lives. The men's past experiences had negatively affected their socioemotional identity and given rise to vulnerabilities which affected their ability to deal with subsequent psychological challenges. They lacked knowledge and skills in identifying and coping with these challenges because they had not been able to accrue these competencies within their cultural environment and normative values restricting emotional expression prevented them from speaking out and seeking help. The main intervention known to them was counselling and this was considered to be both ineffective and sited within a feminine discourse and therefore almost never availed of. In this way their position prior to the suicide attempt was akin to Nelson's (2001) description of damaged identities, identities defined by those with the power to speak for them and to constrain the scope of their actions. As Nelson suggests, these men would have needed a powerful counter-story to redress this perception but they had limited access, for cultural and socioeconomic reasons, to alternative versions of life and they lacked the confidence to enact a different masculinity in their present environment. As will become apparent in the next chapter it was possible to break free from these despairing narratives and identities but this was dependent on resources and the degree of agency still available to them.

Larry

Larry's story exemplifies how long and silent the road to suicide can be yet the decision to act can be quite spontaneous. Larry was mentioned in Chapter 3 in relation to the culture of masculinity operating within his home. He had a relatively secure upbringing but he had always had a difficult relationship with this father and as a result he left home in his teens, began a relationship and subsequently had children. When interviewed, he was in his late twenties and had made the second of two near-lethal attempts at suicide within a short period of time. Although he had a long-term partner and children Larry had developed a solitary and emotionally detached existence from his family. He was employed, worked long hours (taking as much overtime as he was offered) and drinking heavily. He was desperately unhappy but didn't understand the nature or origins of his misery or how to address it. He described a phase of intense despondency lasting over five years but it was clear from his narrative that he had been unhappy for a much longer period. While in the hospital he would begin to categorise his difficulties as depression but up to this he had never considered seeking medical or other assistance and increasingly began to believe that improvement was impossible and that happiness would always elude him. He was aware that he was dependent on alcohol and referred to the fact that he and other men commonly used alcohol to cope with unhappiness. Prior to his first suicide attempt he made what he now identified as a significant move towards suicidal action, a kind of rehearsal for the main act, but this went largely unrecognised or at least was not addressed by his family. It was noted by his boss, a man who also had problems with alcohol, and who appeared to take a paternal interest in Larry. Yet, while the boss's intervention was important he did not, in keeping with their relationship and the view of masculinity they both shared, discuss the issue with Larry or advise him to seek help. In this way Larry remained at high risk of suicide and with little possibility of this situation changing.

> ***Do you remember when you first felt like this?***
> *The first time I suppose that anything happened that was say out of the ordinary was, I was going back to work one day. I left the house as normal, I worked in* (place named) *and I just didn't go back to work. I had a car then and I just drove up the mountains and stayed there for two days in the car. I actually did nothing. I went to a place I knew and as I say it was in the mountains. It was somewhere in* (place named). *It was winter. I know it was cold so where I was you wouldn't get any people. In the summertime it would be packed. Even now I don't really know why I did it because I was actually on my way to work. I came off* (place named) *and I was heading towards work and I just couldn't be bothered. My partner didn't know where I was. Nobody knew. I don't really know why. I came back and went back to work. My boss asked. My boss came out to the house actually and he asked me what was wrong but he just told them in work that I was sick and that was it and he said just come back.*
>
> ***And what did you say to your partner?***
> *I just said I wanted to go away for a while. It wasn't something we really talked about. Not really. More my fault I suppose.*

As Larry's story illustrates, men can experience difficulties both expressing distress and in being heard when they are attempting, perhaps subliminally, to communicate their suffering. In this way, the participants frequently slipped through a potentially protective family network because they did not want to, or felt they could not, divulge difficulties. Yet, it was clear that men were sometimes sending out critical signs of distress and these warning signals were missed by partners, family and friends. This was due, in part, to the prevailing emotional culture as well as to the concealing practices and structures they had set up to protect themselves. Men such as Larry had disconnected emotionally, had few if any close friends, and had developed a lifestyle which was quite marginal from their families. Their objective in doing this was to create sufficient distance from their social circle to shield themselves from unmasking and, as they viewed it, in order to survive emotionally. If they had friends they were unlikely to share their distress with them, especially if they were male friends, for the reasons discussed in Chapter 2. These participants were operating within a socioemotional culture which was not attuned or receptive to receiving distress cues from men while, at the same time, the men were actively hiding this distress. They connected emotional distress to vulnerability and to the feminine and sometimes to psychiatric disorder and all were equally unacceptable and stigmatising for men in the cultural environment they inhabited. In these circumstances, the usual option was to try to keep going, maintain a front of normality and cope by self-medicating with alcohol. In this way, their pathways to suicide were facilitated over time by a lack of space to emote and disclose and by the use of alcohol to sustain these performances. They were however susceptible to ongoing challenges and negative events. Although a precipitating event was not required to move them towards the ultimate step such an occurrence generally accelerated the movement towards suicidal action. When they entered the phase of heightened risk the need to end the anguish they were experiencing became a critical factor. Larry had been at this stage for some time and the (second) suicide action, when it occurred, was quite spontaneous and did not involve a triggering event.

> *I wasn't happy. No, there wasn't really a build-up. As I said, you don't see a future. …I had no problem with work. I don't know, I just didn't feel….*
>
> ***Was there anything that precipitated it?***
> *No. I went into town. I was drinking a lot. But I drink a lot anyway. Or I did up to recently. So that day was no different to any other day. I was drunk. But if I did it every time I was drunk I would have done it a hundred times. I was on the quays and was waiting to get the bus to go out to* (names place) *and I went down to what I thought was far enough down the* (names river). *Obviously the further you go down, the less people and I just took off my jacket and took off my watch. I don't know what happened. The next thing I knew I was in the hospital. When I came around I was in the Accident and Emergency and there was just a doctor there and she told me that I'd been pulled out of the* (names river). *That was it. I don't know what happened. I don't know what happened in between.*

When you jumped in, did you want to kill yourself?
Oh yeah, absolutely, and the only thing that I regret is that I didn't, maybe not now but even so, it wouldn't even bother me now. That was the second time. The first time, it was the previous year. I jumped off a bridge. I was in (name of hospital) for five weeks. *That was more planned.*

Ben

Ben was in his mid-twenties and lived in the family home and this was his first suicide attempt. As with Larry, there was no specific event preceding the attempt and, as his account suggests, the decision to complete suicide concerned a general disappointment about his life. He felt his life was going nowhere and that there was nothing he could do to improve the situation and he had been thinking about suicide for some time. He described the suicide attempt as resulting from a gradual build-up of despondency over some years which was partly related to unfulfilled academic and career aspirations. He had successfully completed second-level schooling but didn't get the grades he needed for his chosen university programme. He did attend another third-level college but found the experience unfulfilling and dropped out after one term. Thereafter his tendency to isolation became more pronounced and he retreated both socially and psychologically. He talked of powerlessness, of an inability to change his life, which he regarded as primarily determined by economic factors, and related his educational 'failure' to this also. He had never been employed, rarely went out and didn't appear to have any friends. Prior to the suicide attempt, he considered he was in an impossible situation in that he didn't have the qualifications which he regarded as essential to success in society and felt he could not return to college to achieve these credentials. His narrative indicated that he may always have been somewhat isolated but more recently he had experienced an increasing sense of disconnection from his family. It appeared he had been moving inexorably towards this point following a kind of social suicide as he removed himself from meaningful social engagement, first from the wider society and subsequently from his family.

Things were probably, things were getting beyond my abilities to deal with it so I just decided to take an overdose. And I thought I wouldn't be here, thought I'd be dead by now. I'm not happy. I'm not happy. There's not a lot I can do until I stop being unhappy.

Has anything happened to make you unhappy?
No. This was, I suppose, a gradual thing over years and years. Its not like one thing happened and that was the end of my world kind of thing. I hadn't been going out and stuff for ten years so it gradually built up over a long time. I've been thinking a long time of dying but I didn't really know how you could commit suicide, that kind of thing, so for a long time I didn't do it, you know. I didn't know how. And obviously I still don't because I'm still alive. I just, I had the opportunity that day kind of thing. I'd been thinking about it for a while but then ended up with loads of pills and stuff around so I decided that I'd take them that night. I thought it'd be better for everybody. …I just didn't think there's any point in continuing on just as I had been, you know, waiting for things to change or whatever. I decided it would be better for everybody. I think I wrote (in a note to his family) *saying I'm sorry about this but it's for the best kind of thing. Something like that. …This situation has been going on for a couple of years now, you know. Be easily going on for another few years. Well, maybe not now but it would have if I hadn't done anything. But that doesn't actually mean it was a big deep thought going into it or anything. …It was just a kind of a conclusion. It was a long process. A wearying-out process. Getting fed up with stuff. Just things, if they're not going right for you, you know.*

The feeling of being low, was that there for some time?
Well it was probably more pessimism. At times, I'd feel slightly optimistic or whatever but then at other times, I'd feel very pessimistic about the future, you know. I mean, like, if they are going against you, you know, and you've no control of them. So, what are you going to do then? Tough luck. … thought I'd do a lot better and stuff but I haven't. If there was like a scale of the person that you could be, kind of thing, and like the best and the worst, I'm like, I suppose, down near the worst. When I was younger, like, I thought I could be up, well say at ten or whatever. Things didn't work out. I didn't really have any specific … well, I thought I'd go to college and the usual, what everybody else does, get married, that kind of stuff. … I suppose school is the thing that leads on to so much. I suppose wealth means that you don't need to worry about basically stupid little things. …I suppose things probably hadn't really

gone my way. I ended up here, basically. If things had been kind of different, if things had gone differently, I'd be in a far better position. Things are out of my control.

There were similar elements in Ben's and Larry's stories. Both had experienced long-term unhappiness and both lived at home—either with parents and siblings (Ben) or with a partner and children (Larry). Yet, despite quite specific indicators of distress, notably Ben's increasing social isolation and in Larry's case, detachment and excessive drinking, the families had not prompted them to seek help. Ben reported that his family were close-knit and supportive and that his mother had been encouraging him to go out more but the family's shocked reaction to his suicide attempt implies they had either unaware of the extent of his unhappiness or they felt unable or unwilling to intervene. Ben suggested that his family should have been aware of his situation but this remark was probably symptomatic of the emotional distance which had developed between them.

How did they react when this happened?
I think they're fairly shocked. Eh, I didn't think they'd probably be as surprised. Hadn't been going out for a while and, eh, I would have thought. I don't know if they know but I think they should really. It's just really, that's what happens when people get low. But they haven't been asking a load of questions or anything like that.

These stories suggest that men in some social environments tend to be left alone even when there are warning signals especially if they give out cues that they want to remain undisturbed. In the aftermath of the suicide attempt Ben was embarrassed, wanted to leave the hospital as soon as possible and showed no desire to engage with therapy and address the difficulties in his life. Larry's aim was to do exactly the same but events took a more positive turn for him (this is discussed in Chapter 5).

What were your feelings when you began to realise where you were?
It was all very surreal, kind of thing. So I just like basically woke up in a hospital, you know, with people all around. It just felt more like a dream. I

suppose a bit embarrassed. I haven't really, I suppose, been reflecting on it. I haven't been thinking about the future. But this is completely different to my normal routine, kind of thing. Because there's no real privacy or anything. I just don't like being surrounded by strangers.

Will you go to somebody for counselling?
Well, I probably will, I don't know. (Name of Staff Member*) is trying to convince me to talk and stuff. I don't really see where it gets you though. You're still in the same place.*

The primary message of these stories is that the decision to complete suicide is rarely if ever sudden or impulsive and the events which are often identified as motivating factors are more likely to be triggering incidents. These points are underlined by Alan's account, provided at interview seven years after the event.

I know why I'm not going to go through it again but I don't know why someone else is going through it and I don't know why people do it but I do know that if somebody said to me that his girlfriend broke up with him and he killed himself well… I don't think you're talking spur of the moment. I don't think you would do it for that reason. Maybe a break-up or something that happened at that moment that's probably why he says 'end it, I can't take anymore' but I think its gone on for ages before. It's a sudden decision there and then but I think… Some people I know say a man from around the corner from me killed himself because his girlfriend left him. I don't believe you can just kill yourself because someone left you. I don't think he killed himself because she left him. I think he killed himself because he just wasn't happy and that was the end of it. I remember when I tried I thought about it all the time. I thought about it for months. I thought about it all the time and then one time I said 'fuck it, I'm going to do it'. It was in me for months.

Entering a Field of Diminishing Possibilities

As the above stories illustrate the participants moved over time towards a critical level of distress about their situation and the strain of suppressing and concealing significant levels of suffering contributed to a feeling of being trapped in an impossible situation. As the chances of a reality check from family, friends or a professional receded and there was no outlet, no way of unburdening themselves, a feeling of panic frequently ensued as distress was now affecting the body in terms of anxiety and sleeplessness. This is when options began to narrow and suicide came to be seen as a viable solution.

> *I couldn't cope with it. I didn't want to live anymore. I just felt I had no choice. I'm not functioning normally. I don't want to spend every day in hell.*
> —Mitch

The men were also restricted in bringing about change in their life situations by a lack of resources, particularly financial and educational capital. Some had considered alternatives such as changing their lifestyle or moving elsewhere but decided this was not feasible. In this way, restricted agency, lack of control over one's life, was a feature of their stories and a similar theme is evident in Redley's (2003) study of those who self-harmed in a disadvantaged community.

As distress increased the notion of suicide was considered and was generally introduced into consciousness slowly and tentatively. As time went on the idea became more definite and specific methods of killing oneself were contemplated, as Matt describes.

> *I have often thought about it over a space of time. As a question to myself. Over a year I suppose. Just a question, a thought really. You might see something on the television, someone's committed suicide and you would think what way would I go about it, think that way, but I didn't think I'd ever do it. The other times were just answering questions in your own head, what was I going to do or how was I going to do it. This time I was giving myself a way of doing it.*

A definite plan for suicidal action was now forming and with no apparent solutions available the men entered a phase in which alternatives were receding while levels of distress were intensifying. This phase has been identified in other studies of suicide (Shneidman 1991; Brownhill et al. 2005). Suicide was now within consciousness but was still a fear-inducing option.

> *You don't have many options and something like that is your best option, your best choice, and you've got the choices but the only good one you have or the best one of them all ... is to end it for yourself, end all your troubles, end all your worries and you'll never have to worry about it again.* —Alex

The participants were now at a critical level of risk when suicidal action had moved beyond the discretionary phase and had come to represent the only way out of their difficulties. A suicide scenario had been created and thoughts of suicide had given way to more serious consideration, and sometimes rehearsal, of the action. There was frequently, as indicated in the narratives, an episode of self-harm during this time which functioned as a type of practice run to test out one's responses and to build up sufficient determination to complete the act. The duration of this phase varied depending on the individual and the circumstances but a tipping point, as described by Byng et al. (2015), could occur at almost any time. Something relatively inconsequential or simply opportunity (as in Larry's case) could now push the participants towards action. Although there was evidence of an impulsive quality to some of the suicidal actions in reality the act had been thought out and planned over some time, occasionally over years. This is illustrated in Gary's account of his sudden compulsion to end his life, although it was the culmination of a long period of unhappiness and frustration about his inability to come out as a gay man.

> *I woke up a bit depressed but it got worse and worse, an overwhelming sadness. I felt I had no one to talk to. I phoned (named person) and he couldn't answer. I just wanted to talk to someone. I just felt very, very, sad. I don't feel that sadness now. It was something that I don't understand. ...I felt no fear. I didn't feel any fear at the time. It was just so overwhelming. ... I just knew what I wanted to do... I just wanted it to be over. I didn't want to be thinking about anything.*

Thoughts of suicide are usually some distance from the action. As many of the participants recounted, the reality of suicide was frightening, both the action itself and the possible physical injuries that might result if one did not succeed. The participants spoke of building up sufficient courage and of urging themselves on to complete the action. In this respect, Firestone (1986) has spoken of a subliminal 'voice', an internal system of hostile thoughts and attitudes, which are involved in the movement towards suicidal action. As with Nelson's (2001) idea of a damaged identity this voice becomes part of a negative concept of self if it goes unchallenged and culminates in 'a rage against the self' (Firestone 1986: 439). As these men lacked an objective view of their predicament, powerful emotions were now in the ascendant. The negative view of themselves, which many had accepted since childhood, came to dominate and the idea of suicide began to seem inevitable. At this point only the action remained and, as Firestone comments, 'the voice' is goading the person to complete the deed. This driving of oneself towards action was apparent in the study and was particularly evident in those who had repeatedly attempted suicide. An element of urgency took over and they described a desire to act decisively and confidently. Alcohol was frequently involved and its main function in this situation was to give courage or anaesthetize feelings.

> *I wasn't in a bad way yesterday or anything like that. I just felt confident enough to do it. Probably drink didn't help but I wouldn't say it had much to do with it. It was more of a painkiller. Up to last night it was an option. It was a choice for me but I didn't want it to be because it's a horrible scary thing to do. I spent the last couple of weeks every once in a while thinking 'how will I write a suicide note?' I was always thinking, contemplating, it but last night I was thinking about how, you know, when something feels right 'do it' you know. One minute I'm sitting down thinking of something and the next minute, 'now is the right time, go do it. Quick before you change your mind'.* —Alex

Their intention in almost all cases was to end their lives and the outcome for all could have been death. The seriousness of their intent was also evident in their reactions when they regained consciousness in the hospital which ranged from amazement, to fear, to relief. Some of those who made the most lethal attempts were glad to be alive.

> *I think I was very close to death. I found it hard to believe that I was alive but I remember feeling glad. I was happy that I was alive.* —Gary

And, while their aim was to complete suicide the primary desire was relief from the emotional anguish and escape from the life they felt had become trapped within. They used the methods which were available to them which did not conform to gender stereotypes in that the majority overdosed with non-prescription drugs (the remainder used methods such as hanging, shooting etc.). The link between method and intent is complex as method is generally determined by availability and lethality cannot be assessed only by reference to the means used. The diversity of methods used in this study, including the techniques used by the participants who later completed suicide, indicate that method is not a robust indicator for predicting intent. The degree of thought and planning is similarly difficult to determine but this study shows clearly that suicide is rarely an impulsive action but occurs in the context of long-term unhappiness and prolonged contemplation of suicide.

The Rationale for Suicide

The principal motives for attempting suicide provided by the men were generalised unhappiness about one's life and the ending of a relationship but the reasons presented were frequently precipitating rather than causative factors. A triggering event was involved in over one-third of cases. Psychiatric symptoms were implicated in only a small number of cases.

Struggling with Relationships

Relationships featured prominently in the men's stories and quite a few related their suicidal action directly to the ending of a relationship. Relationships were replete with tensions. Relationships were a key marker of masculinity for heterosexual men and were especially significant for men who had sought emotional support in a partnership when this was lacking in their upbringing. These background issues made emotional attachment more essential to their psychological wellbeing and the termination of a relationship had strong symbolic meaning for these men. There were, in addition, unhappy relationships which men felt unable to leave and there were gay men who were prevented from accessing relationships because they lived in a cultural environment which devalued their sexual orientation.

Fergus, Dermot and Ronan

The link between childhood insecurities and current loss, which featured in many of these lives was evident in Fergus's story, which was introduced in Chapter 2. Fergus was in his twenties and the father of a young child and his girlfriend has just ended their relationship. The loss of his child and of his only confidant was devastating for Fergus. Early in his narrative Fergus linked this loss to his childhood and specifically the rejection he had suffered from his father. His parents were unmarried when he was born but while they subsequently married the marriage had always been acrimonious. Fergus appears to have been a scapegoat for his father's unhappiness and throughout his life, he had to endure insinuations from his father about his parentage. This had caused immense hurt, isolated Fergus from his younger siblings and he left home in his teens to escape from this situation. Despite these challenges, Fergus had managed to do well in school and in work terms. According to Fergus, the suicide attempt followed a build-up of multiple factors, including the ending of the relationship by his partner. He had been trying to manage financial and emotional challenges and increasingly was coming to believe that the basis for these efforts, the relationship, was not going to continue. As he recounts, there had been another episode of self-harm some months previously which was a common feature of the men's stories and may have been preparatory to this more serious action.

> ***Is this the first time you've felt like this?***
> *No, it's the second time I've tried to do something. Sorry.*
>
> ***And when was the last time?***
> *Just over a year ago. It was only a half-hearted kind of attempt.*

Dermot's relationship had also ended and this signified a more general sense of failure in terms of relationships and underlined his deficits as a man. In his background, there was also a question mark over his parentage and he also shared with Fergus a difficult relationship with his father and, similarly, had always felt marginalised within his family. The possibility that he had a different biological father had increased his anxieties about his identity. These background factors contributed to Dermot's emotional isolation and his reluctance to disclose the difficulties he was experiencing. Following the relationship break-up, his feelings of desperation grew, he left work and became increasingly isolated. At interview, Dermot downplayed the episode and gave the impression of someone who worked assiduously to conceal his pain as well as to please people. He laughed constantly and nervously and was somewhat deferential, ways of behaving he has undoubtedly had to perfect from an early age to cope with feelings of non-acceptance in his home.

I am interested in hearing how you came to be here.
Mmmm. Took a load of tablets. Just woke up in the morning, I just took loads of tablets and went to bed. Just overdosed. Just too much pressure. (Laughs)

And what sort of pressure was it?
Ah, just little things like emm, girlfriend trouble. Just, just, pressure. Just it all built up. I'm not a person to tell people about things, I just kind of bottle everything up and… (Laughs)

So there was a series of things that happened?
Yeah. It was one after the other and it just built up.

So give me an idea of what was going on, what was building up.
Emm, my ex-girlfriend (mentions specific reason for breakup)… *Things like that, just… I was gutted over it, you know. And I had a car accident last year, set me back a bit. I just was affected about going out. There's a road there and I won't go up that road for near death. I won't go up near the road where I had the crash; it just scares the living hell out of me. Few things like that.*

What would you say affected you most?
Well, I'm out of work now, for the last two months, I'm going through a kind of a lazy patch. Just getting run down or whatever, because you're depressed. There were arguments at home and everything because I wasn't getting out of bed. Things like that just build up. Just sometimes I just have the energy to

get up and other days I just couldn't be bothered getting out of bed. And then there'd be arguments at home.

And how long have you been feeling like that?
Emm, last three months, I suppose. Ah just, just the way things are building up. Mmmm. No money, like. [Laughs] That's an awful thing, I have no money. No money, no independence you know. I don't like sponging off other people. (Laughs) *That was embarrassing.*

When did the relationship end?
That was about six months ago.

Did you see it as a serious relationship?
Well, not serious serious but serious as a (mentions period of time) *is serious. I trusted her. I don't trust many people. I trusted her and she let me down.*

Is that your first experience of somebody letting you down like that?
No, not really. I don't have great luck with women now.

Why do you think that is?
I don't know. I just, something in me, whatever. I don't know. …I'm a nice enough fella, like it just, that's probably why, that's what the problem is. Be too nice to them. (I'm) A bit different. Probably a bit of a feminine side of me. [Laughs]

What's the feminine side?
Ah, just, most fellas probably just go out and try and meet as many girls as possible in a night. If I was with a girl I would just, you know, have a few drinks and go home. You know. Just the way I always was. Just quiet. I'm probably just too nice for people, you know. I treat them well and they probably don't want to be treated that well, you know. As the old saying goes, some girls like the rough. [Laughs] You know.

Did you feel rejected when she did that?
Not rejected but just hurt I suppose. Trust is a big thing for me.

And how would you know if you could trust someone?
You'll never know if you can trust someone, that's the thing. You just feel that you can trust someone but they can always let you down as I found out. It makes you cautious.

Were you able to tell anyone about the way you have been feeling over the last few months?
No, not really.

Dermot then described the events leading up to the suicide attempt and its aftermath.

> ***And what were you thinking that day?***
> *Nothing much, just like, I don't know how to explain, just nothing [Laughs]. Just in a depressive mood and decided to take the tablets. Just felt life was crap. [Laughs] …They said I took enough tablets to knock out a horse. [Laughs] I just, I went out, I had about four pints, I think it was. Came home about two o'clock in the morning. I don't do much, like, I just, I don't have the energy to do anything. I just, I lost interest in a lot of stuff. [Laughs]*
>
> ***When you came around and realised that you were in here, how did you feel?***
> *Emm, don't know. Kind of sad, kind of, I was kind of disappointed, because I was hoping that, because I took the tablets that night when I went to bed and I was hoping that I wouldn't wake up in the morning…but I did. [Laughs]. …Just thinking.*
>
> ***And what have you been thinking?***
> *Ah, nothing much. Just, just trying to get better. [Laughs]*

Complicated family relationships, including complex father–son interactions, were central to the two stories outlined above. Both men wanted stronger bonds with their fathers but this became increasingly difficult as time went on and for Fergus involved the ultimate rejection, with his father disowning him as his child. Yet these men had positive elements in common including their resilience in the face of emotional abuse, they didn't misuse alcohol or drugs nor did they engage in risk behaviour. They were capable of love and care and had sought trusting, caring, relationships to compensate for the lack of care in their young lives. These early experiences had resulted in emotional insecurities which made them especially vulnerable when the relationship ended. Their emotional pain had not been relieved over time and, in fact, had intensified in the wake of recent negative occurrences. They had not felt able to confide their difficulties either now or in the past and in this way their vulnerabilities had not been addressed. Many of these issues are also apparent in Ronan's story.

Ronan had been feeling increasingly helpless about his life over a number of years and the recent break-up of a relationship had increased his belief that he was destined to be continually unhappy. The negative issues in his life had been combined into a broad, despairing, narrative which had become increasing fixed as time went on and he viewed ending his life as the only viable option. His family background was problematic as his father was an alcoholic and Ronan had feared his violent moods as a child. Relations with his mother were better but it was not a confiding relationship. School was unhappy as he was bullied which increased his determination to develop a strong body which would project strength. He had successfully completed second level but did not follow his desired career due, he says, to a lack of confidence and he had a perception of himself as timid and ineffectual. As with Dermot, Ronan had self-harmed some months before this suicide attempt.

Tell me why you were admitted here?
I just felt awful about everything, just wanted to end it and tried to OD.

What led up to that?
Just numerous. Just not happy with the way I wanted my life to be. It's not going to be the way I want it. Just giving up. I finished a relationship with a girl. I didn't want to go on. She finished it. She told me (mentions period of time) *ago. She said she just wanted to be friends basically.*

How did you react to that?
Just crying and saying give me a chance.

Has anything like that ever happened to you before?
Yeah. About four months ago I did the same. For a variety of reasons.

Was it the same person again?
It wasn't just that. It wasn't the cause of it. It was just numerous things.

These suicidal narratives were linked to the need to have an intimate, trusting, relationship with another human and about seeking emotional care and support which had often been denied to them growing up. They were generally quite resilient people who had reacted intensely to the ending of a partnership and they were aware of the symbolic nature of the loss and were insightful about the underlying landscape of insecurity which had formed part of their identities. They were also affected by changing relationship norms, particularly the fluidity of partnerships and the increasing equality, sexual and otherwise, of women. Within this scenario maintaining stable emotional links, which these men desperately sought, was becoming more challenging. Relationships were problematic in various ways and some participants were involved in partnerships they felt they could not leave, as in David's case.

David

David, who was in his late twenties, had not been expected to survive his suicidal action and still had extensive injuries. The background feature was a relationship which he desperately wanted to leave. He had begun this relationship following the break-up of a long-term partnership. David recounted that both he and the woman viewed this relationship as a relatively casual affair but when her family objected to the relationship he felt it would be disloyal to leave her. They lived in a place where there was a good deal of surveillance and his suicide attempt followed an incident involving her family. At this point, David decided to end his life as he became convinced that this course of action was the only possible way to escape the unhappy situation. He described experiencing panic but he felt unable to talk to his friends, due to embarrassment, nor to his family because there had been tensions in the past. Seeking professional help had not occurred to him.

> *When I was living with this girl I was just getting a lot of hassle. They disowned her and I didn't want to leave her because they wouldn't talk to her. There was a lot of pressure. All the hassle I was getting. I felt a bit trapped all the time because she had no family. I felt guilty about that all the time. It was hard. We had no one helping us out if you know what I mean. She used to wonder why I was so bothered about it but I couldn't ignore it. I couldn't handle it. Just stupid things and eventually I just couldn't handle it. I exploded. I was just getting grief from her family and I didn't want to retaliate back or do anything. …I didn't want to walk out and leave her. There was a lot of pressure.*

Do you have any idea now why you took it that way?
I felt trapped. I didn't know what to do. That was the only thing I could think of doing. I didn't want to do anything. …I'm feeling a lot better in myself yeah. I'm totally disappointed that I let it all get to me, doing what I did and for not reacting differently. Things are a lot different now. I'm away from all that. It built up over a long time. It changed the way you look at things. Everything was kind of hopeless, grief. I did everything I could.

If you were in that situation again what would you do?
I'd never let myself get into that situation again.

How would you say you cope with things usually, apart from that?
Ok. I had no worries to talk of.

Did your friends know you were under pressure?
They couldn't understand why I was sitting down and taking it all. But what can you do? Now I can laugh and ignore them. A few of them (friends) *have come up to see me. They just couldn't believe what had happened.*

Did you say anything to your family?
No. You feel you're letting them down at home. They're disappointed or something. I've learned a lot like over the last fortnight.

Did you ever think of looking for help?
I thought of it but I didn't do it.

How did your own family respond?
Shock. I think they knew what was wrong but they didn't realise how serious it was.

And had you talked to anyone about this?
Not really, no.

David's family background has been referred to previously and this impacted significantly on how he dealt with the relationship problem as well as his distress. There was no outlet for discussion of emotional issues within the home and David also felt constrained because he was the eldest and believed he had to give leadership and protection when his father was drinking heavily. David's father gave up alcohol when David was an adolescent and subsequently became a caring father and good provider but David found it hard to put aside the pain and turmoil he and the rest of the family had had to endure in the past. Conflict and feelings of rejection remained part of their interaction and impacted on his life in that he described an oppositional dynamic, if his father wanted him to do something he would do something contrary to this. This influenced his decision to leave school early, his temporary involvement in risk behaviour, and the pattern of his relationships. He entered a relationship in his late teens and had a child but this relationship ended, he suggested, because he was too young to take on the responsibility of fatherhood although he maintained contact with his child.

David's reaction to the episode was similar to other men I interviewed from a rural background. Their understanding of masculinity and appropriate masculine behaviour was more rigid than those from urban backgrounds. They were more likely to obscure their feelings about the suicidal event and generally constructed the incident as an aberration which was unlikely to re-occur and did not require any deep understanding or counselling to decipher. There was an understanding of vulnerability and pain but this did not amount to an explanatory discourse around their actions. There was also a fear of connecting their action to a psychiatric discourse as where David lived patients who attended the local psychiatric hospital were identified as a population apart. His brief encounter with the local hospital before he was transferred to a major trauma centre filled him with apprehension and he had no intention of attending there for follow-up care. For these reasons, he refused the counselling offered and intended to put the incident behind him and get on with his life. Yet, he was happy to be interviewed as he felt his story might help others faced with similar difficulties.

Unlike David, who had sought to escape a relationship, others had difficulty in accessing partnerships and following their sexual orientation. In this way Gary wanted to live openly as a gay man but feared the consequences of doing so in his neighbourhood.

Gary

Gary was in his early twenties and his suicidal act would be described in the medical literature as 'near fatal' in that the chances of surviving such an attempt are extremely rare. Much of the pressure in his life was around his inability to live openly as a gay man. Gary knew he was gay from a very early age but carefully concealed this from his family and circle of friends. This situation might have continued indefinitely but Gary 'fell in love' and wanted to include his boyfriend more visibly in his life. However, his tentative moves to introduce his partner to his family were opposed and in desperation he decided to kill himself. His parents had separated when he was young and he lived with his grandparents. He got on well with his grandparents but they were beginning to suspect the true nature of his relationship with his boyfriend and had tried to prevent him visiting the house. Alongside this, Gary was coping with a number of other stresses, including longterm family issues, and these pressures contributed to what he described as an overwhelming desire to escape the mental anguish. His story of near-tragedy indicates that an intervention, having someone to talk to, could potentially interrupt even the most serious of suicidal actions.

> ***So you didn't have anyone to talk to?***
> *No, I didn't have anyone and I just wanted to sit down and talk. I just didn't want to think. And if I was dead I wouldn't think. I wanted to get away from everything. I was in bits. At that time it was all very confusing and it wasn't reality. I just didn't want to … And I knew that (boyfriend) would be there in the evening time but at the time he was going through things where he needed to chill … I was drinking every day for about two months before the attempt, every single day, and that doesn't help.*

Gary described the experience of growing up gay in a working-class community where traditional ideologies of masculinity prevailed. He described working hard at concealing his sexuality, projecting an acceptable version of maleness and continually monitoring his performance. Gary liked his friends and his community and found it difficult to live two separate lives, conducting a heterosexual performance among his friends while his homosexual life was confined to another part of the city.

> ***Were you ever able to tell your school friends?***
> *No, I could never tell. Because I think they see you different. I feel it's something, they act towards me different. Mostly men. Probably mostly men.*

When did you feel ready to be open about being gay?
I really knew that I definitely was one hundred percent gay because I fell in love and I love him to bits and that's when I .... He thought I was open but I was the very same. None of my friends know.

Was there anyone else that knew you were gay?
At the time no.

Was that one of the pressures you're talking about?
Pressure and frustration as well. You could never kind of come out like normal couples. Even having a drink or something. You'd be kind of wary that you're been looked on too much. Be paranoid.

You like socialising with your local group?
Yeah.

Is your partner part of that?
Yeah.

Do the group know he's gay?
No. I can't really say because we're together so much that people are asking questions more and more.

Were there any other pressures?
I was a lot more depressed than I am now. Seriously so. There was a lot happening with my grandparents and they were really coming down with pressure, putting pressure on me. I think my granda kind of had a clue. 'Why is this bloke coming and being so close'. He actually told me. He said I don't want anybody here after such a time. He told me that when he was young that he had a kind of similar experience, he said he went through that stage. He just felt very uncomfortable. My grandfather is very set in his ways. Hardworking.

Does that mean that in a way he knows?
In a way he knows and in a way he doesn't. Ah they know.

Do you think he's going to be more open now?
He's trying to be.

And they're open to your partner coming to visit?
Ah he definitely is now.

How do you feel about being gay now?
I feel more comfortable about it now. I just feel more comfortable. I feel a bit different, the way we don't have to do anything we don't want to do or tell anybody what we don't want to.

The factors cited by these respondents relate to important issues concerning masculinity and sexuality. The narratives feature sensitive, loving and responsibility masculinities, men who sought and were willing to respond with, love and care. These stories also attest to a much more fluid relationship and sexual landscape than traditional frameworks of masculinity imply. The narratives provide a link between traditional masculinities and suicide in terms of the constricting social and emotional discourse attached to this form of masculinity. This hegemonic-type manhood set out rigid parameters and unrealistic aspirations for men to attain. Men, even within similar communities, vary greatly but the findings of this study signify that men, despite their misgivings, felt significant pressure to conform to this model of masculinity because it was the acceptable masculine narrative. This compliance had much to do with the sometimes violent regulation (described in Chapter 3) which underpinned the normative masculinity. The negative effects of masculinity were also evident among those men who attempted suicide for less specific reasons than those described above.

Desperation and Anger

It was clear that for some of the men interviewed their lives generally had become a problem with the various issues difficult for them to disentangle. Their narratives implied a combination of difficulties building up over years to a point which they could no longer cope. The most identifiable category were those whose lives had become enmeshed in alcoholism, drugs and risk behaviour and who had become increasingly desperate about their situation. This group of men often had a history of long-term risk behaviour, usually from their early teens, and had become increasingly unhappy, and angry, about their situation. There were strong themes of self-loathing and of being trapped in a life from which they could not escape and they had come to view suicide as the only action available to them. These participants were more likely to have a history of repeated suicide attempts and their suicidal actions were less connected to identifiable triggering or causal features. This group of men adhered to a pattern of suicidal behaviour which is generally associated with females, with consistent self-harming (interspersed with more serious suicide episodes), and the methods they tended to us (overdosing with drugs) also put them within this category. Yet, they also typified many extreme features of hegemonic masculinity.

Sean, Dale, Rory and Rob

Sean had made numerous self-harming and suicide attempts, by his own count there were at least twenty episodes. Some were very serious attempts, others less so. He had begun self-harming in his early teens and on the first occasion he cut his wrists having seen another man do so during a group drinking session. He said he experienced a sense of relief after doing this and this set a pattern for his subsequent self-harming. In this way, his behaviour had definite parallels with stereotypical views of females who self-harm. He had sought help intermittently within the health services but had never engaged consistently with treatment. His usual pattern was to present to Accident and Emergency departments following a suicide attempt.

> *Pressure, that's exactly what it is. It's pressure that builds up and builds up and builds up and I find the only way of relieving pressure is to take it out on myself. I'm not going to take it out on anybody else because it's not their problem. It's not their fault that I've no money. It's my fault that I've no money so I tend to take it out on myself and I have damaged myself. I've damaged my liver. My liver is in an awful state from taking overdoses. My arms are in bits.*

In common with other men in this section Sean left school early because of disruptive behaviour, had a very inconsistent work history and was a heavy user of alcohol and drugs. He had had a number of serious relationships and one of these partnerships had ended in the previous year but he said this wasn't the motivation for his suicide attempt. His father was an alcoholic who had been violent to both Sean and his mother. Themes of powerlessness loomed large in his account of childhood, of having to be a silent witness to the physical abuse of his mother, and yet wanting to have a father figure. When he was a child he says he hated and feared his father and abhorred the violence and other deprivations his mother had to suffer. He still lived with his father and said he no longer feared him although his father remained an alcoholic and the relationship was not close. His childhood experiences continued to trouble him but he was reluctant to delve into his past and had resisted counselling. Sean's way of dealing with distress was to self-medicate with drugs and take it out on the body.

> *Family problems and stuff like that. My father. I don't get on with him. I can't seem to get on with him at all. He used to kill her* (mother) *in front of us. And we could do nothing to get him to stop. We were fairly young at the time - six or seven. I felt bad. There was nothing I could do. Hiding away. I just felt bad. And then we started growing up, he started hitting on us and we started to go for him then. But he'd only do it in the house because he was afraid that he himself might be caught. …All I remember is him roaring all the time. Yeah it was frightening. …He's a problem, he's a Dr Jekyll, Mr Hyde, and if he has a few drinks he goes off the head and when he has no drink he's a totally different man.*

Dale was in his twenties and had a partner and children. He appeared to have a relatively stable home life and mentioned a number of times that his partner had always been supportive. He was the eldest in the family, was particularly close to his mother growing up but his relationship with his father was problematic. In common with Sean, he had dropped out of school early as life outside school appeared much more attractive and he became involved in substance misuse and risk behaviour. He described himself at this time as 'uncontrollable'.

> *I was never any good in school. Never liked school. I dropped out. I just did not like school. There was too much happening outside school that was more interesting than in school at the time. I was mad into horses and we used to go off robbing horses all the time. Then I was just uncontrollable. Out the window at night and nothing could hold me back. Lock me in the room and I'd get out the window.*

He began the relationship with his partner in his late teens and appeared to settle somewhat following this. However, Dale's substance misuse and his destructive behaviour had escalated in the previous two years and these actions were generally followed by guilt when he realised the upset his behaviour caused to his family. He couldn't understand why he behaved in this way and felt he couldn't stop. Although he mentioned that he suffered from depression this was not a clinical diagnosis assigned to him. He described his actions as precipitated by erratic mood swings, driven by rage and desperation and exacerbated by drugs and alcohol. He spoke with urgency and desperation about his life which he described as out of control and he had attempted suicide a number of times. The precipitant for the most recent suicide attempt was an incident which he was involved in which was likely to impact negatively on him and his family.

> *Ordinary people at home and family and friends, they don't suffer from depression, they don't understand what depression is, how bad it can be and how down it can make you feel and how in a matter of ten or fifteen minutes you can go from normal to a state of anger and then go into a downer, what I call a downer, that you don't care about anything, you just really do not care what happens at all. The worry part goes out of your head. And when I drink on top of that or if I drank and that came on top of me when I had the drink on me, that's when I become suicidal and I wouldn't think twice and I don't ever think twice but it's the time when I do think that second time is when I would take the rope back off my neck, when I think of my children or my partner. They only have to spring to mind once and something will tell me to stop what I'm doing because it's wrong, it's not right.*
>
> ***Was there ever a period when you felt good?***
> *Probably five weeks would be the most – four or five weeks. It can happen every couple of months, I get a spell of…, everything would be going right for me and I'd be just happy. But I always go back and I always fuck up again somewhere, always. You'd be guaranteed, it's just a matter of when. I never got down like this before in my life. I never knew what it was like to feel this low. As I said the word depression frightened me. I thought that happened to older people. …It was building up and it came with the alcohol. It came with things that I would be doing on alcohol and stupid things I'd do with drink on me and the guilt after the next day when you wake up and your memory starts coming back to you. You're doing this, you're after doing that, you were fighting or something that you've done with the alcohol or said something that you shouldn't have said and that feeling that you get after that, when you're*

starting to sober, it's horrible. I drink a lot. At one consumption I would take in a lot of alcohol. I just don't know when to stop. …Anger turning into depression. It starts with anger then I probably do something in the anger that will make me feel guilty and that will send me further down. And when I mix alcohol with that, it's ….(knocks on table).

Why do you get angry?
I don't know. It's like a frustration. Quick, instant. From quite normal to quite narky in two seconds. It's so quick. That's what frightens me. How I can change so quick. And I can change from good to bad very quick and then it takes me a good long time to get from bad back down to normal again. …I just want to be happy. I just want to be normal.

What's a normal person?
Somebody who doesn't go around with ropes in their car and who doesn't (refers to recent incident). *I don't think I'm normal anyway. I think if I was normal I wouldn't be sitting here. I wouldn't be in the situation I am today because I would have been able to do my daily things yesterday which I should have done with my partner and my kids and I shouldn't be here in* (name of hospital) *if I was normal. So it's not just being a man. There's plenty of men out there with* (mentions number of children) *kids that hold their chin up high and hold down a good job and are always there for their kids and their partner and you can see it genuinely that they all love each other.*

Was there anything this time that caused you do this?
It's usually when I argue with the partner. I can't handle that. I just can't handle that, fighting with my partner. I have a drink problem as well.

What was the argument about?
Ah it's me all the time, it's me all the time. How hurtful I can be. How hurtful I am. And angry. Things I say. Unimaginable things. Really hurtful to my partner when I'm fighting with her. And it's that guilt feeling after doing that that makes me go really, really, bad. It's that guilty feeling and I just can't handle that. It will probably take a couple of days for that to pass but then I could be great for a few weeks or a couple of weeks and something will start again and I'll be off again. It just seems to be a pattern that I'm in. Bottle. Fight with (partner). *Grab a rope and hang. It's sort of like that. …I don't know why, why this streak is in me. Ninety percent of the time I'm alright as a person. I'm an alright bloke, I get on with people, I can talk to people, I respect people. …She's not the problem in this relationship, it's me all the time.*

> *It's me who starts the arguments, it's me who finishes them and it's me who goes off stupid drunk. It's all my fault.*

In line with other men in this category, Dale was preoccupied with suicide and reported that suicidal thoughts were consistently in his head. The constant deliberations about suicide appeared to be part of a build-up to completion as suicide had come to be seen as the only meaningful option left. Yet while suicide represented escape from uncomfortable feelings and the seeming uncontrollability of his life he was fearful of taking this ultimate action. The connection to his family prevented him from completing suicide but, as with many of the men who were essentially pushing themselves towards suicide, they feared the action and its finality or the negative implications if they survived. This vacillation around suicide was evident in the narratives of these men and was demonstrated in the urgency of their delivery and the desperation in their voices. These men were within a high-risk phase for suicide but this was difficult to detect because they had built up a pattern of repeated self-harm and heavy substance misuse over a long period of time. Triggering events did not feature as prominently in these men's suicidal actions, in contrast to those who had made only one suicide attempt. At the same time, their lives tended to abound with negative events, largely caused by themselves. In the same way, the movement towards the suicide attempt for Dale involved a long build-up but the pace of desperation was now quickening and his family's continuing support and tolerance seemed to be the only factor protecting him from ending his life.

> *I tried to kill myself a number of times. I was in here last* (month mentioned) *on an overdose of (mentions drug). I never took the stuff before in my life and I drank the whole bottle of it and I was an OD and I came in here and got pumped and that was one time. It's usually ropes after that. I done the rope thing before that but June was really … and … when I try and when I'm going to make up my mind that I'm going somewhere, I'm going to do this today, today is the day I'm going to kill myself, tonight I'm going to kill myself, something always happens to stop me. The word suicide used to frighten me – to take your own life – how could a person do that? I used to think 'how could you kill yourself, you must be able to get help, there must be people out there*

that can help you' and the whole lot but when you get depressed, that all goes out the window, you don't care. You feel so low, you feel as if there's no point in going on. What's the point? This is going to happen again and you're going to feel this. You don't want to live the rest of your life like this, well I don't. It's very hard. I don't like myself being like this. I try to fight it. I try to cut it out of the back of my head. And it just doesn't work, nothing happens. You won't snap out of it until it takes its course and then only for I have somebody and I have people close to me, I'd be dead a long time ago. …When you've alcohol in you system you'll do things that you would never dream of doing when you're sober…I don't even drink every day. It's just when I drink I just don't stop. I went up to the mountains with a rope, (mentions drugs and alcohol). *Took them all, every one. So done that, drank that and came back down for vengeance on somebody. Somebody is getting the anger, somebody was getting it. …I'm full of anger, yeah.*

Why?
I don't know. I don't know where it's coming from.

Although Dale reported that he felt desperate about this life he was unwilling to take the steps necessary to address this. He would not attend counselling for his alcohol addiction although he said he had attended these services in the past and found them helpful. Now the support network, specifically his partner and parents who had buttressed him against the impact of his actions, had become less tolerant of his behaviour and this was driving him to a point of extreme despondency. The possibility that he might lose these important sources of support increased his anxiety.

She's (his partner) *sick of me. I'd say she's sick of it.*

How does she react when something like this happens?
There you go again, same old fucking pattern. Things are great for a few weeks and then he goes and he fucks up again, that's what she usually says to me which is true but nothing this bad has ever happened as what happened yesterday. …The children are sick of me as well. The children are sick of me because they've seen too much. I just can't go on anymore like this, it has to stop. I can't go through this again. I have to do something. I just want to love my partner and love my children and just get on with life. I can't seem to do it with alcohol?

The other two men in this group, Rory and Rob, had similar backgrounds with difficulties in school followed by substance (mainly alcohol) misuse and risk behaviour. They had not experienced particular adversity in childhood but heavy drinking and some violence was a feature in their families. Violence figured prominently in their adult lives and, in common with Dale, the predominant emotions for these men at interview were anger and desperation. They exhibited what might be described as an extreme, hard, form of hegemonic masculinity. They were similarly sceptical about treatment and had never engaged in a consistent way. The modus operandi, in line with Sean and Dale, was to make frequent visits to Accident and Emergency Departments and then fail to turn up for follow-up appointments. Rory and Rob shared with Dale a strong element of self-disgust and a preoccupation with suicide. Rory claimed to have had a desire to complete suicide from an early age. He had made a number of suicide attempts and these attempts had increased in severity in recent times. Recently he had been indicating to friends that he was determined to kill himself. The narratives of the two men appeared frighteningly similar in terms of the urgency and desperation exhibited.

> *I don't see a future in anything. … This little black spot that's inside of me and holds me back. I don't know what it is. That's the depression. I don't know if it is depression or it's just hatred for myself. Self-destructive. I don't know. But whatever it is, it's holding me back big time. If I really wanted to be dead I could have done it successfully. Take this from day to day. Take it from minute to minute. Because the way I see it is if I really want to be dead I'd go out to the* (mentions place) *and go in front of a truck because you're not going to get up. There's no doctor in the world going to save you so why don't I do that. … Yesterday I did* (mentions drug). *Two or three days before that I was only after been let out because I set fire to my apartment. I barricaded myself inside, blocked all the entrances with tables and chairs, lit it with petrol but the fire brigade still got me. Before that I OD'd on* (mentions drug) *again. I've OD'd loads of times. I've tried to kill myself since I was about six. I've had thoughts of it since I was about four. They thought I was silly at that stage, 'he's exaggerating that, it's just the way his mind is working' but I know for a fact that it was my earliest memory. Your very early memories are just pictures, they're just photographs. My very earliest is a picture of the sitting room*

> *covered in glass and the shine off the glass and me standing in the hall. It was a fight that was going on and I'm not supposed to be listening to the fight that was going on. It was my mam and dad fighting and I stood there protecting my little brother who was in the cot. ...I felt panicky. The very same panicky feeling that I have now I had then.*
>
> ***What happened before you were admitted?***
> *No difference to any other day. Just feeling the usual. I'm at the stage now and I think I've been at the stage..... it has to be about thirteen, fourteen, years now, since I was about fifteen, I've had a constant, I just wish I was dead. I don't wear a seat belt, I drive the car a hundred miles an hour. ... Just no regard for myself at all. No self-respect, I hate myself. I look at the mirror, I used to spit in the mirror when I looked at myself. Total self-hatred. All these years I've come up with more excuses and I've blamed more people. I've blamed my family and ... that maybe I was abused as a child and I've blocked that out but I think maybe I'm just using that because it answers the problem. I may have been depressed but I never showed it, nobody ever knew it. It was just building up and building up for nineteen years and I never showed it at all. I was always very quiet. I was just a quiet lad, very shy. And then one day I snapped and all the aggression came out and I* (describes violent attack). *I almost killed him. But it was a wake-up call ...it was like waking up out of a dream. ...I can't get over it now. It still kills me.*

Despite their violent actions, it appeared that anger and aggression were adopted by these men as survival mechanisms, as part of a front to hide the fear they felt in the dangerous environments they inhabited. The idea of imprisonment terrified them. Their families were also losing patience with their behaviour and the fear of losing this support was causing additional anguish.

> *They told me they want me out of the house now. They've had enough of all these suicide attempts, it's driving them up the wall. My da is suffering terrible with the worry and my ma just sits around crying. It's very hard on them. I don't blame them. They've just had it up to their eyeballs. Years of it.* —Rory

The men in this category had features in common, particularly risk and violent behaviour as well as dependency on alcohol and or drugs. Each had reached, according to their own accounts, a very low level of meaningful socioemotional existence. They still retained a level of social contact but emotionally they felt desperate and imprisoned by their lives. They were at very high risk of completing suicide as the magical transformative intervention they wanted was unlikely and alternatives such as treatment were more challenging and less attractive. They felt their lives out of control yet many of their present difficulties arose from their own violent actions fuelled mainly by excess alcohol. They felt a significant level of self-disgust about their behaviour yet they continued to act in a self-destructive way and, critically, they appeared to be driving themselves towards suicide, urging themselves to take this final step. Many of the features these men exhibited are not consistent with theoretical representations of the typical man who completes suicide, a person who makes a strong, rational, choice about suicidal action for external reasons. These men veered persistently between self-harm and more serious attempts, felt constantly powerless and were full of self-hatred. When they reached the point of suicide they were not engaging in an heroic act but had reached this moment slowly and agonisingly by internalising negative views of themselves and by turning the strength of these emotions onto the body. These men had followed a slow, protracted, route to chronic unhappiness to a point where they felt powerless to change things. This combination of substance (particularly alcohol) misuse, crime, and periodic self-harm frequently resulted in a physical and emotional downward spiral as it was not a life which could be endured indefinitely. For these men suicidal action represented a relief of sorts and an attempt to control rather than be controlled by events and their lives were preoccupied with rehearsing the only solution they felt was available to them.

Psychiatric Disorder

A small number of the men were directly affected by serious, ongoing, psychiatric illness and were diagnosed as such. Although depression was cited by many of the subjects as the reason for the attempt this term was used in a very general way and would not always have amounted to a diagnosis of clinical depression. The majority of the participants were diagnosed (if at all) as having mild depression and or anxiety. The term depression was cited most frequently and it seemed to the only psychological concept they were familiar with. Psychosis was present in a small number of cases and one of these was drug-related. There was also one example of brain-injury following an accident which had resulted in significant alterations in the respondent's behaviour and he had made a number of impulsive suicide attempts. This man was atypical of the entire sample across a range of factors. He appeared to have had a stable happy life before the accident and continued to have a close and loving relationship with both his parents. Overall, psychiatric disorder, at a clinical level of severity, was implicated in only a minority of cases which places suicidal action more realistically within a sociocultural discourse.

Summary

Suicide is a complex phenomenon as the narratives presented here demonstrate. While the decision to attempt suicide was often impulsive, thoughts of suicide and more definite plans were generally present for a considerable period. Many of the men spoke of an opportunity presenting itself and of having the confidence to act at that particular time. If there was a precipitant it often had symbolic rather than causative relevance and relatively minor events could take on particular significance. The men's determination to end their lives was apparent from their narratives as well as the detail of the action and the methods they used. Method did not conform to the stereotypical gender pattern in that the majority of the men used methods which are traditionally regarded as 'female' methods and are sometimes associated with less serious attempts. Method is closely linked to availability and the so-called less lethal methods can represent serious intent and or a rehearsal for a future, fatal, action. The men's reactions when they realised they were alive varied although many were relieved, which reflects other findings (O'Donnell et al. 1996). The main reasons provided for the suicide attempt included generalised unhappiness and the ending of a relationship, both of which have been cited in other studies of suicidal behaviour (Redley 2003; Fincham et al. 2011). Psychiatric disorder, at a clinical level of severity, was implicated in a small number of cases. The findings refute gendered explanations for male suicide and suggest that suicidal action is rarely the result of a single event or problem but represents a cluster of issues which have developed over a long period of time. A clustering of risk factors and reduced opportunities were apparent in some of the lives and transitional points such as leaving school were times when problems seemed to accumulate. In this way, causation cannot be assumed to relate only to events which occur prior to a suicide and generalising from such events can provide an inaccurate profile of the person's motivations. Emotional pain, which had been concealed over time, was a significant feature and many of the men linked their present distress to painful, unresolved, issues in their past. For a specific group of men, their lives in a more general sense had become a problem. These men's narratives implied a combination of difficulties, especially substance misuse and risk behaviour, building up over years to a point where they could no longer cope and they felt trapped in these lives. A theme of powerlessness emerged forcefully in these narratives and the suicidal act was sometimes constructed as the only powerful action remaining, a theme identified in other studies (Gaines 1991; Redley 2003; Weaver 2009). These stories are presented as narratives around suicide which relate more crucially to social and cultural factors than psychiatric disorder. The context of suicide, and the reasons why suicide is contemplated are linked to societal scripts about suicide, to features of identity and to gender and specifically the performance of conventional or hegemonic masculinities.

References

Atkinson, M. (2011). *Deconstructing men and masculinities*. London: Oxford University Press.

Brownhill, S., Wilhelm, K., Barclay, L., & Schmied, V. (2005). Big build: Hidden depression in men. *Australian and New Zealand Journal of Psychiatry, 39*, 921–931.

Byng, R., Howerton, A., Owens, C. V., & Campbell, J. (2015). Pathways to suicide attempts among male offenders: The role of agency. *Sociology of Health & Illness, 37*(6), 936–951.

Canetto, S. S. (1992). She died for love and he for glory: Gender myths of suicidal behaviour. *Omega, 26*(1), 1–17.

Chandler, M. J., & Lalonde, C. E. (1998). Cultural continuity as a hedge against suicide in Canada's First Nations. *Transcultural Psychiatry, 35*(2), 193–211.

Cleary, A. (2012). Suicidal action, emotional expression, and the performance of masculinities. *Social Science and Medicine, 74,* 498–505.

Coyle, J., & MacWhannell, D. (2002). The importance of 'morality' in the social construction of suicide in Scottish newspapers. *Sociology of Health & Illness, 24*(6), 689–713.

Durkheim, E. (1951). *Suicide: A study in sociology* (R. Spaulding, Trans.). London: Routledge & Kegan Paul.

Fincham, B., Langer, S., Scourfield, J., & Shiner, M. (2011). *Understanding suicide: A sociological autopsy.* Houndmills and Basingstoke: Palgrave Macmillan.

Firestone, R. W. (1986). The "inner voice" and suicide. *Psychotherapy, 23*(3), 439–447.

Gaines, D. (1991). *Teenage wasteland: Suburbia's dead end kid.* Chicago: University of Chicago Press.

Hamdi, E., Price, S., Qassem, T., Amin, Y., & Jones, D. (2008). Suicides not in contact with mental health services: Risk indicators and determinants of referral. *Journal of Mental Health, 17*(4), 398–409.

Inckle, K. (2014). Strong and silent: Men, masculinity, and self-injury. *Men and Masculinities, 17*(1), 3–21.

Kushner, H. I. (1995). Women and suicidal behavior: Epidemiology, gender and lethality in historical perspective. In S. S. Canetto & D. Lester (Eds.), *Women and suicidal behavior.* New York: Springer.

Lorent, V., Kunst, A. E., Huisman, M., Costa, G., & Mackenbach, J. (2005). Socio-economic inequalities in suicide: A European comparative study. *British Journal of Psychiatry, 187,* 49–54.

Nelson, H. L. (2001). *Damaged identities: Narrative repair.* Ithaca and London: Cornell University Press.

O'Donnell, I., Falmer, R., & Catalán, J. (1996). Explaining suicide: The views of survivors of serious suicide attempts. *British Journal of Psychiatry, 168,* 780–786.

Owens, C., Booth, N., Briscoe, M., & Lloyd, K. (2003). Suicide outside the care of mental health services: A case-controlled psychological autopsy study. *Crisis: The Journal of Crisis Intervention and Suicide Prevention, 24*(3), 113–121.

Page, A., Morrell, S., Hobbs, C., Carter, F., Dudley, M., Duflou, J., et al. (2014). Suicide in young adults: Psychiatric and socio-economic factors from a case-control study. *BMC Psychiatry, 14*(1), 68.

Patterson, A. A., & Holden, R. R. (2012). Psychache and suicide ideation among men who are homeless: A test of Shneidman's model. *Suicide & Life Threatening Behaviour, 42*(2), 147–156.

Redley, M. (2003). Towards a new perspective on deliberate self-harm in an area of multiple deprivation. *Sociology of Health & Illness, 25*(4), 348–373.

Rehkopf, D. H., & Buka, S. L. (2006). The association between suicide and the socio-economic characteristics of geographical areas: A systematic review. *Psychological Medicine, 36*(2), 145–157.

Russell, S. T., & Toomey, R. B. (2012). Men's sexual orientation and suicide: Evidence for US adolescent-specific risk. *Social Science and Medicine, 74*(4), 523–529.

Shneidman, E. S. (1991). The commonalities of suicide across the life span. In A. A. Leenaars (Ed.), *Life span perspectives of suicide: Time-lines in the suicide process* (p. 39). New York: Plenum Press.

Thorne, B. (1993). *Gender play: Girls and boys in school.* New Brunswick, NJ: Rutgers University Press.

Weaver, J. C. (2009). *A sadly troubled history: The meanings of suicide in the modern age*. Montreal: McGill-Queen's University Press.

5

Survivors and Casualties

This chapter considers the men's longer term progress based on two follow-up points after the baseline episode and interview. A detailed study was carried out approximately seven years after the suicide attempt which gathered data on morbidity, mortality and service take-up and a small number of follow-up interviews were also undertaken at this point. A further inquiry, based on mortality data only, was carried out eight years later. The total follow-up period was therefore fifteen years. The analysis presented here is based on data collected at these two points and a re-examination of the baseline interviews in light of the findings. The focus is on establishing patterns and distinguishing between those who repeated or completed suicide and those who made no further attempts. It is an attempt to map relevant factors within the context of a small scale, qualitative, study as well as the meanings and motivations attached to the suicidal action.

A. Cleary, *The Gendered Landscape of Suicide*,
https://doi.org/10.1007/978-3-030-16634-2_5

Surviving, Repeating, and Completing Suicide

A high percentage, up to fifty per cent, of those who self-harm will repeat this behaviour (Zahl and Hawton 2004) and those who repeat are significantly more likely to complete suicide, a risk which is greatest in the short term but continues for many years (Hawton et al. 2003). Approximately one half of those who die by suicide have a history of self-harm (Hawton and van Heeringen 2009) and the risk of completion is substantially greater for males and for those who make a medically serious suicide attempt (Gibb et al. 2005; Beautrais 2003). A suicide attempt is therefore a powerful predictor of completed suicide and this was borne out in this study. Twenty-six men (50% of the participants) subsequently repeated and of this group, eight men completed suicide (a further participant died from physical causes). The repetition rate for suicide attempts is comparable to other studies but the rate for completion (15.4%) represents a relatively high level of suicide in a follow-up study and is attributable to the inclusion criteria of males only and the restriction to clinically serious attempts (Beautrais 2003). Risk for repetition and completion of suicide was greatest in the short term but continued for many years (the range was six months to fourteen years).

Those who repeated (including those who completed) and those who made no further attempts differed in terms of important characteristics even within this relatively small sample. These variations are considered in more detail below but in general those who repeated, and especially those who completed suicide, tended to have problems that were more wide-ranging than those experienced by the non-repeat category. The repeat grouping also had less resources in that they exhibited lower levels of educational attainment, were more likely to work in unskilled or casual employment, to have been in trouble with the law and to have misused alcohol and or drugs. Some of these factors have been identified in other research but this inquiry implies a more nuanced picture in terms of vulnerability and risk. In this way, the repeat and non-repeat groups were not homogenous categories but contained a number of subgroups and the meaning of the suicidal action varied across these categories. The non-repeat group varied in terms of their attitude to the episode, specifically whether the event had a cathartic effect which allowed them to reassess their social and emotional lives. The most obvious division in the repeat group was between those who completed suicide and those who did not but the repeat survivor group was also split between men who made only one further attempt and those who made a number of subsequent attempts. The men who completed suicide were a relatively small group but patterns as well as variations were discernable. As elsewhere, repetition of suicide increased risk for completion as did narratives of hopelessness expressed at the baseline interview.

There were, in addition, differences relating to gender and emotional factors. They all conformed, to some extent, to a type of masculinity which was traditional or hegemonic in type and this constricted the expression of emotions and the communication of distress and vulnerability. However adherence to this model varied and those who performed a more extreme version of this masculinity were particularly at risk of repeating and completing suicide. This masculinity orientation tended to occur in combination with a lack of educational and other resources which reduced the possibility of access to alternative forms of manhood. Another issue which related to high risk for completion of suicide was a perceived inability to find a meaningful gender space within the cultural environment they inhabited. Many of the men felt different to their peers, using normative markers of masculinity to evaluate their lives and behaviour, but a small number of men experienced this difference more acutely and the result was profound, intractable, unhappiness.

Survivors' Stories: Moving on from a Suicide Attempt

Twenty-six men, one half of the sample, made no further suicide attempts. There were no age differences between this group and those who repeated (understandable due to the age criteria applied in the study) but the index episode was much more likely to have been their first suicide attempt (54% of the repeat group had made an attempt prior to the index episode in contrast to 15% of the non-repeat category). The non-repeat participants were more likely to have higher educational attainment and a more stable employment history. These are important elements discriminating between the repeat and non-repeat groups as in this study the majority of the participants came from low socioeconomic backgrounds which is a general marker for suicidal behaviour (Lorent et al. 2005). Lethality of method and level of intent did not differ greatly between the two groups and neither did the prevalence of mental illness as only a small number of the men had an ongoing, serious, psychiatric disorder. Although alcohol (and drugs) was commonly used to cope with distressing symptoms the non-repeat group were much less likely to be engaged in chronic alcohol misuse and or serious drug taking and or to have been in trouble with the law. Another difference between the two groups related to the type of issue or situation which they implicated in the suicidal action. As outlined in Chapter 4, there were two main categories in relation to motivation. The first classification concerned relatively discrete difficulties such as relationship breakdown or a restriction in terms of one's sexuality. Relationship breakdown as a motivating factor tended to dominate in the non-repeat group. The second motivation category involved unhappiness which was more nebulous in terms of type and causation. Almost all of the participants had issues in their background and, in fact, the non-repeat group had experienced more adversity in childhood than those who repeated and or completed. In this way, the past and present difficulties of the non-repeat group were perhaps more identifiable and or circumscribed and this may have made these issues more amenable to resolution. These men also appeared to have a potentially positive feature in their backgrounds in that their father was more likely to have been present during their childhood.

As these findings imply, the suicidal episode for the non-repeat group generally represented a divergence from their usual life and behaviour and this, along with the resources they had, helped them to adjust and move on. These men were vulnerable from past experiences yet they were comparatively resilient people in that they had managed to accrue educational and other resources and on the surface lived fairly ordinary lives. Concealment of distress was common to all but once these men revealed the stressful situation they were able to move from despair and panic towards a more objective assessment of the issue and towards some level of hope for the future. The suicide attempt interrupted the concealment of emotional pain which had been building over time and the support of family members which usually followed also helped to ameliorate painful issues, some of which were family-related. These individuals belonged to families where there had often been significant problems but in a number of cases these difficulties had been resolved, for example, a father's recovery from alcoholism although, as indicated above, a residue of anger remained around these experiences. In other situations the suicide attempt acted as a catalyst for change in facilitating emotional expression within the family. Parents, and especially fathers, were prompted to change their usual emotional styles and demonstrate care and family members sometimes disclosed their own problems and mental health challenges. Change also occurred in relation to accepting a man's sexual orientation. This does not imply that life improved dramatically for these men following the suicide attempt but the action, and more particularly their survival, resulted in a positive outcome. When these changes occurred within a fairly constant life this helped the men to move on but moving on rarely involved a complete re-evaluation of one's life and attitudes.

Continuing adherence to prevailing gender norms deterred the majority of the men, including those within this relatively successful group, from embarking on a more comprehensive appraisal of the issues which had contributed to the suicide attempt. Instead, they tended to compartmentalise the situation and focus on other, more positive, elements in their lives. For these men there were two levels to their emotional lives—the surface level which was relatively constant and which they managed fairly competently and the deeper level which was much more unpredictable and volatile and which they had tried, and failed, to control during the crisis which led to the suicide attempt. In the aftermath of the suicide attempt, the majority of these men were content to work at the surface level and leave the deeper elements untouched which underlines the strength of gender and emotional norms.

Expectations relating to masculinity had contributed to these men's suicide attempt in that restrictions on the expression of emotional pain had allowed problems which could have been ameliorated to escalate over time. In the midst of the crisis, they identified painful issues and emotions in their background and conceded that repressing these feelings had been detrimental to their wellbeing. However, exploring the origins of their pain and vulnerability was moving into entirely untested waters and the majority of the men were reluctant to do so and reverted to more conventional ideals of manhood as they moved on with their lives.

A suicide attempt, even a near-fatal episode, does not necessarily result in catharsis as is evident in this and other studies (O'Donnell et al. 1996). While the suicide attempt prompted a good deal of self-reflection and prompted almost all the men to make some changes in their lives this did not usually involve delving deeply into the underlying reasons for their unhappiness via counselling or psychotherapy. There was a spectrum of attitudes—from the small number of men, such as Myles, who were reluctant to speak about the incident ('*It just happened*') to those who wanted to explore their motivations and make radical changes in their lives. On discharge from hospital all the participants were referred to psychiatric aftercare services but one third never presented and of the group who did take up a service offered, less than half attended for six months or more (Cleary 2017). The latter group included those who had a recognisable mental illness and already had regular contact with the psychiatric services. The take-up of aftercare services, except for those with an established psychiatric condition, was not related to repeating or non-repeating but reflected the men's knowledge about, and attitudes to, mental health issues and available treatment options. While many of the participants did incorporate concepts such as depression into their stories very few constructed their problems as a psychiatric condition and this influenced their attitude to treatment. They generally regarded psychiatric treatment as directed at an entirely different population i.e. those with serious, long-term, mental disorder and the fact that many were treated within the general hospital (with visits from the liaison team) encouraged this view. They were sceptical about, or actively disliked, the interventions on offer, especially counselling, but some did take medication, at least in the short term as this was regarded as acceptable. Their construction of the problem was social rather than psychiatric and the majority of these men believed that practical change (moving away, starting another career or relationship, etc.) rather than specialist help was required. This fitted with their re-constructed view of the episode as a reaction to a difficult period, as a temporary lapse in terms of control of one's life. They felt they could manage things on their own, now that the crisis was past and things were 'out in the open'.

Kieran and Matt

Kieran and Matt represented the group who wanted to put the episode aside and move on with their lives as quickly as possible. Both men had a relatively constant upbringing, had successfully completed second level schooling and there was no history of alcohol or drug misuse nor risk behaviour. Kieran, had experienced sexual abuse in his childhood and the suicide attempt followed the break-up of a long-term relationship. Matt had attempted suicide following the collapse of his business and there were longer term issues related to self-confidence and bullying which made him conscious of strength and competence and fearful of weakness and failure. This was their only suicidal action and occurred in an adult life with relatively good resources and social support. Kieran had been overwhelmed by anxiety at the realisation that his relationship was over but in its aftermath, he viewed this reaction as an uncharacteristic but understandable response to the break-up. Matt's construction of the event was similar and both men wanted to put the episode behind them and start afresh in another country. Themes of rejection and perceived failure, resonating with childhood experiences, occurred in many of the stories but they were similarly dealt with, by addressing the event that had occurred, rather than the underlying issues. Their focus was on practical considerations rather than the emotional implications of moving on, although this left them vulnerable to future challenges.

> *A new life. I feel it's what I want, to get this out of the way before I relax again. Break away and start again and not do what I did. Leave what I've done behind me. I'm fairly strong anyway. I will get through it, I know I*

> *will, I'll be fine. But I just feel that I want to go away with my partner and be happy for a while. Take some time out, rest and bounce back and have a look around and do more research and maybe look back at what I did and see where I went wrong and if I ever wanted to start something again, where would I go.*—Matt

Less frequently, the suicidal action was viewed as a critical moment, as an opportunity to address underlying problems and start rebuilding one's emotional life. For a minority of the men, the suicidal action, or more specifically its aftermath, represented this kind of life-changing moment. Those who were able to construct a broader explanation for their unhappiness were able to go beyond the constraints of their present lives. This involved being able to envisage other forms of masculinity and thereby creating a new, hitherto unknown, socioemotional, space. Although this process was rare among this group of men when it did occur it resulted in transformative change for individuals such as Larry.

Larry

Larry has been mentioned a number of times in this book. He had had a long-term partner and children, a well-paid job and comparatively good educational resources. He had had a relatively uneventful upbringing but had a difficult relationship with his father and for this reason had left home in his late teens. He described his family background as authoritarian and one in which issues were not discussed and he harboured strong feelings of anger towards his father who he felt was responsible for this regime. Larry described himself as a loner but in recent years his social isolation had become more extreme. He had grown increasingly unhappy and detached from his family and this despondency extended to his life more generally. He had attempted suicide twice, had been hospitalised on both occasions, and had refused counselling and out-patient care following the initial attempt. According to his own account Larry didn't envisage a solution to his problems and intended to complete suicide in the future.

I never spoke to people. Not only did I not want to but a lot of it I didn't even realise. Like, you shove it away and its there but you haven't forgotten about it. It is harder for men because I think men… If I had said a few years ago to somebody that I was depressed they probably would have said 'cop on to yourself' and that would have been it whereas if a woman said it, it would be taken more seriously. Even if a man says he has a pain in his shoulder he will work with it whereas a woman will just go to the doctor. I think its that people think that men shouldn't have this kind of pain. Just you're supposed to go through your life and you're supposed to be able to cope with it as a man. You're supposed to be there for other people, your family.

Not everyone is able to do that.
Oh yeah, I know that. I know that now. It's easy to say that now.

Larry's story exemplifies many of the issues considered in this text, an upbringing within a conventional discourse of masculinity which did not provide space to learn about, nor express, emotions. He drew his ideas about appropriate emotional discourse from this environment and despite his assertion that he was comfortable with being detached in this way, his account is underpinned by resentment at not having a voice, at not being heard, and at not having a meaningful relationship with his father. Yet, as he admitted, he adopted many of his father's conventional views as well as his behaviour and most notably, his drinking habits. Larry expressed traditional views about gender and associated disclosing distress with a feminine discourse and that men, no matter how despairing, had to be stoical and deal with problems on their own.

I still think that the man goes out to work and the woman raises the children – maybe not the way people used to think years ago. I still have the ideas that I brought with me from when I was young and she (ex-partner) *has the same ideas. …We just sort of took up that way. I used to think that I did my job and that was it. As long as the money was there at the end of the week that was my job finished. I sort of slipped into that role. The way I was raised. … There's always going to be that thing there, the man is the head of the house no matter what happens. A man has to work. If a man doesn't work he's lazy and that will always be the case. People will always think that, whereas it won't be the same for a woman. The gap between men and women used to be always in the workplace. That's been bridged but the gap between men and women in the home, that hasn't been bridged.*

Larry felt he should have been satisfied with his life but he described a growing sense of desperation over recent years and of living life in a never-ending, state of misery. He tried to survive by drinking and had developed a serious alcohol dependency. Larry became convinced this despair could not be ameliorated and after the first suicide attempt, which involved significant physical injuries, he left the hospital and refused follow-up counselling. He ended his relationship at this point but came to realise that the relationship was not the underlying cause of his unhappiness. One year later, when his desperation again reached a critical level he made a further attempt to complete suicide. Following this episode, and emergency admission to hospital, the attending doctor recommended admission to a psychiatric unit near his home. At that point Larry, who deeply regretted the 'failure' of his suicide attempt, was adamant that he didn't want to receive any form of intervention but to ensure a quick discharge from the hospital he agreed to go for treatment. Once discharged, he defaulted on his promise but was followed up by the local services and at that point he agreed to be admitted to hospital.

> *I was referred here by a psychiatrist in* (name of hospital) *and the reason I ended up there was because I tried to kill myself. I was only in* (name of hospital) *for a short time and they sent me here but I didn't come. The only reason I agreed to come here was because the doctor in the (name of hospital) told me I would have to go to hospital so I just agreed to get out of the hospital. I didn't go there so they persevered and the second time they asked me to go to the hospital I did.*

This account demonstrates how easily men like Larry are lost to the services following a suicide attempt and how difficult it is to get them to engage with treatment yet it also implies that personal contact can work. The hospital admission changed Larry's worldview. Witnessing and engaging with other men with similar problems had a decisive effect and the hospital environment provided a safe, therapeutic, space to consider his life as well as time-out from a seemingly intractable situation.

What do you think helped you?
Going to hospital for a start. I suppose in a way it was admitting to myself this is not just going to go away. Before I always thought I could do it on my own. Obviously I can't. …It wasn't until the Saturday when I was looking at people who were going around and some people were heavily sedated for different reasons and I was looking at that and thought 'I'd hate being drugged like that' and it took me until the Saturday to realise 'hang on a second, I am like that'. It doesn't hit home. It (hospitalisation) *gives you a chance to think about your situation in a totally artificial environment where you don't have to worry about anything. It's just totally different to real life really but it just woke me up a bit, well it woke me up a lot. I saw about five or six different doctors when I was in there, everyone asked me all the same questions. It's not that you get used to it. The more you talk about it, the longer you go on and start to bore people. I spoke about things that I hadn't spoken about ever. I didn't ever tell someone I know but it's alright telling a stranger or it's different. This was different. When I did give up drinking the first time I went to* (Name of Substance Misuse Centre). *I went on their programme and I saw a counsellor there as well and I did that for a while. But this was different. I don't really know why. Maybe it's because I was older. Maybe it's because I was worse than before. A lot of the problems that I had, a lot of them I have sort of put a label on them and said 'right if I give up drinking that's it, everything will be alright' and I think that is another reason why it didn't work the first time because no matter what you do, be it drugs or an addiction to anything, if you give it up and think that your life is all of a sudden going to become rosy you're fooling yourself. And so aside from that there were a couple of things that were wrong in my life that I never thought were there. I don't know what was wrong. I had everything I ever wanted. Nice house, nice car, good job, everything should have been alright but it wasn't. It wasn't enough. By enough I don't mean bigger house or a nicer car, I mean it wasn't fulfilling. I wasn't getting any satisfaction, I was just going from day to day. It wasn't enough, it still isn't.*

Did you come to any other conclusions when you were in there?
It's good to see that you're not the only one for a start. Also, especially the way the wards are split up there's probably an equal number of men and women which surprised me. I'd expect more women in there because women talk about it. If there's something wrong with a woman she goes to the doctor, if there's something wrong with a man he'll hope it will go away. By the time men go

> *to the doctor they are riddled with cancer or something. You hear more about women, you don't hear about men because they don't talk about it, you don't expect them to be in hospital. I looked on it and I look at it now, this is my last chance very much so. This has to work. It's not a case of if it doesn't work because… I know now that if I hadn't gone in when I did, and again they didn't force me to go in but so many people have said there are brilliant doctors and they can't all be wrong. I realised then while I was in there that I wouldn't be sitting here now, I'd probably be dead, there'd be a strong possibility - maybe not a hundred per cent but I'd say very strong. …I'm at a stage where if you're going to start rebuilding your life, you have to start now, it takes a long time. It took me a long time to get where I was. …Now, I'm not happy, let's put it that way but I'm not depressed either or sad or whatever. Just sort of in limbo.*

In Larry's story there is a combination of personal, familial and gender constrictions which prevented him from finding a space to develop alternative modes of thinking and feeling. There were difficulties in his life which he was unable to resolve and over time this led to the despair which almost ended his life. In line with many other participants his unhappiness originated in childhood when he began suppressing feelings of anger and rejection. Now single, Larry intended leaving the country to start again and as he moved forward with his life he described himself as in a liminal type space but with some hope for the future. The hospital admission was a critical intervention for Larry as, along with therapy, it provided knowledge which helped him to understand and reframe his unhappiness and allowed him a way forward. He was also capable of taking on a new discourse and had sufficient resources, educational and otherwise, to implement this change. Guy, who was similarly in the non-repeat group, and was re-interviewed some years later, also achieved significant change in his life.

Guy

In his initial interview Guy presented as angry and resentful about his life and this was directed particularly at his father and the teachers who, he felt, had failed to protect him from prolonged victimisation in school. He had also experienced a good deal of rejection from females and some of his anger was directed at women generally who he regarded as having the gender flexibility denied to him. At that time Guy felt rejected by his peers and by women because he considered he was insufficiently masculine and was angry at his father who he felt should have ensured he had sufficient masculine knowledge to survive in school and elsewhere. He had been bullied in school and this had a significant impact on his self-confidence.

> *I couldn't realise my hopes for myself so basically I set a high target for myself but every time I received a bad grade this diminished me with respect to my projected self and as my condition and quality of mind deteriorated there was an ever increasing disparity between what I wanted to achieve and what I was actually achieving and this was untenable.*

A relationship issue was the trigger for Guy's suicide attempt but, as he explained in the follow-up interview, the episode was connected to more general unhappiness and he had been thinking about suicide for some time. He had a relatively secure background but a somewhat problematic relationship with his father who had conventional ideas about masculinity. Guy didn't conform to the strong masculinity required in his family nor in his school, where he was systematically bullied over many years, and he felt different to his working-class peers because of his academic aspirations. He described the challenges of growing up in a cultural environment where hard masculinities predominated and of being part of a school system which did not encourage academic excellence and progression to university. Guy believed that university would provide him with a more flexibility masculine environment as well as allow him to progress academically. When Guy was re-interviewed seven years after the suicide attempt, and had successfully completed a university degree, he still looked back on his school experience with 'fear and pain' but he had advanced significantly in his life. He had found a more acceptable social, emotional and intellectual space. Achieving a university degree had contributed greatly to his self-esteem as had the social environment of the college. While before his suicide attempt he had been '*very despairing about life and how futile it was*', he now felt more in control and was hopeful about the future.

Along with other study participants who had successfully moved on with their lives, he didn't claim to have a perfect life but felt that he was in a much better place.

> *I was happy I got a* (Degree grade awarded) *but looking back it didn't seem like an accomplishment. I saw it as a chapter in a book. Turn the page, lets go to the next bit. I didn't feel any sort of great sense of achievement. …So generally speaking I don't feel that particularly satisfied. Life seems to be a sort of procession of unmet desires or desires that when you have achieved them they don't satisfy you anymore. Like going to college. I'm happy that I achieved that (but) the main reason for going there was to prove to myself I could do it so the fact that I can't get a job in the present climate doesn't really change anything other than the fact that it's kind of ironic. Yeah, well I'm hoping something will happen in the future.*

According to Guy's account, finding a more fluid cultural setting had allowed him to attain an acceptable level of happiness and achieve an important ambition in his life. He believed this was made possible mainly because he had gone to university and successfully completed the academic programme and gained social acceptance—which had eluded him through his school life. He still attended the psychiatric out-patient services irregularly but viewed these services as contributing little to his wellbeing and progress.

> *You have things like a clinic which should help people but its not really helping people, its just aiding them at their level of misery. What amazes me about this concept is that people come with a problem and they just give you drugs and the medication to help you survive so its like an acceptable level of misery. 'Can you cope with it, we'll give you the tablets, keep you above the threshold' but the actual solution and problem-solving never enters their minds. Generally you have to go crazy before they take any notice of you. Having said that some people do get something out of it.*

These stories demonstrate that a suicide attempt can be a critical juncture in one's life and these men subsequently took action to change elements in their lives. The majority of the men did not access a different place but they make some adjustments in their thinking and gained some degree of knowledge about their emotional lives. In this way they accepted a relationship was over, accessed a more flexible gender/sexual environment and or they engaged with treatment. Although the narratives recounting the suicidal episode were replete with despair and feelings of loss and panic they subsequently managed to achieve a degree of contentment and control in their lives. Reflecting on the crisis from a safe distance they had drawn a boundary around the event, which facilitated problem-solving and moving on, and were drawing on new support networks and they were adamant that it would not occur again.

Repeating Suicide

One half (twenty-six) of the study participants repeated the suicidal behaviour and of these, eight men completed suicide. There was evidence of more severe and chronic substance misuse problems among these men as well as evidence of risk and criminal behaviour but, interestingly, the family backgrounds of the repeat group appeared to be less problematic in terms of adversity than the non-repeat group. They were, however, more likely to have a father absent in childhood. Participants who completed suicide are considered separately below and there were some important variations between those who repeated and survived. The most obvious distinguishing feature in this category was the number of subsequent episodes and in this sense the repeat survivors were divided into two groups—those who made only one further attempt (eight men) and those who had multiple episodes (ten participants). The degree of intent and lethality involved in the subsequent action varied and some of the repeat behaviour is more properly defined as self-harm. This was true for Alan and Gary who both self-harmed on one occasion only after the baseline suicide attempt but are included in this discussion for methodological accuracy. In line with some of the other men who repeated only once they resembled the non-repeat group but with a longer period of instability in their lives. As with the non-repeat category, an event or discrete situation had motivated the original suicide attempt and in Alan's and Gary's case the trigger was their inability to publicly express their sexuality. Alan was interviewed in the follow-up study and his story is included here.

Alan

Alan was about to leave secondary school when he was first interviewed. He wanted to go to university but this had become increasingly unlikely when his school work deteriorated as his distress increased. He used non-prescribed drugs intermittently which had caused conflict with his parents but he was not involved in other risk behaviour. Although Alan had a circle of friends and got on well socially he had always felt different to his peers in the working-class neighbourhood he lived in and had been subjected to homophobic bullying since he was a young child. His parents had separated when he was young and his relationship with his mother, with whom he lived, was problematic. He described his father, with whom he maintained regular contact, as caring and supportive but he had not confided in any of his family about his sexuality nor about his increasing despair. There had been a considerable build-up of pressure in the previous year as he faced final exams and the prospect of going to university receded. He associated university with gender and sexual freedom and his desire to leave his present life was so great that he had become immobilised by anxiety and could not study.

Alan had a period of adjustment after the baseline suicide attempt and in the follow-up interview he described a phase of multi-drug use and an episode of self-harm during this time. He mentioned that he took some time to come to terms with his sexuality and find a meaningful place to express this identity but thereafter, by his own account, he did reasonably well. His story is therefore about finding an acceptable socioemotional space. In the initial interview he had attributed the suicide attempt to feeling overwhelmed with sadness about family problems and life generally but his subsequent account of the suicidal action was more definitively related to his sexuality. Alan had not mentioned that he was gay when initially interviewed, in fact he made a point of denying this, but at the follow-up interview he was open about his sexuality and attributed the initial episode to a build-up of unhappiness because he felt unable to reveal that he was gay to his family and friends.

Do you remember that time?
I do remember that time. Very long ago. Don't really talk about it anymore. That was a bit of a mad time for me. Afterwards, now I'm better, now I'm grand. I had some difficult times between then and now. My early twenties got a bit out of control for a couple of years. Got into partying. A lot of drugs and drink. Now I'm grand. I've got a fulltime job. I hate my job but it's a job.

Did the crisis happen when you were doing your Leaving Certificate?
I think it just kind of surfaced then. I think it was there for a long time. I don't really remember much about it. I just remember lying in bed for two days straight. I don't remember much of the treatment or anything like that. I can't really remember much of the time. I remember the time, I don't remember much of the details.

Alan described growing up gay in a working-class neighbourhood, in a narrative which mirrored Gary's account, and told of always 'performing straight' and the dread of unmasking in the context of constant surveillance and homophobic jokes. He felt unable to tell his family and his friends about his sexuality and was subjected to homophobic abuse in school and in the neighbourhood. At that time an alternative masculine world seemed beyond reach to Alan. He didn't know anyone who was gay and, unlike Gary who was somewhat older, had never visited gay bars or clubs. His only point of reference was university where he believed gender was more fluid and homosexuality accepted.

I'd say it's a lot easier now and its only seven years in the difference. I'd say it's a lot easier but there's people, young teenage fellas, who are suffering from depression. Its hard. I don't think depression has anything to do with the situation. I think when you're in there you just can't get out of it.

Did you feel you couldn't get away?
Yeah, I remember feeling like that. And I remember a couple of years afterwards when, as I said, I went through a bad patch, it was just… I was taking drugs every weekend, drinking, going from Friday until Monday and sometimes you would be like 'Oh my God' because I was just thinking 'I'm feeling like I used to feel'. I had to stop. Back then it was really hard. It was a bit manic, a mental time for me. I love my life. I love being able to go out anytime I want to. …when I was younger I would always look at them and

> *going 'I wish I was them, I wish I was straight. I wish I had a girlfriend or I wish I could do this or do that'. Now I'm looking at some of them coming to me and saying 'we wish we could go out during the week and stay out all night and not have to worry about coming home'. The tables have kind of turned a bit. And in a way I'd love to have a family and kids way way in the future. I'm talking about way into the future. …I'm glad I'm not one of them because they're the same as we used to be. They all still hang around with each other and they are all still friends with each other and they don't have anyone different in their lives. …I just look at them and I'm so happy and so glad that I'm not part of that group anymore.*

Apart from moving into a different cultural environment Alan attributed his progress to support from friends and to '*just getting on with it*'. He described continuing challenges but it was clear that his life had improved in many ways. He had left home and now lived alone but his family were supportive and he had a network of friends and had some relationships. He had accessed a world he felt unattainable when first interviewed. Both Alan's and Gary's stories resonate with research findings about a critical period, in terms of risk for suicide, for young LGBT people which, if negotiated successfully, results in the lowering of risk into adulthood (Russell and Toomey 2012). These men's distress was related to their exclusion from the predominant masculinity in their communities which they did not feel able to publicly reject and to a lack of financial and educational resources which would have allowed them to move away. Once these men found an appropriate socioemotional space their lives normalised and, while ongoing issues remained, despair dissolved. Alan had reached a level of confidence about his identity and his sexuality, societal attitudes to homosexuality had shifted, and his positive state of mind was reflected in his reason for participating in the follow-up study—to help others in a similar situation.

> *I wouldn't say it's very happy. It's very hard but it's just 'cop on', just get on with it. It's still very hard for me. Still, sometimes I don't want to get out of bed. It's not going to change. I have great friends. Best friends, the best friends in the world and if I get down I speak to them. I speak to them every day. It keeps me happy.*

You see your friends as important in terms of moving on?
Ah yeah, because they have their problems and I have my problems and we all seem to sort out each other's problems and it's like kind of just a laugh.

When you were (age mentioned) did you have that group of friends?
No, I didn't know any of them.

Who did you confide in at that time?
No one.

You told me that you were bullied because of the way you spoke.
Yeah, because I'm obviously gay, yeah.

I remember you didn't feel ready to say that when I first met you.
You didn't see (mentions age) *year olds being gay back then but now you do and the gay community has an outreach programme for people at that age. I didn't have that back then.*

Do you think that contributed to you feeling bad at that time?
I think it was just something that was wrong with me. Obviously being gay was a big factor and not getting on with my mum was probably a big thing but I think it was just a thing that I wasn't healthy, just wasn't happy in myself.

What brought you through this?
The friends I have now, they weren't there when I was going through this. I don't know what brought me through it. I could say my family because I actually realised then… I always thought I did'nt get on with my family. We still don't get on but there'd be a lot of people disappointed if I weren't here. And I love them and I can't do that to them. I thought (at that time) 'they'll be sad for a while and they'll get over it' but actually I don't think they would. I know they wouldn't.

If you knew somebody at that age with the same kind of challenges that you had what would you advise them to do?
I don't think you can. No matter what anybody ever said to me, I just didn't care. You could have said anything to me. I just wouldn't care. I'm just like… I hated everyone for trying to help me. Then you realise. I will never forget. I was just lying in bed for two days in a state. I couldn't talk, I wouldn't talk, and my mam never leaving my side. I just think back and say 'poor woman, what did I do to her?' You can't turn round and say to them 'think of your family, they are going to miss you because back in my head I'm thinking they'll

> *get over it. I just describe my life back them as a mess. You against the world, everyone hates me. Looking back I wish I could say to everyone 'it's like a circle. Once you get through it, it will be grand' but you can't say that. I say that to my friends all the time when they're feeling depressed or anything like that, I say 'you'll be grand. You'll be grand in a couple of days'. If they had said that to me 'you'll be grand in a couple of years' I was like 'fuck off'. It was like it was never going to end.*

Alan describes how he was on medication for some time after the suicide attempt but he then decided to stop this treatment and take steps himself to get better.

> *I just said I'm not going to take pills for the rest of my life. So I just stopped. I don't know if they helped me. I don't know if they didn't help me. …I'd rather just have the attitude to get over it. I'm just me. I find it very difficult sometimes and you could catch me on the phone to a friend crying my eyes out for no reason whatsoever. You actually just need to talk to someone. That's extremely important.*

Chronic Disorder: Mental Illness and Substance Misuse

In contrast to the group described above, ten of the men in the repeat survivor category made a number of subsequent suicide attempts and they differed from others who repeated and survived in a number of important ways. There were more chronic, long-term, problems evident among this group and this was reflected in their motivations for the suicide attempt. This group contained two subsets, men who were addicted to drugs and those with long-term psychiatric conditions.

None of the men with serious or consistent psychiatric illness completed suicide despite the fact that high risk is associated with this profile. These participants made multiple subsequent attempts and the person with the highest number of repeat attempts was in this group. This category of men was different from the other participants in the study in that they attended the psychiatric services regularly, more usually as out-patients or as day-hospital patients, and their care extended beyond clinical issues in that they had participated in courses and work experience organised by the services. In this way, the follow-up care of these men was much more regular and comprehensive than that available to the other men in that it related to their lives generally. Two of these participants were interviewed in the follow-up study and their stories illustrate the challenge of mental illness. Both Charlie and Cian, who had serious, long-term, psychiatric conditions had a history of multiple suicide attempts since they were first interviewed as well as numerous hospital admissions. They described their symptoms and their lives as much more stable at this point. Although Cian reported that his mood could be erratic and that he felt '*sometimes good and sometimes bad*' the hallucinatory symptoms which made his life so difficult in the past had eased since he was first interviewed.

> *I just wanted to die. I was living in hell. This feeling was unbelievable. It really was unbelievable. But the thing is it was all in my head. My family kept telling me and I kept telling them 'its not in my head' And I'd be sitting there and looking to see if the telly was making any messages to me. …At the moment now I'm alright. I don't get that feeling anymore so I'm sort of saying 'yeah, my life is getting back together again. I'm not having these feelings. I can watch the telly, I can listen to the radio, I can have a talk with my family, talk with the nurses. But I hope I don't get that feeling again, you know that way.*

This group also tended to have family support but the assistance which appeared to be critical in preventing suicide came from the psychiatric services. These men were atypical in that they had a serious mental disorder, a label which they understood and accepted, while the majority of the men were careful to distance themselves and their problems from a psychiatric discourse. Those who had a serious psychiatric disorder represented a potentially high-risk group as evidenced by the number and intensity of their subsequent suicide attempts yet they all survived. They seemed to have been protected over time by services which provided long-term, consistent, care while most of the other participants were reluctant to engage in any level of such care. In this way the men with serious psychiatric disorder differed from others in the sample in that they maintained regular contact with the services. For other men in the repeat survivor group, contact with the services, if it occurred at all implied intermittent attendance and more usually presentation to Accident and Emergency departments following a crisis.

The second subset of consistent repeaters contained men who were involved in serious drug-taking and were also atypical in a number of ways. They had generally dropped out of school at a young age and became involved in drugs and moved on later to more serious levels of addiction. At this point they generally lived out of home as they were frequently forced to leave the family home by their parents due to the addiction and some were homeless. A few of these participants appeared to have undiagnosed educational challenges which may have contributed to leaving school without qualifications. They began to lose educational and other capital as it was accrued by others, which had long-term implications in terms of leaving drug addiction behind, and having to live on the edge of society changed these men in significant ways. The link between drug-taking and criminal activity was apparent and their experiences had thought them to trust few people. Some had spent time in prison and, along with others who had experienced the prison system, they detested and feared it. Overall, they appeared to be a comparatively normal group of men who had been thrown off course by their addiction to drugs yet they now represented a definite at-risk group as some of their profiles resembled those who subsequently died by suicide. Those with family contact or partners and the few who managed to remain employed were less vulnerable but this depended on their ability to retain these resources and thus prevent further slippage into marginalisation.

The Casualties

Those who completed suicide, although a relatively small group, demonstrated some commonalities as well as distinctive elements compared to others in the sample. Some specific features (mainly biographical facts) relating to this group cannot be cited as it might identify the men concerned but in general, they were slightly older than the others, all had attempted suicide before the index attempt, had expressed strong intent in the original study and had had a number of subsequent episodes. They resembled, in terms of their educational and work background, the profile of the group described above in that they had lower educational attainment (in terms of length of time at school and exams completed) than other participants and inconsistent work histories. Only one of these men had successfully completed the Leaving Certificate examination and three had dropped out of school before taking any exams which implies that they may also have had educational challenges. Some had been engaged in risk behaviour from an early age and had been in trouble with the law (including imprisonment) and almost all were misusing (primarily) alcohol and sometimes drugs. Despite this, there were potentially positive elements in their lives. The men who completed suicide generally experienced lower levels of childhood adversity than the non-repeat group (and the repeat survivor category) and, in line with this, included a number of men who came from seemingly secure backgrounds and had good support from their families. Two of the men were in long-term relationships and five were fathers and therefore, in the Durkheimian sense, were more integrated than those who were unattached. Yet, they were more likely than the other groups to have experienced a father absent while growing up and while there was family support some of these men had come to feel that they were a burden on their families and others felt trapped within unhappy relationships. Despite these trends there were two distinct groups among those who completed suicide—those who conformed to the risk profile outlined above who tended to perform a hard, violent, masculinity and a minority who had more stable lives and work histories who found the prevailing masculinity overly rigid.

Risk Takers and Hard Masculinities

Substance misuse was common across this group and alcohol was more likely to be the drug of addiction. They had usually been involved in long-term risk behaviour and criminality and violence was a feature of their biographies. The motives they gave for the baseline suicidal action related to general unhappiness and dissatisfaction with their lives and this was usually accompanied by a feeling that they could not alter the situation. There was an element of reality in this perception in that their lives had become so enmeshed in addiction and violence that amelioration of their situation seemed improbable. They were somewhat older than the other participants and therefore were dealing with long-term despondency which they felt increasingly unable to address and change. Extreme desperation and helplessness was evident in their narratives and alcohol dependency added a particular intensity to these men's feelings of hopelessness. Some of these men presented at interview with anger amounting to a rage against the world. They blamed themselves for their behaviour but believed only external, unknown, factors would ameliorate their situation. While they had all engaged with the services at some point, generally for alcohol misuse, they resisted interventions which would involve real behaviour change specifically giving up alcohol. In the aftermath of the baseline suicide attempt they did not avail of treatment other than intermittent presentations to the Accident and Emergency and continued to repeat the same behaviour. This angry, sometimes violent, subgroup represented a kind of endpoint of hegemonic masculinity in terms of the channelling of negative emotion into destructive behaviours. Influenced by a cultural environment which extolled hard masculinity, and frequently lacking intellectual and vocational resources, they ran into a kind of social and emotional dead end with increasing use of alcohol and violence. Three men (Dale, Rory, and Rob) exemplified this group and their narratives focused on the negative effect of alcohol, a preoccupation with self-destruction and the inevitability of suicide.

Dale, Rory, and Rob

Dale recounted a background of heavy drinking and involvement in risk behaviour from early adolescence. At interview he described constant thoughts of suicide which he attributed to a cycle of alcohol misuse and destructive behaviour followed by guilt. Dale felt hat he could not break this destructive cycle and that treatment was unlikely to help him. He had been referred to an alcohol dependency programme in the past but had dropped out. Following the baseline suicide attempt, Dale made a further attempt and subsequently completed suicide.

> *You don't care. You feel so low, you feel as if there's no point in going on. What's the point? This is going to happen again and you're going to feel this. You don't want to live the rest of your life like this. Well I don't. It's very hard. I don't like myself being like this. I try to fight it. I try to cut it out of the back of my head and it just doesn't work, nothing happens. You won't snap out of it until it takes its course. …when I'm going to make up my mind that I'm going somewhere, I'm going to do this today, today is the day I'm going to kill myself, tonight I'm going to kill myself, something always happens to stop me. It would go out of your mind, the bad feeling would pass but it always comes back.*

Rory had a very similar background to Dale in that he had dropped out of school early and had a history of risk behaviour and alcohol misuse from an early age. He had been in prison, had found it extremely difficult to cope and had attempted suicide while incarcerated (*…because I couldn't cope with jail)*. He thought about suicide constantly, spoke as if his own self-destruction was inevitable and mentioned that he had told a friend *I'll be dead in the next couple of months* which turned out to be an accurate prediction.

When I interviewed Rob he had had numerous admissions to hospital and had attempted suicide on a number of occasions. Following the interview he again had a series of hospital admissions, mainly for alcoholism, and then completed suicide. At interview he appeared to have reached an intense level of desperation. He felt his life had become intolerable and, as with Dale and Rory, was actively rehearsing ways of escaping from this despair. His adult life had started out in a positive way in that he had a relatively high level of academic achievement but in the last few years his life had spiraled down into alcoholism and then violence and he has been in prison on a number of occasions. He reported that his father and most of his family drank heavily. Rob had been drinking alcohol from an early age but in his twenties his consumption of alcohol had significantly increased and he found it difficult to keep a job and maintain a relationship. He had no faith in treatment—he had refused to attend an alcohol programme and believed he could not give up alcohol.

> ***Why did you do this?***
> *Because I feel like killing myself. I'm happy trying to kill myself. Quite happy just to leave the planet and just go. Just go away because I'm just fed up with it. Just sick of it. Just drinking and drinking and more drinking and they won't let me drink at home so that's why I'm out here. I was in jail this year and before this year I was in jail and I was in* (hospital named). *I was in* (prison named) *over the last year. All because of drink. …I want to die. …I've just had enough. All I do is drink. I go drinking just to kill the pain. Just feeling depressed and sad. It gives me back. It gives me something. The drink does something to me. …I don't want to go on any other way. I want to go on to die. …Because when you reach a certain level and you want to die the drink doesn't matter anymore.*

For these participants suicide had come to represent the only way of exiting a cycle of unhappiness and self-destruction. As the narratives attest, their lives had become intolerable and they could not envisage feeling better. They considered themselves to be beyond help, as with the respondents studied by Hume and Platt (2007). While other participants moved on from the suicide attempt these men were hampered by a lack of economic and educational resources, their addiction to alcohol and the violence which often ensued from this. Repetition of suicidal behaviour had added another layer of desperation to their lives. As time went on the support of family and others, which provided critical protection for many of these men, inevitably decreased and left them even more vulnerable to suicide. In the end their decision to end their lives might be viewed as an effort to end unbearable emotional pain and to save their families further distress (and this was indicated in a note left by one of the men). As their words illustrate they had already begun the process of normalising suicide and were goading themselves towards the final action as Byng et al. (2015) has described. This group appeared to be confined by conventional or hegemonic masculinity and had channelled their distress via rage and anger, as described by Scheff (1997). Their gender background and training was one in which strength was extoled and weakness vilified for males. It was unlikely, given their lack of educational opportunities and movement into early risk behaviour that they would have been able to disclose psychological difficulties.

As they moved further along the road in terms of risk behaviour and violence the possibility of finding a way out of their unhappiness decreased. In this way, these men repeated their destructive behaviours over and over and this increased their anger and frustration (and guilt) and made interventions less likely. As time elapsed they became overwhelmed by these emotions of anger and self-disgust and suicide appeared to be one of the few remaining options available to them. As their narratives imply they had narrowed their options to this and had begun to urge themselves towards self-destruction, a feature described in other studies (Firestone 1986). Yet, there were indications that an intervention earlier in their lives, such as a more relevant educational programme and or timely attention to their drinking, would have made a critical difference. In this way there were individual issues involved, especially educational and related challenges, which had impacted on their early lives. There was also the influence of the particular gender environments and the masculinity training they had received and in these settings conventional or hegemonic masculinity values dominated. In this way, these men might be viewed as casualties of extreme masculinity in that they had adopted a hard, violent, masculinity although there were many indications that this was performed at surface level. They demonstrated abundant examples of normal emotions including the desire, as well as the ability, to care and be cared for and they were very fearful of other, violent, masculinities. At this point in their lives their perspectives had narrowed considerably and their attitudes had become quite rigid and this inflexibility made access to alternative ways of being a man difficult but certainly not impossible.

Trapped Masculinities

The second subset of men who completed suicide were constrained by conventional forms of masculinity but their profiles, as well as the predominant themes, contrasted significantly with the above group. Their emotional biographies were dominated not by anger but by fear and repression and a clear theme in their lives was being unable to find an acceptable, meaningful, space within the environment of traditional masculinity which they inhabited. Many of the men in this study struggled with conventional forms of masculinity and some, often painfully, had accessed more receptive gender environments. Frank and Leo felt unable or unwilling to do this.

Frank and Leo

Frank was in a long-term relationship and was a caring father. He had a wide circle of friends and was strongly connected to his family of origin. In his background were two near-fatal suicide attempts carried out over a relatively short period of time and a history of serious alcohol misuse. Despite the lethality of these attempts, Frank was unclear about the reasons why he wanted to end his life and following the initial episode he refused the counselling offered and continued to drink heavily. The implication was that Frank was in serious ongoing distress but was either unaware of what was causing this unhappiness or had chosen to conceal the underlying causes. He was a friendly, engaging, interviewee and was happy to discuss issues, especially the physical impact of the suicide attempt, but when it came to the detail of what had preceded the action, and the emotions surrounding it, Frank became noticeably uneasy. He presented as fearful and somewhat anxious rather than sad. He did indicate that dissatisfaction with his relationship was a major contributiing factor to his unhappiness and he mentioned that he had entered this partnership against his better judgement. Yet, he was unwilling to engage in counselling which might have ameliorated the situation or provided a way out of the relationship. He may have been reluctant to leave the relationship because of his children (he spoke of the hurt he might cause them if he left the family home) and or because he came from a close-knit, traditional, family background. There may also have other factors involved as there were indications that Frank was gay and was unwilling to accept and or to disclose this. There were clues to this in his narrative, particularly in relation to the vagueness which surrounded his motivations for two very serious suicide attempts, which contrasted with the intensity of his negative feelings about his relationship. He declared that he would die if he had to return to live with his partner yet he could not pinpoint any specific problem and stated that there was nothing particularly wrong with the partnership.

Frank's behaviour contrasted with that of another participant (Larry) whom he shared a number of features with. Larry had also been in an unhappy relationship for some years and, like Frank, had developed a serious drinking problem and both had made two extremely serious suicide attempts over a relatively short period of time. These men had entered relationships and become fathers at a relatively early age but maintained an emotional distance from their partners and structured their lives so that they would not be questioned about their behaviour or feelings. Despite the lethality of method and intent involved in Larry's suicide attempts he survived and moved on with his life largely because he availed of the opportunity to explore the underlying causes of his unhappiness. Frank, however, was adamantly opposed to counselling or therapy of any kind. There were other men in the study who had experienced significant difficulties in disclosing their sexuality but once they did so their lives improved considerably. Frank may have decided that this option was too difficult to contemplate. Unlike the other men cited here whose lives changed when they spoke about their unhappiness and accepted help, Frank left the hospital after a second near-fatal suicide attempt and refused the follow-up supports offered.

Leo was similarly prevented from accessing the life he desired. He was interviewed following his first serious suicide attempt although he mentioned he had self-harmed in the previous year. He came from a relatively secure background and he was in regular employment. He grew up in a family and a neighbourhood where traditional, strong, masculinity was the norm and, in this respect, Leo had always felt different to the males in his family and in the neighbourhood. In many ways he didn't want to be like these men but he struggled to find an alternative masculine identity and role model within this cultural environment. He spoke at length about his creative interests and although he had accessed alternative spaces and masculinities in the past he lacked the self-confidence to follow this though. He was convinced that only a transformation of his identity and or his life would bring happiness. In this way his narrative was underpinned by the desire to escape from the rigidity of his present life but also by feelings of masculine inadequacy and of having to re-invent himself in order to fit it. In contrast to other participants such as Guy, whose life goal (to go to university) was more specific, Leo's issues were broader and the solutions more complex.

I was drinking and I suffer from depression. As far as I know anyway I suffer from depression. It's been going on for the past few years. …I cannot be happy for more than a day and then something else is going to happen. I have my moments. I do have my great moments. No matter what I do I know it's going to go downhill anyway. Something has to happen that just ruins everything. … Things just get on top of you. Small things. It's everything. It's always building up. Everything is just coming at me. I know everything is just getting to me. I know someone says 'find out what's wrong with you and fix it' but you can't go back in time… You have to reinvent yourself. It's weird to say but you have to change your whole personality. … It's like being trapped. Did you ever have that feeling that like you felt you didn't really belong where you are? It's kind of like that. Sounds weird but maybe I shouldn't have been born or something.

How would you reinvent yourself?
I reckon that if I went off for a year somewhere and came back than you kind of change your whole personality. Not change yourself but people will look at you different. It's weird to say but you have to change your whole personality. …I just think I have to leave or something. I have to go. I just want to go. I just want to leave, just go away, see how I am and then I could come back and then I can be, kind of change myself, be different.

What sort of person would you become?
A person who was always laughing like I always try and do. I always think that's the real me sometimes. …Someone who doesn't do this anyway. In a sense I'm probably saying I wish I had taken more pills because I wouldn't have to go home and listen to everyone crying over me, talking shit. I hate that. …its stupid isn't it. If you're going to kill yourself do it properly. If you're going to do it again, go and do it. I'm not playing around. I don't mean to worry you or anything but if you're going to do it, don't cry for help, that's one mistake. Bleeding arseholes. Anyone who does this is stupid. What's the point of putting your family through the likes of this twice, three times, eight times. Do it. Never have a fear and then you'll be gone and you won't have to put them through this over and over again because it's selfish. It's just stupid.

There were many examples in this sample of participants who felt different to other men in their communities. This made them feel isolated as the masculine culture these men lived within was superficially homogenous and there was a lack of alternative masculine voices and role models. Public conformity to conventional masculinity was the norm and difference was not communicated or shared, at least among these men and the males they interacted with. Frank and Leo are extreme examples of this silent conspiracy which made men feel they should all be alike and which prevented them from visualising an acceptable social and emotional future. Some participants did manage to find this space and their situations altered for the better but others were unwilling to make significant changes in their lives. Men such as Frank and Leo were perhaps too fearful to go beyond the prevailing gender norms.

Summary

The participants in this study all made serious suicide attempts, a substantial number repeated and eight men completed suicide. This represents a comparatively high rate for completion of suicide and is related to the inclusion criteria, in particular serious intent at the index attempt (Beautrais 2003). Psychiatric disorder was not a critical feature but substance, especially alcohol, misuse was prevalent as noted in other studies (Seguin et al. 2006). The socioeconomic profile of the study participants confirms other research findings that suicide is more prevalent in lower socioeconomic groups (Lorent et al. 2005; Baudelot and Establet 2008). Yet, those who attempt suicide in these environments are not a homogenous population and there were distinct differences between those who repeated and those who did not. Participants who did not repeat had more positive features in their lives, for example, higher educational attainment, and less negative attributes such as involvement in risk and criminal behaviour. They also differed in terms of the motivation for the suicidal action in that specific issues or situations featured more often in their narratives. The fact that their problems was more identifiable and circumscribed probably made it easier to address or at least draw a boundary around the issue and move on. Those who repeated, and especially those who completed, suicide tended to have problems which extended to their lives more generally while at the same time they had less resources to ameliorate these difficulties. It was also apparent that feelings of despair in the context of substance misuse and risk behaviour took on a particular potency as time passed and the potential for change receded. Suicide occurs when there appears to be no available pathway to a tolerable existence (Cavan 1965) and those who completed suicide were identifiable in terms of despairing narratives and hopelessness, which is an important predictor of suicidality (Kuo et al. 2004). This is supported in this study along with an understanding of how hopelessness is exacerbated by alcohol misuse (Conner and Duberstein 2004). The life situations of those who completed suicide had become unrelenting bleak and they felt unable to action a way out of this situation. The men who did not repeat were able to regain some element of agency in their lives and the resources they had assisted them in doing this. Yet few were willing to attempt an extensive re-evaluation of their socioemotional life in that the majority did not wish to address the deeper issues in their biography which had created the vulnerabilities which formed the backdrop to the suicide attempt and this decision was influenced by the prevailing masculinity discourse.

References

Baudelot, C., & Establet, R. (2008). *Suicide: The hidden side of modernity*. Cambridge: Polity Press.

Beautrais, A. L. (2003). Subsequent mortality in medically serious suicide attempts: A 5 year follow-up. *Australian and New Zealand Journal of Psychiatry, 37*, 595–599.

Byng, R., Howerton, A., Owens, C. V., & Campbell, J. (2015). Pathways to suicide attempts among male offenders: The role of agency. *Sociology of Health & Illness, 37*(6), 936–951.

Cavan, R. S. (1965). *Suicide*. New York: Russell and Russell.

Cleary, A. (2017). Help-seeking patterns and attitudes to treatment amongst men who attempted suicide. *Journal of Mental Health, 26*(3), 220–224.

Conner, K. R., & Duberstein, P. R. (2004). Predisposing and precipitating factors for suicide among alcoholics: Empirical review and conceptual integration. *Alcoholism, Clinical and Experimental Research, 28*(5 Supplement), 6S–17S.

Firestone, R. W. (1986). The "Inner Voice" and suicide. *Psychotherapy, 23*(3), 439–447.

Gibb, S. J., Beautrais, A. L., & Fergusson, D. M. (2005). Mortality and further suicidal behaviour after an index suicide attempt: A 10-year study. *Australian and New Zealand Journal of Psychiatry, 39*(1–2), 95–100.

Hawton, K., & van Heeringen, K. (2009). Suicide. *The Lancet, 373*(9672), 1372–1381.

Hawton, K., Zahl, D., & Weatherall, R. (2003). Suicide following deliberate self-harm: Long-term follow-up of patients who presented to a general hospital. *British Journal of Psychiatry, 182*, 537–542.

Hume, M., & Platt, S. (2007). Appropriate interventions for the prevention and management of self-harm: A qualitative exploration of service-users views. *BMC Public Health, 7*, 9.

Kuo, W., Gallo, J. J., & Eaton, W. W. (2004). Hopelessness, depression, substance disorder, and suicidality: A 13-year community-based study. *Social Psychiatry and Psychiatric Epidemiology, 39*, 497–501.

Lorent, V., Kunst, A. E., Huisman, M., et al. (2005). Socio-economic inequalities in suicide: A European comparative study. *British Journal of Psychiatry, 187*, 49–54.

O'Donnell, I., Falmer, R., & Catalán, J. (1996). Explaining suicide: The views of survivors of serious suicide attempts. *British Journal of Psychiatry, 168*, 780–786.

Russell, S. T., & Toomey, R. B. (2012). Men's sexual orientation and suicide: Evidence for US adolescent-specific risk. *Social Science and Medicine, 74*(4), 523–529.

Scheff, T. (1997). *Emotions, the social bond, and human reality*. Cambridge: Cambridge University Press.

Seguin, M., Lesage, A., Chawky, N., et al. (2006). Suicide cases in New Brunswick from April 2002 to May 2003: The importance of better recognizing substance and mood disorder comorbidity. *Canadian Journal of Psychiatry, 51*, 581–586.

Zahl, D., & Hawton, K. (2004). Repetition of deliberate self-harm and subsequent suicide risk: A long-term follow-up study in 11,583 patients. *British Journal of Psychiatry, 185*, 70–75.

6

Conclusions: The Social and Emotional Landscape of Suicide

Despite the public health importance of suicide, and its historical significance within the discipline, there has been relatively little sociological interest in this topic in the past five decades. Disciplines such as psychology and medicine now dominate this research area and sociological work tends to be in line with Durkheim (1951) in using a macro-level, statistical, approach. These investigations provide important information relating to suicidal behaviour but for conceptual and methodological reasons offer little insight into the process and motivation involved in suicide. Suicide has moved increasingly outside the clinical domain and a significant number of men who complete suicide are not in contact with the services and do not have a psychiatric diagnosis (Owens et al. 2003; Hamdi et al. 2008). In this way, service-based samples are not generally representative of those who complete suicide. The methodologies used in medical and psychological studies are also problematic in that they operate at a broad, statistical, level which may obscure the nuances of such an individual and relatively infrequent action.

Durkheim's theories have been challenged but his basic premise, that suicide is primarily a social story, remains intact and this is the framework for this study and the starting point for these concluding remarks.

A. Cleary, *The Gendered Landscape of Suicide*,
https://doi.org/10.1007/978-3-030-16634-2_6

Culture exerts an important influence on suicide and cultural scripts relating to suicide tend to have a gender dimension which is the second theoretical building block for this inquiry. Gender is a frequently referenced but still largely underdeveloped concept which runs through suicide statistics across the world and through history. Gender represents the cultural attributes assigned to males and females based on their biological sex. The concept of gender has featured consistently in studies of suicidal behaviour but is usually operationalised in terms of sex differences, with males and females constructed as singular as well as distinctive entities, although gender is more accurately represented in fluid terms (Thorne 1993; Butler 2004). Studies using sex-difference frameworks have failed to account for considerable discrepancies in male and female suicide rates across the world as well as within similar societies. In many cultures men outnumber women in terms of completed suicide but the reverse is true elsewhere and within similar cultural settings some groups of men have significantly higher susceptibility to suicide compared to other male groups.

The third explanatory concept employed in this study is emotions, a concept which has featured infrequently in suicide research despite the importance of feelings in the process of suicide (Abrutyn and Mueller 2014). Within cultures norms relating to emotions and the expression of feelings are developed with gender and socioeconomic connotations and these seep down to individual lives in various ways and at different levels of influence (Hochschild 1979; Kemper 1981). Cultural groups share ideas about gender-appropriate ways to feel, and especially to express, emotions and while these ideas are interpreted differently people tend to remain, as this study illustrates, within the normative gender parameters. Emotions have been regulated through history and while there is a more flexible emotional terrain in place today emotion cultures still retain gender and class dimensions which restrict the expression of feelings (Shields 2007). In this way the landscape of emotions is uneven and all individuals do not have the same degree of expressive freedom. The ability 'to speak from the heart', as Stephanie Shields (2007) refers to this capacity, is not equally available to all and was severely restrained for the men in this study.

Over five decades ago, Douglas (1967) remarked that a meaningful analysis of suicide should be based on the definitions supplied by the social actors involved but few studies have attempted this. Qualitative investigations of suicidal behaviour are rare (Wray et al. 2011). There is in-depth work which has provided important detail on why individuals in disadvantaged communities opt for suicidal behaviour but this was based on a wide spectrum of self-harm (Redley 2003). Other qualitative research has used relatives' and coroners' reports as well as notes left by the deceased to understand suicidal motivations (Fincham et al. 2011). These accounts, as the present study illustrates, are subject to error in relation to men and written documentation is left by a minority of those who kill themselves (O'Donnell et al. 1993). As Douglas (1967) implied, the closest one can come to examining the meanings people attach to suicidal action is to speak with those who made a clinically serious or near-fatal suicide attempt and this is the approach used in this study. The sample used in this inquiry, young males, was chosen because they are a high-risk group in both Europe and the United States and because of the paucity of qualitative accounts of male suicidal behaviour from a masculinity perspective. The participants recounted their stories in unstructured interviews conducted soon after the suicide attempt and this format allowed them to provide information according to their own understanding of the action.

These men's accounts produced distinctive stories and biographies but the narratives combined in thematic ways to support the idea that suicidal behaviour is primarily a sociological rather than a medical or psychiatric narrative. The findings highlight vulnerable male lives in contemporary society and indicate particular practices and subgroups of men who require attention in terms of suicide prevention. The study confirms that risk is associated with lower socioeconomic groupings and provides more detail about susceptibility to suicide in this social setting. The participants came from a variety of backgrounds but the majority were from broadly working-class settings and shared characteristics with the socioeconomic category most likely to attempt and complete suicide (Lorent et al. 2005). In thisstudy the association between lower socioeconomic grouping and suicidal behaviour is explained in terms of the existence of emotion discourses which constrained the expression of distress for men in these settings and a lack of resources to access alternative environments. This vulnerability to suicide is not conclusive or fixed in that the majority of men from similar backgrounds do not attempt or complete suicide and many of the men in this study were able to move on successfully with their lives. Yet, the fact that a comparatively high number of the participants later completed suicide allows us to follow a line in some men's lives from the difficulties they experienced to unbearable emotional pain and to self-destruction. The findings convey a narrative of hurt, fearful and restrained lives, of people who experienced suffering superimposed on earlier trauma and who were unable to speak about their pain. These men did not speak about their problems because they felt that such a conversation was unacceptable in the context of prevailing masculinity norms which censured the expression of feelings associated with sentiments other than strength. They felt pressure to follow this conventional or hegemonic construction of masculinity because these ideas were absorbed early in their lives within the home and enforced, sometimes severely, in the school and the neighbourhood. Many had been victimised in school and were aware of the implications of deviating from the normative masculinity. In private they lived out a different scenario for pain and vulnerability was a silent, secretive, affair for men in these communities. These masculinity perspectives were contested and many of the men were aware of, and some had sought out, alternative forms of manhood but they maintained at least superficial adherence to the local gender discourse.

For the men in this study norms of traditional masculinity provided a narrow behavioural and emotional terrain to operate within, impeded knowledge of their emotional needs and acted as a barrier to accessing help. They were restricted in expressing distress because they perceived such feelings as associated with vulnerability and weakness and, as female emotions, and this was a view shared, at least publicly, by family, friends and other men in their locality. They had difficulty in identifying symptoms as they were unfamiliar with psychological discourses and did not frame their issues within an illness discourse. Treatment was not sought because of the fear of exposure and or because the therapies on offer did not appeal and these are themes which feature in other studies (Addis and Mahalik 2003; River 2018). In the absence of disclosure and a therapeutic intervention, alcohol provided a culturally acceptable form of masking problems which prolonged the men's suffering and placed them at greater risk of suicidal behaviour. The extent of concealment in this study, as well as the methods used to deal with emotional pain, help to decipher the paradox of higher rates of reported distress for women but higher levels of completed suicide for men. In reality, certain male emotions remain invisible in some cultural settings where hegemonic-type constructs discourage the public expression of specific feelings. That men experience intense feelings of despair, sadness and inadequacy is clear from these men's narratives and their accounts challenge simple dualistic categorizations of male and female emotions. Despite the existence of gendered accounts in the literature and elsewhere, feelings do not divide neatly along male/female lines. In the context of a critical moment following the suicide attempt, these men produced long, emotion-laden, narratives although a few retained a degree of adherence to hegemonic masculinity norms in an attempt to portray strength in the face of adversity. These emotionally restrictive environments fostered the denial and suppression of normal emotions and resulted in significant, long-lasting, anguish for these men. They questioned the prevailing masculinity but in the context of surveillance and the absence of alternative models this form of masculinity became the basis of their gender identity and they experienced shame and isolation because they could not live up to its principles. There were men who felt trapped by the prevailing masculinity but were fearful of adopting alternative versions of manhood or the normative codes were so deeply embedded that accessing other gender identities was unimaginable. Men who personified an extreme, hard, version of masculinity also felt trapped in lives dominated by anger and violence which had frequently begun via early experiences of inadequate educational formats and escape into risk environments and behaviour. And throughout the narratives alcohol consumption was used to stave off feelings of sadness and desperation, to try to survive emotionally and socially.

These ideas about masculinity were instilled in childhood and fathers were key influencers in terms of the men's gender outlook. Almost all the participants grew up in a family environment where the normative expectations defined manhood in traditional, conventional, terms emphasising strength and restricting the expression of vulnerability. Fathers formed a central and iconic position in these men's lives and were usually their first and primary role models for masculinity. Fathers generally followed traditional masculinity codes and this linked them in a distinct way to their male children but worked against the development of emotional bonds between fathers and sons. The men wanted to be affirmed and cared for by their fathers but close relationships were rarely achieved between fathers and sons given the barriers to emotional engagement which prevailed. Relationships with fathers, both inside and outside the home, were frequently problematic and some were underpinned by paternal hostility and rejection. Father–son interaction emerged as a compelling theme in the study and underlines the significance of emotional engagement between fathers and sons (Lamb and Lewis 2010). It was the nature of the relationship between father and son, rather than the father's presence or absence from the home, that was critical. The imparting of conventional ideas about gender does not imply that a child's sense of self will be negatively affected. Young males are commonly exposed to similar gender regulations and survive this but these men faced particular family difficulties in childhood which made father–son relations especially difficult.

Many of the participants had experienced adversity and trauma in childhood which affected their social and emotional lives and continued to impact on them as adults. Violence, often related to alcoholism, featured in a number of the families and the men were victims of this plus other forms of maltreatment growing up. The men's narratives attest to the suffering they experienced as a result of this abuse but they were prevented from expressing this pain. They felt they could not speak about these issues within the family and the majority did not have an outlet to do so outside the home. These situations were especially difficult when the father was the perpetrator of the maltreatment. Unexpressed and unresolved childhood issues were therefore important in these men's lives and this operated in the context of the masculinity norms in place within the family. Males were expected to be tough and stoical and father–son relationships were rarely close and sometimes underpinned by anger and hostility. Nurturance and care was missing or withheld by fathers either because the father was unable or unwilling to care. The background story frequently appeared to be one of a father who had been inadequately nurtured or traumatised himself who was now unable to care for his own son, of fathers who sometimes passed on their own feelings of unhappiness and rejection to their sons. Hurt and pain, and the methods of dealing with these feelings, moved through generations of men in this study. The prevalence of paternal alcohol dependency, along with other clues in the men's narratives, imply cross-generational adherence to a model of masculinity which suppressed emotions and sometimes channelled distress via alcoholism and violence. The restrictive emotional culture in place in these homes and communities, and the barriers to engagement it gave rise to, was passed on from fathers to their sons. This was apparent in the way the men dealt with problems in their own lives despite the fact that they generally distanced themselves from the attitudes and the practices of the father. Yet, in the aftermath of the suicide attempt conventional masculinity practices were often disassembled and fathers demonstrated care and affection for their sons.

The pathway to suicide was generally long and protracted and did not fit the description of an impulsive act, a feature often ascribed to male suicide in the literature. There was prolonged distress, linked to concealment, and the movement towards suicide quickened as despair increased and they sought to end the misery and pain. In some cases, the suicide attempt was triggered by a specific event but if there was a precipitant it often had symbolic rather than causative relevance. While the decision to carry out the suicidal action at a particular moment was often spontaneous, thoughts of suicide and plans were in place for some time. The participants spoke of an opportunity presenting itself and of having the confidence to act at that particular moment. As these findings indicate, suicidal action is rarely the result of a single event or problem but represents a cluster of interlinked issues drawn out over a longer time period. The main reasons provided for the suicide attempt included generalised unhappiness and the ending of a relationship which have been implicated in other studies (Fincham et al. 2011; Knizek and Hjelmeland 2018). In this way, the issues which formed the background to the suicidal decisions were out of line with historical constructions of male suicide. These men were responding to loss and more fundamentally to a human need to form close emotionally meaningful relationships with others.

The men's determination to end their lives was apparent from their accounts but method did not always conform to the stereotypical gender pattern in that the majority of the men used techniques which are traditionally regarded as less lethal or as 'female' methods. Method and intent are difficult to disentangle but method is closely linked to availability and the so-called less harmful methods can represent serious intent and or a rehearsal for a future, fatal, action. While alcohol and drugs were employed over time to cope with distress alcohol was used at the endpoint to embolden oneself for the suicidal action. Psychiatric disorder, at a clinical level of severity, was implicated in a small number of cases. The men's reactions when they realised they were alive varied from regret to relief, findings which are reflected in similar work (O'Donnell et al. 1996). Knowledge of suicidal behaviour was widespread—from personal contact and in the neighbourhood as well as from the media and they were aware of a male predominance in suicide. The picture was one of drawing from an existing and widely available script around suicide.

When the participants were followed up seven years later, half of the men had made further suicide attempts and six of these men had completed suicide. When the remaining group of men were tracked fifteen years after the initial interview two further men had completed suicide in the interim period which confirms that risk continues for a considerable time (Gibb et al. 2005). The rate for repetition is comparable to other studies but the level of completion is higher than similar research investigations (Beautrais 2003, 2004). Those who made no further attempts tended to have more resources, for example, higher educational attainment and stable employment, than those who repeated and less negative features, such as alcohol dependency, in their lives. The motivating factors for the baseline suicide attempt also differed for the repeat and non-repeat groups. While long-term issues were implicated in most of the stories a triggering event or discrete situation was more likely to feature in the narratives of the non-repeat group. The fact that the precipitating event or situation was circumscribed in this way probably made it more amenable to resolution or at least for them to draw a boundary around it, as many of them did, and move on with their lives. The non-repeat group had experienced higher levels of adversity in childhood and while this had had a negative impact on their lives the issues involved were often quite specific and in some cases had been resolved, for example, a number of previously alcoholic fathers had ceased drinking. This group of men had backgrounds which made them especially vulnerable to loss and similar setbacks but they had relatively stable lives and comparatively good resources and supports. The suicide attempt also disrupted the intense anxiety which resulted from concealing these problems and family and friends generally provided good support in its aftermath.

The men who repeated, and especially those who completed suicide, tended to have problems that enveloped their lives more comprehensively but different patterns were evident within these categories. The group who repeated and survived was divided equally between those who made one subsequent attempt and those who had a pattern of repeat episodes. Those who had one repeat episode resembled the non-repeat group in many respects and the fact that the subsequent attempt was generally not as serious seemed to imply that these men required a longer adjustment time (or a particular type of therapeutic intervention) in dealing with the issues of their lives. The men who made a number of suicide attempts had quite a different profile and included men with a serious psychiatric illness. Despite the fact that this group are recognised as a high-risk category and in this study had very high rates of repetition, none of these men completed suicide. These participants, unlike the rest of the sample, had regular contact with the mental health services and this may have provided protection for this group.

Those who completed suicide, despite the relatively small number involved, were not a uniform category either and contained two quite distinct groupings. The larger category contained men who had problems which were extensive and serious in that violence was frequently involved. At the same time they had less resources, individual and otherwise, to address these problems. These issues were connected in that the men tended to have a personal history which featured an accumulation of negative features from an early age, starting with an early exit from school and increasing involvement in risk behaviour. At this point in their lives they were heavily dependent on alcohol, and violence was a common behaviour. They did have one ostensible resource in that they generally had strong connections to family. However, this finding underlines the problematic nature of using concepts such as the family and marriage as indicators of integration. The social attachment implied by family membership and marriage can contribute to wellbeing but may also cause significant unhappiness as this and other studies of suicide have indicated (Pearson and Liu 2002; Wu 2009). There were men who felt trapped in relationships but for other participants connection to family was a significant and positive feature in their lives. Yet, as time went on the shame and guilt associated their behaviour introduced an element of burden in terms of these relationships. Family connections were often the only meaningful connection in these men's lives and disapproval from this source mattered as did witnessing the obvious negative impact their behaviour was having on family members. Guilt and shame mixed with 'uncontrollable' anger and violence was a toxic psychological mix as their stories imply. These men adhered to an extreme, hard, form of masculinity and had always relied on a performance of strength in their lives but now this life had become unendurable and they displayed an intense form of hopelessness. With minimum experience of self-reflection and little confidence in treatment interventions they were unlikely to resurrect agency. In reality, they generally coped with rising levels of distress by intensifying their alcohol consumption and aggressive behaviour.

The lives of the men who completed suicide were significantly affected by alcohol dependency and it was apparent that feelings of hopelessness, in the context of alcohol misuse and risk behaviour, took on a particular potency as time passed and the potential for change receded. These participants were identifiable in terms of the severity and duration of negative factors and the despairing narratives which were especially intense among those who subsequently died by suicide. They felt their options had reduced, support systems had weakened and feelings of hopelessness, which is an important predictor of suicide

(Kuo et al. 2004), had become overwhelming. That hopelessness is a contributing factor to suicide is supported in this study, along with an understanding of how hopelessness is exacerbated by chronic alcohol misuse (Conner et al. 2003; Conner and Duberstein 2004). The life situations of these men had become unrelentingly bleak and they felt unable to action a way out of this situation. Agency was restricted as cycles of despair and habitual suicide attempts continued and they became locked into a cycle of despondency and self-destructive behaviour. In this context, a meaningful life had come to seem an impossible aspiration and ending their lives as an inevitable and possibly comforting prospect (Gaines 1998).

The second group of men who completed suicide had very different profiles and at surface level appeared to have relatively stable lives with good levels of support. Not living the life they desired was a theme shared by many of the men in this study but those who were able to envisage alternatives and had sufficient resources did relatively well following the suicide attempt. However resources included the confidence to go beyond the life they knew and not all were willing or able to do this. These issues featured in the lives of the remaining men who completed suicide. These men had resources and supports in their lives and none had a psychiatric condition but they were confined by conventional notions of masculinity to a more significant degree than many others. They found the normative masculinity extremely challenging and even suffocating but they felt unable to take on an alternative identity. They were opposed to therapy but in their case the resistance to therapy contained an added dimension in that they feared what therapy might uncover and or that it might force change. In circumstances of continuing concealment they were unlikely to address the issues which had given rise to the suicide attempt. While all the men in this study were constrained by the prevailing masculinity it can be tentatively suggested that the men who completed suicide were, albeit in very different ways, more extensively constricted by conventional forms of masculinity.

As this discussion implies those who complete suicide are not a homogenous population and those who repeat or make single attempts similarly differ from each other. Yet there are patterns within these groupings and this was also apparent in their attitudes to recovery.

A therapeutic intervention, having a space to explore the issues of their lives, would have helped all these men and it would probably have prevented a number of participants from completing suicide. This did not happen due to the men's unwillingness to engage in therapy as well as their antipathy to the therapies available. In their narratives the participants were able to identify problem areas and even vulnerabilities but the majority did not want to explore the issues which had created these vulnerabilities. They were particularly affected by relationship breakdown but few wanted to consider the wider implications of this. Engaging with one's emotional life in this way represented a type of masculinity they were unfamiliar with and in the aftermath of the suicide attempt only a minority of the participants availed of follow-up treatment (Cleary 2017). A number of men did opt for therapy and they were able to reconstruct their emotional lives and find more flexible places to enact masculinity and sexuality. Various elements of therapy probably contributed to this but a defining issue was the realisation that other men had similar problems, that they were not alone. This exposure to the reality of men's lives usually began in the psychiatric unit or hospital which was a place they generally sought to avoid. The majority of participants were opposed to 'talking' therapies but if they did engage it frequently resulted in a significant change in outlook and helped some men to construct a way out of an intractable problem or situation of unhappiness. This occurred for participants who had adamantly resisted such interventions in the past and implies that the challenge is connecting men to this assistance as well as the more general issue of the suitable of the interventions on offer.

These stories of suicide map out the important socioemotional issues of these men's lives. Those contemplating suicide are influenced by general attitudes to the practice within their society and by the gender connotations embedded in this societal script. Every suicide is different as it features a unique individual who experiences life in a distinct way but people draw on cultural, including gender, guidelines for these actions and this is true also of decisions relating to ending one's life. Why people decide to complete suicide is the culmination of a complex mix of individual and group factors which come together at a particular time and place. Historically, suicide has tended to be constructed as a masculine practice which implied strength and courage and remnants of these ideas were evident in these men's stories and presentations. Conventional or hegemonic masculinity norms created a particular socioemotional environment which denied these men a space to express normal emotions, to talk about pain, and they grew into adulthood without a language of, nor a space to express, suffering. Resolving problems was especially challenging in this environment. More generally, the normative masculinity set out unattainable social and emotional objectives for these men and when they faltered in these goals they were denounced and their dissent silenced. Alternative forms of manhood were invisible or existed in other, inaccessible, environments and in this context they were convinced that they were deficient and incompetent men which underlines the strength of the prevailing masculinity ideology.

The narratives and scenarios presented in this study are contrary to gendered or stereotypic views about men and emotions as well as suicidal behaviour. The participants were individuals with painful memories and limited opportunities to address these issues within their families or social networks and as they grew this distress became more embedded and affected their ability to cope with problems. Contrary to conventional gender ideas they channelled painful emotions internally and much less frequently in external ways via aggression and violence. They wanted to speak about their distress but felt they could not do so and this separated them from their male peers in that they were convinced that other men lived happy, contented, lives. Emotions and emotional needs featured significantly in their lives. They sought emotionally responsive relationships with fathers and care from partners and experienced intense feelings of sadness when this was denied or lost.

Masculinity is diverse and fluid and hegemonic masculinity may be a diffuse and possibly waning concept yet elements of this form of manhood were identifiable among the men in this study. This does not imply that hegemonic masculinity is a consistent or uncontested concept but masculinities of various kinds can attain relative stability in some social contexts (Connell 2002). The participants were usually aware that these masculinity norms were discretionary but they exercised strong control over their behaviour because they feared the implications of discarding these conventions. In general, these men were performing hegemonic-type masculinity rather than conforming to hegemonic ideals. There were also structural constraints which worked alongside the cultural barriers in these men's lives in that they did not have the resources to go beyond these restrictions and find another socioemotional and gender space. Education, which can operate as a positive, moderating, feature in these circumstances did not, in general, deliver for these men. Higher levels of wealth and education open up channels of knowledge, and access to various forms of social and emotional capital (Baudelot and Establet 2008) but these men did not have easy access to these forms of capital. Middle-class males are not immune to the kind of distress described here but, in relation to suicide, they tend to inhabit less risky environments than the men in this study (Helliwell 2007).

These stories are presented as narratives around suicide which relate more crucially to social and cultural factors than to psychiatric disorder. The backdrop to suicidal behaviour is its popular currency and knowledge of suicidal behaviour is now widespread. Suicidal behaviour is linked to socioeconomic factors as well as to cultural, specifically gender, expectations and a socioemotional explanation is required to explain the links between these features. Young men who lack socioeconomic and emotional flexibility and who are constrained by models of masculinity that inhibit the expression of distress are more likely to write this pain on the body. Yet, even within gender restrictive environments, people differ in how they deal with challenges and emotional difficulties and the outlets which are available to them vary. Many young people experience similar life events but do not move towards suicide but the emotional and social restrictions these men experienced occurred in the context of other, more prolonged, challenges and this was key to understanding the depth and persistence of their distress. In this situation, relatively common difficulties were transformed into a basis for ending one's life. These men therefore represent a particular group of men who did not find adequate respite from their suffering but they are certainly not an unusual group of men. In this study it is possible to see what began as normal, albeit uncomfortable, emotions, channelled in negative ways due to a lack of recognition, disclosure and intervention. In this way, not all men are vulnerable to suicide, nor are all men from low socioeconomic environments. Men can, and do, share their problems with others and seek help and men can provide comprehensive accounts of their emotional lives, as this research illustrates. There was no evidence in this inquiry of innate or male-specific emotions or of particular male vulnerabilities but there were cultural restrictions relating to the expression of feelings for men. The study demonstrates an uneven landscape in relation to emotions, that the expression of emotions is not equally fluid throughout society. There are environments where emotions are constrained for men and this containment of emotion is unhealthy and can have lethal effects for some men. In this way suicide may represent the externalised cost to particular societies of the repression of normal emotions, the non-acknowledgement of a human need (Hochschild 2010).

References

Abrutyn, S., & Mueller, A. S. (2014). The socioemotional foundations of suicide: A microsociological view of Durkheim's suicide. *Sociological Theory, 32*(4), 327–351.

Addis, M. E., & Mahalik, J. R. (2003). Men, masculinity, and the contexts of help seeking. *American Psychologist, 58*(1), 5–14.

Baudelot, C., & Establet, R. (2008). *Suicide: The hidden side of modernity.* Cambridge: Polity Press.

Beautrais, A. L. (2003). Subsequent mortality in medically serious suicide attempts: A 5 year follow-up. *Australian and New Zealand Journal of Psychiatry, 37,* 595–599.

Beautrais, A. L. (2004). Further suicidal behaviour among medically serious suicide attempters. *Suicide and Life Threatening Behaviour, 34*(1), 1–11.

Butler, J. (2004). *Undoing gender.* New York and London: Routledge.

Cleary, A. (2017). Help-seeking patterns and attitudes to treatment amongst men who attempted suicide. *Journal of Mental Health, 26*(3), 220–224.

Connell, R. W. (2002). *Gender: Short introduction.* Cambridge: Polity Press.

Conner, K. R., Beautrais, A. L., & Conwell, Y. (2003). Risk factors for suicide and medically serious suicide attempts among alcoholics: An analysis of Canterbury Suicide Project data. *Journal of Studies on Alcohol, 64*(4), 551–554.

Conner, K. R., & Duberstein, P. R. (2004). Predisposing and precipitating factors for suicide among alcoholics: Empirical review and conceptual integration. *Alcoholism, Clinical and Experimental Research, 28*(5 Supplement), 6S–17S.

Douglas, J. D. (1967). *The social meanings of suicide*. Princeton, NJ: Princeton University Press.

Durkheim, E. (1951). *Suicide: A study in sociology* (R. Spaulding, Trans.). London: Routledge & Kegan Paul.

Fincham, B., Langer, S., Scourfield, J., et al. (2011). *Understanding suicide: A sociological autopsy*. Basingstoke: Palgrave Macmillan.

Gaines, D. (1998). *Teenage wasteland: Suburbia's dead end kid*. Chicago: University of Chicago Press.

Gibb, S. J., Beautrais, A. L., & Fergusson, D. M. (2005). Mortality and further suicidal behaviour after an index suicide attempt: A 10-year study. *Australian and New Zealand Journal of Psychiatry, 39*(1–2), 95–100.

Hamdi, E., Price, S., Qassem, T., et al. (2008). Suicides not in contact with mental health services: Risk indicators and determinants of referral. *Journal of Mental Health, 17*(4), 398–409.

Helliwell, J. F. (2007). Well-being and social capital: Does suicide pose a puzzle? *Social Indicators Research, 81*, 455–496.

Hochschild, A. R. (1979). Emotion work, feeling rules, and social structure. *American Journal of Sociology, 85*, 551–575.

Hochschild, A. R. (2010). *Personal communication*.

Kemper, T. D. (1981). Social constructivist and positivist approaches to the sociology of emotions. *American Journal of Sociology, 87*, 336–361.

Knizek, B. L., & Hjelmeland, H. (2018). To die or not to die: A qualitative study of men's suicidality in Norway. *BMC Psychiatry, 18*, 263. https://doi.org/10.1186/s12888-018-1843-3.

Kuo, W., Gallo, J. J., & Eaton, W. W. (2004). Hopelessness, depression, substance disorder, and suicidality: A 13-year community-based study. *Social Psychiatry and Psychiatric Epidemiology, 39*, 497–501.

Lamb, M. E. & Lewis, C. (2010). The development and significance of father-child relationships in two-parent families. In M. E. Lamb (Ed.), *The role of the father in child development* (4th ed.). New York: Wiley.

Lorent, V., Kunst, A. E., Huisman, M., et al. (2005). Socio-economic inequalities in suicide: A European comparative study. *British Journal of Psychiatry, 187*, 49–54.

O'Donnell, I., Farmer, R., & Catalán, J. (1993). Suicide notes. *British Journal of Psychiatry, 163,* 45–48.

O'Donnell, I., Falmer, R., & Catalán, J. (1996). Explaining suicide: The views of survivors of serious suicide attempts. *British Journal of Psychiatry, 168,* 780–786.

Owens, C., Booth, N., & Briscoe, M. (2003). Suicide outside the care of mental health services: A case-controlled psychological autopsy study. *Crisis: The Journal of Crisis Intervention and Suicide Prevention, 24*(3), 113–121.

Pearson, V., & Liu, M. (2002). Ling's death: An ethnography of a Chinese women's suicide. *Suicide and Life-Threatening Behaviour, 32*(4), 347–358.

Redley, M. (2003). Towards a new perspective on deliberate self-harm in an area of multiple deprivation. *Sociology of Health & Illness, 25*(4), 348–373.

River, J. (2018). Diverse and dynamic interactions: A model of suicidal men's help seeking as it relates to health services. *American Journal of Men's Health, 12*(1), 150–159.

Shields, S. A. (2007). Passionate men, emotional women: Psychology constructs gender in the late 19th century. *History of Psychology, 10*(2), 92–110.

Thorne, B. (1993). *Gender play: Girls and boys in school.* New Brunswick, NJ: Rutgers University Press.

Wray, M., Colen, C., & Pescosolido, B. (2011). The sociology of suicide. *Annual Review of Sociology, 37,* 505–528.

Wu, F. (2009). *Suicide and justice: A Chinese perspective.* Contemporary China Series. New York: Routledge.

7

Postscript: Lessons for Prevention

Suicidal behaviour is more generally a social phenomenon, a view supported by this and other research. Suicide has many variations and manifestations at individual level including mental disorder but at group level it is more about social than psychiatric factors. One's identity and what gives meaning to one's life is constructed in a sociocultural context and suicide can occur when life has ceased to be meaningful in these terms. Suicide remains a very unique, infrequent and individual action and this has sometimes led to a view that identifying the wide variety of potential risk is an impossible task and not cost effective. Yet, as this relatively small study demonstrates, patterns can be identified which connect to particular groups with specific prevention and intervention needs. These trends are evident because as social beings we connect and share ideas with others in our community and this is true also in relation to decisions around suicidal action. Cultural and subcultural narratives, which have gender and other components, influence who will move towards, and how they will enact, suicidal action. Accepting the primarily social basis to suicide is key to understanding the phenomenon and over-medicalised perceptions of suicide may impede understanding and prevention (Gavin and Rogers 2006). This and

A. Cleary, *The Gendered Landscape of Suicide*,
https://doi.org/10.1007/978-3-030-16634-2_7

other research indicates multiple populations and diverse levels of risk which are unlikely to be reached via conventional services (Hamdi et al. 2008). While this implies a broad span of risk it also suggests a variety of prevention and intervention possibilities. Probably more than any other health issue, suicide prevention should involve community participation and better outcomes are likely to be achieved by a co-ordinated, multilevel approach which combines Public Health campaigns with customised treatment programmes alongside community interventions.

Suicide is not a sudden impulsive action but, as this study indicates, is a relatively long, well-thought-out, process although there can be a rapid build-up to action. Impulsivity should not be inferred from the apparent suddenness of the action and causation cannot be assumed to relate only to events which occur prior to a suicide. The processing period involved in suicide is taken up with contemplating suicide and weighing the various possibilities and when suicide begins to take precedence over other options, developing a plan that gives reality to these thoughts. This knowledge about the progression of suicidal action presents opportunities for specific strategies and interventions to address the various phases.

Gender has been an enduring theme in suicide research but requires more accurate consideration and application to benefit prevention and intervention strategies. At present gender is operationalised in Public Health messages and service environments in very broad and somewhat simplistic ways. Men are not a unitary group and male groupings vary greatly in terms of resources and in their attitudes to health and importantly, in terms of their risk for suicide. The prevailing idea that all men are susceptible to suicide is inaccurate, wasteful of resources and a notion best omitted from Public Health discourse. Men can be proactive about their mental health and engage in therapy when required but some groups of men are challenged by these issues. The way people deal with matters relating to health and wellbeing is shaped by the cultural and socioeconomic environment they live in and this will influence whether a man seeks help when in distress as well as the form of his presentation. In some communities, disclosing problems infringes prevailing masculinity norms and men are reluctant to speak about problems and may adopt maladaptive coping methods. Men adhere to these masculinity beliefs with varying degrees of conviction but in this study adherence to these values was associated with ongoing suffering and movement towards suicidal action. Men in some communities therefore may experience restrictions in terms of expressing and reporting problems and this knowledge should inform health strategies and services. One of the principal messages of this research relates to the ability and freedom to speak about one's feelings and find an adequate response and the health services can help to facilitate this. However, this requires customised messages for specific male groups rather than targeting all men. Health-related initiatives which aim to encourage help-seeking need to be grounded in local knowledge and use local influencers. Campaigns and programmes which appeal to men in these communities to abandon particular masculinity beliefs and practices are unlikely to be effective without this local knowledge and input.

The extensive narratives provided by the participants in this study confirm the range and depth of men's emotions as well their competency in describing their feelings. Participants also engaged in therapy and a therapeutic intervention had a transformative impact on some individuals in this study and prevented as least one man from completing suicide. Mental Health Service support also provided protection to those with serious mental disorder, a group generally recognised as a high-risk category in terms of completing suicide. However, connecting men to treatment, as this study also implies, is not an easy task and even a seemingly cathartic event such as a near-fatal suicide attempt did not induce the majority of the participants to engage in longer-term treatment despite its potential benefits. They were however more inclined to take up treatment when there was personal contact or follow-up by staff, a point noted in other research (Jordan et al. 2012).

The accessibility of the mental health services to men has been questioned in several studies and various solutions advanced. Many of these proposals have focused on modifying existing services to make them more attractive for men but more comprehensive changes, including masculinity-specific strategies and programmes, have also been advocated (Primack et al. 2010; Seidler et al. 2017). According to Seidler et al. (2017) existing initiatives targeting men's health are ill-defined and not grounded in empirical knowledge and the lack of evaluation means that their usefulness remains context-specific (Seidler et al. 2017). Having an effective blueprint for men's health, which is grounded more realistically in men's experiences and reflects the diversity of men's lives, would, they suggest, assist the various levels of the health services from policymakers to service providers.

Primary care services represent a critical setting for reaching at-risk men and moving them towards an intervention. A significant number of men who are contemplating suicide do not present to the services beforehand but if they do they are more likely to attend a General Practitioner who are not necessarily skilled in identifying suicidal ideation in men (Lemieux et al. 2014). This may be due to a dependence on standardised risk assessments which probably have limited efficacy in relation to the wide span of risk which presents in these settings (Knizek and Hjelmeland 2018). Men who are at risk do not always fit with identifiable suicide risk indicators and stereotypic views relating to men and their emotions could also be screening out vulnerable subjects. If health care workers are to respond effectively to men's accounts of their difficulties, they should resist conventional gender and other categorisations (Schwab et al. 2016). Some men may continue to obscure their suffering or make inadvertent appeals for help, as they did in this study, and health professionals need to be alert to this. Frontline hospital staff need to be more knowledgeable about, and sensitive to, the spectrum of suicidal behaviour (Farrelly et al. 2015; Hadfield et al. 2009). Those who work in Accident and Emergency Departments are in a critical setting in relation to suicide risk and they need training in identifying less obvious forms of risk. Men are increasingly likely to self-harm, they are not a typical men, and this practice is an important marker for completing suicide (Griffin et al. 2018).

This research has identified a number of subgroups which require specific attention in terms of prevention and intervention. A large category in this study were men who were affected by problems concerning relationships and their vulnerability had emerged from long-term issues and was exacerbated by concealment of distress. This category of men, who made only one suicide attempt, could be targeted via Public Health messages about wellbeing which are gender and culture sensitive as well as by local, customised, programmes of intervention. Particular vulnerabilities exist for men around relationships which may entail focused programmes (Scourfield and Evans 2014) and there are prevention needs relating to specific groups and critical risk periods, for example, those with LGBT identities require special focus in adolescence and young adulthood (Russell and Toomey 2012). Those who repeat suicide include those with long-term mental disorder and this group appear to be receiving relatively good support from the existing services. Another category within the repeat group are men who need a specific, concentrated, intervention to halt repetition before it becomes a longstanding pattern. The remaining group amongst the repeaters contained the most at-risk men in terms of completing suicide and vulnerability was importantly related to substance misuse, specifically alcohol dependency, which is known to increase risk for suicide (Conner and Duberstein 2004). Finding suitable treatment interventions for some of the men who died would have been challenging because of the duration and diversity of their problems and effective treatment interventions need to be directed at men in the early stages of alcohol dependency.

Individual narratives tell us what is wrong with personal lives but combined they indicate what is important within and across society. Socioeconomic factors are importantly related to suicide and risk is associated with low levels of economic and social capital. Lack of economic and social resources impede life chances in a material way and also impact negatively on one's identity (Baudelot and Establet 2008) and while these matters are challenging to resolve they cannot be ignored. The findings of this and other studies imply that limited resources and restricted access to alternative lifestyles and ideas increases the chance of moving towards suicide. The ability to access other gender spaces and ideas would have prevented some of the men in this study from attempting suicide but this was not a feasible option for the majority. They lacked financial resources and many had experienced an educational system which had failed to cater adequately for their needs. Those who were academically able were not facilitated in accessing third level and those with educational challenges were easily lost to the system. The evidence in relation to bullying was disturbing and indicates that the educational system has an important role to play in extending ideas about masculinity.

Building a positive sense of identity requires affirmation of self and having structures and resources which support this. Many of the men in this study were denied this within their families and within the school system. Rather than one system acting to ameliorate deficits in the other some participants had to contend with challenges in both settings. Families and particularly fathers are another broad but significant link in the chain of prevention. Adversity in childhood does not necessarily lead to suicidal behaviour but if children have no respite from suffering and have to deny and suppress the emotions connected with this pain it is likely to have a negative outcome in terms of wellbeing. This study points to the benefits of close, nurturing, relationships between fathers and sons and the negative impact of paternal indifference and rejection. Fathers who emotionally engage with and affirm their children enhance their wellbeing (Lamb and Lewis 2010). Fathers who endorse masculinity discourses which foster suppression of emotional needs are unlikely to contribute positively to their sons' health. A notable aspect of this research was the way in which unhappiness and maladaptive methods of dealing with emotional pain moved through the male line in families. In this way the benefits of emotionally engaged fatherhood need wider attention and Public Health campaigns which incorporate fathers speaking about these issues could be a way of starting a public conversation about the matter. Local influencers could also make a significant contribution to this discussion.

Public education is also required which helps family, friends and community recognise warning signals of distress. Men experience difficulty in reporting distress but also in having their difficulties recognised by family and friends (Sweeney et al. 2015). A Public Health campaign directed at specific groups and settings, for example secondary-level school pupils and workplaces, would increase lay knowledge of suicide and alert people to signals of vulnerability. The media can be a very positive force in terms of prevention when reporting operates according to guidelines and avoids providing insensitive or gendered information about suicide (Coyle and MacWhammell 2002; Gould et al. 2003). The linking of suicide to all men as a singular group may influence men who don't see a future and feel they have few options. As these comments imply there is a task for policymakers to rethink the issue of men's mental health and wellbeing and for the Health Services to provide treatment interventions which represent the reality and variety of masculinity practices within our society. And, as the issue of suicide and its prevention extends beyond these arenas, giving men hope remains a broad but compelling challenge for society generally.

References

Baudelot, C., & Establet, R. (2008). *Suicide: The hidden side of modernity*. Cambridge: Polity Press.

Conner, K. R., & Duberstein, P. R. (2004). Predisposing and precipitating factors for suicide among alcoholics: Empirical review and conceptual integration. *Alcoholism, Clinical and Experimental Research, 28*(5 Supplement), 6S–17S.

Coyle, J., & MacWhannell, D. (2002). The importance of 'morality' in the social construction of suicide in Scottish newspapers. *Sociology of Health & Illness, 24*(6), 689–713.

Farrelly, S., Jeffery, D., Rüsch, N., Williams, P., Thornicroft, G., Clement, S., et al. (2015). The link between mental health-related discrimination and suicidality: Service user perspectives. *Psychological Medicine, 45*, 2013–2022.

Gavin, G., & Rogers, A. (2006). Narratives of suicide in psychological autopsy: Bringing lay knowledge back in. *Journal of Mental Health, 15*(2), 135–144.

Gould, M., Jamieson, P., & Romer, D. (2003). Media contagion and suicide among the young. *American Behavioral Scientist, 46*(9), 1269–1284.

Griffin, E., Dillon, C. B., McTernan, N., Arensman, E., Williamson, E., Perry, I. J., et al. (2018). *National self-harm registry Ireland annual report 2017*. Cork: National Suicide Research Foundation.

Hadfield, J., Brown, D., Pembroke, L., & Hayward, M. (2009). Analysis of accident and emergency doctors' responses to treating people who self-harm. *Qualitative Health Research, 19*(6), 755–765.

Hamdi, E., Price, S., Qassem, T., Amin, Y., & Jones, D. (2008). Suicides not in contact with mental health services: Risk indicators and determinants of referral. *Journal of Mental Health, 17*(4), 398–409.

Jordan, J., McKenna, H., Keeney, S., Cutcliffe, J., Stevenson, C., Slater, P., et al. (2012). Providing meaningful care: Learning from the experiences of suicidal young men. *Qualitative Health Research, 22*(9), 1207–1219.

Knizek, B. L., & Hjelmeland, H. (2018). To die or not to die: A qualitative study of men's suicidality in Norway. *BMC Psychiatry, 18,* 263. https://doi.org/10.1186/s12888-018-1843-3.

Lamb, M. E., & Lewis, C. (2010). The development and significance of father-child relationships in two-parent families. In M. E. Lamb (Ed.), *The role of the father in child development* (4th ed.). New York: Wiley.

Lemieux, A. M., Saman, D. M., & Lutfiyya, M. N. (2014). Men and suicide in primary care. *Disease-a-Month, 60,* 155–161.

Primack, J. M., Addis, M. E., Sydek, M., & Milleer, I. W. (2010). The men's stress workshop: A gender-sensitive treatment for depressed men. *Cognitive and Behavioural Practice, 17*(1), 77–87.

Russell, S. T., & Toomey, R. B. (2012). Men's sexual orientation and suicide: Evidence for US adolescent-specific risk. *Social Science and Medicine, 74*(4), 523–529.

Schwab, J. R., Addis, M. E., Reigeluth, C. S., & Berger, J. L. (2016). Silence and (in)visibility in men's accounts of coping with stressful life events. *Gender and Society, 30*(2), 289–311.

Scourfield, J., & Evans, R. (2014). Why might men be more at risk of suicide after a relationship breakdown? Sociological insights. *American Journal of Men's Health, 9*(5), 380–384.

Seidler, Z. E., Rice, S. M., & River, J. (2017). Men's mental health services: The care for a masculinities model. *The Journal of Men's Studies, 26*(1), 92–104.

Sweeney, L., Owens, C., & Malone, K. (2015). Communication and interpretation of emotional distress within the friendships of young Irish men prior to suicide: A qualitative study. *Health and Social Care in the Community, 23*(2), 150–158.

References

Abrutyn, S., & Mueller, A. S. (2014). The socioemotional foundations of suicide: A microsociological view of Durkheim's suicide. *Sociological Theory, 32*(4), 327–351.

Addis, M. E., & Mahalik, J. R. (2003). Men, masculinity, and the contexts of help seeking. *American Psychologist, 58*(1), 5–14.

Afifi, T. O., Boman, J., Fleisher, W., & Sareen, J. (2009). The relationship between child abuse, parental divorce, and lifetime mental disorders and suicidality in a nationally representative adult sample. *Child Abuse & Neglect, 33*(3), 139–147.

Andriolo, K. R. (1998). Gender and the cultural construction of good and bad suicides. *Suicide and Life Threatening Behaviour, 28*(1), 37–49.

Atkinson, J. M. (1978). *Discovering suicide*. London and Basingtoke: Macmillan.

Atkinson, M. (2011). *Deconstructing men and masculinities*. London: Oxford University Press.

Baechler, J. (1979). *Suicides* (B. Cooper, Trans.). New York: Basic Books.

Baudelot, C., & Establet, R. (2008). *Suicide: The hidden side of modernity*. Cambridge: Polity Press.

Beautrais, A. L. (2003). Subsequent mortality in medically serious suicide attempts: A 5 year follow-up. *Australian and New Zealand Journal of Psychiatry, 37*(5), 595–599.

A. Cleary, *The Gendered Landscape of Suicide*,
https://doi.org/10.1007/978-3-030-16634-2

Beautrais, A. L. (2004). Further suicidal behaviour among medically serious suicide attempters. *Suicide and Life Threatening Behaviour, 34*(1), 1–11.

Booth, A., Scott, M. E., & King, V. (2010). Father residence and adolescent problem behaviour: Are youth always better off in two-parent families? *Journal of Family Issues, 31*(5), 585–605.

Bourdieu, P. (1998). *Practical reason: On the theory of action*. Stanford, CA: Stanford University Press.

Bronte-Tinkew, J., Moore, K. A., & Carrano, J. (2006). The father-child relationship, parenting styles, and adolescent risk behaviours in intact families. *Journal of Family Issues, 27*(6), 850–881.

Brownhill, S., Wilhelm, K., Barclay, L., & Schmied, V. (2005). Big build: Hidden depression in men. *Australian and New Zealand Journal of Psychiatry, 39*(10), 921–931.

Butler, J. (2004). *Undoing gender*. New York and London: Routledge.

Byng, R., Howerton, A., Owens, C. V., & Campbell, J. (2015). Pathways to suicide attempts among male offenders: The role of agency. *Sociology of Health & Illness, 37*(6), 936–951.

Canetto, S. S. (1992). She died for love and he for glory: Gender myths of suicidal behaviour. *Omega, 26*(1), 1–17.

Canetto, S. S. (1997). Meanings of gender and suicidal behaviour during adolescence. *Suicide and Life-Threatening Behaviour, 27*(4), 339–351.

Cavan, R. S. (1965). *Suicide*. New York: Russell and Russell.

Chandler, M. J., & Lalonde, C. E. (1998). Cultural continuity as a hedge against suicide in Canada's First Nations. *Transcultural Psychiatry, 35*(2), 193–211.

Clancy, P., & Wall, J. (2000). *Social background of higher education entrants*. Dublin: Higher Education Authority.

Cleary, A. (2012). Suicidal action, emotional expression, and the performance of masculinities. *Social Science & Medicine, 74*(4), 498–505.

Cleary, A. (2017). Help-seeking patterns and attitudes to treatment amongst men who attempted suicide. *Journal of Mental Health, 26*(3), 220–224.

Cleary, A., Feeney, M., & Macken-Walsh, A. (2012). Pain and distress in rural Ireland: A qualitative study of suicidal behaviour among men in rural areas. *Teagasc* (Agriculture and Food Authority).

Cochrane, S. V., & Rabinowitz, F. E. (2000). *Men and depression*. San Diego: Academic.

Connell, R. W. (1995). *Masculinities*. Berkeley: University of California Press.

Connell, R. W. (2002). *Gender: Short introduction*. Cambridge: Polity Press.

Connell, R. W., & Messerschmidt, J. W. (2005). Hegemonic masculinity: Rethinking the concept. *Gender & Society, 19*(6), 829–859.

Conner, K. R., Beautrais, A. L., & Conwell, Y. (2003). Risk factors for suicide and medically serious suicide attempts among alcoholics: An analysis of Canterbury Suicide Project data. *Journal of Studies on Alcohol, 64*(4), 551–554.

Conner, K. R., & Duberstein, P. R. (2004). Predisposing and precipitating factors for suicide among alcoholics: Empirical review and conceptual integration. *Alcoholism: Clinical and Experimental Research, 28*(5 Supplement), 6S–17S.

Counts, D. S. (1991). Suicide in different ages from a cross-cultural perspective. In A. A. Leenaars (Ed.), *Life-span perspectives on suicide*. Boston, MA: Springer.

Courtenay, W. H. (2000). Constructions of masculinity and their influence on men's well-being: A theory of gender and health. *Social Science & Medicine, 50*(10), 1385–1401.

Coyle, J., & MacWhannell, D. (2002). The importance of 'morality' in the social construction of suicide in Scottish newspapers. *Sociology of Health and Illness, 24*(6), 689–713.

Dognin, J. S., & Chen, C. K. (2018). The secret sorrows of men: Impact of dynamic interpersonal therapy on 'masculine depression'. *Psychoanalytic Psychotherapy, 32*(2), 181–196.

Douglas, J. D. (1967). *The social meanings of suicide*. Princeton, NJ: Princeton University Press.

Dube, S. R., Anda, R.F., Felitte, V. J., Chapman, D. P., Williamson, D. F., & Giles, W. H. (2001). Childhood abuse, household dysfunction, and the risk of attempted suicide throughout the life span: Findings from the Adverse Childhood Experiences Study. *JAMA, 286*(24), 3089–3096.

Durkheim, E. (1951). Suicide: A study in sociology (R. Spaulding, Trans.). London: Routledge and Kegan Paul.

Elias, N. (1939). *The civilising process: Sociogenetic and psychogenetic investigations*. Oxford: Blackwell.

Emslie, C., Ridge, D., Ziebland, S., & Hunt, K. (2007). Exploring men's and women's experiences of depression and engagement with health professionals: More similarities than differences? A qualitative interview study. *BioMed Central Family Practice, 8*(1), 43.

Enns, M. W., Cox, B. J., Afifi, T. O., De Graaf, R., Ten Have, M., & Sareen, J. (2006). Childhood adversities and risk for suicidal ideation and attempts: A longitudinal population-based study. *Psychological Medicine, 36*(12), 1769–1778.

Farrelly, S., Jeffery, D., Rusch, N., Williams, P., Thornicroft, G., & Clement, S. (2015). The link between mental health-related discrimination and suicidality: Service user perspectives. *Psychological Medicine, 45*(10), 2013–2022.

Fergusson, D. M., Woodward, L. J., & Horwood, L. J. (2000). Risk factors and life processes associated with the onset of suicidal behaviour during adolescence and early adulthood. *Psychological Medicine, 30*(1), 23–39.

Fincham, B., Langer, S., Scourfield, J., & Shiner, M. (2011). *Understanding suicide: A sociological autopsy*. Houndmills and Basingstoke: Palgrave Macmillan.

Firestone, R. W. (1986). The "inner voice" and suicide. *Psychotherapy, 23*(3), 439–447.

Frank, A. (1996). Reconciliatory alchemy: Bodies, narrative and power. *Body & Society, 2*(3), 53–71.

Gaines, D. (1991). *Teenage wasteland: Suburbia's dead end kid*. Chicago: University of Chicago Press.

Gavin, G., & Rogers, A. (2006). Narratives of suicide in psychological autopsy: Bringing lay knowledge back in. *Journal of Mental Health, 15*(2), 135–144.

Gibb, S. J., Beautrais, A. L., & Fergusson, D. M. (2005). Mortality and further suicidal behaviour after an index suicide attempt: A 10-year study. *Australian and New Zealand Journal of Psychiatry, 39*(1–2), 95–100.

Goffman, E. (1968). *Asylums*. Harmondsworth: Penguin Books.

Gould, M., Jamieson, P., & Romer, D. (2003). Media contagion and suicide among the young. *American Behavioral Scientist, 46*(9), 1269–1284.

Griffin, E., Dillon, C. B., McTernan, N., Arensman, E., Williamson, E., Perry, I. J., et al. (2018). *National self-Harm registry Ireland annual report 2017*. Cork: National Suicide Research Foundation.

Hadfield, J., Brown, D., Pembroke, L., & Hayward, M. (2009). Analysis of accident and emergency doctors' responses to treating people who self-harm. *Qualitative Health Research, 19*(6), 755–765.

Hamdi, E., Price, S., Qassem, T., Amin, Y., & Jones, D. (2008). Suicides not in contact with mental health services: Risk indicators and determinants of referral. *Journal of Mental Health, 17*(4), 398–409.

Hanlon, N. (2009). Caregiving masculinities: An exploratory analysis. In K. Lynch, J. Baker, & M. Lyons (Eds.), *Affective equality: Love, care, and injustice* (pp. 180–198). London: Palgrave Macmillan.

Hawton, K., & van Heeringen, K. (2009). Suicide. *The Lancet, 373*(9672), 1372–1381.

Hawton, K., Zahl, D., & Weatherall, R. (2003). Suicide following deliberate self-harm: Long-term follow-up of patients who presented to a general hospital. *British Journal of Psychiatry, 182*(6), 537–542.

Helliwell, J. F. (2007). Well-being and social capital: Does suicide pose a puzzle? *Social Indicators Research, 81*(3), 455–496.

Hochschild, A. R. (1979). Emotion work, feeling rules, and social structure. *American Journal of Sociology, 85*(3), 551–575.

Hochschild, A. R. (2010). *Personal communication.*

Hochschild, A. R. (2012). *The managed heart: The commercialisation of human feeling*. Berkeley: University of California Press.

Holmes, M. (2015). Men's emotions: Heteromasculinity, emotional reflexivity, and intimate relationships. *Men and Masculinities, 18*(2), 176–192.

Hume, M., & Platt, S. (2007). Appropriate interventions for the prevention and management of self-harm: A qualitative exploration of service-users views. *BMC Public Health, 7*(1), 9.

Inckle, K. (2014). Strong and silent: Men, masculinity, and self-injury. *Men and Masculinities, 17*(1), 3–21.

Jacobs, J. (1967). A phenomenological study of suicide notes. *Social Problems, 15*(1), 60–70.

Jefferson, T. (2002). Subordinating hegemonic masculinity. *Theoretical Criminology, 6*(1), 63–88.

Joe, S., & Kaplan, M. S. (2001). Suicide among African American men. *Suicide and Life Threatening Behaviour, 31*(Supplement 1) (Spring), 106–121.

Johnson, J. G., Cohen, P., Gould, M. S., Kasen, S., Brown, J., & Brook, J. S. (2002). Childhood adversities, interpersonal difficulties and risk for suicide attempts during late adolescence and early adulthood. *Archives of General Psychiatry, 59*(8), 741–749.

Jordan, J., McKenna, H., Keeney, S., Cutcliffe, J., Stevenson, C., Slater, P., et al. (2012). Providing meaningful care: Learning from the experiences of suicidal young men. *Qualitative Health Research, 22*(9), 1207–1219.

Kemper, T. D. (1981). Social constructivist and positivist approaches to the sociology of emotions. *American Journal of Sociology, 87,* 336–361.

Kimmel, M. (1994). Masculinity as homophobia. In H. Brod & M. Kaufman (Eds.), *Theorising masculinities* (pp. 119–141). London: Sage.

Knizek, B. L., & Hjelmeland, H. (2018). To die or not to die: A qualitative study of men's suicidality in Norway. *BMC Psychiatry, 18*(1), 263. https://doi.org/10.1186/s12888-018-1843-3.

Kuo, W., Gallo, J. J., & Eaton, W. W. (2004). Hopelessness, depression, substance disorder, and suicidality: A 13-year community-based study. *Social Psychiatry and Psychiatric Epidemiology, 39*(6), 497–501.

Kushner, H. I. (1995). Women and suicidal behavior: Epidemiology, gender and lethality in historical perspective. In S. S. Canetto & D. Lester (Eds.), *Women and suicidal behavior.* New York: Springer.

Lamb, M. E. (2010). *The role of the father in child development.* Hoboken, NJ: Wiley.

Lamb, M. E., & Lewis, C. (2010). The development and significance of father-child relationships in two-parent families. In M. E. Lamb (Ed.), *The role of the father in child development* (4th ed.). New York: Wiley.

Lee, S. (2000, September 9). *Suicide in China—International patterns* (BMJ letter).

Lemieux, A. M., Saman, D. M., & Lutfiyya, M. N. (2014). Men and suicide in primary care. *Disease-a-Month, 60*(4), 155–161.

Lester, D. (1988). Youth suicide: A cross-cultural perspective. *Adolescence, 22*(92), 955–958.

Lorent, V., Kunst, A. E., Huisman, M., Costa, G., & Mackenbach, J. (2005). Socio-economic inequalities in suicide: A European comparative study. *British Journal of Psychiatry, 187,* 49–54.

Loukas, A., Fitzgerald, H. E., Zucker, R. A., & von Eye, A. (2001). Parental alcoholism and co-occurring antisocial behavior: Prospective relationships to externalizing behavior problems in their young sons. *Journal of Abnormal Child Pschology, 29*(2), 91–106.

MacDonald, M., & Murphy, T. (1990). *Sleepless souls: Suicide in early modern England.* Oxford studies in social history. Oxford: Clarendon Press.

Mäkinen, I. H. (2000). Eastern European transition and suicide mortality. *Social Science & Medicine, 51*(9), 1405–1420.

Mäkinen, I. H. (2006). Suicide mortality of Eastern European regions before and after the Communist period. *Social Science & Medicine, 63*(2), 307–319.

Martin, L. A., Neighbors, H. W., & Griffith, D. M. (2013). The experience of symptoms of depression in men vs women: Analysis of the National Comorbidity Survey Replication. *JAMA Psychiatry, 70*(10), 1100–1106.

Marusic, A., Petrovic, A., & Zorko, M. (2008). Does suicide know the points of the compass? *International Journal of Social Psychiatry, 54*(5), 387–389.

Mayer, P., & Ziaian, T. (2002). Suicide, gender, and age variations in India: Are women in Indian society protected from suicide? *Crisis, 23*(3), 98–103.

Middleton, N., Sterne, J. A., & Gunnell, D. (2006). The geography of despair among 15–44-year-old men in England and Wales: Putting suicide on the map. *Journal Epidemiology & Community Health, 60*(12), 1040–1047.

Mills, C. W. (1959). *The sociological imagination*. Oxford: Oxford University Press.

Molner, B., Berkman, L. F., & Buka, S. L. (2001). Psychopathology, childhood sexual abuse and other childhood adversities: Relative links to subsequent suicidal behaviour in the US. *Psychological Medicine, 31*(6), 965–977.

Moore, B. (2018). *Transitions toward equality: A sociological analysis of contemporary fatherhood* (Unpublished doctoral thesis). University College Dublin, Dublin, Ireland.

Mueller, A. S., & Abrutyn, S. (2016). Adolescents under pressure: A new Durkheimian framework for understanding adolescent suicide in a cohesive community. *American Sociological Review, 81*(5), 877–899.

Nardi, P. M. (1992). Seamless souls: An introduction to men's friendships. In P. M. Nardi (Ed.), *Men's friendships*. Newbury Park, CA: Sage.

Nelson, H. L. (2001). *Damaged identities: Narrative repair*. Ithaca and London: Cornell University Press.

Ní Laoire, C. (2001). A matter of life and death? Men, masculinities and staying 'behind' in rural Ireland. *Sociologia Ruralis, 41*(2), 220–236.

Nolan, P. D., Triplett, J., & McDonough, S. (2010). Sociology's suicide: A forensic autopsy. *The American Sociologist, 41*(3), 292–305.

O'Brien, R., Hunt, K., & Hart, G. (2005). 'It's caveman stuff, but that is to a certain extent how guys still operate': Men's accounts of masculinity and help seeking. *Social Science & Medicine, 61*(3), 503–516.

O'Donnell, I., Farmer, R., & Catalán, J. (1993). Suicide notes. *British Journal of Psychiatry, 163*(1), 45–48.

O'Donnell, I., Farmer, R., & Catalán, J. (1996). Explaining suicide: The views of survivors of serious suicide attempts. *British Journal of Psychiatry, 168*(6), 780–786.

Owens, C., Booth, N., & Briscoe, M. (2003). Suicide outside the care of mental health services: A case-controlled psychological autopsy study. *Crisis: The Journal of Crisis Intervention and Suicide Prevention, 24*(3), 113–121.

Page, A., Morrell, S., Hobbs, C., Carter, F., Dudley, M., Duflou, J., et al. (2014). Suicide in young adults: Psychiatric and socio-economic factors from a case-control study. *BMC Psychiatry, 14*(1), 68.

Paperno, I. (1997). *Suicide as a cultural institution in Dostoevsky's Russia*. Ithaca, NY: Cornell University Press.

Parsons, T., & Bales, R. F. (1955). *Family, socialization and interaction process.* Glencoe, Illinois: The Free Press.

Patterson, A. A., & Holden, R. R. (2012). Psychache and suicide ideation among men who are homeless: A test of Shneidman's model. *Suicide & Life Threatening Behaviour, 42*(2), 147–156.

Pearson, V., & Liu, M. (2002). Ling's death: An ethnography of a Chinese women's suicide. *Suicide and Life-Threatening Behaviour, 32*(4), 347–358.

Pease, B. (2000). Beyond the father wound: Memory-work and the deconstruction of the father-son relationship. *Australian and New Zealand Journal of Family Therapy, 21*(1), 9–15.

Pescosolido, B., & Georgianna, S. (1989). Durkheim, suicide and religion: Toward a network theory of suicide. *American Sociological Review, 54*(1), 33–48.

Phillips, M. R., Xianyun, L., & Yanping, Z. (2002). Suicide rates in China, 1995–99. *The Lancet, 359*, 835–840.

Pleck, J. H. (2010). Fatherhood and masculinity. In M. E. Lamb (Ed.), *The role of the father in child development* (5th ed., pp. 27–57). New York: Wiley.

Pleck, J., & Marsiglio, W. (2010). Fatherhood and masculinity. In M. E. Lamb (Ed.), *The role of the father in child development.* Hoboken, NJ: Wiley.

Primack, J. M., Addis, M. E., Syzdek, M., & Miller, I. W. (2010). The men's stress workshop: A gender-sensitive treatment for depressed men. *Cognitive and Behavioural Practice, 17*(1), 77–87.

Pritchard, C., & Baldwin, D. S. (2002). Elderly suicide rates in Asian and English-speaking countries. *Acta Psychiatrica Scandinavica, 105*(4), 271–275.

Reddy, W. (2001). *The navigation of feeling: A framework for the history of emotions.* Cambridge: Cambridge University Press.

Redley, M. (2003). Towards a new perspective on deliberate self-harm in an area of multiple deprivation. *Sociology of Health & Illness, 25*(4), 348–373.

Rehkopf, D. H., & Buka, S. L. (2006). The association between suicide and the socio-economic characteristics of geographical areas: A systematic review. *Psychological Medicine, 36*(2), 145–157.

River, J. (2018). Diverse and dynamic interactions: A model of suicidal men's help seeking as it relates to health services. *American Journal of Men's Health, 12*(1), 150–159.

Robertson, S. (2006). Health an interdisciplinary 'not living live in too much of an excess': Lay men understanding health and well-being. *Health: In Interdisciplinary Journal for the Social Study of Health, Illness and Medicine, 10*(2), 175–189.

Russell, S. T., & Toomey, R. B. (2012). Men's sexual orientation and suicide: Evidence for US adolescent-specific risk. *Social Science & Medicine, 74*(4), 523–529.

Scheff, T. (1997). *Emotions, the social bond, and human reality*. Cambridge: Cambridge University Press.

Schwab, J. R., Addis, M. E., Reigeluth, C. S., & Berger, J. L. (2016). Silence and (in)visibility in men's accounts of coping with stressful life events. *Gender and Society, 30*(2), 289–311.

Scourfield, J., & Evans, R. (2014). Why might men be more at risk of suicide after a relationship breakdown? *Sociological Insights, American Journal of Men's Health, 9*(5), 380–384.

Seale, C., & Charteris-Black, J. (2008). The interaction of class and gender in illness narratives. *Sociology, 42*(3), 453–469.

Seguin, M., Lesage, A., Chawky, N., Guy, A., Daigle, F., Girard, G., et al. (2006) Suicide cases in New Brunswick from April 2002 to May 2003: The importance of better recognizing substance and mood disorder comorbidity. *Canadian Journal of Psychiatry, 51*(9), 581–586.

Seidler, Z. E., Rice, S. M., & River, J. (2017). Men's mental health services: The care for a masculinities model. *The Journal of Men's Studies, 26*(1), 92–104.

Seymour-Smith, S., Weatherall, M., & Phoenix, A. (2002). 'My wife ordered me to come!': A discursive analysis of doctors' and nurses' accounts of men's use of general practitioners. *Journal of Health Psychology, 7*(3), 253–267.

Shields, S. A. (2007). Passionate men, emotional women: Psychology constructs gender in the late 19th century. *History of Psychology, 10*(2), 92–110.

Shneidman, E. S. (1991). The commonalities of suicide across the life span. In A. A. Leenaars (Ed.), *Life span perspectives of suicide: Time-lines in the suicide process* (p. 39). New York: Plenum Press.

Simon, R. W., & Nath, A. (2004). Gender and emotion in the United States: Do men and women differ in self-reports of feelings and expressive behavior? *American Journal Sociology, 109*(5), 1137–1176.

Southworth, P. M. (2016). Hegemonic masculinity and suicide: A review of the literature. *The European Health Psychologist, 18*(1), 7–12.

Sterns, P. N. (1994). *American Cool: Constructing a twentieth-century emotional style*. New York: New York University Press.

Strauss, A., & Corbin, J. (1998). *Basics of qualitative research: Techniques and procedures for developing grounded theory*. Thousand Oaks, CA: Sage.

Sweeney, L., Owens, C., & Malone, K. (2015). Communication and interpretation of emotional distress within the friendships of young Irish men prior to suicide: A qualitative study. *Health & Social Care in the Community, 23*(2), 150–158.

Tarlow, S. (2000). The archaeology of emotion and affect. *Annual Review of Archaeology, 41*(1), 169–185.

Thorne, B. (1993). *Gender play: Girls and boys in school.* New Brunswick, NJ: Rutgers University Press.

Tönnies, F. (1957). *Community and society: Gemeinschaft und Gesellschaft* (Charles P. Loomis, Ed. and Trans.). East Lansing: The Michigan State University Press.

Travis, R. (1990). Halbwachs and Durkheim: A test of two theories of suicide. *The British Journal of Sociology, 41*(2), 225–243.

Van de Velde, S., Bracke, P., & Levecque, K. (2010). Gender differences in depression in 23 countries. Cross-national variation in the gender gap in depression. *Social Science & Medicine, 71,* 305–313.

Van de Velde, S., Huijts, T., Bracke, P., & Bambra, C. (2013). Micro-level gender equality and depression in men and women in Europe. *Sociology of Health & Illness, 35*(5), 682–698.

Van Tubergen, F., Te Grotenhuis, M., & Ultee, W. (2005). Denomination, religious context, and suicide: Neo-Durkheimian multilevel explanations tested with individual and contextual data. *American Journal of Sociology, 111*(3), 797–823.

Videon, T. M. (2005). Parent-child relations and children's psychological well-being: Do dads matter? *Journal of Family Issues, 26*(1), 55–78.

Wagner, B., Silverman, M. C., & Martin, C. E. (2003). Family factors in youth suicidal behaviors. *American Behavioral Scientist, 46*(9), 1171–1191.

Weaver, J. C. (2009). *A sadly troubled history: The meanings of suicide in the modern age*. Montreal: McGill-Queen's University Press.

Weitoft, G. R., Hjern, A., Haglund, B., & Rosén, M. (2003). Mortality, severe morbidity, and injury in children living with single parents in Sweden: A population-based study. *The Lancet, 361*(9354), 289–295.

Wetherall, M., & Edley, N. (1999). Negotiating hegemonic masculinity: Imaginary positions and psycho-discursive practices. *Feminism & Psychology, 9*(3), 335–356.

Wexler, L. M. (2006). Inupiat youth suicide and culture loss: Changing community conversations for prevention. *Social Science and Medicine, 63*(11), 2938–2948.

Whipple, S. C., & Noble, E. P. (1991). Personality characteristics of alcoholic fathers and their sons. *Journal of Studies on Alcohol, 52*(4), 331–337.

Willis, L. A., Coombs, D. W., & Cockerham, W. C. (2002). Ready to die: A postmodern interpretation of the increase in African-American adolescent male suicide. *Social Science & Medicine, 22*(6), 907–920.

Wissow, L. S., Walkup, J., Barlow, A., Reid, R., & Kane, S. (2001). Cluster and regional influences on suicide in a Southwestern American Indian tribe. *Social Science and Medicine, 53*(9), 1115–1124.

World Health Organisation. (2014). *Preventing suicide: A global imperative.* Geneva: WHO.

Wouters, C. (2007). *Informalisation: Manners and emotions since 1890.* London: Sage.

Wray, M., Colen, C., & Pescosolido, B. (2011). The sociology of suicide. *Annual Review of Sociology, 37*(1), 505–528.

Wu, F. (2009). *Suicide and justice: A Chinese perspective.* Contemporary China Series. New York: Routledge.

Zahl, D., & Hawton, K. (2004). Repetition of deliberate self-harm and subsequent suicide risk: A long-term follow-up study in 11,583 patients. *British Journal of Psychiatry, 185,* 70–75.

Index

A

Abrutyn, S. 18, 172
Addis, M.E. 56, 59, 175
Adversity in childhood 18, 42, 62, 63, 129, 140, 179, 194. *See also* Childhood, adversity, Maltreatment
  and link to suicide 18, 27
Afifi, T.O. 62, 63
African-American males – suicide rates compared to White males 6
Aftermath of the suicide attempt 58, 106, 141, 177, 182
Age
  age profile of suicide 26, 27, 98, 158
  older people and suicide 8, 18, 26
  younger people and suicide 62, 184
Alaskan people – suicide rates 6
Alcohol
  addiction 128
  contribution to suicide attempt 3, 9
  dependency 57, 130, 146, 160, 177, 178, 180, 193
  and drugs 57, 123, 140, 178
  method of coping with distress 14. *See also* Self-medicating with alcohol
  misuse 14, 115, 129, 131, 138, 140, 160, 161, 164, 167, 168, 180, 181
Alcoholism 72, 80, 82, 83, 92, 122, 141, 161, 176, 177
  parental alcoholism 82

A. Cleary, *The Gendered Landscape of Suicide*,
https://doi.org/10.1007/978-3-030-16634-2

Altruistic suicide 4
Anda, R.F. 62
Andriolo, K.R. 3
Anger 12, 17, 67, 73, 80, 92, 125, 126, 128–130, 144, 148, 149, 160, 162, 163, 175, 177, 180
Anguish 27, 46, 62, 66, 100, 103, 111, 130, 175
Anomic suicide 4
Anxiety 40, 42, 49, 57
Arensman, E. 12, 192
Asian countries
  male-female suicide rates 10
Atkinson, J.M. 2
Atkinson, M. 98
Attempted suicide 12, 42, 45, 47, 64, 98, 99, 110, 122, 125, 143, 144, 158, 161
Austria – rates of suicide 5

B

Baechler, J. 1, 2
Baldwin, D.S. 6, 10
Bales, R.F. 15
Barclay, L. 14, 36, 108
Barlow, A. 6
Barriers 54, 59, 66, 69, 75, 174, 176, 177, 184
  to accessing/seeking help 59
  to knowledge about emotion/s 16
Baseline study 20, 25
Baudelot, C. 6–8, 17, 167, 184, 193
Beautrais, A.L. 138, 167, 178
Berger, J.L. 44, 54, 192
Berkman, L.F. 62
Binary classifications of males and females 11
Biological characteristics/factors 11
Boman, J. 62, 63
Booth, A. 69
Booth, N. 69
Bourdieu, P. 8, 18
Bracke, P. 17
Briscoe, M. 3, 97, 171
Bronte-Tinkew, J. 69
Brothers 66–69, 75, 79
Brown, D. 192
Brownhill, S. 14, 36, 108
Buka, S.L. 98
Bullying 88, 89, 92, 143, 152, 193. *See also* victimisation
Butler, J. 172
Byng, R. 109, 162

C

Campbell, J. 109, 162
Canetto, S.S. 12, 98
Capital 7, 91, 108, 158, 184
  economic 91
  emotional 184
  social 8, 193
Carrano, J. 69
Carter, F. 98
Casualties 158, 163. *See also* Survivors – comparison with those who repeated and completed
Catalán, J. 2, 132, 142, 173, 178
Catholics 4, 6
Cavan, R.S. 9, 168
Central Statistics Office (CSO) 19, 23, 24
Chandler, M.J. 6, 99
Charteris-Black, J. 56

Chawky, N. 167
Child abuse 38. *See also* Maltreatment; Sexual abuse
as contributing factor to suicide 42, 44, 62, 63, 78, 80, 130, 143
Childhood
adversity 24, 62, 159
childhood experiences 45, 124, 143
childhood insecurities 38, 112
unresolved childhood experiences 45
China
male-female suicide patterns 6
reasons for higher rates of female suicide 12
study of suicide in 7, 10
Cities 8, 91, 120
Clancy, P. 26
Class 3, 13, 15, 16, 27, 36, 88, 89, 91, 92, 120, 149, 152, 153, 172, 173. *See also* Working class
and attitudes to help-seeking 13, 14, 191
and suicide 3, 97
Cleary, A. 12–14, 36, 37, 54, 98, 142, 182
Cochrane, S.V. 36
Cockerham, W.C. 6
Cohen, P. 70
Colen, C. 10, 173
Community/communities 6, 14, 16, 17, 19, 27, 36, 37, 46, 87, 88, 93, 108, 120, 154, 155, 167, 173, 174, 189–191, 194
Completed suicide 19, 23–25, 27, 98, 111, 137–139, 151, 156, 159–161, 163, 167, 168, 172, 174, 175, 178–181
completion of suicide 12, 138, 139, 167
Completing suicide 192
Concealing
emotional pain 44, 46, 47
performances 54
practices 102
re sexuality 120
Confiding relationship/s 68, 92, 116
Connell, R.W. 12, 13, 24, 36, 183
Conner, K.R. 168, 181, 193
Context of suicide 133
Conventional masculinity/ies 13, 65, 70, 93, 165, 177, 181. *See also* Hegemonic masculinity/ies
confined by 181
conformity to 167
Conwell, Y. 181
Coombs, D.W. 6
Corbin, J. 24
Costa, G. 7, 17, 18, 98, 140, 167, 173
Counselling 83, 100, 107, 119, 124, 128, 142, 144, 146, 164, 165
Counts, D.S. 2
Courtenay, W.H. 12
Cox, B.J. 62
Coyle, J. 98, 194
Crisis of masculinity
link with suicide rates 98
Cross-generational factors 177
Cultural 2, 3, 7, 8, 13, 14, 16–18, 26, 35–37, 46, 47, 58, 61, 62, 74, 84, 85, 92, 97, 100, 103,

112, 139, 149, 150, 154, 160, 172, 175, 182, 184, 185, 189, 190
factors 4, 6, 10, 133, 184
norms 46, 47, 172
script/s re suicide 10, 172
Culture 1, 3, 11, 17, 35–37, 91, 97, 99, 101, 167, 172, 192
influence on suicide rates 3, 97, 172
and suicide 2, 3, 27, 99

D

Damaged identities 100, 110
Data analysis 24
Deaths by suicide 2
Decision/s re suicide/suicidal action 47, 97, 177, 189
Defining suicide 2
Depression 3, 17, 56–58, 68, 97, 101, 125, 126, 129, 131, 132, 142, 153, 166
Despair 58, 100, 116, 141, 145, 146, 148, 149, 151, 152, 154, 161, 168, 175, 177, 180, 181
despairing narratives 99, 101, 168
Despondency 101, 104, 128, 144, 160, 181
Developed countries – suicide rate 6
Dillon, C.B. 12, 192
Disguised forms of suicide 3
Distress
critical level of 107
disclosure of 14
expression of 17, 174, 184
persistence of 184
Distribution of suicide
changes in 20th century 7
Douglas, J.D. 9, 18, 24, 27, 37, 173
Drugs 3. *See also* Alcohol
and alcohol 14, 38, 42, 57, 123, 125, 128, 130, 138, 140, 159, 178
dependency on 57, 130
misuse of 14, 79, 115, 138, 140, 143
Dualistic categorizations
of male and female emotions 58, 175
Dube, S.R. 62
Duberstein, P.R. 168, 181, 193
Dublin 20
Dudley, M. 98
Duflou, J. 98
Durkheim, E. 3–9, 11, 15, 17, 19, 26, 97, 98, 159, 171
Durkheimian model 9
theory of suicide 9
types of suicide 4

E

Eastern Europe – suicide rates 6
Eaton, W.W. 168, 180
Economic factors – and suicide 9, 18. *See also* Socioeconomic factors
Edley, N. 13
Education
attainment 26, 38, 40, 54, 63, 74, 138, 140, 159, 167, 178
educational disadvantage 7
educational resources 7, 93, 144, 154, 162
Egoistic suicide 4

Elias, N. 16
Emotional communities 16. *See also* Emotional culture/s
Emotional culture/s 14, 16, 18, 27, 37, 46, 64, 93, 102, 177. *See also* Emotional communities
Emotional engagement 53, 66, 70, 71, 92, 176
  between fathers and sons 66, 92, 176
  and relationships 44, 70, 87, 183
Emotional expression
  gender differences 35
  and masculinity 46, 53
  restrictions on 92, 142
Emotionally restrictive environments 175
Emotional pain
  concealing 46, 47
  suppression of 175, 194
  unbearable 17, 19, 162, 174
Emotions
  and class 15
  discharging painful 17
  display of 12, 36, 67
  expression of 16–18, 36, 46, 47, 53, 66, 69, 92, 100, 139, 141, 142, 172, 185
  and gender 13, 15, 16, 18, 19, 27, 37, 62, 64, 68, 92, 139, 141, 172
  invisibility of 58, 175
  norms relating to 14
  regulation of 176
  restriction of 92, 142, 184
  unitary notion of male and female emotions 11, 15, 36
Employment
  skilled 26
  skilled manual 26
  unemployment 7, 18
Emslie, C. 13
Enns, M.W. 62
Escape
  from mental anguish 120
  from pain 44
  from present life 152, 166
Establet, R. 6–8, 17, 167, 184, 193
Ethics 25
Ethnic minorities - suicide rates 99
Evans, R. 193
Expression of emotions – gender differences re 35
  discouraged 16, 175
  social class influences 16, 36

F

Falmer, R. 2, 132, 142, 173, 178
Family
  background 40, 64, 116, 118, 144, 151, 164
  problems 124, 152
  as site for acquiring masculinity 65
  support 64, 157, 159
Farrelly, S. 192
Fatalistic suicide 4
Father/s
  absent 85, 151, 159
  conflict with 70, 76, 80, 118
  contact with 40, 63, 119
  emotional engagement with sons 53, 66, 70, 71, 87, 92, 176
  influence of 53, 65, 67, 69–71, 87, 119, 176

rejection by 38, 73, 112, 115, 176, 177, 194
relationship/s with 24, 39, 42, 68–71, 73, 74, 79, 80, 85, 101, 112, 115, 119, 124, 144, 145, 149, 159, 161, 164, 165, 176, 177, 183, 194
as role model/s 65, 70, 77, 176
Fear/fearful 5, 38, 44, 45, 50, 52, 53, 56, 57, 59, 62, 69, 76, 80, 82–84, 93, 109, 110, 119, 124, 127, 130, 143, 149, 163, 164, 166, 167, 174, 175, 183
Feeling rules 17, 18, 27, 46
Feelings
anaesthetising 57, 110
concealment of 13, 36, 175
contained 38
control of 17, 54
of desperation 37, 113, 160, 175
expression of 3, 93, 172, 174, 175
painful 40, 59
repression of 75, 93
of sadness 12, 37, 40, 175, 183
Feeney, M. 12–14, 36, 37, 54, 98
Felitte, V.J. 62
Female suicide rates 10, 98, 172
Feminine discourse 13, 100, 145
Fergusson, D.M. 70
Fincham, B. 98, 132, 173, 178
Finland - rates of suicide in 20th century 5
Firestone, R.W. 110, 163
First Nation groups (Canada) - suicide rates 6
Fitzgerald, H.E. 83
Follow-up study 25, 138, 151, 154, 157
France – rates of suicide in 20th century 5
Frank, A. 17, 56, 82, 83, 164, 165, 167
Friendship/s 53, 70

G

Gaines, D. 133, 181
Gallo, J.J. 168, 181
Gavin, G. 189
Gay 87, 88, 109, 112, 119–121, 152, 153, 155, 164
fear of being identified as 88
identity 88
Gemeinschaft 5
Gender
discourse 174
expectations 16, 53, 54, 62, 184
norms 12, 14, 37, 44, 50, 141, 167
and suicide 10, 15, 18, 20, 27, 98, 133, 172, 190, 194
Gender differences
and emotion 35
and psychological health 162
and suicide rates 35
Gendered ideas/notions 12, 15, 61
and emotions 12, 15, 35, 36
and suicide 11, 15, 35, 61, 108
Gender-specific 15, 16, 46
emotions 15, 16
motivations for suicide 98
Generalised unhappiness 111, 132, 177
General Practitioners 192
Georgianna, S. 7

Germany – rates of suicide in 20th century 5
Gesellscahaft 5
Gibb, S.J. 138, 178
Goffman, E. 21
Gould, M. 194
Gould, M.S. 70
Great Britain – rates of suicide in 20th century 5
Griffin, E. 12, 192
Guilt 17, 73, 117, 125, 126, 160, 163, 180
Gunnell, D. 18

H

Hadfield, J. 192
Haglund, B. 85
Halbwachs 9
Hamdi, E. 3, 97, 171, 190
Hanlon, N. 70
Hart, G. 13
Hawton, K. 138
Hegemonic masculinity/ies 92. *See also* Masculinity/masculinities
  confined within 13
  performing 133
  and stoicism 92
  and strength 12, 175, 183
Helliwell, J.F. 5–8, 184
Help-seeking 13, 14, 191
  attitudes to 13, 14, 191
  male and female differences 14, 191
High-risk
  groups 157, 173
  phase 127
  re suicide 127
Historical constructions of suicide 61, 178
Hjelmeland, H. 178, 192
Hjern, A. 85
Hobbs, C. 98
Hochschild, A.R. 14, 16, 18, 24, 36, 172, 185
Holden, R.R. 99
Holmes, M. 17, 37
Homosexuality 88, 90, 153, 154. *See also* Gay; LGBT groups
Hopelessness 38, 39, 63, 139, 160, 168, 180
  alcohol dependency 160, 180
Horwood, L.J. 70
Howerton, A. 109, 162
Huijts, T. 17
Huisman, M. 7, 17, 18, 98, 140, 167, 173
Hume, M. 162
Hunt, K. 13

I

Identity 4, 47, 72, 76, 113, 133, 152, 154, 175, 181, 189, 193, 194
  masculine 14, 47, 93
  social 7
Impulsivity and suicide 11, 97, 99, 190
In care 40, 43, 73, 78, 79
Inckle, K. 12, 98
India – male:female suicide rates 10
Industrialisation 16
Insecurity/ies 43, 64, 79, 86, 92, 115, 117
Integration 4, 7, 9, 180

difficulties of operationalising concept 9
new forms in 20th century 7, 9
and suicide 4, 9
Intent 2, 20, 22, 110, 111, 132, 140, 151, 158, 165, 167, 178
International suicide rates 5, 10
Intervention/s 8, 59, 100, 101, 120, 131, 142, 146, 148, 160, 163, 175, 179, 180, 182, 185, 189–193, 195
Interviews 18–25, 27, 37, 38, 40, 42, 54, 56, 99, 107, 113, 129, 137, 148, 149, 152, 160, 161, 173, 178
Ireland 3, 20, 23, 26

J

Jacobs, J. 9
Jamieson, P. 194
Japan – suicide patterns 6
Jefferson, T. 13
Jeffery, D. 192
Jihad 3
Joe, S. 7, 14, 36
Johnson, J.G. 70
Jordan, J. 191

K

Kaplan, M.S. 7, 14, 36
Keeney, S. 191
Kemper, T.D. 16, 18, 36, 172
Kimmel, M. 12, 36, 49, 62
King, V. 69
Knizek, B.L. 178, 192
Kunst, A.E. 7, 18, 98, 140, 167, 173
Kuo, W. 168, 181
Kushner, H.I. 9, 11, 97, 98

L

Lalonde, C.E. 6, 99
Lamb, M.E. 69, 70, 176, 194
Langer, S. 98, 132, 173, 178
Lee, S. 10
Lemieux, A.M. 192
Lesage, A. 167
Le Suicide 3, 4
Lethality 2, 111, 140, 151, 164, 165
Lethal methods 132
Levecque, K. 17
Lewis, C. 70, 176, 194
LGBT groups – suicide rates 99
Liu, M. 10, 180
Lorent, V. 7, 17, 18, 98, 140, 167, 173
Loss 40, 49, 50, 63, 72, 86, 98, 112, 116, 151, 178, 179
and ending of relationship 40
Loukas, A. 82
Lutfiyya, M.N. 192

M

MacDonald, M. 2, 3
Mackenbach, J. 7, 18, 98, 140, 167, 173
Macken-Walsh, A. 12–14, 36, 37, 54, 98
MacWhannell, D. 98
Mahalik, J.R. 56, 59, 175
Mäkinen, I.H. 5, 6
Male suicide

male:female suicide rates 10, 98, 172
predominance of 61, 178
variation across male groupings 18, 61
Malone, K. 194
Maltreatment 62, 84, 176
Marriage 9, 74, 112, 180
and suicide 9, 180
Marsiglio, W. 70
Martin, C.E. 62, 69, 70
Marusic, A. 6
Masculine
appropriate behaviour 25, 66, 119
and regulation of behaviour 69, 87, 122
unacceptable behaviour 53, 88, 174
Masculinity/ies
alternative 92, 93, 100, 139, 165, 167, 174, 175, 183
codes 53, 69, 175, 176
conventional 12, 66, 120, 122, 139, 163, 165, 174, 176
diverse 13, 61, 183
hard 120, 129, 159, 160, 163, 175, 180
hegemonic 12–14, 36, 52, 59, 62, 92, 122, 123, 129, 133, 160, 162, 163, 174, 175, 183, 184
normative 44, 68, 76, 87, 92, 139, 174–176, 181, 183
norms 44, 46, 47, 49, 50, 53, 59, 66, 90, 141, 174–176, 183, 190
prevailing 44, 49, 50, 59, 69, 87, 89, 93, 159, 168, 174, 175, 181, 183, 190
rigid interpretation of 87
rules 50, 53, 59, 87
and suicide/suicidal behaviour 12, 18, 24, 35, 70, 85, 122, 162, 173, 184, 194
and suicide scripts 3, 10, 12, 15, 37, 69, 93, 133
traditional 12, 14, 66, 120, 122, 139, 164, 165, 174, 176
Mayer, P. 10
McDonough, S. 9
McKenna, H. 191
McTernan, N. 12, 192
Meaning 2, 3, 14, 16, 18, 19, 25, 37, 86, 111, 137, 173, 189
and suicide 2
Meaning of suicide 2, 18, 37, 99, 139, 173
Medical/biomedicine explanations for suicide 97
Mediterranean Region – suicide rates 6
Men
and emotions 12, 13, 15–17, 35, 37, 183, 185
as susceptible to suicide 61, 190
unitary notion of 11, 15, 36
Mental Health Services 179, 191
Messerschmidt, J.W. 12, 13, 36
Method and suicide 26, 165
Methodology of study 19, 21, 27, 171
Middleton, N. 18
Mills, C.W. 14
Modernisation 5
Molner, B. 62
Moore, B. 70
Moore, K.A. 69

Morrell, S. 98
Mortality data 19, 23, 24, 137
Mothers – relationship with 116, 124, 152
Motivation/s for suicide attempt 19, 21, 98, 123, 137, 156, 164, 167, 171, 173
Mueller, A.S. 18, 172
Murphy, T. 2, 3

N

Nardi, P.M. 53
Narratives 12, 18, 22, 24, 25, 27, 37, 44–46, 58, 62, 69, 70, 73, 76, 82, 99, 109, 116, 122, 127, 129, 132, 133, 151, 160, 162, 163, 167, 173, 175–177, 179, 180, 182–184, 189, 191, 193
  and suicide attempt 18, 27, 37, 87, 104
Narrowing of options 108
Nath, A. 17, 36
Native Americans – suicide rates 6
Near-fatal suicide attempt/s 56, 164, 165, 173, 191
Neighbourhood/s 26, 50, 68, 69, 74, 87, 119, 152, 153, 165, 174, 178
Nelson, H.L. 100, 110
Ní Laoire, C. 8
Noble, E.P. 82
Nolan, P.D. 9
Norms
  and expression of suffering 14
  and masculinity 49, 50, 53, 90, 174, 175, 177, 183, 190
Northern European countries - suicide rates 6

O

O'Brien, R. 13
O'Donnell, I. 2, 132, 142, 173, 178
Olds, J. 15
Overdose (OD) 26, 105, 116, 127, 129
Owens, C. 3, 97, 171
Owens, C.V. 109, 162

P

Page, A. 98
Panic 42, 108, 117, 141, 151
  panic attack 43, 57
Paperno, I. 3
Paradox of suicide 6, 11, 175
Parental separation/divorce 40, 42, 77, 85, 120, 152
  and suicide 120, 152
Parsons, T. 15
Paternal alcoholism 68, 82, 92
Pathway/s to suicide/suicidal action 24, 46, 99, 103, 177
Patterson, A.A. 98
Pearson, V. 10, 180
Pease, B. 85
Pembroke, L. 192
Perry, I.J. 12, 192
Pescosolido, B. 10, 173
Petrovic, A. 6
Phillips, M.R. 10
Phoenix, A. 13
Physical abuse 80, 83, 123
Platt, S. 162
Pleck, J. 70
Political hunger strikes 3
Powerlessness 10, 62, 80, 100, 104, 123, 133
Precipitating event 103, 179. *See also* Triggering event

Prevention 8, 19, 173, 189, 190, 192–195
Price, S. 3, 97, 171, 190
Primack, J.M. 191
Pritchard, C. 6, 10
Protective factors 9, 127
  and suicide 9, 127
Protestants 5, 6
Pseudonyms 25
Psychiatric
  discourse 119, 157
  disorder 52, 103, 132, 133, 140, 157, 167, 178, 184
  hospital 119
  illness 131, 156, 179
  services 142, 156, 157
  unit 20, 52, 146, 182
Psychological difficulties 13, 53
  recognising 56
  reporting 17, 36
Public Health 171, 190
  campaigns 190, 194
  messages 190, 192

Q

Qassem, T. 3, 97, 171, 190

R

Rabinowitz, F.E. 17
Rage 110, 125, 160, 162
Reddy, W. 16
Redley, M. 108, 132, 133, 173
Rehkopf, D.H. 98
Reigeluth, C.S. 44, 54, 192
Rejection 73–75, 86, 112, 115, 119, 143, 148, 176, 177, 194
  by father 38, 73, 112, 115, 194
  by peers 12, 149
Relationship
  ending of 38, 40, 44, 64, 78, 111, 112, 132, 177
  relationship breakup and suicide 44, 113, 116
  with family 24, 39, 47, 68, 71, 74, 80, 115, 117, 120, 124, 154, 177, 180
  with fathers 70, 71, 85, 176, 183
  with partners 39, 45, 47, 64, 79, 83, 112, 117, 119, 123, 124, 165
Religion 4–7
Repetition of suicide
  comparison of those who repeated/did not repeat 138, 140, 159, 179
  rate 138, 178, 179
  repeat group 139, 140, 151, 193
Research methods and suicide 11, 85, 138, 154, 167
  qualitative 10
  quantitative 9
Resources
  economic 7, 193
  educational 44, 93, 139, 141, 144, 154, 162
  lack of 108, 138, 139
  social 193
Rice, S.M. 191
Ridge, D. 13
Risk 9
  and suicide 6, 8, 12, 14, 37, 59, 61–63, 85, 99, 102, 109, 131, 138, 139, 154, 175, 190, 192, 193
  categories of 16
Risk behaviour 115, 119, 122, 124, 129, 133, 143, 152, 159, 160, 162, 168

River, J. 52, 59, 175
Robertson, S. 14
Rogers, A. 189
Romer, D. 194
Rural areas and suicide rates 10
Rusch, N. 192
Russell, S.T. 99, 154, 193
Russia 3, 5, 6
explanations for suicide in 19th and 20th centuries 3
suicide rates 3, 5, 6

S

Saman, D.M. 192
Scandinavia – rates of suicide in 20th century 5
Scheff, T. 14, 17, 162
School 42, 45, 48, 53, 63, 69, 72, 75, 79, 81, 87, 89–91, 93, 105, 112, 116, 119, 123, 124, 129, 133, 148–150, 152, 153, 158, 159, 161, 174, 180, 194
and bullying/victimisation 89, 90, 152
regulation of masculine behaviour 87, 89
Schwab, J.R. 44, 54, 192
Scott, M.E. 69
Scourfield, J. 193
Seale, C. 56
Seguin, M. 167
Seidler, Z.E. 191
Self-blame 41, 86, 90
Self-esteem 75, 83, 84, 92, 149
Self-harm 12, 23, 38, 40, 47, 108, 109, 112, 116, 123, 127, 131, 138, 151, 152, 173, 192
Self-medicating with alcohol 57, 103
Sex-difference research 15, 36
Sexual abuse 44, 62, 63, 143
Sexuality 87, 90, 122, 140, 151–154, 165, 182
Seymour-Smith, S. 13
Shame 17, 74, 175, 180
Shields, S.A. 13, 15, 35, 172
Shneidman, E.S. 17, 108
Silverman, M.C. 62, 69, 70
Simon, R.W. 17, 36
Societal scripts 133, 182
and suicide 133, 182
Sociocultural basis to suicide 9, 35
Socioeconomic 7, 13, 14, 18, 26, 27, 37, 91, 98, 100, 140, 167, 172, 173, 184, 185, 190, 193
discrepancies in suicide rates 6, 7
factors re suicide 3, 8, 11, 26, 27, 35, 97, 184
Socioemotional framework for understanding suicide 10, 17, 27
Sociological
interest in topic of suicide 3, 4
study of emotions 18
understanding of suicide 4, 10
Southworth, P.M. 13
Stereotypical 123, 132
gendered 11, 132, 178
ideas about suicide 35, 61
Sterne, J.A. 18
Sterns, P.N. 16
Strauss, A. 24
Strength
displays of 12, 59
links between strength and masculinity 48

performance of 65, 180
projecting an image of 47
Structural factors 18, 99
constraints 184
Substance misuse 14, 17, 36, 52, 124, 127, 133, 147, 151, 156, 159, 168, 193. *See also* Alcohol and drug misuse
as masking diagnosis for depression in men 17, 36
Suicide
biomedical explanations for 3, 97
completing 57, 127, 131, 138, 139, 182, 191, 193
context and meaning of 10, 97, 99, 133, 175, 181, 189
and emotions 14, 15, 18, 27, 35, 37, 38, 46, 58, 98, 100, 110, 129, 131, 142, 163, 172, 175, 184, 185, 191
as impulsive action 42, 99, 111, 190
as a male practice 35, 61
motivations for 19, 21, 56, 98, 137, 156, 164, 173
pathways to 99, 103
patterns of 1, 3–5, 8, 10, 26, 37, 137, 139, 181, 189
plan/s 108, 132, 177, 190
preoccupation with 129, 160
rates 3–12, 17, 20, 26, 27, 35, 97–99, 138, 167, 172, 175
repeating 57, 138, 139, 151
and risk 6, 8, 9, 12, 14, 16, 37, 59, 61–63, 85, 99, 102, 109, 138, 139, 151, 154, 156, 159, 161, 173, 175, 190–193
sociological understanding of 4
as way of exiting cycle of unhappiness 162
Suicide attempt 18–20, 24, 27, 37, 38, 40, 41, 45, 48, 54–56, 68, 73, 75–77, 82, 83, 86, 99–101, 104, 106, 112, 115–117, 122, 123, 125, 127, 129, 132, 138, 139, 141, 142, 146, 149, 150, 156, 157, 160, 162, 164, 165, 168, 173, 175, 177–179, 181
Suicide notes 110
Suicide rates 4–10, 26, 99
comparison between East and West 6
patterns 4, 5, 8, 10, 26
Support
and family 64, 106, 124, 127, 141, 152, 154, 157, 159, 162, 179
and friends 44, 64, 154, 179
networks 128, 151, 154, 183
Surveillance of behaviour 53
by peers 12, 62
Survivors – comparison with those who repeated and completed 139, 151
Sweeney, L. 194
Sydek, M. 191

T

Tarlow, S. 16
Te Grotenhuis, M. 6
Thorne, B. 98, 172
Tönnies, F. 5
Toomey, R.B. 99, 154, 193
Trapped – feeling of being 107
Travis, R. 9

Treatment
antipathy to available 182
reasons for not seeking 131, 142
take-up of 19, 142
Triggering event 103, 111, 127, 179. *See also* Precipitating event
Triplett, J. 9
Trouble with the law 26, 138, 140, 159
Twenty-first century – suicide patterns 6, 19
Typical men 192

U

Ultee, W. 6
Undetermined deaths 2, 23
Unhappiness
concealing 41, 46, 47
intergenerational 74, 92
long-term 39, 106
United States – suicide rate 6, 7
Unresolved suffering 99, 100

V

Values
adherence to traditional values and suicide 5, 7
and suicide 6
Van de Velde, S. 17
van Heeringen, K. 138
Van Tubergen, F. 6
Victimisation 84, 89, 90, 92, 148. *See also* Bullying
Videon, T.M. 69
Violence 68, 69, 74, 80, 83, 84, 92, 123, 129, 159–163, 175–177, 179, 180, 183
paternal 80, 82, 83

W

Wagner, B. 62, 69, 70
Walkup, J. 6
Wall, J. 26
Weakness 12, 13, 36, 44, 51, 59, 92, 98, 143, 162, 174
and masculinity 69
Wealth – as protective factor re suicide 7, 9, 98
Weatherall, M. 13
Weatherall, R. 138
Weaver, J.C. 1, 9, 14, 15, 133
Weber 9
Weitoft, G.R. 85
Wellbeing 1, 6, 12, 65, 70, 85, 98, 111, 142, 150, 180, 194, 195
influences on 14, 64
Western ideas
and emotions 15, 35
and men 15
and suicide 35
Wetherall, M. 13
Wexler, L.M. 6
Whipple, S.C. 82
White US males – rate of suicide 6
comparison with African-American males 6
Wilhelm, K. 108
Williamson, E. 12, 192
Willis, LA. 6
Wissow, L.S. 6
Women 10–13, 15, 17, 35, 46, 49, 50, 54, 61, 69, 97, 117, 145, 147, 149, 172, 175
in China 10
and suicide rates 10–12

Woodward, L.J. 70
Working class
  background 92, 173
  communities 120
  and help-seeking practices 120
  and masculinities 120
World Health Organisation (WHO) 1
Wouters, C. 16
Wray, M. 10, 173
Wu, F. 7, 10, 180

X
Xianyun, L. 10

Y
Yanping, Z. 10

Z
Zahl, D. 138
Ziaian, T. 10
Ziebland, S. 13
Zorko, M. 6
Zucker, R.A. 82